W9-AAE-512

The
Holt
Handbook

Sixth Edition

The
Holt
Handbook

Sixth Edition

LAURIE G. KIRSZNER
University of the Sciences in Philadelphia

STEPHEN R. MANDELL
Drexel University

HARCOURT COLLEGE PUBLISHERS

FORT WORTH   PHILADELPHIA   SAN DIEGO
NEW YORK   ORLANDO   AUSTIN   SAN ANTONIO
TORONTO   MONTREAL   LONDON   SYDNEY   TOKYO

Publisher	Earl McPeek
Market Strategist	Katrina Byrd
Developmental Editor	Camille Adkins
Project Editor	Jon Davies
Art Director	Vicki Whistler
Production Manager	Linda McMillan

ISBN: 0-15-506600-5
Library of Congress Catalog Card Number: 00-111782

Copyright © 2002, 1999, 1995, 1992, 1986 by Harcourt, Inc.

Address for Domestic Orders
Harcourt College Publishers, 6277 Sea Harbor Drive, Orlando, FL 32887-6777
800-782-4479

Address for International Orders
International Customer Service
Harcourt, Inc., 6277 Sea Harbor Drive, Orlando, FL 32887-6777
407-345-3800
(fax) 407-345-4060
(e-mail) hbintl@harcourt.com

Address for Editorial Correspondence
Harcourt College Publishers, 301 Commerce Street, Suite 3700, Fort Worth, TX 76102

Web Site Address
http://www.harcourtcollege.com

Harcourt College Publishers will provide complimentary supplements or supplement packages to those adopters qualified under our adoption policy. Please contact your sales representative to learn how you qualify. If as an adopter or potential user you receive supplements you do not need, please return them to your sales representative or send them to: Attn: Returns Department, Troy Warehouse, 465 South Lincoln Drive, Troy, MO 63379.

Printed in the United States of America
1 2 3 4 5 6 7 8 9 0 039 9 8 7 6 5 4 3 2
Harcourt College Publishers

PREFACE

Our goal for the sixth edition of *The Holt Handbook* is the same as it was for the first edition: to create a writer's handbook that serves as a classroom text, as a comprehensive reference, and as a writer's companion. In preparing the first edition, we concentrated on making the book inviting, accessible, useful, and clear for both teachers and students. In the sixth edition, we have kept these goals in mind, adding distinctive new design features and fine-tuning established ones in order to make information even easier to locate than before. As a result, the sixth edition of *The Holt Handbook* is the most accessible hardback college handbook currently on the market.

Although *The Holt Handbook*, Sixth Edition, is grounded in the most up-to-date research in composition, it is also informed by our many years of classroom experience. As teachers, we continue to search for what works for our students, giving them what they need to succeed in college and beyond. Our hope is that the sixth edition continues to reflect our commitment to our teaching and to our students—some of whose writing appears on its pages. With its logical organization, its process approach to writing, its encouraging tone, and its focus on student writing, we believe that *The Holt Handbook* is an excellent choice for today's students and teachers.

The Holt Handbook, Sixth Edition, is writing centered, and it puts writing first. It is a classroom text, a reference book, and—above all—a writing companion that students can turn to again and again for advice and guidance as they write in college and beyond. We continue to believe that we have an obligation to give not just the rule but the rationale behind it. Accordingly, we are careful to explain the principles that writers must understand if they are to make informed choices about grammar, usage, rhetoric, and style. The result is a book that students and instructors can continue to use with ease, with confidence, and (we hope) with pleasure.

What Do Teachers and Students Like about *The Holt Handbook?*

- *An Attractive Design That Makes the Book Accessible and Easy to Use*   A concise **Guide to the Plan of the Book** appears on the inside front cover to facilitate reference. Taupe **Close-Up boxes,** which appear throughout the text, focus on special problems; they are identified by a magnifying glass icon. **Checklists** provide concise guidance for writers; these are taupe and are distinguished by a check mark icon. Taupe **computer boxes,** distinguished by a computer icon, highlight information students will use as they write with their computers, and blue lines enclose **boxed lists and charts** and other information that students are likely to turn to on a regular basis. **Cross-references,** which direct users to related discussions in other parts of the book, are indicated by small blue "buttons" in the margin keyed to "hypertext links" (blue, underlined in blue) in the text. Throughout the text, headings are clear and descriptive and positioned logically on the page.

- *A Detailed Four-Chapter Treatment of the Writing Process* The treatment of writing in the sixth edition is lucid and easy to follow. All prewriting activities and drafts related to the student essay "My Problem: Escaping the Sterotype of the 'Model Minority'" appear in a single chapter, "Writer's Notebook: Composing an Essay."

- *A Full Chapter on Rhetorical Patterns for Essay Development* Unique in college-level handbooks, "Essay Patterns and Purposes" (Chapter 5) explains the use of eight patterns of development and illustrates each in an annotated student essay.

- *An Extensive Treatment of Critical Thinking and Argument* A three-chapter sequence discusses critical-thinking and active-reading strategies and explains inductive and deductive reasoning as well as the Toulmin model and Rogerian argument. Chapter 9, "Writing an Argumentative Essay," spotlights a student paper, "The Returning Student: Older is Definitely Better," which uses both print and electronic sources to support an argumentative thesis.

- *Comprehensive Coverage of the Research Process* The Holt Handbook includes the most complete treatment of research available in a college handbook, with nine chapters that guide students through every aspect of the reseach process. A separate chapter is devoted to MLA documentation, and two chapters focus on using and evaluating Internet sources. The reseach section ends with Chapter 18, "Research Notebook: A Student's Process," which follows a student's progress from assignment to final paper.

- *A Chapter on Avoiding Plagiarism* A full chapter on avoiding plagiarism underscores its importance for students and helps them understand the ethics of acknowledging both print and Internet sources.

- *A Detailed Treatment of Grammar, Style, and Mechanics with Special Focus on Grammar "Hot Spots"* Part 4, "Solving Common Sentence Problems," provides especially full treatment of the problems teachers and students struggle with most: sentence fragments, comma splices and fused sentences, faulty modification, faulty parallelism, and awkwardly worded sentences.

- *A Section on Writing in the Disciplines* This section, which begins with a chapter devoted to the differences among various disciplines, includes chapter-length discussions of writing in the humanities, the social sciences, and the natural and applied sciences. The section also contains a chapter on writing essay exams, a chapter on writing about literature, and a chapter on writing for the workplace.
- *Advice on Computer Strategies Integrated throughout the Text* Special computer boxes provide advice on writing. In addition, discussions throughout the text reflect the importance of electronic resources in the research and writing process.
- *A Discussion of Document Design and Manuscript Format* Chapter 55 discusses the basic principles of document design, highlighting the use of headings, lists, and visuals (tables, graphs, diagrams, and photographs). This chapter also includes the MLA and APA guidelines for manuscript preparation.
- *A Chapter on English for Speakers of Other Languages (ESL)* Chapter 56 offers students a context for understanding English grammar by contrasting its rules to those of the students' own languages. This unique approach is designed to be of interest to native as well as nonnative speakers of English.

What's New in the 6th Edition of *The Holt Handbook?*

- *A Concise Color-Coded Guide to the Plan of the Book* On the inside front cover, a concise reference guide to the book, color-coded to the book's individual sections, now gets students right into the text.
- *FAQs (Frequently Asked Questions)* Frequently asked questions now appear at the beginning of each chapter. These FAQs address the problems that students encounter most often, and because they are phrased in the students' own language, they enable them to find answers without knowing technical or grammatical terminology. Each FAQ is cross-referenced to a page where the answer is marked with a question mark icon.
- *URLs (Electronic Addresses)* URLs for relevant Web sites have been added to most chapters, enabling students to use the Internet to find additional information about the topics discussed in *The Holt Handbook.*
- *ESL Icons* Special ESL icons direct students to material in Chapter 56, "English for Speakers of Other Languages."
- *A New Organization that Emphasizes the "Writing First" Orientation of the Book* The nine-chapter research section now follows

the composing an essay section to highlight the relationship between writing an essay and writing a research paper.

- *New Student Research Paper*   Chapter 18, "Research Notebook: A Student's Process," presents a new research assignment and a new annotated research paper, "The Great Digital Divide."
- *MLA Documentation in a Separate Chapter*   To facilitate use and eliminate confusion, MLA documentation now appears in its own chapter with a black bar at outside edge of the page to enable quick access.
- *Expanded Coverage of Documentation*   The treatment of documenting electronic sources has been significantly expanded and updated—especially in Chapter 16, "MLA Documentation."
- *A Chapter on Evaluating Web Sites*   New to this edition is Chapter 13, "Evaluating Web Sites," which contains guidelines for assessing the purpose, content, and format of Web sites.
- *A Discussion on How to Create a Web Page*   Chapter 55, "Document Design and Manuscript Format," now explains and illustrates the process of creating and designing a personal Web page.

Ancillary Package

With this edition, an even more comprehensive ancillary package is available for students and instructors.

The following support materials for instructors and students are available to adopters of *The Holt Handbook,* Sixth Edition. Instructors should contact their Harcourt Brace representatives for more information.

For Instructors

Instructor's Guide—Answers to exercises in the handbook, additional exercises with answers, abstracts of articles, suggestions for relating theory and scholarship to classroom activities, computer and Internet tips, quotations, classroom activities, and teaching strategies

Test Package—A complete testing program, cross-referenced to *The Holt Handbook,* Sixth Edition, including general grammar proficiency tests; diagnostic tests; practice tests for CLAST, TASP, and the Tennessee Proficiency Examination; and a bank of eight hundred testing items for skills development, diagnostic evaluation, and state exam preparation. Also available in Windows and Macintosh versions (see the list of electonic supplements)

The Harcourt Guide to Teaching First-Year Composition—An introduction to the basics of teaching writing, with essay examples from students, and a comprehensive bibliography for further study

The Harcourt Guide to Teaching Writing with Computers—Techniques for teaching writing in networked and nonnetworked computer environments, including tips for teaching Internet research

The Harcourt Guide to Writing across the Curriculum—A brief history of Writing across the Curriculum, plus strategies for launching a WAC program, including tips for designing writing assignments

The Harcourt Guide to Peer Tutoring—A Guide for Writers and Peer Editors—An introduction to peer consulting pedagogy and practice, with readings from such rhetoricians and composition theorists as Kenneth Bruffee, Peter Elbow, and Mina Shaughnessey

The Harcourt Sourcebook for Teachers of Writing—A collection of articles by composition scholars, considering such rhetoric and composition issues and trends as analyzing audience, teaching community-based writing, and assigning expressive essays

For Students

The Harcourt Guide to Documentation and Writing in the Disciplines—Full introductions to writing in the humanities, the social sciences, and the natural sciences, with model papers typical of the work students will be expected to submit in each discipline

Supplementary Exercises—A collection of grammar and composition exercises for students who need reinforcement of basic skills; designed for use with *The Holt Handbook,* Sixth Edition

The Holt Composition Workbook, Form A—A full-length workbook intended for first-year students; designed for use with *The Holt Handbook,* Sixth Edition, or on its own

The Holt Composition Workbook, Form B—A full-length workbook intended for developmental as well as first-year students; designed for use with *The Holt Handbook,* Sixth Edition, or on its own

The Holt Guide to the Internet—An overview of the Internet, its components, and its purposes, including but not limited to research

Working Together: A Collaboration Writing Guide—A guide for student writers working constructively in small groups, intended to make each group session productive and satisfying for all participants

Preparing for the TASP—A guide that enables students to connect sample test material to explanations and exercises available in the handbook

Preparing for the CLAST—A guide that enables students to connect sample test material to explanations and exercises available in the handbook

Electronic Supplements

The Holt Handbook CD-ROM—The full text of the handbook on CD-ROM

The Writer's Resources—An interactive multimedia program that provides students with a wide range of guidance and support, including three sections: Skills, Writing Elements, and Rhetorical Patterns

Electronic Test Package—A complete testing program in Windows or Macintosh format, cross-referenced to *The Holt Handbook,* Sixth Edition, including general grammar proficiency tests; diagnostic tests; practice tests for CLAST, TASP, and the Tennessee Proficiency Examination; and a bank of eight hundred testing items for skills development, diagnostic evaluation, and state exam preparation. Also available in a print version (see the list of instructor supplements)

Transparency Masters—A collection of images from *The Holt Handbook,* Sixth Edition, to be downloaded from *The Holt Handbook* Web site

Acknowledgments

We thank the following reviewers for their advice on the development of the sixth edition:

Marilyn Cleland, Purdue University Calumet
Elizabeth Curtin, Salisbury State University
Julie Fenlen, Joliet Junior College
Carolyn Hooker, Spartanburg Technical College
Linda LaPointe, St. Petersburg Junior College
Sue Mattheny, Pasco-Hernando Community College
Sarah McGaughlin, Texas Tech University
Roxanne Munch, Joliet Junior College
Ron Smith, University of North Alabama
Bill Yarrow, Joliet Junior College

We are particularly grateful to Roxanne Munch of Joliet Junior College for her contributions to Chapter 13, "Evaluating Web Sites."

We thank the following colleagues for their help in the development of the fifth edition: Patricia Arnott, University of Delaware; Michel de Benedictis, Miami-Dade Community College; Kay Bosgraaf, Montgomery College; Larry Bromley, University of Texas at Arlington; Beth Brunk, University of Texas at Arlington; Daniel Butcher, Southeastern Louisiana University; Linda Daigle, Houston Community College Central; Dani Day, University of Texas at Arlington; Scott Douglass,

Chattanooga State Technical Community College; Eleanor Gaunder, University of North Alabama; Jacqueline Goffe-McNish, Dutchess Community College; Lori Gravley, Western New England College; Stephen Harding, University of Texas at Arlington; Sydney Harrison, Manatee Community College; Peggy Jolly, University of Alabama at Birmingham; Michael Lèger, University of Texas at Arlington; Richard Louth, Southeastern Louisiana University; Quentin Martin, Loyola University of Chicago; Nellie McCrory, Gaston College; Nancy McGee, Detroit College of Business; Clyde Moneyhun, Youngstown State University; Judy Pearce, Montgomery College; Russ Pottle, Southeastern Louisiana University; Carol Clark Powell, University of Texas at El Paso; Audrey Wick, University of Texas at Arlington; and Jeff Wiemelt, Southeastern Louisiana University.

We also thank the following reviewers for their sound advice on the development of the fourth edition: Henry Castillo, Temple Junior College; Laurie Chesley, Grand Valley State University; Scott Douglass, Chattanooga State Technical Community College; Maurice R. Duperre, Midlands Technical College; Nancy Ellis, Mississippi State University; Jane Frick, Missouri Western State University; G. Dale Gleason, Hutchinson Community College; Maureen Hoag, Wichita State University; Susan B. Jackson, Spartanburg Technical College; Anne Maxham-Kastrinos, Washington State University; J. L. McClure, Kirkwood Community College; John Pennington, St. Norbert College; Robert Perry, Lock Haven University of Pennsylvania; Robbie C. Pinter, Belmont University; Mary Sue Ply, Southeastern Louisiana University; Linda Rollins, Motlow State Community College; Laura Ross, Seminole Community College; Anne B. Slater, Frederick Community College; Connie White, Salisbury State University; and Karen W. Willingham, Pensacola Junior College.

We express our appreciation to the following reviewers of the third edition: Lynne Diane Beene, University of New Mexico, Albuquerque; Elizabeth Bell, University of South Carolina; Jon Bentley, Albuquerque Technical-Vocational Institute; Debra Boyd, Winthrop College; Judith Burdan, University of North Carolina/Chapel Hill; Phyllis Burke, Hartnell College; Sandra Frisch, Mira Costa College; Gerald Gordon, Black Hills State University; Mamie Hixson, University of West Florida; Sue Ellen Holbrook, Southern Connecticut State University; Linda Hunt, Whitworth College; Rebecca Innocent, Southern Methodist University; Gloria John, Catonsville Community College; Gloria Johnson, Tennessee State University; Suzanne Liggett, Montgomery College; Richard Pepp, Massasoit Community College; Robert Peterson, Middle Tennessee State University; Randy Popkin, Tarleton State University; Nancy Posselt, Midlands

Technical College; George Redmond, Benedict College; Terry Roberts, University of North Carolina/Chapel Hill; Linda Rollins, Motlow State Community College; Gary Sattelmeyer, Trident Technical College; Father Joseph Scallon, Creighton University; Emily Seelbinder, Queens College; Cynthia Smith, University of West Florida; Bill Stiffler, Harford Community College; Nancy Thompson, University of South Carolina/Columbia; Kathleen Tickner, Brevard Community College; Warren Westcott, Frances Marion College; Connie White, Salisbury State University; and Helen Yanko, California State University/Fullerton.

We also thank the following colleagues for their valuable comments on the development of the first and second editions: Chris Abbott, University of Pittsburgh; Virginia Allen, Iowa State University; Stanley Archer, Texas A & M University; Lois Avery, Houston Community College; Rance G. Baker, Alamo Community College; Julia Bates, St. Mary's College of Maryland; John G. Bayer, St. Louis Community College/Meramec; Larry Beason, Texas A & M University; Al Bell, St. Louis Community College at Florissant Valley; Debra Boyd, Winthrop College; Margaret A. Bretschneider, Lakeland Community College; Pat Bridges, Grand Valley State College; Alma Bryant, University of South Florida; Wayne Buchman, Rose State College; David Carlson, Springfield College; Patricia Carter, George Washington University; Faye Chandler, Pasadena City College; Peggy Cole, Arapahoe Community College; Sarah H. Collins, Rochester Institute of Technology; Charles Dodson, University of North Carolina/Wilmington; Margaret Gage, Northern Illinois University; Sharon Gibson, University of Louisville; Owen Gilman, St. Joseph's University; Margaret Goddin, Davis and Elkins College; Ruth Greenberg, University of Louisville; George Haich, Georgia State University; Robert E. Haines, Hillsborough Community College; Ruth Hamilton, Northern Illinois University; Iris Hart, Santa Fe Community College; John Harwood, Penn State University; Michael Herzog, Gonzaga University; Clela Hoggatt, Los Angeles Mission College; Keith N. Hull, University of Wyoming/Laramie; Anne Jackets, Everett Community College; Zena Jacobs, Polytechnic Institute of New York; LaVinia Jennings, University of North Carolina/Chapel Hill; D. G. Kehl, Arizona State University; Philip Keith, St. Cloud State University; George Kennedy, Washington State University; William King, Bethel College; Edward Kline, University of Notre Dame; Susan Landstrom, University of North Carolina/Chapel Hill; Marie Logye, Rutgers University; Helen Marlborough, DePaul University; Nancy Martinez, University of New Mexico/Valencia; Marsha McDonald, Belmont College; Vivien Minshull-Ford, Wichita State University; Robert Moore, SUNY/Oswego; George Murphy, Villanova University; Robert Noreen, California State University/Northridge; L. Sam

Phillips, Gaston College; William Pierce, Prince George's Community College; Robbie Pinter, Belmont College; Nancy Posselt, Midlands Technical College; Robert Post, Kalamazoo Valley Community College; Richard N. Ramsey, Indiana University/Purdue University; Mike Riherd, Pasadena City College; Emily Seelbinder, Wake Forest University; Charles Staats, Broward Community College/North; Frank Steele, Western Kentucky University; Barbara Stevenson, Kennesaw College; Jim Stick, Des Moines Area Community College; James Sodon, St. Louis Community College at Florissant Valley; Josephine K. Tarvers, Rutgers University; Kathleen Tickner, Brevard Community College/Melbourne; George Trail, University of Houston; Daryl Troyer, El Paso Community College; Ben Vasta, Camden County Community College; Connie White, Salisbury State College; Joyce Williams, Jefferson State Junior College; Branson Woodard, Liberty University; and Peter Zoller, Wichita State University.

Among the many people at Harcourt who contributed to this project, we would like to single out Julie McBurney for carrying forward Harcourt's extraordinary commitment to the book.

In addition, we want to acknowledge the very vital day-to-day (sometimes minute-to-minute) contributions of an amazing person: Camille Adkins. Camille, our friend as well as our developmental editor, brought to the project a winning combination: a delightfully droll sense of humor and a pragmatic yet creative editorial approach. We would also like to thank Jon Davies, our project editor, who somehow managed to maintain both high standards and incredible patience.

Once again, we would like to thank our families—Mark, Adam, and Rebecca Kirszner and Demi, David, and Sarah Mandell—who gave us no editorial assistance, did not type the manuscript, and offered no helpful suggestions, but who managed to put up with the general chaos for the duration of another edition.

Finally, we would like to thank each other for making this book a collaboration in the truest sense.

CONTENTS

Contents

Contents

PART 1

COMPOSING AN ESSAY

CHAPTER 1

PLANNING AN ESSAY

? FREQUENTLY ASKED QUESTIONS

Where do I start?   (p. 4)
What does my instructor expect?   (p. 7)
How do I choose a topic?   (p. 10)
How do I find ideas to write about?   (p. 12)

1a   Understanding the Writing Process

Writing enables you to discover ideas, make connections, and see from new perspectives. In this sense, writing is a demanding, creative process of thinking and learning—about yourself, about others, and about your world. In another sense, writing is a tool that empowers you: it enables you to participate in the ongoing dialogue among people who "talk" to each other in letters, newsgroups, memos, petitions, reports, articles, editorials, and books.

Writing is also a constant process of decision making, of selecting, deleting, and rearranging material.

THE WRITING PROCESS

Planning: Consider your purpose, audience, and tone; choose your topic; discover ideas to write about.

Shaping: Decide how to organize your material.

Drafting: Write your first draft.

Revising: "Re-see" what you have written; write additional drafts.

Editing: Check grammar, spelling, punctuation, and mechanics.

Proofreading: Check for typographical errors.

Getting Started (Princeton U.)
   http://webware.princeton.edu/Writing/wc4a.htm
Coping with Writing Anxiety (Purdue)
   http://owl.english.purdue.edu/handouts/general/gl_anxiety.html

The neatly defined stages listed above communicate neither the complexity nor the flexibility of the writing process. These stages actually overlap: as you look for ideas, you may begin to shape your material; as you shape your material, you may begin to write; as you write a draft, you may reorganize your ideas; as you revise, you continue to discover new material. Moreover, these stages are repeated again and again throughout the writing process.

During your college years and in the years that follow, you will develop your own version of the writing process and use it whenever you write, adapting it to the audience, purpose, and writing situation at hand.

EXERCISE 1

Write a paragraph in which you describe your own writing process. What do you do first? What steps do you return to again and again? Which stages do you find most enjoyable? Which do you find most frustrating?

1b Getting Started

Writing presents many situations in which you must **think critically**: make judgments, weigh alternatives, analyze, compare, question, evaluate, and engage in other decision-making activities. Virtually all writing demands that you make informed choices about your subject matter and about the way you present your ideas.

Planning your essay—thinking about what you want to say and how you want to say it—begins well before you actually put your thoughts on paper in any organized way. This planning is as important a part of the writing process as the writing itself.

(1) Determining Your Purpose

Your **purpose** is what you want to accomplish when you write. In general, you write to *express emotions,* to *inform,* or to *persuade.*

Writing to Express Emotions   In diaries and journals, writers explore ideas and feelings to make sense of their experiences; in autobiographical memoirs and in personal letters, they communicate their emotions and reactions to others.

At the age of five, six, well past the time when most other children no longer easily notice the difference between sounds uttered at home and words spoken in public, I had a different experience. I lived in a world magically compounded of sounds. I remained a child longer than most; I lingered too long, poised at the edge of language—often frightened by the sounds of *los gringos,* delighted by the sounds of Spanish at home. I shared with my family a language that was startlingly different from that used in the great city around us. (Richard Rodriguez, *Aria: A Memoir of a Bilingual Childhood*)

Writing to Inform   In newspaper articles, writers report information, communicating to readers; in reference books, instruction manuals, textbooks, and the like, writers provide definitions and explain concepts or processes, trying to help readers see relationships and understand ideas.

Most tarantulas live in the tropics, but several species occur in the temperate zone and a few are common in the southern U.S. Some varieties are large and have powerful fangs with which they can inflict a deep wound. These formidable-looking spiders do not, however, attack man; you can hold one in your hand, if you are gentle, without being bitten. Their bite is dangerous only to insects and small mammals such as mice; for man it is no worse than a hornet's sting. (Alexander Petrunkevitch, "The Spider and the Wasp")

Writing to Persuade   In proposals, editorials, and position papers, writers try to convince readers to accept their position on an issue.

Testing and contact tracing may lead to a person's being deprived of a job, health insurance, housing and privacy, many civil libertarians fear. These are valid and grave concerns. But we can find ways to protect civil rights without sacrificing public health. A major AIDS-prevention campaign ought to be accompanied by intensive public education about the ways the illness is *not* transmitted, by additional safeguards on data banks and by greater penalties for those who abuse HIV victims. It may be harsh to say, but the fact that an individual may suffer as a result of doing what is right does not make doing so less of an imperative. (Amitai Etzioni, "HIV Sufferers Have a Responsibility")

Your purpose for writing determines the material you choose and the way you arrange and express it. For instance, a memoir written by an adult remembering summer camp might *express emotions* about the difficulties experienced during a month away from home, exploring memories of mosquitoes, poison ivy, institutional food, shaving cream fights, and so on. A magazine article about summer camps could *inform*, explaining how camping has changed in the past twenty years, for example. Such an article would present facts and statistics straightforwardly, objectively describing such features as recreational programs and sports facilities. An advertising brochure designed to recruit potential campers could *persuade* by enumerating the benefits of the camping experience. Such a brochure would stress positive details—the opportunity to meet new friends, for example—and deemphasize the possibilities of homesickness and rainy weather. In each case, purpose determines what material is selected and how it is presented.

Whenever you write, you may be guided by one of these three general purposes—in college writing, for example, your purpose is most often to inform or to persuade—or you may have other, more specific aims or a combination of purposes.

✔ CHECKLIST: DETERMINING YOUR PURPOSE

Is your purpose:

- ✔ to express emotions?
- ✔ to inform?
- ✔ to persuade?
- ✔ to explain?
- ✔ to amuse or entertain?
- ✔ to evaluate?
- ✔ to discover?
- ✔ to analyze?
- ✔ to debunk?
- ✔ to draw comparisons?
- ✔ to make an analogy?
- ✔ to define?
- ✔ to criticize?
- ✔ to satirize?
- ✔ to speculate?
- ✔ to warn?
- ✔ to reassure?
- ✔ to take a stand?
- ✔ to identify problems?
- ✔ to suggest solutions?
- ✔ to identify causes?
- ✔ to predict effects?
- ✔ to reflect?
- ✔ to interpret?
- ✔ to instruct?

---

(2) Identifying Your Audience

Because writing is often such a solitary activity, it is easy to forget about your audience. But except for diaries and journals, everything you write addresses an **audience**—a particular set of readers.

At different times, in different roles, you address a variety of audiences. As a citizen, consumer, or member of a community, civic, political, or religious group, you may respond to pressing social, economic, or political issues by writing letters to a newspaper editor, to a public official, to a representative of a special interest group or a business, or to another recipient you do not know well or at all. In your personal life, you may write notes and e-mail messages to friends and family. As an employee, you may write letters, memos, and reports to your superiors, to staff members you supervise, or to workers on your level; you may also be called on to address customers or critics, board members or stockholders, funding agencies or the general public. As a student, you write essays, reports, and other papers addressed to one or more instructors and sometimes to other students or to outside evaluators.

As you move through the stages of the writing process, you shape your paper increasingly in terms of what you believe your audience needs and expects. Your assessment of your readers' interests, educational level, **biases**, and expectations determines not only the information you include but also your emphasis, the arrangement of your material, and the style or tone you adopt.

The Academic Audience   As a student, you most often write for an audience of one: the instructor who assigns the paper. Instructors want to know what you know and whether you can express what you know clearly and accurately. They assign written work to encourage you to use **critical thinking** skills, so the way you organize and express your ideas can be as important as the ideas themselves.

As a group, instructors have certain expectations. They expect correct information, standard grammar and correct spelling, and a logical presentation of ideas. They also expect you to define your terms and to support your generalizations with specifics.

If you are writing in an instructor's academic field, you can omit long overviews and basic definitions. Remember, however, that outside their areas of expertise, most instructors are simply general readers. If you think you may know more about a subject than your instructor does, be sure to provide background, supplying the definitions, examples, and analogies that will make your ideas clear.

NOTE: Keep in mind that because different academic **disciplines** have their own document design formats, documentation styles, methods of reporting data, technical vocabularies, and stylistic conventions, instructors' expectations may vary according to their discipline.

> ✔ **CHECKLIST: IDENTIFYING YOUR AUDIENCE**
>
> ✔ Who will read your paper?
> ✔ What are your audience's needs? Expectations? Biases? Interests?
> ✔ Does your audience need you to supply definitions? Overviews?
>   Examples? Analogies?
> ✔ What does your audience expect in terms of document design?
>   Format? Documentation style? Method of collecting and report-
>   ing data? Use of formulas and symbols or specialized vocabulary?

(3) Setting Your Tone

Tone conveys your attitude. The attitude, or mood, that you adopt as you write may be serious or frivolous, respectful or condescending, intimate or detached. Because tone tells your readers how you feel about your material, it must remain consistent with your purpose and your audience as you write and revise.

Your tone also reveals how you feel toward your readers—sympathetic or superior, concerned or indifferent, friendly or critical. For instance, if you identify with your readers or feel close to them, you use a personal and conversational tone. When you address a general reader indirectly or anonymously, you use a more distant, formal tone.

When your audience is an instructor and your purpose is to inform (as is often the case in college writing situations), you should generally use an objective tone—neither too personal and informal nor too detached and formal—as the following student paragraph does.

> One of the major characteristics of streptococci is that they are gram-positive. This means that after a series of dyes and rinses they take on a violet color. (Gram-negative organisms take on a red color.) Streptococci are also nonspore forming and nonmotile. Most strains produce a protective shield called a capsule. They use organic substances instead of oxygen for their metabolism. This process is called fermentation.

An English composition assignment asking students to write a short, informal essay expressing their feelings about the worst job they ever had calls for an entirely different tone. In the paragraph that follows, the student's tone effectively conveys his attitude toward his job, and his use of the first person encourages audience identification. Sarcastic comments ("good little laborer," "Now here comes the excitement!") contribute to the informal effect.

Every day I followed the same boring, monotonous routine. After clocking in like a good little laborer, I proceeded over to a gray file cabinet, forced open the half-caved-in doors, and removed a staple gun, various packs of size cards, and a blue ballpoint pen. Now here comes the excitement! Each farmer had a specific number assigned to his name. As his cucumbers were being sorted according to their particular size, they were loaded into two-hundred-pound bins, which I had to label with a stapled size card with the farmer's number on it. I had to complete a specific size card for every bin containing that size cucumber. Doesn't it sound wonderful? Any second grader could have handled it. And all the time I worked, the machinery moaned and rattled and the odor of cucumbers filled the air.

In a letter applying for a job, however, the same student would have a different purpose—and, therefore, would use a different tone. In this situation, his distance from his audience and his desire to impress readers with his qualifications would call for a much more objective and straightforward tone.

My primary duty at Germaine Produce was to label cucumbers as they were sorted into bins. I was responsible for making sure each two-hundred-pound bin bore the name of the farmer who had grown those cucumbers and also for keeping track of the cucumbers' sizes. Accuracy was extremely important in this task.

EXERCISE 2

1. Focus on a book that you liked or disliked very much. How would you write about the book in each of the following writing situations? Consider how each writing situation would affect your choice of content, style, organization, tone, and emphasis.

   - A journal entry recording your informal impressions of the book
   - An exam question that asks you to summarize the book's main idea
   - A book review for a composition class in which you evaluate the book's strengths and weaknesses
   - A letter in which you try to convince your local school board that the book should (or should not) be purchased for a public high school's library
   - An editorial for your school newspaper in which you try to persuade other students that the book is worth reading

2. Choose one of the writing situations listed above, and write one paragraph in response to the specified assignment.

(4) Analyzing Your Assignment

Before you begin writing, be sure you understand the exact requirements of your assignment, and keep these guidelines in mind as you write and revise. Don't make any guesses—and don't assume anything. Ask questions, and be sure you understand the answers.

✔ CHECKLIST: ANALYZING YOUR ASSIGNMENT

✔ Has your instructor assigned a specific topic, or are you free to choose your own?
✔ What is the word, paragraph, or page limit?
✔ How much time do you have to complete your assignment?
✔ Will you get feedback from other students or from your instructor? Will anyone review your drafts?
✔ Does the assignment require research?
✔ If the assignment requires a specific format, do you know what its conventions are?

 ## (5) Choosing a Topic

**See
56b
ESL**

If your instructor permits you to choose a topic, be sure to choose one you know something about—or, at least, one you want to learn about. Perhaps a class discussion or reading assignment will suggest a **topic**; maybe you have seen a movie or television program or had a conversation (or even an argument) about an interesting subject.

Most of the time your instructor will steer you toward a topic by giving you an assignment that poses a question for you to answer; specifies a length, format, and subject; or gives a list of subjects from which to choose.

How did the boundaries of Europe change after World War I? (Poses a question)

Write a two-page critical analysis of a film. (Specifies length, format, and general subject)

Write an essay explaining the significance of one of these court decisions: *Marbury v. Madison, Baker v. Carr, Brown v. Board of Education, Roe v. Wade.* (Gives list of specific subjects from which to choose)

Even if your instructor gives you an assignment, however, you cannot start to write immediately. First, you must narrow the assignment to a topic that suits your purpose and audience.

NARROWING AN ASSIGNMENT

Course	*Assignment*	*Topic*
American History	Analyze the effects of a social program on one segment of American society.	How did the GI Bill of Rights affect American servicewomen?
Sociology	Identify and evaluate the success of one resource available to the homeless population of one major American city.	The role of the Salvation Army in meeting the needs of Chicago's homeless
Psychology	Write a three- to five-page paper assessing one method of treating depression.	Animal-assisted therapy for severely depressed patients
Composition	Write an essay about your childhood.	My parents' divorce

---

EXERCISE 3

Read the following excerpt from Ron Kovic's autobiographical *Born on the Fourth of July.* Then, list ten possible essay topics about your own childhood suggested by Kovic's memories of his. (Your assignment is to write a three-page essay about your childhood; your purpose is to give your audience—your composition instructor—a vivid sense of what some aspect of your childhood was like.) Finally, choose the one topic that you feel best qualified to write about, and explain why you selected it.

When we weren't down at the field or watching the Yankees on TV, we were playing whiffle ball and climbing trees checking out birds' nests, going down to Fly Beach in Mrs. Zimmer's old car that honked the horn every time it turned the corner, diving underwater with our masks, kicking with our rubber frog's feet, then running in and out of our sprinklers when we got home, waiting for our turn in the shower. And during the summer nights we were all over the neighborhood, from Bobby's house to Kenny's, throwing gliders, doing handstands and backflips off fences, riding to the woods at the end of the block on our bikes, making rafts, building tree forts, jumping across the streams with tree branches, walking and balancing along the back fence like Houdini, hopping along the slate path all around the back yard seeing how far we could go on one foot.

And I ran wherever I went. Down to school, the candy store, to the deli, buying baseball cards and Bazooka bubblegum that had the little fortunes at the bottom of the cartoons.

When the Fourth of July came, there were fireworks going off all over the neighborhood. It was the most exciting time of year for me next to Christmas. Being born on the exact same day as my country I thought was really great. I was so proud. And every Fourth of July, I had a birthday party and all my friends would come over with birthday presents and we'd put on silly hats and blow these horns my dad brought home from the A&P. We'd eat lots of ice cream and watermelon and I'd open up all the presents and blow out the candles on the big red, white, and blue birthday cake and then we'd all sing "Happy Birthday" and "I'm a Yankee Doodle Dandy." At night everyone would pile into Bobby's mother's old car and we'd go down to the drive-in, where we'd watch the fireworks display. Before the movie started, we'd all get out and sit up on the roof of the car with our blankets wrapped around us watching the rockets and Roman candles going up and exploding into fountains of rainbow colors, and later after Mrs. Zimmer dropped me off, I'd lie on my bed feeling a little sad that it all had to end so soon. As I closed my eyes I could still hear strings of firecrackers and cherry bombs going off all over the neighborhood [. . .].

❓ (6) Finding Something to Say

After you have a topic, you can begin to collect ideas for your paper, using one (or several) of the strategies discussed in the pages that follow. (Each of these strategies is illustrated in Chapter **4.**) Note that many of these activities for finding something to say can (with your instructor's permission) be done in collaboration with other students.

Reading and Observing   The best way to find material to write about is to open your mind to new ideas. As you read textbooks, magazines, and newspapers or browse the **Internet**, be on the lookout for ideas that relate to your topic, and make a point of talking informally with friends or family about it.

Films, television programs, interviews, telephone calls, letters, and questionnaires can also provide material. But be sure your instructor permits such research—and remember to document ideas that are not your own. If you do not, you will be committing **plagiarism**.

Keeping a Journal   Many professional writers keep **journals,** writing in them regularly whether or not they have a specific project in mind. Such a collection of thoughts and ideas can be a valuable resource when you run short of material. Journals, unlike diaries, do more than simply record personal experiences and reactions. In a journal, you explore ideas; you think on paper, asking questions and drawing conclusions. You might, for example, analyze your position on a political issue, try to solve an ethical problem, or trace the evolution of your ideas about an academic assignment. You can also record quotations that have special meaning to you or make notes about your reactions to important news events, films, or conversations. A good journal is a scrapbook of ideas that you can leaf through in search of new material and new ways of looking at old material. The important thing is to *write regularly*—every day if possible—so that when a provocative idea comes along, you won't miss the opportunity to record it. (A sample journal entry appears on pages 45–46.)

Freewriting   Another strategy that can help you discover ideas is **freewriting.** Freewriting is comparable to the stretching exercises that athletes do to warm up. A relatively formless, low-key activity, it is also serious preparation for the highly focused, sometimes strenuous, work that lies ahead. When you freewrite, you let yourself go and write non-stop about anything that comes to mind, moving as quickly as you can. Give yourself a set period of time—say, five minutes—and don't stop to worry about punctuation, spelling, or grammar, or about where your mind is wandering. This strategy encourages your mind to make free associations; thus, it helps you to discover ideas you probably aren't even aware you have. When your time is up, look over what you have written and underline, bracket, or star the most promising ideas. You can then use each of these ideas as the center of a focused freewriting exercise.

When you do **focused freewriting,** you zero in on your topic. Here too you write without stopping to reconsider or reread, so you have no time for counterproductive reactions—no time to be self-conscious about style or form, to worry about the relevance of your ideas, or to count how many words you have and panic about how many more you think you need. At its best, focused freewriting can suggest new details, a new approach to your topic, or even a more interesting topic. (Sample freewriting exercises appear on pages 46–47.)

Brainstorming   One of the most useful ways to accumulate ideas is by brainstorming. This strategy enables you to recall pieces of information and to see connections among them.

When you **brainstorm,** you list all the points you can think of that seem pertinent to your topic, writing down ideas—comments, questions, single words, symbols, or diagrams—as quickly as you can, without pausing to consider their relevance or trying to understand their significance. (A sample brainstorming exercise appears on page 47.)

USING YOUR COMPUTER TO GENERATE IDEAS

You can keep a computer journal, and you can also use your computer for freewriting and brainstorming.

When you freewrite or write a journal entry, try turning down the brightness of the monitor, leaving the screen blank to eliminate distractions and encourage spontaneity.

When you brainstorm, type your notes randomly. Later, after you print them out, you can add further notes and graphic elements (arrows, circles, and so on) to indicate parallels and connections.

Clustering   **Clustering**—sometimes called *webbing* or *mapping*—is similar to brainstorming. As with brainstorming, you don't need to worry about writing complete sentences, and you jot ideas down quickly, without pausing to evaluate their usefulness or to analyze their logical relationships to other ideas. However, clustering encourages you to explore your topic in a somewhat more systematic (and more visual) manner.

Begin making a cluster diagram by writing your topic in the center of a sheet of paper. Then, surround your topic with related ideas as they

Freewriting (Lynchburg College in Virginia)
  http://www.lynchburg.edu/public/writcntr/guide/drafting/freewrit.htm/

occur to you, moving outward from the general topic in the center and writing down increasingly specific ideas and details as you move toward the edges of the page. Eventually, following the path of one idea at a time, you create a diagram (often lopsided rather than symmetrical) that arranges ideas on spokes or branches radiating out from the center (your topic). (A sample cluster diagram appears on page 48.)

Asking Journalistic Questions   **Journalistic questions** offer a more structured way of finding something to say about your topic. (This process is illustrated on page 49.) Your answers to these questions will enable you to explore your topic in an orderly and systematic fashion.

This strategy involves asking six simple questions: *Who? What? Why? Where? When?* and *How?* Journalists often ask these questions to assure themselves that they have explored all angles of a story, and you can use these questions to see whether you have considered all aspects of your topic.

JOURNALISTIC QUESTIONS

Who?   Why?   When?
What?   Where?   How?

Asking In-Depth Questions   If you have time, you can ask a series of more focused questions about your topic. These in-depth questions not only can give you a great deal of information but also can suggest ways for you to eventually shape your ideas into paragraphs and **essays**.

See Ch. 5

IN-DEPTH QUESTIONS

What happened?
When did it happen?
Where did it happen?
} Suggest <u>narration</u> (an account of your first day of school; a summary of Emily Dickinson's life)

What does it look like?
What does it sound like, smell like, taste like, or feel like?
} Suggest <u>description</u> (of the Louvre; of the electron microscope)

What are some typical cases or examples of it?
} Suggests <u>exemplification</u> (three infant day-care settings; four popular fad diets)

(continued on the following page)

(continued from the previous page)

How did it happen? What makes it work? How is it made?	Suggest <u>process</u> (how to apply for financial aid; how a bill becomes a law)
Why did it happen? What caused it? What does it cause? What are its effects?	Suggest <u>cause and effect</u> (events leading to the Korean War; the results of Prohibition; the impact of a new math curriculum on slow learners
How is it like other things? How is it different from other things?	Suggest <u>comparison and contrast</u> (of the popular music of the 1950s and 1960s; of two paintings)
What are its parts or types? Can they be separated or grouped? Do they fall into a logical order? Can they be categorized?	Suggest <u>division and classification</u> (components of the catalytic converter; kinds of occupational therapy; kinds of dietary supplements)
What is it? How does it resemble other members of its class? How does it differ from other members of its class?	Suggest <u>definition</u> (What is Marxism? What is photosynthesis? What is schizophrenia?)

EXERCISE 4

List all the sources you encounter in one day (people, books, magazines, observations, and so on) that could provide you with useful information for the essay you are writing.

EXERCISE 5

Make a cluster diagram and brainstorming notes for the topic you selected in Exercise 3. If you have trouble thinking of material to write about, try freewriting. Then, write a journal entry assessing your progress and evaluating the different strategies for finding something to say. Which strategy worked best for you? Why?

EXERCISE 6

Using the question strategies described on pages 15–16 to supplement the work you did in Exercises 4 and 5, continue generating material for a short essay on your topic from Exercise 3.

CHAPTER 2

SHAPING YOUR MATERIAL

? FREQUENTLY ASKED QUESTIONS

How do I arrange my ideas into an essay?
(p. 17)
What is a thesis? (p. 18)
Where should I place my thesis statement?
(p. 18)
Do I need an outline? (p. 25)

2a Grouping Ideas: Making a Topic Tree

After you have gathered material for your essay and begun to see the direction your ideas are taking, you start to sift through these ideas and choose those you can use in your essay. At this point you may find it useful to make a **topic tree,** a diagram that enables you to arrange material logically and to see relationships among ideas.

✔ CHECKLIST: MAKING A TOPIC TREE

- ✔ Review all your notes carefully.
- ✔ Decide on three or four general categories that best suit your material.
- ✔ Write or type these categories across the top of a piece of paper.
- ✔ Review your notes again to help you select ideas and details that fall within each category.
- ✔ List each idea from your notes under an appropriate heading, moving from general information to increasingly specific details as you work down the page.
- ✔ Draw lines to indicate relationships between ideas in each category.

As you review the material in your notes, and perhaps add new material, you will add, delete, and rearrange the items on the branches of your topic tree. Your completed tree will help you develop a tentative thesis and organize supporting information in your essay. If you go on to prepare an **informal outline**, each branch of your topic tree will probably

See
2c

correspond to one of your outline's major divisions. (A sample topic tree appears on page 50.)

EXERCISE 1

Reread your notes from the work you did for Exercises 3, 5, and 6 in Chapter **1.** Use this material to help you construct a topic tree.

2b Developing a Thesis

Your **thesis** is the main idea of your essay, the central point your essay supports.

(1) Understanding Thesis and Support

The concept of **thesis and support**—stating the **thesis,** or main idea, and then supplying information that explains and develops it—is central to a good deal of the writing you will do in college.

See 6f2–3 As the following diagram illustrates, the essays you will write will consist of an **introductory paragraph**, which opens your essay and states your thesis; a **concluding paragraph**, which closes your essay and gives it a sense of completion, perhaps restating your thesis; and a number of **body paragraphs,** which provide the support for your thesis statement.

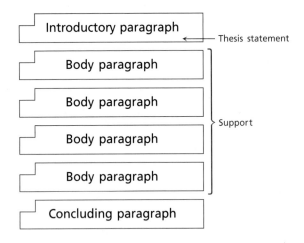

(2) Stating Your Thesis

See 56c ESL An effective **thesis statement** has four characteristics.

1. **An effective thesis statement clearly communicates your essay's main idea.** It tells readers not only what your essay's topic is, but also how you will approach that topic and what you will say about it. Thus, your thesis statement reflects your essay's **purpose**.

See
1b1

2. **An effective thesis statement is more than a general subject, a statement of fact, or an announcement of your intent.**

Subject	Statement of Fact	Announcement
The Draft	The United States currently has no peacetime draft.	In this essay, I will reconsider our country's need for a draft.

Thesis statement Once the military draft may have been necessary to keep the armed forces strong; however, today's all-volunteer force has eliminated the need for a draft.

3. **An effective thesis statement is carefully worded.** Because it communicates your paper's main idea, your thesis statement should be clearly and accurately worded, with careful phrasing that makes your meaning apparent to your readers. Your thesis statement—usually expressed in a single concise sentence—should be direct and straightforward, including no vague or abstract language, overly complex terminology, or unnecessary details that might confuse or mislead readers.

CLOSE UP   **AVOIDING VAGUE LANGUAGE**

Do not use vague phrases, such as *centers on, deals with, involves, revolves around, has a lot to do with,* and *is primarily concerned with.* Be direct and forceful.

INEFFECTIVE THESIS STATEMENT: The real problem in our schools does not *revolve around* the absence of nationwide goals and standards; the problem *is primarily concerned with* the absence of resources with which to implement them.

EFFECTIVE THESIS STATEMENT: The real problem in our schools *is* not the absence of nationwide goals and standards; the problem *is* the absence of resources with which to implement them.

4. **Finally, an effective thesis statement suggests your essay's direction, emphasis, and scope.** Your thesis statement should not make promises that your essay will not fulfill. It should suggest how your ideas are related, in what order your major points should be discussed, and where you should place your emphasis, as the following thesis statement does.

> Widely ridiculed as escape reading, romance novels are becoming increasingly important as a proving ground for many never-before-published writers and, more significantly, as a showcase for strong heroines.

This thesis statement tells readers that the essay to follow will focus on two major new roles of the romance novel: providing markets for new writers and (more important) presenting strong female characters; it also suggests that the role of the romance novel as escapist fiction will be treated briefly. This effective thesis statement, as the diagram below shows, even suggests the order in which the various ideas will be discussed.

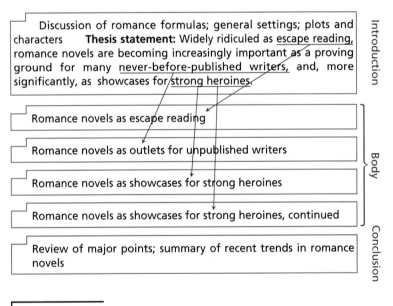

Developing a Thesis (Princeton)
  http://web.princeton.edu/sites/writing/wc4c.htm
Strategies for Writing Thesis Statements (U. of Wisc.)
  http://instruct1.cit.cornell.edu/courses/hist100.96/ThesisStatements.html

USING ORIGINAL PHRASING

One of the simplest kinds of thesis statements to write is also one of the dullest and most mechanical: the "three points" (or "four reasons" or "five examples") thesis. This thesis statement enumerates each of the specific points to be discussed ("Hot air ballooning is an exciting sport for three reasons: x, y, and z"), and the paper that follows goes on to cover each of these points, using the same tired language: "The first reason hot air ballooning is so exciting is x"; "Another reason is y"; "The most important reason is z." This kind of formulaic thesis statement can be a very useful strategy for a rough draft, but as you revise, you should try to substitute fresher, more interesting, and more original language.

✔ CHECKLIST: STATING YOUR THESIS

- ✔ Does your thesis statement clearly communicate your essay's main idea? Does it suggest the approach you will take toward your material? Does it reflect your essay's purpose?
- ✔ Is your thesis statement more than a subject, a statement of fact, or an announcement of your intent?
- ✔ Is your thesis statement carefully worded?
- ✔ Does your thesis statement suggest your essay's direction, emphasis, and scope?

(3) Revising Your Thesis Statement

Occasionally—especially if you know a lot about your topic—you may begin writing with a thesis in mind. Most often, however, your thesis evolves out of the reading, questioning, and grouping of ideas that you do during the planning stage of the writing process.

The thesis statement that you develop as you plan your essay is only tentative. As you write and rewrite, you often think of new ideas and see new connections; as a result, you may modify your essay's direction, emphasis, and scope several times, and if you do so, you must reword your thesis statement as well. Notice how the following thesis statements changed as the writers moved through successive drafts of their essays.

REVISING YOUR THESIS STATEMENT

Tentative Thesis Statement (rough draft)	*Revised Thesis Statement (final draft)*
Professional sports can easily be corrupted by organized crime.	Although supporters of legalized sports betting argue that organized crime cannot make inroads into professional sports, the way in which underworld figures compromised the 1919 World Series suggests the opposite.
Laboratory courses provide valuable educational experiences.	By providing students with the actual experience of doing scientific work, laboratory courses encourage precise thinking, careful observation, and creativity.
It is difficult to understand Henry James's short novel *The Turn of the Screw* without examining the personality of the governess.	A careful reading of Henry James's *The Turn of the Screw* suggests that the governess is an unreliable narrator, incapable of distinguishing appearance from reality.

(4) Using a Thesis Statement to Shape Your Essay

The wording of your thesis statement often suggests not only a possible order and emphasis for your essay's ideas, but also a specific **pattern of development**—*narration, description, exemplification, process, cause and effect, comparison and contrast, division and classification,* or *definition.* These familiar patterns may also shape individual paragraphs of your essay.

Thesis Statement	*Pattern of Development*
As the months went by and I grew more and more involved with the developmentally delayed children at the Learning Center, I came to see how important it is to treat every child as an individual.	Narration

Looking around the room where I had spent my childhood, I realized that every object I saw told me I was now an adult.

Description

The risk-taking behavior that has characterized the past decade can be illustrated by the increasing interest and involvement in such high-risk sports as mountain biking, ice climbing, sky diving, and bungee jumping.

Exemplification

Armed forces basic training programs take recruits through a series of tasks designed to build camaraderie as well as skills and confidence.

Process

The exceptionally high birthrate of the post-World War II years had many significant social and economic consequences.

Cause and Effect

Although people who live in cities and people who live in small towns have some obvious basic similarities, their views on issues like crime, waste disposal, farm subsidies, and educational vouchers tend to be very different.

Comparison and Contrast

The section of the proposal that recommends establishing satellite health centers is quite promising; unfortunately, however, the sections that call for the creation of alternative educational programs, job training, and low-income housing are seriously flawed.

Division and Classification

Thesis Statement	*Pattern of Development*
Until quite recently, most people assumed that rape was an act perpetrated by a stranger, but today's wider definition encompasses acquaintance rape as well.	Definition

EXERCISE 2

Analyze the following items and explain why none of them qualifies as an effective thesis statement. How could each be improved?

1. In this essay, I will examine the environmental effects of residential and commercial development on the coastal regions of the United States.
2. Residential and commercial development in the coastal regions of the United States
3. How to avoid coastal overdevelopment
4. Coastal Development: Pro and Con
5. Residential and commercial development of America's coastal regions benefits some people, but it has some disadvantages.
6. The environmentalists' position on coastal development
7. More and more coastal regions in the United States are being overdeveloped.
8. Residential and commercial development guidelines need to be developed for coastal regions of the United States.
9. Coastal development is causing beach erosion.
10. At one time I enjoyed walking on the beach, but commercial and residential development has ruined the experience for me.

EXERCISE 3

For three of the following topics, formulate a clearly worded thesis statement.

1. A literary work that has influenced your thinking
2. Cheating in college
3. The validity of SAT scores as the basis for college admissions
4. Should women in the military serve in combat?
5. Private versus public education

6. Should college health clinics provide birth control services?
7. Is governmental censorship of art justified?
8. The role of the individual in saving the earth
9. The portrayal of an ethnic group in film or television
10. Should smoking be banned from all public places?

EXERCISE 4

Review the topic tree you made in Exercise 1. Use it to help you to develop a thesis for an essay on the topic you chose in Exercise 3 in Chapter **1.**

2c Preparing an Informal Outline

Once you have a thesis statement, you may want to prepare an informal outline. An **outline** is a blueprint for an essay, a plan that gives you more detailed, specific guidance than a thesis statement does. You don't always need to prepare an outline; a short essay on a topic with which you are very familiar may require nothing beyond a thesis statement and a list of three or four main supporting points. Often, however, you will find that you need the additional help of an **informal outline,** one that arranges your essay's main points and supporting ideas and details in an informal but orderly way to guide you as you write. (A sample informal outline appears on pages 51–52.)

✔ **CHECKLIST: PREPARING AN INFORMAL OUTLINE**

✔ Copy down the categories and subcategories from your **topic tree**.

✔ Arrange the categories and subcategories in the order in which you plan to discuss them.

✔ Expand the outline with additional material from your notes, adding any new points that come to mind.

See 2a

NOTE: For a short paper, an informal outline is usually sufficient. Sometimes, however—particularly when you are writing a long or complex essay—you will need to construct a **formal outline**, which indicates both the exact order of all the ideas you will explore and the relationship of those ideas to one another.

See 3c3

EXERCISE 5

Find an editorial in the newspaper. Then, prepare an informal outline that includes all the writer's main points and supporting ideas. (Use the model outline in **4b3** as a guide.)

EXERCISE 6

Prepare an informal outline for the paper you have been developing in Chapters **1** and **2.**

Outlining (Purdue)
   http://owl.english.purdue.edu/Handouts/General/GL_Outlin.html

CHAPTER 3

DRAFTING AND REVISING

? FREQUENTLY ASKED QUESTIONS

How do I revise my drafts?   (p. 30)
What's the difference between *revising* and *editing?*   (p. 40)
How much can I rely on spell checkers and grammar checkers?   (p. 42)
How do I find a title for my paper?   (p. 42)

3a Writing a Rough Draft

(1) Understanding Drafting

As its name implies, a rough draft is far from perfect; in fact, it usually includes false starts, irrelevant information, and unrelated details. At this stage, though, the absence of focus and order is not a problem. You write your rough draft simply to get your ideas down on paper so that you can react to them. You should expect to add or delete words, to reword sentences, to rethink ideas, and to reorder paragraphs. You should also expect to discover some new ideas—or even to take an unexpected detour.

When you write your rough draft, concentrate on the body of your essay, and don't waste time mapping out your introduction and conclusion. The effort to write appropriate and effective opening and closing paragraphs will slow you down; besides, these paragraphs are likely to change substantially in subsequent drafts. For now, focus on drafting the support paragraphs of your essay. (A sample rough draft appears on pages 52–53.)

(2) Developing Drafting Strategies

Taking a practical and systematic approach to your first draft will greatly simplify the revision process.

STRATEGIES FOR WRITING A ROUGH DRAFT

- **Prepare your work area.** Once you begin to write, you should not have to stop because you need a sharp pencil, better lighting, important notes, or anything else.
- **Fight writer's block.** An inability to start (or continue) writing, **writer's block** is usually caused by fear that you will not write well or that you have nothing to say. If you really don't feel ready to write, take a short break. If you decide that you really don't have enough ideas to get you started, return to one of the strategies for <u>finding something to say</u>.
- **Get your ideas down on paper as quickly as you can.** Don't worry about sentence structure, about spelling and punctuation, or about finding exactly the right word—just write. Writing quickly helps you uncover new ideas and new connections between ideas. You may find that following an informal outline enables you to move smoothly from one point to the next, but if you find this structure too confining, go ahead and write without consulting your outline.
- **Take regular breaks as you write.** Try writing one section of your essay at a time. When you have completed a section—for example, one paragraph—take a break. Your mind may continue to focus on your assignment while you do other things. When you return to your essay, writing may be easier.
- **Leave yourself enough time to revise.** All writing benefits from revision, so be sure you have time to reconsider your work and to write as many drafts as you need.

See
1b6

You should always approach your rough draft (as well as all subsequent drafts before the one you hand in for a grade) as something you know you will revise. This means taking three steps to make your draft physically receptive to revision.

1. Triple-space your draft. (If you handwrite your draft, write on every other line.) This makes errors more obvious and also gives you plenty of room to add new material or to try out new versions of sentences.
2. If you do a handwritten draft, be sure you write on only one side of a sheet of paper so you can reread your pages side by side. Writing on only one side also permits you to cut and paste without destroying

material on the other side of the page. This strategy gives you the flexibility to keep reorganizing the sections or paragraphs of your paper until you find their most effective arrangement.

3. Finally, develop a system of symbols, each designating a different type of revision. For instance, you can circle individual words or box longer groups of words (or even entire paragraphs) that you want to relocate. You can use an arrow to indicate the new location, or you can use matching numbers or letters to indicate how you want to re-arrange ideas. When you want to add words, use a caret like this.

DRAFTING YOUR ESSAY

Because it is much more difficult to see errors on the computer screen than on hard copy, it is a good idea to print out every draft so that you can revise on paper rather than on the screen, making revisions by hand on your printed draft and then returning to the computer to type these changes into your document. If you do revise directly on the computer screen, be very careful not to delete any material that you may need later; instead, move this material to the end of your document so that you can assess its usefulness later on and retrieve it if necessary. As you type your drafts, get into the habit of including notes to yourself in parentheses or brackets, perhaps highlighting these comments and questions by using boldface or italic type.

EXERCISE 1

Write a rough draft of the essay you began planning in Chapter **1**.

3b Revising Your Drafts

(1) Understanding Revision

Revision is a process you engage in from the moment you begin to discover ideas for your essay. As you work, you are constantly rethinking your ideas and reconsidering their relevance, their relative importance, the logical and sequential relationships between them, and the patterns in which you arrange them. Revision is a creative part of the writing process, and everyone does it somewhat differently. You will have to experiment to find the techniques that work best for you.

Inexperienced writers often do little more than change a word here and there, correct grammatical or mechanical errors, or reprint their papers to make them neater. Experienced writers, however, expect revision to involve a major reworking of their papers, so they are willing to rethink a thesis statement or even to completely rewrite and rearrange an essay.

(2) Moving from Rough to Final Draft

Often, you write your rough draft without thinking much about your audience. When you revise, however, you should begin to make the kinds of changes that your readers need in order to understand and appreciate your ideas. Thus, revision should reflect not only your private criticism of your first draft but also your anticipation of your readers' needs and reactions.

✔ CHECKLIST: REVISING TO ACCOMMODATE YOUR READERS

- ✔ **Present one idea at a time and summarize when necessary.** When you overload your paper with more information than readers can take in, you lose their attention. Readers should not have to backtrack constantly to understand your message.
- ✔ **Organize your ideas clearly.** Readers expect your essay to do what your thesis statement says it will do, with major points introduced in a logical order and supported in your body paragraphs.
- ✔ **Provide clear signals to establish coherence.** Repeating key points, constructing clear topic sentences, using **transitional words and phrases** to link ideas logically, and providing verbal cues that indicate the precise relationships among ideas all help provide continuity and coherence.

See
6c2

As you revise successive drafts of your essay, you should shift your focus from larger elements, such as overall structure and content, to increasingly smaller elements. (You can see the progression of the revision process through several drafts in the work of the student writer in **4c**.)

Revising Your Rough Draft   After you finish your rough draft, set it aside for a day or two if you can. When you return to it, focus on only a few areas at a time. As you review this first draft, evaluate the thesis-and-support structure of your essay and your paper's general organization. Once you feel satisfied that your thesis statement says what you want it to say and that your essay's content supports this thesis and is logically arranged, you can turn your attention to other matters.

As you reread this draft, you may want to consult the questions in the "Revising the Whole Essay" checklist on page 37. If you have the benefit of a collaborative revision session or of a conference with your instructor, consider your readers' comments carefully, focusing for now on their suggestions about content, organization, and thesis and support.

Writing and Revising Additional Drafts   After you have read over your rough draft several times, marking it up with notes and outlining plans for revision, you are ready to write a second draft.

As you assess this draft, as well as any drafts that follow, you will narrow your focus to your essay's individual paragraphs, sentences, and words; if you like, you can use the "Revising Paragraphs," "Revising Sentence Style," and "Revising Word Choice" checklists on pages 38–39 to guide your revision.

Preparing a Final Draft   Once you have revised your drafts to your satisfaction, two final tasks remain: **editing** and **proofreading** your paper.

See
3d

3c   Using Revision Strategies

Everyone revises differently, and every writing task demands a slightly different process of revision. Four strategies in particular can help you revise at any stage of the writing process. (These strategies are illustrated in Chapter **4**.)

(1) Doing Collaborative Revision

Instead of trying to imagine an audience for your paper, you can address a real audience, doing **collaborative revision** by asking friends, classmates, or family members to read your draft and comment on it (with your instructor's permission, of course). Collaborative revision can also be more formal. Your instructor may conduct the class as a workshop, assigning students to work in groups to critique other students' essays, perhaps answering such questions as those included in the checklist below.

✔ CHECKLIST: DOING COLLABORATIVE REVISION

- ✔ What is the essay about? Does the topic fulfill the requirements of the assignment?
- ✔ What is the essay's main idea? Is the thesis clearly worded? If not, how can the wording be improved?
- ✔ Is the essay arranged logically? Do the body paragraphs appear in an appropriate order?
- ✔ What ideas support the thesis? Does each body paragraph develop one of these ideas?
- ✔ Is any necessary information missing? Identify any areas that seem to need further development. Is any information irrelevant? If so, suggest possible deletions.
- ✔ Can you think of any ideas or examples from your own reading, experience, or observations that would strengthen the writer's essay?
- ✔ Can you follow the writer's ideas? If not, would clearer connections between sentences or paragraphs be helpful? If so, where are such connections needed?
- ✔ Is the introductory paragraph interesting to you? Would another opening strategy be more effective?
- ✔ Does the conclusion leave you with a sense of closure? Would another concluding strategy be more effective?
- ✔ Is anything unclear or confusing?
- ✔ What is the essay's greatest strength?
- ✔ What is the essay's greatest weakness?

---

(2) Using Instructors' Comments

Instructors' comments—in correction symbols, in marginal comments, or in conferences—can also help you revise.

Correction Symbols   Your instructor may indicate concerns about style, grammar, mechanics, or punctuation by using the correction symbols listed on the inside back cover of this book. Instead of correcting a problem, the instructor will simply identify it and supply the number of the section in this handbook that deals with the error. After reading the appropriate pages, you should be able to make the necessary corrections on your own. For example, the symbol and number beside the following sentence referred a student to **29f2,** the section in the handbook that discusses sexist usage.

DRAFT WITH INSTRUCTOR'S COMMENT: Equal access to jobs is a desirable goal for all mankind.   *Sexist Usage—see 29f2*

After reading section **29f2,** the student made the following change.

REVISED: Equal access to jobs is a desirable goal for everyone.

(For examples of an instructor's use of correction symbols on a student paper, see **4c3.**)

Marginal Comments   Instructors frequently make marginal comments on your essays to suggest changes in content or structure. Such comments may ask you to add supporting information or to arrange paragraphs differently within the essay, or they may recommend stylistic changes, such as more varied sentences. Marginal comments may also question your logic, suggest a more explicit thesis statement, ask for clearer transitions, or propose a new direction for a discussion. In some cases, you can consider these comments to be suggestions rather than corrections. You may decide to incorporate these ideas into a revised draft of your essay, and then again, you may not. In all instances, however, you should consider your instructor's comments seriously. (A student draft with marginal comments appears in **4c3.**)

Conferences   Many instructors require or encourage one-on-one conferences, and you should certainly schedule a conference if you can. (Some instructors also use **e-mail** to answer questions and offer feedback at various points in the writing process.) During a conference, you can respond to your instructor's questions and ask for clarification of marginal comments. If a certain section of your paper is a problem, use your conference time to focus on it, perhaps asking for help in sharpening your thesis or choosing more accurate words.

See
12a1

✔ CHECKLIST: PREPARING FOR A CONFERENCE

- ✔ Make an appointment.
- ✔ Read your paper carefully before coming to the conference.
- ✔ Prepare a list of questions.
- ✔ Bring your draft to the conference.
- ✔ Take notes as you discuss your paper.
- ✔ Participate actively.

(3) Making a Formal Outline

Making a formal outline can help you to plan and shape a draft before you write it, but an outline can also guide you as you revise, helping you to check the structure of a draft that you have already completed.

Outlining can be helpful early in the revision process, when you are reworking the larger structural elements of your essay, or later on, when you are checking the logic of a completed draft. For example, a formal outline reveals at once whether points are irrelevant or poorly placed—or, worse, missing. It also reveals the hierarchy of your ideas—which points are dominant and which are subordinate.

A **formal outline** uses a system of letters and numbers to indicate the order of your ideas and the relationship of main ideas to supporting details. A formal outline is more polished and more detailed than an **informal outline**. It is more strictly parallel and more precise, pays more attention to form, and presents points in the exact order in which you plan to present them in your draft.

A formal outline may be a **topic outline,** in which each entry is a single word or a short phrase, or a **sentence outline,** in which each entry is a complete sentence. (A sentence outline is a more fully developed guide for your paper: you have a head start on your paper when you are able to use the sentences of your outline in your draft. Because it is so polished and complete, however, a sentence outline is more difficult and time consuming to construct, especially at an early stage of the writing process.)

Formal outlines conform to specific conventions of structure, content, and style. If you follow the conventions of outlining carefully, your formal outline can help you make sure that your paper presents all relevant ideas in an effective order, with appropriate emphasis.

THE CONVENTIONS OF OUTLINING

Structure

- Outline format should be followed strictly.

    I. First major point of your paper
      A. First subpoint
      B. Next subpoint
        1. First supporting example
        2. Next supporting example
          a. First specific detail
          b. Next specific detail
    II. Second major point

- Headings should not overlap.
- No heading should have a single subheading. (A category cannot be subdivided into one part.)
- Each entry should be preceded by an appropriate letter or number, followed by a period.
- The first word of each entry should be capitalized.

Content

- Outline should include the paper's thesis statement.
- Outline should cover only the body of the essay, not the introductory or concluding paragraphs.
- Headings should be concise and specific.
- Headings should be descriptive, clearly related to the topic to which they refer.

Style

- Headings of the same rank should be grammatically parallel.
- Sentence outlines should use complete sentences, with all sentences in the same tense.
- In a sentence outline, each entry should end with a period.
- Topic outlines should use words or short phrases, with all headings of the same rank using the same parts of speech.
- In a topic outline, entries should not end with periods.

The page that follows presents side-by-side topic and sentence outlines of this chapter. (An additional topic outline appears on pages 61–62; an additional sentence outline appears on pages 62–64.)

Topic Outline of Chapter 3—Writing and Revising

I. Writing a rough draft
   A. Understanding drafting
   B. Developing drafting strategies
II. Revising your drafts
   A. Understanding revision
   B. Moving from rough to final draft
      1. Revising your rough draft
      2. Writing and revising additional drafts
      3. Preparing a final draft
III. Using revision strategies
   A. Doing collaborative revision
   B. Using instructor comments
      1. Using correction symbols
      2. Using marginal comments
      3. Using conferences
   C. Making a formal outline
   D. Using checklists
IV. Editing and proofreading

Sentence Outline of Chapter 3—Writing and Revising

I. Before you revise, you must write a rough draft.
   A. In a rough draft, your purpose is to get ideas down on paper.
   B. As you draft, take a practical and systematic approach to the process.
II. Once you have completed your first draft, you can begin to revise.
   A. Understand that revision is a natural part of the writing process.
   B. As you move from rough to final draft, narrow your focus.
      1. When you reread your rough draft, focus on content and organization.
      2. When you revise additional drafts, focus on paragraphs, sentences, and words.
      3. When you prepare your final draft, focus on editing and proofreading.
III. Certain specific strategies can aid the revision process.
   A. Collaborative revision is one useful revision strategy.
   B. Instructor comments can also guide your revision.
      1. Instructors often use correction symbols to refer you to specific sections of your handbook.
      2. Instructors also write marginal comments on your essays.
      3. Finally, instructors offer suggestions in conferences.
   C. A formal outline is another helpful revision strategy.
   D. Checklists can also help you to revise.
IV. The last stage of the writing process is editing and proofreading your paper.
   A. When you edit, scrutinize grammar, punctuation, mechanics, and spelling.
   B. When you proofread, check for typographical errors.

(4) Using Checklists

A **revision checklist**—one that your instructor prepares or one that you develop yourself—enables you to examine your writing systematically by helping you to focus on revising one element at a time. Depending on the problems you have and the amount of time you have to deal with them, you can survey your paper using all the questions on a checklist or only some of them.

The four revision checklists that follow are keyed to sections of this text. They parallel the normal revision process, moving from the most global to the most specific concerns. As your understanding of the writing process increases and you become better able to assess the strengths and weaknesses of your writing, you may want to add items to (or delete items from) one or more of the checklists. You can also use your instructors' comments to tailor these checklists to your own needs.

✔ CHECKLIST: REVISING THE WHOLE ESSAY

- ✔ Is your tone consistent with your purpose? (See **1b3.**)
- ✔ Have you maintained an appropriate distance from your readers? (See **1b3.**)
- ✔ Are thesis and support logically related, with each body paragraph supporting your thesis statement? (See **2b1.**)
- ✔ Is your thesis statement clearly and specifically worded? (See **2b2.**)
- ✔ Have you discussed everything promised in your thesis statement? (See **2b2.**)
- ✔ Have you deleted irrelevant points? (See **2b2.**)
- ✔ Have you presented your ideas in a logical sequence? Can you think of a different arrangement that might be more appropriate for your purpose? (See **2b4.**)
- ✔ Do clear transitions between paragraphs allow your readers to follow your essay's structure? (See **6c6.**)
- ✔ Does your essay follow a particular pattern of development? (See Ch. **5.**)

✔ CHECKLIST: REVISING PARAGRAPHS

✔ Does each body paragraph have one main idea? (See **6b**.)

✔ Are topic sentences clearly worded and logically related to your thesis? (See **6b1**.)

✔ Are your body paragraphs adequately developed? (See **6e**.)

✔ Does your introductory paragraph arouse reader interest and prepare readers for what is to come? (See **6f2**.)

✔ Does each body paragraph have a clear organizing principle? (See **6c1**.)

✔ Are the relationships of sentences within paragraphs clear? (See **6c2–5**.)

✔ Are your paragraphs arranged according to familiar patterns of development? (See **6e**.)

✔ Does your concluding paragraph sum up your main points? (See **6f3**.)

✔ Have you provided transitional paragraphs where necessary? (See **6f1**.)

✔ CHECKLIST: REVISING SENTENCE STYLE

✔ Have you strengthened sentences with repetition, balance, and parallelism? (See **21c–d, 27a**.)

✔ Have you avoided overloading sentences with too many clauses? (See **22c**.)

✔ Have you used correct sentence structure? (See Chs. **24** and **25**.)

✔ Have you placed modifiers clearly and logically? (See Ch. **26**.)

✔ Have you avoided potentially confusing shifts in tense, voice, mood, person, or number? (See **28a–d**.)

✔ Are your sentences constructed logically? (See **28f–h**.)

✔ Have you used emphatic word order? (See **21a**.)

✔ Have you used sentence structure to signal the relative importance of clauses in a sentence and their logical relationship to one another? (See **21b**.)

✔ Have you eliminated nonessential words and unnecessary repetition? (See **22a–b**.)

✔ Have you varied your sentence structure? (See Ch. **23**.)

✔ Have you combined sentences where ideas are closely related? (See **23b**.)

✔ CHECKLIST: REVISING WORD CHOICE

✔ Is your level of diction appropriate for your audience and your purpose? (See **29a–b.**)

✔ Have you selected words that accurately reflect your intentions? (See **29b1.**)

✔ Have you chosen words that are specific, concrete, and unambiguous? (See **29b3–4.**)

✔ Have you enriched your writing with figurative language? (See **29d.**)

✔ Have you eliminated jargon, neologisms, pretentious diction, clichés, ineffective figures of speech, and offensive language from your writing? (See **29c, 29e–f.**)

EXERCISE 2

Revise your rough draft, using one or more of the strategies for revision discussed in **3c.** Focus on your paper's thesis and support and on content and arrangement of ideas. Try not to worry now about stylistic issues, such as sentence variety and word choice.

EXERCISE 3

Review the second draft of your paper, this time focusing on paragraphing, topic sentences, and transitions, and on the way you structure your sentences and select your words. If possible, ask a friend to read your draft and to respond to the collaborative revision questions in **3c1.** Then, revise your draft, incorporating any suggestions you find helpful.

EXERCISE 4

Using the revision checklists in **3c4** as a guide, create a customized checklist—one that reflects the specific concerns that you need to consider when you revise an essay. Then, revise your essay according to this checklist.

❓ 3d Editing and Proofreading

The last stage of the writing process is editing and proofreading your paper.

Editing When you **edit,** you concentrate on grammar and spelling, punctuation and mechanics. You will have done some of this work as you revised previous drafts of your paper, but now your *focus* is on editing. Approach your work critically, reading each sentence carefully. As you proceed, consult the items on the editing checklist on page 41. Keep your preliminary notes and drafts and reference books (such as this handbook and a current dictionary) nearby as you edit.

EDITING AND PROOFREADING

- As you edit and proofread, try looking at only a small portion of text at a time. If your software allows you to split the screen and create another window, create one so small that you can see only one or two lines of text. If you use this technique, you can dramatically reduce the number of surface-level errors in your paper.
- Use the *search* or *find* command to look for words or phrases in usage errors you commonly make—for instance, confusing *it's* with *its, lay* with *lie, effect* with *affect, their* with *there,* or *too* with *to.* You can also locate inadvertent use of <u>sexist language</u> by searching for words like *he, his, him,* or *man.*
- Keep in mind that neatness does not equal correctness. The computer's ability to produce neat-looking text can disguise flaws that might otherwise be readily apparent.

See
29f2

Proofreading After you have completed your editing, print a final draft. Now you must proofread, rereading every word carefully to make sure neither you nor your computer missed any errors. You must also make sure the final typed copy of your paper conforms to your instructor's format requirements.

✔ CHECKLIST: EDITING AND PROOFREADING

GRAMMAR

✔ Have you used the appropriate case for each pronoun? (See **33a–b.**)
✔ Are pronoun references clear and unambiguous? (See **33c.**)
✔ Are verb forms correct? (See **34a.**)
✔ Are tense, mood, and voice of verbs logical and appropriate? (See **34b–d.**)
✔ Do subjects and verbs agree? (See **35a.**)
✔ Do pronouns and antecedents agree? (See **35b.**)
✔ Are adjectives and adverbs used correctly? (See **36a–e.**)

PUNCTUATION

✔ Is end punctuation used correctly? (See Ch. **37.**)
✔ Are commas used correctly? (See Ch. **38.**)
✔ Are semicolons used correctly? (See Ch. **39.**)
✔ Are apostrophes used correctly? (See Ch. **40.**)
✔ Are quotation marks used where they are required? (See Ch. **41.**)
✔ Are quotation marks used correctly with other punctuation marks? (See **41d.**)
✔ Are other punctuation marks—colons, dashes, parentheses, brackets, slashes, and ellipses—used correctly? (See Ch. **42.**)

MECHANICS

✔ Is capitalization consistent with standard English usage? (See Ch. **43.**)
✔ Are italics used correctly? (See Ch. **44.**)
✔ Are hyphens used where required and placed correctly within and between words? (See Ch. **45.**)
✔ Are abbreviations used where convention calls for their use? (See Ch. **46.**)
✔ Are numerals and spelled-out numbers used appropriately? (See Ch. **47.**)

SPELLING

✔ Are all words spelled correctly? (Run a spell check, and check a dictionary if necessary.)

Proofreading (Bowling Green)
http://www.bgsu.edu/departments/writing-lab/goproofreading.html

USING SPELL CHECKERS AND GRAMMAR CHECKERS

Spell checkers and grammar checkers can make the process of editing and proofreading your papers a lot easier. Remember, though, that both have limitations. Neither a spell checker nor a grammar checker is a substitute for careful editing and proofreading.

- **Spell checkers** A spell checker simply identifies strings of letters it does not recognize; it does *not* distinguish between homophones or spot every typographical error. For example, it does not recognize *there* in "They forgot there books" as incorrect, nor does it spot a typo that produces a correctly spelled word, such as *word* for *work* or *thing* for *think*. Moreover, a spell checker is not likely to include every word you might use. For technical terms, proper nouns, and foreign words, for example, a spell checker may not be much help.

- **Grammar checkers** Grammar checkers are not always accurate. For example, they may identify a long sentence as a run-on when it is in fact grammatically correct, and they generally advise against using passive voice—even in contexts where it is appropriate. Moreover, grammar checkers do not always supply answers; often, they ask questions—for example, whether *which* should be *that* or *which* preceded by a comma—that you must answer, based on what you know or what you can find out. In short, grammar checkers can guide your editing, but you yourself must always be the one who decides when a sentence is (or is not) correct.

  CHOOSING A TITLE

When you are ready to decide on a title for your essay, keep these points in mind.

- A title should be descriptive, giving readers an accurate sense of your essay's focus. Whenever possible, include one or more of the key words and phrases that are central to your paper.

- A title's wording can echo the wording of your assignment, reminding you (and your instructor) that you have not lost sight of it.
- Ideally, a title should arouse interest, perhaps by using a provocative question or a suitable quotation (or, if appropriate, by introducing a note of controversy).

ASSIGNMENT: Write about a problem faced on college campuses today.

TOPIC: Free speech on campus

POSSIBLE TITLES:

Free Speech: A Problem for Today's Colleges (descriptive; echoes wording of assignment and includes key words of essay)

How Free Should Free Speech on Campus Be? (provocative question)

The Right to "Shout 'Fire' in a Crowded Theater" (quotation)

Hate Speech: A Dangerous Abuse of Free Speech on Campus (controversial position)

EXERCISE 5

Using the editing checklist on page 41 as a guide, edit your essay. Then, prepare a final draft, being sure to proofread it carefully, and give it an appropriate title.

EXERCISE 6

Review your response to Exercise 1 in Chapter **1.** How has your personal writing process changed since you wrote that response?

Introductions, Conclusions, and Titles (George Mason U.)
   http://www.gmu.edu/departments/writingcenter/handouts/introcon.html

CHAPTER 4

WRITER'S NOTEBOOK: COMPOSING AN ESSAY

This chapter follows the writing process of Nguyen Dao, a first-year composition student. Nguyen's instructor gave the class the following assignment.

> Write a short essay about a problem you face that you believe is unique to you. Be sure that your essay has a clearly stated thesis and that it helps readers to understand your problem and why it troubles you.

The instructor gave the class two weeks to complete the assignment and did not permit students to do research. She explained that she was going to require some collaborative work, so Nguyen knew that his classmates would read and react to his paper.

Because this paper was the class's first full-length assignment, the instructor asked students to take a systematic approach to the writing process, experimenting with different kinds of activities designed to help them plan, shape, write, and revise their essays. Although not all these strategies would work equally well for each student or each topic, she wanted students to discover which activities worked best for them. For this reason, she asked them to write a brief reaction to each activity after completing it. In addition to illustrating Nguyen Dao's writing process, the pages that follow include his reactions (in italics).

4a   Planning an Essay

(1) Choosing a Topic

Thinking up possible topics wasn't too hard. I've had plenty of problems lately. Some topics I thought about were specific things, like the trouble I had convincing my parents to let me live at school, and my decision to study political science and give up the idea of being a doctor. I also thought about more general, long-standing problems: dealing with my parents' strict rules and their limited English skills. I saw all these different problems as related to my being Asian American. Then this made me think about the problem of how Asian Americans are always stereotyped as family oriented, science oriented, or success oriented, which is not always true. Dealing with what people expect of me—because I'm supposed to be a "typical Asian" or "model minority"—is a problem I've always faced.

(2) Finding Something to Say

Reading and Observing

Writing about a problem I face that's unique to me isn't something I need to do any reading about. I know all about being stereotyped. I've had this problem for almost 19 years. I figured it would be a good idea to listen more closely to the kind of things people say about Asians all the time (the things I usually tune out) on TV or even right to my face. One thing I heard was the idea that Asians come to the US and take unskilled entry-level jobs away from American citizens. (Someone on talk radio was really steamed about this.) Maybe I can use this idea—maybe not.

Keeping a Journal

I really hated the idea of writing in a journal, but I guess it works. When I reread my first entry, it helped to remind me that my paper didn't have to be a confession or an argument about what's wrong with my life.

JOURNAL ENTRY   ❓

I'm not really comfortable writing about being Asian American, but I have to admit it's a good topic for a paper about a problem I have. A lot of my problems seem to come from the ideas about what other people think Asians are supposed to do or be. But I don't want to get too personal because other people are going to read what I write, and it could get embarrassing. I don't want them to know about fights I have with my parents over what they think a good Asian son should be. It's like in that story where the Chinese mother tells her daughter there are two kinds of daughters—obedient ones and the other kind: "Americans." I don't feel like analyzing my whole family in public. What I want to do is write about just the pressures on Asians in general and mention a few things about my own life to support these general ideas.

Freewriting

I liked the idea about not having to worry about grammar, spelling, etc. Still, I felt pretty self-conscious doing freewriting, but I actually got one idea I might be able to use in my paper—the fact that Asians are expected to be certain things and not others.

FREEWRITING (EXCERPT)

I really don't want to do this freewriting, but I have to—I'm being forced—I have no choice, but it seems stupid. If I have ideas they'll come and if not they won't. I don't see why I need an idea anyway—I wish she'd just say write about your summer vacation like they did in high school, and I'd write about Colorado last summer and the mountains and that lake I can't remember the name but we had a boat and I could see—This is too hard. I need to write about Asians, but there weren't any Asians in that town on that lake. People looked at me like someone from outer space half the time. I wonder what they thought, or who they thought I was.

FOCUSED FREEWRITING (EXCERPT)

Being Asian in the Colorado mountains—wondering whether people thought I was a Japanese tourist—Asian cowboy—Asian hiker/athlete/mountain man. People never expect Asians to be athletes. Just engineers or violinists. Or maybe own fruit stands or be kung fu teachers. Being a teacher could be good for me—being a role model for kids, showing them other things to be.

Brainstorming

This is the way I like to think up ideas—moving around a page, starting and stopping when I feel like it instead of writing in sentences and paragraphs. It's good for me because I lose patience if I don't get ideas right away. I don't see anything I can use, though, except maybe the idea of the math/science stereotype.

BRAINSTORMING NOTES

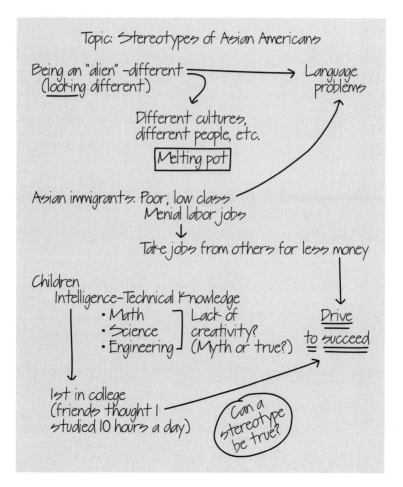

? *Clustering*

This didn't take much time at all, and it showed me that I have basically three parts to my topic—stereotypes about Asian immigrants, stereotypes about their children, and ideas about myself. I'm not sure yet how this all fits together.

CLUSTER DIAGRAM

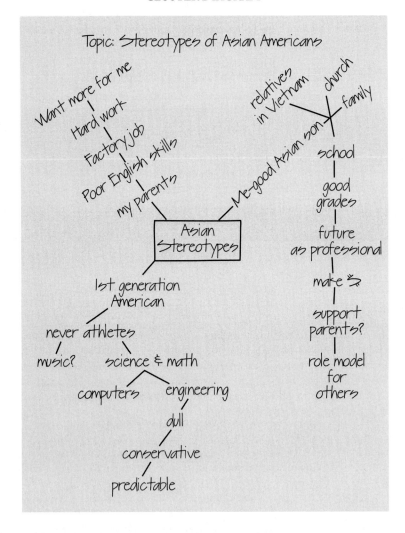

Topic: Stereotypes of Asian Americans

Want more for me — Hard work — Factory job — Poor English skills — my parents

relatives in Vietnam — church — family

Me-good Asian son

Asian Stereotypes

school — good grades — future as professional — make $ — support parents? — role model for others

1st generation American

never athletes — music? — science & math — computers — engineering — dull — conservative — predictable

Asking Questions

These questions took a lot of time, but they did help me to see a possible shape for my essay. I thought the questions that explored the reasons for stereotyping were the most interesting (although probably the hardest to answer).

JOURNALISTIC QUESTIONS

Who stereotypes Asian Americans? Who suffers from this?

What is a stereotype? What exactly is an Asian? (Vietnamese, Chinese, Korean, Japanese, Indian?) What is an Asian American? What is an American?

Why do people stereotype others? Why do they stereotype Asians? Why do people expect so much of Asians? Why do we ourselves accept these stereotypes? Why do we use them?

Where does most stereotyping occur? (In places where a lot of Asians live? In places where hardly any live?) Where do stereotypes appear? (In newspapers? On TV? In casual conversation?)

How has the stereotype of the "typical Asian" changed over the years? How are immigrants seen? How are their children seen? How do people see me? How are various kinds of Asians alike? How are they different?

IN-DEPTH QUESTIONS (EXCERPT)

What are some typical cases or examples of stereotyping of Asian Americans? (suggests exemplification)

Asians are seen as good in math, science, engineering, and computers.

Everyone thinks I study all day.

People think my parents make me work hard.

What causes such stereotyping? (suggests cause and effect)

People don't understand other cultures. There are a lot of different kinds of people in the United States, so we have a lot of confusion and conflict.

4b   Shaping Your Material

(1) Grouping Ideas: Making a Topic Tree

This diagram showed some true ideas as well as some inaccurate stereotypes. Obviously, there are *some things Asian Americans have in common. I'll have to be careful to distinguish between stereotype and reality in my paper.*

TOPIC TREE

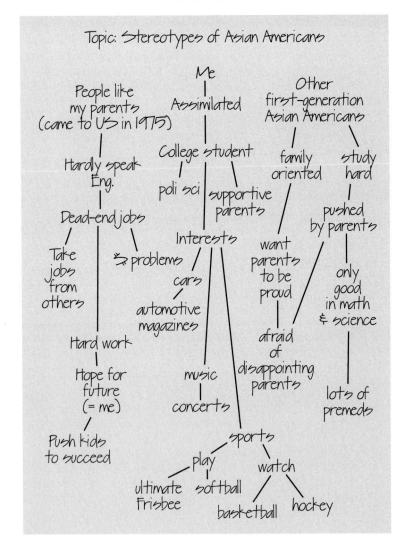

(2) Developing a Thesis

I tried some other ways to word my tentative thesis, but I wanted to make sure it included the most important ideas I was going to talk about—that I'm Asian American, that people stereotype me, and that this is a problem. This thesis seemed to do all that. It seemed to suggest I could include some examples of things that happened to me or things other people assume about me. And I could also dig into some causes and effects, explaining why this stereotyping has been a problem. This thesis was pretty specific and to the point, not too wordy or general. So, I thought I'd stick with it for the time being.

TENTATIVE THESIS STATEMENT

As an Asian American, I am frequently a victim of ethnic stereotyping, and this has been a serious problem for me.

(3) Preparing an Informal Outline

My outline seemed kind of short, even after I added a category (Reality) that wasn't on my topic tree, but I thought I could follow it pretty easily as I wrote my rough draft, maybe getting a paragraph out of each section.

INFORMAL OUTLINE

Asian-American Stereotypes

<u>Thesis statement:</u> As an Asian American, I am frequently a victim of ethnic stereotyping, and this has been a serious problem for me.

Stereotypes of Asian immigrants
    –Poor English
    –Can't use skills and education here
    –Low-paid jobs
        –Sacrifice for children
        –Take from US citizens
Stereotypes of children of Asian immigrants
    –Hard workers
    –Study hard
        –Pushed by parents
    –Focus on math and science
        –Premed

Stereotypes applied to me
    –Science major
    –Forced to study all day
      –No social life
Reality
    –I have outside interests
    –I'm not premed
    –My parents don't push me

4c Drafting and Revising

(1) Writing a Rough Draft

As I wrote my first draft, I tried to write quickly. Still, I checked my outline as I wrote so that I wouldn't wander off my topic.

ROUGH DRAFT

Asian-American Stereotypes

The United States prides itself on being the "melting pot" of the world. However, in reality, the abundance of different cultures in America often causes misunderstandings and even conflicts within the society. These misunderstandings and conflicts result from the society's lack of knowledge about other cultures. As an Asian American, I am frequently a victim of ethnic stereotyping, and this has been a serious problem for me.

It has been within the last twenty years or so that the United States has seen a large rise in the number of Asian immigrants. First-generation immigrants are seen as an underclass of poor who struggle in low-paying jobs so their children will have a better future. Many accuse immigrants of accepting less pay for their work than the established majority is willing to accept, thus putting the established majority out of work. Although it is true that most newly arrived

Asians do seek low-paying, low-skill jobs, they are just following the same trend that other immigrant groups followed when they first arrived in the United States. Because the first generation of Asian Americans have poorly developed skills in English, they are forced into jobs that do not require those skills. Many Asians received degrees from institutions in their native countries or received advanced training of some kind but cannot use those skills in the United States.

Asian-American children are seen as hard workers who are pushed by their families to succeed. Asian children are seen as intelligent, but only in scientific and technical knowledge. The media likes to point to the facts that most Asians succeed only in the math, science, and engineering fields and that there is an inordinate number of Asian college students who identify themselves as "premed."

In my personal experience, in college, many of my friends assume that I am either a science or an engineering major and that my parents force me to study five to ten hours a day. They believe that I sacrifice all my free time and social life in pursuit of a high grade point average.

In fact, I am a political science major. I also like to go to basketball games, listen to music, and read automotive magazines, just like other college students I know. My parents do encourage me to do well in school because they see that education is a stepping-stone to social class mobility; however, I am lucky because my parents do not push me in one direction or another, as some of my Asian friends' parents do. Many of my friends do not realize that just two or three generations ago, their parents and grandparents were going through the same process of social adjustment that all immigrants endure.

It is important to remember that not all Asians fit into the overachieving, success-oriented stereotype.

This first draft really only got me started writing. I wrote a short introduction to get into the subject and identify my problem, but I really didn't have a clear idea of where my paper was headed or how I was going to support my points. I thought I might like to compare my experiences with the experiences of other ethnic groups, particularly other minorities that are like Asians. I also saw that I had to revise my thesis statement to make it more focused on the problems that stereotyping causes.

(2) Revising the Rough Draft

When I met with my collaborative revision group to discuss my draft, people said I had a good topic. They liked the idea that I was going to talk about stereotypes instead of more common problems like grades, money, or family. Also, they didn't know much about Asian Americans, so they thought my paper could be pretty interesting. But they said what I had so far wasn't specific enough and wasn't really focused on my problem. I mostly talk about society in general or Asians in general. They said I should put in examples from my own experiences (which I was planning on doing anyway, but I forgot).

People in the group also talked about their own problems with being stereotyped. It's not just Asians—someone in my group said people always assume she's on a scholarship because she's African American, but her parents own a business. A football player said his professors always assume he's dumb (which I admit I assumed too). I thought if I asked around, I could find other examples, and I thought I might be able to use some of them in my next draft.

ROUGH DRAFT WITH STUDENT'S REVISIONS

The unique characteristic of American culture is its genuine desire to understand & embrace the wide range of traditions and values of its people.

The United States prides itself on being the "melting pot" of the

—a nation where diverse cultures intermingle to form a unique and enlightened society.

world. However, in reality, the abundance of different cultures in

America often causes misunderstandings and even conflicts within the

society. These misunderstandings and conflicts result from the society's

still, as

lack of knowledge about other cultures. ~~As~~ an Asian American, I am frequently a victim of ethnic stereotyping, [People keep trying to make me something I'm not, and this is] and this has been a serious problem for me.

It has been within the last twenty years or so that the United States has seen a large rise in the number of Asian immigrants. First-generation immigrants are seen as an underclass of poor [people] who struggle in low-paying jobs so that their children will have a better future. Many accuse immigrants of accepting less [lower] pay for their work than [other American citizens are] the established majority is willing to accept, thus putting the established majority out of work. Although it is true that most newly arrived Asians do seek low-paying, low-skill jobs, they are just following the same trend [road] that other immigrant groups followed when they first arrived in the United States. [The Irish who escaped the potato famines came to the United States without many advanced skills. To this day, many Latinos come to the United States in search of a better life with] Because the first generation of Asian Americans [my parents included,] have poorly developed skills in English, [little more than the shirts on their backs.] they are forced into jobs that do not require those skills. Many Asians received degrees from institutions in their native countries or received advanced training of some kind but cannot use those skills in the United States. [Therefore, they have no choice but to accept whatever low-paying job they can get—not to steal jobs from others, but to survive.]

[Along with the generalization of Asian-Americans as low-skilled workers comes the notion that] Asian-American children are seen as hard workers who are pushed by their families to succeed. Asian children are seen as intelligent, but only in [terms of] scientific and technical knowledge. The media likes to point to the facts that most Asians succeed only in the math, science, and engineering fields and that there is an inordinate [a great] number of Asian college students who identify themselves as "premed." [What the media seems to forget is that other immigrant groups also seem to prize success above all else.]

In my personal experience, in college, many of my friends assume that I am either a science or an engineering major and that my parents force me to study five to ten hours a day. They believe that I sacrifice all my free time and my social life in pursuit of a high grade point average. [My friends are quite surprised when I tell them that I take drawing classes and that I am majoring in political science—not as a stepping-stone into law, but as a study of man & society.]

∧Add new ¶ here

In fact, I am a political science major. I also like to go to basketball games, listen to music, and read automotive magazines, just like other college students I know. My parents do encourage me to do well in school because they see that education is a stepping-stone to social class mobility; however, I am lucky because my parents do not push me in one direction or another, as many of my Asian friends' parents do. Many of my friends do not realize that just two or three generations ago, their parents and grandparents were going through the same process of social adjustment that all immigrants endure.

It is important to remember that ~~not all Asians~~ fit into the overachieving, success-oriented stereotype. When any child comes from an economically disadvantaged background, many times they must sacrifice their academic pursuits in order to support their families. Also, as Asians, particularly the children, become more integrated into the society, the traditional Asian values of hard work & familial obligations will certainly clash with the American pursuits of recreation & individualism. The resolution of that conflict will add yet another facet to the complexity of America's society.

(most people don't) these cultural stereotypes. For example, not all Asians fit

This practice of assuming that people of similar ethnic backgrounds share certain traits is certainly not limited to Asian Americans. African-American students complain people expect them to be athletes, to like rap music, to be on scholarship, to be from single-parent families—even to be gang members. Athletes say people expect them to be dumb jocks, to drink a lot, and to mistreat their girlfriends. Latinos say people assume that their parents are immigrants and that they speak Spanish better than English. Business majors say people think they're politically conservative and not creative. Engineering students are expected to be dull & wear pocket protectors. Women are supposed to be weak in math & science. Overweight people are expected to be class clowns. In fact, my friends (of all ethnic groups) buy their clothes where I do, & we listen to the same music & laugh at the same jokes. But outsiders don't know this. They have different expectations for each of us, & these expectations are based on culture, not ability.

Revising this draft took a lot of time. I'd triple-spaced so I had room to write in ideas, but I think I might have gotten carried away, adding everything everyone suggested in class, plus every detail that occurred to me on my own. I'm kind of worried about handing it in—she's going to hate it.

(3) Writing a Second Draft

Even though I had reservations about this draft, I typed in my changes, printed it out, and handed it in.

SECOND DRAFT WITH INSTRUCTOR'S COMMENTS

The Danger of Stereotypes

The United States prides itself on being the "melting pot" of the world—a nation where diverse cultures intermingle to form a unique and enlightened society. However, in reality, the abundance of different cultures in America often causes misunderstandings and even conflicts within the society. These misunderstandings result from the society's lack of knowledge about other cultures. The unique characteristic of American culture is its genuine desire to understand and embrace the wide range of traditions and values of its people.

Still, as an Asian American, I am a victim of ethnic stereotyping: *Can you sharpen the thesis so it takes a stand?* people keep trying to make me something I'm not, and this is a *Why is stereotyping a problem?* serious problem for me. *Wordy—see 22a*

It has been within the last twenty years or so that the United States has seen a large rise in the number of Asian immigrants. First-generation immigrants are seen as an underclass of poor people who struggle in low-paying jobs so that their children will have a better future. Many are angry at immigrants, accusing them of accepting lower pay for their work than other American citizens are willing to *Good background. But you might condense ¶s 2 & 3 a bit. You're wandering from* accept, thus putting the established majority out of work. *your topic.*

Although it is true that most newly arrived Asians do seek low-paid, low-skill jobs, they are just following the same road that other immigrant groups followed when they first arrived in the United States. The Irish who escaped the potato famines came to the United

States without many advanced skills. To this day, many Latinos come
cliché (See 29c4.) Also   you may be guilty of stereotyping here.
to the United States in search of a better life with little more than the
shirts on their backs. Because the first generation of Asian Americans,
my parents included, have poorly developed skills in English, they are
forced into jobs that do not require those skills. Many Asians received
degrees from institutions in their native countries or received
pronoun ref—see 32b
advanced training of some kind but cannot use those skills in the
United States. Therefore, they have no choice but to accept whatever low-
paying job they can get—not to steal jobs from others, but to survive.

Along with the view of the first-generation Asian Americans as
low-skilled workers comes the notion that Asian-American children
are hard workers who are pushed by their families to succeed. Asian
children are seen as intelligent, but only in terms of scientific and
technical knowledge. The media likes to point to the facts that most
Asians succeed only in math, science, and engineering and that a
great number of Asian college students identify themselves as
agreement—see 35ab
"premed." What the media seems to forget is that other immigrant
(Media = plural; medium = singular)
groups also seem to prize success above all else.
Wordy—see 22a
In my personal experience, in college, many of my friends
assume that I am either a science or an engineering major and that
my parents force me to study five to ten hours a day. They believe
that I sacrifice all my free time and my social life in pursuit of a high
grade point average. My friends are really surprised when I tell them
that I take drawing classes and that I am majoring in political
science—not as a stepping-stone into law school, but as a study of
sexist language
man and society.   *See 29f2*

This practice of assuming that people of similar ethnic
backgrounds share certain traits is certainly not limited to

Asian Americans. African-American students complain people expect
them to be athletes, to like rap music, to be on scholarship, to be
from single-parent families—even to be gang members. Athletes say
people expect them to be dumb jocks, to drink a lot, and to mistreat
their girlfriends. Latinos say people assume that their parents are
immigrants and that they speak Spanish better than English. Business
majors say people think they're politically conservative and not
Are you sure you need all this? Your focus in this paper is on
creative. Engineering students are expected to be dull and wear
ethnic (specifically Asian) stereotypes, remember?
pocket protectors. Women are supposed to be weak in math and
science. Overweight people are expected to be class clowns. In fact,
my friends (of all ethnic groups) buy their clothes where I do, and we
listen to the same music and laugh at the same jokes. But outsiders
don't know this. They have different expectations for each of us, and
these expectations are based on culture, not ability.
good point—but wordy (see 22a)
It is important to remember that most people do not fit these
cultural stereotypes. For example, not all Asians fit into the overachieving,
success-oriented stereotype. When any child comes from an economically
agreement
disadvantaged background, many times they must sacrifice their
Are you sure this is what you   *see 35b*
academic pursuits in order to support their families. Also, as Asians,
want to leave your readers with?
particularly the children, become more integrated into the society, the
It doesn't really address your
traditional Asian values of hard work and familial obligations will
essay's main point.
certainly clash with the American pursuits of recreation and
individualism. The resolution of that conflict will add yet another facet
to the complexity of America's society.
*I like what you've done here, but something important is still missing. You
really do need more examples from your own experience. Also, think about
this question before our conference on Tuesday: Exactly why are the
stereotypes you enumerate so harmful, so damaging? This idea needs to be
developed in some detail (it's really the heart of your paper), and it should
certainly be addressed in your thesis statement and conclusion as well.*

When I reread my second draft before I handed it in, my two biggest worries were that it had too many ideas in it and that it didn't sound like me. Still, I liked it better than the rough draft—especially the material in paragraphs 5 and 6, which my collaborative revision group wanted me to add. Now I thought I might like to add something about how I've been limited by my own preconceptions. For example, I did start out as a premed student, although I'm now a political science major. Another idea I might want to look into is that many Asians, including some of my friends, are now reconsidering whether the drive for success is worth the price. I saw this as an interesting possibility, but I felt as if I was trying to do too much. Was I writing about my own personal problem (the conflict between what people expect a good Asian boy to do vs. what I want to do) or about a problem in US society? Was I going to deal with all *stereotypes*? All *ethnic* stereotypes? Or only Asian-American stereotypes?

My conference with Professor Cross, and her comments on my draft, helped me solve some of my problems and get my assignment into focus. It also brought up some new problems. First, she reminded me that my paper was supposed to be only two to three pages long (something I was starting to forget), so I should stop looking for new material and start sorting through what I had. She said that my knowledge of the Asian-American experience was my paper's biggest strength, but that I was going in too many directions at once. She thought all the stuff in paragraph 6 was interesting, but she said it didn't really fit if my paper was going to be on Asians and on the problems I face. I hate to take this paragraph out, but I guess she's right. She wants me to revise my thesis statement so it takes a stand about why and how *stereotyping has been damaging to me (and, for the same reasons, to other people). Then, of course, I'll have to add support based on what I know firsthand.

This all makes sense, but it means I'll have to take out some of the background on immigrants in paragraphs 2 and 3 and cut most of paragraph 6. I won't have anything left! Now I'll have to list and explain the problems I have, telling why they're problems, and I'll also have to redo my introduction and conclusion so they fit with the new ideas. It sounds like a lot of work.

(4) Revising the Second Draft

To move from this second draft to what I hoped would be my final draft, I had to get a clear sense of what to cross out, what to keep, and what to add. Professor Cross thought that making a formal outline of this draft could help me to see which ideas worked well together and which ones just floated.

I started by outlining my second draft, the one with all the problems, hoping that a topic outline would show me the relationships (if any) among my ideas and give me some idea about what to do next.

TOPIC OUTLINE ❓

The Danger of Stereotypes

Thesis statement: As an Asian American, I am a victim of ethnic stereotyping: people keep trying to make me something I'm not, and this is a problem for me.

I. Stereotypes of Asian immigrants
   A. Underclass
      1. Struggle in low-paying jobs
      2. Hope children will do better
   B. Displace Americans
      1. Accept low pay
      2. Put others out of work
II. Reality
   A. Similar to unskilled Irish immigrants
   B. Similar to poor Latino immigrants
   C. Limited
      1. Poor English skills
      2. Useless degrees
III. Stereotypes of immigrants' children
   A. Work habits
      1. Work hard
      2. Pushed by parents
   B. Intelligence
      1. Highly intelligent
      2. Scientific and technical knowledge
         a. Math and science
         b. Premed
IV. My experience
   A. Stereotypes applied to me
      1. Science/engineering major
      2. Forced to study
         a. No free time
         b. No social life
   B. Reality
      1. Drawing classes
      2. Political science major

   V. Other inaccurate stereotypes
      A. African Americans
         1. Athletic
         2. Like rap music
         3. On scholarship
         4. From single-parent families
         5. Gang members
      B. Athletes
         1. Dumb
         2. Drinkers
         3. Mistreat girlfriends
      C. Latinos
         1. Immigrants
         2. Poor English
      D. Business majors
         1. Politically conservative
         2. Not creative
      E. Engineering students
         1. Dull
         2. Wear pocket protectors
      F. Women
      G. Overweight people

   Outlining this draft showed me what Professor Cross had been trying to tell me: my paper was really unbalanced, with some areas underdeveloped and others overstuffed. (Most of the information, in fact, wasn't even about Asians.) After I finished the outline, I went through it again, indicating with x's and check marks what to keep and what to drop and making notes about what to add to my next draft.

   Now I was finally ready to make an outline to guide my final draft. At this point, I thought the effort of a sentence outline would really pay off because I might be able to use sentences from my outline in my paper.

❓ **SENTENCE OUTLINE**

   My Problem: Escaping the Stereotype of the "Model Minority"

   <u>Thesis statement:</u> Such stereotypes are not only limiting to me, but also dangerous to the nation because they challenge the image of the United States as a place where people can be whatever they want to be.

I. Asian Americans are stereotyped.
  A. First-generation immigrants are seen as a struggling underclass.
    1. They are viewed as poor and underpaid.
    2. They are viewed as hardworking.
    3. They are viewed as sacrificing for their children.
  B. Their children are seen as hard workers.
    1. They are viewed as driven.
      a. They need to succeed.
      b. They are pushed by their parents.
    2. They are viewed as intelligent.
      a. They excel only in scientific and technical fields.
      b. They are good only in math, science, and engineering.
      c. Many are premed.
  C. These traits are not limited to Asian Americans.
    1. Other immigrant groups also value success.
    2. Everyone seeks the American Dream.
II. Because I am Asian American I am unfairly stereotyped.
  A. I am viewed as a robot.
    1. People assume I am a science or engineering major.
    2. People assume my parents make me study.
    3. People assume I have no social life.
  B. Such stereotypes are inaccurate.
    1. I take drawing classes.
    2. I am a political science major.
    3. I am not quiet or shy.
    4. I do not play a musical instrument.
    5. I do not live in Chinatown.
III. These stereotypes have negative consequences for me.
  A. Teachers have unreasonable expectations for me.
    1. Teachers expect me to do well in certain areas.
      a. They have encouraged me to take AP math and science.
      b. They have encouraged me to try out for band.
      c. They have encouraged me to take an advanced computer seminar.
      d. They have encouraged me to join the chess club.
    2. Teachers do not expect me to do well in other areas.
      a. They do not expect me to be an athlete.
      b. They do not expect me to be a writer.
      c. They do not expect me to be a debater.
  B. I have conformed to their expectations.
IV. Similar stereotypes limit other groups' options.
  A. Stereotypes determine people's career paths.
    1. Teachers, bosses, and parents steer us in certain directions.

    2. We ourselves make choices based on stereotypes.
  B. Even in school, students are expected to follow certain predetermined paths.
V. Most people do not fit these cultural stereotypes.
  A. Stereotypes are invalid for Asians.
    1. Children of recent Asian immigrants do work and study hard.
    2. Even when they become assimilated, they retain Asian values.
      a. They work hard.
      b. They have obligations to their families.
    3. However, they also acquire the American drive for individuality.
  B. Stereotypes are invalid for other groups.

(5) Preparing a Final Draft

Even as I started to turn my paper into something I could hand in, I still worried that it didn't really sound like me. I didn't want to make my paper too informal, but I did want it to be a little less stiff. As I added information to my draft, though, I found that my style was becoming more relaxed and natural—maybe because the information was about me, not about people in general. The opening and closing paragraphs were still a little distant, but somehow that seemed to make sense, giving my personal problem some context.

Before I typed my final draft, I decided to change my title to something more specific, something that connected my paper to the assignment. After I finished printing out this final draft, I read it through one more time—and noticed a few typos. So I corrected them and printed it out again—and then I had a really final draft.

FINAL DRAFT　❓

Dao 1

Nguyen Dao

Professor Cross

English 101

10 October 2000

My Problem:

Escaping the Stereotype of the "Model Minority"

The United States prides itself on being a nation where
diverse cultures intermingle to form a unique and enlightened
society. However, in reality, the existence of so many different
cultures in America often causes misunderstandings within the
society. These misunderstandings result from most people's
lack of knowledge about other cultures. The unique
characteristic of American culture is its genuine desire to
understand and embrace the wide range of traditions and
values of its people. Still, as an Asian American, I am
frequently confronted with other people's ideas about who I
am and how I should behave. Such stereotypes are not only
limiting to me, but also dangerous to the nation because they
challenge the image of the United States as a place where
people can be whatever they want to be.

Within the last twenty years, the United States has
experienced a sharp rise in the number of Asian immigrants,
and these immigrants, and their children, are stereotyped.

(margin notes:)

Introductory paragraph presents basic background

Thesis statement

First body paragraph: Common stereotypes applied to Asian Americans

Dao 2

First-generation immigrants are seen as an underclass of poor people who struggle in low-paying jobs, working long hours so that their children will have a better future. Along with the view of the first-generation Asian Americans as driven, low-skilled workers comes the notion that all Asian-American children are hard workers who are pushed by their families to succeed. Asian children are seen as intelligent, but only in terms of scientific and technical knowledge. The media like to point out that most Asians succeed only in math, science, and engineering and that a disproportionately large number of Asian college students identify themselves as premed. What the media seem to forget is that many other immigrant groups also value success. In a larger sense, America has always been seen as the land of opportunity, where everyone is in search of the American Dream.

Second body paragraph: Stereotype applied to student himself

Many of my college friends assume that I am some kind of robot. They think that I must be either a science or an engineering major and that my parents force me to study many hours each day. They believe that I sacrifice all my free time and my social life in pursuit of a high grade point average. Naturally, these assumptions are incorrect. My friends are really surprised when I tell them that I take drawing classes and that I am majoring in political science—not as a stepping-stone into law school, but as a foundation for a liberal arts education. They are also surprised to find that I am not particularly quiet or shy,

Dao 3

that I do not play a musical instrument, and that I do not live in Chinatown. (I don't know why this surprises people; I'm not even Chinese.)

I try to see these stereotypes as harmless, but they aren't. Even neutral or positive stereotypes can have negative consequences. For example, teachers have always had unreasonably high expectations for me, and these expectations have created pressure for academic success. And even though teachers expect me to do well, they expect me to excel only in certain areas. So, they have encouraged me to take AP math and science classes, try out for band, sign up for an advanced computer seminar, and join the chess club. No one has ever suggested that I (or any other Asian American I know) pursue athletics, creative writing, or debating. I spent my high school years trying to be what other people wanted me to be, and I got to be pretty good at it.

Third body paragraph: Negative effects of stereotypes on student

I realize now, however, that I have been limited and that similar stereotypes also limit the options that other groups have. The law says we can choose our activities and choose our careers, but things do not always work out that way. Often, because of long-held stereotypes, we are gently steered (by peers, teachers, bosses, parents, and even by ourselves) in a certain direction, toward some options and away from others. We may have come a long way from the time when African Americans were expected to be domestics

Fourth body paragraph: Negative effects of stereotypes on society

Dao 4

or blue-collar workers, Latinos to be migrant farmers or gardeners, and Asians to be restaurant workers. But at the college, high school, and even elementary school levels, students are expected to follow certain predetermined paths, and too often these expectations are based on culture, not on interests or abilities.

Most people do not fit these cultural stereotypes. For example, not all Asians fit into the overachieving, success

Conclusion   oriented mold. When children come from an economically disadvantaged background, as the children of some recent Asian immigrants do, they must work hard and study hard. But this situation is only temporary. As Asian children become more assimilated into American society, they do retain the traditional Asian values of hard work and family obligations—but they also acquire the American drive for individualism. I know from my own experience that the stereotypes applied to Asians are not accurate. In the same way, people of other ethnic groups know that the cultural stereotypes applied to them are not valid. My problem is not just <u>my</u> problem because ethnic and cultural stereotypes are never harmless. Whenever someone is stereotyped, that person has fewer choices. And freedom to choose our futures, to be whoever we want to be, is what living in the United States is supposed to be all about.

CHAPTER 5

ESSAY PATTERNS AND PURPOSES

? FREQUENTLY ASKED QUESTIONS

How do I decide which pattern to use to structure my paper? (p. 69)
How do I organize a comparison-and-contrast paper? (p. 87)

Writers have many options for arranging material within an essay. The pattern of development you choose is determined by your **purpose**, which in college writing is often stated in (or suggested by) your assignment. For example, if your assignment is to analyze the events that led to the Spanish-American War, you may use a **cause-and-effect** pattern; if your assignment is to evaluate the relative merits of two systems of government, you may use **comparison and contrast;** if your assignment is to reflect on an experience, you may use **narration** or **description;** and if your assignment is to persuade readers that a literary work's reputation is not deserved, you may use **exemplification.** In each case, of course, you have other options as well, and many essays combine several patterns of development. (The same patterns used to structure essays can also be used as **patterns of paragraph development**.)

5a Writing Narrative Essays

A **narrative** essay tells a story by presenting events in chronological (time) order. Sometimes a narrative begins in the middle of a story, or even at the end, and then moves back to the beginning. Most narrative essays, however, move in a logical, orderly sequence from beginning to end, from first event to last. Clear transitional words and phrases (*later, after that*) and time markers (*in 1990, two years earlier, the next day*) establish the chronological sequence and the relationship of each event to the others.

(1) Using Narration

You use narration in a variety of college writing situations—for example, when you review a novel's plot, when you write a case study, when you summarize your employment history in a letter of application for a job, when you present background on a history examination, when you recount personal experiences in a journal, or when you write an autobiographical essay.

Any assignment that asks you to *tell, trace, summarize the events, present the background,* or *outline* may call for narration. Here are some typical assignments that might suggest narrative writing.

- *Trace* the events that led the Food and Drug Administration to ban thalidomide in this country. (Public health paper)
- *Summarize* the incidents that immediately preceded the French Revolution. (History exam)
- *Present some background* to show why nineteenth-century British workers were receptive to the ideas of social reformers like Robert Owen. (Political science exam)
- *Outline* the plot of Jane Austen's novel *Sense and Sensibility.* (English literature quiz)

(2) Student Essay: Narration

The following student essay was written by Gary McManus for a composition course. The instructor asked each student to interview a relative and to write a brief family history based on the interview.

My Family History

Introduction (identifies subject; gives background)

On October 7, I interviewed my father, John McManus, about my family history. Although he knew more about his own ancestors than my mother's, he was able to give me valuable details about both sides of my family. The family history, as I have reconstructed it, shows me that although some of my relatives experienced the financial

Thesis statement

hardships and prejudice common to many other immigrants, many members of my family were lucky enough to achieve success.

My grandmother on my father's side was born in Newry, Ireland, in poverty caused by the potato famine. When she was a child, her father, a sea captain, took his family to Liverpool, England, so he could find work. While in England, my grandmother McManus was constantly teased by the English children because of her Irish-Catholic ancestry. When she was eighteen, she came alone to the United States to visit a distant cousin in Baltimore, Maryland. At the time she had no way of knowing that she would never return home. In Baltimore she met her future husband, and they were married a year later.

Events presented in sequence

My grandfather McManus was born and raised in the Baltimore area and came from a well-to-do family. His uncle invented the bottle cap (before this, people used corks) and was president of the Crown Cork and Seal Bottle Company. One of my grandfather's aunts was a judge in juvenile court in Boston—no minor achievement for a woman in the late 1880s. Another of his uncles was an architect who designed several of Boston's churches. He had trouble getting other commissions, however, because of discrimination against the Irish. At that time, it was common in Boston to see signs in shop windows saying "Workers needed—N.I.N.A." (No Irish Need Apply). As an officer in the US Army, my grandfather McManus fought in the Spanish-American War in the Philippines in the 1890s and later during the Boxer Rebellion in China. During his military career, he served under both General Arthur MacArthur and his son General Douglas MacArthur.

During World War I, from 1918 to 1919, a terrible influenza epidemic killed millions worldwide and hundreds of thousands in the United States. So many people died that there were not enough gravediggers to bury the dead. Squads of men would go from house to house in many cities on the east coast, collecting the bodies of

Narrative continues

those who had died. Two of my grandparents' children died from influenza during the epidemic. One son only six years old died early one day just after sunrise, and later that evening their two-year-old daughter died in her sleep.

Shift to mother's family   My mother's family settled in Irish neighborhoods in Washington, DC, where my great-grandfather, John Howard, owned a livery stable. His son, my great-uncle Lee, was a US attorney and judge who was known as one of the most influential Irish-American men in the District of Columbia. Because he had grown up poor and had to work to put himself through law school, he was sympathetic to the poor and often went to great lengths to find them employment.

My maternal grandfather, a builder, was among the first to attempt to organize his fellow workers. Eventually he became a union official for the AFL. He would have advanced much higher in the union if he had renounced Catholicism and joined the Masons, but he refused.

Conclusion   Many Irish immigrants in the late 1880s and early 1900s became priests, policemen, and blue-collar workers. That was as far as many of them could go because the anti-Irish prejudice that prevailed at this time severely limited their opportunities. In spite of some problems, however, many members of my family carved out good lives in this country.

EXERCISE 1

Write a narrative essay on one of the following topics.

- Interview an older relative or friend and write an account of his or her childhood.
- Retell a favorite short story or fairy tale from memory.
- Write the biography of a word. Look up a word in the *Oxford English Dictionary,* and write a narrative account of its development from its first use in English to its present meaning in modern usage.

5b   Writing Descriptive Essays

A **descriptive** essay communicates to readers how something looks, sounds, smells, tastes, or feels. The most natural arrangement of details in a description reflects the way you actually look at a person, scene, or object: near to far, top to bottom, side to side, or front to back. This arrangement of details is made clear by transitions that identify precise spatial relationships: *next to, near, beside, under, above,* and so on.

NOTE: Sometimes a descriptive essay does not have an explicitly stated thesis statement. In such cases, it is unified by a **dominant impression**—the effect created by all the details in the description.

(1) Using Description

Description plays an important role in college writing. For example, technical reports, lab reports, case studies, and field notes all depend upon precise description. In addition, on a European history exam you might have to describe the scene of a famous battle, and in an American literature paper you might have to describe the setting of a play or novel. In other situations, too, description is necessary—for example, for presenting your reactions to a painting or a musical composition.

The following assignments are typical of those you may encounter.

- Describe the structures you observed during your dissection of the reproductive system of the fetal pig. (Biology laboratory manual)
- Describe the English political system at the time of the American Revolution. (European history midterm)
- Write an essay in which you describe one character in the novel *The Color Purple.* (American literature paper)
- In a short essay, describe Titian's use of color in his *Madonna with Members of the Pesaro Family.* (Art history exam)

(2) Student Essay: Description

Barbara Quercetti, a student in a composition course, wrote this essay in response to an assignment asking her to describe a place that had made a strong impression on her. She based her descriptive essay largely on her own firsthand observations of her subject. (A few factual details were taken from an informational brochure that she picked up at the site.)

A Newport Mansion

Located on Ochre Point Avenue in Newport, Rhode Island, The Breakers is a mansion presently owned by the Preservation Society of Newport County. The mansion was built in 1895 for Cornelius Vanderbilt, the financier who accumulated the renowned Vanderbilt fortune. This house, like other Newport mansions, was used only during the three summer months, when the Newport social season was at its peak. The architect, Richard Morris Hunt, modeled The Breakers after an Italian Renaissance Palace. Presently, The Breakers is one of Newport's most popular tourist attractions because its

extravagant architecture and opulent appointments call up a time of lost elegance.

As you approach the grounds of the mansion, you see enormous black wrought iron gates that are thirty feet high at the center point and weigh seven tons. The arched top of the gates is decorated with very elaborate scroll work, and this arch pattern is repeated throughout the exterior and interior of the mansion. To either side of the gates are two twenty-foot-high square posts, each with a black wrought iron lantern also decorated with scroll work. The buff Indian limestone that is used for the posts is also used for the facade of The Breakers.

Standing in front of the mansion, you see that although none of the faces of The Breakers is identical, each relates to the others. The first story of each exterior wall is made up of a series of arches, with the interior of each arch inlaid with ceramic tiles. Supporting the arches are round columns with Greek Ionic capitals. Each facade is three complete stories high, except for the east side, which has a terrace above the second-story level. This terrace is one of three that give a panoramic view of the Atlantic Ocean. The other two terraces are located on the north side of The Breakers. One, at the first-story level, extends out to the garden area. The other terrace is above the first-story level. The south face of the mansion has a semicircular protrusion that forms an open one-story foyer. The entire building is decorated with ornate figures sculpted by Karl Bitter.

As you enter The Breakers, you see that the interior is as exquisite as the exterior. The first room that you encounter is the Great Hall or reception room, which is also decorated with intricately carved stone and marble. The Great Hall rises nearly fifty feet and is the largest room in any of the Newport mansions. Its ceiling is covered with geometric patterns of fourteen-karat-gold gilding that run over the entire surface. There are eight chandeliers, each suspended by a single metal rod. The second story of the room is an open balcony with a black wrought iron railing that repeats the scroll work pattern of the entrance gates. The railing is divided into sections by two-story-high square stone columns with Ionic capitals. These Greek Ionic columns are similar to those used on the exterior of the mansion. The railing continues along the side of the royal red carpeted stairs to the first floor. Surrounding the room is a series of arches, each situated between two of the two-story-high columns. Floor-length royal red tie-back draperies hang inside the arches. The wood parquet floor is covered with Persian area rugs, and potted ferns at the base of each column add a touch of greenery to the room.

View of interior: Great Hall

Walking through the Great Hall, you come to an equally impressive dining room that is also two full stories high. Lavish decorations fill the room, which is lined with two-story-high columns with arches in between. The columns are red alabaster with bronze Corinthian capitals. As in the Great Hall, royal red tie-back draperies

View of interior: dining room

hang inside the arches. Above each arch is a gilded cornice around which is a ceiling arch containing life-sized sculptured figures. Four huge crystal chandeliers hang down the length of the room. On the west wall, there is only one arch, and this outlines a blue carved Venetian marble fireplace. The room is richly furnished with antique European furniture, and the wood parquet floor is covered with Persian carpets. A solid oak dining table ten feet by ten feet square dominates the center of the room.

Conclusion

Restatement
of thesis

The Newport social season is now part of America's past, and so are the individuals who spent millions for a summer residence. But The Breakers remains one of the grandest mansions of the area. Now a tourist attraction, it retains its popularity because it stands as a reminder to us of a time when America was rapidly expanding and life in Newport was a good deal more extravagant than it is today.

EXERCISE 2

Write a descriptive essay on one of the following topics.

- Describe a person, place, or object that has had a significant impact on you.
- Write a description of a room in your house or a place in your neighborhood.
- Visit a local museum or a site of historical interest, and describe one exhibit or display.

5c Writing Exemplification Essays

Exemplification essays support a thesis statement with a series of specific examples (or, sometimes, with a single extended example). These examples can be drawn from personal observation or experience or from the facts and opinions you gather through research. Within the essay, examples are linked to one another and to the thesis statement with clear transitional words and phrases: *the first example, another reason, in addition, finally,* and so on.

(1) Using Exemplification

Exemplification is basic to most college writing assignments. In fact, any time you are called upon to give a specific example of a more general principle, you use exemplification. The following assignments are typical of those you may encounter.

- Discuss three examples of *film noir.* (Film midterm)
- Write an essay in which you illustrate the following statement by the literary critic John Tytell: "Although the Beat movement lacked any shared platform such as the Imagist or surrealist manifestoes, it nonetheless cohered as a literary group." (Literature paper)
- In what ways does existentialism confront the problem of personal action in a universe devoid of purpose? (Philosophy final)
- Discuss four technological advances that took place during the Renaissance. (History of science paper)
- Identify and discuss three examples that Glazer and Moynihan give to support their thesis that in New York City and in much of the United States, the melting pot does not exist. (Sociology midterm)

(2) Student Essay: Exemplification

The following paper on a life-changing accident was written for a composition course by Felicia Marianni, who supports her thesis statement with a variety of examples from her own experience.

A New Experience

The ability to see is not often thought of as a privilege. In fact, in   Introduction

daily life, it is rarely even acknowledged. Unlike most other people,

however, I understand how important sight is because I recently lost

part of my vision because of my own carelessness. Impatient to remove my contact lenses one evening, I borrowed an unmarked bottle of solution that was lying on a shelf in the dorm bathroom. Unaware that the liquid was not saline but hydrogen peroxide, I woke up the next morning with my eyes stinging. I had chemically burned both eyes, causing a hemorrhage.

Fortunately, the damage turned out to be both minimal and temporary. I did not lose my sight completely; I only lost clarity—that is, the ability to see distinct, sharp lines. I was not isolated in a world of blackness or of lights and shadows. I was able to see colors.

Thesis statement

Nevertheless, my world was "fuzzy," and this caused a lot of problems that adversely affected my feelings of security and of self.

First group of examples

Problems that I had never anticipated coping with now plagued me. For example, reading even for short periods of time strained my eyes and gave me headaches. I could not recognize my friends from a distance of more than a couple of feet. Friends thought I was behaving rudely if I didn't stop to chat, unaware that if I had recognized them, I certainly would have stopped to say hello. Stairways became dangerous, for it was difficult to determine where one step ended and the next began. Sometimes, in the evening after a rainy afternoon, I could not determine whether a dark area in front of me was a puddle or just a shadow, and I must have looked strange to onlookers who saw me skirt a pool of darkness as if I were afraid to get my feet wet.

Second group of examples

Not only did letters in a book and human faces become distorted, but the beauty of nature did, too. As the hours and the days passed, I missed being able to see clear outlines of trees against the sky; all I could see was something greenish fading to brown as it neared the ground. I longed to see separate blades of grass rather than a mass of green beside the grayish strip that I knew to be pavement. If I heard a bird chirping, I was not able to find the source of the sound. I missed shapes of clouds shifting and changing above me. When it rained, I could not see reflections in puddles.

I also missed being able to see the cityscape that I had learned to integrate into my field of experience. After my accident, I could no longer discern the sharp edges of the sides of the buildings; for example, I saw a large reddish blur instead of a red-brick building. The beauty of the arching skeleton of a bridge had turned into a jumble of disconnected shapes. I was aching to see the real features of the people hurrying around me and the intricate architecture of public statues. But none of this was possible.

Third group of examples

After a week and a half of limited vision, I recovered. My first reaction to "seeing again" was disbelief. When I went outside and looked around, my vision was still blurred, but this time with tears. Now, I appreciate every new day that I can wake up and put in my contact lenses, or put on my glasses, to see everything clearly. But the world will never look as beautiful to me as it did when I saw it anew for the first time.

Conclusion

Restatement of major point

EXERCISE 3

Write an exemplification essay on one of the following topics.

- Discuss the merits of television. Use specific examples from your own experience to support your thesis.
- Explain how several incidents at a family dinner or a neighborhood gathering revealed the social attitudes of the people who attended it.
- Discuss three things that you would like to change in your home, school, or job.

5d Writing Process Essays

A **process** essay explains how to do something or how something works. It presents a series of steps in strict chronological order, using transitional words such as *first, then, next, after this,* and *finally* to link steps in the process.

Some process essays are **instructions,** providing all the specific information that enables readers to perform a procedure themselves. Instructions use commands and the present tense. Other process essays simply explain the process to readers, with no expectation that they will actually perform it. These process essays may use first or third person and past tense (for a process that has been completed) or present tense (for a process that occurs regularly).

(1) Using Process

Academic situations frequently call for process explanations and sometimes for instructions. In scientific and technical writing, you may describe how an apparatus works or how a procedure is carried out. Occasionally, you may even write a set of instructions telling your readers how to duplicate your procedure. In the humanities, you might have to write a proposal for a research paper in which you explain how you plan to carry out your research. Here are some typical assignments that call for a process pattern of development.

- Explain how an amendment is added to the Constitution. (Political science quiz)
- Review the stages that each of the Old English long vowels went through during the Great Vowel Shift. (Examination in history of the English language)
- Outline the steps in the process of mitosis. (Biology lab quiz)
- Write a set of instructions that outlines a treatment plan for a patient complaining of lower back pain. (Physical therapy paper)

(2) Student Essay: Process

Richard Patrone, a student in a course in animal biology, submitted the following laboratory report. In writing up his experiment, he was careful to provide an exact record of what he did in order to give readers the information they would need to understand his procedure.

Background

Based on the postulation that pollen contains an anticarcinogenic principle that can be added to food, an experiment was set up in which female mice, fed with pollenized food, were checked for delays in the appearance of spontaneous mammary tumors. Mice used in the study were bred from a subline of the C_3H strain, which develops palpable tumors at between 18 and 25 weeks of age.

Introduction

Procedure

First, 10 mice were set aside as controls, to be fed only unpollenized food (Purina Laboratory Chow). Next, the pollen suspension was prepared: one gram of bee-gathered pollen was ground and then mixed with 50 ml of distilled water. Two different mixtures were then prepared using this pollen suspension. One mixture consisted of 6 lb of food with a 36 ml dosage of pollen suspension (1 part pollen per 3,800 parts food), and one consisted of 6 lb of lab chow with an 8 ml dosage of suspension (1 part pollen per 120,000 parts food). Each of these two mixtures was then fed to a different group of 10 mice. The mice were weighed weekly, and the amount of food eaten was recorded. As soon as estrus began, vaginal smears of each mouse were made daily and examined microscopically for the presence of cornified cells.

Steps in the process

Results

The experimental results indicated that the development of mammary tumors in C_3H mice was delayed 10 to 12 weeks with the ingestion of pollenized food.

Conclusion

EXERCISE 4

Write a process essay on one of the following topics.

- Explain your typical writing process. Then, rewrite the explanation as a set of instructions.
- Write a detailed set of instructions for playing any computer game or board game whose rules you know well.
- Think about a time when you had to complete a complicated transaction that involved dealing with bureaucratic red tape—applying for a student loan or getting your driver's license, for instance. List the steps you went through, and then write an explanation of the process.

5e Writing Cause-and-Effect Essays

Cause-and-effect essays explore causes or predict or describe results; sometimes a single cause-and-effect essay does both. Because cause-and-effect relationships are often quite complex, clear, specific transitional words and phrases such as *one cause, another cause, a more important result, because,* and *as a result* are essential.

(1) Using Cause and Effect

Many of your course assignments call for writing that examines causes, predicts effects, or does both. Language like "How did X affect Y?" "What were the contributing factors?" "Describe some side effects," "What caused X?" "What were the results of X?" and "Why did X happen?" suggests cause-and-effect writing. Here are some typical assignments.

- Identify and explain some factors that contributed to the stock market crash of 1987. (Economics essay)
- Describe some of the possible side effects of dialysis. (Nursing exam)
- How have geologic changes affected the productivity of Pennsylvania soil? (Agronomy project)
- What factors led to the wave of eastern European immigration to this country at the end of the nineteenth century? (American history exam)
- How did Ernest Hemingway's experiences during World War I influence his writing? (American literature paper)

(2) Student Essay: Cause and Effect

Michael Liebman wrote the essay that follows for a class in elementary education. The assignment was "Identify the causes of a social problem of concern to both parents and educators, and analyze the effects of this problem, making some recommendations about how the problem can be solved." Michael decided to examine the positive and negative effects on children of being left on their own after school.

The Latchkey Children

In recent years, the expanding economy and wider employment opportunities for women have combined to lead more and more mothers of school-aged children to return to work. In fact, more than half of the mothers of school-aged children are now employed, and the two-paycheck family has become the norm. As a result, many children are now left unsupervised between 3 and 6 p.m. every day. The lack of much-needed after-school programs has left some families in cities and suburbs alike with no other alternative but to leave the children on their own and hope for the best. Luckily, many of the children seem to manage very well.

Introduction (States primary cause: working parents)

Thesis statement

The negative effects of the latchkey trend are fairly easily perceived. Many parents' firm rules—don't use the stove, don't open the door for anyone, don't let telephone callers know you are alone—have made some children (especially those without siblings) fearful and jittery. These children may also become very lonely in an empty house or apartment. Because many working parents do not allow their children's friends to visit when no adult is present, their children may spend hours with no company but the television set. A lonely, frightened child turning to the TV for comfort and companionship is a common stereotype of the latchkey child. Fortunately, however, it is for the most part not an accurate one.

Negative effects

Other possible negative effects   The latchkey phenomenon has the potential to have some even more disturbing effects on children. Parents and teachers worry that unattended children will be more vulnerable to violent crimes, especially sexual assaults and kidnapping. They also fear the children will be unable to protect themselves in case of fire or other disaster. Parents have been concerned as well that young adolescents left alone will be free to experiment with sex, drugs, and alcohol. But these fears have not been substantiated by statistical data.

First positive effect   Surprisingly enough, in fact, many positive results have actually been observed—positive both for the children and parents involved and for our society as a whole. One such positive result has been the response of the many schools across the country that have instituted courses in "survival skills." In these courses, boys and girls as young as ten learn such skills as cleaning, cooking, and sewing; consumerism; safety and first aid; and how to care for younger siblings. The focus of the home economics courses in these schools has changed as the students' needs have, and the trend toward these "domestic survival courses" seems to be spreading.

Second positive effect   Perhaps the most significant positive effect has been a subtle one: the emotional strengths so often observed in the latchkey children. As they learn to fend for themselves, and take pride in doing so, their self-esteem increases. Educators cite these children as more self-reliant, more mature, more confident; parents add that they are also more cooperative around the house. Of course it is still too early to tell whether the latchkey trend will produce a generation of more independent, self-reliant adults, but it is certainly a possibility.

Clearly, the latchkey syndrome has negative as well as positive   Conclusion
results, but the answer is not to have parents leave the workforce. For
the majority of working parents, especially in single-parent families,
working is an economic necessity. Parents should be able to remain
employed, and most of their children will benefit—though some,
inevitably, will suffer. The best solution would be the continued
development of government-subsidized programs to meet the needs of
the latchkey child. Most important among these would be supervised
after-school programs, perhaps utilizing school buildings and facilities.
Communities and private industry can also contribute--the former by
establishing networks of "block parents" and information and referral
services, the latter by offering "flextime" as an option for working
parents. Most latchkey children are managing quite well, but their lives
and their parents' lives can—and should—be made a lot easier.

EXERCISE 5

Write a cause-and-effect essay on one of the following topics.

- Discuss the likely effects on your present life of one of the following
  situations: losing your scholarship, loan, or job; becoming a parent;
  failing a course; inheriting ten thousand dollars.
- The rights of adopted children are under a good deal of scrutiny
  lately. Although adoptees have long been denied information about
  their parentage, many people think they should have the right to
  know the identities of their biological parents. Explore the possible effects on *one* of the following groups of opening adoption files: adoptive parents, foster parents, parents who give their children up for
  adoption, or adopted children.
- What led you to come to the school you now attend? For instance,
  were you influenced by the school's size, location, or course offer-
  ings? By your friends' choices? By your parents' wishes? By your financial situation?

5f   Writing Comparison-and-Contrast Essays

Comparison-and-contrast essays explain how two subjects are alike or different; sometimes a single comparison-and-contrast essay examines both similarities and differences. The two subjects being compared or contrasted must have a clear **basis for comparison.** That is, they must have qualities or elements in common that make the comparison or contrast logical. Similarities and differences are identified with appropriate transitional words and phrases, such as *similarly* and *likewise* for comparison and *however* and *in contrast* for contrast. These transitions can also signal movement from one subject to another.

(1) Using Comparison and Contrast

Instructors often ask you to use comparison and contrast in answering examination questions.

- Compare and contrast the Neoclassic and Romantic views of nature. (Literature)
- Discuss the similarities and differences of the insanity defenses for murder under the M'Naghten test and the Durham rule. (Criminology)
- What are the advantages and disadvantages of load and no-load mutual funds? (Personal finance)
- Examine the benefits and liabilities of team-taught and individual teacher-centered classrooms. (Educational methods)
- How did Darwin and Lamarck differ on the subject of mutability of the species? (Biology)

Each of these assignments provides you with cues that tell you how to treat your material. Certain words and phrases—*compare and contrast, similarities and differences, advantages and disadvantages,* and *benefits and liabilities*—indicate that you should use comparison and contrast to structure your answer.

Many other situations also call for comparison and contrast. For example, if your supervisor on a work-study project asked you to write a report discussing the feasibility of two types of insulation, cellulose and urethane foam, you would use comparison and contrast to organize your ideas.

(2) Student Essay: Comparison and Contrast

When asked by his composition instructor to compare any two subjects, Alan Escobero, a professed expert on arcade games, used a **point-by-point comparison** to present his ideas—that is, he alternated be-

See 6e6

tween subjects, making a point about one subject and then making a comparable point about the other subject. (A **subject-by-subject comparison** treats one subject in full and then moves on to discuss the other subject in full.)

Arcade Wars

Long ago, in a time more innocent than ours, pinball aficionados were content to while away the hours watching silver balls bounce frenetically through a maze of bumpers and flashing lights. That, of course, was in the pre-Space Invader era, before solid-state technology revolutionized the coin-operated game industry and challenged pinball machines with computerized video games. Currently, pinball and video games are locked in deadly combat in arcades across the country for dominance of a multimillion-dollar market. How this battle will be won or lost depends, to a great extent, on how enthusiasts react to two entirely different game formats.

Pinball machines have a long history. They can be traced back to a popular nineteenth-century game that was played on a table and was similar to pool. The original pinball game, a board with a coin chute and variations on the placement of holes, went through a swift period of change. New machines had new scoring and play attraction features. Pinball games as we now know them got their start in the late 1930s and within a few years developed into the flippers, bumpers, and flashing lights we know today.

Video games had their start in the solid-state technology that was a spinoff of the space program and computer research. The first video game, called Pong, appeared in 1972 and had a television screen and a handheld control. This simple machine, which at first was viewed by pinball manufacturers as a curiosity, eventually revolutionized the industry and prepared the way for the games that

Introduction

Thesis statement

History (Pinball machines)

History (Video games)

followed. Current video games combine intellectual strategies with realistic visual effects.

Players
(Pinball
machines)

Pinball players are mainly young males. Players who talk about how they feel playing pinball say that they get great satisfaction from beating the machine. Some say that pinball challenges their skill and enables them to beat a machine on its own terms. Obviously the game provides a release of frustration, a challenge, and an opportunity to win—all very important. It also stimulates the senses with buzzers, gongs, voices, and electronic effects. One habitual player sums up the attraction of pinball games when he says, "When you play, nothing else counts. It's just you and the machine."

Players (Video
games)

Computerized video games attract a different type of player, as a trip to a downtown arcade any weekday at lunchtime will show. Standing beside the usual crowd of teenagers are groups of young executives. And no wonder, for video games draw you into a world that lets your imagination run wild. They can give a player the sense of piloting a starship or the thrill of snowboarding down a realistic mountain trail. The most popular—for example, Tekkan, Mace, and Mortal Kombat—allow you to work out your most violent and aggressive fantasies.

Restatement
of thesis

It is too soon to tell who will win the technological war that is presently being fought in arcades. The stakes are high, for a good machine can take in hundreds of dollars a week. Presently, both pinball and video game designers are planning new and spectacular games. But even the most eager pinball players believe that video games will eventually triumph. Pinball is still a game of silver balls being bounced by flippers and bumpers, but video games are constantly evolving as computer technology develops. Possibly the most important difference between the two is that when you play a   Concluding
summary

pinball machine, you only push around a ball, but when you play a

video game, you fight for a galaxy.

EXERCISE 6

Write a comparison-and-contrast essay on one of the following topics. (You may write either a subject-by-subject or a point-by-point comparison.)

- Compare any two athletes, movie or TV stars, writers, or musicians.
- Write an essay about a disillusioning experience you have had. Contrast your original view of what you expected with your feelings after you were disillusioned.
- Explain the differences between the best and worst classes or teachers you have had in your academic career.

5g   Writing Division-and-Classification Essays

A **division-and-classification** essay **divides** (breaks a subject into its component parts) and **classifies** (groups individual terms into categories). Division and classification are closely related processes. For example, when you *divide* the English language into three historical categories (Old English, Middle English, Modern English) you can then *classify* examples of specific linguistic characteristics by assigning them to the appropriate historical period. Transitional words and phrases help to distinguish categories from one another: *one kind, another group, a related category, the most important component.*

(1) Using Division and Classification

You divide and classify information every time you write an academic paper: you *divide* your subject into possible topics, you *classify* your notes into categories, and you *divide* your paper into paragraphs.

Division and classification are also called for in specific academic situations. For example, when you study a laboratory animal, you may arrange your observations in categories that reflect the animal's systems: digestive, circulatory, nervous, and so on. When you write a book review, you may organize your information into sections devoted to plot, the author's previously published works, and your evaluation of the book you are reviewing. Assignments like the following are typical of the many that call for division and classification.

- The English language is constantly in the process of acquiring new words. Write an essay in which you classify some of the many examples of these coinages and adaptations into at least five distinct categories. (History of language midterm)
- Discuss recurrent themes in James Baldwin's novels, short stories, and essays. (American literature research paper)
- Analyze the workings of the federal court system, paying special attention to the relationship between the lower courts, the appellate courts, and the Supreme Court. (Take-home exam in American government)
- Write a detailed report analyzing the possible roles of each member of the management team during the proposed reorganization of the credit department. (Business management report)
- Explain in general terms how the most common orchestral instruments are classified, making sure you provide examples of instruments in each group. (Introduction to music quiz)

(2) Student Essay: Division and Classification

Robin Twery used division and classification to structure the following written version of a presentation she gave to her public speaking class. Before writing out her speech, she made an informal outline that enabled her to establish categories and clarify the relationship of one category to another. (Information was adapted from notes she took in her geology class.)

Classes of Rocks

Introduction
(Lists
categories)

To most people, rocks are distinguished from one another only by size: some are big; others are little. But actually, rocks are divided into three general classes: igneous rocks, sedimentary rocks, and metamorphic rocks.

Igneous rocks were once molten rock; now they have cooled First category
down and solidified. Igneous rocks, like the one I'm holding up now,
may be intrusive or extrusive. Intrusive igneous rocks, in their molten
state, forced their way into other rocks and cooled and hardened there,
sometimes forming very large masses called batholiths. These batholiths
are frequently made up of granite, a crystalline rock. Some other
intrusive igneous rocks can form between other rocks in the form of sills
or dikes. Other igneous rocks are extrusive; that is, they are formed
when molten rock is driven out onto the surface of the earth to cool
and harden. The molten rock that flows along the earth's surface
is lava. The bits of molten rock that are extruded into the air solidify
in the air and fall to the ground in the form of volcanic ash and
cinder.

Sedimentary rocks are formed when other rocks break apart. Second category
Pieces of rock, borne by water or wind, are deposited in the form of
sediments. After a time, these particles are consolidated into rock.
Sedimentary rocks may be classified according to the size of the grains
of which they are composed, ranging from coarse gravel to finer sand,
silt, or clay to fine lime and marl. As you can see in this picture,
sedimentary rocks are usually deposited in layers (strata), with the
oldest sediments on the bottom and the most recent on top.

The final category, metamorphic rock, has been subjected to Third category
great heat and pressure. Metamorphic rocks have been buried under
other rocks so that their structures and their mineral components have
been altered by the weight of the layers above and the high
temperatures to which they are exposed under the earth. An example
of a metamorphic rock is the crystalline rock called gneiss, which is
now being passed around the room.

Conclusion   The next time you take a walk, you can look for igneous, sedimentary, and metamorphic rocks. Now that you know that not all rocks are alike, I hope you will look at them in a different way.

EXERCISE 7

Write a division-and-classification essay on one of the following topics.

- Every social group is governed by a hierarchy, a system whereby individuals or groups of people are ranked at different levels according to their relative importance in the group. Choose one group you know well—your extended family, the population of your school, the people on your street, fellow members of a special interest group to which you belong, coworkers at your place of employment—and place individuals within the hierarchy. Explain why each person ranks where he or she does according to your scheme.
- Itemize the contents of your desk, the surface as well as the drawers, and classify the items into categories. Then, describe an ideal organization pattern for a college student's desk, adding any items you think are needed in each category.

5h   Writing Definition Essays

A **formal definition** includes the term being defined, the class to which it belongs, and the details that distinguish it from the other members of its class.

(term)   (class)   (details)
Carbon is a nonmetallic element occurring as diamond, graphite, and charcoal.

A **definition** essay develops a formal definition with narration, description, exemplification, process, cause and effect, comparison and contrast, or division and classification—or any combination of these patterns. In addition, it may examine the origin of a term by using an **analogy** or by using negation (telling what a term is *not*).

See 6e6

(1) Using Definition

In academic writing, you must define your terms to demonstrate to your audience that you know what you are talking about and to clarify crucial concepts or terms. Following are some typical assignments calling for definition.

- The WPA: History, Operation, and Contributions (American history research paper)
- The villanelle in French and American Poetry (Comparative literature paper)
- Distinguish between the Organic and International schools of modern architecture. (Architecture exam)
- What is a colluvial soil? (Agronomy quiz)
- Define the school of painting known as Fauvism, paying particular attention to the early work of Matisse. (History of art midterm)
- Identify and define four of the following: anorexia, autism, schizophrenia, agoraphobia, paranoia, manic depression, dyssymbolia. (Psychology quiz)

(2) Student Essay: Definition

In response to the **exam question** "Choose one early-twentieth-century American social or political movement and briefly discuss its purpose, its leading supporters, and their social or political contribution," Suzanne Bohrer chose to write on the muckrakers. In defining the term *muckraker,* she decided to include a formal definition, provide a brief explanation of the term's origin, and expand the basic definition to discuss the movement's role in American social and political history.

See Ch. 52

Muckrakers were early-twentieth-century reformers whose mission was to look for and uncover political and business corruption. The term <u>muckraker</u>, which referred to the "man with a muckrake" in John Bunyan's <u>Pilgrim's Progress</u>, was first used in a pejorative sense by Theodore Roosevelt, whose opinion of the muckrakers was that they were biased and overreacting. The movement began about 1902 and died down by 1917. Despite its brief duration, however, it had a significant impact on the political, commercial, and even literary climate of the period.

Introduction
(Includes formal definition and origin of term)

Thesis statement

First point—
movement's
influence
reflected in
magazines

Many popular magazines featured articles whose purpose was to expose corruption. Some of these muckraking periodicals included The Arena , Everybody's, The Independent, and McClure's. Lincoln Steffens, managing editor of McClure's (and later associate editor of American Magazine and Everybody's), was an important leader of the muckraking movement. Some of his exposés were collected in his 1904 book The Shame of the Cities and in two other volumes, and his 1931 autobiography also discusses the corruption he uncovered and the development of the muckraking movement. Ida Tarbell, another noted muckraker, wrote a number of articles for McClure's, some of which were gathered in her 1904 book The History of the Standard Oil Company.

Second
point—
movement's
influence
reflected in
fiction of
D. G. Phillips

Muckraking appeared in fiction as well. David Graham Phillips, who began his career as a newspaperman, went on to write muckraking magazine articles and eventually novels about contemporary economic, political, and social problems, such as insurance scandals, state and municipal corruption, shady Wall Street dealings, slum life, and women's emancipation.

Third (and
most
important)
point—
movement's
influence
reflected in
The Jungle

Perhaps the best-known muckraking novel was Upton Sinclair's The Jungle, the 1906 exposé of the Chicago meatpacking industry. The novel focuses on an immigrant family and sympathetically and realistically describes their struggles with loan sharks and others who take advantage of their innocence. More importantly, Sinclair graphically describes the brutal working conditions of those who find work in the stockyards. Sinclair's description of the main character's work in the fertilizer plant is particularly gruesome; at the novel's end, this man turns to socialism.

With the muckrakers featured prominently in fiction, magazines, Conclusion and newspapers—especially the New York <u>World</u> and the Kansas City <u>Star</u>—some results were forthcoming. Perhaps the most far-reaching was the pure-food legislation of 1906, supposedly a direct result of Roosevelt's reading of <u>The Jungle</u>. In any case, the muckrakers helped to nourish the growing tradition of social reform in America.

EXERCISE 8

Write a definition essay on one of the following topics.

- Select a term or concept that is central to an understanding of one of your courses other than English composition. Explain the term or concept to someone who has not yet taken the course.
- Choose a word or phrase that has a strong emotional meaning to almost everyone—*patriotism* or *family values*, for example—and interview five people from different age groups and backgrounds, asking each what the term means. Use their responses to write a definition essay developed with a series of examples.

✔ CHECKLIST: PATTERNS OF ESSAY DEVELOPMENT

- ✔ **Narration**   Have you discussed enough events to enable readers to understand what occurred? Have you supported your thesis statement with specific details and dialogue?
- ✔ **Description**   Have you supplied enough detail about what things look like, sound like, smell like, taste like, and feel like? Will your readers be able to visualize the person, object, or setting that your essay describes?
- ✔ **Exemplification**   Have you presented enough examples to support your essay's thesis? If you have used a single extended example, will readers understand how it supports the essay's thesis?

continued on the following page

continued from the previous page

✔ **Process**　Have you presented enough steps to enable readers to understand how the process is performed? Is the sequence of steps clear? If you are writing instructions, have you included enough explanation—as well as reminders and warnings—to enable readers to perform the process efficiently and safely?

✔ **Cause and Effect**　Have you identified enough causes (subtle as well as obvious, minor as well as major) to enable readers to understand why something occurred? Have you identified enough effects to show the significance of the causes and the impact they had?

✔ **Comparison and Contrast**　Have you supplied a sufficient number of details to illustrate each of the subjects in the comparison? Have you presented a similar number of details for each subject?

✔ **Division and Classification**　Have you presented enough information to enable readers to identify each category and distinguish one from another?

✔ **Definition**　Have you presented enough detail (examples, analogies, and so on) to enable readers to understand the term you are defining and to distinguish it from others in its class?

CHAPTER 6

WRITING PARAGRAPHS

? FREQUENTLY ASKED QUESTIONS

When do I begin a new paragraph?   (p. 97)
What is a topic sentence?   (p. 98)
What transitional words and phrases can I use
   to make my paragraphs flow?   (p. 105)
How do I know if I have enough
   information to support my paragraph's
   main idea?   (p. 111)
How do I write a good introduction for my
   paper?   (p. 124)
How do I write an effective conclusion?
   (p. 127)

A **paragraph** is a group of related sentences. It may be complete in itself or part of a longer piece of writing.

WHEN TO PARAGRAPH

- Begin a new paragraph whenever you move from one major point to another.
- Begin a new paragraph whenever you move your readers from one time period or location to another.
- Begin a new paragraph whenever you introduce a new step in a process or sequence.
- Begin a new paragraph when you want to emphasize important ideas.
- Begin a new paragraph every time a new person speaks.
- Begin a new paragraph to signal the end of your introduction and the beginning of your conclusion.

Paragraphs (from Harvard U.)
   http://www.fas.harvard.edu/~wricntr/para.html
Writing Topic Sentences
   http://www.uottawa.ca/academic/arts/writcent/hypergrammar/partopic.html

6a   Charting Paragraph Structure

Charting a paragraph helps you see its underlying structure. By charting your paragraphs, you can make certain that each one is **unified**, **coherent**, and **well developed**.

Begin charting by assigning the sentence that expresses the main idea of the paragraph to level 1. (If no sentence in the paragraph expresses the main idea, compose a sentence that does.) Then, indent and assign to level 2 more specific sentences, those that qualify or limit the main idea. Indent again and assign to level 3 any sentences that support level-2 sentences. Do this for every sentence in the paragraph, assigning increasingly higher numbers to more specific sentences.

Notice in the following paragraph how the first sentence (level 1) introduces the topic of the paragraph by stating the main idea. Each level-2 sentence restricts the topic by explaining this idea. Finally, the level-3 sentences illustrate the points made in the level-2 sentences.

> 1 My grandmother told me that fifty years ago life was not easy for a girl in rural Italy.
>> 2 At the age of six, a girl was expected to help her mother with household chores.
>>> 3 Girls of this age were no longer permitted to play games or to indulge in childish activities.
>> 2 At the age of twelve, a girl assumed most of the responsibilities of an adult.
>>> 3 She worked in the fields, prepared meals, carried water, and took care of the younger children.
>>> 3 It was an unusual family that allowed a girl to enroll in one of the few convent schools that took peasant children.

NOTE: A logically constructed paragraph has only one level-1 sentence. If your charting reveals more than one level-1 sentence, you need to **revise** your paragraph, perhaps dividing it into two paragraphs.

6b   Writing Unified Paragraphs

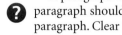

A paragraph is **unified** when its sentences develop a single idea. Each paragraph should have a **topic sentence** that states the main idea of the paragraph. Clear topic sentences help readers follow your discussion and enable you to make sure that your paragraphs are unified.

(1) Using Topic Sentences

Topic sentences can be placed at the beginning, in the middle, or at the end of a paragraph. In some cases, the paragraph's main idea is implied, and so there is no stated topic sentence.

Topic Sentence at the Beginning   A topic sentence at the beginning of a paragraph tells readers what to expect and helps them to understand your paragraph's main idea immediately.

<u>I was a listening child, careful to hear the very different sounds of Spanish and English.</u> Wide-eyed with hearing, I'd listen to sounds more than words. First, there were English *(gringo)* sounds. So many words were still unknown that when the butcher or the lady at the drugstore said something to me, exotic polysyllabic sounds would bloom in the midst of their sentences. Often the speech of people in public seemed to me very loud, booming with confidence. The man behind the counter would literally ask, "What can I do for you?" But by being so firm and so clear, the sound of his voice said that he was a *gringo;* he belonged in public society. (Richard Rodriguez, *Aria: A Memoir of a Bilingual Childhood*)

Topic Sentence in the Middle   A topic sentence in the middle of a paragraph leads readers to the main idea gradually or gives background information before you state and support your main idea.

African-American servicemen have played a role in the US military since revolutionary times. In the years before World War II, however, they were employed chiefly as truck drivers, quartermasters, bakers, and cooks. Then, in July 1941, a program was set up at Alabama's Tuskegee Institute to train black fighter pilots. Eventually, nearly one thousand flyers—about half of whom fought overseas—were trained there; sixty-six of these men were killed in action. <u>Ironically, even as African-American servicemen were fighting valiantly against fascism in Europe, they continued to experience discrimination in the US military</u>. Black officers encountered hostility and even violence at officers' clubs. Enlisted men and women were frequently the target of bigoted remarks. Throughout the war, in fact, African-American servicemen were placed in separate, all-black units. This segregation was official army policy until 1948, when President Harry S. Truman signed an executive order to desegregate the military. (Student Writer)

Topic Sentence at the End   Occasionally, particularly if you are presenting an unusual or hard-to-accept idea, you may decide to place a topic sentence at the end of a paragraph. If you present a logical chain of reasoning and *then* state your conclusion in the topic sentence, you are more likely to convince readers that your conclusion is reasonable.

These sprays, dusts and aerosols are now applied almost universally to farms, gardens, forests, and homes—nonselective chemicals that have the power to kill every insect, the "good" and the "bad," to still the song of birds and the leaping of fish in the streams, to coat the leaves with a deadly film, and to linger on in soil—all this though the intended target may be only a few weeds or insects. Can anyone believe it is possible to lay down such a barrage of poisons on the surface without making it unfit for life? They should not be called "insecticides," but "biocides." (Rachel Carson, "The Obligation to Endure," *Silent Spring*)

Main Idea Implied   In some situations, you may not need a topic sentence—for example, if an explicit topic sentence would seem forced or unnatural, as it might in some narrative or descriptive paragraphs. Even in such cases, your paragraph must have a clear, unifying idea. In the following paragraph, for example, the author wants readers to conclude for themselves (as she did) that because she was female, she was considered inferior.

I am eight years old and a tomboy. I have a cowboy hat, cowboy boots, checkered shirt and pants, all red. My playmates are my brothers, two and four years older than I. Their colors are black and green, the only difference in the way we are dressed. On Saturday nights we all go to the picture show, even my mother; Westerns are her favorite kind of movie. Back home, "on the ranch," we pretend we are Tom Mix, Hopalong Cassidy, Lash LaRue (we've even named one of our dogs Lash LaRue); we chase each other for hours rustling cattle, being outlaws, delivering damsels from distress. Then my parents decide to buy my brothers guns. These are not "real" guns. They shoot "BBs," copper pellets my brothers say will kill birds. Because I am a girl, I do not get a gun. Instantly I am relegated to the position of Indian. Now there appears a great distance between us. They shoot and shoot at everything with their new guns. I try to keep up with my bow and arrows. (Alice Walker, "Beauty: When the Other Dancer Is the Self," *In Search of Our Mothers' Gardens*)

(2) Revising for Unity

Each sentence in a paragraph should support its main idea, whether that idea is stated or implied. The following paragraph is not unified because it includes sentences that do not support the main idea.

> <u>One of the first problems that students have is learning to use a computer.</u> All students were required to buy a computer before school started. Throughout the first semester, we took a special course to teach us to use a computer. My notebook computer has a large memory and can do word processing and spreadsheets. It has a hard drive and a modem. My parents were happy that I had a computer, but they were concerned about the price. Tuition was high, and when they added in the price of the computer, it was almost out of reach. To offset expenses, I got a part-time job in the school library. Now I am determined to overcome "computer anxiety" and to master my computer by the end of the semester. (Student Writer)

The lack of unity in the preceding paragraph becomes obvious when you **chart** its structure.

See
6a

1 One of the first problems that students have is learning to use a computer.
  2 All students were required to buy a computer before school started.
    3 Throughout the first semester, we took a special course to teach us to use a computer.
1 My notebook computer has a large memory and can do word processing and spreadsheets.
  2 It has a hard drive and a modem.
1 My parents were happy that I had a computer, but they were concerned about the price.
  2 Tuition was high, and when they added in the price of the computer, it was almost out of reach.
    3 To offset expenses, I got a part-time job in the school library.
1 Now I am determined to overcome "computer anxiety" and to master my computer by the end of the semester.

Each level-1 sentence represents a topic that could be developed in its own paragraph; in other words, this paragraph has not one but four topic sentences. Instead of writing one unified paragraph, the writer has made a series of false starts.

After the writer decided what his main idea actually was, he deleted the sentences about his parents' financial situation and the computer's characteristics, keeping only those details related to the main idea (expressed in his topic sentence).

<u>One of the first problems that I had as a college student was learning to use my computer.</u> All first-year students were required to buy a computer before school started. Throughout the first semester, we took a special course to teach us to use the computer. In theory this system sounded fine, but in my case it was a disaster. In the first place, the closest I had ever come to a computer was the handheld calculator I used in math class. In the second place, I could not type. And to make matters worse, many of the people in my computer orientation course already knew how to operate a computer. By the end of the first week, I was convinced that I would never be able to work with my computer.

EXERCISE 1

Each of the following paragraphs is unified by one main idea, but that idea is not explicitly stated. Identify the main idea of each paragraph, write a topic sentence that expresses it, and decide where in the paragraph to place it.

A. The narrator in Ellison's novel leaves an all-black college in the South to seek his fortune—and his identity—in the North. Throughout the story, he experiences bigotry in all forms. Blacks as well as whites, friends as well as enemies, treat him according to their preconceived notions of what he should be, or how he can help to advance their causes. Clearly this is a book about racial prejudice. However, on another level, *Invisible Man* is more than the account of a young African American's initiation into the harsh realities of life in the United States before the civil rights movement. The narrator calls himself invisible because others refuse to see him. He becomes so alienated from society—black and white—that he chooses to live in isolation. But, when he has learned to see himself clearly, he will emerge demanding that others see him, too.

B. "Lite" can mean that a product has fewer calories, or less fat, or less sodium, or it can simply mean that the product has a "light" color, texture, or taste. It may also mean none of these. Food can be advertised as 86 percent fat free when it is actually 50 percent fat because the term "fat free" is based on weight, and fat is extremely light. Another misleading term is "no cholesterol," which is found on some products that never had any cholesterol in the first place. Peanut

82-85

103-109

butter, for example, contains no cholesterol—a fact that manufacturers have recently made an issue—but it is very high in fat and so would not be a very good food for most dieters. Sodium labeling presents still another problem. The terms "sodium free," "very low sodium," "low sodium," "reduced sodium," and "no salt added" have very specific meanings, frequently not explained on the packages on which they appear.

6c Writing Coherent Paragraphs

A paragraph is **coherent** if its sentences are logically related to one another. You can achieve coherence by arranging details according to an organizing principle, by using transitional words and phrases, by using pronouns, by using parallel structure, and by repeating key words and phrases.

(1) Arranging Details

Even if its sentences are all about the same subject, a paragraph lacks coherence if the sentences are not arranged according to a general organizing principle—*spatial, chronological,* or *logical.*

Spatial order establishes the perspective from which readers will view details. For example, an object or scene can be viewed from top to bottom or from near to far. Spatial order is central to paragraphs that use **description**. Notice how the following descriptive paragraph begins on top of a hill, moves down to a valley, follows a river through the valley into the distance, and then moves to a point behind the speaker, where Mount Adams stands.

See
6e2

> East of us rose another hill like ours. Between the hills, far below, was the highway which threaded south into the valley. This was the Yakima valley; I had never seen it before. It is justly famous for its beauty, like every planted valley. It extended south into the horizon, a distant dream of a valley, a Shangri-la. All its hundreds of low, golden slopes bore orchards. Among the orchards were towns, and roads, and plowed and fallow fields. Through the valley wandered a thin, shining river; from the river extended fine, frozen irrigation ditches. Distance blurred and blued the sight, so that the whole valley looked like a thickness or sediment at the bottom of the sky. Directly behind us was more sky, and empty lowlands blued by

distance, and Mount Adams. Mount Adams was an enormous, snow-covered volcanic cone rising flat, like so much scenery. (Annie Dillard, "Total Eclipse")

Chronological order presents details in sequence, using transitional words and phrases that establish the sequence of events—*at first, yesterday, later,* and so on. Chronological order is central to paragraphs that use **narration** and **process**. The following narrative paragraph gains coherence from the orderly sequence of events.

They married in February, 1921, and began farming. Their first baby, a daughter, was born in January, 1922, when my mother was 26 years old. The second baby, a son, was born in March, 1923. They were renting farms; my father, besides working his own fields, also was a hired man for two other farmers. They had no capital initially, and had to gain it slowly, working from dawn until midnight every day. My town-bred mother learned to set hens and raise chickens, feed pigs, milk cows, plant and harvest a garden, and can every fruit and vegetable she could scrounge. She carried water nearly a quarter of a mile from the well to fill her wash boilers in order to do her laundry on a scrub board. She learned to shuck grain, feed threshers, shuck and husk corn, feed corn pickers. In September, 1925, the third baby came, and in June, 1927, the fourth child—both daughters. In 1930, my parents had enough money to buy their own farm, and that March they moved all their livestock and belongings themselves, 55 miles over rutted, muddy roads. (Donna Smith-Yackel, "My Mother Never Worked")

Logical order presents ideas in terms of their logical relationship to one another. For example, the ideas in a paragraph may move from *general to specific,* as in the conventional topic-sentence-at-the-beginning paragraph, or the ideas may progress from *specific to general,* as they do when the topic sentence appears at the end of the paragraph. A writer may also choose to begin with the *least important* idea and move to the *most important.* The following paragraph moves from a *general* statement about the need to address the problem of the injury rate in boxing to *specific* solutions.

Several reforms would help solve the problem of the high injury rate in boxing. First, all boxers should wear protective equipment—head gear and kidney protectors, for example. This equipment is required in amateur boxing and should be required in professional boxing. Second, the object of boxing should be to score points, not to knock out opponents. An increased glove weight would make knockouts almost impossible. And finally, all fights should be limited to ten rounds. Studies show that most serious injuries occur in boxing between the eleventh and fifteenth rounds—when the boxers are tired and vulnerable. By limiting the number of rounds a boxer could fight, officials could substantially reduce the number of serious injuries. (Student Writer)

(2) Using Transitional Words and Phrases

Transitional words and phrases clarify the relationships between sentences in a paragraph by identifying spatial, chronological, and logical connections. (These words and phrases are also used to achieve **coherence between paragraphs** in an essay.) In the following paragraph, such words and phrases as *after, finally, once again,* and *in the end* identify the order in which events occurred.

See 6c6

Napoleon certainly made a change for the worse by leaving his small kingdom of Elba. After Waterloo, he went back to Paris, and he abdicated for a second time. A hundred days after his return from Elba, he fled to Rochfort in hope of escaping to America. Finally, he gave himself up to the English captain of the ship *Bellerophon.* Once again, he suggested that the Prince Regent grant him asylum, and once again, he was refused. In the end, all he saw of England was the Devon coast and Plymouth Sound as he passed on to the remote island of St. Helena. After six years of exile, he died on May 5, 1821, at the age of fifty-two. (Norman Mackenzie, *The Escape from Elba*)

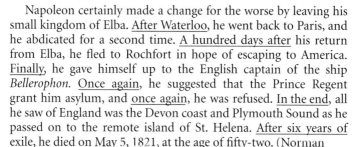

USING TRANSITIONAL WORDS AND PHRASES

To Signal Sequence or Addition

again	in addition
also	last
and	next
besides	one . . . another
finally	still
first . . . second . . . third	too
furthermore	

continued on the following page

Writing Transitions
   http:www.unc.edu/depts/wcweb/handouts/transitions.html

continued from the previous page

To Signal Time

afterward	in the meantime
as soon as	later
at first	meanwhile
at length	next
at the same time	now
before	soon
earlier	subsequently
eventually	then
finally	until
immediately	

To Signal Comparison

also	likewise
by the same token	similarly
in comparison	

To Signal Contrast

although	nevertheless
but	nonetheless
despite	on the contrary
even though	on the one hand ...
however	on the other hand
in contrast	still
instead	whereas
meanwhile	yet

To Signal Examples

for example	specifically
for instance	thus
namely	

To Signal Narrowing of Focus

after all	in particular
indeed	specifically
in fact	that is
in other words	

> ### To Signal Conclusions or Summaries
>
> | | |
> |---|---|
> | as a result | in summary |
> | consequently | therefore |
> | in conclusion | thus |
> | in other words | to conclude |
>
> ### To Signal Concession
>
> | | |
> |---|---|
> | admittedly | naturally |
> | certainly | of course |
> | granted | |
>
> ### To Signal Causes or Effects
>
> | | |
> |---|---|
> | accordingly | since |
> | as a result | so |
> | because | then |
> | consequently | therefore |
> | hence | |

(3) Using Pronouns

By referring to nouns or other pronouns, **pronouns** establish connections between sentences. Clear, well-placed **pronoun references**, such as those in the following paragraph, help to make a paragraph's ideas easier to follow.

See
33c

> Like Martin Luther, John Calvin wanted to return to the principles of early Christianity described in the New Testament. Martin Luther founded the evangelical churches in Germany and Scandinavia, and John Calvin founded a number of reformed churches in other countries. A third Protestant branch, episcopacy, developed in England. Its members rejected the word *Protestant* because they agreed with Roman Catholicism on most points. All these sects rejected the primacy of the pope. They accepted the Bible as the only source of revealed truth, and they held that faith, not good works, defined a person's relationship to God. (Student Writer)

(4) Using Parallel Structure

Parallelism—the use of similar grammatical constructions to reinforce similar ideas—can help to increase the coherence of a paragraph.

See
21c;
27a

Note in the following paragraph how parallel constructions (that begin with "He was . . .") link Thomas Jefferson's accomplishments:

Thomas Jefferson was born in 1743 and died at Monticello, Virginia, on July 4, 1826. During his eighty-four years, he accomplished a number of things. Although best known for his draft of the Declaration of Independence, Jefferson was a man of many talents who had a wide intellectual range. He was a patriot who was one of the revolutionary founders of the United States. He was a reformer who, when he was governor of Virginia, drafted the Statute for Religious Freedom. He was an innovator who drafted an ordinance for governing the West and devised the first decimal monetary system. He was a president who abolished internal taxes, reduced the national debt, and made the Louisiana Purchase. And, finally, he was an architect who designed Monticello and the University of Virginia. (Student Writer)

(5) Repeating Key Words and Phrases

Repeating **key words and phrases**—those essential to meaning—throughout a paragraph connects the sentences to one another and to the paragraph's main idea. The following paragraph repeats the key word *mercury* to help readers focus on the subject.

Mercury poisoning is a problem that has long been recognized. "Mad as a hatter" refers to the condition prevalent among nineteenth-century workers who were exposed to mercury during the manufacturing of felt hats. Workers in many other industries, such as mining, chemicals, and dentistry, were similarly affected. In the 1950s and 1960s, there were cases of mercury poisoning in Minamata, Japan. Research showed that there were high levels of mercury pollution in streams and lakes surrounding the village. In the United States, this problem came to light in 1969 when a New Mexico family got sick from eating food tainted with mercury. Since then pesticides containing mercury have been withdrawn from the market, and chemical wastes can no longer be dumped into the ocean. (Student Writer)

Notice that to avoid monotony the writer sometimes refers indirectly to the subject of the paragraph with such phrases as *similarly affected* and *this problem.*

(6) Achieving Coherence between Paragraphs

The strategies you use to establish coherence within paragraphs may also be used to link paragraphs in an essay. In addition to these strategies, you can use topic sentences to connect paragraphs. You can also use a **transitional paragraph** as a bridge between two paragraphs.

See
6f1

The following group of related paragraphs shows how some of the preceding strategies work together to create a coherent unit.

> <u>A language may borrow a word directly or indirectly.</u> A direct borrowing means that the borrowed item is a native word in the language it is borrowed from. *Festa* was borrowed directly from French and can be traced back to Latin *festa.* On the other hand, the word *algebra* was borrowed from Spanish, which in turn borrowed it from Arabic. Thus *algebra* was indirectly borrowed from Arabic, with Spanish as an intermediary.
>
> <u>Some languages are heavy borrowers.</u> Albanian has borrowed so heavily that few native words are retained. On the other hand, most Native American languages have borrowed little from their neighbors.
>
> <u>English has borrowed extensively.</u> Of the 20,000 or so words in common use, about three-fifths are borrowed. Of the 500 most frequently used words, however, only two-sevenths are borrowed, and because these "common" words are used over and over again in sentences, the actual frequency of appearance of native words is about 80 percent. Morphemes such as *and, be, have, it, of, the, to, will, you, on, that,* and *is* are all native to English. (Victoria Fromkin and Robert Rodman, *An Introduction to Language*)

These paragraphs are arranged according to a logical organizing principle, moving from the general concept of borrowing words to a specific discussion of English. In addition, each topic sentence repeats a variation of the word group *A language may borrow.* Throughout the three paragraphs, some form of this key phrase (as well as *word* and the names of various languages) appears in almost every sentence.

EXERCISE 2

A. Read the following paragraph, and determine how the author achieves coherence. Identify parallel elements, pronouns, repeated words, and transitional words and phrases that link sentences.

Some years ago the old elevated railway in Philadelphia was torn down and replaced by the subway system. This ancient El with its barnlike stations containing nut-vending machines and scattered food scraps had, for generations, been the favorite feeding ground of flocks of pigeons, generally one flock to a station along the route of the El. Hundreds of pigeons were dependent upon the system. They flapped in and out of its stanchions and steel work or gathered in watchful little audiences about the feet of anyone who rattled the peanut-vending machines. They even watched people who jingled change in their hands, and prospected for food under the feet of the crowds who gathered between trains. Probably very few among the waiting people who tossed a crumb to an eager pigeon realized that this El was like a food-bearing river, and that the life which haunted its banks was dependent upon the running of the trains with their human freight. (Loren Eiseley, *The Night Country*)

B. Revise the following paragraph to make it more coherent.

The theory of continental drift was first put forward by Alfred Wegener in 1912. The continents fit together like a gigantic jigsaw puzzle. The opposing Atlantic coasts, especially South America and Africa, seem to have been attached. He believed that at one time, probably 225 million years ago, there was one supercontinent. This continent broke into parts that drifted into their present positions. The theory stirred controversy during the 1920s and eventually was ridiculed by the scientific community. In 1954, the theory was revived. The theory of continental drift is accepted as a reasonable geological explanation of the continental system. (Student Writer)

EXERCISE 3

Read the following group of related paragraphs. Then, revise as necessary to increase coherence among paragraphs.

Leave It to Beaver and *Father Knows Best* were typical of the late 1950s and early 1960s. Both were popular during a time when middle-class mothers stayed home to raise their children while fathers went to "the office." The Beaver's mother, June Cleaver, always wore a dress and high heels, even when she vacuumed. So did Margaret Anderson, the mother on *Father Knows Best*. Wally and the Beaver lived a picture-perfect small-town life, and Betty, Bud, and Kathy never had a problem that father Jim Anderson couldn't solve.

The Brady Bunch featured six children and the typical Mom-at-home and Dad-at-work combination. Of course, Carol Brady did wear pants, and the Bradys were what today would be called a "blended family." Nevertheless, *The Brady Bunch* presented a hopelessly idealized picture of upper-middle-class suburban life. The Brady kids lived in a large split-level house, went on vacations, had two loving parents, and even had a live-in maid, the ever-faithful, wisecracking Alice. Everyone in town was heterosexual, employed, able-bodied, and white.

The Cosby Show was extremely popular. It featured two professional parents, a doctor and a lawyer. They lived in a townhouse with original art on the walls, and money never seemed to be a problem. In addition to warm relationships with their siblings, the Huxtable children also had close ties to their grandparents. *The Cosby Show* did introduce problems, such as son Theo's dyslexia, but in many ways it replicated the 1950s formula. Even in the 1980s, it seemed, father still knew best.

6d Writing Well-Developed Paragraphs

A paragraph is **well developed** when it includes all the information—  examples, statistics, expert opinion, and so on—that readers need to understand and accept its main idea.

WELL-DEVELOPED PARAGRAPHS

Keep in mind that length does not determine whether a paragraph is well developed. The amount and kind of support you need depends on your audience, your purpose, and your paragraph's main idea.

- **Identify your audience.** Will readers be familiar with your subject? Given the needs of your audience, is your paragraph well developed?
- **Identify your purpose.** Should the paragraph give readers a general overview of your topic, or should it present detailed information? Given your purpose, is your paragraph well developed?
- **Identify your paragraph's main idea.** Do you need to explain it more fully? Do you need another example, a statistic, an anecdote, or expert opinion? Given the complexity and scope of your main idea, is your paragraph well developed?

(1) Testing for Adequate Development

Just as **charting paragraph structure** can help you see whether a paragraph is unified, it can also help you determine whether the paragraph is well developed. At first glance, the following paragraph may seem adequately developed.

> From Thanksgiving until Christmas, children and their parents are bombarded by ads for violent toys and games. Toy manufacturers persist in thinking that only toys that appeal to children's aggressiveness will sell. Despite claims that they (unlike action toys) have educational value, video games have escalated the level of violence. The real question is why parents continue to buy these violent toys and games for their children.

Charting the underlying structure of the paragraph, however, reveals a problem.

> 1 From Thanksgiving until Christmas, children and their parents are bombarded by ads for violent toys and games.
>> 2 Toy manufacturers persist in thinking that only toys that appeal to children's aggressiveness will sell.
>> 2 Despite claims that they (unlike action toys) have educational value, video games have escalated the level of violence.
>> 2 The real question is why parents continue to buy these violent toys and games for their children.

Upon closer examination, we see that the paragraph does not contain enough support to convince readers that children and parents are "bombarded by ads for violent toys." The first sentence of this paragraph, the topic sentence, is a level-1 sentence. The level-2 sentences do qualify this topic sentence, but the paragraph offers no level-3 sentences (specific examples). What kinds of toys appeal to a child's aggressive tendencies? What particular video games does the writer object to?

(2) Revising Undeveloped Paragraphs

You can improve undeveloped paragraphs like the preceding one by adding specific examples that illustrate the statements made in the level-2 sentences.

> From Thanksgiving until Christmas, children and their parents are bombarded by ads for violent toys and games. Toy manufacturers persist in thinking that only toys that appeal to children's aggres-

siveness will sell. *One television commercial features a commando team that attacks and captures a miniature enemy base. Toy soldiers wear realistic uniforms and carry automatic rifles, pistols, knives, grenades, and ammunition. Another commercial shows laughing children shooting one another with plastic rocket launchers and tanklike vehicles.* Despite claims that they (unlike action toys) have educational value, video games have escalated the level of violence. *The most popular video games involve children in strikingly realistic combat simulations. One game lets children search out and destroy enemy fighters on the ground and in the air. Other best-selling games graphically simulate hand-to-hand combat on city streets and feature dismembered bodies and the sound of breaking bones.* The real question is why parents continue to buy these violent toys and games for their children.

← Examples

← Examples

You can use expert opinion and statistics to develop the paragraph further.

From Thanksgiving to Christmas, children are bombarded by ads for violent toys and games. Toy manufacturers persist in thinking that only toys that appeal to children's aggressiveness will sell. *The president of one large toy company recently observed that in spite of what people may say, they buy action toys. This is why toy companies spend so much money on commercials that promote them* (Wilson 54). One such television commercial features a commando team that attacks and captures a miniature enemy base. Toy soldiers wear realistic uniforms and carry automatic rifles, pistols, knives, grenades, and ammunition. Another commercial shows laughing children shooting one another with plastic rocket launchers and tanklike vehicles. Despite claims that they (unlike action toys) have educational value, video games have escalated the level of violence. *A parents' watchdog group has estimated that during the past three years, violent video games have increased sales by almost 20 percent* ("Action Toys Sell" 17). The most popular video games involve children in strikingly realistic combat situations. One game lets children search out and destroy enemy fighters on the ground and in the air. Other best-selling games graphically simulate hand-to-hand combat on city streets and feature dismembered bodies and chilling sound effects. The real question is why parents continue to buy these violent toys and games for their children.

← Expert
opinion

← Statistic

Along with several specific examples, this revised paragraph includes an expert opinion—a statement by a toy manufacturer—and a statistic that shows the extent to which sales of violent video games have increased.

(Notice that the writer documents both the expert opinion and the statistic because she got them from outside sources.)

The following paragraph is also inadequately developed.

> Handheld calculators have made it impossible for people to think. People have lost their ability to solve simple problems in their minds without using a piece of equipment that does the work for them. Calculators have become too controlling over our intellect. Without calculators, many people would be unable to function.

Once you chart the paragraph's structure, the problem becomes clear.

1 Handheld calculators have made it difficult for many students to think independently.
1 People have lost their ability to think without using a piece of equipment that does the work for them.
1 Calculators have become too controlling over our intellect.
1 Without calculators, most of us would be unable to function.

This paragraph contains only level-1 sentences. In other words, it keeps making the same general point over and over again. Because it never develops this point, the paragraph goes nowhere. By editing the first sentence into a topic sentence, editing the second sentence so it restricts the topic sentence, and adding supporting detail, the writer expands the discussion and makes this paragraph much more convincing.

> Handheld calculators have made it difficult for many people to think independently. They have lost their ability to solve simple problems without using a piece of equipment that does the work for them. Recently, when my math instructor told our class to put away our calculators and take a test, some of the students were unable to solve the problems or to do simple calculations in their heads. Formal studies have shown similar results. In one college, for example, Domb reports that a number of students in physics, chemistry, and accounting classes were unable to do simple problems, even though they were able to use calculators to do complex tasks. Shockingly, 22 percent of the students had difficulty calculating 17 percent of $21 or estimating the yearly interest on a car loan. Domb concludes that the extensive use of calculators has made it unnecessary for students to master the basics of mathematics (43).

Anecdote →
Example →
Statistic →
Expert →
opinion

EXERCISE 4

Write a paragraph for two of the following topic sentences. Make sure you include all the examples and other support necessary to develop the paragraph adequately. Assume that you are writing your paragraph for the members of your composition class.

1. First-year students can take specific steps to make sure that they are successful in college.
2. Setting up a first apartment can be quite a challenge.
3. Whenever I get depressed, I think of _____, and I feel better.
4. The person I admire the most is _____.
5. If I won the lottery, I would do three things.

EXERCISE 5

Chart each of the paragraphs that you wrote for Exercise 4. If your charting indicates that you have not adequately developed a paragraph, revise it, adding the necessary detail.

6e   Patterns of Paragraph Development

Patterns of paragraph development—*narration, exemplification,* and so on—like **essay patterns**, reflect the way a writer arranges material to express ideas most effectively.

See
Ch. 5

(1) Narration

Narrative paragraphs tell a story, with words and phrases moving readers from one time period to another.

My academic career almost ended as soon as it began when, three weeks after I arrived at college, I decided to pledge a fraternity. By midterms, I was wearing a straw hat and saying "Yes sir" to every fraternity brother I met. When classes were over, I ran errands for the fraternity members, and after dinner I socialized and worked on projects with the other people in my pledge class. In between these activities, I tried to study. Somehow I managed to write papers, take tests, and attend lectures. By the end of the semester, though, my grades had slipped, and I was exhausted. It was then that I began to ask myself some important questions. I realized that I wanted to be popular, but not at the expense of my grades and my future career. At the beginning of my second semester, I dropped out of the fraternity and got a job in the biology lab. Looking back, I realize that it was then that I actually began to grow up. (Student Writer)

(2) Description

Descriptive paragraphs convey how something looks, sounds, smells, tastes, or feels. Transitional words and phrases clarify the spatial relationships.

> When you are inside the jungle, away from the river, the trees vault out of sight. It is hard to remember to look up the long trunks and see the fans, strips, fronds, and sprays of glossy leaves. Inside the jungle you are more likely to notice the snarl of climbers and creepers round the trees' boles, the flowering bromeliads and epiphytes in every bough's crook, and the fantastic silk-cotton tree trunks thirty or forty feet across, trunks buttressed in flanges of wood whose curves can make three high walls of a room—a shady, loamy-aired room where you would gladly live, or die. Butterflies, iridescent blue, striped, or clear-winged, thread the jungle paths at eye level. And at your feet is a swath of ants bearing triangular bits of green leaf. The ants with their leaves look like a wide fleet of sailing dinghies—but they don't quit. In either direction they wobble over the jungle floor as far as the eye can see. I followed them off the path as far as I dared, and never saw an end to ants or to those luffing chips of green they bore. (Annie Dillard, "In the Jungle")

(3) Exemplification

Exemplification paragraphs use specific illustrations to clarify a general statement. Most exemplification paragraphs, like the following, use several examples to support the topic sentence (others may use a single extended example).

> Illiterates cannot travel freely. When they attempt to do so, they encounter risks that few of us can dream of. They cannot read traffic signs and, while they often learn to recognize and to decipher symbols, they cannot manage street names which they haven't seen before. The same is true for bus and subway stops. While ingenuity can sometimes help a man or woman to discern directions from familiar landmarks, buildings, cemeteries, churches, and the like, most illiterates are virtually immobilized. They seldom wander past the streets and neighborhoods they know. Geographical paralysis becomes a bitter metaphor for

their entire existence. They are immobilized in almost every sense we can imagine. They can't move up. They can't move out. They cannot see beyond. Illiterates may take an oral test for drivers' permits in most sections of America. It is a questionable concession. Where will they go? How will they get there? How will they get home? Could it be that some of us might like it better if they stayed where they belong? (Jonathan Kozol, *Illiterate America*)

(4) Process

Process paragraphs describe how something works, presenting a series of steps in strict chronological order. The topic sentence identifies the process, and the rest of the paragraph presents the steps involved.

Members of the court have disclosed, however, the general way the conference is conducted. It begins at ten A.M. and usually runs on until late afternoon. At the start each justice, when he enters the room, shakes hands with all others there (thirty-six handshakes altogether). The custom, dating back generations, is evidently designed to begin the meeting at a friendly level, no matter how heated the intellectual differences may be. The conference takes up, first, the applications for review—a few appeals, many more petitions for certiorari. Those on the Appellate Docket, the regular paid cases, are considered first, then the pauper's applications on the Miscellaneous Docket. (If any of these are granted, they are then transferred to the Appellate Docket.) After this the justices consider, and vote on, all the cases argued during the preceding Monday through Thursday. These are tentative votes, which may be and quite often are changed as the opinion is written and the problem thought through more deeply. There may be further discussion at later conferences before the opinion is handed down. (Anthony Lewis, *Gideon's Trumpet*)

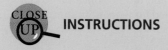 **INSTRUCTIONS**

When a process paragraph presents instructions to enable readers to actually perform the process, it is written in the present tense and in the **imperative mood**—"*Remove* the cover . . . and *check* the valve."

See
28c

(5) Cause and Effect

Cause-and-effect paragraphs explore why events occur and what happens as a result of them.

Some paragraphs examine causes.

> The main reason that a young baby sucks his thumb seems to be that he hasn't had enough sucking at the breast or bottle to satisfy his sucking needs. Dr. David Levy pointed out that babies who are fed every 3 hours don't suck their thumbs as much as babies fed every 4 hours, and that babies who have cut down on nursing time from 20 minutes to 10 minutes [. . .] are more likely to suck their thumbs than babies who still have to work for 20 minutes. Dr. Levy fed a litter of puppies with a medicine dropper so that they had no chance to suck during their feedings. They acted just the same as babies who don't get enough chance to suck at feeding time. They sucked their own and each other's paws and skin so hard that the fur came off. (Benjamin Spock, *Baby and Child Care*)

Other paragraphs focus on effects.

> On December 8, 1941, the day after the Japanese attack on Pearl Harbor in Hawaii, my grandfather barricaded himself with his family—my grandmother, my teenage mother, her two sisters and two brothers—inside of his home in La'ie, a sugar plantation village on Oahu's North Shore. This was my maternal grandfather, a man most villagers called by his last name, Kubota. It could mean either "Wayside Field" or else "Broken Dreams," depending on which ideograms he used. Kubota ran La'ie's general store, and the previous night, after a long day of bad news on the radio, some locals had come by, pounded on the front door, and made threats. One was said to have brandished a machete. They were angry and shocked, as the whole nation was in the aftermath of the surprise attack. Kubota was one of the few Japanese Americans in the village and president of the local Japanese language school. He had become a target for their rage and suspicion. A wise man, he locked all his doors and windows and did not open his store the next day, but stayed closed and waited for news from some official. (Garrett Hongo, "Kubota")

(6) Comparison and Contrast

Comparison-and-contrast paragraphs examine the similarities among and differences between two subjects. Comparison emphasizes similarities; contrast emphasizes differences.

Comparison-and-contrast paragraphs can be organized in one of two ways. In some comparison-and-contrast paragraphs, the subjects are compared **point by point:** the paragraph alternates points about one subject with comparable points about the other subject.

> There are two Americas. One is the America of Lincoln and Adlai Stevenson; the other is the America of Teddy Roosevelt and the modern superpatriots. One is generous and humane, the other narrowly egotistical; one is self-critical, the other self-righteous; one is sensible, the other romantic; one is good-humored, the other solemn; one is inquiring, the other pontificating; one is moderate, the other filled with passionate intensity; one is judicious and the other arrogant in the use of great power. (J. William Fulbright, *The Arrogance of Power*)

Other paragraphs, **subject-by-subject** comparisons, treat one subject completely and then move on to the other subject. In the following paragraph, notice how the writer shifts from one subject to the other with the transitional word *however.*

> First, it is important to note that men and women regard conversation quite differently. For women it is a passion, a sport, an activity even more important to life than eating because it doesn't involve weight gain. The first sign of closeness among women is when they find themselves engaging in endless, secretless rounds of conversation with one another. And as soon as a woman begins to relax and feel comfortable in a relationship with a man, she tries to have that type of conversation with him as well. However, the first sign that a man is feeling close to a woman is when he admits that he'd rather she please quiet down so he can hear the TV. A man who feels truly intimate with a woman often reserves for her and her alone the precious gift of one-word answers. Everyone knows that the surest way to spot a successful long-term relationship is to look around a restaurant for the table where no one is talking. Ah [. . .] now *that's* real love. (Merrill Markoe, "Men, Women, and Conversation")

An **analogy** is a special kind of comparison that explains an unfamiliar concept or object by likening it to a familiar one. Here the writer uses the behavior of people to explain the behavior of ants.

> Ants are so much like human beings as to be an embarrassment. They farm fungi, raise aphids as livestock, launch armies into wars, use chemical sprays to alarm and confuse enemies, capture slaves. The families of weaver ants engage in child labor,

holding their larvae like shuttles to spin out the thread that sews the leaves together for their fungus gardens. They exchange information ceaselessly. They do everything but watch television. (Lewis Thomas, "On Societies as Organisms")

(7) Division and Classification

Division paragraphs take a single item and break it into its components.

> The blood can be divided into four distinct components: plasma, red cells, white cells, and platelets. Plasma is 90 percent water and holds a great number of substances in suspension. It contains proteins, sugars, fat, and inorganic salts. Plasma also contains urea and other by-products from the breaking down of proteins, hormones, enzymes, and dissolved gases. In addition, plasma contains the red blood cells that give it color, the white cells, and the platelets. The red cells are most numerous; they get oxygen from the lungs and release it in the tissues. The less numerous white cells are part of the body's defense against invading organisms. The platelets, which occur in almost the same number as white cells, are responsible for clotting. (Student Writer)

Classification paragraphs take many separate items and group them into categories according to qualities or characteristics they share.

> Charles Babbage, an English mathematician, reflecting in 1830 on what he saw as the decline of science at the time, distinguished among three major kinds of scientific fraud. He called the first "forging," by which he meant complete fabrication—the recording of observations that were never made. The second category he called "trimming"; this consists of manipulating the data to make them look better, or, as Babbage wrote, "in clipping off little bits here and there from those observations which differ most in *excess* from the mean and in sticking them on to those which are too small." His third category was data selection, which he called "cooking"—the choosing of those data that fitted the researcher's hypothesis and the discarding of those that did not. To this day, the serious discussion of scientific fraud has not improved on Babbage's typology. (Morton Hunt, *New York Times Magazine*)

(8) Definition

A **formal definition** includes the term defined, the class to which it belongs, and the details that distinguish it from other members of its class.

(term) (class to which it belongs)
Carbon is a nonmetallic element

(distinguishing details)
sometimes occurring as diamond.

Definition paragraphs develop the formal definition with other patterns, defining *happiness,* for instance by telling a story (narration), or defining a diesel engine by telling how it works (process).

The following paragraph begins with a straightforward definition of *gadget* and then cites an example.

A gadget is nearly always novel in design or concept and it often has no proper name. For example, the semaphore which signals the arrival of the mail in our rural mailbox certainly has no proper name. It is a contrivance consisting of a piece of shingle. Call it what you like, it saves us frequent frustrating trips to the mailbox in winter when you have to dress up and wade through snow to get there. That's a gadget! *(Smithsonian)*

✔ CHECKLIST: DEVELOPING PARAGRAPHS

✔ **Narration** Do you present enough explanation to enable readers to understand the events you discuss? Do you support your main idea with descriptive details?

✔ **Description** Do you supply enough detail about what things look like, sound like, smell like, taste like, and feel like? Will your readers be able to visualize the person, object, or setting that your paragraph describes?

✔ **Exemplification** Do you present enough individual examples to support your paragraph's main idea? If you use a single extended example, is it developed in enough detail to enable readers to understand how it supports the paragraph's main idea?

✔ **Process** Do you present enough steps to enable readers to understand how the process is performed? Is the sequence of steps clear? If you are writing instructions, do you include enough explanation—as well as reminders and warnings—to enable readers to perform the process?

✔ **Cause and Effect** Do you identify enough causes (subtle as well as obvious, minor as well as major) to enable readers to understand why something occurred? Do you identify enough effects to show the significance of the causes and the impact they had?

continued on the following page

continued from the previous page

✔ **Comparison and Contrast**   Do you supply a sufficient number of details to illustrate and characterize each of the subjects in the comparison? Do you present a similar number of details for each subject? Do you discuss the same or similar details for each subject?

✔ **Division and Classification**   Do you present enough information to enable readers to identify each category and distinguish one from another?

✔ **Definition**   Do you present enough support (examples, analogies, descriptive details, and so on) to enable readers to understand the term you are defining and to distinguish it from others in its class?

EXERCISE 6

Determine one possible pattern of development for a paragraph on each of these topics. Then, write a paragraph on one of the topics.

1. What success is (or is not)
2. How to write a résumé
3. The kinds of people who listen to radio talk shows
4. My worst date
5. American versus Japanese education
6. The connection between stress and the immune system
7. Budgeting money wisely
8. Self-confidence
9. Preparing for the perfect vacation
10. Drinking and driving

EXERCISE 7

A. Read each of the following paragraphs, and then answer these questions: In general terms, how could each paragraph be developed further? What pattern of development might be used in each case?

B. Choose one paragraph, and rewrite it to develop it further.

1. Many new words and expressions have entered the English language in the last ten years or so. Some of them come from the world of computers. Others come from popular music. Still others have politics as their source. There are even some expressions that have their origins in films or television shows.

2. Making a good spaghetti sauce is not a particularly challenging task. First, assemble the basic ingredients: garlic, onion, mushrooms, green pepper, and ground beef. Sauté these ingredients in a large saucepan. Then, add canned tomatoes, tomato paste, and water, and stir. At this point, you are ready to add the spices: oregano, parsley, basil, and salt and pepper. Don't forget a bay leaf! Simmer for about two hours, and serve over spaghetti.

3. High school and college are not at all alike. Courses are a lot easier in high school, and the course load is lighter. In college, teachers expect more from students; they expect higher quality work, and they assign more of it. Assignments tend to be more difficult and more comprehensive, and deadlines are usually shorter. Finally, college students tend to be more focused on a particular course of study—even a particular career—than high school students are.

6f Writing Special Kinds of Paragraphs

So far this chapter has focused on **body paragraphs,** the paragraphs that carry the weight of your essay's discussion. Other kinds of paragraphs have specialized functions in an essay.

(1) Transitional Paragraphs

A **transitional paragraph** connects one section of the essay to another.

At their simplest, transitional paragraphs can be single sentences that move readers from one point to the next.

Let us examine this point further.

This idea works better in theory than in practice.

We need to begin with a few examples.

More often, writers use a transitional paragraph to present a concise summary of what they have already said before moving on to a new point. The following transitional paragraph uses a series of questions to sum up some of the ideas the writer has been discussing. In the next part of his essay, he goes on to answer these questions.

Can we bleed off the mass of humanity to other worlds? Right now the number of human beings on Earth is increasing by 80 million per year, and each year that number goes up by 1 and a fraction percent. Can we really suppose that we can send 80 million people per year to the Moon, Mars, and elsewhere, and engineer those worlds to support those people? And even so, nearly remain in the same place ourselves? (Isaac Asimov, "The Case against Man")

(2) Introductory Paragraphs

An **introductory paragraph** prepares readers for the essay to follow. It typically introduces the subject, narrows it, and then states the essay's thesis.

> Christine was just a girl in one of my classes. I never knew much about her except that she was strange. She didn't talk much. Her hair was dyed black and purple, and she wore heavy black boots and a black turtleneck sweater, even in the summer. She was attractive—in spite of the ring she wore through her left eyebrow—but she never seemed to care what the rest of us thought about her. Like the rest of my classmates, I didn't really want to get close to her. It was only when we were assigned to do our chemistry project together that I began to understand why Christine dressed the way she did. (Student Writer)

To arouse their audience's interest, writers may vary this direct approach by using one of the following introductory strategies.

STRATEGIES FOR EFFECTIVE INTRODUCTIONS

Quotation or Series of Quotations

> When Mary Cassatt's father was told of her decision to become a painter, he said: "I would rather see you dead." When Edgar Degas saw a show of Cassatt's etchings, his response was: "I am not willing to admit that a woman can draw that well." When she returned to Philadelphia after twenty-eight years abroad, having achieved renown as an Impressionist painter and the esteem of Degas, Huysmans, Pissarro, and Berthe Morisot, the *Philadelphia Ledger* reported: "Mary Cassatt, sister of Mr. Cassatt, president of the Pennsylvania Railroad, returned from Europe yesterday. She has been studying painting in France and owns the smallest Pekingese dog in the world." (Mary Gordon, "Mary Cassatt")

Introductions, Conclusions, and Titles
http://www.gmu.edu/departments/writingcenter/handouts/introcon.html

Question or Series of Questions

Of all the disputes agitating the American campus, the one that seems to me especially significant is that over "the canon." What should be taught in the humanities and social sciences, especially in introductory courses? What is the place of the classics? How shall we respond to those professors who attack "Eurocentrism" and advocate "multiculturalism"? This is not the sort of tedious quarrel that now and then flutters through the academy; it involves matters of public urgency. I propose to see this dispute, at first, through a narrow, even sectarian lens, with the hope that you will come to accept my reasons for doing so. (Irving Howe, "The Value of the Canon")

Definition

Moles are collections of cells that can appear on any part of the body. With occasional exceptions, moles are absent at birth. They first appear in the early years of life, between ages two and six. Frequently, moles appear at puberty. New moles, however, can continue to appear throughout life. During pregnancy, new moles may appear and old ones darken. There are three major designations of moles, each with its own unique distinguishing characteristics. (Student Writer)

Unusual Comparison

Once a long time ago, people had special little boxes called refrigerators in which milk, meat, and eggs could be kept cool. The grandchildren of these simple devices are large enough to store whole cows, and they reach temperatures comparable to those at the South Pole. Their operating costs increase each year, and they are so complicated that few home handymen attempt to repair them on their own. Why has this change in size and complexity occurred in America? It has not taken place in many areas of the technologically advanced world (the average West German refrigerator is about a yard high and less than a yard wide, yet refrigeration technology in Germany is quite advanced). Do we really need (or even want) all that space and cold? (Appletree Rodden, "Why Smaller Refrigerators Can Preserve the Human Race")

continued on the following page

continued from the previous page

Controversial Statement

Something had to replace the threat of communism, and at last a workable substitute is at hand. "Multiculturalism," as the new menace is known, has been denounced in the media recently as the new McCarthyism, the new fundamentalism, even the new totalitarianism—take your choice. According to its critics, who include a flock of tenured conservative scholars, multiculturalism aims to toss out what it sees as the Eurocentric bias in education and replace Plato with Ntozake Shange and traditional math with the Yoruba number system. And that's just the beginning. The Jacobins of the multiculturalist movement, who are described derisively as P.C., or politically correct, are said to have launched a campus reign of terror against those who slip and innocently say "freshman" instead of "freshperson," "Indian" instead of "Native American" or, may the Goddess forgive them, "disabled" instead of "differently abled." (Barbara Ehrenreich, "Teach Diversity—with a Smile")

 INTRODUCTORY PARAGRAPHS

Avoid introductory paragraphs that simply announce your subject ("In my paper, I will talk about Lady Macbeth") or that undercut your credibility ("I don't know much about alternative energy sources, but I would like to present my opinion about the subject").

✔ CHECKLIST: REVISING INTRODUCTIONS

  ✔ Does your introduction include your essay's thesis statement?
  ✔ Does it lead naturally into the body of your essay?
  ✔ Does it arouse your readers' interest?
  ✔ Does it avoid statements that simply announce your subject or that undercut your credibility?

(3) Concluding Paragraphs

A **concluding paragraph** typically begins with specifics—reviewing the essay's main points, for example—and then moves to more general statements. Whenever possible, it should end with a sentence that readers will remember.

> As an Arab-American, I feel I have the best of two worlds. I'm proud to be part of the melting pot, proud to contribute to the tremendous diversity of cultures, customs and traditions that makes this country unique. But Arab-bashing—public acceptance of hatred and bigotry—is something no American can be proud of. (Ellen Mansoor Collier, "I Am Not a Terrorist")

Writers may also use one of the following concluding strategies.

STRATEGIES FOR EFFECTIVE CONCLUSIONS

Prediction

> Looking ahead, [we see that] prospects may not be quite as dismal as they seem. As a matter of fact, we are not doing so badly. It is something of a miracle that creatures who evolved as nomads in an intimate, small-band, wide-open-spaces context manage to get along at all villagers or surrounded by strangers in cubicle apartments. Considering that our genius as a species is adaptability, we may yet learn to live closer and closer to one another, if not in utter peace, then far more peacefully than we do today. (John Pheiffer, "Seeking Peace, Making War")

Opinion

> A piece of writing is never finished. It is delivered to a deadline, torn out of the typewriter on demand, sent off with a sense of accomplishment and shame and pride and frustration. If only there were a couple more days, time for just another run at it, perhaps then. . . . (Donald Murray, "The Maker's Eye: Revising Your Own Manuscripts")

continued on the following page

continued from the previous page

Quotation

When we let freedom ring, when we let it ring from every village and every hamlet, from every state and every city, we will be able to speed up that day when all of God's children, black men and white men, Jews and Gentiles, Protestants and Catholics, will be able to join hands and sing in the words of the old Negro spiritual, "Free at last! Free at last! Thank God almighty, we are free at last!" (Martin Luther King, Jr., "I Have a Dream")

 CONCLUDING PARAGRAPHS

Avoid concluding paragraphs that introduce new points or go off in new directions. Because it is your last word, a weak or uninteresting conclusion detracts from an otherwise strong essay. Do not just repeat your introduction in different words, and do not apologize or in any way cast doubt on your concluding points ("I may not be an expert" or "At least, this is my opinion").

✔ CHECKLIST: REVISING CONCLUSIONS

- ✔ Does your conclusion remind readers of the primary focus of your essay?
- ✔ Does it review your essay's main points?
- ✔ Does it end memorably?
- ✔ Does it do more than repeat the introduction?
- ✔ Does it avoid apologies?

STUDENT WRITER AT WORK

Writing Paragraphs

The following draft of a student essay has weak body paragraphs. Rewrite these paragraphs so that they are unified, coherent, and well developed. (You may want to chart these paragraphs before you begin to revise them.)

Oh, How Things Have Changed!

When my grandfather was supporting his family in 1950, a good job was easy to find. World War II was over, and the United States was experiencing an unprecedented economic boom. The American Dream was alive and well, and people thought they were living in a land of unlimited opportunity. Even though many people did not get past high school, they still got jobs that enabled them to marry and make a down payment on a house. Today, the situation is different. Education, even a college degree, no longer ensures a high-paying job. Now, it takes two people working full-time to provide the lifestyle that people used to maintain with one salary. What has changed? Actually, a number of factors have helped to create the present job climate in the United States.

Currently, there are too many people who are qualified for jobs and not enough good jobs to go around. In order to get a good job, a person must be the best. Even many qualified people are being laid off. Companies are now hiring young, inexperienced people because they work for less. High-paid positions are very hard to find.

The current corporate trend to downsize has also contributed to the decline in jobs. In order to cut expenses, many companies have laid off workers. Some companies have laid off thousands of workers, while others have laid off just a few. Whatever the number, the results are the same. People are out of work.

To keep their costs down, some companies have moved their operations to foreign countries where wages are a fraction of those in the United States. General Motors has plants in South America. Many national chains, such as The Gap, buy clothes from manufacturers who have relocated to Southeast Asia. Recently, I bought a pair of shoes and was surprised to see that they were made in China. American workers may have trouble getting manufacturing jobs as long as this situation exists.

Finally, companies no longer see their workers as valued employees. Too often, upper-level managers treat workers as if they were less than human. Workers are seen as numbers on a balance sheet and treated as if they had no feelings. Even workers who have been with a company for twenty years or more are not safe. They can lose their jobs as easily as someone who has been with the company for just a short time.

The employment situation that existed in the 1950s will never return. Too much has changed since then. Many businesses have become international and feel no loyalty to the United States or its workers. The result is that profit seems to be the only thing that motivates corporate executives. Certainly there are some executives who have supported their workers, but they are the exceptions. Unless our government does something to protect its workers, the United States not only will continue to lose manufacturing jobs, but also will be dependent on the rest of the world for its clothes, its appliances, and its transportation. This is a situation that neither the country nor its workers can afford.

CHAPTER 7

THINKING, READING, AND WRITING CRITICALLY

❓ FREQUENTLY ASKED QUESTIONS

What is critical thinking? (p. 131)
How do I tell the difference between a fact
and an opinion? (p. 132)
How do I know if the evidence a writer
presents is reliable? (p. 134)
How can I tell if a writer is biased? (p. 135)
What is active reading? (p. 139)
What is a critical response and how do I
write one? (p. 147)

When you **read critically,** your goal should be to assess the writer's credibility and to evaluate (sometimes in writing) the soundness of his or her ideas. To do this, you must be willing to think critically and to use active reading strategies.

7a Thinking Critically

As you read, you must **think critically** about the ideas you encounter ❓ and consider the merits of opposing points of view. In addition, you must remain open-minded, realizing that a text may challenge your beliefs and expose your biases.

Critical Thinking (USML)
    http://www.umsl.edu/~klein/Critical_Thinking.html
Critical Thinking (Humboldt)
    http:www.humboldt.edu/~act/

THINKING CRITICALLY

When you approach a text, you should agree to the following conditions:

- Keep an open mind.
- Withhold judgment.
- Acknowledge your own limitations and biases as a reader.
- Consider the possible reactions and questions of other readers—both to the text and to your ideas.

To evaluate the effectiveness of a writer's argument, you must understand the difference between *fact* and *opinion.*

(1) Distinguishing Fact from Opinion

A **fact** is a verifiable statement that something is true or that something occurred. An **opinion** is a conclusion or belief that can never be substantiated beyond any doubt and is, therefore, debatable.

FACT: Measles is a potentially deadly disease.

OPINION: All children should be vaccinated against measles.

An opinion may be *supported* or *unsupported.*

UNSUPPORTED OPINION: All children in Pennsylvania should be vaccinated against measles.

SUPPORTED OPINION: Despite the fact that an effective measles vaccine is widely available, several unvaccinated Pennsylvania children have died of measles each year since 1992. States that have instituted vaccination programs have had no deaths in the same period. For this reason, all children in Pennsylvania should be vaccinated against measles.

As these examples show, supported opinion is more convincing than unsupported opinion. Remember, however, that supporting evidence can only make a statement more convincing; it cannot turn an opinion into a fact.

KINDS OF SUPPORTING EVIDENCE

Examples

The American Civil Liberties Union is an organization that has been unfairly characterized as left wing. It is true that it has opposed prayer in the public schools, defended conscientious objectors, and challenged police methods of conducting questioning and searches of suspects. However, it has also backed the anti-abortion group Operation Rescue in a police brutality suit and presented a legal brief in support of a Republican politician accused of violating an ethics law.

Statistics

A recent National Institute of Mental Health study concludes that mentally ill people account for more than 30 percent of the homeless population (27). Because so many homeless people have psychiatric disabilities, the federal government should seriously consider expanding the state mental hospital system.

Expert Testimony

Clearly no young soldier ever really escapes the emotional consequences of war. As William Manchester, noted historian and World War II combat veteran, observes in his essay "Okinawa: The Bloodiest Battle of All," "the invisible wounds remain" (72).

EXERCISE 1

Some of the following statements are facts; others are opinions. Identify each fact with the letter *F* and each opinion with the letter *O*. Then, consider what kind of evidence, if any, could support each opinion.

1. The incidence of violent crime fell in the first six months of this year.
2. New gun laws and more police officers led to a decrease in crime early in the year.
3. The television rating system uses a system similar to the familiar movie rating codes to let parents know how appropriate a certain show might be for their children.

4. The new television rating system would be better if it gave specifics about the violence, sexual innuendo, and language content in rated television programs.
5. Affirmative action laws and policies have helped women and minority group members advance in the workplace.
6. Affirmative action policies have outlived their usefulness.
7. Women who work are better off today than they were twenty years ago.
8. The wage gap between men and women in similar jobs is smaller now than it was twenty years ago.
9. The Charles River and Boston Harbor currently test much lower for common pollutants than they did ten years ago.
10. We don't need to worry about environmental legislation anymore because we've made great advances in cleaning up our environment.

❓ (2) Evaluating Supporting Evidence

The more reliable the supporting **evidence**—examples, statistics, or expert testimony—the more willing readers will be to accept it. No matter what kind of evidence writers use, however, it must be *accurate, sufficient, representative,* and *relevant.*

Evidence is likely to be **accurate** if it comes from a trustworthy source. Such a source quotes *exactly* and does not present remarks out of context. It also presents examples, statistics, and expert testimony fairly, drawing them from other reliable sources.

For evidence to be **sufficient,** a writer must present an adequate amount of evidence. It is not enough, for instance, for a writer to cite just one example in an attempt to demonstrate that most poor women do not receive adequate prenatal care. Similarly, the opinions of a single expert, no matter how reputable, are not enough to support this idea.

Writers should also select evidence that is **representative** of a fair range of sources and viewpoints; they should not choose evidence that supports their arguments and ignore evidence that does not. In other words, they should not permit their biases to govern their choice of evidence. For example, a writer who is arguing that Asian immigrants have had great success in achieving professional status in the United States must draw from the experience of a range of Asian immigrant groups—Vietnamese, Chinese, Japanese, Indian, and Korean, for example—and a representative sample of professions—law, medicine, teaching, and so forth. No matter how accurate the information or how numerous the examples, a writer cannot draw a general conclusion about Asian professionals by citing examples that apply only to Chinese doctors.

Finally, evidence must be **relevant**—that is, it must apply to the case being discussed. For example, you cannot support the position that the United States should send medical aid to developing nations by citing examples that apply only to our own nation's health-care system.

EXERCISE 2

Read the following student paragraph and evaluate its supporting evidence.

> The United States is becoming more and more violent every day. I was talking to my friend Gayle, and she mentioned that a guy her roommate knows was attacked at dusk and had his skull crushed by the barrel of a gun. Later she heard that he was in the hospital with a blood clot in his brain. Two friends of mine were walking home from a party when they were attacked by armed men right outside the A-Plus Mini Market. These two examples make it very clear to me how violent our nation is becoming. My English professor, who is in his fifties, remembers a few similar violent incidents occurring when he was growing up, and he was even mugged in London last year. He believes that if London police carried guns, the city would be safer. Two of the twenty-five people in our class have been the victims of violent crime, and I feel lucky that I am not one of them.

(3) Detecting Bias

A **bias** is a predisposition to think a certain way. A writer is biased when he or she bases conclusions on preconceived ideas rather than on evidence. As a critical reader, you should be aware that bias may sometimes lead a writer to see only what he or she wants to see and to select evidence that supports one conclusion over all others.

Some bias that you will encounter in your reading will be obvious and easy to detect.

- **A writer's stated beliefs.** In a recent article about the Middle East, a writer declared herself a strong supporter of the Palestinian position. This statement should tell readers that it is unlikely that she will present an unbiased view of Israel's policies in the West Bank. Although the writer may offer an interesting perspective, she will probably *not* present a *balanced* view of the subject.
- **Sexist or racist statements.** A writer who assumes that all engineers are male and that all nurses are female reflects a clear bias. A researcher who states that certain racial groups are intellectually superior to others is also presenting a biased view.

- **Slanted language.** Writers can use slanted language to influence readers' reactions. For example, saying "The politician presented an *impassioned* speech" gives one impression; saying "The politician delivered a *diatribe*" gives another.
- **Tone.** The tone of a piece of writing indicates a writer's attitude toward readers or toward his or her subject. In many cases, the tone of an essay can alert you to the possibility that the writer is slanting his or her case. An angry writer, for example, might not be able or willing to present an accurate summary of an opponent's position, and an apologetic writer might inadvertently dilute the strength of his or her case in an attempt to avoid offending readers.
- **Choice of evidence.** As you read, try to evaluate a writer's use of **evidence**. Frequently, the examples selected reveal the writer's biases—that is, a writer may include only examples that support a point and may leave out examples that might contradict it.

- **Choice of experts.** A writer should cite experts who represent a fair range of opinion. If, for instance, a writer assessing the president's economic policies toward Japan includes only statements by economists who advocate protectionism, he or she is presenting a biased case.

Remember, too, that your *own* biases can affect your reaction to a text—how you interpret a writer's ideas, whether you are convinced by what you read, and whether you react with sympathy or anger, for example. When you read, then, it is important to remain aware of your own values and beliefs and alert to how they may affect your reactions.

(4) Recognizing Faulty Reasoning

As a critical reader, you should carefully scrutinize a writer's **reasoning**. The connection between evidence and conclusions should be clear, and the writer's inferences should be based on a logical chain of reasoning, with no missing links or unwarranted conclusions.

(5) Recognizing Logical Fallacies

Writers who use **logical fallacies**—flawed arguments—cannot be trusted. A writer who uses these fallacies inadvertently is not thinking clearly or logically; a writer who uses them intentionally is trying to deceive readers.

(6) Recognizing Unfair Appeals

See
9b3

Writers should make every effort to be **fair**. **Unfair appeals**—appeals to a reader's prejudices or fears—should cause you to question a writer's motives and credibility.

✔ CHECKLIST: READING CRITICALLY

✔ Are the writer's statements supported primarily by fact or by opinion? Does the writer present opinion as fact?

✔ Does the writer offer supporting evidence for his or her statements? What kind of evidence is provided? How convincing is it?

✔ Is the evidence accurate? Sufficient? Representative? Relevant?

✔ Does the writer display any bias? If so, is the bias revealed through language, tone, or choice of evidence?

✔ Does the writer present a balanced picture of the issue?

✔ Are any alternative viewpoints overlooked?

✔ Does the writer omit pertinent examples?

✔ Do your reactions reveal biases in your own thinking?

✔ Does the writer challenge your own values, beliefs, and assumptions?

✔ Does the writer use faulty reasoning?

✔ Does the writer use logical fallacies?

✔ Does the writer use unfair appeals, such as appeals to prejudice or fear?

EXERCISE 3

Read the following excerpt from a statement on comparable worth, a method by which some people seek to balance inequities in jobs occupied primarily by women. First, identify the facts and opinions in the excerpt. Then, evaluate the quantity and quality of the writer's supporting evidence and try to determine what biases, if any, she has. Finally, evaluate the writer's reasoning, identifying logical fallacies and unfair appeals. Use the questions in the preceding checklist as a guide.

My name is Phyllis Schlafly, president of Eagle Forum, a national profamily organization. I am a lawyer, writer, and homemaker.

We oppose the concept called *comparable worth* for two principal reasons: (*a*) it's unfair to men and (*b*) it's unfair to women.

The comparable worth advocates are trying to freeze the wages of blue-collar men while forcing employers to raise the wages of *some* white- and pink-collar women above marketplace rates. According to the comparable worth rationale, blue-collar men are overpaid and their wages should be frozen until white- and pink-collar women have their wages artificially raised to the same level. The proof that this is really what the comparable worth debate is all about is in both their rhetoric and their statistics.

I've been debating feminists and listening to their arguments for more than a decade. It is impossible to overlook their rhetoric of envy. I've heard feminist leaders say hundreds of times, "It isn't fair that the man with a high school education earns more money than the woman who graduated from college or nursing or secretarial school." That complaint means that the feminists believe that truck drivers, electricians, plumbers, mechanics, highway workers, maintenance men, policemen, and firemen earn more money than feminists think they are worth. And how do the feminists judge "worth"? By paper credentials instead of by apprenticeship and hard work and by ignoring physical risk and unpleasant working conditions.

So the feminists have devised the slogan *comparable worth* to make the blue-collar man feel guilty for earning more money than women with paper credentials and to trick him into accepting a government-enforced wage freeze while all available funds are used to raise the wages of *some* women.

Statistical proof that the aim of comparable worth is to reduce the relative earning power of blue-collar men is abundantly available in the job evaluations commissioned and approved by the comparable worth advocates. You can prove this to yourself by making a job-by-job examination of *any* study or evaluation made with the approval of comparable worth advocates; it is always an elaborate scheme to devalue the blue-collar man.

For example, look at the Willis evaluation used in the famous case called *AFSCME v. State of Washington*. Willis determined that the electricians and truck drivers were overvalued by the state and that their "worth" was really far less than the "worth" of a registered nurse. More precisely, Willis produced an evaluation chart on which the registered nurse was worth 573 points, whereas the electrician was worth only 193 points (one-third of the nurse), while the truck driver was only worth 97 points (one-sixth of the nurse).

The federal court accepted the Willis evaluation as though it were some kind of divine law (refusing to listen to the Richard Jeanneret "PAQ" evaluation, which produced very different estimates of "worth"). The federal court decision (unless it is overturned on appeal) means that the electricians and the truck drivers will probably have their salaries frozen until the state finds a way to pay the registered nurse three times and six times as much, respectively. [In a September 4, 1985, decision, the Ninth US Circuit Court of Appeals overturned the decision.]

(Phyllis Schlafly, "Comparable Worth: Unfair to Men and Women")

7b   Reading Actively

Central to becoming a critical reader is learning the techniques of active reading. **Active reading** means reading with pen in hand, physically marking the text. As you do so, you distinguish important points from not-so-important ones; identify parallels; and connect causes with effects and generalizations with specific examples.

(1) Previewing

The first time you encounter a text, you should **preview** it—that is, skim it to get a sense of the author's subject and emphasis.

When you preview a *book,* begin by looking at its table of contents, especially at the sections that pertain to your topic. A quick glance at the index will reveal the kind and amount of coverage the book gives to subjects that may be important to you. As you leaf through the chapters, look at pictures, graphs, or tables, reading the captions that appear with them.

When you preview a *magazine article,* scan the introductory and concluding paragraphs for summaries of the author's main points. (Journal articles in the sciences and social sciences often begin with summaries called **abstracts**.) Thesis statements, topic sentences, repeated key terms, transitional words and phrases, and transitional paragraphs can also help you to identify the points a writer is making. In addition, look for the visual cues—such as headings and lists—that writers use to emphasize ideas.

(2) Highlighting

When you have finished previewing a work, highlight it to identify the writer's key points and their relationships to one another. As you **highlight,** use symbols and underlining to identify important ideas. (If you are working with library material, photocopy the pages you need and then highlight them.) Be sure to use symbols that you will understand when you reread your material later on.

The Reading Comprehension Page (Muskingum College)
  http://muskingum.edu/~cal/database/reading.html
How to Get the Most out of Reading Non-Fiction (U. Mich.)
  http://www.si.umich.edu/~pne/read.a.book.htm

✔ **CHECKLIST: USING HIGHLIGHTING SYMBOLS**

✔ Underline to indicate information you should read again.
✔ Box or circle key words or important phrases.
✔ Put question marks next to confusing passages, unclear points, or words you need to look up.
✔ Draw lines or arrows to show connections between ideas.
✔ Number points that appear in sequence.
✔ Draw a vertical line in the margin to set off an important section of text.
✔ Star especially important ideas.

The student who highlighted the following passage used the symbols listed in the checklist above to help her isolate the author's key ideas and clarify the progression of ideas in the passage.

☆　Public zoos came into existence at the beginning of the period which was to see the disappearance of animals from daily life. The zoo to which people go to meet animals, to observe them, to see
☆ them, is, in fact, a monument to the impossibility of such encounters. Modern zoos are an epitaph to a relationship which was as old as man. They are not seen as such because the wrong questions have been addressed to zoos.

　　When they were founded—the London Zoo in 1828, the Jardin
①　des Plantes in 1793, the Berlin Zoo in 1844—they brought considerable prestige to the national capitals. The prestige was not so different from that which had accrued to the private royal menageries. These menageries, along with gold plate, architecture, orchestras, players, furnishings, dwarfs, acrobats, uniforms, horses, art and food, had been demonstrations of an emperor's or king's power
②　and wealth. Likewise in the 19th century, public zoos were an endorsement of modern colonial power. The capturing of the animals was a symbolic representation of the conquest of all distant and exotic lands. "Explorers" proved their patriotism by sending home a tiger or an elephant. The gift of an exotic animal to the metropolitan zoo became a token in subservient diplomatic relations.

　　Yet, like every other 19th century public institution, the zoo, however supportive of the ideology of imperialism, had to claim an independent and civic function. The claim was that it was another kind of museum, whose purpose was to further knowledge and public enlightenment. And so the first questions asked of zoos belonged to natural history; it was then thought possible to study the natural life of animals even in such unnatural conditions. A century later, more sophisticated zoologists such as Konrad Lorenz ?? asked behavioristic and ethological questions, the claimed purpose of which was to discover more about the springs of human action through the study of animals under experimental conditions. (John Berger, *About Looking*)

Once this student highlighted the passage, she went on to record her re-actions to its ideas in the form of marginal **annotations**.

EXERCISE 4

Preview the following passage, and then read it more carefully, highlighting it to help you understand the writer's ideas. Then, compare your highlighting with a classmate's. When you are satisfied that you have identified the most important ideas and that you both understand the passage, work together to answer the following questions:

What is the writer's subject?
What is the writer's most important point?
Which points are related?
What is their relationship to one another?
How does the writer make connections among related ideas clear?

My father loved to tell the story of how he got into college. It was 1947 and my father, poor, black and brilliant, was a 15-year-old high school senior in rural Sylvester, Ga. One day he was called into the principal's office to meet a visiting state education official, a white bureaucrat who had learned of my father's academic prowess. The state, the official said, had decided that it wanted to send "a nigra" to college. "You can go to any college in the state," the official told my father. "Except [. . .] for the University of Georgia, Georgia Tech, Georgia A & M, Emory [. . .]."

My father was happy and proud to attend Atlanta's Morehouse, perhaps the finest black college in America. But there was always a trace of bitterness when he told this story since his choice of college had, in effect, been made for him.

Times had changed when I applied to college in 1978. Thanks to my father's success as a financial consultant, I grew up in a solidly middle-class home in the Bronx, and, thanks largely to the social advances wrought by the civil rights movement, I was able to attend private school and get into Harvard.

I arrived in Cambridge just as the national backlash against affirmative action was gaining momentum. Many critics were suggesting that African-Americans were inherently inferior students, below the standards of the great universities. I found this argument fatuous, particularly when I encountered some of the less illustrious white students who had allegedly been accepted on "merit." There was, for example, the charming, wealthy young man I'll call "Ted." Intellectually incurious, struggling in most of his courses, Ted said he had been rejected by every college to which he had applied, except Harvard, the alma mater of his father and grandfather.

Ted was what is known as a "legacy." According to Harvard's dean of admissions, William Fitzsimmons, approximately 40 percent of alumni children who apply are admitted each year as against 14 percent of nonalumni applicants.

So Ted and I were beneficiaries of two different forms of affirmative action. He was accepted largely because his forebears had attended Harvard. I was accepted largely because my father had been denied the chance to apply to any predominantly white universities. Yet the type of affirmative action that benefited me is relentlessly assailed while the more venerable form of preferential treatment that Ted enjoyed goes virtually unchallenged.

Whether one is listening to Clarence Thomas's tortuous rationalizations about how he didn't really benefit from affirmative action, or George Bush's railing against racial quotas, which have never been widely supported by Americans, white or black, the underlying message is the same: were it not for affirmative action, America would function as a perfect meritocracy.

Of course there are people of all backgrounds who have succeeded solely through talent and perseverance. But at least as many have been assisted by personal connections, old-boy networks, family ties and the benefits traditionally accorded certain, primarily white, primarily male segments of the American population. Why, in the interminable debate over affirmative action, have these historic advantages generally been brushed aside?

I am not suggesting that most "legacies" or other beneficiaries of long-established de facto affirmative action programs are unqualified for the placements and positions they get. Most of the "legacies" I met at Harvard did just fine there, but so did the great majority of African-Americans. The difference was that the "legacies" were not stigmatized by their extra edge and the black students were.

(Jake Lamar, "Whose Legacy Is It, Anyway?")

(3) Annotating

After you have read through a reading selection once, start to read more critically. At this stage, you should **annotate** the pages, recording your reactions to what you read. This process of recording notes in the margins or between the lines will help you understand the writer's ideas and your own reactions to those ideas.

Some of your responses may be relatively straightforward. For example, you may define new words, identify unfamiliar references, or jot down brief summaries. Other responses may be more personal. For example, you may identify a parallel between your own experience and one described in the reading selection, or you may record your opinion of the writer's position. Still other annotations may require you to think critically, identifying points that confirm (or dispute) your own ideas, questioning the appropriateness or accuracy of the writer's support, uncovering the writer's biases or **faulty reasoning**, or even questioning (or challenging) the writer's conclusion.

See
8c

The following passage illustrates a student's annotations of an article about the decline of American public schools.

One of the most compelling arguments about the Vietnam War is that it lasted as long as it did because of its "classist" nature. The central thesis is that because neither the decision makers in the government *nor anyone they knew* had children fighting and dying in Vietnam, they had no personal incentive to bring the war to a halt. The government's generous college-deferment system, steeped as it was in class distinctions, allowed the white middle class to avoid the tragic consequences of the war. And the people who did the fighting and dying in place of the college-deferred were those whose voices were least heard in Washington: the poor and the disenfranchised.

I bring this up because I believe that the decline of the public schools is rooted in the same cause. Just as with the Vietnam War, as soon as the middle class no longer had a stake in the public schools, the surest pressure on school systems to provide a decent education instantly disappeared. Once the middle class was gone, no mayor was going to get booted out of office because the schools were bad. No incompetent teacher had to worry about angry parents calling for his or her head "downtown." No third-rate educationalist at the local teachers college had to fear having his or her methods criticized by anyone that mattered.

Is this comparison valid? (seems forced)

bias

The analogy to the Vietnam War can be extended even to the extent of the denial. It amuses me sometimes to hear people like myself decry the state of the public schools. We bemoan the lack of

Who are these people? Does he really represent them?

money, the decaying facilities, the absurd credentialism, the high foolishness of the school boards. We applaud the burgeoning reform movement. And everything we say is deeply, undeniably true. We can see every problem with the schools clearly except one: the fact that our decision to abandon the schools has helped create all the other problems. One small example: In the early 1980s, Massachusetts passed one of those tax cap measures, called Proposition 2 1/2, which has turned out to be a force for genuine evil in the public schools. Would Proposition 2 1/2 have passed had the middle class still had a stake in the schools? I wonder. I also wonder whether 20 years from now, in the next round of breast-beating memoirs, the exodus of the white middle class from the public schools will finally be seen for what it was. Individually, every parent's rationale made impeccable sense—"I can't deprive my children of a decent education"—but collectively, it was a deeply destructive act.

The main reason the white middle class fled, of course, is race, or more precisely, the complicated admixture of race and class and good intentions gone awry. The fundamental good intention—which even today strikes one as both moral and right—was to integrate the public classroom, and in so doing, to equalize the resources available to all school children. In Boston, this was done through enforced busing. In Washington, it was done through a series of judicial edicts that attempted to spread the good teachers and resources throughout the system. In other big city districts, judges weren't involved; school committees, seeing the handwriting on the wall, tried to do it themselves.

However moral the intent, the result almost always was the same. The white middle class left. The historic parental vigilance I mentioned earlier had had a lot to do with creating the two-tiered system—one in which schools attended by the kids of the white middle class had better teachers, better equipment, better everything than those attended by the kids of the poor. This did not happen because the white middle-class parents were racists, necessarily; it happened because they knew how to manipulate the system and were willing to do so on behalf of their kids. Their neighborhood schools became little havens of decent education, and they didn't much care what happened in the other public schools.

In retrospect, this behavior, though perfectly understandable, was tragically short-sighted. When the judicial fiats made those safe havens untenable, the white middle class quickly discovered what the poor had always known: There weren't enough good teachers, decent equipment, and so forth to go around. For that matter, there weren't even enough good students to go around;

Is this "one small example" enough to support his claim?

bias

Oversimplification–Do all parents have the same motives?

Is this a valid assumption?

Why does he assume intent was "good" + "moral"? Is he right?

Interesting point—but is it true?

Slanted language (over emotional) generalization?

along with everything else, middle-class parents had to start worrying about whether their kids were going to be mugged in school.

Slanted language (over emotional)

Faced with the (grim) fact that their children's education was
quickly deteriorating, middle-class parents essentially had two
choices: They could stay and pour the energy that had once gone
into improving the neighborhood school into improving the entire school system—a frightening task, to be sure. Or they could
leave. (Invariably,) they chose the latter.

Either/or fallacy? Were there other choices?

Oversimpli-ication? No exceptions?

And it wasn't just the white middle class that fled. The black middle class, and even the black poor who were especially ambitious for
their children, were getting out as fast as they could too, though not
to the suburbs. They headed mainly for the parochial schools, which
subsequently became integration's great success story, even as the
public schools became integration's great failure. (Joseph Nocera,
"How the Middle Class Has Helped Ruin the Public Schools")

As she read and reread the article, the student referred to the "Checklist: Reading Critically" on page 137 and recorded her reactions in the
form of annotations. When she finished her annotations, the student was
ready to draw her ideas together and write a **critical response** to the text.

See 7c

EXERCISE 5

Read the following short article, highlighting it as you read. Then, read
the questions that follow the article. Reread the article, recording your
reactions in the form of annotations. Finally, answer the questions.

"Go to Wall Street," my classmates said.
"Go to Wall Street," my professor advised.
"Go to Wall Street," my father threatened.
Whenever I tell people about my career indecisiveness, their an-
swer is always the same: Get a blueprint for life and get one fast.
Perhaps I'm simply too immature, but I think 20 is far too young
to set my life in stone.
Nobody mentioned any award for being the first to have a white
picket fence, 2.4 screaming kids and a spanking new Ford station
wagon.
What's wrong with uncertainty, with exploring multiple options in multiple fields? What's wrong with writing, "Heck, I don't
know" under the "objective" section of my résumé?
Parents, professors, recruiters and even other students seem to
think there's a lot wrong with it. And they are all pressuring me to
launch a career prematurely.

My sociology professor warns that my generation will be the first in American history not to be more successful than our parents' generation. This depressing thought drives college students to think of success as something that must be achieved at all costs as soon as possible.

My father wants me to emulate his success: Every family wants its children to improve the family fortune. I feel that desire myself, but I realize I don't need to do it by age 25.

This pressure to do better, to compete with the achievements of our parents in a rapidly changing world, has forced my generation to pursue definitive, lifelong career paths at far too young an age. Many of my friends who have graduated in recent years are already miserably unhappy.

My professors encourage such pre-professionalism. In upper level finance classes, the discussion is extremely career-oriented. "Learn to do this and you'll be paid more" is the theme of many a lecture. Never is there any talk of actually enjoying the exercise.

Nationwide, universities are finally taking steps in the right direction by re-emphasizing the study of liberal arts and a return to the classics. If only job recruiters for Wall Street firms would do the same.

"Get your M.B.A. as soon as possible and you'll have a jump on the competition," said one overly zealous recruiter from Goldman Sachs. Learning for learning's sake was completely forgotten: Goldman Sachs refused to interview anybody without a high grade-point average, regardless of the courses composing that average.

In other interviews, it is expected that you know exactly what you want to do or you won't be hired. "Finance?" they say, "What kind of finance?"

A recruiter at Dean Witter Reynolds said investment banking demands 80 to 100 hours of work per week. I don't see how anyone will ever find time to enjoy the gobs of money they'll be making.

The worst news came from a partner at Salomon Brothers. He told me no one was happy there, and if they said they were, they're lying. He said you come in, make a lot of money and leave as fast as you can.

Two recent Wharton alumni, scarcely two years older than I, spoke at Donaldson, Lufkin & Jenrette's presentation. Their jokes about not having a life outside the office were only partially in jest.

Yet, students can't wait to play this corporate charade. They don ties and jackets and tote briefcases to class.

It is not just business students who are obsessed with their careers. The five other people who live in my house are not undergraduate business majors, but all five plan to attend graduate school next year. How is it possible that, without one iota of real work experience, these people are willing to commit themselves to years of intensive study in one narrow field?

Mom, dad, grandpa, recruiters, professors, fellow students: I implore you to leave me alone.

Now is my chance to explore, to spend time pursuing interests simply because they make me happy and not because they fill my wallet. I don't want to waste my youth toiling at a miserable job. I want to make the right decisions about my future.

Who knows, I may even end up on Wall Street.

(Michael Finkel, "Undecided—and Proud of It")

1. What is the writer's main point?
2. How does he support this point?
3. Is his supporting evidence primarily fact or opinion? Does he support his opinions? Is the support convincing?
4. Where does the writer use expert testimony? How convincing are the experts he cites?
5. Should the writer have used other kinds of support? For example, should he have used statistics? If so, where? What kind of statistical evidence might have made his case more convincing?
6. Does the writer's choice of examples reveal any biases? What leads you to your conclusion?
7. The writer is a student at an Ivy League university. Do you think this status might give him a limited or an unrealistic view of college students' professional options?
8. The writer is a college senior. Do his age and his lack of experience in the working world make his article less credible to you?
9. Do you have any biases against the writer based on your assessment of his economic status, social class, or educational level?

7c Writing a Critical Response

After you have read a text critically, you can draw your reactions together by writing a critical response.

Before you begin writing your critical response, review your annotations. Carefully reconsider your judgments and reactions to the text in light of any biases that you may have uncovered in your own thinking.

See
14a

See
14b

See
Chs.
16–17

Begin writing your critical response by identifying the text you are evaluating and **summarizing** its main point. Next, present your evaluation of the text and the support for your position: summarize and respond to the writer's key points one by one, carefully **paraphrasing** ideas and supporting your judgments with specific examples from the text and the ideas that you wrote down as you annotated. As in any essay, you must supply the logical and sequential links (transitions, topic sentences, and so on) that will help your readers follow the progression of your ideas. Conclude by restating your evaluation of the text. When you have finished, reread what you have written, making sure that it is as accurate, clear, and fair as possible. Be sure to **document** all words and ideas that you borrow from your source.

Following is a student's critical response to Joseph Nocera's "How the Middle Class Has Helped Ruin the Public Schools," an annotated section of which is reproduced on pages 143–45.

Identification
of text

Summary of
text's position

Statement of
critical
reaction to
the text

Support:
summary and
evaluation of
writer's key
points (¶2–4)

In his article "How the Middle Class Has Helped Ruin the Public Schools," first published in the February 1989 issue of The Washington Monthly and later reprinted in the September/October 1990 Utne Reader, Joseph Nocera tries to have it both ways. He is confessing the guilt he feels for contributing to the decline of public education, and he is attacking those middle-class parents who have made the same choices he has made. What he seems to be asking his audience to do is to feel both sympathy and outrage toward parents in this situation. This is asking a lot.

Early in his essay, Nocera tells readers that he moved to a small town because of its good public schools—which he attributes to "a large group of white middle-class parents deeply involved in the public school system" (67). He cites the "outrages" of public schools in Boston, Washington, and New York and concludes that "The destruction of the large public school systems in America is one of the great tragedies of our time" (67). Then, he apologetically explains that he has chosen, for the sake of his children's education, "not to stand

and fight" (68). After all, he argues, "Parents aren't willing to sacrifice their children on the altar of their social principles" (71). Throughout the essay, he seems to assume that his readers will agree with him simply because he is an ordinary middle-class parent.

Admitting that, as this typical middle-class parent, he has options that poor parents do not have, Nocera tries to justify his private decision despite the widespread public disaster that he admits it has helped to create. In doing so, he reveals his biases. At various points in his discussion, he attacks the courts, unions, bureaucrats, and school committees. He talks about the nation's problems, but all his examples are drawn from the urban Northeast, particularly Boston. He also suggests that any middle-class parents who, unlike himself, keep their children in public schools are sacrificing their children's education for some abstract social principles. This conclusion ignores the fact that some parents may consider the understanding of such social principles to be a valuable part of their children's education. In addition, not all urban public schools provide an inferior education. Finally, he reveals a racial bias when he makes the assumption that white middle-class students (and parents) are the most valuable in a school system and that without them the system is doomed.

Nocera's reasoning is sometimes faulty. For instance, when he says, "Since the white middle class left, the system [in Boston] has simply fallen apart. Can this be sheer coincidence? I think not" (71), he is making a sweeping (and unsupported) generalization. He is also assuming that either white flight or coincidence—and no other factor—must have caused the schools' decline. Similarly, when he says the middle class could either try to improve the whole system or abandon it, he ignores the possibility of other options—such as working to improve one particular school in a system.

Restatement
of critical
reaction to
the text

Generalizations and oversimplifications like these reduce a complex issue to a simplistic, either-or situation. Given this limited perspective, it is not surprising that Nocera can offer no solution. Predictably, he believes that change should come not from people like him but rather from those outside the system. In his conclusion, Nocera reveals that what he is really looking for is not a platform from which to effect change but an opportunity for confession and a plea for forgiveness.

✔ **CHECKLIST: WRITING A CRITICAL RESPONSE**

BEFORE WRITING:
✔ Review your annotations.
✔ Reconsider your judgments about the text in light of your own biases.

IN YOUR CRITICAL RESPONSE:
✔ Identify your text and summarize its main point.
✔ Present your evaluation of the text.
✔ Summarize and evaluate the writer's key points, using paraphrase and quotation as needed.
✔ Restate your critical response to the text.
✔ Reread what you have written, checking for accuracy, clarity, and fairness.
✔ Document any words or ideas that you borrowed from a source.

EXERCISE 6

The following letter (*Utne Reader,* November/December 1990) was written by a Denver parent in response to Nocera's essay (pp. 143–45). Putting yourself in Nocera's place, write a brief critical response to the letter. Use the checklist above to guide you.

Multicultural Education

I believe Joseph Nocera's article is entirely accurate except for one major flaw. That flaw is the belief that sending your children to urban public schools is "sacrificing them." I believe it is in their best interest to do so.

I am a parent of four children in the Denver public school system. I have observed all of the rationalizations described in Nocera's article as dozens of good white liberals in our integrated neighborhood have fled to the suburbs and private schools. For years I tried to appeal to their altruism to support the schools. Then I realized that the reason I was sending my kids to the public schools was not "a sacrifice for my social principles" as Nocera would have us believe, but was actually because I knew it was in their own best interest, to help them learn how to relate and function within a multicultural, multiracial environment. Let me illustrate this point with personal anecdotes.

My son, who is a good fourth-grade student, asked why our friend's son was leaving our public school. I told him it was because "his parents didn't want him to be the only white boy in his class." Then I asked him, "Has that ever happened to you?" He pondered a moment and then said, "I don't think so. I can't remember." Actually, only the year before, he was the only white boy in his third-grade class, but he obviously had overcome any anxiety or prejudice or even awareness of this recent experience.

My daughter, who is a straight-A seventh grader, asked me, "What is an ethnic minority?" I explained that it was a small minority group like blacks. She said with a totally straight face, "Come on, Dad, blacks aren't a minority." In her world they aren't.

Duane Gall
Denver, CO

CHAPTER 8

THINKING LOGICALLY

Arguments must be based on logical reasoning. The two most common methods of reasoning are *induction* and *deduction*. Quite often writers use a combination of inductive and deductive reasoning in their arguments.

8a   Reasoning Inductively

(1) Moving from Observations to Conclusion

Inductive reasoning moves from specific facts, observations, or experiences to a general conclusion. Writers use inductive reasoning when they address a skeptical audience that requires a lot of evidence before it will accept a conclusion. You can see how inductive reasoning operates by studying the following list of statements that focus on the relationship between SAT scores and admissions at one liberal arts college.

- The SAT is an admission requirement for all applicants.
- High school grades and rank in class are also examined.
- Nonacademic factors, such as sports, activities, and interests, are taken into account as well.
- Special attention is given to the applications of athletes, minorities, and children of alumni.
- Fewer than 52 percent of applicants for a recent class with SAT verbal scores between 600 and 700 were accepted.
- Fewer than 39 percent of applicants with similar math scores were accepted.

Logic in Argumentation (Purdue)
   http://owl.english.purdue.edu/handouts/general/gl_argpers.html

- Approximately 18 percent of applications with SAT verbal scores between 450 and 520 and about 19 percent of applicants with similar SAT math scores were admitted.

After reading the preceding statements, you can use inductive reasoning to draw the general conclusion that although important, SAT scores are not necessarily the most important factor that determines whether a student is admitted.

(2) Making Inferences

No matter how much evidence is presented, an inductive conclusion is never certain, only probable. It is arrived at by making an **inference**, a statement about the unknown based on the known. Naturally, the more observations you make, the narrower the gap between your observations and your conclusion. Even so, absolute certainty is not possible. The best you can do is present a convincing conclusion to your readers.

For example, suppose a student in a summer internship program is told to research a way her state could eliminate the many bottles and cans that litter its towns and roadways. Her reading suggests a number of possible actions. The state could hire unemployed teenagers to pick up the litter. It could also use brightly colored refuse containers to encourage people to dispose of bottles and cans properly. Finally, the state could require a deposit from all those who buy beverages in bottles or cans. Reviewing her reading, the student finds that the first two solutions have had no long-term effect on litter in states that tried them. However, mandatory deposit regulations, along with the outlawing of plastic beverage containers, have significantly decreased the number of bottles and cans in the two states that instituted such measures. Still, because the conditions in the student's state are not exactly the same as those in the states she studied, she must make a leap from the known—the states she studied—to the unknown—the situation in her state. By means of inductive reasoning, the student is able to infer that a mandatory deposit law could be a good solution to the problem.

EXERCISE 1

Read the following paragraph and answer the questions that follow it.

Americans are becoming more ecologically aware with each passing year, but their awareness may be limited. Most people know about the destruction of rain forests in South America, for example, or the vanishing African elephant, but few realize what is going on in their own backyards in the name of progress. Even people who are knowledgeable about such topics as the plight of the wild mustang, the dangers of toxic waste disposal, and acid rain frequently fail to realize either the existence or the importance of "smaller" ecological issues. The wetlands are a good case in point. In recent decades, more than 500,000 acres of wetlands a year have been filled, and it seems unlikely that the future will see any great change. What has happened in recent times is that United States wetlands are filled in one area and "restored" in another area, a practice that is legal according to Section 404 of the Clean Water Act and one that does in fact result in "no net loss" of wetlands. Few see the problems with this. To most, wetlands are mere swamps, and getting rid of swamps is viewed as something positive. In addition, the wetlands typically contain few spectacular species—the sort of glamour animals, such as condors and grizzlies, that easily attract publicity and sympathy. Instead, they contain boring specimens of flora and fauna unlikely to generate great concern among the masses. Yet the delicate balance of the ecosystem *is* upset by the elimination or "rearrangement" of such marshy areas. True, cosmically speaking, it matters little if one organism (or many) is wiped out. But even obscure subspecies might provide some much-needed product or information in the future. We should not forget that penicillin was made from a lowly mold.

Which of the following statements can be inferred from the paragraph?

1. The loss of even a single species may be disastrous to the ecosystem of the wetlands.
2. Even though the wetlands are considered swamps, most people are very concerned about their fate.
3. Section 404 of the Clean Water Act is not sufficient to protect the wetlands.
4. Few Americans are concerned about environmental issues.
5. Most people would agree that the destruction of rain forests is worse than the destruction of the wetlands.

8b Reasoning Deductively

See
Ch. 9

Deductive reasoning moves from a generalization believed to be true or self-evident to a more specific conclusion. Writers use deductive reasoning (most often in **argumentative essays**) when they address an audience that is more likely to be influenced by logic than by evidence. The process of deduction has traditionally been illustrated with a **syllogism,** a three-part set of statements or propositions that includes a **major premise,** a **minor premise,** and a **conclusion.**

> MAJOR PREMISE: All books from that store are new.
>
> MINOR PREMISE: These books are from that store.
>
> CONCLUSION: Therefore, these books are new.

The major premise of a syllogism makes a general statement that the writer believes to be true. The minor premise presents a specific example of the belief that is stated in the major premise. If the reasoning is sound, the conclusion should follow from the two premises. (Note that these two premises contain all the information expressed in the conclusion; that is, the conclusion introduces no terms that have not already appeared in the major and minor premises.) The strength of a deductive argument is that if readers accept the premises, they usually grant the conclusion.

 USING SYLLOGISMS

You can use a syllogism when you plan an essay (to test the validity of your points), or you can use it as a revision strategy (to test your logic). In either case, the syllogism enables you to express your deductive argument in its most basic form and to see whether it makes sense.

(1) Constructing Valid Syllogisms

A syllogism is **valid** (or logical) when its conclusion follows from its premises. A syllogism is **true** when it makes accurate claims—that is, when the information it contains is consistent with the facts. To be **sound,** a syllogism must be both valid and true. However, a syllogism may be valid without being true or true without being valid. The following syllogism, for example, is valid but not true.

> MAJOR PREMISE: All politicians are male.
>
> MINOR PREMISE: Barbara Boxer is a politician.
>
> CONCLUSION: Therefore, Barbara Boxer is male.

As odd as it may seem, this syllogism is valid. In the major premise, the phrase *all politicians* establishes that the entire class *politicians* is male. After Barbara Boxer is identified as a politician, the conclusion that she is male automatically follows—but, in fact, she is not. Because the major premise of this syllogism is not true, no conclusion based upon it can be true. Even though the logic of the syllogism is correct, its conclusion is not.

Just as a syllogism can be valid but not true, it can also be true but not valid. In each of the following situations, the structure of the syllogism undercuts its logic.

Syllogism with an Illogical Middle Term   A syllogism with an illogical middle term cannot have a valid conclusion. The **middle term** of a syllogism is the term that appears in both the major and minor premises but not in the conclusion. A rule of logic is that the middle term of a syllogism must refer to *all* members of the group.

Invalid Syllogism

MAJOR PREMISE: All fathers are male.

MINOR PREMISE: Bill Cosby is a male.

CONCLUSION: Therefore, Bill Cosby is a father.

Even though the premises of this syllogism are true, the conclusion is illogical. *Males* is used as the middle term (that is, it appears in both the major and minor premises), but because *male* does not refer to *all males,* it cannot logically function as the middle term. For this reason, the conclusion—"Bill Cosby is a father"—does not follow, and so the syllogism is invalid.

Valid Syllogism

MAJOR PREMISE: All fathers are male.

MINOR PREMISE: Bill Cosby is a father.

CONCLUSION: Therefore, Bill Cosby is a male.

Here the term *fathers* refers to all fathers; therefore, it can logically function as the middle term. Because of this, the conclusion—"Bill Cosby is male"—logically follows.

Syllogism with a Term Whose Meaning Shifts   A syllogism in which the meaning of a key term shifts cannot have a valid conclusion.

Invalid Syllogism

MAJOR PREMISE: Only man contemplates the future.

MINOR PREMISE: No woman is a man.

CONCLUSION: Therefore, no woman contemplates the future.

In the major premise, *man* denotes all human beings. In the minor premise, however, *man* denotes a person who is male. You can avoid this problem by making certain that the meaning of each key term in the major premise remains the same throughout the syllogism.

Valid Syllogism

MAJOR PREMISE: Only human beings contemplate the future.

MINOR PREMISE: No dog is a human being.

CONCLUSION: Therefore, no dog contemplates the future.

Syllogisms with Negative Premises   A syllogism in which *one* of the premises is negative can only have a negative conclusion.

Invalid Syllogism

MAJOR PREMISE: No person may be denied employment because of a physical disability.

MINOR PREMISE: Deaf persons have a physical disability.

CONCLUSION: Therefore, a deaf person may be denied employment because of a physical disability.

Because the major premise of the preceding syllogism is negative (*"No person . . ."*), the only conclusion possible is a negative one. ("Therefore, *no* deaf person may be denied employment . . .).

A syllogism in which *both* premises are negative cannot have a valid conclusion.

Invalid Syllogism

MAJOR PREMISE: Injured workers may not be denied workers' compensation.

MINOR PREMISE: Frank is not an injured worker.

CONCLUSION: Therefore, Frank may not be denied workers' compensation.

In the preceding syllogism, both the major and minor premises are negative. As they now stand, the two premises cannot yield a valid conclusion. (How, for example, can Frank get workers' compensation if he is *not* an injured worker?)

If a syllogism is to yield a valid conclusion, only one of its premises may be negative.

Valid Syllogism

MAJOR PREMISE: Injured workers may not be denied workers' compensation.

MINOR PREMISE: Frank is an injured worker.

CONCLUSION: Therefore, Frank may not be denied workers' compensation.

(2) Recognizing Enthymemes

An **enthymeme** is a syllogism in which one of the premises—often the major premise—is unstated. Enthymemes often occur as sentences containing words that signal conclusions—*therefore, consequently, for this reason, for, so, since,* or *because.*

Melissa is on the Dean's List; therefore, she is a good student.

The preceding sentence contains the minor premise and the conclusion of a syllogism. The reader must fill in the missing major premise in order to complete the syllogism and see whether or not the reasoning is logical.

MAJOR PREMISE: All those on the Dean's List are good students.

MINOR PREMISE: Melissa is on the Dean's List.

CONCLUSION: Therefore, Melissa is a good student.

Some writers deliberately leave premises unstated in an attempt to influence an audience unfairly, keeping their basic assumptions ambiguous or pretending that assumptions are so self-evident that they need not be stated. Whenever you identify an enthymeme, try to supply the missing premise and then determine whether the enthymeme is logical.

REVIEW: INDUCTIVE AND DEDUCTIVE REASONING

Inductive

1. Begins with specific observations.
2. Moves from the specific to the general.
3. Conclusion is probable, never certain.
4. Progresses by means of inference.
5. Draws a conclusion about the unknown based on what is known.

Deductive

1. Begins with a general statement or proposition.
2. Moves from the general to the specific.
3. Conclusion can be logical or illogical.
4. Progresses by means of the syllogism.
5. Draws a necessary conclusion about the known based on what is known.

---

(3) Using Toulmin Logic

Philosopher Stephen Toulmin has introduced another method for structuring arguments. **Toulmin logic** divides arguments into three parts: *the claim, the grounds,* and *the warrant.*

- **The claim** is the main point that the writer makes in the essay.
- **The grounds** are the evidence and reasons on which the claim is based. They are the support that the writer uses to bolster the claim.
- **The warrant** is the assumption that links the claim to the data. It shows how the evidence supports the claim.

In its simplest terms, an argument following Toulmin's pattern would look like this.

(Grounds)   (Claim)
Jane graduated from medical school. ──┬── Jane is a doctor.
                    (Warrant)   │
           A person who graduates from medical
                    school is a doctor.

Notice that the claim presents a specific situation, whereas the warrant is a general principle that can apply to a number of situations. In this sense, the warrant is similar to the major premise of a syllogism, and the claim is similar to the conclusion. (The grounds are the premises from which the claim is derived or the premises that make the claim probable or possible.)

In addition to suggesting a general way of structuring arguments, Toulmin logic offers a way of identifying and assessing an argument's assumptions.

- A warrant based on **authority** is based on the credibility of the person making the argument.
- A warrant based on **substance** is based on the reliability of the evidence.
- A warrant based on **motivation** is based on the values and beliefs of the writer and the readers.

Toulmin logic is an alternative method of constructing arguments. Far from replacing inductive and deductive logic, it provides another way of clarifying the major elements of an argument. Even so, it still relies on inductive and deductive reasoning: you arrive at your claim by moving *inductively* from your reading, and the relationship of your grounds and warrant to your claim is *deductive*.

EXERCISE 2

Read this essay carefully.

A nation succeeds only if the vast majority of its citizens succeed. It therefore stands to reason that with immigrants accounting for about 40 percent of our population growth, the future economic and social success of the United States is bound up with the success of these new Americans. Demography, in a word, is destiny.

This is an important principle to keep in mind as we try to come to grips with the problems and opportunities presented by the flood of legal and illegal immigrants from Mexico and other parts of South and Central America, who now constitute by far our largest immigrant group.

How are we doing in our efforts to assimilate these largely Hispanic newcomers and provide them with a bright future? Some signs are disturbing.

John Garcia, associate professor of political science at the University of Arizona, writing in *International Migration Review*, finds that the average rate of naturalization of Mexican immigrants is one-tenth that of other immigrant naturalization rates. The Select Commission on Immigration and Refugee Policy made a similar finding. Increasingly, immigrants are separated from everyone else by language, geography, ethnicity and class.

The future success of this country is closely linked to the ability of our immigrants to succeed. Yet 50 percent of our children of Hispanic background do not graduate from high school. Hispanic students score 100 points under the average student on Scholastic Aptitude Test scores. Hispanics have much higher rates of poverty, illiteracy and need for welfare than the national average. This engenders social crisis.

Not all the indicators of assimilation are pessimistic: the success of many Indochinese immigrants has been gratifying. But the warning signs of nonassimilation are increasing and ominous.

America must make sure the melting pot continues to melt: immigrants must become Americans. Seymour Martin Lipset, professor of political science and sociology at the Hoover Institution, Stanford University, observes: "The history of bilingual and bicultural societies that do not assimilate are histories of turmoil, tension and tragedy. Canada, Belgium, Malaysia, Lebanon—all face crises of national existence in which minorities press for autonomy, if not independence. Pakistan and Cyprus have divided. Nigeria suppressed an ethnic rebellion. France faces difficulties with its Basques, Bretons and Corsicans."

The United States is at a crossroads. If it does not consciously move toward greater integration, it will inevitably drift toward more fragmentation. It will either have to do better in assimilating all of the other peoples in its boundaries or it will witness increasing alienation and fragmentation. Cultural divisiveness is not a bedrock upon which a nation can be built. It is inherently unstable.

The nation faces a staggering social agenda. We have not adequately integrated blacks into our economy and society. Our education system is rightly described as "a rising tide of mediocrity." We have the most violent society in the industrial world; we have startlingly high rates of illiteracy, illegitimacy and welfare recipients.

It bespeaks a hubris to madly rush, with these unfinished social agendas, into accepting more immigrants and refugees than all of the rest of the world and then to still hope to keep a common agenda.

America can accept additional immigrants, but we must be sure that they become American. We can be a Joseph's coat of many nations, but we must be unified. One of the common glues that hold us together is language—the English language.

We should be color-blind but linguistically cohesive. We should be a rainbow but not a cacophony. We should welcome different peoples but not adopt different languages. We can teach English through bilingual education, but we should take great care not to become a bilingual society.

(Richard D. Lamm, "English Comes First")

A. Answer the following questions about the essay.

1. Former Colorado governor Richard D. Lamm relies on a number of unstated premises about his subject that he expects his audience to accept. What are some of these premises?
2. What kinds of information does Lamm use to support his position?
3. Where does Lamm state his conclusion? Restate the conclusion in your own words.
4. In paragraph 1, Lamm uses deductive reasoning. Express this reasoning as a syllogism.
5. Express the syllogism in paragraph 1 in terms of Toulmin logic.

B. Evaluate the reasoning in the following statements. (If the statement is in the form of an enthymeme, supply the missing term before evaluating it.)

1. All immigrants should speak English. If they do not, they are not real Americans.
2. Richard D. Lamm was born in the United States and grew up in an English-speaking household. Therefore, he has no credibility on the subject of bilingualism.
3. Spanish-speaking immigrants should be required by law to learn English. After all, most eastern European immigrants who came to this country early in the twentieth century learned English.
4. If immigrants do not care enough about our country to learn English, we should not allow them to become citizens.
5. Some immigrants have become financially successful even though they did not learn English. Obviously, then, learning English does not increase an immigrant's chances for success.
6. All Cuban immigrants speak Spanish. Former Secretary of Housing and Urban Development Henry Cisneros speaks Spanish, so he must be a Cuban immigrant.
7. As sociologist Seymour Martin Lipset points out, bilingual societies can be threatened by tension and political unrest. Therefore, it is important that immigrants not be bilingual.

8c   Recognizing Logical Fallacies

Fallacies are flawed arguments. Unscrupulous writers often use logical fallacies to manipulate readers, appealing to prejudices and fears, for example, instead of to reason. But even when you write with the best of intentions and the greatest care, you may accidentally include fallacies. When readers detect fallacies, they may conclude that you are illogical—or worse yet, dishonest.

(1) Hasty Generalization

A **hasty generalization** is a form of improper induction. It draws a conclusion based on too little evidence. For example, one disappointing performance by an elected official is not enough to warrant the statement that you will never vote again. Similarly, you cannot conclude that two bad teachers do not indicate a bad school, or that one or two rejection letters mean that new writers cannot get their work published.

(2) Sweeping Generalization

A **sweeping generalization** is a statement that cannot be adequately supported no matter how much evidence is supplied. **Absolute statements,** for example, are so sweeping that they allow for no exceptions.

Everyone should exercise.

Certainly, most people would agree that regular exercise promotes good health. This does not mean, however, that *all* people should exercise. For example, what if a person has a severe heart condition? To avoid making statements that cannot be supported, you should be careful to qualify your statements. For example, you might say, "Most people benefit from regular exercise." The easiest way to identify absolute statements is to examine each use of such words as *always, all, never,* and *everyone*. In many cases, such a word as *often, seldom, some,* or *most* will be more accurate.

Stereotypes are sweeping generalizations about the members of a race, religion, gender, nationality, or other group. Because such generalizations are almost never accurate, they undercut the credibility of those who make them.

Logical Fallacies (or Errors in Thinking)
   http://www.intrepidsoftware.com/fallacy/toc.htm
Avoiding Common Errors in Logic and Reasoning (Princeton U.)
   http://web.princeton.edu/sites/writing/logic-re.htm

(3) Equivocation

Equivocation occurs when the meaning of a key word or phrase shifts during an argument.

It is not in the public interest for the public to lose interest in politics.

Although clever, the shift in meaning of the term *public interest* clouds this issue.

(4) The Either/Or Fallacy

The **either/or fallacy** occurs when a complex situation is presented as if it has only two sides. If you ask whether the policies of the United States toward Latin America are beneficial or harmful, you acknowledge only two possibilities, ruling out all others. In fact, the policies of the United States toward some Latin American countries may be beneficial, but US policies toward others may be harmful. Do not misrepresent issues by making them more simple than they actually are.

(5) The *Post Hoc* Fallacy *(post hoc, ergo propter hoc)*

Post hoc, ergo propter hoc is Latin for "after this, therefore because of this." The *post hoc* **fallacy** occurs when you mistakenly infer that because one event follows another, the first event *caused* the second. For example, after the United States sold wheat to Russia, the price of wheat and wheat products rose dramatically. Many people blamed the wheat sale for this rapid increase. One event followed the other closely in time, so people falsely assumed that the first event caused the second. In fact, a complicated series of farm price controls that had been in effect for years was responsible for the increase in wheat prices.

(6) Begging the Question

Begging the question (also known as **circular reasoning**) occurs when a writer states a debatable premise as if it were true. Often this fallacy occurs when a person incorrectly assumes that a proposition is so obvious that it needs no proof.

Sadistic experiments on animals should be stopped because they clearly constitute cruel and unusual punishment.

Certainly, sadistic experimentation is cruel. What has to be proven, however, is that the experiments on animals to which the writer refers actually are sadistic.

(7) False Analogy

Analogies—extended comparisons—enable a writer to explain something unfamiliar by comparing it to something familiar. Skillfully used, an analogy can be quite effective, as when a student illustrates her frustration with the registration process at her college by comparing students to rats in a maze. In an argument, however, an analogy alone establishes nothing; it is no substitute for evidence.

A **false analogy** (or *faulty analogy*) assumes that because issues or concepts are similar in some ways, they are similar in other ways. On a television talk show, a psychologist who was asked to explain why people commit crimes gave the following response.

> People commit crimes because they are weak and selfish. They are like pregnant women who know they shouldn't smoke but do anyway. They have a craving that they have to give in to. The answer is not to punish criminals, but to understand their behavior and to try to change it.

Admittedly, the analogy between criminals and pregnant women who smoke is convincing. However, it oversimplifies the issue. A pregnant woman does not intend to harm her unborn child by smoking; many criminals do intend to harm their victims. To undercut the psychologist's argument, you need only point out the shortcomings of his analogy.

(8) Red Herring

The **red herring** fallacy occurs when a writer changes the subject to distract readers from the issue. Consider the statement, "This company may charge high prices, but it gives a great deal of money to charity each year." The latter issue has nothing to do with the former; still, it manages to obscure the real issue.

(9) Argument to Ignorance
(*argumentum ad ignorantiam*)

The **argument to ignorance** fallacy occurs when a writer says that something is true because it cannot be proved false or vice versa. This fallacy occurred during a debate about a policy allowing children who have AIDS to attend public school. A parent asked a doctor, "How can you tell me to put my child in danger by sending him to a school with a child with AIDS? After all, doctors can't say for sure that my son won't catch AIDS, can they?" In other words, the parent was saying, "My son could contract AIDS from another child in school because you can't prove that he cannot." As persuasive as this line of reasoning can sometimes be, it is logically flawed: no evidence has been presented to support the speaker's conclusion.

(10) The Bandwagon Fallacy

The **bandwagon fallacy** occurs when a writer tries to establish that something is true because everyone believes it is. For example, a newspaper editorial made the statement, "Everyone knows that eating too much candy makes a child hyperactive." Instead of providing evidence to support this claim, the editorial relied on an appeal to numbers.

(11) Skewed Sample

A **skewed sample** occurs when a statistical sample is collected so that it will lead to one conclusion rather than another. To present accurate results, a statistical sample should be *representative;* that is, it should be typical of the broader population it represents. For example, census questions asked only in English would skew results in favor of English-speaking respondents.

(12) You Also *(tu quoque)*

The **you also** fallacy occurs when a writer argues that a point has no merit because the person making it does not follow his or her own advice. Such an argument is irrelevant because it focuses attention on the person rather than on the issue being debated.

How can government economists advise Americans to save? Look at how much money the government spent last year.

(13) Argument to the Person *(ad hominem)*

Arguments *ad hominem* attack a person rather than an issue. By attacking an opponent, these arguments turn attention away from the real issues.

That woman has criticized the president's commitment to preserving social security. But she believes in parapsychology. She thinks that she can communicate with the dead.

(14) Argument to the People *(ad populum)*

Arguments *ad populum* appeal to people's prejudices. A senatorial candidate seeking support in a state whose textile industry has been hurt by foreign competition may allude to "foreigners who are attempting to overrun our shores." By exploiting the prejudices of the audience, the candidate tries to avoid the concrete issues of the campaign.

✔ CHECKLIST: LOGICAL FALLACIES

✔ **Hasty Generalization**   A conclusion based on too little evidence

✔ **Sweeping Generalization**   A statement that cannot be supported no matter how much evidence is supplied

✔ **Equivocation**   A shift in the meaning of a key word during an argument

✔ **Either/Or Fallacy**   A complex issue treated as if it has only two sides

✔ *Post Hoc* **Fallacy**   An unjustified link between cause and effect

✔ **Begging the Question**   A debatable premise stated as if it were true

✔ **False Analogy**   An assumption that because things are similar in some ways, they are similar in other ways

✔ **Red Herring**   A change in subject to distract an audience

✔ **Argument to Ignorance**   A claim that something is true because it cannot be proved false, or vice versa

✔ **Bandwagon Fallacy**   An attempt to establish that something is true because everyone believes it is true

✔ **Skewed Sample**   A statistical sample that favors one population over another

✔ **You Also Fallacy**   A claim that a position is not valid because the person advocating it does not follow it

✔ **Argument to the Person**   An attack on the person and not the issue

✔ **Argument to the People**   An appeal to the prejudices of the people

EXERCISE 3

Identify the logical fallacies in the following statements. In each case, name the fallacy and rewrite the statement to correct the problem.

1. Membership in the Coalition against Pornography has more than quadrupled since the 1980s. Convenience stores in many parts of the country have limited their selection of pornography and, in many cases, taken pornography off the shelves. In 1995, the defense appropriations bill included a ban on the sale of pornography on military

installations. The American public clearly believes that pornography has a harmful effect on its audience.

2. With people like Larry Flynt and Hugh Hefner arguing that pornography is harmless, you know that pornography is causing its readers to live immoral lifestyles.

3. The Republican Party and conservative thinkers are all for the free market when the issue is environmental degradation, but they'll be the first ones to call for a limit to what can be shown on movies, television, and the Internet.

4. Television is out of control. There is more foul language, sex, and sexual innuendo on television than there has ever been before. The effects of this obscene and pornographic material have been clearly documented in studies that proved that serial killers and other criminals were much more likely to be regular consumers of pornographic materials.

5. We know that television causes children to be more violent. So what can we use to rein in television? The V-chip, television ratings, and more governmental control of television content will help us reduce violence.

6. Study after study has been completed, and none of the researchers has presented incontrovertible evidence that rap music causes an increase in violent behavior among its listeners.

7. A boy in Idaho set fire to his family's home after watching an episode of *Beavis and Butthead*. From this incident, we can see that television has a negative influence on children's behavior.

8. We want our children to grow up in safe neighborhoods. We'd like to see less violence in the schools and on the playgrounds. We'd like to be less fearful when we have to go out at night. If we stop polluting our culture with violent images from television and popular music, we can reclaim our communities and our children.

9. Ted Bundy and Richard Ramirez, two of the most violent serial killers ever caught, both used pornography regularly. Pornography caused them to kill women.

10. Some people believe that violence on television affects children and want the government to find ways to limit violence. Others believe that children are unaffected by the violence they see on television. I don't think violence on television causes children to become violent.

EXERCISE 4

Read the following excerpt. Identify as many logical fallacies as you can. Then, write a letter to the author pointing out the fallacies and explaining how they weaken his argument.

Hunting and eating a free-roaming wild deer is one thing; slaughtering and eating a [wounded] deer is another.

The point [. . .] is that—despite what our enemies are saying—hunters are just as compassionate as the next fellow. It hurts us to see an animal suffer, and when we can help an animal in need, we go out of our way to do whatever we can.

A case in point is the story [. . .] about SCI Alaska vice president Dave Campbell's efforts to help a cow moose. That animal had carried a poorly shot arrow in its body for weeks until Campbell saw it and made certain it got help.

Despite how some media handled that story, there is no irony in hunters coming to the rescue of the same species we hunt.

We do it all the time.

A story of hunters showing compassion for an animal is something you'll never see in *The Bunny Huggers' Gazette* (yes, there *is* such a publication. It's a bimonthly magazine produced on newsprint. According to the publisher's statement, it provides information about vegetarianism, and "organizations, protests, boycotts or legislation on behalf of animal liberation [. . .]").

Among the protests announced in the June issue of *BHG* are boycotts against the countries of Ireland and Spain, the states and provinces of the Yukon Territory, Alberta, British Columbia, Pennsylvania and Alaska, the companies of American Express, Anheuser-Busch, Bausch & Lomb, Bloomingdale's, Coca-Cola Products, Coors, Gillette, Hartz, L'Oreal, McDonald's, Mellon Bank, Northwest Airlines, Pocono Mountain resorts and a host of others.

Interestingly, *BHG* tells how a subscribing group, Life Net of Montezuma, New Mexico, has petitioned the US Forest Service to close portions of the San Juan and Rio Grande National Forests between April and November to all entry "to provide as much protection as possible" for grizzly bears that may still exist there. Another subscriber, Predator Project of Bozeman, Montana, is asking that the entire North Cascades region be closed to coyote hunting because gray wolves might be killed by "sportsmen (who) may not be able to tell the difference between a coyote and a wolf."

Although it's not a new idea, another subscriber, Prairie Dog Rescue, is urging persons who are opposed to hunting to apply for limited quota hunting permits because "one permit in peaceful hands means one less opportunity for a hunter to kill."

And if you ever doubted that the vegetarian/animal rights herd is a wacko bunch, then consider the magazine's review of *Human*

Tissue, A Neglected Experimental Resource. According to the review, the 24-page essay encourages using human tissues to test "medicines and other substances, any of which would save animals' lives."
(Bill Roberts, "The World of Hunting")

EXERCISE 5

The following statements provide the claim and the grounds for an argument. Identify the claim and the grounds. Then supply the warrant.

> EXAMPLE:　Cigarette smoking should be illegal because it isn't healthful.
> **CLAIM:** Cigarette smoking should be illegal.
> **GROUNDS:** Cigarette smoking isn't healthful.
> **WARRANT:** Things that aren't healthful should be illegal.

1. Buy this car because it has a powerful engine.
2. Karate is good for overactive kids because it teaches them to control their bodies.
3. Legal immigrants contribute to the economy by paying taxes, so they should be allowed to receive welfare and Medicare benefits.
4. Sports figures shouldn't be paid so much because their work doesn't contribute to the betterment of society.
5. Because it takes a long time to complete the income tax forms required by the IRS, we should change the current tax system to a flat tax system.

CHAPTER 9

WRITING AN ARGUMENTATIVE ESSAY

? FREQUENTLY ASKED QUESTIONS

How do I know if a topic is suitable for an argumentative essay? (p. 171)

How do I make sure that I have an argumentative thesis? (p. 173)

How should I deal with opposing arguments? (p. 174)

How can I convince readers that I'm someone they should listen to? (p. 176)

How can I be sure I'm being fair? (p. 178)

How should I organize my argumentative essay? (p. 180)

For most people, the true test of their critical thinking skills comes when they write an argumentative essay, one that takes a position on an issue and uses logic and evidence to convince readers. When you write an argumentative essay, you follow the same process you use when you write any **essay**. The special demands of argument, though, require you to use some additional strategies to make your ideas convincing to readers.

See Chs. 1–4

9a Planning an Argumentative Essay

(1) Choosing a Debatable Topic

Because an argumentative essay attempts to change the way people think, it must focus on a **debatable topic,** one about which reasonable

Writing an Argument Paper (Muskingum College)
   http://muskingum.edu/~cal/database/writing.html#Argument
Writing Argumentative Essays
   http://www2.rscc.cc.tn.us/~jordan_jj/OWL/Argumentation.html

people disagree. Factual statements—those about which reasonable people do *not* disagree—are, therefore, not suitable for argument.

FACT: Many countries hold political prisoners.

DEBATABLE TOPIC: The United States *should not* trade with countries that hold political prisoners.

FACT: First-year students are not required to purchase a meal plan from the university.

DEBATABLE TOPIC: First-year students *should* be required to purchase a meal plan from the university.

In addition to being debatable, your topic should be one about which you know something. The more evidence you can provide, the more likely you are to influence your audience. General knowledge is seldom convincing by itself, however, so you will probably have to do some **research**.

Your topic should also be narrow enough so that you can write about it within your page limit. After all, in your argumentative essay, you will have to develop your own ideas and present supporting evidence, while also pointing out the strengths and weaknesses of opposing arguments. If your topic is too broad, you will not be able to cover it in enough detail.

Finally, keep in mind that some topics—such as "The Need for Gun Control" or "The Effectiveness of the Death Penalty"—have been discussed and written about so often that you will probably not be able to say anything new or interesting about them. Such topics usually inspire tired, uninteresting essays that add little or nothing to a reader's understanding of an issue. Instead of relying on an overused topic, choose one that enables you to contribute something new to the debate.

(2) Developing an Argumentative Thesis

After you have chosen a topic, your next step is to state your position in an **argumentative thesis,** one that takes a strong stand about your topic. Properly worded, this thesis statement lays the foundation for the rest of your argument.

One way to make sure that your thesis statement actually does take a stand is to formulate an **antithesis,** a statement that takes an arguable position opposite from yours. If you can create an antithesis, your thesis statement takes a stand. If you cannot, your statement needs further revision to make it argumentative.

Thesis Statement: Term limits would improve government by bringing people with fresh ideas into office every few years.

Antithesis: Term limits would harm government because elected officials would always be inexperienced.

 DEVELOPING AN ARGUMENTATIVE THESIS

You can determine if your argumentative thesis is effective by asking the following questions.

- Is your thesis one with which reasonable people would disagree?
- Can you think of arguments against your thesis?
- Can your thesis be supported by evidence?
- Does your thesis make clear to readers what position you are taking?

Whenever possible, test a tentative thesis statement on classmates— either informally in classroom conversations or formally in collaborative work. You may also want to talk to your instructor, do some reading about your topic, or do research in the **library** or on the **Internet**. Your goal should be to get a grasp of your topic so you can make an informed statement about it.

 See 11a

 See Ch. 12

(3) Defining Your Terms

Be sure to define any potentially ambiguous terms you use in your argument; after all, the soundness of an entire argument may hinge on the definition of a word that may mean one thing to one person and another thing to someone else. In the United States, *democratic* elections involve the selection of government officials by popular vote. In other countries, rulers have used the same term to describe elections in which only one candidate has run or in which several candidates—all from the same party—have run. For this reason, when you use a term such as *democratic,* you should make sure that your readers know exactly what you mean.

In some cases, you may want to use a formal definition in your essay. Instead of quoting from a dictionary, however, you may want to develop an extended **definition** that includes examples from your own experience or reading. Not only can it be tailored to the specific issue you are

 See 6e8

writing about but it also can provide much more specific information than a dictionary definition.

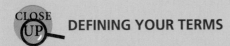 **DEFINING YOUR TERMS**

> Be careful to use precise terms in your thesis statement, avoiding vague and judgmental words, such as *wrong, bad, good, right,* and *immoral.*
>
> **VAGUE:** Censorship of the Internet would be wrong.
>
> **CLEARER:** Censorship of the Internet would unfairly limit free speech.

(4) Considering Your Audience

As you plan your essay, keep a specific **audience** in mind. Are your readers unbiased observers or people deeply concerned about the issue you plan to discuss? Can they be cast in a specific role—concerned parents, victims of discrimination, irate consumers—or are they so diverse that they cannot be categorized? If you cannot be certain who your readers are, you will have to direct your arguments to a general audience.

Always assume a skeptical audience. Even if your readers are sympathetic to your position, you cannot assume that they will accept your ideas without question. The strategies you use to convince your readers will vary according to your relationship with them. Sympathetic readers may need to see only that your argument is logical and that your evidence is solid. Skeptical readers may need a good deal of reassurance that you understand their concerns and that you concede some of their points. However, you may never be able to convince hostile readers that your conclusion is valid. The best you can hope for is that these readers will acknowledge the strength of your argument.

❓ (5) Refuting Opposing Arguments

As you develop your argument, you must **refute**—that is, disprove—opposing arguments by showing that they are untrue, unfair, illogical, unimportant, or irrelevant. By refuting an opposing view, you weaken it and make it less credible to readers. In the following paragraph, a student refutes the argument that Sea World should keep whales in captivity.

Of course, some will say that Sea World wants to capture only a few whales, as George Will points out in his commentary in *Newsweek.* Unfortunately, Will downplays the fact that Sea World wants to capture a hundred whales, not just "a few." And, after releasing ninety of these whales, Sea World intends to keep ten for "further work." At hearings in Seattle last week, several noted marine biologists went on record as condemning Sea World's research program.

When an opponent's position is so strong that it cannot be refuted, concede the point and then, if possible, discuss its limitations. Martin Luther King, Jr., uses this tactic in his "Letter from Birmingham Jail."

You express a great deal of anxiety over our willingness to break laws. This is certainly a legitimate concern. Since we so diligently urge people to obey the Supreme Court's decision of 1954 outlawing segregation in the public schools, at first glance it may seem rather paradoxical for us consciously to break laws. One may well ask: "How can you advocate breaking some laws and obeying others?" The answer lies in the fact that there are two types of laws: just and unjust. I would be the first to advocate obeying just laws. Conversely, one has a moral responsibility to disobey unjust laws. I would agree with St. Augustine that "an unjust law is no law at all."

NOTE: When you acknowledge an opposing view, do not distort it or present it as ridiculously weak. This tactic, called creating a **straw man,** can seriously undermine your credibility.

EXERCISE 1

Make two columns by drawing a line down the center of a piece of paper. Choose one of the following five statements, and list the arguments in favor of it in one column and the arguments against it in the other column. Then, choose one position and write a paragraph or two supporting it. Be sure to refute the arguments against your position.

1. Public school students should have to wear school uniforms.
2. The federal government should limit the amount of violence shown on television.
3. All health-care workers should be required to take a yearly AIDS test.
4. Retirees making more than $50,000 a year should not be eligible for Social Security benefits.
5. Colleges and universities should provide free child care for students with children.

9b Using Evidence and Establishing Credibility

(1) Using Evidence

Most arguments are built on **assertions**—claims that you make about a debatable topic—backed by **evidence**—supporting information, in the form of examples, statistics, or expert opinion. You could, for instance, assert that law-enforcement officials are beginning to win the war against violent crime. You could then support this assertion by referring to a government report stating that violent crime in several of the largest US cities has decreased during the past few years. This report would be one piece of persuasive evidence.

Only assertions that are *self-evident* ("All human beings are mortal"), *true by definition* (2 + 2 = 4), or *factual* ("The Atlantic Ocean separates England and the United States") need no proof. All other kinds of assertions require support.

NOTE: Remember that you never prove a thesis conclusively—if you did, there would be no argument. The best you can do is to provide enough evidence to establish a high probability that your thesis is correct or reasonable.

❓ (2) Establishing Credibility

Clear reasoning, compelling evidence, and strong refutations go a long way toward making an argument solid. But these elements are not sufficient in themselves to create a convincing argument. In order to convince readers, you have to satisfy them that you are someone they should listen to—in other words, that you have **credibility.**

Certain individuals, of course, bring credibility with them every time they speak. When a Nobel Prize winner in physics makes a speech about the need to control proliferation of nuclear weapons, we assume that he or she speaks with authority. But most people do not have this kind of credibility and therefore must work to establish it—by *establishing common ground, demonstrating knowledge,* and *maintaining a reasonable tone.*

Establishing Common Ground   When you write an argument, it is tempting to go on the attack, emphasizing the differences between your position and those of your opponents. Writers of effective arguments know they can gain a greater advantage by establishing common ground between their opponents and themselves.

One way to avoid a confrontational stance, and thereby increase your credibility, is to use the techniques of **Rogerian argument,** based on the work of the psychologist Carl Rogers. According to Rogers, you should think of the members of your audience as colleagues with whom you must collaborate to find solutions to problems. Instead of verbally assaulting them, you should emphasize points of agreement. In this way, you establish common ground and work toward a resolution of the problem you are discussing.

Demonstrating Knowledge   Including relevant personal experiences in your argumentative essay can show readers that you know a lot about your subject and thus can give you authority. Describing your observations at a National Rifle Association conference, for example, can give you authority in an essay arguing for (or against) gun control.

You can also establish credibility by showing you have done research into a subject. By referring to important sources of information and by documenting your information, you show readers that you have done the necessary background work. Including references to several sources—not just one—suggests that you have a balanced knowledge of your subject. Questionable sources, inaccurate documentation, and factual errors can undermine an argument. For many readers, an undocumented quotation or even an incorrect date can call an entire argument into question.

Maintaining a Reasonable Tone   Your tone is almost as important as the information you convey. Talk *to* your readers, not *at* them. If you lecture your readers or appear to talk down to them, you will alienate them. Remember that readers are more likely to respond to a writer who is conciliatory than to one who is insulting.

As you write your essay, be sure to use moderate language. Such words and phrases as *never, all,* and *in every case* can make your claims seem exaggerated and unrealistic. Learn to qualify your statements so that they seem reasonable. The statement "Euthanasia is never acceptable," for example, leaves you no room for compromise. A more conciliatory statement might be "In cases of extreme suffering, one can understand a patient's desire for death, but in most cases, the moral, social, and legal implications of euthanasia make it unacceptable."

✔ CHECKLIST: ESTABLISHING YOUR CREDIBILITY

ESTABLISH COMMON GROUND
- ✔ Identify the various sides of the issue.
- ✔ Identify the points on which you and your readers agree.
- ✔ Work these areas of agreement into your argument.

DEMONSTRATE KNOWLEDGE
- ✔ Include relevant personal experiences.
- ✔ Include relevant special knowledge of your subject.
- ✔ Refer to sources.

MAINTAIN A REASONABLE TONE
- ✔ Avoid talking down to your readers.
- ✔ Use moderate language, and avoid exaggerated claims.

❓ (3) Being Fair

Argument promotes one point of view, so it is seldom objective. However, college writing requires that you stay within the bounds of fairness. To be sure that the support for your argument is not misleading or distorted, you should take the following steps.

Avoid Distorting Evidence   Distortion is misrepresentation. Writers sometimes intentionally misrepresent their opponents' views by exaggerating them and then attacking this extreme position. For example, a governor of a northeastern state proposed requiring unmarried mothers receiving welfare to identify their children's fathers and supply information about them. Instead of challenging this proposal on its own merits, a critic distorted the governor's position and attacked it unfairly.

What is the governor's next idea in his headlong rush to embrace the extreme right-wing position? A program of tattoos for welfare mothers? A badge sewn on to their clothing identifying them as welfare recipients? Creation of colonies, similar to leper colonies, where welfare recipients would be forced to live? How about an involuntary relocation program into camps?

Avoid Quoting Out of Context   A writer or speaker quotes out of context by taking someone's words from their original setting and using them in another. When you select certain statements and ignore others, you can change the meaning of what someone has said or implied.

> MR. N, TOWNSHIP RESIDENT: I don't know why you are opposing the new highway. According to your own statements, the highway will increase land values and bring more business into the area.

> MS. L, TOWNSHIP SUPERVISOR: I think you should look at my statements more carefully. I have a copy of the paper that printed my interview, and what I said was [*reading*]: "The highway will increase land values a bit and bring some business to the area. But at what cost? One hundred and fifty families will be displaced, and the highway will divide our township in half." My comments were not meant to support the new highway but to underscore the problems that its construction will cause.

By repeating only some of Ms. L's remarks, Mr. N altered her meaning to suit his purpose. In context, Ms. L's words indicate that although she concedes the highway's few benefits, she believes that its drawbacks outweigh them.

Avoid Slanting   When you select only information that supports your case and ignore information that does not, you are guilty of slanting supporting information. Inflammatory language is another form of slanting that creates bias in your writing. A national magazine slanted its information, to say the least, when it described a person accused of a crime as "a hulk of a man who looks as if he could burn out somebody's eyes with a propane torch." Although one-sided presentations frequently appear in newspapers and magazines, you should avoid such distortions in your argumentative essays.

Avoid Using Unfair Appeals   Traditionally, writers of arguments use three kinds of appeals to influence readers: the **logical appeal** addresses an audience's sense of reason; the **emotional appeal** plays on the emotions of a reader; and the **ethical appeal** calls the reader's attention to the credibility of the writer.

Problems arise when these appeals are used unfairly. For example, writers can use **fallacies** to fool readers into thinking that a conclusion is logical when it is not. Writers can also employ inappropriate emotional appeals—to prejudice or fear, for example—to influence readers. And finally, writers can use their credentials in one area of expertise to bolster their stature in another area that they are not qualified to discuss.

See
8c

9c   Organizing an Argumentative Essay

In its simplest form, an argument consists of a thesis statement and supporting evidence. However, argumentative essays frequently include additional elements calculated to win audience approval and overcome potential opposition.

ELEMENTS OF AN ARGUMENTATIVE ESSAY

Introduction

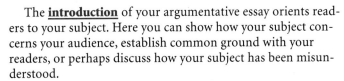

See
6f2

The **introduction** of your argumentative essay orients readers to your subject. Here you can show how your subject concerns your audience, establish common ground with your readers, or perhaps discuss how your subject has been misunderstood.

Background

In this section, you briefly present a narrative of past events, an overview of others' opinions on the issue, definitions of key terms, or a review of basic facts.

Thesis Statement

Your thesis statement can appear anywhere in your argumentative essay. Most often, you present your thesis in your introduction. However, in highly controversial arguments—those to which you believe your readers might react negatively—you may postpone stating your thesis until later in your essay, after you have made your arguments in support of the thesis.

Arguments in Support of Your Thesis

This section presents arguments that support your thesis and the evidence to support them. Often, you begin with your weakest argument and work up to your strongest. If all your arguments are equally strong, you might begin with those points with which your readers are already familiar (and which they are therefore likely to accept) and then move on to relatively unfamiliar ideas.

Refutation of Opposing Arguments

In an argumentative essay, you summarize and refute the arguments against your thesis. If you do not address these opposing arguments, doubts about your case will remain in the minds of your readers. If the opposing arguments are relatively weak, refute them after you have made your case. However, if the opposing arguments are strong, you may want to concede their strengths and then discuss their limitations before you present your own points.

Conclusion

Often, the **conclusion** restates the major arguments in support of your thesis. Your conclusion can also summarize key points, restate your thesis, remind readers of the weaknesses of opposing arguments, or underscore the logic of your position. Many writers like to end their arguments with a strong last line, such as a quotation or a statement that captures the intensity of the argument.

See
6f3

9d Writing and Revising an Argumentative Essay

(1) Writing an Argumentative Essay

The following student essay includes many of the elements discussed in this chapter. The student, Samantha Masterton, was asked to write an argumentative essay, drawing her supporting evidence from her own knowledge and experience as well as from other sources.

Masterton 1

Samantha Masterton

Professor Wade

English 102

15 March 2000

The Returning Student:

Older Is Definitely Better

Introduction

After graduating from high school, young people must decide what they want to do with the rest of their lives. Many graduates (often without much thought) decide to continue their education uninterrupted, and they go on to college. This group of teenagers makes up what many see as the typical first-year college student. Recently, however, this stereotype has been challenged by an influx of older students into American colleges and universities. Not only do these students make a valuable contribution to the schools they attend, but they also offer an alternative to young people who go to college simply because it is the thing to do. A few years off

Thesis statement

between high school and college can give many—perhaps most—students the life experience they need to appreciate the value of higher education.

Background statement

The college experience of an eighteen-year-old is quite different from that of an older student. The typical teenager is often concerned with things other than cracking books—going to parties, dating, and testing personal limits, for example. Although the maturation process from teenager to adult is

Masterton 2

something we must all go through, college is not necessarily the appropriate place for this to occur. My experience as an adult enrolled in a university has convinced me that many students would benefit from delaying entry into college. I almost never see older students cutting lectures or not studying. Most have saved for tuition and want to get their money's worth, just as I do. Many are also balancing the demands of home and work to attend classes, and they know how important it is to do well.

Generally, young people just out of high school have not been challenged by real-world situations that include meeting deadlines and setting priorities. Younger college students often find themselves hopelessly behind or scrambling at the last minute simply because they have not learned how to budget their time. Although success in college depends on the ability to set realistic goals and organize time and materials, college itself does little to help students develop these skills. On the contrary, the workplace—where reward and punishment are usually immediate and tangible—is the best place to learn such lessons. Working teaches the basics that college takes for granted: the value of punctuality and attendance, the importance of respect for superiors and colleagues, and the need for establishing priorities and meeting deadlines.

The adult student who has gained experience in the workplace has advantages over the younger student. In general,

Argument in support of thesis

Argument in support of thesis

Masterton 3

the older student enrolls in college with a definite course of
study in mind. As Laura Mansnerus reports in her article
"A Milieu Apart," for the older student, "college is no longer a
stage of life but a place to do work" (17). For the adult student,
then, college becomes an extension of work rather than a place
to discover what work will be. This greater sense of purpose is
not lost on college instructors. Dr. Laurin Porter, Assistant
Professor of English at the University of Texas at Arlington,
echoes the sentiments of many of her colleagues when she
says, "Returning older students, by and large, seem more
focused, more sure of their goals, and more highly motivated."

*Argument in
support of
thesis*   Given their age and greater experience, older students
bring more into the classroom than younger students do.
Eighteen-year-olds have been driving for only a year or two;
they have just earned the right to vote; and they usually have
not lived on their own. They cannot be expected to have
formulated definite goals or developed firm ideas about
themselves or about the world in which they live. In contrast,
older students have generally had a variety of real-life
experiences. Most have worked for several years; many have
started families. Their years in the "real world" have helped
them to become more focused and more responsible than
they were when they graduated from high school. As a result,
they are better prepared for college. Thus, they not only bring
more into the classroom, but also take more out of it.

Masterton 4

Of course, postponing college for a few years is not for Refutation of opposing argument everyone. There are certainly some teenagers who have a definite sense of purpose and a maturity well beyond their years, and these individuals might benefit from an early college experience, so that they can get a head start on their careers. Charles Woodward, a law librarian, went to college directly after high school, and for him the experience was positive. "I was serious about learning, and I loved my subject," he said. "I felt fortunate that I knew what I wanted from college and from life." For the most part, though, students are not like Woodward; they graduate from high school without any clear sense of purpose. For this reason, it makes sense for most students to stay away from college until they are mature enough to benefit from the experience.

Granted, some older students do have difficulties when Refutation of opposing argument they return to college. Because these students have been out of school so long, they may have difficulty studying and adapting to the routines of academic life. Some older students may even feel ill at ease because they are in class with students who are many years younger than they are and because they are too busy to participate in extracurricular activities. As I have seen, though, these problems soon disappear. After a few weeks, older students get into the swing of things and adapt to college. They make friends, get used to studying, and even begin to participate in campus life.

Masterton 5

Conclusion   All things considered, higher education is wasted on the
young, who are either too immature or too unfocused to take
advantage of it. Taking a few years off between college and
high school would give these students the breathing room they
need to make the most of a college education. The increasing
numbers of older students returning to college would seem to
indicate that many students are taking this path. According to
one study, 45 percent of the students enrolled in American
colleges in 1987 were twenty-five years of age or older
(Aslanian 57). Older students such as these have taken time off
to serve in the military, to work, or to raise a family. Many have
traveled, engaged in informal study, and taken the time to
grow up. By the time they get to college they have defined
their goals and made a commitment to achieve them. It is clear
that postponing college for a few years can result in a better
educational experience for both students and teachers. As Dr.
Porter says, when the older student brings more life experience
into the classroom, "everyone benefits."

Masterton 6

Works Cited

Aslanian, Carol B. "The Changing Face of American

Works Cited
list begins new
page

    Campuses." <u>USA Today Magazine</u> May 1991: 57–59.

Mansnerus, Laura. "A Milieu Apart." <u>New York Times</u> 4 Aug.

    1991, late ed.: A7.

Porter, Laurin. Personal interview. 23 Feb. 2000.

Woodward, Charles B. Personal interview. 25 Feb. 2000.

(2) Revising an Argumentative Essay

When you **revise** your argumentative essay, you use the same strate-gies you use for any essay. In addition, you concentrate on some specific concerns, which are listed in the following checklist.

See 3c

✔ CHECKLIST: ARGUMENTATIVE ESSAYS

✔ Is your topic debatable?
✔ Does your essay develop an argumentative thesis?
✔ Have you adequately defined the terms you use in your argument?
✔ Have you considered the opinions, attitudes, and values of your audience?
✔ Have you identified and refuted opposing arguments?
✔ Have you supported your assertions with evidence?
✔ Have you established your credibility?
✔ Have you documented all information that is not your own?
✔ Have you been fair?
✔ Have you constructed your arguments logically?
✔ Have you avoided logical fallacies?
✔ Have you provided your readers with enough background information?
✔ Have you presented your points clearly and organized them logically?
✔ Have you written an interesting introduction and a strong conclusion?

USING TRANSITIONS IN ARGUMENTATIVE ESSAYS

Argumentative essays should include transitional words and phrases to indicate which paragraphs are *arguments in support of the thesis,* which are *refutations* of arguments that oppose the the-sis, and which are *conclusions.*

Arguments in support of thesis	Accordingly, because, for example, for instance, in general, given, generally, since

continued on the following page

continued from the previous page

Refutations	Although, admittedly, certainly, despite, granted, in all fairness, naturally, nonetheless, of course
Conclusions	All things considered, as a result, in conclusion, in summary, therefore, thus

EXERCISE 2

Samantha Masterton deleted the following paragraph from her essay "The Returning Student: Older Is Definitely Better." Was Samantha right to delete it? Is it relevant? Logical? If it belongs in the essay, where would it go? Does it need any revision?

The dedication of adult students is evident in the varied roles they must play. Many of the adults who return to school are seeking to increase their earning power. They have established themselves in the working world, only to find they cannot advance without more education or a graduate degree. The dual-income family structure enables many of these adults to return to school, but it is unrealistic for them to put their well-established lives on hold while they pursue their education. In addition to the rigors of college, older students are often juggling homes, families, and jobs. However, adult students make up in determination what they lack in time. In contrast, younger students often lack the essential motivation to succeed in school. Teenagers in college often have no clear idea of why they are there and, lacking this sense of purpose, may do poorly even though they have comparatively few outside distractions.

STUDENT WRITER AT WORK

Writing an Argumentative Essay

Revise the following draft of an argumentative essay, paying particular attention to the essay's logic, its use of support, and the writer's efforts to establish credibility. Be prepared to identify the changes you made and to explain how they make the essay more convincing. If necessary, revise further to strengthen coherence, unity, and style.

Television Violence: Let Us Exercise Our Choice

Television began as what many people thought was a fad. Now, over fifty years later, it is the subject of arguments and controversy. There are even some activist groups who spend all their time protesting television's role in society. The weirdest of these groups is definitely the one that attacks television for being too violent. As far as I am concerned, these people should find better things to do with their time. There is nothing wrong with American television that a little bit of parental supervision wouldn't fix.

The best argument against these protest groups is that television gives people what they want. I am not an expert on the subject, but I do know that the broadcasting industry is a business, a very serious business. Television programming has to give people what they want, or else they won't watch it. This is a fact that many of the so-called experts forget. If the television networks followed the advice of the protestors, they would be out of business within a year.

Another argument against the protest groups is that the First Amendment of the US Constitution guarantees all citizens the right of free speech. I am a citizen, so I should be able to watch whatever I want to. If these protestors do not want to watch violent programs, let them change the channel or turn off their sets. The Founding Fathers realized that an informed citizenry is the best defense against tyranny. Look at some of the countries that control the programs that citizens are able to watch. In Iran and in China, for example, people see only what the government wants them to see. A citizen can be put into prison if he or she is caught watching an illegal program. Is this where our country is heading?

Certainly, American society is too violent. No one can deny this fact, but we cannot blame all the problems of American society on television violence. As far as I know, there is absolutely no proof that the violence that people see on television causes them to act violently. Violence in society is probably caused by a number of things—drugs, the proliferation of guns, and unemployment, for example. Before focusing on violence on television, the protestors should address these things. Protestors should also remember that television shows don't kill people; people kill people. Obviously the protestors are forgetting this important fact.

All things considered, the solution to violence on television is simple: parents should monitor what their children watch. If they don't like what their children are watching, they should change the channel or turn off the television. There is no reason why the majority of television watchers—who are for the most part law-abiding people—should have to stop watching programs they like. I for one do not want some protestor telling me what I can or cannot watch, and if, by chance, these protestors do succeed in eliminating all violence, the result will be television programming that is boring, and television, the vast wasteland, will suddenly be turned into the dull wasteland.

PART 2

RESEARCH

CHAPTER 10

WRITING A RESEARCH PAPER

? FREQUENTLY ASKED QUESTIONS

How do I plan a research project?   (p. 194)
How do I keep track of all my sources?
   (p. 200)
What format should I use for taking notes?
   (p. 205)
Why can't I just photocopy or print out the
   information I need instead of taking
   notes?   (p. 207)
How do I turn my notes into an outline?
   (p. 210)

Research is the systematic study and investigation of a topic outside your own experience and knowledge. When you do research, you move from what you know about a topic to what you do not know.

Doing research means more than just reading about other people's ideas; when you undertake a research project, you become involved in a process that requires you to **think critically**, evaluating and interpreting the ideas explored in your sources and formulating ideas of your own. Research is rewarding, but it is also demanding and time consuming. It requires discipline, strategic planning, careful time management, and a constant willingness to rethink ideas and reshape discussions. It is precisely because the research process encourages you to develop this kind of focus that instructors assign research papers.

See
7a

Researchpaper.com
   http://www.researchpaper.com/

? **THE RESEARCH PROCESS**

Activity	Date Due	Date Completed
Choose a Topic 10a	_____	_____
Map Out a Search Strategy 10b	_____	_____
Do Exploratory Research and Formulate a Research Question 10c	_____	_____
Assemble a Working Bibliography 10d	_____	_____
Develop a Tentative Thesis 10e	_____	_____
Do Focused Research 10f	_____	_____
Take Notes 10g	_____	_____
Decide on a Thesis 10h	_____	_____
Prepare a Formal Outline 10i	_____	_____
Write a Rough Draft 10j	_____	_____
Revise Your Drafts 10k	_____	_____
Prepare a Final Draft 10l	_____	_____

10a Moving from Assignment to Topic

(1) Understanding Your Assignment

Every research paper begins with an assignment. Before you can find a direction for your research, you must be sure you understand the exact requirements of this assignment.

✔ CHECKLIST: UNDERSTANDING YOUR ASSIGNMENT

✔ Has your instructor provided a list of possible topics, or are you expected to select a topic on your own?
✔ Is your purpose to explain or to persuade?

✔ Is your audience your instructor? Your fellow students? Both? Someone else?

✔ Can you assume your audience knows a lot (or just a little) about your topic?

✔ When is the completed research paper due?

✔ About how long should it be?

✔ Will you be given a specific research schedule to follow, or are you expected to set your own schedule?

✔ Is collaborative work permitted? Is it encouraged? If so, at what stages of the research process?

✔ Does your instructor expect you to keep your notes on note cards? In a computer file?

✔ Does your instructor expect you to prepare a formal outline?

✔ Are instructor-student conferences required?

✔ Will your instructor review notes, outlines, or drafts with you at regular intervals?

✔ Does your instructor require you to do research in the library, or can you also gather information outside the library?

✔ Are you expected to use your library's electronic resources?

✔ Are you expected to do research on the Internet?

✔ Does your instructor require you to keep a research notebook?

✔ What manuscript guidelines and documentation style are you to follow?

✔ What help is available to you—from your instructor, other students, experts on your topic, community resources, your library staff?

(2) Choosing a Topic

Once you understand the requirements and scope of your assignment, you need to find a direction for your research. You begin this task by focusing on a topic you can explore within the boundaries of your assignment.

In many cases, your instructor will help you to choose a topic, either by providing a list of suitable topics or by suggesting a general subject area—a famous trial, an event that happened on the day you were born, a problem on your college campus. Even in these instances, you will still need to choose one of the topics or narrow the subject area: decide on one trial, one event, one problem.

Researchpaper.com's "Idea (Topic) Directory"
   http://www.researchpaper.com/directory.html
Steps in the Research Process (Ohiolink)
   http://karn.ohiolink.edu/~sg-ysu/process.html

If your instructor prefers that you select a topic entirely on your own, your task is somewhat more difficult: you must consider a number of different topics and weigh both their suitability for research and your interest in them. You decide on a topic for your paper in much the same way you decide on a topic for a short essay: you brainstorm, ask questions, talk to people, and read. With a research paper, however, you know from the start that you will examine not only your own ideas on a topic but also the ideas of others.

As you look for a suitable topic, keep the following guidelines in mind.

✔ CHECKLIST: CHOOSING A RESEARCH TOPIC

- ✔ **Are you genuinely interested in your research topic?** Remember that you will be deeply involved with the topic you select for weeks—perhaps even for an entire semester. If you lose interest in your topic, you are likely to see your research as a tedious chore rather than as an opportunity to discover new information, new associations, and new insights.

- ✔ **Is your topic suitable for research?** Topics limited to your personal experience and those based on value judgments are not suitable for research. For example, "The superiority of Freud's work to Jung's" might sound promising, but no amount of research can establish that one person's work is "better" than another's.

- ✔ **Are the boundaries of your research topic appropriate?** A research topic should be neither too broad nor too narrow. "Julius and Ethel Rosenberg: Atomic Spies or FBI Scapegoats?" is far too broad a topic for a ten-page—or even a one-hundred-page—treatment, and "One piece of evidence that played a decisive role in establishing the Rosenbergs' guilt" would probably be too narrow for a ten-page research paper. But how one newspaper reported the Rosenbergs' espionage trial or how a particular group of people (government employees, peace activists, or college students, for example) reacted at the time to the couple's 1953 execution might work well.

- ✔ **Can your topic be researched in a library to which you have access?** For instance, the library of an engineering or a business school may not have a large collection of books of literary criticism; the library of a small liberal arts college may not have extensive resources for researching technical or medical topics. (Of course, if you have access to the Internet or to specialized databases, your options are greatly increased.)

(3) Starting a Research Notebook

Keeping a **research notebook,** a combination journal of your reactions and log of your progress, is an important part of the research process. A research notebook maps out your direction and keeps you on track; throughout the research process, it helps you define and redefine the boundaries of your assignment.

In this notebook, you can record lists of things to do, sources to check, leads to follow up on, appointments, possible community contacts, questions to which you would like to find answers, stray ideas, possible thesis statements or titles, and so on. Be sure to date your entries and to check off and date work completed.

Some students use a spiral notebook that includes pockets to hold notes and bibliography cards. Others find a small assignment book more convenient. Still others prefer to use a special computer file for this purpose. Whatever form your research notebook takes, it can be a useful record of what has been done and what is left to do.

EXERCISE 1

Using your own instructor's guidelines for selecting a research topic, choose a topic for your paper. Then, start a research notebook by entering information about your assignment, schedule, and topic.

10b Mapping Out a Search Strategy

Once you have found a topic to write about, plan your search strategy. A **search strategy,** a systematic process of locating and evaluating source material, reflects the way research works: you begin by doing exploratory research, looking at general reference works that give you a broad overview of your topic, and progress to focused research, consulting more specialized reference works as well as books and articles on your topic.

Not so long ago, searching for source material meant spending long hours in the library flipping through card catalogs, examining heavy reference volumes, and hunting for books in the stacks. Technology, however, has dramatically changed the way research is conducted. For

Research and Writing, Step-by-Step (Internet Public Library)
   http://www.ipl.org/teen/aplus/stepfirst.htm
The Research Rubric
   http://www.bham.wednet.edu/mod8cyl.htm

SEARCH STRATEGY: THE PROCESS OF RESEARCH

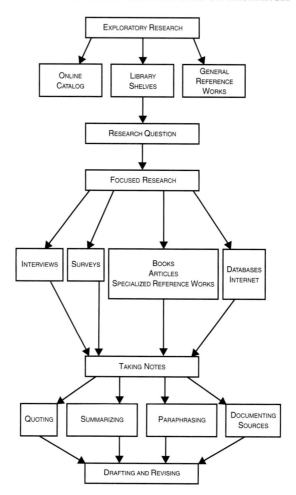

See 11a1

example, library card catalogs have largely given way to computerized or **online catalogs** that can be searched at terminals located throughout the library or, in some cases, at home on a personal computer. In addition, many reference works—indexes, bibliographies, encyclopedias, and other works that serve as starting points for research—are also available in computerized or electronic formats. The "wiring" of school and community libraries means that today, students and professionals engaged in research find themselves spending a great deal of time in front of a computer, particularly during the exploratory stage of the research process. Note, however, that although the way in which research materials are located and accessed has changed, the research process itself has not. Whether you are working with **print sources** (books, journals, magazines) or **electronic resources** (online catalogs, databases, the Internet), in the library or at your home computer, you need to follow a systematic process.

The diagram on page 198 is a general model of a search strategy that you can customize (perhaps with the help of your instructor or reference librarian) so that it suits the research project you are working on.

10c Doing Exploratory Research and Formulating a Research Question

(1) Doing Exploratory Research

Exploratory research helps you get an overview of your topic and an understanding of its possibilities. One way to explore your topic is to discuss your ideas with others. Teachers, librarians, family, and friends may all suggest possible sources—sometimes unexpected or unconventional ones—for your paper. Another way to explore your topic is to skim general reference works—encyclopedias, for example—in your college library or online.

(2) Formulating a Research Question

As you do exploratory research, your goal is to formulate a **research question,** the question you want your research paper to answer. A research question helps you to decide which sources to seek out, which to examine first, which to examine in depth, and which to skip entirely. The answer to your research question will be your paper's **thesis statement**.

Your assignment determines whether your paper will explain something to readers or persuade them, and your research question should reflect this general purpose. For example, the question "What characteristics do horror movies of the 1990s have in common?" calls for an informative paper. However, the question "Does the explicit violence in horror movies of the 1990s affect the behavior of adolescent viewers?" calls for a persuasive paper.

10d Assembling a Working Bibliography

As soon as you begin the process of exploratory research, start assembling a **working bibliography** for your paper. As you examine each source, record *complete* bibliographic information as well as a brief evaluation on an index card or in a computer file. Continue to add this kind of information for each source as you move from exploratory to focused research. This working bibliography will be the basis for your **Works Cited list**, which includes all the books, articles, and other materials that you have cited in your paper.

See 16b

 CLOSE UP **ASSEMBLING A WORKING BIBLIOGRAPHY**

As you record bibliographic information for your sources, include the following information:

See 11b2

Book   Author(s); title (underlined or in italics); **call number** (for future reference); city of publication; publisher; date of publication; brief evaluation

Article   Author(s); title of article (in quotation marks); title of journal (underlined or in italics); volume number; date; inclusive page numbers; electronic address (if applicable); brief evaluation

---

Also keep records of interviews (including telephone and e-mail interviews), meetings, lectures, films, and other nonprint sources of information, as well as of electronic sources. For each source, include not only basic identifying details—such as the date of an interview, the call number of a library book, the address (URL) of an Internet source, or the author of an article accessed from a database—but also a brief evaluation. You might also include comments about the kind of information the source contains, the amount of information offered, its relevance to your topic, and its limitations—whether it is biased or outdated, for instance.

As you go about collecting sources and building your working bibliography, be careful to monitor the quality and relevance of all the materials you examine. For more on evaluating library sources, see **11c;** for guidelines on evaluating Internet sources, see Chapter **13.**

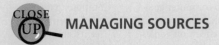

CLOSE UP MANAGING SOURCES

Making informed choices early in the research process will save you a lot of time in the long run, so don't collect sources first and assess their usefulness later. Before you check a book out of the library, photocopy a journal article, or download text, take the time to consider its relevance to your topic. Resist the temptation to check out every book that mentions your subject, photocopy page after page of perhaps only marginally useful articles, or download material from every electronic source to which you have access. After all, you will eventually have to read all these sources and take detailed notes on them. If you have too many sources, you will be overwhelmed, unable to remember why a particular idea or a certain article seemed important.

EXERCISE 2

Consulting the diagram on p. 198, map out a search strategy for your research project. Next, do exploratory research to find a research question for your paper, carefully evaluating the relevance and usefulness of each source. Then, compile a working bibliography. When you have finished, reevaluate your sources and plan additional research if necessary.

10e   Developing a Tentative Thesis

Your **tentative thesis** is a preliminary statement of what you think your research will support. This statement, which you will eventually refine into a **thesis statement**, should be the answer to your research question.

See
10h

DEVELOPING A TENTATIVE THESIS

Subject Area

Computer technology

Topic	*Research Question*	*Tentative Thesis*
The possible negative effects of computer games on adolescents	Do computer games have any negative effects on adolescents?	Computer games interfere with adolescents' ability to learn.

Subject Area

Feminism

Topic	*Research Question*	*Tentative Thesis*
The relationship between the feminist movement and the use of sexist language	What is the relationship between the feminist movement and the use of sexist language?	The feminist movement is largely responsible for the decline of sexist language.

Subject Area

Mood-altering drugs

Topic	*Research Question*	*Tentative Thesis*
The use of mood-altering drugs in state mental hospitals	How has the use of mood-altering drugs affected patients in state mental hospitals?	The use of mood-altering drugs has changed the population of state mental hospitals.

EXERCISE 3

Following your instructor's guidelines, develop a tentative thesis for your research paper.

10f Doing Focused Research

Once you have decided on a tentative thesis, you are ready to begin your focused research and note taking.

During exploratory research, you build your basic knowledge of your topic as you work toward formulating a research question. During **focused research**, you keep this research question in mind as you approach your source material with more narrowly focused objectives. Now you fill in the specific details—facts, examples, statistics, definitions, quotations—you will need to support your ideas. You do this by consulting **specialized reference works** and by reading books and journal articles written by experts on your topic. You may also have to conduct an **interview** or a **survey**. The nature, depth, and scope of your focused research will depend on your assignment and your topic as well as on more practical matters, such as the amount of time you have and the availability of research materials.

See 11b

See 11b1

See 11d2–3

(1) Reading Sources

As you read, use **active reading** strategies: preview each source, skimming it quickly; then read it carefully, highlighting potentially useful material. Be sure to **think critically**: distinguish fact from opinion and evaluate writers' support carefully. Remain alert to bias, faulty reasoning, logical fallacies, and unfair appeals.

See 7b

See 7a

It is important to evaluate the potential usefulness of each source as quickly as possible so you do not waste time reading irrelevant material. Before you begin, survey the work carefully. Check a book's index and the headings and subheadings in the table of contents to determine which pages to read thoroughly and which to skim, and look carefully at abstracts and headings of articles. These strategies will enable you to evaluate each source's usefulness to you as efficiently as possible. (For more on evaluating library sources, see **11c;** for information on evaluating Internet sources, see Chapter **13.**)

As you look for sources, explore as many different viewpoints as possible. (Reading just the sources that present a single viewpoint will not give you the perspective you need to develop a balanced view of your topic.) You should also locate more sources than you actually intend to use in your paper because one or more of the sources you find may turn out to be one-sided, outdated, unreliable, biased, superficial, or irrelevant—and therefore unusable.

(2) Distinguishing between Primary and Secondary Sources

An important step in the process of focused research is determining whether you are reading a **primary** or a **secondary source**—that is, whether you are considering original documents and observations or interpretations of those documents and observations.

PRIMARY SOURCE: United States Constitution, Amendment XIV (Ratified July 9, 1868). Section I.

All persons born or naturalized in the United States, and subject to the jurisdiction thereof, are citizens of the United States and the state wherein they reside. No state shall make or enforce any law which shall abridge the privileges or immunities of citizens of the United States; nor shall any state deprive any person of life, liberty, or property, without the process of law; nor deny to any person within its jurisdiction the equal protection of the laws.

SECONDARY SOURCE: Paula S. Rothenberg, *Racism and Sexism: An Integrated Study.*

Congress passed the Fourteenth Amendment [. . .] in July 1868. This amendment, which continues to play a major role in contemporary legal battles over discrimination, includes a number of important provisions. It explicitly extends citizenship to all those born or naturalized in the United States and guarantees all citizens due process and "equal protection" of the law.

For many research projects, primary sources, such as letters, speeches, and data from questionnaires, are essential. However, secondary sources, which provide insights and interpretations of scholars, can also be valuable. Keep in mind, though, that the farther you get from the primary source, the more chances exist for inaccuracies caused by researchers' inadvertent distortions and misinterpretations.

PRIMARY AND SECONDARY SOURCES

Primary Source	*Secondary Source*
Novel, poem	Literary criticism
Diary, autobiography	Biography
Letters, historical documents, oral testimony	Historical commentary
	Editorial
Newspaper report	Social science article
Raw data from questionnaires	Scientific article
Observation/experiment	Review
Television show/film	Case study
Interview	

Primary vs. Secondary Sources (U. of Toronto)
   http://library.scar.utoronto.ca/Bladen_Library/reference/Research101/
   htmldoc/primary.htm

10g   Taking Notes

Take careful notes as you do research, and be sure to take notes on nonprint as well as print sources. And remember, if you discover a promising new source during the note-taking process, record full source information in your **working bibliography** immediately.

As you **take notes**, your goal is flexibility: you want to be able to arrange and rearrange information easily and efficiently. If you take notes by hand, you may decide to use the time-tested index card system. If you do, be sure to use a separate index card for each piece of information rather than running several ideas together on a single card. If you do your note-taking on your computer, keep your notes distinct from one another rather than collecting all information from a single source under one general heading. (Examples of two formats for notes appear in **18g.**)

Each piece of information you record—in the form of a **summary**, a **paraphrase**, or a **quotation**—should be accompanied by a short descriptive heading that indicates its relevance to some aspect of your topic. Because you will use these headings to guide you as you construct your outline and organize your notes, they should be as specific as possible. Labeling every note for a paper on the "digital divide" created by the Internet *digital divide* or *Internet,* for example, will not prove very helpful later on. More focused headings—*dangers of digital divide* or *government's steps to narrow gap,* for instance—will be much more useful.

Each note should accurately identify the source of the information you are recording. You need not write out the complete citation, but you must include enough information to identify your source. For example, *Gibbs and Smith 5* would be enough to send you back to your working bibliography card or file, where you can find the complete documentation for Mark Gibbs and Richard Smith's *Navigating the Internet.* (If you use more than one source by the same author, you need a more complete reference.)

Each note should also include a brief comment that makes clear your reasons for recording the information and identifies what you think it will contribute to your paper. This comment (placed in brackets so you will know it expresses your own ideas, not those of your source) should establish the purpose of your note—what you think it can explain, support, clarify, describe, or contradict—and perhaps suggest its relationship to other notes or other sources. Any questions you have about the source information can also be included in your comment.

TAKING NOTES

Note-taking software can make it easy for you to record and organize information, allowing you to enter notes (quotations, summaries, paraphrases, or your own comments), pictures, or tables; to sort and categorize your material; and even to print out the information in order on computerized note cards. If you do not have access to such software, type each note under an appropriate heading on a separate page. When you finish taking notes and print out the individual pages, you will find that keeping notes distinct from one another makes it easy for you to sort notes into categories as well as to add and delete bits of information and to experiment with different sequences of ideas.

✔ CHECKLIST: TAKING NOTES

- ✔ **Identify the source of each piece of information clearly and completely.** Even if the source is sitting on your bookshelf or stored in your computer's hard drive, include full source information with each note.
- ✔ **Include everything now that you will need later** to understand your note—names, dates, places, connections with other notes—and to remember why you recorded it.
- ✔ **Distinguish quotations from paraphrases and summaries and your own ideas from those of your sources.** If you copy a source's words, place them in quotation marks. (If you take notes by hand, circle the quotation marks; if you type your notes, put the quotation marks in boldface.) If you write down your own ideas, enclose them in brackets—and, if you are taking notes on a computer, italicize them as well. These techniques will help eliminate accidental plagiarism in your paper.
- ✔ **Put an author's comments into your own words whenever possible,** summarizing and paraphrasing material as well as adding your own observations and analyses. Not only will this strategy save you time later on, but it will also help you understand your sources and evaluate their usefulness now, when you still have time to find additional sources to substitute if necessary.
- ✔ **Copy an author's comments accurately,** using the exact words, spelling, punctuation marks, and capitalization.

Photocopies and Computer Printouts Many researchers routinely photocopy useful portions of books or articles or print out parts of electronic sources. As long as you are careful to accurately record the bibliographic information for the source, this is a useful and time-saving strategy. As you prepare to photocopy or print out material, however, keep the following guidelines in mind.

> ### ✔ CHECKLIST: WORKING WITH PHOTOCOPIES AND COMPUTER PRINTOUTS
>
> ✔ Record full and accurate source information, including the page numbers, electronic addresses (URLs), and any other relevant information, on the first page of each copy.
> ✔ Clip or staple together consecutive pages of a single source.
> ✔ Do not copy a source without reminding yourself—*in writing*—why you are doing so. In pencil or on removable self-stick notes, record your initial responses to the source's ideas, jot down cross-references to other works or notes, and highlight important sections.
> ✔ Photocopying can be time consuming and expensive, so try to avoid copying material that is only marginally relevant to your paper.
> ✔ Keep photocopies and printouts in a file so you'll be able to find them when you need them.

Photocopies and computer printouts are no substitute for notes. In fact, copying information is only the first step in the process of taking thorough, careful notes on a source. You should be especially careful not to allow the ease and efficiency of copying to encourage you to postpone decisions about the usefulness of your information. Remember, you can easily accumulate so many pages that it will be almost impossible to keep track of all your information.

You should also keep in mind that photocopies and printouts do not have the flexibility of notes you take yourself because a single page of text may include information that should be earmarked for several different sections of your paper. This lack of flexibility makes it difficult for you to arrange source material into any meaningful order.

Finally, remember that the annotations you make on photocopies and printouts are usually not focused or polished enough to be incorporated directly into your paper. You will still have to paraphrase and summarize your source's ideas and make connections among them. Therefore, you should approach a photocopy or printout just as you approach any other print source—as material that you will read, highlight, annotate, and take notes about.

EXERCISE 4

Begin focused research for your paper, reading sources carefully and taking notes as you read. Remember, your notes should include paraphrase, summary, and your own observations and analysis as well as quotations.

10h Deciding On a Thesis

After you have finished your focused research and note-taking, you must refine your tentative thesis into a carefully worded sentence that expresses a conclusion your research can support. This **thesis statement** should be more detailed than your tentative thesis, accurately conveying the direction, emphasis, and scope of your paper.

Deciding On a Thesis

Tentative Thesis	*Thesis Statement*
Computer games interfere with adolescents' ability to learn.	Because they teach players to expect immediate gratification, computer games interfere with adolescents' ability to learn.
The feminist movement is largely responsible for the decline of sexist language.	By raising public awareness of careless language habits and changing the image of women, the feminist movement has helped to bring about a decline of sexist language.
The use of mood-altering drugs has changed the population of state mental hospitals.	It is the development of psychotropic (mood-altering) drugs, not advances in psychotherapy, that has made possible the release of large numbers of patients from state hospitals into the community.

If your thesis statement does not express a conclusion your research can support, you should revise it. Reviewing your notes carefully, perhaps grouping information in different ways, may help you to decide on a suitable thesis. Or you may try other techniques—for instance, brainstorming or freewriting with your research question as a starting point.

EXERCISE 5

Read the following passages. Assume you are writing a research paper on the influences that shaped young writers in the 1920s. What possible thesis statements could be supported by the information in these passages?

1. Yet in spite of their opportunities and their achievements the generation deserved for a long time the adjective [lost] that Gertrude Stein had applied to it. The reasons aren't hard to find. It was lost, first of all, because it was uprooted, schooled away and almost wrenched away from its attachment to any region or tradition. It was lost because its training had prepared it for another world that existed after the war (and because the war prepared it only for travel and excitement). It was lost because it tried to live in exile. It was lost because it accepted no older guides to conduct and because it formed a false picture of society and the writer's place in it. The generation belonged to a period of transition from values already fixed to values that had to be created. (Malcolm Cowley, *Exile's Return*)

2. The 1920s were a time least likely to produce substantial support among intellectuals for any sound, rational, and logical program. Prewar stability and convention were condemned because all evidences of stability seemed illusory and artificial. The very lively and active interest in science was perhaps the decade's most substantial contribution to modern civilization. Yet in this case as well, achievement became a symbol of disorder and a source of disenchantment. (Frederick J. Hoffman, *The 20's*)

3. Societies do not give up old ideals and attitudes easily; the conflicts between the representatives of the older elements of traditional American culture and the prophets of the new day were at times as bitter as they were extensive. Such matters as religion, marriage, and moral standards, as well as the issues over race, prohibition, and immigration were at the heart of the conflict. (Introduction to *The Twenties*, ed. George E. Mowry)

EXERCISE 6

Carefully read over all the notes you have collected during your focused research, and develop a thesis statement for your paper.

10i   Preparing a Formal Outline

By the time you have completed your focused research and note-taking, you will have accumulated a good many notes. These notes will probably be arranged haphazardly, perhaps in the order in which you took them—and perhaps in no order at all. Before you can write a rough draft, you will need to make some sense out of all these notes, and you do this by sorting and organizing them. By identifying categories and subcategories of information, you begin to see the emerging shape of your paper and are able to construct a formal outline that reflects this shape.

Although most students will not prepare an outline when planning a short essay, a formal outline is essential for a longer or more complex writing project. A **formal outline** indicates not only the exact order in which you will present your ideas but also the relationship of main ideas to supporting details.

Whether they are <u>topic outlines</u> or <u>sentence outlines</u>, formal outlines conform to specific conventions of structure, content, and style. (An example of a topic outline appears in **18i;** a sentence outline appears at the beginning of the sample student research paper in **18m.**) If you follow the conventions of outlining carefully, your outline can help you to plan a research paper in which you cover all relevant ideas in an effective order with appropriate emphasis.

See
3c3

  ✔ CHECKLIST: PREPARING A FORMAL OUTLINE

✔ Make sure that each note expresses only one general idea. If this is not the case, recopy any unrelated information, creating a separate note.

✔ Check that the heading for each note specifically characterizes the information it includes. If it does not, change the heading.

✔ Sort your notes by their headings, keeping a miscellaneous pile for notes that do not seem to fit into any category.

✔ Check your categories for balance. If most of your notes fall into one or two categories, rewrite some of your headings to create narrower, more focused categories. If you have only one or two notes in a category, you'll need to do additional research or treat that topic only briefly (or not at all).

✔ Organize the individual notes within each group, adding more specific subheads to your headings and arranging ideas in an order that highlights the most important points and subordinates lesser ones. Set aside any notes that do not fit into your emerging scheme.

✔ Decide on a logical order in which to discuss your paper's major points.

✔ Write out your formal outline with divisions and subdivisions corresponding to your headings.

✔ Review your completed outline to determine whether you have placed too much emphasis on a relatively unimportant idea, whether ideas are illogically placed, or whether overlapping discussions turn up at different points.

OUTLINING

Before you begin writing, create a separate file for each major section of your outline. Then, copy your notes into these files in the order in which you intend to use them. You can print out each file as you need it and use it for a guide as you write.

Remember that the outline you construct at this stage is only a guide for you to follow as you draft your paper; it is likely to change as you write and revise. The final outline, written after your paper is complete, will reflect what you have written and serve as a guide for your readers.

EXERCISE 7

Review your notes carefully. Then, sort and group them into categories and construct a topic outline for your paper.

10j Writing a Rough Draft

When you are ready to write your **rough draft**, arrange your notes in the order in which you intend to use them. Follow your outline as you write, using your notes as you need them.
See 3a

To make it easy for you to revise later on, triple-space your draft. Be careful to copy your source information fully and accurately on this and every subsequent draft, placing the documentation as close as possible to the material it identifies.

DRAFTING

You can use a split screen or multiple windows to view your notes as you draft your paper. You can also copy the material that you need from your notes and then insert it into the text of your paper. (As you copy, be especially careful that you do not unintentionally commit **plagiarism**.)

See
Ch. 15

Once you begin drafting, you'll find that the time you spent taking careful, accurate notes and preparing an outline will pay off. Even so, do not expect to write the whole draft in a single sitting. Developing one major heading from your outline is a realistic goal for a morning or afternoon of writing.

Each paragraph will probably correspond to one major point of your outline, at least in this draft. (Later on, you may make changes.) As you write, supply transitions between sentences and paragraphs. These transitions need not be polished; you will refine them in subsequent drafts. But if you leave them out entirely at this stage, you may lose track of the logical and sequential links between ideas, and this will make revision difficult.

If words do not come easily, freewriting for a short period may help. Sometimes leaving your paper for five or ten minutes gives you a fresh view of your material. Another strategy for avoiding writer's block is beginning your drafting with the section for which you have the most material.

See
3b

Remember, the purpose of the rough draft is to get ideas down on paper so that you can react to them. You should *expect* to **revise**, so postpone making precise word choices and refining style. As you draft, jot down questions to yourself, and note points that need further clarification (you can bracket those ideas or print them in boldface on a typed draft, or you can write them on self-stick notes). Leave space for material you plan to add, and bracket phrases or whole sections that you think you may later decide to move or delete. In other words, lay the groundwork for a major revision. Remember that even though you are guided by an outline and notes, you are not bound to follow their content or sequence exactly. As you write, new ideas or new connections among ideas may occur to you. If you find yourself deviating from your thesis or outline, reexamine them to see whether the departure is justified.

(1) Shaping the Parts of the Paper

Like any other essay, a research paper has an introduction, a body, and a conclusion, but in your rough draft, you should concentrate on developing the body of your paper. You should not spend time planning an introduction or conclusion at this stage. Your ideas will change as you write, and you will want to revise your opening and closing paragraphs later to reflect these changes.

Introduction   In your **introduction,** you identify your topic and establish how you will approach it. Your **introduction** also includes your thesis statement, which expresses the position you will support in the rest of the paper. Sometimes the introductory paragraphs briefly summarize your major supporting points (the major divisions of your outline) in the order in which you will present them. Such a preview of your thesis and support provides a smooth transition into the body of your paper. Your introduction can also present an overview of the problem you will discuss or summarize research already done on your topic. In your rough draft, however, an undeveloped introduction is perfectly acceptable; in fact, your thesis statement alone can serve as a placeholder for a more polished introduction.

Body   As you draft the **body** of your paper, indicate its direction with strong **topic sentences** that correspond to the divisions of your outline.

> Today, many people believe the Internet has ushered in a new age, one in which this instant communication will bring people closer together and eventually even eliminate national boundaries.

You can also use **headings** if they are a convention of the discipline in which you are writing.

> Reactions from Public Officials
>
> Many public officials recognize the potential danger of the "digital divide," and they are taking steps to narrow the gap.

Even in your rough draft, carefully worded headings and topic sentences will help you keep your discussion under control.

Use different **patterns of development** to shape the individual sections of your paper, and be sure to connect ideas with clear transitions. If necessary, connect two sections of your paper with a **transitional paragraph** that shows their relationship.

Conclusion The **conclusion** of a research paper often restates the thesis. This is especially important in a long paper because by the time your readers get to the end, they may have lost sight of your paper's main point. Your **conclusion** can also include a summary of your key ideas, a call for action, or perhaps an apt quotation. In your rough draft, however, your concluding paragraph is usually very brief.

See
6f3

(2) Working Source Material into Your Paper

In the body of your paper, you evaluate and interpret your sources, comparing different ideas and assessing conflicting points of view. As a writer, your job is to draw your own conclusions, **synthesizing** information from various sources into a paper that presents a coherent, original view of your topic to your readers.

See
14d3

Your source material must be smoothly integrated into your paper, with the relationships among various sources (and between those sources' ideas and your own) clearly and accurately identified. If two sources present conflicting interpretations, you must be especially careful to use precise language and accurate transitions to make the contrast apparent (for instance, "Although Gore is optimistic, recent studies suggest . . ."). When two sources agree, you should make this clear (for example, "Like Belluck, Gates believes . . ." or "Commerce Department statistics confirm Gates's point"). Such phrasing will provide a context for your own comments and conclusions. If different sources present complementary information about a subject, blend details from the sources *carefully*, keeping track of which details come from which source, to reveal the complete picture.

EXERCISE 8

Write a draft of your paper, being careful to incorporate source material smoothly and to record source information accurately. Begin drafting with the section for which you have the most material.

10k Revising Your Drafts

A good way to begin revising is to check whether your thesis is still appropriate for your paper. Make an outline of your completed draft, and compare it with the outline you made before you began the draft. If you find significant differences, you may have to revise your thesis or rewrite sections of your paper.

As you review your drafts, follow the **revision** procedures that apply to any paper. In addition, try to answer the following questions, which apply specifically to research papers.
See
3b–c

✔ CHECKLIST: REVISING A RESEARCH PAPER

✔ Should you do more research to find support for certain points?
✔ Do you need to reorder the major sections of your paper?
✔ Should you rearrange the order in which you present your points within those sections?
✔ Do you need to add section headings? Transitional paragraphs?
✔ Have you **integrated source material** smoothly into your paper?
✔ Do you introduce source material with running acknowledgments?
✔ Are quotations blended with paraphrase, summary, and your own observations and reactions?
✔ Have you avoided **plagiarism** by carefully documenting all borrowed ideas?
✔ Have you analyzed and interpreted the ideas of others rather than simply stringing those ideas together?
✔ Do your own ideas—not those of your sources—define the focus of your discussion?

See
14d

See
15b

If your instructor allows **collaborative revision**, take advantage of it. As you move from rough to final draft, you should think more and more about your readers' reactions. Testing out others' reactions to a draft can be extremely helpful.

See
3c1

You will probably take your paper through several drafts, changing different parts of it each time or working on one part over and over again. After revising each draft thoroughly, print out a corrected version and make additional corrections by hand on that draft before typing the next version.

 REVISING

When you finish revising your paper, copy the file containing your working bibliography, and insert it at the end of your paper. Delete any irrelevant entries, and use the bibliographic information

continued on the following page

continued from the following page

to help you compile your Works Cited list. (Make sure that the format of the entries on your Works Cited list conforms to the documentation style you are using.)

NOTE: A variety of Web sites may be useful to you as you go through the research process. For a list of such sites, see *The Holt Handbook* Web site at http://www.harcourtcollege.com/english/comp/holt/.

EXERCISE 9

Following the guidelines in **10k** and **3c,** revise your research paper until you are ready to prepare a final draft.

10l   Preparing a Final Draft

See
3d

Before you print out the final version of your paper, you will need to **edit and proofread** not just the paper itself but also your outline and your Works Cited list. Before you do so, stop for a moment to consider your paper's **title.** It should be descriptive enough to tell your readers what your paper is about, and it should create interest in your subject. Your title should also be consistent with the purpose and tone of your paper. (You would hardly want a humorous title for a paper about the death penalty or world hunger.) Finally, your title should be engaging and to the point—and perhaps even provocative. Often a quotation from one of your sources will suggest a likely title.

When you are satisfied with your title, read your paper through one last time, proofreading for grammar, spelling, or typing errors you may have missed. Pay particular attention to parenthetical documentation and Works Cited entries. (Remember that every error undermines your credibility.) Once you are satisfied that your paper is as accurate as you can make it, you are ready to print it out and hand it in.

EXERCISE 10

Prepare a sentence outline and a Works Cited list for your research paper. (Section **3c3** explains and illustrates the specific conventions of sentence outlines; **16b** illustrates MLA Works Cited list format.) Then, edit and proofread your paper, outline, and Works Cited list; decide on a title; and type your paper according to the format your instructor requires. Proofread your typed copy carefully before you hand it in.

CHAPTER 11

DOING LIBRARY AND FIELD RESEARCH

❓ FREQUENTLY ASKED QUESTIONS

Can I use the Internet for all my research?
  (p. 217)
What strategies should I use when I do
  research in the library?   (p. 218)
How do I use the library's online catalog?
  (p. 219)
What electronic resources can I use to find
  information about my topic?   (p. 223)
How do I find articles in the library?   (p. 227)
What online indexes should I use?   (p. 229)
How do I get a book that my school library
  does not own?   (p. 231)
How do I evaluate the books and articles
  that I find in the library?   (p. 232)
How should I conduct an interview?   (p. 237)

Even though the nature of research has changed and the research options available to you have increased, the traditional place to begin your papers remains the same—the library. It gives you access to material you cannot get anywhere else—even on the Internet. You can also obtain a good deal of useful information outside the library by engaging in **field research**—observing people, places, objects, and events; by conducting an interview; and by conducting a survey.

 See 11d

11a   Doing Exploratory Research in the Library

Modern college libraries offer you access to many of the print and electronic sources that you will need to begin your research. For example, you can begin your **exploratory research** in the library by consulting general encyclopedias, dictionaries, and bibliographies. It is also the See 10c1

See 10f

place to find the many resources you will use during **focused research**— for example, periodical indexes, articles, and books. Your visit to the library will be most successful, however, if you have a clear idea of where to begin once you get there.

STRATEGIES FOR DOING LIBRARY RESEARCH

Before You Start:

- Know your library's physical layout. (Take a tour of the library if one is offered.)
- Familiarize yourself with the library's holdings.
- Find out if your college library has a guide to its resources.
- Meet with a reference librarian or your instructor if you have questions.
- Be sure you know the library's hours.

As You Do Research:

- Copy down or print out the complete publication information—author, title, volume number, date of publication, and page numbers—that you will need to locate a particular source.
- Remember how to distinguish between a book and a periodical citation: a periodical citation includes an article title set in quotation marks as well as the underlined periodical title.
- Get a copy of the guidelines that your library provides to explain how to use its electronic resources. Attend an orientation session if your library offers one.

See 11a4

NOTE: Doing library research may mean visiting the library to look through print sources or **electronic resources**. It may also mean accessing your library's holdings through your own computer at home or in your dorm or from a computer terminal on your campus.

---

(1) Using Online Catalogs

Most college and university libraries—and a growing number of regional and community libraries—have abandoned print catalog systems in favor of **online catalogs**—computer databases that list all the books, articles, and other materials held by the library.

You access an online catalog by using one of the computer terminals located throughout the library and typing in certain words or phrases—*search terms* or *options*—that enable you to find the information you need. If you have never used an online catalog, ask your reference librarian for help.

When you search the online catalog for information about your topic, you may conduct either a *keyword search* or a *subject search*. (Later on in the research process, when you know more precisely what you are looking for, you can search for a particular book by entering its title or author.)

Conducting a Keyword Search   When you carry out a **keyword search,** you enter into the computer a term or terms associated with your topic. The computer then retrieves articles that contain those words in their bibliographic citations or abstracts. The more precise your search terms are, the more specific and useful the information you will retrieve. (Combining keywords with AND, OR, and NOT allows you to narrow or broaden your search. This technique is called conducting a **Boolean search**.)

See
12b3

✔ CHECKLIST: KEYWORD DOS AND DON'TS

When conducting a keyword search, remember the following hints:

- ✔ Use precise, specific keywords to differentiate your topic from similar topics.
- ✔ Enter both singular and plural keywords when appropriate—*printing press* and *printing presses,* for example.
- ✔ Enter both abbreviations and their full-word equivalents (for example, *US* and *United States*).
- ✔ Remember to try variant spellings (for example, *color* and *colour*).
- ✔ Don't use too long a string of keywords. If you do, you will retrieve large amounts of irrelevant material.

Conducting a Subject Search   When you carry out a **subject search,** you enter specific subject headings into the computer. The subject categories in a library are most often arranged according to headings

Library of Congress Searchable Catalog
    http://lcweb.loc.gov/catalog/
Academic Libraries—US (searchable)
    http://sunsite.berkeley.edu/Libweb/Academic_main.html
Public Libraries—US
    http://www.publiclibraries.com
Web Resources by Paper Topic (St. Ambrose University, IA)
    http://www.sau.edu/bestinfo/Hot/Hotindex.htm

established in the five-volume manual *Library of Congress Subject Headings,* sometimes referred to as the "big red books," which are held at the reference desk of your library. Although it may be possible to guess at a subject heading, your search will be more successful if you consult these volumes to help you identify the exact words you need.

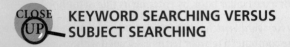

KEYWORD SEARCHING VERSUS SUBJECT SEARCHING

Keyword Searching	*Subject Searching*
• Searches many fields	• Searches only a specific field
• Any significant word or phrase can be used	• Only the specific words listed in the *Library of Congress Subject Headings* can be used
• Retrieves large number of items	• Retrieves small number of items
• May retrieve many irrelevant items	• Retrieves few irrelevant items

USING LIBRARY WEB PAGES

Many college and university libraries have Web pages that enable users to access their online catalogs from a dorm room or from any computer connected to the Internet. Ask at your library for the appropriate Web address.

You can also browse the online catalogs of major research libraries, such as the Library of Congress, the New York Public Library, or the list of academic libraries maintained by the University of California. Although you may not be able to access subscription-only databases or indexes, searching a research library's catalog can give you an overview of the sources available for your topic and the bibliographic information you can use to request material via **interlibrary loan**.

See
11b4

(2) Browsing

Browsing through the stacks in your library can help you narrow your topic to a research question. Knowing how libraries arrange their books will enable you to find the area in which you are interested.

 LIBRARY MATERIALS

The Circulating Collection
- Books (hardback and paperback)—novels, how-to manuals, biographies, and so on
- Periodicals—newspapers, magazines, and journals in hard copy and online indexes.
- CDs, audiotapes, and videotapes—music, films, speeches, and so on
- Large-print books and books-on-tape

The Reference Collection
- Dictionaries, encyclopedias, handbooks, and atlases provide facts and background information.
- Bibliographies and indexes tell you what source material is available for the subject you are researching.
- Special subject guides help you find detailed information quickly.

(3) Consulting General Reference Works

General reference works, which provide a broad overview of a particular subject, can be helpful when you are exploring possible research topics. You can learn key facts and specific terminology as well as find dates, places, and people. In addition, general reference works often include bibliographies that you can use later on when you do focused research. The following reference works, many of which are available in electronic form as well as in print, are useful for exploratory research.

General Encyclopedias General multivolume encyclopedias, such as *Encyclopedia Americana, Collier's Encyclopedia,* and *The New Encyclopaedia Britannica* (also available on CD-ROM as well as on the World Wide Web at <http://www.britannica.com>), are a good place to begin.

To get a quick overview of your topic, use a one-volume general encyclopedia, such as *The New Columbia Encyclopedia* or *The Random House Encyclopedia.* Remember, though, that one-volume general encyclopedias do not contain the cross-references and in-depth bibliographical information provided by multivolume encyclopedias.

 USING ENCYCLOPEDIAS

Articles in encyclopedias aimed at general readers are usually not detailed enough for a college-level research paper. Articles in specialized encyclopedias, dictionaries, and bibliographies, however, are aimed at a more advanced audience. For this reason, they are more likely to be appropriate for your research.

Specialized Encyclopedias, Dictionaries, and Bibliographies   These specialized reference works contain in-depth articles focusing on a single subject area. Specialized reference works are listed in Robert Balay's *Guide to Reference Books,* available at the reference desk in most libraries.

General Bibliographies   General bibliographies list books available in a wide variety of fields.

   Books in Print. An index of authors and titles of books in print in the United States. The *Subject Guide to Books in Print* indexes books according to subject area.

   The Bibliographic Index. A tool for locating bibliographies.

Biographical References   Biographical reference books provide information about people's lives as well as bibliographic listings. The *Biography and Genealogy Master Index* is a good place to begin when you know very little about a person's life.

   Living Persons
   Who's Who in America. Gives concise biographical information about prominent Americans.

   Who's Who. Collects concise biographical facts about notable British men and women.

   Current Biography. Includes articles on people of many nationalities.

Deceased Persons

Dictionary of American Biography. Considered the best of American biographical dictionaries. Includes articles on over thirteen thousand Americans.

Dictionary of National Biography. The most important reference work for British biography.

Webster's Biographical Dictionary. Perhaps the most widely used biographical reference work. Includes people from all periods and places.

Who Was When? A Dictionary of Contemporaries. A reference source for historical biography; covers 500 BC through the early 1970s.

Who Was Who in America. Consists of eleven volumes covering 1607 to 1985, a historical volume covering 1607 to 1896, and an index volume.

(4) Using Electronic Resources ❓

Today's libraries have electronic resources that enable you to find much more current information than that found in print sources. Computer terminals and printers, located throughout the library, enable you to access this material.

Online databases **Online databases** offer citations of books; articles in journals, magazines, and newspapers; and reports. Once you have searched the databases and found the right information, you can print out the bibliographic citations, abstracts, and sometimes even full text (see Figure 1 on page 224). In some cases, you may be able to download the information onto one of your own disks.

Different libraries offer different databases. For example, LEXIS focuses on law and NEXIS focuses on business. Your library may also offer online services that enable you to access a large number of databases. For example, DIALOG contains ERIC (education), PsychINFO (psychology), the *MLA International Bibliography* (literature), News-Bank (periodicals), and the Government Printing Office Monthly Catalog.

Online Periodical Indexes **Online periodical indexes** list articles that are available in general interest magazines, such as *Time, Newsweek, National Geographic,* or *Harper's.* The most common is the periodical index *Readers' Guide to Periodical Literature,* which you

Date   Volume   Number   Page

Title: A year of Web pages for every class. (UCLA policy reviewed)

Periodical: The Chronicle of Higher Education, May 15, 1998 v44 n36 pA29.

Author: Jeffrey R. Young

Abstract: The University of California at Los Angeles debates the use of Web pages for classroom use, unwilling to force instructors to offer online course descriptions and discussions with students. Some administrators and students argue Web pages are not worth the money they cost while others support the "Instructional Enhancement Initiative" which strives to intertwine technology and university life.

Subjects: Internet - Usage
Universities and colleges - Innovations

Features: photograph; illustration
Figure 1   Online database printout

have probably used before. (Be aware that because the *Readers' Guide* indexes only periodicals aimed at a popular audience, it may not be appropriate for your research. Remember, however, that although you may not be able to use articles from this index in your research paper, you can use them to help gather background information about your topic.) Other general indexes include the *Magazine Index,* the *New York Times Index,* and *InfoTrac.*

CD-ROMs   Many of the databases available online are also available on CD-ROM. In some cases, libraries subscribe to a CD-ROM service or database the same way they do to a printed index or journal, and they receive updates periodically. In other cases, reference books available in print are also published on CD-ROMs—for example, the *Oxford English Dictionary* and the *Encyclopaedia Britannica.* Many libraries offer individual workstations where CD-ROMs can be loaded and the information can be viewed and printed out.

```
TI:   Curfews and delinquency in major american cities
AU:   Ruefle, -William; Reynolds, -Kenneth-Mike
SO:   Crime-and-Delinquency.  V.41 July 95 p. 347-63
PY:   1995
AN:   95035204
```
Figure 2 CD-ROM Database Printout

11b Doing Focused Research in the Library

Once you have completed your exploratory research and formulated your **research question**, it is time to move to focused research. During **focused research**, you examine the specialized reference works, books, and articles devoted specifically to your topic. You may also need to make use of the special services that many college libraries provide.

(1) Consulting Specialized Reference Works

During your exploratory research, you use general reference works to help you narrow your topic and formulate your research question. Now you can access specialized works to find facts, examples, statistics, definitions, and quotations. The following reference works—many of which are available on CD-ROM or online as well as in print versions—are most useful for focused research.

Unabridged Dictionaries **Unabridged dictionaries**, such as the *Oxford English Dictionary,* are comprehensive works that give detailed information about words.

Special Dictionaries These dictionaries focus on such topics as usage, synonyms, slang and idioms, etymologies, and foreign terms. Some specialized dictionaries focus on specific academic **disciplines**.

Yearbooks and Almanacs A **yearbook** is an annual publication that updates factual and statistical information already published in a reference source. An **almanac** provides lists, charts, and statistics about a wide variety of subjects.

World Almanac. Includes statistics about government, population, sports, and many other subjects. Published annually since 1868.

Information Please Almanac. Could be used to supplement the *World Almanac* (each work includes information unavailable in the other). Published annually since 1947.

Facts on File. Covering 1940 to the present, this work offers digests of important news stories from metropolitan newspapers.

Editorials on File. Reprints important editorials from American and Canadian newspapers.

Statistical Abstract of the United States. Summarizes the statistics gathered by the US government. Published annually.

Atlases   An **atlas** contains maps and charts as well as historical, cultural, political, and economic information.

National Geographic Society. *National Geographic Atlas of the World.* The most up-to-date atlas available.

Rand McNally Cosmopolitan World Atlas. A modern and extremely legible medium-sized atlas.

Times, London. *The Times Atlas of the World* (5 vols.). Considered one of the best large world atlases.

We the People: An Atlas of America's Ethnic Diversity. Presents information about specific ethnic groups. Maps show immigration routes and settlement patterns.

Shepherd, William Robert. *Historical Atlas,* 9th ed. Covers period from 2000 BC to 1955. Excellent maps show war campaigns and development of commerce.

Quotation Books   A **quotation book** contains numerous quotations on a wide variety of subjects. Such quotations can be useful for your paper's introductory and concluding paragraphs.

Bartlett's Familiar Quotations. Quotations are arranged chronologically by author.

The Home Book of Quotations. Quotations are arranged by subject. An author index and a keyword index are also included.

(2) Consulting Books

The online catalog gives you the information you need—specifically, the call numbers—for locating specific titles. A **call number** is like a book's address in the library: it tells you exactly where to find the book you are looking for.

Subject Search: College Sports--Economic Aspects--United States

Call Number: 796.06073D

Author: Dealy, Francis X.

Title: Win at any cost: the sell out of college athletics

Publisher: Carol	Publication Date: 1990
Edition: First edition	Type/Language: Book/English
ISBN/ISSN: 1-55972-052-2	Description: 230 pages, illustrated

Figure 3 Online Catalog Entry

✔ CHECKLIST: TRACKING DOWN A MISSING SOURCE

PROBLEM	POSSIBLE SOLUTION
✔ Book has been checked out of library.	Consult person at circulation desk.
✔ Book is not in library's collection.	Check other nearby libraries. Ask instructor if he or she owns a copy. Arrange for interlibrary loan (if time permits).
✔ Journal is not in library's collection/article is ripped out of journal.	Arrange for interlibrary loan (if time permits). Check to see whether article is available in a full-text database. Ask librarian whether article has been reprinted as part of a collection.

(3) Consulting Articles

A **periodical** is a newspaper, magazine, scholarly journal, or other publication that is published at regular intervals (weekly, monthly, or quarterly). Articles in scholarly journals can be the best, most reliable sources you can find on a subject; they provide current information and are written by experts on the topic. Because these journals focus on a particular subject area, they can provide in-depth analysis.

Periodical indexes list articles from a selected group of magazines, newspapers, or scholarly journals. These indexes may be available in your library in bound volumes, on microfilm or microfiche, and on CD-ROM; however, many libraries offer them online. These online indexes are updated frequently and provide the most current information available.

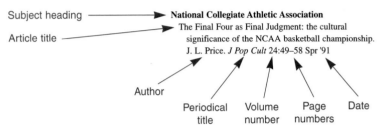

Figure 4 Citation from Periodical Index

There are two basic types of indexes and abstracts: general indexes and specialized indexes. **General indexes** lead you to articles in newspapers and popular magazines. Because these periodicals are aimed at general audiences and assume no expert knowledge, they are most useful during exploratory research. More useful at the focused research stage are **specialized indexes,** which lead you to articles in professional and scholarly journals. Many of the articles listed in such indexes assume expert knowledge, but some are accessible to general readers. For information about specialized indexes used in specific disciplines, see Part **8.**

Abstracting services are a type of specialized index. In addition to providing citations for journal articles, abstracting services include **abstracts,** brief summaries of the articles' major points. For information about abstracting services used in specific disciplines, see Part **8.**

How to Find Articles (U. of Toronto)
  http://library.scar.utoronto.ca/Bladen_Library/reference/findarticles.htm

CHOOSING THE RIGHT INDEX

Choosing the right index for your research saves you time and energy by allowing you to find articles written about your subject. Following is a selection of indexes (available in electronic and in print form) for specific discipline categories:

Category	Description
Readers' Guide to Periodical Literature	General index, all topics
Social Science Index	Political science, psychology, sociology, history, sports
Humanities Index	Music, literature, film, arts
General Science Index	Science, nursing, medicine, health
Business Index	Business
Biology and Agricultural Index	Agriculture, ecology, forestry

FREQUENTLY USED ONLINE INDEXES

Index	Description
Dow Jones Interactive	Full text of articles from US newspapers and trade journals
Ebscohost	Database system for thousands of periodical articles

continued on the following page

General Reference Resources (CMU)
  http://eserver.org/reference/
Selected Web Resources by Academic Subject (Georgetown U.)
  http://gulib.lausun.georgetown.edu/swr/
Internet Public Library—Serials (Magazines)
  http://www.ipl.org/reading/serials/

continued from the previous page

Index	Description
ERIC	Largest index of education-related journal articles and reports in the world
FirstSearch	Abstracts and some full-text files in news and current events
LEXIS-NEXIS	Wide range of full-text local, national, and international publications on law and business
New York Times Index	Article summaries, from 1918 to the present
Reuters Business Briefings	Full-text articles from newspapers, newswires, and magazines
SearchBank	General reference and academic topic databases
Uncover	Tables of contents for 14,000 periodicals
Wall Street Journal Index	Article citations, 1955–1992 (continued by Dow Jones Interactive)

Remember to examine your library's print indexes as well as electronic ones (many important articles predate the present computer indexes). Check with your librarian if you are unsure where to find these volumes.

Microfilm and Microfiche Extremely small images of pages of a periodical may be stored on microfilm. (You need a microfilm scanner to read or photocopy the pages.) Microfiche is similar to microfilm, but images are on a 5-by-7-inch sheet of film and are scanned with a microfiche reader.

(4) Using Special Library Services

As you do focused research, ask your librarian about any of the following special services you plan to use.

Internet Public Library—Newspapers
   http:www.ipl.org/reading/news
Encyclopaedia Britannica Online
   http:www.eb.com:180/
(U.S.) Government Information Locator Service
   http://www.gils.net/

CLOSE UP SPECIAL LIBRARY SERVICES

- **Interlibrary Loans** Your library may be part of a library system that allows loans of books from one location to another. If this is the case, a loan of a book usually takes no more than a day or two. However, be sure to check with your librarian. If the loan takes longer, you may not be able to take advantage of this service unless you initiate the loan early in your research.
- **Special Collections** Your library may house special collections of books, manuscripts, or documents. In addition, churches, ethnic societies, historical trusts, and museums sometimes have material that you cannot find anywhere else.
- **Government Documents** Federal, state, and local governments publish a variety of print and electronic materials, ranging from consumer information to detailed statistical reports. A large university library may have a separate government documents area with its own catalog or index. The *Monthly Catalog of U.S. Government Publications* may be located either there or among the indexes in the reference area.
- **Vertical File** The vertical file includes pamphlets from a variety of organizations and interest groups, newspaper clippings, and other material collected by librarians because of its relevance to the research interests of your college's population.

EXERCISE 1

Which library research sources would you consult to find the following information?

1. A discussion of Maxine Hong Kingston's *China Men* (1980)
2. A government publication about how to heat your home with solar energy
3. Biographical information about the American anthropologist Margaret Mead
4. Books about Margaret Mead and her work
5. Organizational literature about what is being done to prevent the killing of wolves in North America
6. Information about the theories of Albert Einstein
7. Current information about the tobacco lobby
8. The address at which to contact A. S. Byatt, a British novelist

9. Whether your college library has *The Human Use of Human Beings*
   by Norbert Wiener
10. Current information about Americorps

11c   Evaluating Library Sources

Whenever you find information in the library, you should take the
time to determine whether the source is reliable. In other words, you
have to **evaluate** it—to assess its usefulness and its reliability.

Print Sources   One efficient way to evaluate a print source and its
author is to ask a librarian or your instructor for an opinion. Remember,
though, that even if a source is highly recommended, it may not suit
your needs.

To assess the usefulness of a print source, ask the following questions.

Is the Source Relevant to Your Topic? How detailed is its treatment
of your subject? Skim a book's table of contents and index for references to your topic. To be of any real help, a book should include a
section or chapter on your topic, not simply a footnote or a brief reference. For articles, read the abstract, or skim the entire article for key
facts, looking closely at section headings, information set in boldface
type, and topic sentences. An article should have your topic as its central subject, or at least as a major concern.

Is the Source Current? The date of publication tells you whether the
information in a book or article is up-to-date. A source's currency is
particularly important for scientific and technological subjects, which
usually demand up-to-date treatment. (A discussion of computer languages written in 1966, for instance, will now be obsolete.) Even in the
humanities, new discoveries and new ways of thinking lead scholars to
reevaluate and modify their ideas.

Some classic works, however, never lose their usefulness. For example, although Edward Gibbon wrote *The History of the Decline and Fall of
the Roman Empire* in the eighteenth century, the book still offers a valuable discussion of the events it describes. Contemporary historians may
have newer information or may interpret events differently, but Gibbon's information is sound, and the book is required reading for anyone
studying Roman history. If a number of your sources cite earlier works,
you should consult those works, regardless of their publication dates.
Do, however, be alert for out-of-date information in such sources.

Is the Source Reliable? Is a piece of writing largely fact or unsubstantiated opinion? Does the author support his or her conclusions thoroughly and appropriately? Is the supporting information balanced? Is the author objective? Here biographical information can be helpful. The source itself may contain such information, sometimes in a separate section, or you can consult a biographical dictionary. Skim the preface to see what the author says about purpose and methods. What do other sources say about the author? Do they consider the author fair? Biased? Compare a few statements with a fairly neutral source—a textbook or an encyclopedia, for instance—to see whether an author seems to be slanting facts.

Is the Source Respected? A contemporary review of a source can help you make this assessment. *Book Review Digest,* available in the reference section of your library, lists popular books that have been reviewed in at least three newspapers or magazines and includes excerpts from representative reviews. A larger number of books are indexed in *Book Review Index.* Although this index contains no excerpts, it does include citations that refer you to the periodicals in which books were reviewed. Book reviews are also available from the *New York Times Book Review*'s Web site <http://www.nytimes.com/books>, which includes text of book reviews the newspaper has published since 1980.

You can also find out about the standing of a source in the scholarly community by consulting a special class of indexes called **citation indexes.** These books list all scholarly articles published in a given year that mention a particular source. Information is listed under the original article, the author of the article in which the original article is mentioned, or the subject. Seeing how often an article is mentioned can help you determine how influential it is. Citation indexes are available for the humanities, the sciences, and the social sciences.

CLOSE UP EVALUATING PRINT SOURCES

Use articles from popular periodicals, such as *Newsweek* and *Sports Illustrated,* with care. Assuming they are current and written by reputable authors, they may be appropriate for your research. But remember that these articles are aimed at a general audience, and not all popular periodicals adhere to the same kind of rigorous standards

continued on the following page

continued from the pervious page

as scholarly publications. Although some popular periodicals—such as *Atlantic Monthly* and *Harper's*—generally contain articles that are reliable and carefully researched, other periodicals may not.

Nonprint Sources **Nonprint sources**—interviews, telephone calls, films, lectures, and so on—must also be evaluated. Here too you should consider the *relevance* of the source—the extent to which it addresses your needs. An expert on family planning who knows little about adolescent health problems may be an excellent source if your paper will focus on changing trends in birth control methods, but not if your paper is about teenage pregnancy.

The *currency* of a nonprint source is also a factor. A 1970 television documentary on the topography of a Pacific island may still be accurate, but a documentary on the lives of its people may not reflect today's conditions at all.

Reliability is important too. Is a radio feature on energy conservation part of a balanced news program, or is it a thinly veiled commercial sponsored by a public utility or a special interest group? Is the material presented by experts in the field or by actors? Check the credits and acknowledgments and read reviews to see which sources were consulted. Do the participants in a panel discussion on global warming agree on the magnitude of the problem, or do they represent different points of view? Is the person you plan to interview fair and impartial or biased on some issues? Try to find out by consulting an instructor in a related field or by reading the person's writings before your interview.

✔ CHECKLIST: EVALUATING LIBRARY SOURCES

✔ How relevant is your source to your needs?
   How detailed is its treatment of your subject?
   Is your topic a major focus of your source?
✔ How current is your source?
   Have recent developments made any parts of your source dated?
   Does your source rely on information from earlier works?
✔ How reliable is your source?
   Is your source largely **fact or opinion**? Are its opinions based on fact?

See
7a1

Is the **supporting evidence** accurate? Does the writer present enough evidence to support his or her position? Does the writer select representative examples?
Does the author of your source reveal any bias?
How respected is your source?
Do other scholars mention your source in their work?

See
7a2

EXERCISE 2

Read the following paragraphs carefully, paying close attention to the information provided about their sources and authors as well as to their content. Decide which sources would be most useful and reliable in supporting the thesis "Winning the right to vote has (or has not) significantly changed the role of women in national politics." Which sources, if any, should be disregarded? Which would you examine first? Be prepared to discuss your decisions.

1. Almost forty years after the adoption of the Nineteenth Amendment, a number of promised or threatened events have failed to materialize. The millennium has not arrived, but neither has the country's social fabric been destroyed. Nor have women organized a political party to elect only women candidates to public office. [. . .] Instead, women have shown the same tendency to divide along orthodox party lines as male voters. (Eleanor Flexner, *Century of Struggle*, Atheneum 1968. *A scholarly treatment of women's roles in America since the* Mayflower, *this book was well reviewed by historians.*)

2. Woman has been the great unpaid laborer of the world, and although within the last two decades a vast number of new employments have been opened to her, statistics prove that in the great majority of these, she is not paid according to the value of the work done, but according to sex. The opening of all industries to women, and the wage question as connected with her, are the most subtle and profound questions of political economy, closely interwoven with the rights of self-government. (Susan B. Anthony; first appeared in Vol. I of *The History of Woman Suffrage;* reprinted in *Voices from Women's Liberation,* ed. Leslie B. Tanner, NAL 1970. *An important figure in the battle for women's suffrage, Susan B. Anthony* [1820–1906] *also lectured and wrote on abolition and temperance.*)

3. Women [. . .] have never been prepared to assume responsibility; we have never been prepared to make demands upon ourselves; we have never been taught to expect the development of what is best in

ourselves because no one has ever expected *anything* of us—or for us. Because no one has ever had any intention of turning over any serious work to us. (Vivian Gornick, "The Next Great Moment in History Is Ours," *Village Voice* 1969. *The* Voice *is a liberal New York City weekly.*)

4. With women as half the country's elected representatives, and a woman President once in a while, the country's *machismo* problems would be greatly reduced. The old-fashioned idea that manhood depends on violence and victory is, after all, an important part of our troubles. [. . .] I'm not saying that women leaders would eliminate violence. We are not more moral than men; we are only uncorrupted by power so far. When we do acquire power, we might turn out to have an equal impulse toward aggression. (Gloria Steinem, "What It Would Be Like if Women Win," *Time* 1970. *Steinem, a well-known feminist and journalist, is one of the founders of* Ms. *magazine.*)

5. Nineteen eighty-two was the year that time ran out for the proposed equal rights amendment. Eleanor Smeal, president of the National Organization for Women, the group that headed the intense 10-year struggle for the ERA, conceded defeat on June 24. Only 24 words in all, the ERA read simply: "Equality of rights under the law shall not be denied or abridged by the United States or by any state on account of sex." Two major opinion polls had reported just weeks before the ERA's defeat that a majority of Americans continued to favor the amendment. (June Foley, "Women 1982: The Year That Time Ran Out," *The World Almanac & Book of Facts*, 1983.)

6. When you think about it, right-wing victories have almost always depended on *turning on* the conservative minority, and *turning off* everybody else. This was done categorically by denying suffrage to black men and to women of all races; physically, by implementing poll taxes and literacy tests; and procedurally, by creating barriers that still make registration and voting a more daunting task here than in any other democracy. It's interesting that the psychological turnoff—the idea that politics is a dirty game, and voting doesn't matter—began to be pushed just as the 1960s civil rights movement was showing the nation that voting could be meaningful. (Gloria Steinem, "Voting as Rebellion," *Ms.* magazine, Sept./Oct. 1996.)

7. It won't happen this year. But the next chance at the White House is only four years away, and more women than you might think are already laying the groundwork for their own presidential bids. Bolstered by changing public attitudes, women in politics no longer assume that the Oval Office will always be a male bastion. In 1936, when George Gallup first asked people whether they would "vote for a woman for president if she qualified in every other respect," 65 percent said they

would not. Back then, women were only slightly more open to the idea than men. Things are far different today. A recent poll shows that 90 percent of Americans, men included, say they could support a woman for president. (*Eleanor Clift and Tom Brazaitis,* Madam President. ©*2000 by Eleanor Clift and Tom Brazaitis by Scribner. The authors profile the women who they say are positioning themselves to be president.*)

11d　Doing Field Research

In addition to using the library's resources, you can find valuable information by doing **field research**—gathering your own information by observing people, places, objects, and events or by conducting an interview or a survey.

(1) Observing People, Places, Objects, and Events

Your own observations can be a useful source of information. For example, an art or a music paper may be enriched by information gathered during a visit to a museum or a concert; an education paper may include a report of a classroom observation; and a psychology or sociology paper may include observations of an individual's behavior or of group dynamics.

✔ CHECKLIST: MAKING OBSERVATIONS

- ✔ Determine in advance what information you hope to gain from your observations.
- ✔ Decide exactly what you want to observe and where you are going to observe it.
- ✔ Bring a small notepad or tape recorder so you can keep a record of your observations.
- ✔ Bring any additional materials you may need—a camera, videocassette recorder, or stopwatch, for example.
- ✔ Copy your observations onto note cards. Include the date, place, and time of your observations.

(2) Conducting an Interview

Interviews often give you material that you cannot get by any other means—for instance, biographical information, a firsthand account of an event, or the opinions of an expert on a particular subject.

The kinds of questions you ask in an interview depend on the information you are seeking. **Open-ended questions,** designed to elicit general information, allow a respondent great flexibility in answering: *"Do you think students today are motivated? Why or why not?"* **Closed-ended questions**—questions intended to elicit specific information—encourage the respondent to focus on a particular aspect of a subject: *"How much money did the government's cost-cutting programs actually save?"*

CONDUCTING AN E-MAIL INTERVIEW

Using e-mail to conduct an interview can save you a great deal of time because your questions are transmitted instantly. Before you send an e-mail message, make sure that the person you want to contact is willing to cooperate. If the person agrees to be interviewed, send a short list of specific questions. After you have received the answers, send a message thanking the person for his or her cooperation.

✔ CHECKLIST: CONDUCTING AN INTERVIEW

✔ Always make an appointment.
✔ Prepare a list of specific questions tailored to the subject matter and to the time limit of your interview.
✔ Do background reading about your topic. Be sure you don't ask for information that you can easily find elsewhere.
✔ Have a pen and paper with you. If you want to tape the interview, get the respondent's permission in advance.
✔ Allow the person you are interviewing to complete an answer before you ask another question.
✔ Take notes, but continue to pay attention as you do so. Occasionally nod or make comments that show you are interested and that encourage the respondent to continue.
✔ Pay attention to the reactions of the respondent.
✔ Be willing to depart from your prepared list of questions to ask follow-up questions.
✔ At the end of the interview, thank the respondent for his or her time and cooperation.
✔ Send a brief note of thanks.

(3) Conducting a Survey

If you are examining a contemporary social, psychological, or economic issue, a **survey** of attitudes or opinions could be indispensable. Begin by identifying the group of people you will poll. This group can be a **convenient sample**—for example, people in your chemistry lecture—or a **random sample**—names chosen from a telephone directory, for instance. When you choose a sample, your goal is to designate a population that is *representative*. You must also have enough respondents to convince readers that your sample is *significant*. If you poll ten people in your French class about an issue of college policy, and your university has ten thousand students, you cannot expect your readers to be convinced by your results.

You should also be sure that your questions are worded clearly and are specifically designed to elicit the kind of information you wish to get. Short-answer or multiple-choice questions, whose responses can be quantified, are much easier to handle than questions that call for paragraph-length answers. Also, be sure that you do not ask so many questions that respondents lose interest and stop answering. Finally, be careful not to ask biased or leading questions.

If your population is your fellow students, you can slip questionnaires under their doors in the residence hall, or you can distribute them in class, if your instructor permits. If your questionnaire is brief, allow respondents a specific amount of time and collect the forms yourself. If filling out forms will take more than a few minutes, request that responses be returned to you—placed in a box set up in a central location, for instance.

Determining exactly what your results tell you is challenging and sometimes unpredictable. For example, even though only 20 percent of your respondents may be fraternity members, the fact that nearly all fraternity members favor restrictions on hazing would be a fairly significant finding.

✔ CHECKLIST: CONDUCTING A SURVEY

- ✔ Determine what you want to know.
- ✔ Select your sample.
- ✔ Design your questions.
- ✔ Type and duplicate the questionnaire.
- ✔ Distribute the questionnaires.
- ✔ Collect the questionnaires.
- ✔ Analyze the responses.
- ✔ Decide how to use the results in your paper.

CHAPTER 12

USING THE INTERNET
FOR RESEARCH

❓   The **Internet** is a vast system of networks that links millions of computers. Because of its size, its diversity, and the technology by which it is driven, the Internet enables people from all over the world to share information and communicate with one another quickly and easily.

Furthermore, because it is inexpensive to publish text, pictures, and sound online (via the Internet), companies, government agencies, libraries, and universities are able to make available to the public vast amounts of information: years' worth of newspaper articles, thousands of pages of scientific papers or government studies, images of all the paintings in a museum—even an entire library of literature. All this information can be accessed and searched for quickly and easily on the Internet.

12a   Using the Internet

As you might imagine, the Internet has revolutionized the way scholars and students conduct research. Still, as one scientist put it, the Internet is "like a vast library with all the books strewn on the floor." This

Guide to Internet Research and Resources
   http://www.miracosta.cc.ca.us/home/gfloren/INTNET.HTM
Internet Research FAQ
   http://www.purefiction.com/pages/res1.htm
Internet Tutorials
   http://library.albany.edu/internet/
Internet Research Tips
   http://library.albany.edu/internet/checklist.html

chapter will help you understand how the various components of the Internet work and how to use the tools available for searching and accessing the Net's wealth of information.

INFORMATION AVAILABLE ON THE INTERNET

- Pending legislation, stock market quotes, research study findings, and other current information
- Information disseminated by individuals, institutions, and corporations that is not published by traditional media
- Online editions of newspapers, magazines, and books
- Internet-only publications about a wide variety of topics, including the Internet itself
- Library catalogs and periodical indexes that can help you locate print resources
- Reference material, including many encyclopedias and almanacs

(1) E-Mail

E-mail (electronic mail) is the most familiar and widely used way to communicate via the Internet. All you need to send and receive e-mail messages is e-mail software and an account with an **Internet Service Provider,** or **ISP** (for example, AOL, Microsoft Network, or ATT WorldNet).

You can use e-mail to talk to friends at different colleges or to relatives at home. In your research, you can use e-mail to communicate with classmates and instructors, to conduct interviews, to follow e-mail links in Web documents, or to transfer word-processing documents or even entire files from one computer to another.

(2) Listservs

Another way to use e-mail to get information is to subscribe to a **Listserv.** Essentially electronic mailing lists, Listservs enable you to communicate

Denison Memorial Library
   http://www.uchsc.edu/library/rules.html
Starting Points for Internet Research (Purdue)
   http://owl.english.purdue.edu/internet/tools/research.html

with a group of people who are interested in a particular topic. In *moderated* Listservs, the person who manages or "moderates" the group e-mails information, often in the form of an electronic digest or a newsletter, to all subscribers on a weekly or monthly basis; in *unmoderated* Listservs, individual subscribers send e-mails to a main e-mail address, and these message are routed to all group members. Anyone who chooses can then continue the discussion or start a new one by sending a message in the same way. With unmoderated Listservs, the general rule is "anything goes"; as a result, subscribers sometimes find themselves overwhelmed with information if they do not check their messages regularly.

NOTE: The material you get from a Listserv is only as good as the person or group that is sending it to you. You should evaluate this information just as you would any other source.

ACCESSING LISTSERVS

To subscribe to a Listserv, you need the electronic address of the group. To find a Listserv, visit the CataList Listserv reference resource at <http://www.lsoft.com/lists/listref.html>. After you have the electronic address, send an e-mail message to the Listserv containing the following message:

Subscribe < name of the list >< first name ><last name >

(3) Newsgroups

See 12a2

Newsgroups are discussion groups that form part of a network called the **Usenet** system. Unlike **Listserv** messages, which are sent to your private e-mail box, Usenet messages are collected on a news server, where anyone with Usenet access can read them. Newsgroups are organized by topics and subtopics. For example, under the topic *science* are subtopics like *research methods, organic chemistry,* and *numeric analysis.* Currently, thousands of newsgroups enable people from all over the world to carry on discussions about subjects from anthropology to stand-up comedy. These groups function like gigantic bulletin boards where users post messages that others read and respond to.

Many postings on newsgroups are simply requests for information. As you explore a research topic, you can use newsgroups to get specific information as well as suggestions about where to look for further information. You can also use newsgroups to get a sense of how others will respond to your ideas before you use them in your paper.

At best, newsgroups provide interesting and current information about a wide variety of subjects. At worst, they supply a daunting amount of information that users have difficultly evaluating. Because the quality of information from newsgroups varies widely, choose your material carefully, remembering to check the reliability of your source the same way you would check any other information you get from the Internet.

ACCESSING NEWSGROUPS

You need a newsreader program to gain access to newsgroups. Most of the software that enables you to access the World Wide Web (browsers or "clients") now comes with built-in newsreaders.

(4) FTP

FTP (file transfer protocol) enables you to transfer documents at high speed from one computer to another. (Note that because many FTP files are compressed—transferred in a nonreadable form—you must have a program, such as *StuffIt Expander,* to make them readable.) There are two kinds of FTP, full-service and anonymous. *Full-service* FTP enables you to access a host computer and to transfer documents from it to your own computer if you have a password. *Anonymous* FTP enables anyone (without a password) to access files from thousands of different computers on the Internet.

With FTP, you can get the full texts of books and articles as well as pictures. In addition, you can download *freeware,* software in the public domain (which you can use without charge), and *shareware,* software that developers allow people to use for a fee. The most common use for FTP is for downloading updates from computer software manufacturers, who often put improved versions of software on their Web sites for FTP transfer.

ACCESSING FTP FILES

You can use a tool called *Archie* to search the Internet for FTP files. You can also download FTP files through a World Wide Web browser, certain Gopher sites (see the following section), or an FTP transfer program, such as *Fetch* for the Macintosh.

(5) Gopher

Gopher is a tool for navigating the Internet. Because Gopher reads text only and does not include complex graphics, using Gopher is often faster than navigating the **World Wide Web**.

See 12b

By presenting items as a series of menu choices, Gopher gives you access to a wide variety of resources all over the world. You can get information about business, medicine, and engineering as well as up-to-the-minute information about the weather. Gopher is also able to provide material from archived newsgroups and electronic books and magazines.

Gopher can be used by individuals who are connected to a mainframe or campus **server** (a computer that provides information to other computers) and can retrieve FTP files. Gopher enables users to retrieve menu information from any server in the worldwide Gopher network.

ACCESSING GOPHER

The tool Veronica (<u>V</u>ery <u>E</u>asy <u>R</u>odent-<u>O</u>riented <u>N</u>et-wide <u>I</u>ndex to <u>C</u>omputerized <u>A</u>rchives) enables users to do a keyword search of the various menus on the Gopher network. After a keyword (or words) is entered into Veronica, it creates a menu of items that contain the keyword or words. When you select an item on the Veronica menu, you are sent to the Gopher site that contains the keyword.

12b   Searching the Web

Although the terms *Internet* and *World Wide Web* are often used interchangeably, they are different. Technically, the **Web** is a smaller network—within the larger network of the **Internet** itself—that consists of millions of hypertext documents or "pages." (**Hypertext** refers to the way in which information in related documents is cross-referenced or "linked.") Most commonly, these pages are written in a computer language called HTML (Hypertext Markup Language) that allows standard text to be combined with images and other media, like audio and video. HTML also makes it possible to link individual documents to any number of others. Links are indicated by underlined words in blue (or another color different from a document's body text); when you use a mouse to click on a link, you are connected to other related documents.

The Web enables you to connect to a vast variety of documents. For example, you can call up a **home page** or **Web page** (an individual document), a **Web site** (a collection of Web pages), a newsgroup, or an FTP site. Government agencies, businesses, universities, libraries, newspapers and magazines, journals, and public interest groups, as well as individuals, all operate their own Web sites. Each of these sites contains hypertext links that can take you to other relevant sites. By using these links, you can "surf the Net," following your interests and moving from one document to another.

ACCESSING THE WEB

You access the Web by means of a program called a **Web browser** (or "client"), which enables you to find information on the Internet by clicking on icons or buttons instead of by typing commands. Two of the most popular Web browsers, which display the full range of **hypermedia** (some combination of text, photos, graphics, sound, and video files integrated into a document) on the Web, are *Netscape Navigator* and *Microsoft Internet Explorer.*

(1) Beginning a Web Search

Begin your World Wide Web search by clicking on your Web browser icon or selecting the browser from the list of programs on your computer. After the program has loaded, you will see a screen that looks similar to the Netscape Navigator screen shown in Figure 1 on page 246.

(2) Entering a Web Address

The most basic way to access information on the Web is to direct your browser to a specific Web page address, called a **URL** (uniform resource locator). (This is like looking for a book in the library after you have its call number.) If you are using Netscape Navigator, select "Open" from the file menu at the top of your browser window; a dialog box will appear (see Figure 1). Next, enter the address you wish to visit (typically, a combination of letters, numbers, and symbols, such as: <http://www.harcourtcollege.com/english/comp/holt/>). Click "Open" on the dialog box, and Navigator will connect you to the page located at that address. From there, you can use hypertext links to go to other parts of the document or to other sites that are related to the one you are exploring.

Netscape
Navigator
home page

Text
field

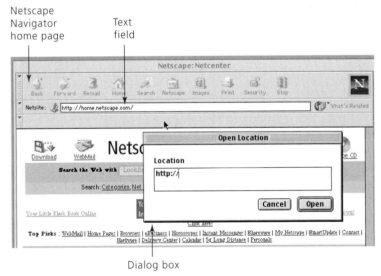

Dialog box

Figure 1 Entering an Address in Navigator

You may also type the URL directly into the text field just below the control panel of your browser window. Use your mouse to highlight the text field, and then type the URL you wish to visit and hit the return key. Your browser will then call up the desired page.

NOTE: Make sure you type the URL *exactly* as it appears, without adding or deleting spaces or punctuation marks. (See **12c** for a list of specific Web sites along with their URLs.)

UNDERSTANDING URLS

The first section of a URL indicates the type of file being accessed. In the address <http://www.harcourtcollege.com/english/comp/holt/>, *http* indicates that the file is in hypertext transfer protocol. After the colon and the two slashes is the name of the host site where the file is stored (<www.harcourtcollege.com/>). The *www* tells the user that the Web site is on the World Wide Web, *harcourtcollege* is the domain name, and *com* shows that this is a commercial institution. Following this section are the directory paths to the files (<english/comp/holt/>).

(3) Using Subject Guides and Search Engines

Another way to locate information on the Web is to use *subject guides* and *search engines*. Although some Web users do not differentiate between the two, there are important differences.

Subject Guides Subject guides are Web sites that list or index Web pages according to subject category or subcategories. Yahoo! (<www.yahoo.com>) is the most popular and well known of the Web's subject guides. Some others are about.com (<www.about.com>) and Look Smart (<www.looksmart.com>).

When you use a subject guide to help you look for information, you click through a hierarchy of subject headings and subheadings until, eventually, you are presented with a list of specific topics that you want to explore (see Figure 2 on page 248). Generally speaking, the goal of subject guides is to direct users to the most useful sites relating to any given subject. In many cases, subject guides provide short blurbs about the sites and pages they index so that you can choose between one site and another. In this way, subject guides are subjective: someone decides whether a particular Web page is indexed or not. Although subject guides are excellent for **exploratory research**, when you move on to **focused research**, you should use a *search engine*.

See
11a–b

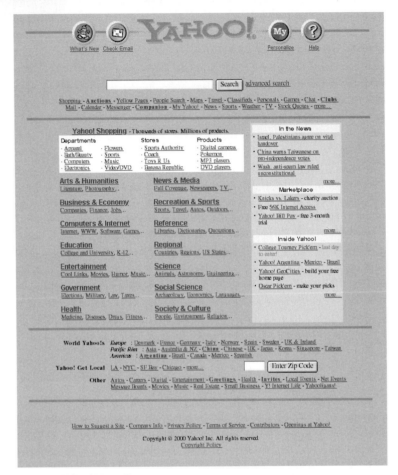

Figure 2 Yahoo! Home Page

Search Engines　A **search engine** is much like the online catalog at your college or local library. On the home page of the search engine you have chosen, you will find a box where you can enter a keyword (or words). When you hit the return key, the search engine retrieves and then displays all the Web pages in its database that match your query. (Note that many search engines offer subject guides on their main pages.)

Alta Vista (<www.altavista.com>) is perhaps the best known search engine, but there are others as well. Some search engines are more user friendly than others; some allow for more sophisticated searching functions; some are updated more frequently; and some are more comprehensive than others. As you try out a number of search engines, you will probably settle on a favorite that you will turn to first whenever you need to find information.

 A GUIDE TO SEARCH ENGINES

Alta Vista (<www.altavista.com>): Good engine for precise searches. Fast and fairly easy to use.

Ask Jeeves (<www.askjeeves.com>): Good beginner's site. Allows you to ask questions to narrow your search. Easy to use, but wording precise questions can be difficult.

Excite (<www.excite.com>): Good for general topics. Search results not always useful.

Hotbot (<www.hotbot.com>): Excellent and fast search engine for locating specific information. Good search options that allow you to fine-tune your searches.

Lycos (<www.lycos.com>): Enables you to search for specific media (graphics, for example). Somewhat small index of Web pages.

Northern Light (<www.northernlight.com>): Searches Web pages but also lists pay-for-view articles not always listed by other search engines. Arranges results under subject headings.

Because even the best search engines search only a fraction of what is on the Web, if you use only one search engine, you will most likely miss much valuable information. It is, therefore, a good idea to repeat each search with several different search engines or to use one of the **metasearch** or **metacrawler** sites that enable you to use several search engines simultaneously.

METASEARCH SITES

CNET Search (<www.search.com/>)

Dogpile (<www.dogpile.com>)

GoHip (<www.gohip.com/>)

Metacrawler (<www.metacrawler.com>)

In addition to the popular, general-purpose search engines and meta-sites, there are numerous search engines devoted entirely to specific subject areas, such as literature, business, sports, and women's issues. Hundreds of specialized search engines are indexed at Allsearchengines.com (<www.allsearchengines.com>).

SPECIALIZED SEARCH ENGINES

Bizbot (business search engine)
http://www.bizbot.net/

FedWorld (U.S. government database and report search engine)
http://www.fedworld.gov/

FindLaw (legal search engine)
http://www.findlaw.com/

HealthFinder (health, nutrition, and diseases information for consumers)
http://www.healthfinder.gov/

The Internet Movie Database (search engine and database for film facts, reviews, and so on)
http://www.imdb.com

Newsbot (news search engine)
http://www.lycos.com/news/

Pilot-Search.com (literary search engine)
http://www.Pilot-Search.com/

SportQuest (sports search engine)
http://www.sportquest.com/

Voice of the Shuttle (humanities search engine)
http://vos.ucsb.edu/

Keep in mind that a search engine retrieves any site in its database on which the keyword (or words) you have typed appear. If, for example, you simply type *Baltimore* in hope of finding information on the city's economy, the search engine will generate an enormous list of pages—well over a million. This list will likely include, along with pages that might be relevant to your research, the home page of the Baltimore Orioles baseball team, as well as many home pages of people who happen to live in Baltimore.

Because searching this way is inefficient and time-consuming, you need to *focus* your search, just as you would with your library's online catalog. You do this by using **search operators,** words and symbols that tell a search engine how to interpret your keywords. One way to use operators to focus your search is to put quotation marks around your search term (type *"Baltimore economy"* rather than *Baltimore economy*). This will direct the search engine to locate only documents containing this phrase.

Another way to focus your search with search operators is to carry out a **Boolean search,** combining keywords with AND, OR, NOT (typed in all capital letters), or a plus or minus sign to restrict the field of titles accessed. (To do this type of searching, you may have to select a search engine's *advanced search* option.) For example, to find Web pages that have to do with Baltimore's economy, type *Baltimore* AND *economy* or *Baltimore + economy*. By doing this, you make sure the documents you receive contain both the keywords *Baltimore* and *economy*. Some search engines allow you to search using three or four keywords (*Baltimore* AND *economy* NOT *agriculture,* for example). Focusing your searches in this way helps you eliminate irrelevant Web pages from your search.

USING SEARCH OPERATORS

" "   Use quotation marks to focus your search: *"Baltimore Economy"*

AND   Use *and* to search for sites that contain both words: *Baltimore* and *Economy*

OR   Use *or* to search for sites that contain either word: *Baltimore* or *Economy*

NOT   Use *not* to exclude the word that comes after the *not*: *Baltimore* and *Economy* not *Agriculture*

+ (plus sign)   Use a plus sign to include the word that comes after it: *Baltimore + Economy*

– (minus sign)   Use a minus sign to exclude the word that comes after it: *Baltimore + Economy – Agriculture*

? ✔ CHECKLIST: TIPS FOR EFFECTIVE SEARCHING

- ✔ **Choose the Right Search Site**   No one all-purpose search site exists. Make sure you review the tips for choosing a search site on pages 247–49. Remember, use a subject guide, such as Yahoo!, for exploratory research and a search engine, such as Alta Vista, for more focused research. Also, don't forget to do a metasearch with a search engine like Metacrawler.
- ✔ **Choose Your Keywords Carefully**   A search engine is only as good as the keywords you use. Choose keywords carefully.
- ✔ **Narrow Your Search**   Use search operators to make your searches more productive. Review the box above before you use any search engine.
- ✔ **Check Your Spelling**   If your search does not yield the results you expect, check to make sure you have spelled your search terms correctly. Even a one-letter mistake can confuse a search engine and cause it to retrieve the wrong information—or no information at all.

✔ **Include Enough Terms**   If you are looking for information on housing, for example, search for several different variations of your keyword: *housing, houses, home buyer, buying houses, residential real estate,* and so on. Some search engines, like Infoseek, automatically search plurals; others do not. Some others, like Alta Vista, automatically search variants of your keyword; others require you to think of the variants by yourself.

✔ **Consult the Help Screen**   Most search engines have a "help" screen. If you have trouble with your search, do not hesitate to consult it. A little time spent here can save you a lot of time later.

✔ **Use More Than One Subject Guide or Search Engine**   Because different subject guides and search engines index different sites, try several when you are looking for results. If one does not yield results after a few tries, switch to another.

✔ **Add Useful Sites to Your Bookmark List**   Whenever you find a particularly useful Web site, add it to your bookmark list so that you can return to the site quickly and easily. If you cannot keep a bookmark list, make sure that you keep an accurate record of URLs. In either case, you may want to make a note of URLs, dates of access, and a short evaluation of each site in your **research notebook**.

See
10a3

12c   Useful Web Sites

The Web sites listed here should prove particularly useful to you as you do Internet research.

Guide to Internet Research and Resources
http://www.miracosta.cc.ca.us/home/gfloren/INTNET.HTM

Information on Evaluating Internet Sources (U. VT)
http://www.lib.vt.edu/research/libinst/evaluating.html

Internet Research FAQ
http://www.purefiction.com/pages/res1.htm

Internet Tutorials
http://www.albany.edu/library/internet/

Internet Research Tips
http://www.albany.edu/library/internet/checklist.html

Starting Points for Internet Research (Purdue)
http://owl.english.purdue.edu/internet/tools/research.html

General Reference Resources (CMU)
http://eserver.org/reference/

Selected Web Resources by Academic Subject (Georgetown U.)
http://gulib.lausun.georgetown.edu/swr/

(US) Government Information Locator Service
http://www.gils.net/

Internet Public Library—Serials (Magazines)
http://www.ipl.org/reading/serials/

Internet Public Library—Newspapers
http://www.ipl.org/reading/news/

Encyclopaedia Britannica Online
www.Britannica.com

Citing Electronic Sources (APA and MLA)
http://www.uvm.edu/~ncrane/estyles/

The World Fact Book
http://www.odci.gov/cia/publications/factbook/

Library of Congress
http://lcweb.loc.gov

Research-It!
http://www.iTools.com/research-it/research-it.html

CHAPTER 13

EVALUATING WEB SITES

❓ FREQUENTLY ASKED QUESTIONS

What does a Web site's URL tell me about its content?   (p. 256)
How can I determine if an anonymous Web source is legitimate?   (p. 259)
What should I keep in mind about a Web site's graphic design?   (p. 262)

Web sites vary greatly in quality and reliability. Because it is so easy for anyone to operate a Web site and thereby publish anything, regardless of quality, critical evaluation of Web-based material is more important than evaluation of more traditional sources of information, such as books and journal articles.

Sources you find on the Web (and on the Internet in general) may present theories, rumors, hearsay, speculation, or even intentional misrepresentations as fact. Sometimes it is difficult to distinguish such questionable information from legitimate material because you do not know your source as well as you might know a reputable journal or magazine. To complicate matters further, unscrupulous individuals can (and sometimes do) represent themselves as respected authorities with impressive credentials, even using the names of other people, and make claims that seem credible but are not.

The proliferation of Web-based information has led to another disturbing problem. Many Web sites freely "borrow" material from other Web sites or from print sources without acknowledging these sources or documenting the information. If you inadvertently use "borrowed" information from one of these sites, you will be guilty of **plagiarism**. The lesson to be learned from this situation is clear: do not use information from questionable Web sites unless you can verify it.

See 15a

Determining the quality of a Web site is crucial if you plan to use it as a source for your research. If you are using a Web site for personal

Information on Evaluating Internet Sources (U. VT)
   http://www.lib.vt.edu/research/libinst/evaluating.html
Tips and Self-Test: Evaluating Internet Sources (Georgetown U. Libraries)
   http://www.library.georgetown.edu/internet/eval.htm#test

information or entertainment, it is probably enough just to be aware of what is legal and what is illegal (for example, you should not download copyrighted software illegally posted on a Web site). However, if you are using the Internet to locate appropriate sources for a research project, you need to be much more careful. To evaluate a Web site, you must look closely at its *purpose, content,* and *format.*

13a   Determining a Web Site's Purpose

In general terms, Web pages may exist *to inform, to persuade,* or *to entertain.* More specifically, a site's purpose may be anything from advocating a political position or selling merchandise to disseminating information or news or even promoting a private agenda. Classifying a site by its purpose is a good first step for determining its credibility because a site whose purpose is not purely informational may not be suitable for research. You can use the following six categories and the questions that follow them to help you classify Web sites.

   UNDERSTANDING URLs

One helpful clue to a Web site's purpose is its URL (Uniform Resource Locator). Here are some common URL endings.

.org = Organization

.com = Business

.edu = Educational institution

.gov = Government

.net = Network

.xx = Two-letter country code, such as .US or .UK

Advocacy   These sites, which may be profit or nonprofit, are usually sponsored by organizations attempting to influence public opinion or to urge action. These sites may represent a large corporation, such as a national political party or candidate, or a special-interest group, such as the National Rifle Association or the Sierra Club. The URLs of these sites are most likely to end in .org.

- Does this site solicit membership and/or money?
- Is this site calling for a particular action?
- Does this site attempt to influence public opinion?

Business/Marketing   These sites are maintained by commercial enterprises attempting to promote or sell products or services. The businesses may exist entirely online, or they may be affiliated with bricks-and-mortar stores or catalog businesses. The URLs of these sites will most likely end in .com.

- Does this site sell goods or services?
- Does this site request demographic information for marketing purposes?
- Does this site take online orders?
- Does this site offer a catalog?

Entertainment   These sites are designed to provide pleasure through humor, the arts, music, or similar endeavors. Some sites exist purely for entertainment, while others may combine entertainment with marketing a product or advocating a viewpoint. The URLs of these sites will have a variety of endings.

- Does this site offer games or activities?
- Does this site offer enticements such as membership in a fan club?
- Does this site use animation, sound files, streaming video, or other audio-video enhancements?

Informational/Reference   These sites present factual information— for example, in online encyclopedias or almanacs. Remember, though, that some of these sites may also be marketing a product or service. The URLs of these sites most likely end in .edu or .gov, but some end in .com.

- Is the information conveyed in the form of tables, statistics, glossaries, or other accepted methods of presenting factual data?
- Does a recognized organization, government agency, or educational institution maintain the site?
- Can the source of the information in the site be verified?

News   These sites provide up-to-the-minute local, national, or international news. Some are affiliated with the print or broadcast media, but others exist only online. The URLs of these sites are likely to end in .com.

- Is the organization responsible for this information a recognized news outlet?
- Does the site clearly separate news from editorial comment?

Personal   Sites maintained by individuals may be published independently or be affiliated with larger institutions. The URLs of these sites will frequently contain a mark called a tilde (~).

- Is the content primarily personal opinion?
- Is the creator of the site identifiable?
- Does an institution or organization sponsor the site?

EXERCISE 1

Examine the home page for the Mothers Against Drunk Driving Web site (Figure 1). Determine which purpose—advocacy, business/marketing, entertainment, information/reference, news, or personal—the site represents.

Figure 1

EXERCISE 2

Work in small groups to select a controversial issue or topic of interest to the class. Then, search the topic on the Internet. Select three to five Web sites on this same topic, and determine each site's purpose.

13b   Evaluating a Web Site's Content

Once you have determined the purpose of a Web site, you should examine its content more closely. If the site exists primarily to entertain, market goods and services, advocate a particular viewpoint, or provide personal information, you should immediately be on the alert for possible biases. Even if the site appears to be informational and possibly suitable for college-level research, you will still have to evaluate its content in terms of *accuracy, credibility, objectivity, currency, coverage or scope,* and *stability.*

Accuracy *Accuracy* refers to the reliability of the material itself and to the use of proper documentation. Keep in mind that factual error—especially errors in facts that are central to the main point of the source—should cause you to question the reliability of the material you are reading.

- Is the text free of errors in sentence structure, usage, and grammar?
- Does the site provide a list of references?
- Are links available to other references?
- Has the author identified himself or herself and provided an e-mail or traditional address?
- Does the author encourage questions and comments?
- Can information be verified in other resources?

Credibility *Credibility* refers to the credentials of the person or organization responsible for the site. Web sites vary greatly in quality and reliability. Those operated by well-known institutions (the Smithsonian or the Department of Health and Human Services, for example) tend to provide highly reliable information and therefore have built-in credibility. Those operated by individuals (private Web pages, for example) are often less reliable. Before using information that you access from a Web site, consider the credibility of both the sponsoring organization and the author of the material.

- What credentials are provided for the author or authors?
- Is the author a recognized authority in his or her field?
- Does the site claim to be **refereed?** In other words, does an editorial board or a group of experts determine whether or not material appears on the Web site, or is this an individual decision?
- Does the sponsoring organization exist apart from its Web presence?
- Does the site display a corporate logo? If so, is this corporation respected?
- Can you determine how long the Web site has existed?

✔ **CHECKLIST: DETERMINING THE LEGITIMACY OF AN ANONYMOUS WEB SOURCE**

When a Web source is anonymous, you have to take special measures to determine its legitimacy. The following strategies can help you get the information you need to judge the legitimacy of an anonymous source.

❓

continued on the following page

The Evaluating Web Resources Homepage (Widener U.)
   http://www2.widener.edu/Wolfgram-Memorial-Library/
   webevaluation/webeval.htm

continued from the previous page

✔ **Post a query.** If you get information from a newsgroup or a Listserv, ask others in the group what they know about the source and its author.

✔ **Follow the links.** Follow the hypertext links in a document to other documents. If the links take you to legitimate sources, you know that the author is aware of these sources of information.

✔ **Do a keyword search.** Do a search using the name of the organization or the article as keywords. Other documents (or citations in other works) may identify the author, and this will help you assess the legitimacy of your source.

Objectivity   Objectivity refers to the degree to which a Web site exhibits bias. Some Web sites make no secret of their biases. They openly advocate a particular point of view or action, or they are clearly trying to sell something. The biases of other Web sites may be harder to identify. For example, a Web site may present itself as a source of factual information when it is actually advocating a political point of view. You need to determine a site's biases before you use material as a resource for academic work.

- Does advertising appear in the text?
- Does a corporation, political organization, or special-interest group sponsor the site?
- Does the site provide links to sites with a political purpose?
- Does the site have an expressed policy concerning the advertising that it exhibits?
- Does the site express a particular viewpoint?

Currency   Currency refers to how up-to-date the Web site is. The easiest way to assess a site's currency is to determine when it was last updated. Keep in mind, however, that even if the date on the site is current, the information that the site contains may not be.

- Is the most recent update available?
- Are all the links to other sites still functioning?
- Is the actual information on the page up-to-date?
- Does the site clearly identify the date it was created and revised?

Coverage or Scope   Coverage, or *scope,* refers to the comprehensiveness of the information on a Web site. More is not necessarily better, but the information provided by some sites may be scanty or incomplete. Others may provide information that is no more than common knowledge. Still others may present discussions aimed at a targeted audience, such as high-school students, which may not be suitable for college-level research.

- Does the site provide wide coverage of the subject matter?
- Does the site provide in-depth coverage?
- Does the site provide information that is not available elsewhere?
- Does the site identify a target audience, particularly by age or grade level? Does the target audience suggest the site is appropriate for your research needs?

Stability   *Stability* means that the site is being maintained and that it will be around when you want to access it again. If you use a Web site that is here today and gone tomorrow, it will be difficult for readers to check your sources or for you to obtain updated information.

- Is the site updated regularly?
- Has the site been active for a long period of time?
- Is an organization or institution committed to financing and maintaining the site?

EXERCISE 3

Examine the home page for the *New York Times* Web site (Figure 2). Use the criteria discussed in **13b** to evaluate its content in terms of accuracy, credibility, objectivity, currency, coverage or scope, and stability.

Figure 2

EXERCISE 4

Select three to five sites that share one of the purposes discussed in **13a**. For example, search for sites offering the same retail product, sites for several comparable colleges within one state, or sites for several weekly magazines or newspapers. Use the criteria outlined in **13b** to help you evaluate the content of the selected sites.

13c   Evaluating a Web Site's Format

Even after you have identified a Web site's purpose and assessed its content, you may still not be sure whether or not it is suitable for your research. **Format**—the way text and graphics are arranged on the page—is another criterion you can use to evaluate a Web site. The main function of a Web site's format is to make navigation easier. Eye-catching visuals, animation, slick graphics, and colorful presentations are no substitute for content.

Organization   *Organization* refers to the way information is structured—with headings, subheadings, hypertext links, and so on. A well-designed Web site is easy to navigate as users move from the home page to more deeply embedded information.

• Does the home page provide all the major headings you need to move easily to the other Web pages?
• Are links clearly and logically worded?
• Can you find what you want without navigating many Web pages or searching many links?

Graphic Design   *Graphic design* refers to the artwork as well as the visual arrangement of text.

• Does the artwork serve a purpose, or is it purely ornamental?
• Is the home page free of clutter?
• Is advertising distinct from information?
• Are pages linked visually through color, logos, or other layout features?

Technical Requirements   *Technical requirements* refer to the software and hardware needed to access a site. Some sites require special software called *plug-ins* (which you can usually download at no cost) that allow you to view streaming video or film clips. Other sites may include extremely large files, such as sound files or text files. Unless you are using a high-speed Internet line, your computer will be tied up for long periods of time while downloading these files.

Navigation or Searchability   Navigation, or *searchability,* refers to how easily you can move through a Web site.

- Is there a site map?
- Are the links clear and easy to identify?
- Does the site require a minimum of scrolling?
- Do the links lead where they claim to lead?
- Do the links lead to pages that are complete rather than under construction?
- Does the site indicate what its icons represent?
- Do links alert you to especially large files?

EXERCISE 5

Examine the home page for the Library of Congress Web site (Figure 3). Use the criteria in **13c** to evaluate its content in terms of organization, graphic design, technical requirements, and navigation or searchability.

The LIBRARY of CONGRESS

SEARCH THE CATALOG | SEARCH OUR WEB SITE | ABOUT OUR SITE

America's Library: New Site for Kids & Families! "Log On ... Play Around ... Learn Something"

USING the LIBRARY
*Catalogs, Collections
& Research
Services*

AMERICAN MEMORY
*America's Story in
Words, Sounds
& Pictures*

THOMAS
*Congress
At Work*

**BICENTENNIAL
1800-2000**
Libraries • Creativity • Liberty

EXHIBITIONS
*An On-Line
Gallery*

**COPYRIGHT
OFFICE**
*Forms &
Information*

HELP & FAQs
General Information

**THE LIBRARY
TODAY**
*News, Events
& More*

Above, the interior of the dome of the Main Reading Room of the Library of Congress

101 INDEPENDENCE AVE. S.E.
WASHINGTON, D.C. 20540
(202) 707-5000

Comments: lcweb@loc.gov

Figure 3

EXERCISE 6

Using the criteria outlined in **13c,** evaluate each of the sites you selected in Exercise 4.

CHAPTER 14

SUMMARIZING, PARAPHRASING, QUOTING, AND SYNTHESIZING

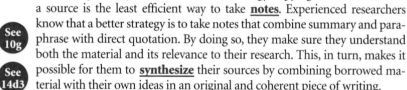

? FREQUENTLY ASKED QUESTIONS

What is the difference between a
   paraphrase and a summary?   (p. 266)
When should I quote a source?   (p. 268)
How do I avoid saying "he said" or "she
   said" every time I use a source?   (p. 270)
How can I make sure readers will be able to
   tell the difference between my ideas and
   those of my source?   (p. 273)

Although it may seem like a sensible strategy, copying down the words of a source is the least efficient way to take **notes**. Experienced researchers know that a better strategy is to take notes that combine summary and paraphrase with direct quotation. By doing so, they make sure they understand both the material and its relevance to their research. This, in turn, makes it possible for them to **synthesize** their sources by combining borrowed material with their own ideas in an original and coherent piece of writing.

See
10g

See
14d3

14a   Writing a Summary

A **summary** is a brief restatement, in your own words, of the main idea of a passage or an article. When you write a summary, you condense the author's ideas into a few concise sentences. A summary is always much shorter than the original because it omits the examples, asides, analogies, and rhetorical strategies that writers use to add emphasis and interest.

When you summarize, use your own words, not the exact language or phrasing of your source. If you think it is necessary to reproduce a distinctive word or phrase, place it in quotation marks; otherwise, you will be committing **plagiarism**. Finally, remember that your summary

See
15a

Summarizing (USCA)
   http://www.usca.sc.edu/writingroom/hos/summarizing.html

should accurately represent the author's ideas and should include only the ideas of your source, not your own interpretations or opinions.

Compare the following three passages. The first is an original source; the second, an unacceptable summary; and the third, an acceptable summary.

ORIGINAL SOURCE:

Today, the First Amendment faces challenges from groups who seek to limit expressions of racism and bigotry. A growing number of legislatures have passed rules against "hate speech"—[speech] that is offensive on the basis of race, ethnicity, gender, or sexual orientation. The rules are intended to promote respect for all people and protect the targets of hurtful words, gestures, or actions.

Legal experts fear these rules may wind up diminishing the rights of all citizens. "The bedrock principle [of our society] is that government may never suppress free speech simply because it goes against what the community would like to hear," says Nadine Strossen, president of the American Civil Liberties Union and professor of constitutional law at New York University Law School. In recent years, for example, the courts have upheld the right of neo-Nazis to march in Jewish neighborhoods; protected cross-burning as a form of free expression; and allowed protesters to burn the American flag. The offensive, ugly, distasteful, or repugnant nature of expression is not reason enough to ban it, courts have said.

But advocates of limits on hate speech note that certain kinds of expression fall outside of First Amendment protection. Courts have ruled that "fighting words"—words intended to provoke immediate violence—or speech that creates a clear and present danger are not protected forms of expression. As the classic argument goes, freedom of speech does not give you the right to yell "Fire!" in a crowded theater. (Sudo, Phil. "Freedom of Hate Speech?" *Scholastic Update* 124.14 [1992]: 17–20)

UNACCEPTABLE SUMMARY: Today, the First Amendment faces challenges from lots of people. Some of these people are legal experts who want to let Nazis march in Jewish neighborhoods. Other people have the sense to realize that some kinds of speech fall outside of First Amendment protection because they create a clear and present danger (Sudo 17).

The preceding unacceptable summary uses words and phrases from the original without placing them in quotation marks. This use constitutes plagiarism. In addition, the summary expresses its writer's opinion ("Other people have the sense to realize . . .").

Compare the unacceptable summary with the following acceptable summary. Notice that the acceptable summary presents an accurate, objective overview of the original without using its exact language or phrasing. (The one distinctive phrase borrowed from the source is placed within quotation marks.)

> **ACCEPTABLE SUMMARY:** The right to freedom of speech, guaranteed by the First Amendment, is becoming more difficult to defend. Some people think that stronger laws against the use of "hate speech" weaken the First Amendment. But others argue that some kinds of speech remain exempt from this protection (Sudo 17).

✔ CHECKLIST: WRITING A SUMMARY

- ✔ Reread your source until you understand it.
- ✔ Write a one-sentence restatement of the main idea.
- ✔ Write your summary, using the one-sentence restatement as your topic sentence. Use your own words and phrasing, not those of your source. Include quotation marks where necessary.
- ✔ Add appropriate documentation.

14b Writing a Paraphrase

A summary conveys just the essence of a source; a **paraphrase** gives a *detailed* restatement of all a source's important ideas. It not only indicates the source's main points, but it also reflects its order, tone, and emphasis. Consequently, a paraphrase can sometimes be as long as the source itself.

When you paraphrase, make certain that you use your own words, except when you want to quote to give readers a sense of the original. If you do include quotations, circle the quotation marks in your notes so that you will not forget them later. Try not to look at the source as you paraphrase—use language and syntax that come naturally to you, and avoid duplicating the wording or sentence structure of the original. Whenever possible, use synonyms that accurately convey the meaning of the original word or phrase. If you cannot think of a synonym for an important term, quote—but remember to document all direct quotations from your source as well as the entire paraphrase. Finally, be sure that your paraphrase reflects only the ideas of your source—not your analysis or interpretation of those ideas.

Following are an original passage, an unacceptable paraphrase, and an acceptable paraphrase.

> **ORIGINAL PASSAGE:**
> When you play a video game, you enter into the world of the programmers who made it. You have to do more than identify with a char-

acter on a screen. You must act for it. Identification through action has a special kind of hold. Like playing a sport, it puts people into a highly focused and highly charged state of mind. For many people, what is being pursued in the video game is not just a score, but an altered state.

The pilot of a race car does not dare to take [. . .] attention off the road. The imperative of total concentration is part of the high. Video games demand the same level of attention. They can give people the feeling of being close to the edge because, as in a dangerous situation, there is no time for rest and the consequences of wandering attention [are] dire. With pinball, a false move can be recuperated. The machine can be shaken, the ball repositioned. In a video game, the program has no tolerance for error, no margin for safety. Players experience their every movement as instantly translated into game action. The game is relentless in its demand that all other time stop and in its demand that the player take full responsibility for every act, a point that players often sum up [with] the phrase "One false move and you're dead." (Turkle, Sherry. *The Second Self: Computers and the Human Spirit.* New York: Simon & Schuster, 1984. 83–84.)

UNACCEPTABLE PARAPHRASE: Playing a video game, you enter into a new world—one the programmer of the game made. You can't just play a video game; you have to identify with it. Your mind goes to a new level, and you are put into a highly focused state of mind.

Just as you would if you were driving a race car or piloting a plane, you must not let your mind wander. Video games demand complete attention. But the sense that at any time you could make one false move and lose is their attraction—at least for me. That is why I like video games more than pinball. Pinball is just too easy. You can always recover. By shaking the machine or quickly operating the flippers, you can save the ball. Video games, however, are not so easy to control. Usually, one slip means that you lose (Turkle 83–84).

The preceding unacceptable paraphrase simply echos the phrasing and syntax of the original, borrowing words and expressions without enclosing them in quotation marks. This constitutes **plagiarism**. In addition, the paraphrase digresses into a discussion of the writer's own views about the relative merits of pinball and video games.

See 15a

Although the following acceptable paraphrase follows the order and emphasis of the original—and even quotes a key phrase—its wording and sentence structure are very different from those of the source. Moreover, it conveys the key ideas of the source and maintains an objective tone.

ACCEPTABLE PARAPHRASE: The programmer defines the reality of the video game. The game forces a player to merge with the character who is part of the game. The character becomes an extension of the player, who determines how he or she will think and act. Like sports, video games put a player into a very intense "altered state" of mind that is the most important part of the activity (Turkle 83).

The total involvement they demand is what attracts many people to video games. These games can simulate the thrill of participating in a dangerous activity without any of the risks. There is no time for rest and no opportunity to correct errors of judgment. Unlike video games, pinball games are forgiving. A player can—within certain limits—manipulate a pinball game to correct minor mistakes. With video games, however, every move has immediate consequences. The game forces a player to adapt to its rules and to act carefully. One mistake can cause the death of the character on the screen and the end of the game (Turkle 83–84).

✔ CHECKLIST: WRITING A PARAPHRASE

- ✔ Reread your source until you understand it.
- ✔ Write your paraphrase, following the order, tone, and emphasis of the original and making sure that you do not use the words or phrasing of the original without enclosing the borrowed material within quotation marks.
- ✔ Add appropriate documentation.

14c   Quoting Sources

When you **quote,** you copy an author's remarks exactly as they appear in a source, word for word and punctuation mark for punctuation mark, enclosing the borrowed words in quotation marks. As a rule, do not quote extensively in a research paper. Numerous quotations interrupt the flow of your discussion and give readers the impression that your paper is just a collection of other people's ideas.

❓ ✔ CHECKLIST: WHEN TO QUOTE

- ✔ Quote when a source's wording or phrasing is so distinctive that a summary or paraphrase would diminish its impact.
- ✔ Quote when a source's words—particularly those of a recognized expert on your subject—will lend authority to your presentation.
- ✔ Quote when an author's words are so concise that paraphrasing would create a long, clumsy, or incoherent phrase or would change the meaning of the original.

> ✔ Quote when you expect to disagree with a source. Using a source's exact words helps convince readers you are being fair.

EXERCISE 1

Choose a debatable issue from the following list.

- Noncitizens' rights to free public education
- Helmet requirements for motorcycle riders
- Community service requirements for college students
- Making English the official language of the United States
- The use of animals in medical experiments
- A constitutional amendment prohibiting the defacing of the American flag

Write a one-sentence *summary* of your own position on the issue; then, interview a classmate and write a one-sentence *summary* of his or her position on the same issue. Be sure each sentence includes the reasons that support the position. Next, locate a source that discusses your issue, and write a *paraphrase* of the writer's position, quoting a few distinctive phrases. Finally, write a single sentence that compares and contrasts the three positions.

EXERCISE 2

Assume that in preparation for a paper on the effects of the rise of the suburbs, you read the following paragraph from the book *Great Expectations: America and the Baby Boom Generation* by Landon Y. Jones. Reread the paragraph, and then write a brief summary. Finally, paraphrase the paragraph, quoting only those words and phrases you consider especially distinctive.

> As an internal migration, the settling of the suburbs was phenomenal. In the twenty years from 1950 to 1970, the population of the suburbs doubled from 36 million to 72 million. No less than 83 percent of the total population growth in the United States during the 1950s was in the suburbs, which were growing fifteen times faster than any other segment of the country. As people packed and moved, the national mobility rate leaped by 50 percent. The only other comparable influx was the wave of European immigrants to the United States around the turn of the century. But as *Fortune* pointed out, more people moved to the suburbs every year than had ever arrived on Ellis Island.

14d Integrating Source Material into Your Writing

Weave paraphrases, summaries, and quotations smoothly into your discussion, adding analysis or explanation to increase coherence and to show why you are using each source. Remember that you are orchestrating a conversation among different speakers, and your own voice should dominate.

CLOSE UP — INTEGRATING SOURCE MATERIAL INTO YOUR WRITING

To avoid monotonous sentence structure, experiment with different methods of integrating source material into your paper.

- Vary the verbs you use to introduce a source's words or ideas (instead of repeating *says*).

acknowledges	discloses	implies
suggests	observes	notes
concludes	believes	comments
insists	explains	claims
predicts	summarizes	illustrates
reports	finds	proposes
warns	concurs	speculates
admits	affirms	indicates

- Vary the placement of the **identifying tag** (the phrase that identifies the source), putting it in the middle or at the end of the quoted material instead of always at the beginning.

QUOTATION WITH IDENTIFYING TAG IN MIDDLE: "A serious problem confronting Amish society from the viewpoint of the Amish themselves," observes Hostetler, "is the threat of absorption into mass society through the values promoted in the public school system" (193).

PARAPHRASE WITH IDENTIFYING TAG AT END: The Amish are also concerned about their children's exposure to the public school system's values, notes Hostetler (193).

(1) Integrating Quotations

Quotations should never be awkwardly dropped into your paper, leaving the exact relationship between the quoted words and your point unclear. Instead, use a brief introductory remark to provide a context for a quotation, quoting only those words you need to make your point.

> **UNACCEPTABLE:** For the Amish, the public school system represents a problem. "A serious problem confronting Amish society from the viewpoint of the Amish themselves is the threat of absorption into mass society through the values promoted in the public school system" (Hostetler 193).

> **ACCEPTABLE:** For the Amish, the public school system is a problem because it represents "the threat of absorption into mass society" (Hostetler 193).

Whenever possible, use a **running acknowledgment** to introduce the source of the quotation.

> **RUNNING ACKNOWLEDGMENT:** As John Hostetler points out, the Amish see the public school system as a problem because it represents "the threat of absorption into mass society" (193).

Substitutions or Additions within Quotations   When you make changes or additions to make a quotation fit into your paper, acknowledge your changes by enclosing them in brackets (not parentheses).

> **ORIGINAL QUOTATION:** "Immediately after her wedding, she and her husband followed tradition and went to visit almost everyone who attended the wedding" (Hostetler 122).

> **QUOTATION REVISED TO MAKE VERB TENSES CONSISTENT:** Nowhere is the Amish dedication to tradition more obvious than in the events surrounding marriage. Right after the wedding celebration the Amish bride and groom "visit almost everyone who [has] attended the wedding" (Hostetler 122).

> **QUOTATION REVISED TO SUPPLY AN ANTECEDENT FOR A PRONOUN:** "Immediately after her wedding, [Sarah] and her husband followed tradition and went to visit almost everyone who attended the wedding" (Hostetler 122).

> **QUOTATION REVISED TO CHANGE AN UPPERCASE TO A LOWERCASE LETTER:** The strength of the Amish community is illustrated by the fact that "[i]mmediately after her wedding, she and her husband followed tradition and went to visit almost everyone who attended the wedding" (Hostetler 122).

Omissions within Quotations When you delete unnecessary or irrelevant words, substitute an **ellipsis** (three spaced periods) for the deleted words.

> ORIGINAL: "Not only have the Amish built and staffed their own elementary and vocational schools, but they have gradually organized on local, state, and national levels to cope with the task of educating their children" (Hostetler 206).

> QUOTATION REVISED TO ELIMINATE UNNECESSARY WORDS: "Not only have the Amish built and staffed their own elementary and vocational schools, but they have gradually organized [. . .] to cope with the task of educating their children" (Hostetler 206).

NOTE: MLA style requires square brackets around ellipses you add to distinguish them from those that appear in the source.

 OMISSIONS WITHIN QUOTATIONS

Be sure you do not misrepresent or distort the meaning of quoted material when you shorten it. For example, do not say, "the Amish have managed to maintain [. . .] their culture" when the original quotation is "the Amish have managed to maintain *parts of* their culture."

Long Quotations Set off a quotation of more than four typed lines of **prose** by indenting it one inch (ten spaces) from the margin. Double-space, do not use quotation marks, and introduce the long quotation with a colon. If you are quoting a single paragraph, do not indent the first line. If you are quoting more than one paragraph, indent the first line of each complete paragraph (including the first one) an additional one-quarter inch (three spaces).

According to Hostetler, the Amish were not always hostile to

public education:

> The one-room rural elementary school served the Amish
>
> community well in a number of ways. As long as it was a

public school, it stood midway between the Amish
community and the world. Its influence was tolerable,
depending upon the degree of influence the Amish were
able to bring to the situation. (196)

(2) Integrating Paraphrases and Summaries

Introduce your paraphrases and summaries with running acknowledgments, and end them with appropriate documentation. By doing so, you make certain that your readers are able to differentiate your own ideas from the ideas of your sources.

MISLEADING (IDEAS OF SOURCE BLEND WITH IDEAS OF WRITER):
Art can be used to uncover many problems that children have at home, in school, or with their friends. For this reason, many therapists use art therapy extensively. Children's views of themselves in society is often reflected by their art style. For example, a cramped, crowded art style using only a portion of the paper shows their limited role (Alschuler 260).

REVISED WITH RUNNING ACKNOWLEDGMENT (IDEAS OF SOURCE DIFFERENTIATED FROM IDEAS OF WRITER): Art can be used to uncover many problems that children have at home, in school, or with their friends. For this reason, many therapists use art therapy extensively. According to William Alschuler in *Art and Self-Image*, children's views of themselves in society are often reflected by their art style. For example, a cramped, crowded art style using only a portion of the paper shows a child's limited role (260).

EXERCISE 3

Look back at the summary and paraphrase you wrote for Exercise 2. Write three possible running acknowledgments for each, varying the verbs you use for attribution and the placement of the identifying tag. Be sure to include appropriate documentation at the end of each passage.

(3) Synthesizing Sources

A **synthesis** uses paraphrase, summary, and quotation to combine material from two or more sources, along with your own ideas, in order to express an original viewpoint. (In this sense, an entire research paper is a synthesis.) You begin synthesizing material by comparing your sources and determining how they are alike and different, where they agree and disagree, and whether they reach the same conclusions. As you identify connections between one source and another or between a source and your own ideas, you develop your own perspective on your subject. It is this viewpoint, summarized in a thesis statement (in the case of an entire paper) or in a topic sentence (in the case of a paragraph), that becomes the focus of your synthesis.

As you write your synthesis, make your points one at a time, and use material from your sources to support these points. Make certain you use running acknowledgments as well as the transitional words and phrases that your readers will need to follow your discussion. Finally, remember that your distinctive viewpoint, not the ideas of your sources, should be central to your discussion.

Following is a synthesis written by a student as part of a research paper:

> Computers have already changed our lives. They carry out (at incredible speed) many of the everyday tasks that make our way of life possible. For example, computer billing, with all its faults, makes modern business possible, and without computers we would not have access to the telephone services or television reception that we take for granted. But computers are more than fast calculators. According to one computer expert, they are well on their way to learning, creating, and someday even thinking (Raphael 21). Another computer expert, Douglas Hofstadter, agrees, saying that someday a computer will have both "will [. . .] and consciousness" (423). It seems likely, then, that as a result of the computer, our culture will change profoundly (Turkle 15).

EXERCISE 4

Write a paragraph that synthesizes the three positions you worked with in Exercise 1. (If you like, you may use the sentence comparing the three positions, drafted in response to Exercise 1, as your topic sentence.)

CHAPTER 15

AVOIDING PLAGIARISM

❓ FREQUENTLY ASKED QUESTIONS

What is plagiarism?   (p. 275)
What material don't I have to document?
   (p. 275)
How can I be sure that I don't plagiarize?
   (p. 279)

15a   Defining Plagiarism

Plagiarism is taking credit for ideas or words that are not your own.
Sometimes plagiarism is intentional, but often it is unintentional—
occurring, for example, when a student pastes a quoted passage from a
computer file directly into a paper and forgets to use quotation marks
and documentation. The best way to avoid plagiarism is to take careful
notes, to distinguish between your ideas and those of your sources, and
to give credit to your sources with **documentation**.

See Chs. 16–17

In general, document all words and ideas borrowed from your sources.
(This rule applies to both print and electronic sources.) Of course, certain
items need not be documented: **common knowledge** (information most
readers probably know), facts available from a variety of reference
sources, familiar sayings and well-known quotations, and the results of
your own original research (interviews and surveys, for example).

Information in dispute or that is one person's original contribution,
however, must be acknowledged. For example, you need not document
the fact that John F. Kennedy graduated from Harvard in 1940 or that he
was elected president in 1960. You must, however, document a historian's
evaluation of Kennedy's performance as president or one researcher's recent statements about his private life.

Plagiarism
   http://www2.rscc.cc.tn.us/~jordan_jj/OWL/Plagiarism.html
Plagiarism
   http://www.indiana.edu/~wts/wts/plagiarism.html

PLAGIARISM AND INTERNET SOURCES

Any time you download text from the Internet, you run the risk of committing unintentional plagiarism. To avoid the possibility of plagiarism, follow these guidelines.

- Download information into individual files so that you can keep track of your sources.
- Do not simply cut and paste blocks of downloaded text into your paper; summarize or paraphrase this material first.
- If you do record the exact words of your source, enclose them in quotation marks.
- Whether your information is from e-mails, discussion groups, Listservs, or World Wide Web sites, give proper credit by documenting the source.

15b Revising to Eliminate Plagiarism

You can avoid plagiarism by using documentation whenever it is required and by adhering to the following guidelines.

(1) Enclose Borrowed Words in Quotation Marks

ORIGINAL: Historically, only a handful of families have dominated the fireworks industry in the West. Details such as chemical recipes and mixing procedures were cloaked in secrecy and passed down from one generation to the next. [. . .] One effect of familial secretiveness is that, until recent decades, basic pyrotechnic research was rarely performed, and even when it was, the results were not generally reported in scientific journals. (Conkling, John A. "Pyrotechnics." *Scientific American* July 1990: 96)

PLAGIARISM: John A. Conkling points out that until recently, little scientific research was done on the chemical properties of fireworks, and when it was, <u>the results were not generally reported in scientific journals</u> (96).

Even though the student writer documented the source of his information, he did not indicate that he borrowed the source's exact words. To correct this problem, the student should either place the borrowed words in quotation marks or paraphrase the source's words.

CORRECT (BORROWED WORDS IN QUOTATION MARKS): John A. Conkling points out that until recently, little scientific research was done on the chemical properties of fireworks, and when it was, "the results were generally not reported in scientific journals" (96).

CORRECT (PARAPHRASE): John A. Conkling points out that research conducted on the chemical composition of fireworks was seldom reported in the scientific literature (96).

(2) Do Not Imitate a Source's Syntax and Phrasing

ORIGINAL: Let's be clear: this wish for politically correct casting goes only one way, the way designed to redress the injuries of centuries. When Pat Carroll, who is a woman, plays Falstaff, who is not, casting is considered a stroke of brilliance. When Josette Simon, who is black, plays Maggie in *After the Fall,* a part Arthur Miller patterned after Marilyn Monroe and which has traditionally been played not by white women, but by blonde white women, it is hailed as a breakthrough.

But when the pendulum moves the other way, the actors' union balks. (Quindlen, Anna. "Error, Stage Left." *New York Times* 12 Aug. 1990, sec. 1: 21)

PLAGIARISM: Let us be honest. The desire for politically appropriate casting goes in only one direction, the direction intended to make up for the damage done over hundreds of years. When Pat Carroll, a female, is cast as Falstaff, a male, the decision is an inspired one. When Josette Simon, a black woman, is cast as Maggie in *After the Fall,* a role Arthur Miller based on Marilyn Monroe and which has usually been played by a woman who is not only white but also blonde, it is considered a major advance.

But when the shoe is on the other foot, the actors' union resists (Quindlen 21).

Although this student documents the passage and does not use the exact words of her source, she closely imitates the original's syntax and phrasing, simply substituting synonyms for the author's words. The student could have avoided plagiarism by changing the syntax as well as the individual words of the original.

CORRECT (PARAPHRASE IN STUDENT'S OWN WORDS; ONE DISTINCTIVE PHRASE PLACED IN QUOTATION MARKS): According to Anna Quindlen, the actors' union supports "politically correct casting" (21) only when it means casting a woman or a minority group member in a role created for a male or a Caucasian. Thus, it is acceptable for actress Pat Carroll to play Falstaff or for black actress Josette Simon to play Marilyn Monroe; in fact, casting decisions such as these are praised. However, when it comes to casting a Caucasian in a role intended for an African American, Asian, or Hispanic, the union objects (21).

(3) Document Statistics Obtained from a Source

ORIGINAL: From the time they [male drivers between sixteen and twenty-four] started to drive, 187 of these drivers (almost two-thirds) reported one or more accidents, with an average of 1.6 per involved driver. Features of 303 accidents are tabulated in Table 2. Almost half of all first accidents occurred before the legal driving age of 18, and the median age of all accidents was 19. (Schuman, Stanley, et al. "Young Male Drivers: Accidents and Violations." *JAMA* 50 [1983]: 1027)

PLAGIARISM: By and large, male drivers between the ages of sixteen and twenty-four accounted for the majority of accidents. Of 303 accidents recorded in Michigan, almost one-half took place before the drivers were legally allowed to drive at eighteen.

Although many people assume that statistics are common knowledge, statistics are usually the result of original research and must therefore be documented. Moreover, readers may need to locate the source of the statistics in order to assess their reliability.

CORRECT: According to one study, male drivers between the ages of sixteen and twenty-four accounted for the majority of accidents. Of 303 accidents recorded, almost one half took place before the drivers were legally allowed to drive at eighteen (Schuman et al. 1027).

(4) Differentiate Your Words and Ideas from Those of Your Source

ORIGINAL: At some colleges and universities traditional survey courses of world and English literature [. . .] have been scrapped or diluted. At others they are in peril. At still others they will be. What replaces them is sometimes a mere option of electives, sometimes "multicultural" courses introducing material from Third World cultures and thinning out an already thin sampling of Western writings, and sometimes courses geared especially to issues of class, race, and gender. Given the notorious lethargy of academic decision making, there has probably been more clamor than change; but if there's enough clamor, there will be change. (Howe, Irving. "The Value of the Canon." *The New Republic* 2 Feb. 1991: 40–47)

PLAGIARISM: Debates about expanding the literary canon take place at many colleges and universities across the United States. At many universities, the Western literature survey courses have been edged out by courses that emphasize minority concerns. These courses are "thinning out an already thin sampling of Western writings" in favor of courses geared especially to issues of "class, race, and gender" (Howe 40).

Because the student who wrote this passage does not differentiate his ideas from those of his source, it appears that only the quotations in his last sentence are borrowed when, in fact, his second sentence also owes a debt to the original. The student should have clearly identified the boundaries of the borrowed material with a running acknowledgment and documentation. In the following correct example, notice that both the summary and the quotation (which always requires a separate parenthetical reference) are documented.

CORRECT: Debates about expanding the literary canon take place at many colleges and universities across the United States. According to the noted critic Irving Howe, at many universities, the Western literature survey courses have been edged out by courses that emphasize minority concerns (40). These courses, says Howe, are "thinning out an already thin sampling of Western writings" in favor of "courses geared especially to issues of class, race, and gender" (40).

✔ CHECKLIST: AVOIDING PLAGIARISM

- ✔ **Take careful notes.** Be sure you have recorded information from your sources carefully and accurately.
- ✔ **In your notes, put all words borrowed from sources inside circled quotation marks** and enclose your own comments within brackets.
- ✔ **In your paper, differentiate your ideas from those of your sources** by clearly introducing borrowed material with a running acknowledgment and by following it with documentation.
- ✔ **Enclose all direct quotations** used in your paper within quotation marks.

continued on the following page

continued from the previous page

✔ **Review paraphrases and summaries in your paper** to make certain they are in your own words and that any distinctive words and phrases from a source are quoted.

✔ **Document all quoted material and all paraphrases and summaries** of your sources.

✔ **Document all facts** that are open to dispute or are not common knowledge.

✔ **Document all opinions, conclusions, figures, tables, statistics, graphs, and charts** taken from a source.

EXERCISE

This student paragraph uses material from three sources, but its author has neglected to cite them. After reading the paragraph and the three sources that follow it, identify material that has been quoted directly from a source. Compare the wording to the original for accuracy and insert quotation marks where necessary, being sure the quoted passages fit smoothly into the paragraph. Next, paraphrase any passages the student did not need to quote, and, after consulting Chapters **16** and **17,** document each piece of information that requires it.

Student Paragraph

Oral history became a legitimate field of study in 1948, when the Oral History Research Office was established by Allan Nevins. Like recordings of presidents' fireside chats and declarations of war, oral history is both oral and historical. But it is more: oral history is the creation of new historical documentation, not the recording or preserving of documentation that already exists. Oral history also tends to be more spontaneous and personal and less formal than ordinary tape recordings. Nevins's purpose was to collect and prepare materials to help future historians to better understand the past. Oral history has enormous potential to do just this because it draws on people's memories of their own lives and deeds and of their associations with particular people, periods, or events. The result, when it is recorded and transcribed, is a valuable new source.

Source 1

When Allan Nevins set up the Oral History Research Office in 1948, he looked upon it as an organization that in a systematic way could obtain from the lips and papers of living Americans who had led significant lives a full record of their participation in the political, economic, and cultural affairs of the nation. His purpose was to prepare such material for the use of future historians. It was his conviction that the individual played an important role in history and that an individual's autobiography might in the future serve as a key to an understanding of contemporary historical movements. (Excerpted from Benison, Saul. "Reflections on Oral History." *The American Archivist* 28.1 [January 1965]: 71)

Source 2

Typically, an oral history project comprises an organized series of interviews with selected individuals or groups in order to create new source materials from the reminiscences of their own life and acts or from their association with a particular person, period, or event. These recollections are recorded on tape and transcribed on a typewriter into sheets of transcript. [. . .] Such oral history may be distinguished from more conventional tape recordings of speeches, lectures, symposia, etc., by the fact that the former creates new sources through the more spontaneous, personal, multi-topical, extended narrative, while the latter utilizes sources in a more formal mode for a specific occasion. (Excerpted from Rumics, Elizabeth. "Oral History: Defining the Term." *Wilson Library Bulletin* 40 [1966]: 602)

Source 3

Oral history, as the term came to be used, is the creation of new historical documentation, not the recording or preserving of documentation—even oral documentation—that already exists. Its purpose is not, like that of the National Voice Library at Michigan State University, to preserve the recordings of fireside chats or presidential declarations of war or James Whitcomb Riley reciting "Little Orphan Annie." These are surely oral and just as surely the stuff of history; but they are not oral history. For this there must be the creation of a new historical document by means of a personal interview. (Excerpted from Hoyle, Norman. "Oral History." *Library Trends* [July 1972]: 61)

CHAPTER 16

MLA DOCUMENTATION

❓ FREQUENTLY ASKED QUESTIONS

How do I place references in my paper?
(p. 282)
What is MLA style?   (p. 283)
How do I list the sources I use in my paper?
(p. 288)
How do I list sources I get from the
Internet?   (p. 298)
What are content notes, and how do I use
them?   (p. 302)

Documentation, the formal acknowledgment of the sources you use in your paper, enables your readers to judge the quality and originality of your work. Different academic disciplines use different documentation styles. This chapter explains and illustrates the documentation style recommended by the Modern Language Association (MLA). Chapter **17** discusses the documentation styles of the American Psychological Association (APA), *The Chicago Manual of Style* (CMS), and the Council of Biology Editors (CBE).

 PLACING PARENTHETICAL REFERENCES

 Place the parenthetical references in your paper with care. Each reference must clearly refer to the information it documents.

- Place documentation after each quotation as well as at the end of each passage of paraphrase or summary. Avoid using a single reference to cover several pieces of information from a variety of different sources.
- Place documentation so that it will not interrupt your discussion—ideally, at the end of a sentence.

> • To differentiate your ideas from those of your sources, place running acknowledgments before, and documentation after, all borrowed material.

MLA style* is required by many teachers of English and other languages as well as teachers in other humanities disciplines. This method of documentation has three parts: *parenthetical references in the text* (also known as *in-text citations*), a *list of works cited*, and *content notes*.

16a   Parenthetical References in the Text

MLA documentation uses **parenthetical references** within the text keyed to a Works Cited list at the end of the paper. A typical reference consists of the author's last name and a page number. (Student papers illustrating MLA style appear in **18m** and **49d1**.)

The colony's religious and political freedom appealed to many idealists

in Europe (Ripley 132).

To distinguish two or more sources by the same author, include an appropriate shortened title in the parenthetical reference after the author's name.

Penn emphasized his religious motivation (Kelley, William Penn 116).

If you state the author's name or the title of the work in your sentence, do not include it in the parenthetical reference that follows.

Penn's political motivation is discussed by Joseph P. Kelley in Pennsylvania,

The Colonial Years, 1681-1776 (44).

MLA Style Guide (Capital Comm.-Tech. College, CT)
   http://webster.commnet.edu/mla.htm
MLA Homepage
   http://www.mla.org/
Dan Kies' Guide to the MLA Style (College of DuPage)
   http://papyr.com/hypertextbooks/eng1_101/mla.htm
MLA Style Documentation (U. Wisc.)
   http://www.wisc.edu/writing/Handbook/DocMLA.html

*MLA documentation style follows the guidelines set in the *MLA Handbook for Writers of Research Papers,* 5th ed. New York: MLA, 1999.

PUNCTUATING WITH PARENTHETICAL REFERENCES: MLA

Paraphrases and summaries Parenthetical references are placed *before* the sentence's end punctuation.

Penn's writings epitomize seventeenth-century religious thought (Dengler and Curtis 72).

Quotations run in with the text Parenthetical references are placed *after* the quotation but *before* the end punctuation.

As Ross says, "Penn followed this conscience in all matters" (127).

See
c1–2

According to Williams, Penn's utopian vision was informed by his Quaker beliefs [. . .]" (72).

Quotations set off from the text When you quote a **long prose passage** or more than three lines of **poetry**, parenthetical references are placed one space *after* the end punctuation.

According to Arthur Smith, William Penn envisioned a state based on his religious principles:

> Pennsylvania would be a commonwealth in which all individuals would follow God's truth and develop according to God's law. For Penn this concept of government was self-evident. It would be a mistake to see Pennsylvania as anything but an expression of Penn's religious beliefs. (314)

DIRECTORY OF PARENTHETICAL REFERENCES

1. A work by a single author
2. A work by two or three authors
3. A work by more than three authors
4. A work in multiple volumes
5. A work without a listed author

6. A work that is one page long
7. An indirect source
8. More than one work
9. A literary work
10. An entire work
11. Two or more authors with the same last name
12. A government document or a corporate author
13. An electronic source

Sample MLA Parenthetical References

1. A Work by a Single Author

Fairy tales reflect the emotions and fears of children (Bettelheim 23).

2. A Work by Two or Three Authors

The historian's main job is to search for clues and solve mysteries

(Davidson and Lytle 6).

With the advent of behaviorism, psychology began a new phase of

inquiry (Cowen, Barbo, and Crum 31-34).

3. A Work by More Than Three Authors

List only the first author, followed by *et al.* ("and others").

The European powers believed they could change the fundamentals of

Muslim existence (Bull et al. 395).

4. A Work in Multiple Volumes

If you list more than one volume of a multivolume work in your
Works Cited list, include the appropriate volume and page number (separated by a colon) in your parenthetical reference.

The French Revolution had a great influence on William Blake (Raine

1: 52-53).

Big Dog Grammar's Quick MLA guide
    http://gabiscott.com/bigdog/mla.htm
Downloadable MLA Style Guide pdf file (Montana State U.)
    http://www.lib.montana.edu/instruct/styles/
Citing Electronic Sources (APA, MLA, and Chicago)
    http://www.lib.uwo.ca/weldon/docs/electronicstyle.html

5. A Work without a Listed Author

Use a shortened version of the title in the parenthetical reference, beginning with the word by which it is alphabetized in the Works Cited list.

In spite of political unrest, Soviet television remained fairly conservative,

ignoring all challenges to the system ("Soviet").

6. A Work That Is One Page Long

Do not include a page reference for a one-page article.

Sixty percent of Arab Americans work in white-collar jobs (El-Badru).

7. An Indirect Source

If you must use a statement by one author that is quoted in the work of another author, indicate that the material is from an indirect source with the abbreviation *qtd. in* ("quoted in").

Wagner stated that myth and history stood before him "with opposing

claims" (qtd. in Thomas 65).

8. More Than One Work

Cite each work as you normally would, separating one from another with a semicolon.

The Brooklyn Bridge has been used as a subject by many American

artists (McCullough 144; Tashjian 58).

See
16c

NOTE: Long parenthetical references distract readers. Whenever possible, present them as **content notes**.

9. A Literary Work

When citing a literary work, it is often helpful to include more than just the author's name and the page number.

In a parenthetical reference to a prose work, begin with the page number, follow it with a semicolon, and then add any additional information that might be necessary.

In Moby Dick, Melville refers to a whaling expedition funded by Louis

XIV of France (151; ch. 24).

In parenthetical references to long poems, cite both division and line numbers, separating them with a period.

In the <u>Aeneid</u>, Virgil describes the ships as cleaving the "green woods

reflected in the calm water" (8.124).

(In this citation, the reference is to book 8, line 124 of the *Aeneid.*)

In citing classic verse plays, omit page numbers and include the act, scene, and line numbers, separated by periods (*Macbeth* 2.2.14–16). In biblical citations, include an abbreviated title, the chapter, and the verse (Gen 5.12).

NOTE: Use arabic rather than roman numerals for act and scene numbers of plays.

10. An Entire Work

When citing an entire work, include the author's name and the work's title in the text of your paper rather than in a parenthetical reference.

Herbert Gans's <u>The Urban Villagers</u> is a study of an Italian-American

neighborhood in Boston.

11. Two or More Authors with the Same Last Name

To distinguish authors with the same last name, include their initials in the parenthetical references.

Recent increases in crime have probably caused thousands of urban

homeowners to install alarms (R. Weishoff 115). Some of these alarms use

sophisticated sensors that were developed by the Army (C. Weishoff 76).

12. A Government Document or a Corporate Author

Cite such works using the organization's name followed by the page number. (American Automobile Association 34). You can avoid long parenthetical references by working the organization's name into the text of your paper.

According to the President's Commission for the Study of Ethical

Problems in Medicine and Biomedical and Behavioral Research, the issues

relating to euthanasia are complicated (76).

13. An Electronic Source

If a reference to an electronic source includes paragraph numbers rather than page numbers, use the abbreviation *par.* or *pars.* and the paragraph number or numbers. If the electronic source has no page or paragraph numbers, cite the work in the text of your paper rather than in a parenthetical reference.

The earliest type of movie censorship came in the form of licensing fees, and in Deer River, Minnesota, "a licensing fee of $200 was deemed not excessive for a town of 1000" (Ernst, par. 20).

In her article "Limited Horizons," Lynne Cheney says that schools do best when students read literature not for what it tells about the workplace, but for its insights into the human condition.

16b   Works Cited List

The **Works Cited list,** which appears at the end of your paper, gives publication information for all the research materials you cite. If your instructor tells you to list all the sources you read, whether you actually cited them or not, give this list the title *Works Consulted.*

✔ CHECKLIST: PREPARING THE MLA WORKS CITED LIST

- ✔ Begin the list of works cited on a new page after the last page of text or content notes, numbered as the next page of the paper.
- ✔ The title *Works Cited* should be centered one inch from the top of the page. Double-space between the title and the first entry.
- ✔ Each item has three divisions—author, title, and publication information. The separation between major divisions is marked by a period and one space.
- ✔ List entries alphabetically according to the author's last name. List the author's full name as it appears on the title page. If a source has no listed author, alphabetize it by the first important word of the title.
- ✔ Type the first line of each entry flush with left-hand margin; indent subsequent lines five spaces (or one-half inch).
- ✔ Double-space within and between entires.

Works Cited Format: MLA

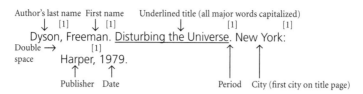

Author's last name First name   Underlined title (all major words capitalized)
    ↓ [1]   ↓ [1]   ↓   [1]   [1]
    Dyson, Freeman. <u>Disturbing the Universe</u>. New York:
Double →   [1]   ↑   ↑
space   Harper, 1979.   │   │
                ↑   ↑   │   │
            Publisher Date   Period   City (first city on title page)

DIRECTORY OF MLA WORKS CITED ENTRIES

Entries for Books

1. A book by one author
2. A book by two or three authors
3. A book by more than three authors
4. Two or more books by the same author
5. An edited book
6. A selection in an anthology
7. More than one essay from the same anthology
8. A multivolume work
9. The foreword, preface, or afterword of a book
10. A short story, play, or poem in an anthology
11. A short story, play, or poem in a collection of an author's work
12. A book with a title within its title
13. A translation
14. A republished book
15. A dissertation (published/unpublished)
16. An article in a reference book (signed/unsigned)
17. A pamphlet
18. A government publication

Entries for Articles

19. An article in a scholarly journal with continuous pagination through an annual volume
20. An article in a scholarly journal with separate pagination in each issue
21. An article in a weekly magazine (signed/unsigned)
22. An article in a monthly magazine
23. An article that is not printed on consecutive pages
24. An article in a newspaper (signed/unsigned)
25. An editorial

26. A letter to the editor
27. A book review
28. An article with a title within its title

Entries for Other Sources

29. A lecture
30. A personal interview
31. A published interview
32. A personal letter
33. A published letter
34. A letter in a library's archives
35. A film
36. A videotape, DVD, or laser disc
37. A radio or television program
38. A recording
39. A cartoon
40. An advertisement

Entries for Electronic Sources

41. A scholarly project or information database
42. A document within a scholarly project or information database
43. A Web site or home page
44. An online book
45. An article in an online scholarly journal
46. An article in an online newspaper
47. An article in an online newsletter
48. An article in an online magazine
49. A review
50. A letter to the editor
51. An article in an online encyclopedia
52. A work from an online service
53. A nonperiodical publication on CD-ROM or diskette
54. A periodical publication on CD-ROM
55. A painting or photograph
56. A map
57. An e-mail
58. An online posting
59. A synchronous communication (MOO or MUD)

Sample MLA Works Cited Entries: Books   Book citations include the author's name; book title (underlined); and publication information (place, publisher, date). Capitalize all major words of the title except articles, coordinating conjunctions, prepositions, and the *to* of an infinitive (unless such a word is the first or last word of the title or subtitle).

NOTE: Do not underline the period that follows a book's title.

1. A Book by One Author

Use a short form of the publisher's name. *Alfred A. Knopf, Inc.*, for example, is shortened to *Knopf*, and *Oxford University Press* becomes *Oxford UP.*

Bettelheim, Bruno. <u>The Uses of Enchantment: The Meaning and Importance of Fairy Tales</u>. New York: Knopf, 1976.

When citing an edition other than the first, indicate the edition number as it appears on the work's title page.

Gans, Herbert J. <u>The Urban Villagers</u>. 2nd ed. New York: Free, 1982.

2. A Book by Two or Three Authors

List the first author last name first. Subsequent authors are listed first name first in the order in which they appear on the title page.

Davidson, James West, and Mark Hamilton Lytle. <u>After the Fact: The Art of Historical Detection</u>. New York: Knopf, 1982.

3. A Book by More Than Three Authors

List only the first author, followed by *et al.* ("and others").

Bull, H., et al. <u>The Near East</u>. New York: Oxford UP, 1990.

4. Two or More Books by the Same Author

List books by the same author in alphabetical order by title. Three unspaced hyphens, followed by a period, take the place of the author's name after the first entry.

Thomas, Lewis. <u>The Lives of a Cell: Notes of a Biology Watcher</u>. New York: Viking, 1974.

---. <u>The Medusa and the Snail: More Notes of a Biology Watcher</u>. New York: Viking, 1979.

If the author is the editor or translator of the second entry, place a comma and the appropriate abbreviation after the hyphens (---, ed.).

5. An Edited Book

An edited book is a work prepared for publication by a person other than the author. If your emphasis is on the *author's* work, begin your citation with the author's name. After the title, include the abbreviation *Ed.* ("Edited by") followed by the name of the editor or editors.

Bartram, William. <u>The Travels of William Bartram</u>. Ed. Mark Van Doren.

New York: Dover, 1955.

If your emphasis is on the *editor's* work, begin your citation with the editor's name followed by the abbreviation *ed.* ("editor") if there is one editor or *eds.* ("editors") if there is more than one.

Van Doren, Mark, ed. <u>The Travels of William Bartram</u>. By William

Bartram. New York: Dover, 1955.

6. A Selection in an Anthology

Supply inclusive page numbers for the entire essay even if you cite only one page in your paper.

Lloyd, G. E. R. "Science and Mathematics." <u>The Legacy of Greece</u>. Ed.

Moses I. Finley. New York: Oxford UP, 1981. 256-300.

7. More Than One Essay from the Same Anthology

List each essay from the same anthology separately, followed by a cross-reference to the entire anthology. Also list complete publication information for the anthology itself.

Bolgar, Robert R. "The Greek Legacy." Finley 429-72.

Finley, Moses I., ed. <u>The Legacy of Greece</u>. New York: Oxford UP, 1981.

Williams, Bernard. "Philosophy." Finley 202-55.

8. A Multivolume Work

When all volumes of a multivolume work have the same title, include the number of the volume you are using.

Raine, Kathleen. <u>Blake and Tradition</u>. Vol. 1. Princeton: Princeton UP,

1968.

When you use two or more volumes, cite the entire work.

Raine, Kathleen. <u>Blake and Tradition</u>. 2 vols. Princeton: Princeton UP,

1968.

If the volume you are using has an individual title, you may cite the title without mentioning any other volumes.

Durant, Will, and Ariel Durant. <u>The Age of Napoleon</u>. New York:

Simon, 1975.

If you wish, however, you may include supplemental information, such as the number of the volume, the title of the entire work, the total number of volumes, and the inclusive publication dates.

Durant, Will, and Ariel Durant. <u>The Age of Napoleon</u>. New York: Simon,

1975. Vol. 11 of <u>The Story of Civilization</u>. 11 vols. 1935-75.

9. The Foreword, Preface, or Afterword of a Book

Taylor, Telford. Preface. <u>Less Than Slaves</u>. By Benjamin B. Ferencz. Cam-

bridge: Harvard UP, 1979. xiii-xxii.

10. A Short Story, Play, or Poem in an Anthology

Chopin, Kate. "The Storm." <u>Literature: Reading, Reacting, Writing</u>. Ed.

Laurie G. Kirszner and Stephen R. Mandell. Compact 4th ed. Fort

Worth: Harcourt, 2000. 138-42.

Shakespeare, William. <u>Othello, The Moor of Venice</u>. <u>Shakespeare: Six

Plays and the Sonnets</u>. Ed. Thomas Marc Parrott and Edward

Hubler. New York: Scribner's, 1956. 145-91.

11. A Short Story, Play, or Poem in a Collection of an Author's Work

Walcott, Derek. "Nearing La Guaira." <u>Selected Poems</u>. New York:

Farrar, 1964. 47-48.

12. A Book with a Title within Its Title

If the book you are citing contains a title that is normally underlined to indicate italics (a novel, play, or long poem, for example), do *not* underline the interior title.

Knoll, Robert E., ed. <u>Storm over</u> The Waste Land. Chicago: Scott, 1964.

If the book you are citing contains a title that is normally enclosed within quotation marks, keep the quotation marks.

Herzog, Alan, ed. <u>Twentieth Century Interpretations of "To a Skylark."</u>

Englewood Cliffs: Prentice, 1975.

13. A Translation

García Márquez, Gabriel. <u>One Hundred Years of Solitude</u>. Trans.

　　　　Gregory Rabassa. New York: Avon, 1991.

14. A Republished Book

Include the original publication date after the title of a republished book—for example, a paperback version of a hardcover book.

Wharton, Edith. <u>The House of Mirth</u>. 1905. New York: Scribner's, 1975.

15. A Dissertation (Published/Unpublished)

For dissertations published by University Microfilms International (UMI), include the order number.

Peterson, Shawn. <u>Loving Mothers and Lost Daughters: Images of</u>

　　　　<u>Female Kinship Relations in Selected Novels of Toni Morrison</u>.

　　　　Diss. U of Oregon, 1993. Ann Arbor: UMI, 1994. 9322935.

NOTE: University Microfilms, which publishes most of the dissertations in the United States, also publishes in CD-ROM. You will find the proper format for citing CD-ROMs on page 301.

Use quotation marks for the title of an unpublished dissertation.

Romero, Yolanda Garcia. "The American Frontier Experience in Twentieth-

　　　　Century Northwest Texas." Diss. Texas Tech U, 1993.

16. An Article in a Reference Book (Signed/Unsigned)

For a signed article, begin with the author's name. When citing relatively unfamiliar reference books, give full publication information.

Drabble, Margaret. "Expressionism." <u>The Oxford Companion to English</u>

　　　　<u>Literature</u>. 5th ed. New York: Oxford UP, 1985.

When citing familiar reference books, do not include publication information. Enter the title of an unsigned article just as it is listed in the reference book. No volume or page numbers are needed.

"Cubism." <u>Encyclopedia Americana</u> 1994 ed.

17. A Pamphlet

If no author is listed, begin with the title (underlined).

<u>Existing Light Photography</u>. Rochester: Kodak, 1989.

18. A Government Publication

If the publication has no listed author, begin with the name of the government, followed by the name of the agency.

United States. Office of Consumer Affairs. <u>1999 Consumer's Resource</u>

<u>Handbook</u>. Washington: GPO, 1999.

Sample MLA Works Cited Entries: Articles   Article citations include the author's name, the title of the article (in quotation marks); the underlined name of the periodical; the month and the year; and the pages on which the full article appears (without the abbreviations *p.* or *pp.*).

NOTE: Abbreviate the names of months—except for May, June, and July—in the Works Cited list (Jan., Feb., Mar., Apr., Aug., Sept., Oct., Nov., Dec.). Spell out the names of all months in the text of your paper.

19. An Article in a Scholarly Journal with Continuous Pagination through an Annual Volume

For an article in a journal with continuous pagination—for example, one in which an issue ends on page 172 and the next issue begins with page 173—include the volume number, followed by the date of publication (in parentheses). Follow the publication date with a colon, a space, and the page numbers.

Huntington, John. "Science Fiction and the Future." <u>College English</u> 37

(1975): 340-58.

20. An Article in a Scholarly Journal with Separate Pagination in Each Issue

For a journal in which each issue begins with page 1, add a period and the issue number after the volume number.

Sipes, R. G. "War, Sports, and Aggression: An Empirical Test of Two

Rival Theories." <u>American Anthropologist</u> 4.2 (1973): 65-84.

21. An Article in a Weekly Magazine (Signed/Unsigned)

In dates, the day precedes the month. For unsigned articles, start with the title of the article.

Traub, James. "The Hearts and Minds of City College." <u>New Yorker</u> 7

June 1993: 42-53.

"Solzhenitsyn: A Candle in the Wind." <u>Time</u> 23 Mar. 1970: 70.

22. An Article in a Monthly Magazine

Roll, Lori. "Careers in Engineering." <u>Working Woman</u> Nov. 1982: 62.

23. An Article That Is Not Printed on Consecutive Pages

When, for example, an article begins on page 15, continues on page 16, and then skips to page 86, include only the first page number and a plus sign.

Griska, Linda. "Stress and Job Performance." <u>Psychology Today</u>

Nov.-Dec. 1995: 120+.

24. An Article in a Newspaper (Signed/Unsigned)

Oates, Joyce Carol. "When Characters from the Page Are Made Flesh

on the Screen." <u>New York Times</u> 23 Mar. 1986, late ed.: C1+.

"Soviet Television." <u>Los Angeles Times</u> 13 Dec. 1990, sec. 2: 3+.

25. An Editorial

"Tough Cops, Not Brutal Cops." Editorial. <u>New York Times</u> 5 May

1994, late ed.: A26.

26. A Letter to the Editor

Bishop, Jennifer. Letter. <u>Philadelphia Inquirer</u> 10 Dec. 1995: A17.

27. A Book Review

Begin with the reviewer's name, followed by the title of the review (if any); then write *Rev. of,* the title of the book reviewed, a comma, the word *by,* and the name of the author. End with publication information.

Fox-Genovese, Elizabeth. "Big Mess on Campus." Rev. of <u>Illiberal</u>

<u>Education: The Politics of Race and Sex on Campus</u>, by Dinesh

D'Souza. <u>Washington Post</u> 15 Apr. 1991, ntnl. weekly ed.: 32.

28. An Article with a Title within Its Title

If the article you are citing contains a title that is normally enclosed within quotation marks, use single quotation marks for the interior title.

Nash, Robert. "About 'The Emperor of Ice Cream.'" <u>Perspectives</u> 7

(1954): 122-24.

If the article you are citing contains a title that is normally underlined to indicate italics, underline it in your Works Cited entry.

Leicester, H. Marshall, Jr. "The Art of Impersonation: A General

Prologue to <u>The Canterbury Tales</u>." <u>PMLA</u> 95 (1980): 213-24.

Sample MLA Works Cited Entries: Other Sources

29. A Lecture

Sandman, Peter. "Communicating Scientific Information."

Communications Seminar, Dept. of Humanities and

Communications. Drexel U, 26 Oct. 1999.

30. A Personal Interview

West, Cornel. Personal interview. 28 Dec. 1998.

Tannen, Deborah. Telephone interview. 8 June 1999.

31. A Published Interview

Stavros, George. "An Interview with Gwendolyn Brooks." <u>Contemporary</u>

<u>Literature</u> 11.1 (Winter 1970): 1-20.

32. A Personal Letter

Tan, Amy. Letter to the author. 7 Apr. 1997.

33. A Published Letter

Joyce, James. "Letter to Louis Gillet." 20 Aug. 1931. <u>James Joyce</u>. By

Richard Ellmann. New York: Oxford UP, 1965. 631.

34. A Letter in a Library's Archives

Stieglitz, Alfred. Letter to Paul Rosenberg. 5 Sept. 1923. Stieglitz

Archive. Yale Lib., New Haven.

35. A Film

Include the title of the film (underlined), the distributor, and the date, along with other information of use to readers, such as the names of the performers, the director, and the writer.

<u>Citizen Kane</u>. Dir. Orson Welles. Perf. Orson Welles, Joseph Cotten,

Dorothy Comingore, and Agnes Moorehead. RKO, 1941.

If you are focusing on the contribution of a particular person, begin with that person's name.

Welles, Orson, dir. <u>Citizen Kane</u>. . . .

36. A Videotape, DVD, or Laser Disc

Cite a videotape, DVD (digital videodisc), or laser disc like a film, but include the medium before the name of the distributor.

<u>Interview with Arthur Miller</u>. Dir. William Schiff. Videocassette. The

    Mosaic Group, 1987.

37. A Radio or Television Program

"Prime Suspect 3." Writ. Lynda La Plante. Perf. Helen Mirren. <u>Mystery!</u>

    PBS. WNET, New York. 28 Apr. 1994.

38. A Recording

List the composer, conductor, or performer (whichever you are emphasizing), followed by the title (and, when citing jacket notes, a description of the material), manufacturer, and year of issue.

Boubill, Alain, and Claude-Michel Schönberg. <u>Miss Saigon</u>. Perf. Lea

    Salonga, Claire Moore, and Jonathan Pryce. Cond. Martin Koch.

    Geffen, 1989.

Marley, Bob. "Crisis." Lyrics. <u>Bob Marley and the Wailers</u>. Kava Island

    Records, 1978.

39. A Cartoon

Trudeau, Garry. "Doonesbury." Cartoon. <u>The Philadelphia Inquirer</u> 19

    July 1999: E 13.

40. An Advertisement

Microsoft. Advertisement. <u>National Review</u> 28 June 1999: 11.

? ***Sample MLA Works Cited Entries: Electronic Sources***   The documentation style for electronic sources presented here conforms to the most recent guidelines published in the *MLA Handbook for Writers of Research Papers* (5th ed.) and found online at <http://mla.org>. (If your instructor prefers that you use Columbia Online Style for citing electronic sources, you can find it at <http://www.cas.usf.edu/english/walker/mla. html>.)

Because the information in electronic sources can change frequently, the version you accessed at the time of your research may not be the version that readers see later. For this reason, MLA recommends that you include *both* the date of the electronic publication (if available) and the date you accessed the source. In addition, MLA suggests that you print out and save the version of the electronic source that you accessed during your research. Finally, MLA recommends that you print the electronic address inside angle brackets to distinguish the address from the punctuation in the rest of the citation. (If you have to carry an electronic address over to the next line, divide it after a slash or, if that is not possible, at some other logical place—after a punctuation mark, for example. Never insert a hyphen at the end of a line—or permit your word processor to insert one.)

NOTE: MLA style recognizes that full source information is not always available. Include in your citation whatever information you can reasonably obtain.

41. A Scholarly Project or Information Database

Philadelphia Writers Project. Ed. Miriam Kotzen Green. May 1998.

Drexel U. 12 June 1999. <http://www.Drexel.edu/letrs/wwp/>.

NOTE: Be sure to give the complete electronic address, including the **access mode identifier** (*http, ftp, gopher, telnet,* or *news*) and all appropriate path and file names.

42. A Document within a Scholarly Project or Information Database

"'D' Day: June 7th, 1944." The History Channel Online. 1999. History

Channel. 7 June 1999 <http://historychannel.com/thisday/today/

997690.html>.

43. A Web Site or Home Page

Wilton, D. D. Wilton's Etymology Page. 15 June 1999

<http://www.wilton.net/Etyma1.htm>.

Gainor, Charles. Home page. 22 July 1999 <http://

www.chass.utoronto.ca:9094/~char/>.

44. On Online Book

Douglass, Frederick. My Bondage and My Freedom. Boston, 1855.

8 June 1999 <gopher://gopher.vt.edu:10024/22/178/3>.

45. An Article in an Online Scholarly Journal

> Dekoven, Marianne. "Utopias Limited: Post-Sixties and Postmodern
>
> > American Fiction." <u>Modern Fiction Studies</u> 41.1 (1995): 13 pp. 17
> >
> > Mar. 1999 <http://muse.jhu.edu/journals/mfs.v041/
> >
> > 41.1dwkovwn.html>.

When you cite information from the print version of an online source, include the publication information for the printed source, the number of pages or paragraphs (if available), and the date you accessed it.

46. An Article in an Online Newspaper

> Lohr, Steve, "Microsoft Goes to Court." <u>New York Times on the Web</u>
>
> > 19 Oct. 1998. 29 Apr. 1999 <http://www.nytimes.com/web/
> >
> > docroot/library.cyber/week/1019business.html>.

47. An Article in an Online Newsletter

> "Unprecedented Cutbacks in History of Science Funding." <u>AIP Center
>
> > for History of Physics</u> 27.2 (Fall 1995). 26 Feb. 1996 <http://
> >
> > www.aip.org/history/fall95.html>.

48. An Article in an Online Magazine

> Weiser, Jay. "The Tyranny of Informality." <u>Time</u> 26 Feb. 1996. 1 Mar. 1999.
>
> > <http://www.enews.com/magazines.tnr/current/022696.3.html>.

49. A Review

> Ebert, Roger. Rev. of <u>Star Wars: Episode I—The Phantom Menace</u>, dir.
>
> > George Lucas. <u>Chicago Sun-Times Online</u> 8 June 1999. 22 June
> >
> > 1999 <http://www.suntimes.com/output/ebert1/08show.html>.

50. A Letter to the Editor

> Chen-Cheng, Henry H. Letter. <u>New York Times on the Web</u> 19 July
>
> > 1999. 19 July 1999 <http://www.nytimes.com/yr/mo/day/letters/
> >
> > lchen-cheng.html>.

51. An Article in an Online Encyclopedia

> "Hawthorne, Nathaniel." <u>Britannica Online</u>. Vers. 98.2. Apr. 1998.
>
> > Encyclopaedia Britannica. 16 May 1998 <http://www.eb.com/>.

52. A Work from an Online Service

You can often access material from online services like America Online and Lexis-Nexis without using a URL. If you access such material by using a keyword, provide the keyword you used at the end of the entry (following the date of access).

"Kafka, Franz." Compton's Encyclopedia Online. Vers. 2.0. 1997.

America Online. 8 June 1998. Keyword: Compton's.

If, instead of using a keyword, you follow a series of paths, list the paths (separated by semicolons).

"Elizabeth Adams." History Resources. 11 Nov. 1997. America Online.

28 June 1999. Path: Research; Biography; Women in Science;

Biographies.

53. A Nonperiodical Publication on CD-ROM or Diskette

Cite a nonperiodical publication on CD-ROM or diskette the same way you would a book, but also include a description of the medium of publication—*CD-ROM* or *Diskette.*

"Windhover." The Oxford English Dictionary. 2nd ed. CD-ROM. Oxford:

Oxford UP, 1992.

"Whitman, Walt." DiscLit: American Authors. Diskette. Boston: Hall,

1993.

54. A Periodical Publication on CD-ROM

Zurbach, Kate. "The Linguistic Roots of Three Terms." Linguistic

Quarterly 37 (1994): 12-47. InfoTrac: Magazine Index Plus.

CD-ROM. Information Access. Jan. 1996.

55. A Painting or Photograph

Lange, Dorothea. Looking at Pictures. 1936. Museum of Mod. Art,

New York. 28 June 1999 <http://moma.org/exhibitions/

lookingatphotographs/lang-fr.html>.

56. A Map

"Philadelphia, Pennsylvania." Map. U. S. Gazetteer. US Census Bureau.

17 July 1999 <http://www.census.gov/cgi-bin/gazetteer>.

57. An E-Mail

Adkins, Camille. E-mail to the author. 28 June 1999.

58. An Online Posting

Gilford, Mary. "Dog Heroes in Children's Literature." Online posting. 17

  Mar. 1999. 12 Apr. 1999 <news: alt.animals.dogs>.

Schiller, Stephen. "Paper Cost and Publishing Costs." Online posting.

  24 Apr. 1999. 17 May 1999. Book Forum. 11 May 1999

  <www.nytimes.com/webin/webx?13A^41356.ee765e/0>.

59. A Synchronous Communication (MOO or MUD)

MOOs (multiuser domain, object oriented) and MUDs (multiuser domain) enable users to communicate in real time. To cite a communication obtained on a MOO or a MUD, give the name (or names) of the writer, a description of the situation, and the form of communication (LinguaMOO).

Guitar, Gwen. Online discussion of Cathy in Emily Brontë's Wuthering

  Heights. 17 Mar. 1999. LinguaMOO. 17 Mar. 1999 <telnet://

  lingua.utdallas.edu:8888>.

NOTE: Using information from Internet sources—especially newsgroups and online forums—always carries some risk. Contributors are not necessarily experts, and, frequently, they are incorrect and misinformed. Unless you can be certain that the information you are obtaining from these sources is reliable, do not use it. You can check the reliability of an Internet source by consulting Chapter **13,** Evaluating Web Sites.

16c   Content Notes

Content notes—multiple bibliographical citations or other material that does not fit smoothly into the text—are indicated by a **superscript** (raised numeral) in the paper. Notes can appear either as footnotes at the bottom of the page or as endnotes on a separate numbered sheet entitled *Notes,* placed after the last page of the paper and before the Works Cited list. Content notes are double-spaced within and between entries.

For Multiple Bibliographic Citations

In the Paper

Many researchers emphasize the necessity of having dying patients share their experiences.[1]

In the Note

[1] Kübler-Ross 27; Stinnette 43; Poston 70; Cohen and Cohen 31-34; Burke 1: 91-95.

For Other Material

In the Paper

The massacre of the Armenians during World War I is an event the survivors could not easily forget.[2]

In the Note

[2] For a firsthand account of these events, see Bedoukian 178-81.

EXERCISE

The following notes identify sources used in a paper on censorship and the Internet. Following the proper format for MLA parenthetical documentation, create a parenthetical reference for each source, and then arrange the sources in the proper order for the Works Cited list. (If your instructor requires a different method of documentation, use that style instead.)

1. Page 72 in a book called Banned in the USA by Herbert N. Foerstel. The book has 231 pages and was published in 1994 by Greenwood Press, located in Westport, Connecticut. The author's name appears in the text of your paper.
2. A statement made by Esther Dyson in her keynote address at the Newspapers 1996 Conference. Her statement is quoted in an article by Jodi B. Cohen called Fighting Online Censorship. The speech has not been printed in any other source. The article is in the April 13, 1996, edition of the weekly business journal Editor & Publisher. Dyson's quotation appears on page 44. The article begins on page 44 and continues on page 60. Dyson's name is mentioned in the text of your paper.

When and What to Footnote (from Harvard)
http://www.fas.harvard.edu/~wricntr/footnote.html

3. If You Don't Love It, Leave It, an essay by Esther Dyson in the New York Times Magazine, July 15, 1995, on pages 26 and 27. Your quotation comes from the second page of the essay. No author's name is mentioned in the text of your paper.

4. An essay by Nat Hentoff entitled Speech Should Not Be Limited on pages 22–26 of the book Censorship: Opposing Viewpoints, edited by Terry O'Neill. The book is published by Greenhaven Press in St. Paul, Minnesota. The publication year is 1985. The quotation you have used is from page 24, and the author is mentioned in the text of your paper.

5. An essay on the Internet called A Parent's Guide to Supervising a Child's Online and Internet Experiences. The document is by Robert Cannon, Esq., and you have Version 1.0 of the essay, which was updated May 10, 1996. Though the essay prints out on four pages, the pages are not numbered. In your paper, you summarize information from the second and third pages of the document. You accessed the information on January 20, 2000, through the library's Internet provider. The author's name is mentioned in the text of your paper.

CHAPTER 17

APA AND OTHER DOCUMENTATION STYLES

? FREQUENTLY ASKED QUESTIONS

When should I use APA documentation style?   (p. 305)

How do I arrange the works in an APA reference list?   (p. 310)

How do I cite an online article?   (p. 314)

When should I use CMS documentation? (p. 315)

When should I use CBE documentation? (p. 323)

What other documentation styles are there? (p. 326)

17a   Using APA Style

The documentation style recommended by the American Psychological Association is used extensively in the social sciences. **APA style**[*] relies

---

American Psychological Association Extension Webpage (WEAPAS)
   http://www.beadsland.com/weapas/

Using APA Sources Wisely (Roane St. CC)
   http://rscc3.rscc.cc.tn.us/~jordan_jj/OWL/UsingSources_APA.html

List of APA Style Resources
   http://www.psychwww.com/resource/apacrib.htm

Downloadable APA Style Guide, pdf file (Montana State U.)
   http://www.lib.montana.edu/instruct/styles/

Citing Electronic Sources (APA, MLA, and Chicago)
   http://www.lib.uwo.ca/weldon/docs/electronicstyle.html

---

[*]APA documentation style follows the guidelines set in the *Publication Manual of the American Psychological Association,* 4th ed. Washington, DC: APA, 1994.

on short parenthetical citations, consisting of the last name of the author, the year of publication, and—for direct quotations only—the page number. These references are keyed to an alphabetical list of references that follows the paper. APA style also permits content notes placed after the last page of the text. (A student paper illustrating the use of APA style appears in **50d.**)

(1) Parenthetical References in the Text

When introducing a quotation, include the author's name and the date in the introductory phrase. Put the page number in parentheses after the quotation.

> According to Weston (1996), children from one-parent homes read at "a significantly lower level than those from two-parent homes" (p. 58).

When introducing a paraphrase or summary, include the author's name and the date either in the introductory phrase or in parentheses at the end of the paraphrase or summary.

> According to Zinn (1995), this program has had success in training teenage fathers to take financial and emotional responsibility for their offspring.

> This program has had success in training teenage fathers to take financial and emotional responsibility for their offspring (Zinn, 1995).

Long quotations (forty words or more) are double-spaced and indented five spaces from the left margin. Parenthetical documentation is placed after the final punctuation.

DIRECTORY OF APA PARENTHETICAL REFERENCES

1. A work by a single author
2. A work by two authors
3. A work by three to five authors
4. A work by six or more authors
5. A work by a corporate author

6. A work with no listed author
7. A personal communication
8. An indirect source
9. A specific part of a source
10. Two or more works within the same parenthetical reference
11. A table

Sample APA In-Text Citations

1. A Work by a Single Author

Supporters of bilingual education programs often speak about the

psychological well-being of the child (Bakka, 1992).

NOTE: When the author's name and date appear in the parenthetical reference, APA style requires a comma between the name and the date.

2. A Work by Two authors

When a work has two authors, cite both names every time you refer to it.

There is growing concern over the use of psychological testing in

elementary schools (Albright & Glennon, 1982).

3. A Work by Three to Five Authors

If a work has more than two but fewer than six authors, mention all names in the first reference. In subsequent references, cite only the first author followed by *et al.* if the reference appears in the same paragraph as the first citation. Add the year if the reference appears in later paragraphs.

First Reference in Paper

(Sparks, Wilson, & Hewitt, 1984)

Subsequent References in the Same Paragraph

(Sparks et al.)

First Reference in Later Paragraphs

(Sparks et al., 1984).

4. A Work by Six or More Authors

When a work has six or more authors, cite the name of the first author followed by *et al.* and the year in all references.

(Miller et al., 1995).

 CITING WORKS BY MULTIPLE AUTHORS

When referring to multiple authors in the text of your paper, join the last two names with *and.*

According to Rosen, Wolfe, and Ziff (1988). . . .

In parenthetical documentation, however, use an **ampersand.**

(Rosen, Wolfe, & Ziff, 1988).

---

5. A Work by a Corporate Author

If the name of a corporate author is long, abbreviate it after the first citation.

First Reference

(National Institute of Mental Health [NIMH], 1994)

Subsequent Reference

(NIMH, 1994)

6. A Work with No Listed Author

If a work has no listed author, cite the first two or three words of the title and the year.

("New Immigration," 1994).

7. A Personal Communication

(R. Takaki, personal communication, October 17, 1996).

NOTE: Cite letters, memos, telephone conversations, personal interviews, e-mail, messages from electronic bulletin boards, and so on only in the text—*not* in the reference list.

8. An Indirect Source

Cogan and Howe offer very different interpretations of the problem (as cited in Swenson, 1990).

9. A Specific Part of a Source

Use abbreviations for the words *page* (p.), *chapter* (chap.), and *section* (sec.).

These theories have an interesting history (Lee, 1966, chap. 2).

10. Two or More Works within the Same Parenthetical Reference

List works by different authors in alphabetical order.

This theory is supported by several studies (Barson & Roth, 1985; Rose, 1987; Tedesco, 1982).

List works by the same author or authors in order of date of publication.

This theory is supported by several studies (Weiss & Elliot, 1982, 1984, 1985).

For works by the same author published in the same year, designate the work whose title comes first alphabetically *a*, the one whose title comes next *b*, and so on; repeat the year in each citation.

This theory is supported by several studies (Hossack, 1985a, 1985b).

11. A Table

If you use a table from a source, give credit to the author in a note at the bottom of the table.

Note. From "Predictors of Employment and Earnings Among JOBS Participants," by P. A. Neenan and D. K. Orthner, 1996, Social Work Research, 20 (4), p. 233.

(2) Reference List

The list of all the sources cited in your paper falls at the end on a new numbered page headed *References* (or *Bibliography* if you are listing all the works you consulted, whether or not you cited them).

✔ **CHECKLIST: PREPARING THE APA REFERENCE LIST**

✔ Begin the reference list on a new page after the last page of text or content notes, numbered as the next page of the paper.
✔ Center the title *References* at the top of the page.
✔ List the items on the reference list alphabetically (with author's last name first).
✔ Indent the first line of each entry five to seven spaces; type subsequent lines flush with the left-hand margin.*
✔ Separate the major divisions of each entry with a period and one space.
✔ Double-space the reference list within and between entries.

Reference List Format: APA

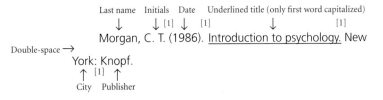

✔ **CHECKLIST: ARRANGING WORKS IN THE APA REFERENCE LIST**

✔ Single-author entries precede multiple-author entries that begin with the same name.

Field, S. (1987).

Field, S., & Levitt, M. P. (1984).

✔ Entries by the same author or authors are arranged according to date of publication, starting with the earliest date.

Ruthenberg, H., & Rubin, R. (1985).

Ruthenberg, H., & Rubin, R. (1987).

*This format is now recommended by the APA for all manuscripts submitted for publication. If your instructor prefers, you may instead type the first line of each entry flush with the left-hand margin and indent subsequent lines three spaces.

✔ Entries with the same author or authors and date of publication are arranged alphabetically according to title.

Wolk, E. M. (1986a). Analysis . . .

Wolk, E. M. (1986b). Hormonal . . .

DIRECTORY OF APA REFERENCE LIST ENTRIES

Entries for Books
1. A book with one author
2. A book with more than one author
3. An edited book
4. A book with no listed author or editor
5. A work in several volumes
6. A work with a corporate author
7. A government report
8. One selection from an anthology
9. An article in a reference book
10. The foreword, preface, or afterword of a book

Entries for Articles
11. An article in a scholarly journal with continuous pagination through an annual volume
12. An article in a scholarly journal with separate pagination in each issue
13. A magazine article
14. A newspaper article (signed/unsigned)
15. A letter to the editor
16. A published letter

Entries for Electronic Sources
17. Online article
18. Abstract on CD-ROM
19. Abstract online
20. Computer software

Sample APA Reference List Entries: Books Capitalize only the first word of the title and subtitle. Underline the entire title, including punctuation, and enclose the date, volume number, and edition number in parentheses. Write out the publisher's name in full.

1. A Book with One Author

> Maslow, A. H. (1974). <u>Toward a psychology of being.</u> Princeton: Van Nostrand.

2. A Book with More Than One Author

List all the authors—by last name and initials—regardless of how many there are.

> Wolfinger, D., Knable, P., Richards, H. L., & Silberger, R. (1990). <u>The chronically unemployed.</u> New York: Berman Press.

3. An Edited Book

> Lewin, K., Lippitt, R., & White. R. K. (Eds.). (1985). <u>Social learning and imitation.</u> New York: Basic Books.

4. A Book with No Listed Author or Editor

> <u>Writing with a computer.</u> (1993). Philadelphia: Drexel Publications.

5. A Work in Several Volumes

> Jones, P. R., & Williams, T. C. (Eds.). (1990-1993). <u>Handbook of therapy</u> (Vols. 1-2). Princeton: Princeton University Press.

6. A Work with a Corporate Author

> League of Women Voters of the United States. (1991). <u>Local league handbook.</u> Washington, DC: Author.

NOTE: When the author and publisher are the same, list *Author* at the end of the citation instead of repeating the publisher's name.

7. A Government Report

> National Institute of Mental Health. (1987). <u>Motion pictures and violence: A summary report of research</u> (DHHS Publication No. ADM 91-22187). Washington, DC: U.S. Government Printing Office.

8. One Selection from an Anthology

> Lorde, A. (1984). Age, race, and class. In P. S. Rothenberg (Ed.), <u>Racism and sexism: An integrated study</u> (pp. 352-360). New York: St. Martin's.

NOTE: A title of a selection in an anthology is not underlined or enclosed in quotation marks. If you cite two or more selections from the same anthology, give the full citation for the anthology in each entry.

9. An Article in a Reference Book

Edwards. P. (Ed.). (1987). Determinism. In The encyclopedia of

philosophy (Vol. 2, pp. 359-373). New York: Macmillan.

10. The Foreword, Preface, or Afterword of a Book

Taylor, T. (1979). Preface. In Less than slaves by Benjamin B.

Ferencz. Cambridge: Harvard University Press.

Sample APA Reference List Entries: Articles　Capitalize only the first word of the title and subtitle. Do not underline the title of the article or enclose it in quotation marks. Give the periodical title in full; underline the title and capitalize all major words. Underline the volume number, as well as the comma that follows it, but not the issue number in parentheses. Give inclusive page numbers. Use *pp.* when referring to page numbers in newspapers and popular magazines, but omit this abbreviation when referring to page numbers in periodicals with volume numbers.

11. An Article in a Scholarly Journal with Continuous Pagination through an Annual Volume

Miller, W. (1969). Violent crimes in city gangs. Journal of Social

Issues, 27, 581-593.

12. An Article in a Scholarly Journal with Separate Pagination in Each Issue

Williams, S., & Cohen, L. R. (1984). Child stress in early learning

situations. American Psychologist, 21 (10), 1-28.

13. A Magazine Article

McCurdy, H. G. (1983, June). Brain mechanisms and intelligence.

Psychology Today, pp. 61-63.

14. A Newspaper Article (Signed/Unsigned)

James, W. R. (1993, November 16). The uninsured and health

care. The Wall Street Journal, pp. A1, A14.

NOTE: Article appears on two nonconsecutive pages.

Study finds many street people mentally ill. (1993, June 7). New York Times, p. A7.

15. A Letter to the Editor

Williams, P. (1993, July 19). Self-fulfilling stereotypes [Letter to the editor]. Los Angeles Times, p. A22.

16. A Published Letter

Joyce, J. (1931). Letter to Louis Gillet. In Richard Ellmann, James Joyce (p. 631). New York: Oxford University Press.

Sample APA Reference List Entries: Electronic Sources

17. Online Article

Farrell, P. D. (1997, March). New high-tech stresses hit traders and investors on the information superhighway. [14 paragraphs.] Wall Street News [Online serial]. Available http:wall-street-news.com/forecasts/stress/stress.html

NOTE: No period follows the electronic address.

18. Abstract on CD-ROM

Guiot, A., & Peterson, B. R. (1995). Forgetfulness and partial cognition. [CD-ROM]. Memory and Cognition, 23, 643-652. Abstract from: SilverPlatter File: PsycLit Item: 90-14321

19. Abstract Online

Guiot, A., & Peterson, B. R. (1995). Forgetfulness and partial cognition. [Online]. Memory and Cognition, 23, 643-652. Abstract from: DIALOG file: PsycINFO Item: 90-14321

20. Computer Software

Sharp, S. (1995). Career Selection Tests (Version 5.0) [Computer software]. Chico, CA: Avocation Software.

NOTE: APA formats for documenting online sources are based on Li and Crane's *Electronic Style: A Guide to Citing Electronic Information.* For the most current information on citing electronic sources, consult the APA Web site (<http://www.apa.org>).

(3) Content Notes

APA format allows, but does not encourage, the use of content notes, indicated by **superscripts** (raised numerals) in the text. The notes are listed on a separate numbered page, entitled *Footnotes,* following the last page of text. Double-space all notes, indenting the first line of each note five to seven spaces and beginning subsequent lines flush left.

17b   Using CMS Format

The Chicago Manual of Style (CMS) is used in history and some social science and humanities disciplines. **CMS format*** has two parts: notes at the end of the paper (endnotes) and a list of bibliographic citations. (Although Chicago style encourages the use of endnotes, it also allows the use of footnotes at the bottom of the page.)

(1) Endnotes and Footnotes

The notes format calls for a **superscript** (raised numeral) in the text after source material you have either quoted or referred to. This numeral, placed after all punctuation marks except dashes, corresponds to the numeral that accompanies the note.

✔ CHECKLIST: PREPARING CMS ENDNOTES

✔ Begin endnotes on a new page after the last page of the paper.
✔ Center the title *Notes* one inch from the top of the page.
✔ Number the page on which the endnotes appear as the next page of the paper.
✔ Type and number notes in the order in which they appear in the paper, beginning with number 1.
✔ Type the note number on (not above) the line, followed by a period and one space.
✔ Indent the first line of each note three spaces; type subsequent lines flush with the left-hand margin.
✔ Double-space within and between entries.

University of Chicago Press Home Page
  http://press-www.uchicago.edu

---

*CMS format follows the guidelines set in *The Chicago Manual of Style,* 14th ed. Chicago: U of Chicago P, 1993.

Endnote and Footnote Format: CMS

In the Text

By November of 1942, the Allies had proof that the Nazis were engaged in the systematic killing of Jews.¹

In the Note

1. David S. Wyman, *The Abandonment of the Jews: America and the Holocaust 1941–1945* (New York: Pantheon Books, 1984), 65.

 SUBSEQUENT REFERENCES

In the first reference to a work, use the full citation; in subsequent references to the same work, list only the author's last name, followed by a comma and a page number.

First Note on Espinoza

1. J. M. Espinoza, *The First Expedition of Vargas in New Mexico, 1692* (Albuquerque: University of New Mexico Press, 1949), 10–12.

Subsequent Note

5. Epinoza, 29.

NOTE: *The Chicago Manual of Style* allows the use of the abbreviation *ibid.* ("in the same place") for subsequent references to the same work as long as there are no intervening references. *Ibid.* takes the place of the author's name and the work's title—but not the page number.

First Note on Espinoza

1. J. M. Espinoza, *The First Expedition of Vargas in New Mexico, 1692* (Albuquerque: University of New Mexico Press, 1949), 10–12.

Subsequent Note

2. Ibid., 23.

Keep in mind, however, that the use of *Ibid.* is giving way to the use of the author's last name and the page number for subsequent references to the same work.

(2) Bibliography

In addition to the heading *Bibliography,* Chicago style allows *Selected Bibliography, Works Cited, Literature Cited, References,* and *Sources Consulted.*

✔ CHECKLIST: PREPARING THE CMS BIBLIOGRAPHY

✔ Type entries on a separate page after the endnotes.
✔ List entries alphabetically according to the author's last name.
✔ Type the first line of each entry flush with the left-hand margin; indent subsequent lines three spaces.
✔ Double-space the bibliography within and between entries.

Bibliography Format: CMS

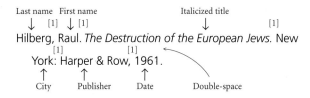

Last name   First name   Italicized title
↓   [1] ↓ [1]   ↓   [1]
Hilberg, Raul. *The Destruction of the European Jews.* New
   [1]   [1]
   York: Harper & Row, 1961.
   ↑   ↑   ↑
   City   Publisher   Date   Double-space

DIRECTORY OF CMS ENDNOTE CITATIONS AND BIBLIOGRAPHY ENTRIES

Entries for Books
1. A book by one author
2. A book by two or three authors
3. A book by more than three authors
4. An edited book
5. A chapter in a book or an essay in an anthology
6. A multivolume work

Entries for Articles
7. An article in a scholarly journal with continuous pagination through an annual volume
8. An article in a scholarly journal with separate pagination in each issue
9. An article in a weekly magazine
10. An article in a monthly magazine
11. An article in a newspaper

Entries for Other Sources
12. A personal interview
13. A published interview
14. A letter
15. A film or videotape
16. A recording

Entries for Electronic Sources
17. Computer software
18. An electronic document

Sample CMS Entries: Books   Capitalize the first, last, and all major words of titles and subtitles. Although underlining to indicate italics is acceptable, Chicago style recommends the use of italics for titles.

1. A Book by One Author
Endnote

1. Herbert J. Gans, *The Urban Villagers,* 2d ed. (New York: Free

Press, 1982), 100.

Bibliography

Gans, Herbert J. *The Urban Villagers.* 2d ed. New York: Free Press, 1982.

2. A Book by Two or Three Authors
Endnote

2. James W. Davidson and Mark Hamilton Lytle, *After the Fact: The

Art of Historical Detection* (New York: Alfred A. Knopf, 1982), 54.

Bibliography

Davidson, James W., and Mark Hamilton Lytle. *After the Fact: The Art of

Historical Detection.* New York: Alfred A. Knopf, 1982.

3. A Book by More Than Three Authors
Endnote

3. Robert E. Spiller et al., eds., *Literary History of the United States*

(New York: Macmillan, 1974), 24.

Bibliography

Spiller, Robert E., et. al., eds. *Literary History of the United States.* New

York: Macmillan, 1974.

4. An Edited Book

Endnote

> 4. William Bartram, *The Travels of William Bartram,* ed. Mark Van Doren (New York: Dover Press, 1955), 85.

Bibliography

> Bartram, William. *The Travels of William Bartram.* Edited by Mark Van Doren. New York: Dover Press, 1955.

5. A Chapter in a Book or an Essay in an Anthology

Endnote

> 5. Peter Kidson, "Architecture and City Planning," in *The Legacy of Greece,* ed. M. I. Finley (New York: Oxford University Press, 1981), 376–400.

Bibliography

> Kidson, Peter. "Architecture and City Planning." In *The Legacy of Greece,* edited by M. I. Finley, 376–400. New York: Oxford University Press, 1981.

6. A Multivolume Work

Endnote

> 6. Kathleen Raine, *Blake and Tradition* (Princeton: Princeton University Press, 1968), 1:143.

Bibliography

> Raine, Kathleen. *Blake and Tradition.* Vol. 1. Princeton: Princeton University Press, 1968.

Sample CMS Entries: Articles

7. An Article in a Scholarly Journal with Continuous Pagination through an Annual Volume

Endnote

> 7. John Huntington, "Science Fiction and the Future," *College English* 37 (fall 1975): 341.

Bibliography

Huntington, John. "Science Fiction and the Future." *College English* 37 (fall 1975): 340–58.

8. An Article in a Scholarly Journal with Separate Pagination in Each Issue

Endnote

8. R. G. Sipes, "War, Sports, and Aggression: An Empirical Test of Two Rival Theories," *American Anthropologist* 4, no. 2 (1973): 80.

Bibliography

Sipes, R. G. "War, Sports, and Aggression: An Empirical Test of Two Rival Theories." *American Anthropologist* 4, no. 2 (1973): 65–84.

9. An Article in a Weekly Magazine

Endnote

9. James Traub, "The Hearts and Minds of City College," *New Yorker,* 7 June 1993, 45.

Bibliography

Traub, James. "The Hearts and Minds of City College." *New Yorker,* 7 June 1993, 42–53.

10. An Article in a Monthly Magazine

Endnote

10. Lori Roll, "Careers in Engineering," *Working Woman,* November 1982, 62.

Bibliography

Roll, Lori. "Careers in Engineering." *Working Woman,* November 1982, 62.

11. An Article in a Newspaper

Endnote

11. Raymond Bonner, "A Guatemalan General's Rise to Power," *New York Times,* 21 July 1982, 3(A).

Bibliography

> Bonner, Raymond. "A Guatemalan General's Rise to Power." *New York*
> *Times,* 21 July 1982, 3(A).

Sample CMS Entries: Other Sources

12. A Personal Interview

Endnote

> 12. Cornel West, interview by author, tape recording, St. Louis, Mo.,
> 8 June 1994.

Bibliography

> West, Cornel. Interview by author. Tape recording. St. Louis, Mo., 8
> June 1994.

13. A Published Interview

Endnote

> 13. Gwendolyn Brooks, interview by George Stravos, *Contemporary*
> *Literature* 11, no. 1 (winter 1970): 12.

Bibliography

> Brooks, Gwendolyn. Interview by George Stravos. *Contemporary*
> *Literature* 11, no. 1 (winter 1970): 1–20.

14. A Letter

Endnote

> 14. Amy Tan, letter to author, 7 April 1990.

Bibliography

> Tan, Amy. Letter to author. 7 April 1990.

15. A Film or Videotape

Endnote

> 15. *Interview with Arthur Miller,* dir. William Schiff, 17 min., The
> Mosaic Group, 1987, videocassette.

Bibliography

> Miller, Arthur. *Interview with Arthur Miller.* Directed by William Schiff.
> 17 min. The Mosaic Group, 1987. Videocassette.

16. A Recording

Endnote

16. Bob Marley, "Crisis," on *Bob Marley and the Wailers,* Kava Island Records compact disk 423 095-3.

Bibliography

Marley, Bob. "Crisis." On *Bob Marley and the Wailers.* Kava Island Records compact disk 423 095-3.

Sample CMS Entries: Electronic Sources

17. Computer Software

Endnote

17. Reunion: The Family Tree Software, vers. 2.0, Macintosh, Lester Productions, Cambridge, Mass.

Bibliography

Reunion: The Family Tree Software. Vers. 2.0, Macintosh. Lester Productions, Cambridge, Mass.

18. An Electronic Document

The Chicago Manual of Style recommends following the guidelines developed by the International Standards Organization (ISO). List the authors, the title, the electronic medium (electronic bulletin board, for example), information about a print version, access dates, and electronic address or location information.

Endnote

18. Arthur Sklar, "Survey of Legal Opinions Regarding the Death Penalty in New Jersey," in NL-KR (Digest vol. 3, no. 2) [electronic bulletin board] (Newark, N.J., 1995 [cited 17 March 1997]); available from nl-kr@cs.newark.edu; INTERNET.

Bibliography

Sklar, Arthur. "Survey of Legal Opinions Regarding the Death Penalty in New Jersey," in NL-KR (Digest vol. 3, no. 2) [electronic bulletin board]. (Newark, N.J., 1995 [cited 17 March 1997]). Available from nl-kr@cs.newark.edu; INTERNET.

17c Using CBE Style

(1) Documentation in the Text

Documentation styles recommended by the Council of Biology Editors (CBE) are used in biology, zoology, physiology, anatomy, and genetics. **CBE Style*** recommends two documentation formats: number-reference and author-year (or name-year).

The Number-Reference Format: The number-reference format calls for either raised numbers in the text of the paper (the preferred form) or numbers inserted parenthetically in the text of the paper.

One study[1] has demonstrated the effect of low dissolved oxygen.

These numbers correspond to a list of references at the end of the paper. If you refer to more than one source in a single note, the numbers are separated by a dash if they are in sequence[2-3] and by a comma if they are not[3,6].

The Author-Year (or Name-Year) Format: This system calls for the author's name and the year of publication to be inserted parenthetically in the text. If the author's name is used to introduce the source material, only the date of publication is needed. When two or more works are cited in the same parentheses, the sources are arranged chronologically (from earliest to latest) and separated by a semicolon.

A great deal of heat is often generated during this process (McGinness 1999).

According to McGinness, a great deal of heat is often generated during this process (1999).

Epidemics can be avoided by taking tissue cultures (Domb 1998) and by intervention with antibiotics (Baldwin and Rigby 1984; Martin and others 1992; Cording 1998).

Council of Biology Editors (CBE) home page
    http://www.cbe.org

*CBE style follows the guidelines set in the style manual of the Council of Biology Editors: *Scientific Style and Format: The CBE Manual for Authors, Editors, and Publishers,* 6th ed. New York: Cambridge UP, 1994.

NOTE: The first citation, *Baldwin and Rigby, 1984,* refers to a work by two authors; the second citation, *Martin and others,* refers to a work by three or more authors.

(2) Reference List

The format of the reference list depends on the documentation format you use. If you use the author-year documentation format, your reference list will resemble the reference list for an **APA** paper. If you use the number-reference documentation style, your sources will be listed by number, in the order in which they appear in your text, on a *References* page. This section presents guidelines for using the number-reference format.

✔ CHECKLIST: PREPARING THE CBE REFERENCE LIST

- ✔ Begin the reference list on a new page after the last page of the paper, numbered as the next page of the paper.
- ✔ Center the title *References, Literature Cited,* or *References Cited* about one inch from the top of the page.
- ✔ List the items in the order in which they appear in the paper, not alphabetically.
- ✔ Number the entries consecutively; type the note numbers on (not above) the line, followed by a period.
- ✔ Type the first line of each entry flush with the left-hand margin; align subsequent lines directly beneath the first letter of the author's last name.
- ✔ Double-space within and between entries.

Reference List Format: CBE

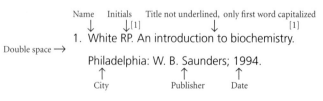

DIRECTORY OF CBE REFERENCE LIST ENTRIES

1. A book with one author
2. A book with more than one author
3. An edited book
4. A specific section of a book
5. A chapter in a book or an essay in an anthology
6. An article in a journal with continuous pagination
7. An article in a journal with separate pagination in each issue
8. An article with no listed author
9. An electronic source

Sample CBE Reference List Entries: Books   List the author or authors (last name first), the title (not underlined, and with only the first word capitalized), the place of publication (followed by a colon), the full name of the publisher (followed by a semicolon), the year (followed by a period), and the total number of pages (followed by a period).

1. A Book with One Author

1. Key K. Plant biology. Fort Worth: Harcourt Brace; 1995. 437 p.

2. A Book with More Than One Author

2. Krause KF, Paterson MK. Tissue culture: methods and application.

New York: Academic Press; 1993. 217 p.

3. An Edited Book

3. Marzacco MP, editor. A survey of biochemistry. New York: Bowker;

1985. 523 p.

4. A Specific Section of a Book

4. Baldwin LD, Rigby CV. A study of animal virology. New York: Wiley;

1984: p 121-33.

5. A Chapter in a Book or an Essay in an Anthology

5. Brydon RB, Ellis J, Scott CD. Cell division and cancer treatment. In

Gotlieb, JM, editor. Current research in cancer treatment. New York:

Springer-Verlag; 1996: p 34-47.

Sample CBE Reference List Entries: Articles   List the author or authors (last name first), the title of the article (with only the first word capitalized), the abbreviated name of the journal (with all major words capitalized, but not underlined), the year (followed by a semicolon), the volume number (followed by a colon), and inclusive page numbers. No spaces separate the year, the volume, and the page numbers.

6. An Article in a Journal with Continuous Pagination

6. Bensley KR. Profiling women physicians. Medica 1985;1:140-5.

7. An Article in a Journal with Separate Pagination in Each Issue

7. Paul DR, Wang AR, Richards L. The human genome project. Sci Am 1995 Sept;285(2):43-52.

8. An Article with No Listed Author

8. [Anonymous]. Developments in microbiology. Int. J. Microbiol 1987;6:234-48.

9. An Electronic Source

List the author or authors, the title (followed by the journal title, along with the date and volume number, in the case of journal articles), the electronic medium [*serial online* for periodicals and *monograph online* for books], the date of publication, the words *Available from* followed by a colon and the electronic address, and the date of access.

9. Bensley KR. Profiling women physicians. Medica [serial online] 1985;1. Available from: ftp.lib.nscu.edu via the INTERNET. Accessed 1997 Feb 18.

17d Using Other Documentation Styles

The following style manuals describe documentation formats used in other disciplines.

Chemistry
Dodd, Janet S. American Chemical Society. *The ACS Guide: A Manual for Authors and Editors.* 2nd ed. Washington: Amer. Chemical Soc., 1997.

Government Documents
Garner, Diane L. *The Complete Guide to Citing Government Information Resources: A Manual for Writers and Librarians.* Rev. Ed. Bethesda: Congressional Information Service, 1993.

Geology
United States Geological Survey. *Suggestions to Authors of the Reports of the United States Geological Survey.* 7th ed. Washington: GPO, 1991.

History
The Chicago Manual of Style. 14th ed. Chicago: U of Chicago P, 1993.

Journalism
Associated Press Staff. *Associated Press Stylebook and Libel Manual.* 32nd ed. New York: Associated Press, 1997.

Law
The Bluebook: A Uniform System of Citation. Comp. Editors of *Columbia Law Review* et al. 16th ed. Cambridge: Harvard Law Rev. Assn., 1996.

Linguistics
Linguistic Society of America. "LSA Style Sheet." Published annually in December issue of the *LSA Bulletin.*

Mathematics
American Mathematical Society. *AMS Author Handbook.* Providence: Amer. Mathematical Soc., 1997.

Medicine
Iverson, Cheryl. *Manual of Style: A Guide for Authors and Editors.* 9th ed. Chicago: Amer. Medical Assn., 1997.

Music
Holman, D. Kirn, ed. *Writing about Music: A Style Sheet from the Editors of 19th-Century Music.* Berkeley: U California P, 1988.

Physics
American Institute of Physics. *AIP Style Manual.* 4th ed. New York: Am. Inst. of Physics, 1990.

Scientific and Technical Writing
Rubens, Philip, ed. *Science and Technical Writing: A Manual of Style.* Fort Worth: Harcourt, 1992.

NOTE: For other guides to style, see John Bruce Howell. *Style Manuals of the English-Speaking World: A Guide.* Phoenix: Oryx, 1983.

CHAPTER 18

RESEARCH NOTEBOOK: A STUDENT'S PROCESS

? FREQUENTLY ASKED QUESTIONS

Kimberly Larsen Romney, a student in a composition class, was given this assignment:

> Write an eight- to twelve-page research paper that takes a position on any issue related to the Internet.

This was to be a full-semester project, so Kim had fourteen weeks in which to research and write the paper. This chapter traces her progress, reproducing (in italics) the comments she made in her research notebook at various stages of the project as well as some examples of her work in progress.

Kim's instructor, Professor Linda Wilson, required regular conferences at which she reviewed students' progress and checked their research notebooks; a segment of the assignment was due at each meeting. At various points in the process, Professor Wilson required collaborative work, and she expected students to use a variety of print, electronic, and nonlibrary sources, particularly Internet sources. With these general guidelines in mind, Kim began to think about her assignment.

18a   Moving from Assignment to Topic

(1) Understanding Your Assignment

Today, Professor Wilson gave our English class an assignment. By the end of the semester, we have to hand in an eight- to twelve-page paper on a controversial issue related to the Internet. We're supposed to explain the issue and present our position. At the end of next week, Professor Wilson will meet with each student in the class to help us decide on a search strategy. In two weeks, we have to turn in an outline of our paper and meet with Professor Wilson again so she can make comments and suggestions. The final paper has to use MLA documentation.

(2) Choosing a Topic

Last year, I volunteered at the YMCA. A local computer company had just donated several computers to the after-school program. It was my job to show the children, most of whom were from low-income families, how to use the computers, specifically the Internet. I was really surprised to see that most of these kids had never been on the Internet before. Recently, I read an article in a magazine about the "digital divide." This term refers to the situation that exists because many people do not have access to computers or to the Internet. I want to find out more about the digital divide, so I'm choosing it as the topic of my paper.

(3) Starting a Research Notebook

Today I started my research notebook. I wrote down my schedule, as well as a few potential sources to check and the name of a library science professor who is an expert on the Internet. I hope to contact him and interview him for my paper.

18b Mapping Out a Search Strategy

Today I met with Professor Wilson to discuss my search strategy. First, she approved my topic. Then, she suggested I start my work by familiarizing myself with the history of the Internet. She suggested I go to the Internet itself for this information. Once I understand the Internet and its history, I can look through current magazines and newspapers in the school library or online for specific information about the digital divide, asking a reference librarian for help if necessary. Professor Wilson also gave me the Web address for the Digital Divide Network, which she thought would be very helpful.

18c Doing Exploratory Research and Formulating a Research Question

(1) Doing Exploratory Research

Today I researched the history of the Internet and found out that it's over thirty years old. I also learned that to compete in today's marketplace, it's essential to understand computers. Those who don't have access to the Internet are going to be left behind. I discussed my topic with a reference librarian, and she directed me to several helpful Web sites. Surprisingly, a friend was able to help me; she gave me a copy of an article about the digital divide from the <u>New York Times</u> that she found on the Web.

(2) Formulating a Research Question

I've been researching my topic for a few days now and have finally decided on my research question: Does the Internet threaten to create a "digital divide?"

18d Assembling a Working Bibliography

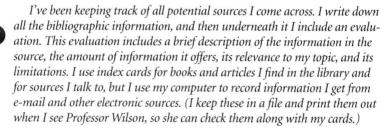

I've been keeping track of all potential sources I come across. I write down all the bibliographic information, and then underneath it I include an evaluation. This evaluation includes a brief description of the information in the source, the amount of information it offers, its relevance to my topic, and its limitations. I use index cards for books and articles I find in the library and for sources I talk to, but I use my computer to record information I get from e-mail and other electronic sources. (I keep these in a file and print them out when I see Professor Wilson, so she can check them along with my cards.)

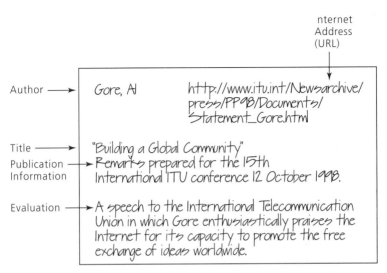

Figure 1 Information for Working Bibliography (on Index Card)

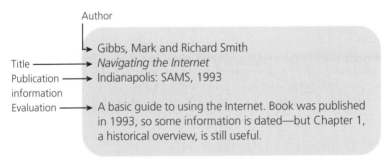

Figure 2 Information for Working Bibliography (in Computer File)

Occasionally, I review my sources and reevaluate them. Today, I decided to remove from my list an article about a company called World-Com and its initiatives to aid those in need of Internet access. It had seemed like a helpful source at first, but the article turned out to be too short, and it didn't include enough specific information about World-Com's programs. I need to find Bill Clinton's 2000 State of the Union Speech. I keep reading that he mentioned the digital divide, but I need to know exactly what he said.

18e   Developing a Tentative Thesis

I've done a lot of research and have decided on a tentative thesis.

The Internet threatens to leave many people behind, creating a

"digital divide."

18f   Doing Focused Research

(1) Reading Sources

To make sure I get everything I can out of each source, I first skim it and then go back and reread it, highlighting the key points. As I read, I ask myself which parts of the information are fact and which are the opinion of the author. This is difficult to do, so I sometimes have to read the information two or three times. Because I know I might find later that some of my sources aren't useful, I'm trying to locate as many sources as I can.

As I gather new sources, I evaluate them using a variety of criteria, according to Professor Wilson's guidelines. For my print sources, I sometimes ask the reference librarian or Professor Wilson whether an author is credible. I also consider how current a source is. I'm trying to find sources no more than a couple of years old (except for sources of background about the Internet). I'm also discarding sources that are mostly opinion. One of my sources is an interview with a library science professor, a reliable source who can give me information for my section on the efforts that public libraries are taking to provide people with Internet access.

(2) Distinguishing between Primary and Secondary Sources

I'm trying to collect both primary and secondary sources. For example, I've found a copy of Clinton's 2000 State of the Union Speech on the Web, and this is a primary source, and I'm also using newspaper articles, which are secondary sources.

18g   Taking Notes

For each source I use, I'm taking notes on index cards or in a computer file.

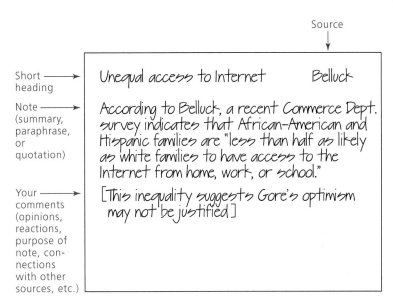

Figure 3 *Notes (on Note Card)*

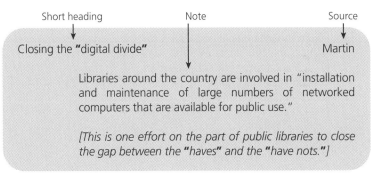

Figure 4 *Notes (in Computer File)*

18h   Deciding on a Thesis

I've revised my tentative thesis so that it clearly communicates my stand on the issue. My final thesis is more specific than my tentative thesis was:

The Internet threatens to leave many people behind, creating two

distinct classes—those who have access and those who do not.

❓ 18i Preparing a Formal Outline

Today I did my outline. Professor Wilson told us that constructing a topic outline now would help us when we wrote our rough draft, so I gathered all my notes together and started arranging them in what I thought was a logical way. I identified the five main topics I want to cover and arranged all my notes into these five categories. Tomorrow I meet with Professor Wilson to go over the outline. If it's okay, I can start to draft my paper.

Thesis Statement: The Internet threatens to leave many people behind, creating two distinct classes—those who have access and those who do not.

I. History of the Internet
   A. ARPANET
   B. Expansion (1972)
   C. HTML
II. Importance of the Internet Today
   A. Empowering Tool
   B. Source of Knowledge and Prosperity
III. Digital Divide
   A. Lack of Access by Poor, Minorities, etc.
   B. Educational and Economic Disadvantages
   C. Widening Gap
IV. Efforts by Government and Others to Close Gap
   A. Clinton's 2000 State of the Union Address
   B. SLD and Neighborhood Networks
   C. Congressional Efforts
   D. Corporations: Power Up
   E. Nonprofits: PBS, Civil Rights Forum
   F. Public Libraries
V. Recommendations for Future
   A. Internet Availability
   B. Training
   C. Targeting the Likely "Have-Nots"

18j Writing a Rough Draft

(1) Shaping the Parts of the Paper

I've discussed my outline with Professor Wilson, and we made a few changes. Now I'm ready to start writing my rough draft.

In my introduction, I'm going to explain the importance of understanding technology in today's society; this will allow me to bring up the digital divide.

In the body of the paper, I plan to start with the history of the Internet and briefly discuss its benefits. Then I'll discuss the Internet's drawbacks, which will allow me to move on to a fuller discussion of the digital divide.

In my conclusion, I'll summarize my ideas and restate my thesis.

(2) Working Source Material into Your Paper

One of the most difficult challenges I've faced is integrating my research into my paper. I've tried to show how each of my sources supports my thesis, and I've also tried to show how sources that agree with one another are related. For example, in my conclusion I show that both Bill Clinton and Dr. Martin (the librarian) believe that it is often everyday problems like damaged phone jacks or not having an appropriate computer table that prevent people from using the Internet. I think this makes my argument that we must solve these minor problems more convincing.

18k Revising the Drafts

When I finished my rough draft, I asked two of my friends to read it. I also took it to the Writing Lab. Having other people review my draft was a big help. For example, the Writing Lab tutor suggested that adding statistics to certain sections of my paper would really strengthen it. (I took her advice, and I added a bar graph, too.)

Rough Draft

A recent survey by the Commerce Department shows that African-American and Hispanic families are "less than half as likely as white families to have access to the Internet from home, work, or school" (Belluck). This disparity exists even at low income levels. According to Belluck, "at the lowest income levels, the gap is great— a child in a low-income white family is three times as likely to have Internet access as a child in a low-income black family."

Revised

A recent survey by the Department of Commerce shows that people with higher annual household incomes and whites are more likely to own a computer than minorities and people from low-income households. Approximately 80 percent of households with incomes of $75,000 or above have computers, compared to 16 percent of households earning $10,000-$15,000. The survey also found that in households with incomes between $15,000 and $34,999, only 23 percent of African-American and 26 percent of Hispanic households have computers, compared to 47 percent of white households. This disparity exists even at household incomes lower than $15,000. According to a New York Times article by Pam Belluck, "at the lowest income levels, the gap is great—a child in a low-income white family is three times as likely to have Internet access as a child in a low-income black family."

18l   Preparing a Final Draft

I've finished my final draft, and I've put together my Works Cited list and prepared my formal outline. I've also decided on a title for my paper: The Great Digital Divide. I'll read through my paper one more time to check for grammar mistakes and typos, and then I'll print it out and turn it in.

18m   The Completed Paper

Kim Romney's completed research paper, "The Great Digital Divide," appears on the pages that follow. The paper, which uses MLA documentation style, is accompanied by a title page, a sentence outline, a notes page, and a Works Cited list.

NOTE: Although MLA style does not require a title page or an outline, many instructors do; for an example of a first page that conforms to MLA style, see **55c.**

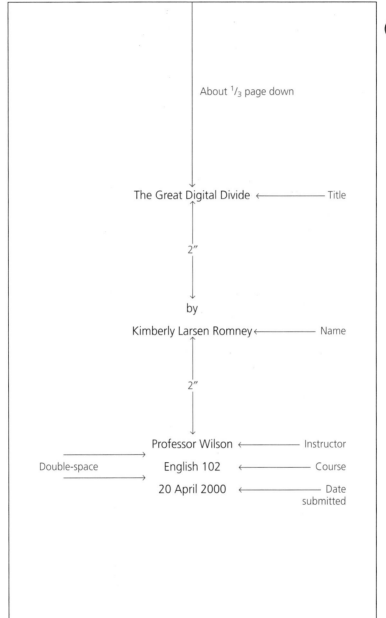

About ⅓ page down

The Great Digital Divide ⟵———— Title

↑
2″
↓

by

Kimberly Larsen Romney ⟵———— Name

↑
2″
↓

Professor Wilson ⟵———— Instructor

Double-space ⟶
⟶

English 102 ⟵———— Course

20 April 2000 ⟵———— Date submitted

½ inch

Romney i

Center ⟶   Outline ⟵——————— Double-space

1 inch

Thesis Statement: The Internet threatens to leave many people behind, creating two distinct classes—those who have access and those who do not.

1 inch → I. The Internet's popularity has soared in recent years, but it has existed for more than thirty years.

    A. The Internet began in 1969 as ARPANET, a communication system designed to survive nuclear attacks.

    B. It was expanded in 1972 into a system of interconnected networks.

    C. In the 1990s, HTML was created to allow information on the Internet to be displayed graphically.

II. Today, many people believe the Internet has ushered in a new age.

    A. Former Vice President Al Gore sees the Internet as an empowering tool.

    B. Gore believes the Internet will bring knowledge and prosperity to the entire world.

III. For many people, however, the benefits of the Internet are not nearly this obvious or far-reaching.

    A. The Internet is still out of reach for many Americans.

        1. Low-income and minority households are less likely than others to have computers.

        2. For minorities, Internet content may be as much of a problem as economics.

    B. People without Internet access have difficulties at school, trouble obtaining employment, and fewer opportunities to save money and time as consumers.

1 inch

Romney ii

    C. The Internet is widening the economic and social divide that already separates Americans.

IV. Public officials, the government, corporations, nonprofit organizations, and public libraries are making efforts to bridge the gap between the "haves" and "have-nots."

    A. President Clinton proposed "to help 5,000 schools a year make immediate and urgent repairs" in his 2000 State of the Union address.

    B. The federal government has launched programs like SLD and Neighborhood Networks to provide free Internet access to impoverished communities.

    C. Congress is making efforts to decrease the gap between the "haves" and the "have-nots."

    D. Corporations are sponsoring programs like Power Up.

    E. Nonprofit organizations like PBS and The Civil Rights Forum are working to raise public awareness.

    F. Public libraries are working to increase public access to the Internet and computers.

V. Despite these efforts, much still needs to be done.

    A. We must make the Internet available to the widest possible audience.

    B. We must provide training to people unfamiliar with the new technology.

    C. We must target low-income and minority families and the elderly for this training.

1 inch

½ inch
Romney 1

The Great Digital Divide ← — Center
← — Double-space

indent
½ inch → Today, a basic understanding of computers and how to use them is necessary for success. For this reason, those who are unfamiliar with modern digital technology find themselves at a great disadvantage when it comes to education and employment. One of the most exciting digital technologies

1 inch → available is the information superhighway—better known as the Internet. The Internet, with its accompanying software and services, is rapidly changing the way we access and see information. Although the Internet offers great promise, it has also created some problems. Perhaps the most serious of these problems is that the Internet threatens to leave many people behind, creating two distinct classes—those who have access and those who do not.

Thesis statement

The Internet's popularity has soared in recent years, but the Internet has existed for more than thirty years. It began in 1969 under the name ARPANET (ARPA stood for Advanced Research Projects Agency, which was part of the United States Department of Defense). During the Cold War, the United States government allocated funds to establish a communication system that would survive a nuclear attack, and ARPANET was created to serve this purpose. The goal was to build a network that would function even if part of it were destroyed. The first ARPANET system consisted of just four connected computers, but by 1972, fifty universities and

¶s 2–4 present background on history of the Internet, summarizing information from two sources.

Romney 2

research facilities (all doing research for the military) were linked (Gibbs and Smith 5).

Beginning in 1972, researchers decided to expand the scope of this project. They wanted to find a way to increase the number of computers that could be on ARPANET. Researchers established a collection of protocols called TCP/IP (Transmission Control Protocol/Internet Protocol). The conversion to TCP/IP, completed in 1983, allowed ARPANET to connect all the new networks (UNIX, USENET, and BITNET, for example) that had come into existence since 1972. This new system was given the name Internet (Wendall).

Finally, in the 1990s, a computer language called HTML (HyperText Markup Language) was created to allow information on the Internet to be displayed graphically. Whereas the older networks on the Internet looked like typed pages, HTML displayed information in a more visually stimulating format. This advance gave rise to the World Wide Web, which allowed users to access text, graphics, sound, and even video while moving from one site to another simply by clicking on a hypertext link. This in turn made the Internet more accessible and aroused unprecedented interest in the new digital technology (Wendall).

Today, many people believe the Internet has ushered in a new age, one in which this instant communication will bring

Romney 3

people closer together and eventually even eliminate
national boundaries. Former Vice President Al Gore takes
this optimistic view, observing that the Internet is a means
"to deepen and extend our oldest and most cherished
global values: rising standards of living and literacy, an ever-
widening circle of freedom, and individual empowerment."
Gore goes on to say that he can see the day when we will
"extend our knowledge and our prosperity to our most
isolated inner cities, to the barrios, the favelas, the colonias,
and our most remote rural villages."

> Material from Internet source, introduced by author's name, does not include a parenthetical reference directing reader to a paragraph or page number because this information was not provided in the electronic text.

For many people, however, the benefits of the Internet are
not nearly this obvious or far-reaching. In fact, despite Gore's
optimistic predictions, the Internet is still out of reach for many
Americans, and this has created what the NAACP and others
have called a "digital divide" ("NAACP Targets Minority Gap"): a
large percentage of the poor, elderly, disabled, and members of
many minority groups are excluded from current technological
advancements, and there is a widening gap between those who
have access to this new technology and those who do not.

> Parenthetical documentation refers to an article accessed from the Internet.

A recent survey by the Department of Commerce shows
that people with higher annual household incomes and whites
are more likely to own computers than minorities and people
from low-income households. Approximately 80 percent of
households with incomes of $75,000 or above have computers,
compared to 16 percent of households earning $10,000-

> Paragraph synthesizes information from a Commerce Department study and a newspaper article.

Romney 4

$15,000. The survey also found that in households with incomes between $15,000 and $34,999, only 23 percent of African-American and 26 percent of Hispanic households have computers, compared to 47 percent of white households. This disparity exists even at incomes lower than $15,000. According to a New York Times article by Pam Belluck, "at the lowest income levels, the gap is great—a child in a low-income white family is three times as likely to have Internet access as a child in a low-income black family."

Graph summarizes relevant data. (AIEA stands for American Indian, Eskimo, Aleut; API stands for Asian Pacific Islander.) Source information is typed directly below the figure. This information does *not* appear in the Works Cited list.

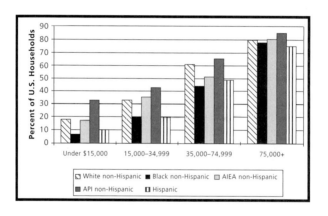

Fig. 1. Percent of U.S. Households with a Computer by Income by Race/Origin, 1998, United States Department of Commerce and National Telecommunications and Information Administration, "Falling through the Net: Defining the Digital Divide," November 1999 <http://www.ntia.doc.gov/ntiahome/fttn99/FTTN_I/Chart-I-14.html>.

Romney 5

Although the Commerce Department study seems to indicate that financial circumstances create the "digital divide," the gap in computer ownership across incomes hints that other factors might be contributing to the disparity. Henry Louis Gates, Jr., argues that bridging the digital divide will "require more than cheap PC's, it will involve content." African Americans are not interested in the Internet, Gates writes, because the content rarely appeals to them. Gates comparesthe lack of interest in the Internet with the history of African-Americans' relationship with the recording industry: "Blacks began to respond to this new medium only when mainstream companies like Columbia Records introduced so-called race records, blues and jazz discs aimed at a nascent African-American market." Gates believes that Web sites that address the needs of African Americans can play the same role that race records did for the music industry. Ignoring this problem, Gates warns, will lead to a form of cyber-segregation that will devastate the African American community.[1]

People without Internet access have difficulty at school, trouble obtaining employment, and fewer opportunities to save money and time as consumers. For example, those to whom the Internet is not available are denied access to special airline discounts, savings on long-distance carriers, and lower prices on computer software. More important, they lack access

Summary of a newspaper op-ed piece includes two quotations. Because source is mentioned frequently in running acknowledgments, no parenthetical references are needed.

Superscript indentifies content note.

Romney 6

to educational and research materials and to jobs posted on the Web. With access to only a portion of available goods and services, people who are off-line do not have the advantages that people who are online can routinely get.

> Their choices will be restricted, and they're going to pay a little bit more for things and they'll have fewer options [. . .] and it's not going to be one of these things where you see the digital homeless on the street, or sleeping on the steps of City Hall. It's going to be an invisible problem. The people who are digitally dispossessed may not even appreciate that they are dispossessed. (Belluck)

Clearly, the Internet is widening the economic and social divide that already separates people in this country.

Many public officials recognize the potential danger of the "digital divide" and are taking steps to narrow the gap. Bill Clinton addressed the technology boom and its effect on education in his 2000 State of the Union speech. According to Clinton, schools need more than software and computers if they are to enter the information age. Many schools, he pointed out, have wiring and walls that must be repaired before students can access the Internet. President Clinton proposed "to help 5,000 schools a year make immediate and urgent repairs [. . .] and [. . .] to help build or modernize 6,000 more, to get students out of trailers and into high-tech

Quotation of more than four lines is typed as a block, indented ten spaces (or one inch) and double spaced with no quotation marks. Parenthetical documentation is placed one space after end punctuation.

Summary of Bill Clinton's remarks on the digital divide includes quoted material. Bracketed ellipses indicate that the student has deleted words from the quotation.

Romney 7

classrooms." The president added, "Opportunity for all requires something else [. . .] having access to a computer and knowing how to use it. That means we must close the digital divide between those who've got the tools and those who don't."

The federal government is making an effort to narrow the "digital divide" by sponsoring several programs aimed at those groups who are in danger of becoming "have-nots." One example of their efforts is the Schools and Libraries Division of the Universal Service Administrative Company. This service, known as SLD, provides eligible schools and libraries with discounted access to telecommunications services, and to the Internet ("The Schools and Libraries Division"). Another government program, Neighborhood Networks, is sponsored by the U.S. Department of Housing and Urban Development (HUD) and works to provide computer-training centers to people living in private homes that are assisted or insured by HUD. Neighborhood Networks offers grants, loans, and volunteer services to support the centers, which are organized by local residents and designed to fit the needs of a particular community. The centers offer a variety of programs, but some include Internet access and computer-use training. As a result of programs like Neighborhood Networks and SLD, the government hopes to target those groups that are at risk of being left behind and provide them with access to the Internet and other technology ("About Neighborhood Networks").

Because no author is listed, parenthetical reference cites a shortened version of the source's title.

Romney 8

Exact wording of a key piece of legislation is quoted to eliminate any possibility of misinterpretation.

Congress, too, is making efforts to decrease the gap between the "haves" and "have-nots." In the Telecommunications Act of 1996, the Federal Communications Commission was directed to "set rules requiring telephone and cable television companies to provide 'universal access' to new services, like the Internet" (Lohr). Legislators hope this language will encourage regulators to "mandate access and cut-rate service for schools and public libraries" (Lohr).[2]

Each quotation requires its own parenthetical reference even though both cite the same source.

Corporations are also concerned with the growing divide between those who have access to the Internet and those who do not. They, too, are sponsoring programs whose goal is to aid the technologically illiterate. A program called Power Up is just one example. Over a dozen corporations, nonprofit organizations, and federal agencies have joined forces to provide Internet access and computer training to children in lower-income communities. One Power Up initiative will use grants from the Waitt Family Foundation and the AOL Foundation to purchase 50,000 computers and 100,000 AOL accounts that will be given to community centers and schools throughout the country (Power Up).

Nonprofit organizations are also entering the war on the "digital divide." In an effort to raise public awareness, the Public Broadcasting Corporation (PBS) created a series called Digital Divide. The series investigates the effects of the "digital divide" in terms of race and gender in the classroom and at

Romney 9

work. For example, the second hour of the series, entitled "Virtual Diversity," examines the way many females and minorities feel alienated from technology. According to this program, the dynamic of a co-ed classroom as well as the lack of appealing content make technology seem inaccessible to both women and minorities. Only by including content that is interesting to women and minorities and changing teaching methods can we make technology and the Internet accessible to these populations (<u>Digital Divide</u>).

Parenthetical documentation cites an Internet source.

    Another nonprofit organization working to bridge the "digital divide" is the Civil Rights Forum, which "works to bring civil rights organizations and community groups into the current debate over the future of our media environment" ("Missions and Goals"). The Civil Rights Forum's main purpose is to raise public awareness, and it does so by conducting research on communications policies, providing educational materials, and creating links between "civil rights groups, communications policy activists, neighborhood technology centers, and the academic community." By opening the discussion of the "digital divide" to civil rights groups, this organization hopes to focus attention on those who may become "have-nots" and to encourage the government, corporations, and individuals to take action ("Mission and Goals").

Paragraph summarizes purpose of CRF, quoting from its mission statement.

    Finally, public libraries are also attempting to address the needs of those without access to computers and the Internet.

Romney 10

Libraries have always been responsible for providing free information to the public, and the Internet and other sources of digital information have presented them with a great challenge. According to Dr. Robert Martin, a professor of library science at Texas Woman's University, libraries are currently making several efforts to bridge the "digital divide." One of these efforts is the "installation and maintenance of large numbers of networked computers that are available for public use" (Martin). These computers can be used in a variety of ways, including accessing the Internet, word processing, and creating spreadsheets.

Although libraries are making many efforts to increase access to the Internet and computers, several obstacles stand in their way. One of the most obvious is funding. Although many libraries receive money from organizations like the Gates Foundation, these programs often "provide only for the initial startup expenses of hardware and software" (Martin). Many libraries actually need funds for more practical problems. As Martin points out, "For some small rural libraries, such simple problems as having a table to put a computer on, or even having space in the library to put the table, are actual and real impediments to expanding digital access." Furthermore, unlike books and other print materials, hardware and software must be updated, and this adds to an already expensive endeavor. Finally, librarians must be trained so that they understand

Running acknowledgments and parenthetical documentation in these two paragraphs refer to an e-mail interview. Each quotation has its own reference.

Romney 11

computer use and can help patrons as they use computers and the Internet: "It is not enough just to have the hardware sitting on the table—it is also imperative to provide training to library staff on using and maintaining the resources" (Martin).

Despite the efforts of government, businesses, and nonprofit organizations, much still needs to be done to ensure that everyone has access to the Internet. First, we must continue efforts to make the Internet available to the widest possible audience. Although public officials, the government, corporations, nonprofit organizations, and public libraries sponsor programs aimed at increasing access, we often overlook the simple and easily solved problems that stand in the way—problems like the damaged walls and phone connections that are keeping many schools from going online and the lack of adequate space or appropriate furniture in libraries. Solving these and similar problems could help widen Internet access. Another way we can make the Internet available to a wider audience is by increasing the variety of content available on the Internet. Although many programs are in place that address access and training needs, little effort has been made to increase the content on the Internet aimed at minorities. We must also continue to provide training to people unfamiliar with new technology, and we must ensure that the instructors

Conclusion recommends solutions for problem of "digital divide." Because paragraph introduces no new material (it summarizes material already discussed and presents student's original conclusions), no documentation is necessary.

Romney 12

who are teaching these new technology skills understand the
equipment and software they are explaining. Finally, we must
target low-income and minority families (particularly those in
rural areas) for this training because these are the most likely
"have-nots." Unless we take steps to make the Internet
available to all, we will quickly become two separate and
unequal societies: one "plugged-in" and privileged and one
"unplugged" and marginalized.

Emphatic final
sentence
echoes the
title.

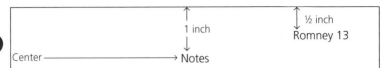

1 inch

½ inch
Romney 13

Center ⟶ Notes

Indents 5 ⟶ [1] Interestingly, Gates also acknowledges that African
spaces
(or   Americans bear some of the responsibility for changing the
½ inch)
          situation.

[2] The Telecommunications Act also established a board

to recommend policies that would preserve and advance

universal service.

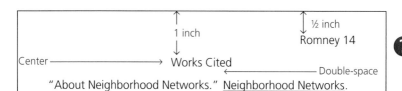

↑
1 inch
↓

↓ ½ inch

Romney 14

Center ——————————→ Works Cited
←—————— Double-space

"About Neighborhood Networks." <u>Neighborhood Networks</u>.

Indents 5 →3 May 2000. 26 June 2000 <http://www.
spaces
(or one-half digitaldividenetwork.org/frameset.adp?url=http%3a%
inch)
2f%2fwww%2ehud%2egov%2fnnw%2fnnwindex%

2ehtml>.

Belluck, Pam. "What Price Will Be Paid by Those Not on the

Net?" <u>New York Times on the Web</u> 22 Sept. 1999.

Long URL
cannot be
divided after a
slash. For this
reason, URL is
broken in
logical places.

26 July 2000 <http://search3.nytimes.com/search/daily/

bin/fastweb?getdoc+site+site+124947+32+wAAA+

What%7EPrice%7Ewill%7Ebe%7EPaid%7Eby%7EThose%

7ENot%7Eon%7Ethe%7ENet>.

Clinton, William J. <u>2000 State of the Union Address</u>.

27 January 2000. 5 July 2000 <http://

www.whitehouse.gov/WH/SOTU00/sotu-text.html>.

<u>Digital Divide</u>. 1 April 2000. 24 June 2000 <http://

www.pbs.org/digitaldivide/about.about.html#series>.

Gates, Henry Louis, Jr. "One Internet, Two Nations." <u>New York</u>

<u>Times</u> 31 October 1999, late ed.: A25.

Gibbs, Mark, and Richard Smith. <u>Navigating the Internet</u>.

Indianapolis: SAMS, 1993.

Gore, Al. "Building a Global Community." Remarks Prepared

for the 15th International ITU Conference. 12 Oct. 1998.

69 pars. 5 July 2000 <http://www.itu.int/Newsarchive/

press/PP98/Documents/Statement_Gore.html>.

Romney 15

Lohr, Steve. "The Great Unplugged Masses Confront the

Future." New York Times on the Web 21 Apr. 1996.

26 July 2000 <http://search3.nytimes.com/search/daily/

bin/fastweb?getdoc+site+site+29519+0+wAAA+The%

7EGreat%7Eunplugged%7EMasses>.

Martin, Robert S., Ph.D. E-mail interview. 7 July 2000.

"Mission and Goals." The Civil Rights Forum. June 2000.

23 June 2000 <http://www.civilrightsforum.org/text/

mission.htm>.

"NAACP Targets Minority Gap in Internet Use, TV Roles."

CNN.Com 13 July 1999. 3 July 2000 <http://

www.cnn.com/US/9907/13/naacp.gap/>.

Power Up. 25 June 2000 <http://

www.digitaldividenetwork.org/

frameset.adp?url=http%3a%2f%2fwww%2epowerup%

2eorg>.

The Schools and Libraries Division (SLD) of the Universal

Service Administrative Company. 6 July 2000. 7 July 2000

<http://www.digitaldividenetwork.org/frameset.adp?

url=http%3a%2f%2fwww%2esl%2euniversalservice%

2eorg%2f>.

Wendall, Kyla. "Internet History." University of Regina Student

Connection Program. 18 Aug. 1997. 27 June 2000

<http://tdi.uregina.ca/~ursc/internet/history.html>.

PART 3

SENTENCE STYLE

CHAPTER 19

BUILDING SIMPLE SENTENCES

? FREQUENTLY ASKED QUESTIONS

What is a phrase? (p. 358)
What is a clause? (p. 359)
How can I compose more interesting simple
   sentences? (p. 361)

A **sentence** is an independent grammatical unit that includes a <u>subject</u> and a <u>predicate</u> and expresses a complete thought.

> <u>The quick brown fox</u> <u>jumped over the lazy dog.</u>

> <u>It</u> <u>came from outer space.</u>

A **simple subject** is a noun or noun substitute (*fox, it*) that tells who or what the sentence is about. A **simple predicate** is a verb or verb phrase (*jumped, came*) that tells or asks something about the subject. The **complete subject** of a sentence includes the simple subject plus all its modifiers (*the quick brown fox*). The **complete predicate** includes the verb or verb phrase as well as all the words associated with it—such as modifiers, objects, and complements (*jumped over the lazy dog, came from outer space*).

19a   Constructing Simple Sentences

A **simple sentence** consists of at least one subject and one predicate. Simple sentences conform to one of five basic patterns.

(1) Subject + Intransitive Verb (s + v)

The most basic simple sentence consists of just a subject and a verb or **verb phrase** (the **<u>main verb</u>** plus all its **<u>auxiliary verbs</u>**).

> ^s   ^v
> <u>The price of gold</u> <u>rose</u>.

> ^s   ^v
> <u>Stock prices</u> <u>may fall</u>.

Here the verbs *rose* and *may fall* are **intransitive**—that is, they do not need an object to complete their meaning.

(2) Subject + Transitive Verb + Direct Object (s + v + do)

Another kind of simple sentence consists of the subject, a transitive verb, and a direct object.

> s v do
> Van Gogh created *The Starry Night.*

> s v do
> Caroline saved Jake.

Here the verbs *created* and *saved* are **transitive**—each requires an object to complete its meaning in the sentence. In each sentence, the **direct object** indicates where the verb's action is directed and *who* or *what* is affected by it.

(3) Subject + Transitive Verb + Direct Object + Object Complement (s + v + do + oc)

Some simple sentences include an **object complement,** which renames or describes the direct object.

> s v do oc
> The class elected Bridget treasurer. (Object complement *treasurer* renames direct object *Bridget.*)

> s v do oc
> I found the exam easy. (Object complement *easy* describes direct object *exam.*)

(4) Subject + Linking Verb + Subject Complement (s + v + sc)

Another kind of simple sentence consists of a subject, a **linking verb** (a verb that connects a subject to its complement), and the **subject complement** (the word or phrase that describes or renames the subject).

See 32c1

> s v sc
> The injection was painless.

> s v sc
> Tony Blair became prime minister.

Note that the linking verb is like an equal sign, equating the subject with its complement (*Tony Blair = prime minister*).

(5) Subject + Transitive Verb + Indirect Object + Direct Object (s + v + io + do)

Some simple sentences include an **indirect object,** which indicates to whom or for whom the verb's action was done.

$$\underset{\text{s}}{\underline{\text{Cyrano}}} \; \underset{\text{v}}{\underline{\text{wrote}}} \; \underset{\text{io}}{\text{Roxanne}} \; \underset{\text{do}}{\text{a poem.}} \; \text{(Cyrano wrote a poem for Roxanne.)}$$

s   v   io   do
The officer handed Frank a ticket. (The officer handed a ticket to Frank.)

EXERCISE 1

In each of the following sentences, underline the subject once and the predicate twice. Then label direct objects, indirect objects, subject complements, and object complements.

sc
EXAMPLE: Isaac Asimov was a science fiction writer.

1. Isaac Asimov first saw science fiction stories in the newsstand of his parents' Brooklyn candy store.
2. He practiced writing by telling his schoolmates stories.
3. Asimov published his first story in *Astounding Science Fiction.*
4. The magazine's editor, John W. Campbell, encouraged Asimov to continue writing.
5. The young writer researched scientific principles to make his stories better.
6. Asimov's "Foundation" series of novels is a "future history."
7. The World Science Fiction Convention awarded the series a Hugo Award.
8. Sometimes Asimov used "Paul French" as a pseudonym.
9. *Biochemistry and Human Metabolism* was Asimov's first nonfiction book.
10. Asimov coined the term *robotics.*

19b   Identifying Phrases and Clauses

Individual words may be combined into *phrases* and *clauses.*

(1) Identifying Phrases

A **phrase** is a group of related words that lacks a subject or predicate or both and functions as a single part of speech. It cannot stand alone as a sentence.

- A **verb phrase** consists of a main verb and all its auxiliary verbs.

  Time <u>is flying</u>.

- A **noun phrase** includes a noun or pronoun plus all related modifiers.

  I'll climb <u>the highest mountain</u>.

- A **prepositional phrase** consists of a preposition, its object, and any modifiers of that object.

  They discussed the ethical implications <u>of the animal studies</u>.

  He was last seen heading <u>into the orange sunset</u>.

- A **verbal phrase** consists of a **verbal** (participle, gerund, or infinitive) and its related objects, modifiers, or complements. A verbal phrase may be a **participial phrase,** a **gerund phrase,** or an **infinitive phrase.**

  <u>Encouraged by the voter turnout</u>, the candidate predicted a victory. (participial phrase)

  <u>Taking it easy</u> always makes sense. (gerund phrase)

  The jury recessed <u>to evaluate the evidence</u>. (infinitive phrase)

- An **absolute phrase** usually consists of a noun and a participle, accompanied by modifiers. It modifies an entire independent clause rather than a particular word or phrase.

  <u>Their toes tapping</u>, they watched the auditions.

(2) Identifying Clauses

A **clause** is a group of related words that includes a subject and a predicate. An **independent** (main) **clause** may stand alone as a sentence, but a **dependent** (subordinate) **clause** cannot. It must always be combined with an independent clause to form a **complex sentence**.

See
20b

[Lucretia Mott was an abolitionist.] [She was also a pioneer for women's rights.] (two independent clauses)

[Lucretia Mott was an abolitionist] [who was also a pioneer for women's rights.] (independent clause, dependent clause)

[Although Lucretia Mott was most widely known for her support of women's rights,] [she was also a prominent abolitionist.] (dependent clause, independent clause)

Dependent clauses may be *adjective, adverb,* or *noun* clauses.

- **Adjective clauses,** sometimes called **relative clauses,** modify nouns or pronouns and always follow the nouns or pronouns they modify. They are introduced by relative pronouns—*that, what, whatever, which, who, whose, whom, whoever,* or *whomever,* or by the adverbs *where* or *when.*

  The television series *M*A*S*H,* which depicted life in an army hospital in Korea during the Korean War, ran for eleven years. (Adjective clause modifies the noun *M*A*S*H.*)

  William Styron's novel *Sophie's Choice* is set in Brooklyn, where the narrator lives in a house painted pink. (Adjective clause modifies the noun *Brooklyn.*)

  NOTE: Some adjective clauses, called **elliptical clauses,** are grammatically incomplete but nevertheless can be easily understood from the context of the sentence. Typically, a part of the subject or predicate or the entire subject or predicate is missing.

  Although [they were] full, they could not resist dessert.

- **Adverb clauses** modify single words (verbs, adjectives, or adverbs), entire phrases, or independent clauses. They are always introduced by subordinating conjunctions. Adverb clauses provide information to answer the questions *how? where? when? why?* and *to what extent?*

  Exhausted after the match was over, Kim decided to take a long nap. (Adverb clause modifies *exhausted,* telling *when* Kim was exhausted.)

  Mark will go wherever there's a party. (Adverb clause modifies *will go,* telling *where* Mark will go.)

  Because 75 percent of its exports are fish products, Iceland's economy is heavily dependent on the fishing industry. (Adverb clause modifies independent clause, telling *why* the fishing industry is so important.)

- **Noun clauses** function as subjects, objects, or complements. A noun clause may be introduced by a relative pronoun or by *whether, when, where, why,* or *how.*

<u>What you see</u> is <u>what you get</u>. (Noun clauses serve as subject and subject complement.)

They finally decided <u>which candidate was most qualified.</u> (Noun clause serves as direct object of verb *decided.*)

EXERCISE 2

Which of the following groups of words are independent clauses? Which are dependent clauses? Which are phrases? Label each word group *IC, DC,* or *P.*

EXAMPLE: Coming through the rye. (P)

1. Beauty is truth.
2. When knights were bold.
3. In a galaxy far away.
4. He saw stars.
5. I hear a symphony.
6. Whenever you're near.
7. The clock struck ten.
8. The red planet.
9. Slowly I turned.
10. For the longest time.

19c   Expanding Simple Sentences

A **simple sentence** is a single independent clause. A simple sentence can consist of just a subject and a verb.

<u>Jessica</u> <u>fell</u>.

Or, a simple sentence can be expanded with modifying words and phrases.

Jessica and her younger sister Victoria almost immediately fell hopelessly in love with the very mysterious Henry Goodyear.

NOTE: Joined with other clauses, simple sentences can be expanded into **compound and complex sentences**.

See
Ch. 20

See
36a

(1) Expanding Simple Sentences with Adjectives and Adverbs

Descriptive **adjectives and adverbs** can expand a simple sentence. Read this sentence again:

Jessica and her younger sister Victoria almost immediately fell hopelessly in love with the very mysterious Henry Goodyear.

Here two adjectives describe nouns.

Adjective	*Noun*
younger	sister
mysterious	Henry Goodyear

Four adverbs describe the action of verbs or modify adjectives or other adverbs.

Adverb	
almost	immediately (adverb)
immediately	fell (verb)
hopelessly	fell (verb)
very	mysterious (adjective)

EXERCISE 3

Label all descriptive adjectives and adverbs in the following sentences

                              adv   adj   adj
EXAMPLE: Marge listened secretly to the quiet conversation at the next table.

1. John swallowed the last of his cold coffee and gently set the thermos down. (Sherman Alexie, *Indian Killer*)
2. Each year I watched the field across from the Store turn caterpillar green, then gradually frosty white. (Maya Angelou, *I Know Why the Caged Bird Sings*)
3. He gingerly held the box and studied the old, familiar pictures. (Alan Lightman, *Good Benito*)
4. Stealthy and alert, he hunkers down like a predator and sneaks right up behind the seal, climbs decisively onto its back, and grips its cheeks in both hands. (Diane Ackerman, *The Rarest of the Rare*)
5. In late mammal times, the body evidently added a third brain. (Robert Bly, *The Sibling Society*)

EXERCISE 4

Using the following sentences as models, write five original simple sentences. Use adverbs and adjectives where the model sentences use them, and then underline and label these modifiers.

adv   adj
EXAMPLE: Manek gazed <u>shyly</u> at the <u>beautiful</u> girl.

adv   adv
The cat ran <u>wildly</u> around the <u>empty</u> house.

1. Walkways from the Washington Monument to the Lincoln Memorial quickly filled.
2. People, shrugging off their winter coats, seemed to step more lightly around the mall.
3. Some sat on benches in carefully pressed white shirts with half-eaten sandwiches in pale hands.
4. Others spun wildly by on bikes or Rollerblades wearing shiny spandex and torn T-shirts, sweatily celebrating the first days of spring.
5. Finally, the cherry blossoms burst into flower.

(2) Expanding Simple Sentences with Nouns and Verbals

Nouns and verbals can help you build richer simple sentences.

Nouns   Nouns can act as adjectives modifying other nouns.

He needed two <u>cake</u> pans for the <u>layer</u> cake.

Verbals   **Verbals,** which include participles, infinitives, and gerunds, may act as modifiers or as nouns.

See
32c2

All the <u>living</u> former presidents attended the funeral. (Present participle acts as adjective.)

The Grand Canyon is the attraction <u>to visit</u>. (Infinitive acts as adjective.)

The puzzle was impossible <u>to solve</u>. (Infinitive acts as adverb.)

When the <u>going</u> gets tough, the tough get going. (Gerund acts as noun.)

<u>To err</u> is human. (Infinitive acts as noun.)

It took me an entire three-hour lab period to identify my <u>unknown</u>. (Past participle acts as noun.)

EXERCISE 5

For additional practice in building simple sentences with individual words, combine each of the following groups of sentences into one simple sentence that contains several modifiers. You will have to add, delete, or reorder words.

EXAMPLE: The night was cold. The night was wet. The night scared them. They were terribly scared.

REVISED: The cold, wet night scared them terribly.

1. The ship landed. The ship was from space. The ship was tremendous. It landed silently.
2. It landed in a field. The field was grassy. The field was deserted.
3. A dog appeared. The dog was tiny. The dog was abandoned. The dog was a stray.
4. The dog was brave. The dog was curious. He approached the spacecraft. The spacecraft was burning. He approached it carefully.
5. A creature emerged from the spaceship. The creature was smiling. He was purple. He emerged slowly.
6. The dog and the alien stared at each other. The dog was little. The alien was purple. They stared meaningfully.
7. The dog and the alien walked. They walked silently. They walked carefully. They walked toward each other.
8. The dog barked. He barked tentatively. He barked questioningly. The dog was uneasy.
9. The alien extended his hand. The alien was grinning. He extended it slowly. The hand was hairy.
10. In his hand was a bag. The bag was made of canvas. The bag was green. The bag was for laundry.

(3) Expanding Simple Sentences with Prepositional Phrases

See 32f

A **preposition** indicates the relationship between a noun or noun substitute and other words in a sentence. A **prepositional phrase** consists of the preposition, its object (the noun or noun substitute), and any modifiers of that object. Prepositional phrases can function in a sentence as *adjectives* or as *adverbs*.

prep   obj

Carry Nation was a crusader <u>for temperance</u>. (Prepositional phrase functions as adjective modifying the noun *crusader*.)

prep   mod   obj
The Madeira River flows <u>into the mighty Amazon</u>. (Prepositional phrase functions as adverb modifying the verb *flows*.)

EXERCISE 6

Read the following sentences. Underline each prepositional phrase, and then connect it with an arrow to the word it modifies. Finally, tell whether each phrase functions as an adjective or an adverb.

EXAMPLE: The porch <u>of her grandmother's house</u> wraps <u>around all three sides</u>.

adj   adv

1. Carol sat on the front porch and rocked in her grandmother's chair.
2. Age had surprised her in the middle of her life, crept up behind her in the mirror, and attacked her at the joints of her knees and hips.
3. Now she sat on the porch—Juliet's balcony in her memories—and felt that it too creaked in the joints.
4. Inside the house, her grandmother slept in a narrow bed under a worn chenille spread, the mattress sagging and spilling over the edges of the frame.
5. The slow rocking of the chair soothed the worries from the edges of Carol's eyes.

EXERCISE 7

For additional practice in using prepositional phrases, combine each pair of sentences to create one simple sentence that includes a prepositional phrase. You may add, delete, or reorder words. Some sentences may have more than one possible correct version.

EXAMPLE: America's drinking water is being contaminated. Toxic substances are contaminating it.

REVISED: America's drinking water is being contaminated by toxic substances.

1. Toxic waste disposal presents a serious problem. Americans have this problem.
2. Hazardous chemicals pose a threat. People are threatened.
3. Some towns, like Times Beach, Missouri, have been completely abandoned. Their residents have abandoned them.

4. Dioxin is one chemical. It has serious toxic effects.
5. Dioxin is highly toxic. The toxicity affects animals and humans.
6. Toxic chemical wastes like dioxin may be found. Over fifty thousand dumps have them.
7. Industrial parks contain toxic wastes. Open pits, ponds, and lagoons are where the toxic substances are.
8. Toxic wastes pose dangers. The land, water, and air are endangered.
9. In addition, toxic substances are a threat. They threaten our public health and our economy.
10. Immediate toxic waste cleanup would be a tremendous benefit. Americans are the ones who would benefit.

(4) Expanding Simple Sentences with Verbal Phrases

See
19b1

A **verbal phrase** consists of a **verbal** (participle, gerund, or infinitive) and its related objects, modifiers, or complements.

Some verbal phrases act as nouns. For example, **gerund phrases,** like gerunds themselves, are always used as nouns. **Infinitive phrases** may also be used as nouns.

<u>Making a living</u> isn't always easy. (Gerund phrase serves as sentence's subject.)

Wendy appreciated <u>Tom's being honest</u>. (Gerund phrase serves as object of verb *appreciated*.)

The entire town was shocked by <u>their breaking up</u>. (Gerund phrase is object of preposition *by*.)

<u>To know him</u> is <u>to love him</u>. (Infinitive phrase *To know him* serves as sentence's subject; infinitive phrase *to love him* is subject complement.)

Other verbal phrases act as modifiers. **Participial phrases** always function as adjectives; **infinitive phrases** may function as adjectives or as adverbs.

<u>Fascinated by Scheherazade's story</u>, they waited anxiously for the next installment. (Participial phrase modifies pronoun *they*.)

It wasn't the ideal time <u>to do homework</u>. (Infinitive phrase modifies noun *time*.)

Henry M. Stanley went to Africa <u>to find Dr. Livingstone</u>. (Infinitive phrase modifies verb *went*.)

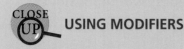

CLOSE UP   **USING MODIFIERS**

See 26a2; 26b1

When you use verbal phrases as modifiers, be especially careful not to create **misplaced modifiers** or **dangling modifiers**.

EXERCISE 8

For practice in using verbal phrases, combine each of these sentence pairs to create one simple sentence that contains a participial phrase, a gerund phrase, or an infinitive phrase. Underline and label the verbal phrase in your sentence. You will have to add, delete, or reorder words, and you may find more than one way to combine each pair.

EXAMPLE: The American labor movement has helped millions of workers. It has won them higher wages and better working conditions.

REVISED: The American labor movement has helped millions of

participial phrase
workers, <u>winning them higher wages and better working conditions.</u>

1. In 1912 the textile workers of Lawrence, Massachusetts, went on strike. They were demonstrating for "Bread and Roses, too."
2. The workers wanted higher wages and better working conditions. They felt trapped in their miserable jobs.
3. Mill workers toiled six days a week. They earned about $1.50 for this.
4. Most of the workers were women and children. They worked up to sixteen hours a day.
5. The mills were dangerous. They were filled with hazards.
6. Many mill workers joined unions. They did this to fight exploitation by their employers.
7. They wanted to improve their lives. This was their goal.
8. Finally, twenty-five thousand workers walked off their jobs. They knew they were risking everything.
9. The police and the state militia were called in. Attacking the strikers was their mission.
10. After sixty-three days, the American Woolen Company surrendered. This ended the strike with a victory for the workers.

(Adapted from William Cahn, *Lawrence 1912: The Bread and Roses Strike*)

(5) Expanding Simple Sentences with Appositives

An **appositive** is a noun or a noun phrase that identifies or renames an adjacent noun or pronoun.

> Farrington hated his boss, <u>a real tyrant</u>. (Appositive *a real tyrant* identifies noun *boss*.)

> <u>A barrier island off the coast of New Jersey</u>, Long Beach Island is a popular vacation spot. (Appositive *A barrier island off the coast of New Jersey* identifies noun *Long Beach Island*.)

NOTE: Appositives are sometimes introduced by the phrases *such as, or, that is, for example,* or *in other words.*

> A regional airline, <u>such as Southwest</u>, frequently accounts for more than half the departures at so-called second-tier airports.

> Rabies, <u>or hydrophobia</u>, was nearly always fatal until Pasteur's work.

For information on punctuating sentences that include appositives, see **38d1.**

EXERCISE 9

For practice in using appositives when you write, build five new simple sentences by combining each of the following pairs, turning one sentence in each pair into an appositive. (Note that each pair can be combined in a variety of different ways and that the appositive can precede or follow the noun it modifies.) You may need to delete or reorder words in some cases.

> EXAMPLE: René Descartes was a noted French philosopher. Descartes is best known for his famous declaration, "I think, therefore I am."

> REVISED: René Descartes, <u>a noted French philosopher</u>, is best known for his famous declaration, "I think, therefore I am."

1. *I Know Why the Caged Bird Sings* is the first book in Maya Angelou's autobiography. It deals primarily with her life as a young girl in Stamps, Arkansas.
2. Catgut is a tough cord generally made from the intestines of sheep. Catgut is used for tennis rackets, for violin strings, and for surgical stitching.
3. Hermes was the messenger of the Greek gods. He is usually portrayed as an athletic youth wearing a cap and winged sandals.

4. Emiliano Zapata was a hero of the Mexican Revolution. He is credited with effecting land reform in his home state of Morelos.
5. Pulsars are celestial objects that emit regular pulses of radiation. Pulsars were discovered in 1967.

(6) Expanding Simple Sentences with Compound Constructions

A **compound construction** consists of two or more grammatically **parallel** items, equivalent in importance. Within simple sentences, compound words or phrases—subjects, predicates, complements, or modifiers—may be joined in one of three ways.

- With commas:

  He took one <u>long</u>, <u>loving</u> look at his '57 Chevy.

- With a **coordinating conjunction**:

  They <u>reeled</u>, <u>whirled</u>, <u>flounced</u>, <u>capered</u>, <u>gamboled</u>, <u>and</u> <u>spun</u>. (Kurt Vonnegut, Jr., "Harrison Bergeron")

- With a pair of **correlative conjunctions** (*both/and, not only/but also, either/or, neither/nor, whether/or*):

  <u>Both milk and carrots</u> contain Vitamin A.

  <u>Neither the twentieth-century poet Sylvia Plath nor the nineteenth-century poet Emily Dickinson</u> achieved recognition during her lifetime.

EXERCISE 10

A. Expand each of the following sentences by using compound subjects and/or predicates.

    EXAMPLE: Bill played guitar.

    REVISED: Bill and Juan played guitar and sang.

B. Then expand your simple sentence with modifying words and phrases, using compound constructions whenever possible.

    EXAMPLE: Despite butterflies in their stomachs and a restless audience, Bill and Juan played guitar and sang.

1. Cortés explored the New World.
2. Virginia Woolf wrote novels.

3. Edison invented the phonograph.
4. PBS airs educational television programming.
5. Thomas Jefferson signed the Declaration of Independence.

EXERCISE 11

To practice building sentences with compound subjects, predicates, and modifiers, combine the following groups of sentences into one.

EXAMPLE: Marion studied. Frank studied. They studied quietly. They studied diligently.

REVISED: Marion and Frank studied quietly and diligently.

1. Robert Ludlum writes best-selling spy thrillers. Tom Clancy writes best-selling spy thrillers. John le Carré writes best-selling spy thrillers.
2. Smoking can cause heart disease. A high-fat, high-cholesterol diet can cause heart disease. Stress can cause heart disease.
3. Walter Mosley and Sue Grafton write detective novels. They both write about "hard-boiled" detectives.
4. Successful rock bands give concerts. They record albums. They make videos. They license merchandise bearing their names and likenesses.
5. Sports superstars like Tiger Woods and Michael Jordan earn additional income by making personal appearances. They earn money by endorsing products.

CHAPTER 20

BUILDING COMPOUND AND COMPLEX SENTENCES

❓ FREQUENTLY ASKED QUESTIONS

How are compound sentences constructed?
  (p. 371)
When should I use a compound sentence?
  (p. 371)
How are complex sentences constructed?
  (p. 374)

20a Building Compound Sentences

A **compound sentence** is created when two or more independent ❓
clauses are joined with *coordinating conjunctions, transitional words or
phrases, correlative conjunctions, semicolons,* or *colons.*

USE COMPOUND SENTENCES   ❓

- to show addition (*and, in addition, not only . . . but also*)
- to show contrast (*but, however*)
- to show cause and effect (*so, therefore, consequently*)
- to present a choice of alternatives (*or, either . . . or*)

---

(1) Using Coordinating Conjunctions

You can join two **independent clauses** with a **coordinating conjunction**—*and, or, nor, but, for, so,* or *yet*—preceded by a comma.

[The cowboy is a workingman], <u>yet</u> [he has little in common with the
urban blue-collar worker]. (John R. Erickson, *The Modern Cowboy*)

[In the fall the war was always there], <u>but</u> [we did not go to it any
more]. (Ernest Hemingway, "In Another Country")

Elementary Rules of Composition for Strunk's *Elements of Style*
  http://www.bartleby.com/141/strunk.html#III

[She carried a thin, small cane made from an umbrella], _and_ [with this she kept tapping the frozen earth in front of her]. (Eudora Welty, "A Worn Path")

(2) Using Transitional Words and Phrases

You can join two independent clauses with a **transitional word or phrase,** preceded by a semicolon (and followed by a comma).

[Aerobic exercise can help lower blood pressure]; _however,_ [those with high blood pressure should still limit salt intake].

[The saxophone does not belong to the brass family]; _in fact,_ [it is a member of the woodwind family].

Commonly used **transitional words and phrases** include **conjunctive adverbs** like _however, therefore, nevertheless, consequently, finally, still,_ and _thus_ and expressions like _for example, in fact, on the other hand,_ and _for instance._

(3) Using Correlative Conjunctions

You can use **correlative conjunctions** to join two independent clauses into a compound sentence.

Either he left his coat in his locker, _or_ he left it on the bus.

(4) Using Semicolons

A **semicolon** can link two closely related independent clauses.

[Alaska is the largest state]; [Rhode Island is the smallest].

[Theodore Roosevelt was president after the Spanish-American War]; [Andrew Johnson was president after the Civil War].

(5) Using Colons

A **colon** can link two independent clauses.

He got his orders: he was to leave for France on Sunday.

They thought they knew the outcome: Truman would lose to Dewey.

EXERCISE 1

After reading the following paragraph, use coordination to build as many compound sentences as you think your readers need to understand the links between ideas. When you have finished, bracket the independent clauses and underline the coordinating conjunctions, correlative conjunctions, or punctuation marks that link clauses.

Paolo Soleri came to the United States from Italy. He came as an apprentice to Frank Lloyd Wright. Frank Lloyd Wright's designs celebrate the suburban lifestyle, with stand-alone homes meant for single families. Soleri's Utopian designs celebrate the city. Soleri believes that suburban lifestyles separate people from true nature. He also believes that our lifestyle separates us from the energy of the city. His first theoretical design was called Mesa City. It proposed to house two million people. Soleri is currently building one of his dream cities, Arcosanti, in the desert outside of Scottsdale, Arizona. This project is funded privately by Soleri. He teaches design and building classes to students who help build the city. The students' tuition helps pay for construction. He also makes wind bells and chimes. He sells these all over the world. The profits further finance Arcosanti. The design for Arcosanti evokes images of colonies erected on space stations. It also resembles the hillside towns in Soleri's home country, Italy. The problems with our current city structures grow each year. People are looking for ways to revitalize the city. Some are looking at Soleri's Arcosanti as a model for sustainable urban development and renewal.

EXERCISE 2

Add appropriate coordinating conjunctions, conjunctive adverbs, or correlative conjunctions as indicated to combine each pair of sentences into one well-constructed compound sentence that retains the meaning of the original pair. Be sure to use correct punctuation.

EXAMPLE: The American population is aging. People seem to be increasingly concerned about what they eat. (coordinating conjunction)

REVISED: The American population is aging, so people seem to be increasingly concerned about what they eat.

1. The average American consumes 128 pounds of sugar each year. Most of us eat much more sugar than any other food additive, including salt. (conjunctive adverb)

2. Many of us are determined to reduce our sugar intake. We have consciously eliminated sweets from our diets. (conjunctive adverb)
3. Unfortunately, sugar is not found only in sweets. It is also found in many processed foods. (correlative conjunction)
4. Processed foods like puddings and cake contain sugar. Foods like ketchup and spaghetti sauce do too. (coordinating conjunction)
5. We are trying to cut down on sugar. We find limiting sugar intake extremely difficult. (coordinating conjunction)
6. Processors may use sugar in foods for taste. They may also use it to help prevent foods from spoiling and to improve the texture and appearance of food. (correlative conjunction)
7. Sugar comes in many different forms. It is easy to overlook on a package label. (coordinating conjunction)
8. Sugar may be called sucrose or fructose. It may also be called corn syrup, corn sugar, brown sugar, honey, or molasses. (coordinating conjunction)
9. No sugar is more nourishing than the others. It really doesn't matter which is consumed. (conjunctive adverb)
10. Sugars contain empty calories. Whenever possible, they should be avoided. (conjunctive adverb)

(Adapted from *Jane Brody's Nutrition Book*)

20b Building Complex Sentences

❓ A **complex sentence** consists of one **independent clause** and at least one **dependent clause.**

A dependent clause cannot stand alone; it must be combined with an independent clause to form a sentence. A **subordinating conjunction** or **relative pronoun** links the independent and dependent clauses and indicates the relationship between them.

        dependent clause   independent clause
[After the town was evacuated], [the hurricane began].

     independent clause   dependent clause
[Officials watched the storm], [which threatened to destroy the town].

Sometimes a dependent clause may be embedded within an independent clause.

          dependent clause
Town officials, [who were very concerned], watched the storm.

FREQUENTLY USED SUBORDINATING CONJUNCTIONS

after	in order that	unless
although	now that	until
as	once	when
as if	rather than	whenever
as though	since	where
because	so that	whereas
before	that	wherever
even though	though	while
if		

RELATIVE PRONOUNS

that	whatever	who (whose, whom)
what	which	whoever (whomever)

EXERCISE 3

Bracket the independent and dependent clauses in the following complex sentences. Then, using these sentences as models, create two new complex sentences in imitation of each. For each set of new sentences, use the same subordinating conjunction or relative pronoun that appears in the original.

1. I said what I meant.
2. Savion Glover is the dancer who best exemplifies the phrase "poetry in motion."
3. Because she was considered a heretic, Joan of Arc was burned at the stake.
4. The oracle at Delphi predicted that Oedipus would murder his father and marry his mother.
5. The ghost vanished before Hamlet could question him further.

EXERCISE 4

Use a subordinating conjunction or relative pronoun to combine each of the following pairs of sentences into one well-constructed complex sentence. The connecting word you select must clarify the relationship between the two sentences. You will have to change or reorder words, and in most cases, you will have a choice of connecting words.

EXAMPLE: Some colleges are tightening admissions requirements. Their pool of students may be growing smaller.

REVISED: Although the pool of students is growing smaller, some colleges are tightening admissions requirements.

1. Many high school graduates are currently out of work. They need new skills for new careers.
2. Talented high school students are usually encouraged to go to college. Some high school graduates are now starting to see that a college education may not guarantee them a job.
3. A college education can cost a student more than $100,000. Vocational education is becoming increasingly important.
4. Vocational students complete their work in less than four years. They can enter the job market more quickly.
5. Nurses' aides, paralegals, travel agents, and computer technicians do not need college degrees. They have little trouble finding work.
6. Some four-year colleges are experiencing growth. Public community colleges and private trade schools are growing much more rapidly.
7. The best vocational schools are responsive to the needs of local businesses. They train students for jobs that actually exist.
8. For instance, a school in Detroit might offer advanced automotive design. A school in New York City might focus on fashion design.
9. Other schools offer courses in horticulture, respiratory therapy, and computer programming. They are able to place their graduates easily.
10. Laid-off workers, returning housewives, recent high school graduates, and even college graduates are reexamining vocational education. They all hope to find rewarding careers.

Note: A **compound-complex sentence** consists of two or more independent clauses and at least one dependent clause.

dependent clause
[When small foreign imports began dominating the US automobile

independent clause   independent clause
industry], [consumers were very responsive], but [American auto workers were dismayed].

Sentence Variety (Rhodes College)
   http://www.rhodes.edu/kamhi/center/gram/variety.html

STUDENT WRITER AT WORK

Building Sentences

A student in a freshman composition class was assigned to interview a grandparent and write a short paper about his or her life. When she set out to turn her grandmother's words into a paper, the student faced a set of choppy notes—words, phrases, and simple sentences—that she had jotted down as her grandmother spoke. She needed to combine these fragments and short sentences into varied, interesting sentences that would establish the relationships among her ideas.

Read the following notes, turn them into complete sentences when necessary, and combine sentences wherever it seems appropriate. Your goal is to build simple, compound, and complex sentences enriched by modifiers—without adding any information. When you have finished, revise further to strengthen coherence, unity, and style.

Notes

67 years old. Born in Lykens, PA (old coal-mining town). Got her first paying job at 13. Her parents lied about her age. Working age was 14. Parents couldn't afford all the mouths they had to feed. Before that, she helped with the housework. At work, she was a maid. Got paid only about a dollar a week. Most of that went to her parents. Ate her meals on job. Worked in house where 3 generations of men lived. They all worked in the mines. Had to get up at 4 a.m. First chore was to make lunch for the men. She'd scrub the metal canteens. Then she'd fill them with water. Then she'd make biscuits and broth. Then she'd start breakfast. Mrs. Muller would help. Cooking for 6 hungry men was a real job. Then she did the breakfast dishes. Then she did the chores. The house had 3 stories. She had to scrub floors, dust, and sweep. It wasn't easy. Then Mrs. Muller would need help patching and darning. She had just enough time to get dinner started. Grabbed her meals after the family finished eating. Had no spare time. When not working she had chores to do at home. In spring and summer she would grow vegetables. Canned vegetables for her family. What was left over, she sold. Got married at 16.

CHAPTER 21

WRITING EMPHATIC SENTENCES

? FREQUENTLY ASKED QUESTIONS

Is it a good idea to begin a sentence with
there is or *there are*?   (p. 379)
Is repeating words and phrases ever a good
idea?   (p. 385)
When is it acceptable to use passive voice?
(p. 387)

In speaking, we emphasize certain ideas and deemphasize others with intonation and gesture; in writing, we convey **emphasis**—the relative importance of ideas—through the selection and arrangement of words.

21a   Conveying Emphasis through Word Order

Readers expect to find key information at the *beginning* or at the *end* of a sentence.

(1) Beginning with Important Ideas

Placing key ideas at the beginning of a sentence stresses their importance. The following sentence places emphasis on the study, not on those who conducted it or those who participated in it.

> In a landmark study of alcoholism, Dr. George Vaillant of Harvard followed two hundred Harvard graduates and four hundred inner-city working-class men from the Boston area.

From Strunk's *Elements of Style*
http://www.bartelby.com/141/strunk.html#18

Rephrasing focuses attention on the researcher, not on the study.

> Dr. George Vaillant of Harvard, in a landmark study of alcoholism, followed two hundred Harvard graduates and four hundred inner-city working-class men from the Boston area.

Situations that demand a straightforward presentation—laboratory reports, memos, technical papers, business correspondence, and the like—call for sentences that present vital information first and qualifiers later.

> Treating cancer with interferon has been the subject of a good deal of research. (emphasizes the treatment, not the research)

> Dividends will be paid if the stockholders agree. (emphasizes the dividends, not the stockholders)

 AVOIDING EMPTY OPENING PHRASES

Placing an empty phrase, such as *there is* or *there are,* at the beginning of a sentence generally weakens the sentence.

UNEMPHATIC: There is heavy emphasis placed on the development of computational skills at MIT.

EMPHATIC: Heavy emphasis is placed on the development of computational skills at MIT.

or

MIT places heavy emphasis on the development of computational skills.

---

(2) Ending with Important Ideas

Placing key elements at the end of a sentence conveys their importance.

Using a Colon or a Dash   A colon or a dash can add emphasis by isolating an important word or phrase at the end of a sentence.

> Beth had always dreamed of owning one special car: a 1953 Corvette.

> The elderly need a good deal of special attention—and they deserve that attention.

PLACING TRANSITIONAL EXPRESSIONS

At the end of a sentence, conjunctive adverbs or other transitional expressions lose their power to indicate the relationship between ideas. Place **transitional words and phrases** earlier, where they can fulfill their purpose and also add emphasis.

LESS EMPHATIC: Smokers do have rights; they should not try to impose their habit on others, however. (conjunctive adverb at end of clause)

MORE EMPHATIC: Smokers do have rights; however, they should not try to impose their habit on others. (conjunctive adverb at beginning of clause)

Using Climactic Word Order **Climactic word order,** the arrangement of a series of items from the least to the most important, places emphasis on the most important idea at the end.

Binge drinking can lead to unwanted pregnancies, car accidents, and even death. (*Death* is the most serious consequence.)

EXERCISE 1

Underline the most important ideas in each sentence of the following paragraph. Then, identify the strategy that the writer used to emphasize those ideas. Are the key ideas placed at the beginning or the end of a sentence? Does the writer use climactic order?

Listening to diatribes by angry callers or ranting about today's news, the talk radio host spreads ideas over the air waves. Every day at the same time, the political talk show host discusses national events and policies, the failures of the opposing view, and the foibles of the individuals who espouse those opposing views. Listening for hours a day, some callers become recognizable contributors to many different talk radio programs. Other listeners are less devoted, tuning in only when they are in the car and never calling to voice their opinions. Political radio hosts usually structure their programs around a specific agenda, espousing the party line and ridiculing the opponent's position. With a style of presentation aimed both at entertainment and information, the host's ideas become caricatures of party positions. Sometimes, in order to keep the information lively and interesting, a host may either state the issues too simply or deliberately mislead the audience. A host can excuse these errors by insisting that the show is harmless: it's for entertainment, not information. Many are concerned about how the political process is affected by this misinformation.

(3) Experimenting with Word Order

In English sentences, the most common word order is subject-verb-object (or subject-verb-complement). When you depart from this expected word order, you call attention to the word, phrase, or clause that you have relocated.

More modest and less inventive than Turner's paintings are John Constable's landscapes.

EXERCISE 2

Revise the following sentences to make them more emphatic. For each, decide which ideas should be highlighted and place these key ideas at sentence beginnings or endings. Use climactic order or depart from conventional word order where appropriate.

1. Police want to upgrade their firepower because criminals are better armed than ever before.
2. A few years ago, felons used so-called Saturday night specials, small-caliber six-shot revolvers.
3. Now, semiautomatic pistols capable of firing fifteen to twenty rounds, along with paramilitary weapons like the AK-47, have replaced these weapons.
4. Police are adopting such weapons as new fast-firing shotguns and 9mm automatic pistols in order to gain an equal footing with their adversaries.
5. Faster reloading and a hair trigger are among the numerous advantages that automatic pistols, the weapons of choice among law-enforcement officers, have over the traditional .38-caliber police revolver.

21b Conveying Emphasis through Sentence Structure

As you write, you can construct sentences that emphasize more important ideas and deemphasize less important ones.

(1) Using Cumulative Sentences

A **cumulative sentence** begins with an independent clause, followed by additional words, phrases, or clauses that expand or develop it.

> She holds me in strong arms, arms that have chopped cotton, dismembered trees, scattered corn for chickens, cradled infants, shaken the daylights out of half-grown upstart teenagers. (Rebecca Hill, *Blue Rise*)

Because it presents its main idea first, a cumulative sentence tends to be clear and straightforward. (Most English sentences are cumulative.)

(2) Using Periodic Sentences

A **periodic sentence** moves from supporting details, expressed in modifying phrases and dependent clauses, to the key idea, which is placed in the independent clause.

> Unlike World Wars I and II, which ended decisively with the unconditional surrender of the United States's enemies, the war in Vietnam did not end when American troops withdrew.

NOTE: In some periodic sentences, the modifying phrase or dependent clause comes between subject and predicate.

> Columbus, after several discouraging and unsuccessful voyages, finally reached America.

EXERCISE 3

A. Bracket the independent clause(s) in each sentence and underline each modifying phrase and dependent clause. Label each sentence cumulative or periodic.

B. Relocate the supporting details to make cumulative sentences periodic and periodic sentences cumulative, adding words or rephrasing to make your meaning clear.

C. Be prepared to explain how your revision changes the emphasis of the original sentence.

> EXAMPLE: Feeling isolated, sad, and frightened, [the small child sat alone in the train depot.] (periodic)

> REVISED: The small child sat alone in the train depot, feeling isolated, sad, and frightened. (cumulative)

1. However different in their educational opportunities, both Jefferson and Lincoln as young men became known to their contemporaries as "hard students." (Douglas L. Wilson, "What Jefferson and Lincoln Read," *Atlantic Monthly*)
2. The road came into being slowly, league by league, river crossing by river crossing. (Stephen Harrigan, "Highway 1," *Texas Monthly*)
3. Without willing it, I had gone from being ignorant of being ignorant to being aware of being aware. (Maya Angelou, *I Know Why the Caged Bird Sings*)

EXERCISE 4

A. Combine each of the following sentence groups into one cumulative sentence, subordinating supporting details to more important ideas.

B. Then, combine each group into one periodic sentence. Each group can be combined in a variety of ways, and you may have to add, delete, change, or reorder words.

C. How do the two versions of the sentence differ in emphasis?

> EXAMPLE: More women than ever before are running for office. They are encouraged by the success of other female candidates.

> CUMULATIVE: More women than ever before are running for office, encouraged by the success of other female candidates.

> PERIODIC: Encouraged by the success of other female candidates, more women than ever before are running for office.

1. Many politicians opposed the MX missile. They believed it was too expensive. They felt that a smaller, single-warhead missile was preferable.
2. Smoking poses a real danger. It is associated with various cancers. It is linked to heart disease and stroke. It threatens even nonsmokers.

3. Infertile couples who want children sometimes go through a series of difficult processes. They may try adoption. They may also try artificial insemination or in vitro fertilization. They may even seek out surrogate mothers.

4. The Thames is a river that meanders through southern England. It has been the inspiration for such literary works as *Alice's Adventures in Wonderland* and *The Wind in the Willows*. It was also captured in paintings by Constable, Turner, and Whistler.

5. Black-footed ferrets are rare North American mammals. They prey on prairie dogs. They are primarily nocturnal. They have black feet and black-tipped tails. Their faces have raccoonlike masks.

EXERCISE 5

Combine each of the following sentence groups into one sentence that subordinates supporting details to the main idea. In each case, create either a periodic or a cumulative sentence, depending on which structure you think will best convey the sentence's emphasis. Add, delete, change, or reorder words when necessary.

EXAMPLE: The fears of today's college students are based on reality. They are afraid there are too many students and too few jobs.

REVISED: The fears of today's college students—that there are too many students and too few jobs—are based on reality. (periodic)

1. Today's college students are under a good deal of stress. Job prospects in some fields are not very good. Financial aid is not as easy to come by as it was in the past.

2. Education has grown very expensive. The job market has become tighter. Pressure to get into graduate and professional schools has increased.

3. Family ties seem to be weakening. Students aren't always able to count on family support.

4. College students have always had problems. Now college counseling centers report more—and more serious—problems.

5. The term *student shock* was coined several years ago. This term describes a syndrome that may include depression, anxiety, headaches, and eating and sleeping disorders.

6. Many students are overwhelmed by the vast array of courses and majors offered at their colleges. They tend to be less decisive. They take longer to choose a major and to complete school.

7. Many drop out of school for brief (or extended) periods or switch majors several times. Many take five years or longer to complete their college education.

8. Some colleges are responding to the pressures that students feel. They hold stress-management workshops and suicide-prevention courses. They advertise the services of their counseling centers. They train students as peer counselors. They improve their vocational counseling services.

21c   Conveying Emphasis through Parallelism and Balance

By reinforcing the correspondence between grammatical elements, **parallelism** adds emphasis to a sentence.

> We seek an individual <u>who is</u> a self-starter, <u>who owns</u> a late-model automobile, and <u>who is</u> willing to work evenings. (classified advertisement)

> <u>Do not pass</u> Go; <u>do not collect</u> $200. (instructions)

> The Faust legend is central <u>in</u> Benét's *The Devil and Daniel Webster,* <u>in</u> Goethe's *Faust,* and <u>in</u> Marlowe's *Dr. Faustus.* (examination answer)

See 27a

A **balanced sentence** is neatly divided between two parallel structures—for example, two independent clauses in a compound sentence. The symmetrical structure of a balanced sentence adds emphasis by highlighting correspondences or contrasts between clauses.

> In the 1950s, the electronic miracle was the television; in the 1980s, the electronic miracle was the computer.

> Alive, the elephant was worth at least a hundred pounds; dead, he would only be worth the value of his tusks, five pounds, possibly. (George Orwell, "Shooting an Elephant")

21d   Conveying Emphasis through Repetition

See 22b

?

<u>Unnecessary repetition</u> makes sentences dull and monotonous as well as wordy. Effective repetition, however, can place emphasis on key words or ideas.

> They decided to begin again: <u>to begin</u> hoping, <u>to begin</u> trying to change, <u>to begin</u> working toward a goal.

During those years when I was just learning to speak, my mother and father addressed me only <u>in Spanish</u>; <u>in Spanish</u> I learned to reply. (Richard Rodriguez, *Aria: A Memoir of a Bilingual Childhood*)

EXERCISE 6

Revise the sentences in this paragraph, using parallelism and balance to highlight corresponding elements and using repetition of key words and phrases to add emphasis. You may combine sentences and add, delete, or reorder words.

Many readers distrust newspapers. They also distrust what they read in magazines. They do not trust what they hear on the radio and what television shows them, either. Of these media, newspapers have been the most responsive to audience criticism. Some newspapers even have ombudsmen. They are supposed to listen to reader complaints. They are also charged with acting on these grievances. One complaint that many people have is that newspapers are inaccurate. Newspapers' disregard for people's privacy is another of many readers' criticisms. Reporters are seen as arrogant, and readers feel that journalists can be unfair. They feel that reporters tend to glorify criminals, and they believe there is a tendency to place too much emphasis on bizarre or offbeat stories. Finally, readers complain about poor writing and editing. Polls show that despite its efforts to respond to reader criticism, the press continues to face hostility. (Adapted from *Newsweek*)

21e   Conveying Emphasis through Active Voice

See 34d

Active voice is generally more emphatic—and more concise—than **passive voice**.

PASSIVE: The prediction that oil prices will rise is being made by economists.

ACTIVE: Economists now predict that oil prices will rise.

The passive voice tends to focus your readers' attention on the action or on its receiver rather than on who is performing it. The receiver of the action is the subject of a passive sentence, so the actor fades into the background (*by economists*) or is omitted (*the prediction is now being made*).

Sometimes, of course, you *want* to stress the action rather than the actor. If so, it makes sense to use the passive voice.

PASSIVE: The West was explored by Lewis and Clark. (stresses the exploration of the West, not who explored it)

ACTIVE: Lewis and Clark explored the West. (stresses the contribution of the explorers)

You also use passive voice when the identity of the person performing the action is irrelevant or unknown (*The course was canceled*). For this reason, the passive voice is frequently used in **scientific** and technical writing.

See Ch. 51

EXERCISE 7

Revise this paragraph to eliminate awkward or excessive use of passive constructions.

Jack Dempsey, the heavyweight champion between 1919 and 1926, had an interesting but uneven career. He was considered one of the greatest boxers of all time. Dempsey began fighting as "Kid Blackie," but his career didn't take off until 1919, when Jack "Doc" Kearns became his manager. Dempsey won the championship when Jess Willard was defeated by him in Toledo, Ohio, in 1919. Dempsey immediately became a popular sports figure; President Franklin D. Roosevelt was one of his biggest fans. Influential friends were made by Jack Dempsey. Boxing lessons were given by him to the actor Rudolph Valentino. He made friends with Douglas Fairbanks, Sr., Damon Runyon, and J. Paul Getty. Hollywood serials were made by Dempsey, but the title was lost by him to Gene Tunney, and Dempsey failed to regain it the following year. After his boxing career declined, a restaurant was opened by Dempsey, and many major sporting events were attended by him. This exposure kept him in the public eye until he lost his restaurant. Jack Dempsey died in 1983.

STUDENT WRITER AT WORK

Writing Emphatic Sentences

Identify the strategies that a freshman composition student has used in this draft to convey his emphasis to readers. Revise the draft to make his emphasis clearer, and then revise again if necessary to strengthen coherence, unity, and style.

"Fight, Fight, Fight for the Home Team"

It is pathetic for an athlete being paid millions of dollars to get into a fight for something so ridiculous as a bad call by a referee or an accidental push by a player. Players have to be tough in order to win. This shouldn't mean they have to be violent, however. The amount of violence increases every day in the world of sports. It is a national embarrassment that this situation exists.

It is a disgrace to see professional athletes getting into fights. This situation occurs in nearly every game. If a fight breaks out at an event, the game is disrupted, the players involved in the altercation are fined, and spectators are disappointed or angry. What does a fight solve, therefore? Nothing. Things are only made worse by fights.

In hockey, there are always fights that break out. These fights aren't even stopped by the referees. The players are allowed to continue beating each other to a pulp instead. The crowd gets into the hitting and checking, and a fight erupts in the stands before you know it. A family can seldom go to a peaceful game without witnessing a fight between players or a riot in the stands.

America's pastime, baseball, can be a beautiful sport to watch. Imagine the crack of the bat, the smell (in some ballparks) of fresh-cut grass, the cheers for a home run, and the sounds of both teams rushing out of the dugouts to the mound to demolish the other team. Fighting shouldn't be part of the game, obviously, but often it seems it is. A batter should just walk it off on the way to first base if he gets hit by a pitch. Usually, he runs after the pitcher, though. Within seconds, the dugouts are empty, and fists are flying on the mound.

Violence is even more obvious in sports like football, lacrosse, boxing, and rugby. It is becoming harder and harder to go to a sporting event and have a plain old-fashioned good time because of all the violence on the field or court. A player can be "bad" or "hungry," but this shouldn't mean getting into violent fights. What ever happened to the spirit of "Buy me some peanuts and Cracker Jack, I don't care if I never get back"?

CHAPTER 22

WRITING CONCISE SENTENCES

❓ FREQUENTLY ASKED QUESTIONS

How can I tell which words I really need in my
sentences and which can be cut? (p. 390)
How do I revise a long, rambling sentence?
(p. 393)

A **concise sentence** contains only the words necessary to make its point. Because it is free of unnecessary words and convoluted constructions, a concise sentence is also clear and emphatic.

22a Eliminating Nonessential Words

A good way to find out which words are essential in a sentence is to underline the key words. Then, decide which of the remaining words are unnecessary, and delete them.

WORDY: It seems to me that it doesn't make sense to allow any bail to be <u>granted</u> to <u>anyone</u> who has ever been <u>convicted</u> of a <u>violent crime</u>.

CONCISE: Bail should not be granted to anyone who has ever been convicted of a violent crime.

Whenever possible, delete nonessential words—*deadwood, utility words,* and *circumlocution*—from your writing.

(1) Deleting Deadwood

Deadwood refers to unnecessary phrases that take up space and add nothing to meaning.

Writing Concise Sentences
   http://webster.commnet.edu/grammar/concise.htm
Eliminating "Word Clutter"
   http://www2.rscc.cc.tn.us/~jordan_jj/OWL/Clutter.html
Eliminating Wordiness (Texas)
   http://uwc.fac.utexas.edu/stu/handouts/wordines.html

WORDY: Sometimes <u>there would be an accumulation of</u> water on the roof.

CONCISE: Sometimes water accumulated on the roof.

WORDY: The two plots <u>are both similar</u> <u>in the way that</u> they trace the characters' increasing rage.

CONCISE: The two plots are similar in that they trace the characters' increasing rage.

WORDY: The only truly tragic character in *Hamlet* <u>would have to be</u> Ophelia.

CONCISE: The only truly tragic character in *Hamlet* is Ophelia.

WORDY: <u>In</u> this article <u>it</u> discusses lead poisoning.

CONCISE: This article discusses lead poisoning.

Many familiar expressions—such as *as the case may be, I feel, it seems to me, all things considered, without a doubt, in conclusion,* and *by way of explanation*—are also deadwood. You may think they balance or fill out a sentence or make your writing sound more authoritative, but they are more likely to distract or annoy your readers than to impress them.

WORDY: <u>In my opinion,</u> I disagree with Thomas's position.

CONCISE: I disagree with Thomas's position.

WORDY: <u>It is important to note that</u> the results were identical in both clinical trials.

CONCISE: The results were identical in both clinical trials.

(2) Deleting or Replacing Utility Words

Utility words are fillers; they contribute nothing to a sentence. Utility words include nouns with imprecise meanings (*factor, kind, type, quality, aspect, thing, sort, field, area, situation,* and so on); adjectives so general that they are almost meaningless (*good, nice, bad, fine, important, significant*); and common adverbs denoting degree (*basically, completely, actually, very, definitely, quite*). Often, you can simply delete a utility word; if you cannot, replace it with a more specific word.

WORDY: The registration <u>situation</u> was disorganized.

CONCISE: Registration was disorganized.

WORDY: It was <u>actually</u> a worthwhile book, but I didn't <u>completely</u> finish it.

CONCISE: It was a worthwhile book, but I didn't finish it.

(3) Avoiding Circumlocution

Using ten words when five will do is called **circumlocution.** Instead of using complicated phrases and rambling constructions, use concrete, specific words and phrases, and come right to the point.

WORDY: The curriculum was <u>of a unique nature</u>.

CONCISE: The curriculum was unique.

WORDY: <u>It is not unlikely that</u> this trend will continue.

CONCISE: This trend will probably continue.

 REVISING WORDY PHRASES

A wordy phrase can almost always be replaced by a more concise, more direct term.

Wordy	Concise
at the present time	now
at this point in time	now
for the purpose of	for
due to the fact that	because
on account of the fact that	because
until such time as	until
in the event that	if
by means of	by
in the vicinity of	near
have the ability to	be able to

 EXERCISE 1

Revise the following paragraph to eliminate deadwood, utility words, and circumlocution. Whenever possible, delete wordy phrases or replace them with more concise expressions.

For all intents and purposes, the shopping mall is no longer an important factor in the American cultural scene. In the '80s, shopping malls became gathering places where teenagers met, walkers came to get in a few miles, and shoppers who were looking for a wide selection and were not concerned about value went to shop. There are several factors that have worked to undermine the mall's popularity. First, due to the fact that today's shoppers are more likely to be interested in value, many of them have headed to the discount stores. Today's shopper is now more likely to shop in discount stores or bulk-buying warehouse stores than in the small, expensive specialty shops in the large shopping malls. Add to this a resurgence of the values of community, and we can see how malls would have to be less attractive than shopping at local stores. Many malls actually have up to 20 percent empty storefronts, and some have had to close down altogether. Others have met the challenge by expanding their roles from shopping centers into community centers. They have added playgrounds for the children and more amusements and restaurants for the adults. They have also appealed to the growing sense of value shopping by giving gift certificates and discounts to shoppers who spend money in their stores. In the early '90s, it seemed as if the huge shopping malls that had become familiar cultural icons were dying out. Now, it looks as if some of those icons just might make it by meeting the challenges and continue to survive as more than just places to shop.

22b   Eliminating Unnecessary Repetition

See
21d

Repetition can make your writing more emphatic, but unnecessary repetition and **redundant** word groups (words or phrases that say the same thing) can obscure your meaning.

You can correct unnecessary repetition by using one of the following strategies.

(1) Substituting a Pronoun

WORDY: Fictional detective <u>Miss Marple</u> has solved many difficult cases. *The Murder at the Vicarage* was one of <u>Miss Marple's</u> most challenging puzzles.

CONCISE: Fictional detective Miss Marple solves many difficult cases. *The Murder at the Vicarage* was one of her most challenging puzzles. (The pronoun *her* is substituted for *Miss Marple*.)

(2) Creating Appositives

See
19c5

WORDY: Red Barber <u>was</u> a sportscaster. He <u>was</u> known for his colorful expressions.

CONCISE: Sportscaster Red Barber was known for his colorful expressions. (**Appositive** eliminates unnecessary repetition.)

(3) Creating Compounds

WORDY: Wendy <u>found the exam difficult</u>, and Karen <u>also found it hard</u>. Ken <u>thought it was tough, too</u>.

CONCISE: Wendy, Karen, and Ken all found the exam difficult. (Compound subject eliminates unnecessary repetition.)

WORDY: *Huckleberry Finn* <u>is</u> an adventure story. <u>It is also</u> a sad account of an abused, neglected child.

CONCISE: *Huckleberry Finn* is both an adventure story and a sad account of an abused, neglected child. (Compound complement eliminates unnecessary repetition.)

WORDY: In 1964, Ted Briggs was discharged from the Air Force. <u>He</u> then got a job with Maxwell Data Processing. <u>He</u> married Susan Thompson that same year.

CONCISE: In 1964, Ted Briggs was discharged from the Air Force, got a job with Maxwell Data Processing, and married Susan Thompson. (Compound predicate eliminates unnecessary repetition.)

(4) Creating Complex Sentences

WORDY: Americans value <u>freedom of speech</u>. <u>Freedom of speech</u> is guaranteed by the First Amendment.

CONCISE: Americans value freedom of speech, which is guaranteed by the First Amendment. (Creating a compound sentence eliminates needless repetition.)

EXERCISE 2

Eliminate any unnecessary repetition of words or ideas in this paragraph. Also revise to eliminate deadwood, utility words, or circumlocution.

For a wide variety of different reasons, more and more people today are choosing a vegetarian diet. There are three kinds of vegetarians: strict vegetarians eat no animal foods at all; lactovegetarians eat dairy products, but they do not eat meat, fish, poultry, or eggs; and ovolactovegetarians eat eggs and dairy products, but they do not eat meat, fish, or poultry. Famous vegetarians include such well-known people as George Bernard Shaw, Leonardo da Vinci, Ralph Waldo Emerson, Henry David Thoreau, and Mahatma Gandhi. Like these well-known vegetarians, the vegetarians of today have good reasons for becoming vegetarians. For instance, some religions recommend a vegetarian diet. Some of these religions are Buddhism, Brahmanism, and Hinduism. Other people turn to vegetarianism for reasons of health or for reasons of hygiene. These people believe that meat is a source of potentially harmful chemicals, and they believe meat contains infectious organisms. Some people feel meat may cause digestive problems and may lead to other difficulties as well. Other vegetarians adhere to a vegetarian diet because they feel it is ecologically wasteful to kill animals after we feed plants to them. These vegetarians believe *we* should eat the plants. Finally, there are facts and evidence to suggest that a vegetarian diet may possibly help people live longer lives. A vegetarian diet may do this by reducing the incidence of heart disease and lessening the incidence of some cancers. (Adapted from *Jane Brody's Nutrition Book*)

22c   Tightening Rambling Sentences

The combination of nonessential words, unnecessary repetition, and complicated syntax creates **rambling sentences.** Revising rambling sentences frequently requires extensive editing.

(1) Eliminating Excessive Coordination

When you string a series of clauses together with coordinating conjunctions, you create a rambling, unfocused **compound sentence** that presents all your ideas as if they have equal weight. To revise such sentences, identify the main idea, state that idea in the independent clause, and then subordinate the supporting details to the main idea.

See 20a

WORDY: Puerto Rico is a large island in the Caribbean, and it is very mountainous, and it has steep slopes, and they fall to gentle plains along the coast.

CONCISE: A large island in the Caribbean, Puerto Rico is very mountainous, with steep slopes falling to gentle plains along the coast. (Puerto Rico's mountainous terrain is the sentence's main idea.)

(2) Eliminating Adjective Clauses

A series of **adjective clauses** is likely to produce a rambling sentence. To revise, substitute more concise modifying words or phrases for the adjective clauses.

WORDY: *Moby-Dick,* which is a novel about a white whale, was written by Herman Melville, who was friendly with Nathaniel Hawthorne, who encouraged him to revise the first draft.

CONCISE: *Moby-Dick,* a novel about a white whale, was written by Herman Melville, who revised the first draft at the urging of his friend Nathaniel Hawthorne.

(3) Eliminating Passive Constructions

Excessive use of the **passive voice** can create rambling sentences. Correct this problem when you revise by changing passive to active voice.

WORDY: The sense of being safe inside an airplane is no longer felt by many people.

CONCISE: Many people no longer feel safe inside an airplane.

WORDY: Water rights are being fought for in court by Indian tribes like the Papago in Arizona and the Pyramid Lake Paiute in Nevada.

CONCISE: Indian tribes like the Papago in Arizona and the Pyramid Lake Paiute in Nevada are fighting in court for water rights.

(4) Eliminating Wordy Prepositional Phrases

When you revise, substitute adjectives or adverbs for wordy **prepositional phrases**.

WORDY: The trip was one of danger but also one of excitement.
CONCISE: The trip was dangerous but exciting.

WORDY: He spoke in a confident manner and with a lot of authority.
CONCISE: He spoke confidently and authoritatively.

(5) Eliminating Wordy Noun Constructions

Substitute strong verbs for wordy noun phrases.

WORDY: <u>The normalization of</u> commercial relations between the United States and China in 1979 led to <u>an increase in</u> trade between the two countries.

CONCISE: When the United States and China <u>normalized</u> commercial relations in 1979, trade between the two countries <u>increased</u>.

WORDY: We have <u>made the decision to</u> postpone the meeting until after <u>the appearance of</u> all the board members.

CONCISE: We have <u>decided</u> to postpone the meeting until all the board members <u>appear</u>.

EXERCISE 3

Revise the rambling sentences in these paragraphs by eliminating excessive coordination, unnecessary use of the passive voice, and overuse of adjective clauses, wordy prepositional phrases, and noun constructions. As you revise, make your sentences more concise by deleting nonessential words and superfluous repetition.

Some colleges that have been in support of fraternities for a number of years are at this time in the process of conducting a reevaluation of the position of those fraternities on campus. In opposition to the fraternities are a fair number of students, faculty members, and administrators who claim fraternities are inherently sexist, which they say makes it impossible for the groups to exist in a coeducational institution, which is supposed to offer equal opportunities for members of both sexes. More and more members of the college community also see fraternities as elitist as well as sexist and favor their abolition. In addition, many point out that fraternities are associated with dangerous practices, such as hazing and alcohol abuse.

However, some students, faculty, and administrators remain whole-heartedly in support of traditional fraternities, which they believe are responsible for helping students make the acquaintance of people and learn the leadership skills that they believe will be of assistance to them in their future lives as adults. Supporters of fraternities believe students should retain the right to make their own social decisions and that joining a fraternity is one of those decisions, and they also believe fraternities are responsible for providing valuable services. Some of these are tutoring, raising money for charity, and running campus escort services. Therefore, these individuals are not of the opinion that the abolition of traditional fraternities makes sense.

STUDENT WRITER AT WORK

Writing Concise Sentences

Revise this excerpt from an essay exam in American literature to make it more concise. After you have done so, revise further if necessary to strengthen coherence, unity, and style.

Oftentimes in the course of a literary work, characters may find themselves misfits in the sense that they do not seem to be a real part of the society in which they find themselves. This problem often leads to a series of genuinely serious and severe problems, conflicts either between the misfits and their own identities or possibly between them and that society into which they so poorly fit.

In "The Minister's Black Veil," Reverend Hooper all of a sudden gives to the townspeople and members of his parish a surprise: a piece of black material that he has wrapped over his face, which causes readers to be as completely and thoroughly confused as the townspeople about the possible reason for the minister's decision to hide his face, until readers learn, in his sermon, that he is covering his face (from God, his fellow man, and himself) to atone for the sins of mankind. As far as readers can tell, they are never quite sure exactly why he is in possession of the notion that this act must be carried out by him, and they are never completely sure whether Reverend Hooper feels this guilt for some sin that may exist in his own past or for those sins that may have been committed by mankind in general, but in any case it is clear that he feels it is his duty to place himself in isolation from the world at large around him. To the reverend, there is no solution to his problem, and he lives his whole entire life wearing the veil. Even after his death, he insists that the veil remain covering his features, for it is said by the reverend that his face must not be revealed on earth.

For Reverend Hooper, a terrible conflict exists within himself, and so Reverend Hooper voluntarily makes himself a misfit even at the expense of losing everything, even his true love Elizabeth.

CHAPTER 23

WRITING VARIED SENTENCES

? FREQUENTLY ASKED QUESTIONS

How do I combine choppy sentences to make my writing "flow"? (p. 401)

How do I revise a string of compound sentences? (p. 402)

How do I revise if all my sentences begin with "I" or another subject? (p. 405)

23a Varying Sentence Length

Using sentences of different lengths in a single passage can make your writing more interesting.

(1) Mixing Long and Short Sentences

A paragraph consisting entirely of short sentences (or entirely of long ones) can be dull.

> Drag racing began in California in the 1940s. It was an alternative to street racing, which was illegal and dangerous. It flourished in the 1950s and 1960s. Eventually, it became almost a rite of passage. Then, during the 1970s, almost one-third of America's racetracks closed. Today, however, drag racing is making a comeback.

Combining some of the paragraph's short sentences into longer ones creates a more interesting passage.

> Drag racing began in California in the 1940s as an alternative to street racing, which was illegal and dangerous. It flourished in the 1950s and 1960s, eventually becoming almost a rite of passage. Then, during the 1970s, almost one-third of America's racetracks closed. Today, however, drag racing is making a comeback.

(2) Following a Long Sentence with a Short One

Another way to add interest is to follow one or more long sentences with a short one. (This strategy also places emphasis on the short sentence.)

> Over the years, vitamin boosters say, a misconception has grown that as long as there are no signs or symptoms of, say, scurvy, then we have all of the vitamin C we need. Although we know how much of a particular vitamin or mineral will prevent clinical disease, we have practically no information on how much is necessary for peak health. In short, we know how sick is sick, but we don't know how well is well. (*Philadelphia Magazine*)

EXERCISE 1

Combine each of the following sentence groups into one long sentence. Then, compose a relatively short sentence to follow each long one. Finally, combine all the sentences into a paragraph, adding a topic sentence and any transitions necessary for coherence. Proofread your paragraph to be sure the sentences are varied in length.

1. Chocolate is composed of more than three hundred compounds. Phenylethylamine is one such compound. Its presence in the brain may be linked to the emotion of falling in love.
2. Americans now consume a good deal of chocolate. On average, they eat more than nine pounds of chocolate per person per year. The typical Belgian, however, consumes almost fifteen pounds per year.
3. In recent years, Americans have begun a serious love affair with chocolate. Elegant chocolate boutiques sell exquisite bonbons by the piece. At least one hotel offers a "chocolate binge" vacation. The bimonthly *Chocolate News* for connoisseurs is flourishing.

(Adapted from *Newsweek*)

23b Combining Choppy Simple Sentences

Strings of short simple sentences can be tedious—and sometimes hard to follow, as this paragraph illustrates.

> John Peter Zenger was a newspaper editor. He waged and won an important battle for freedom of the press in America. He criticized the policies of the British governor. He was charged with criminal libel as a result. Zenger's lawyers were disbarred. Andrew Hamilton

defended him. Hamilton convinced the jury that Zenger's criticisms were true. Therefore, the statements were not libelous.

You can revise choppy sentences like these by using *coordination, subordination,* or *embedding* to combine them with adjacent sentences.

(1) Using Coordination

Coordination pairs similar elements—words, phrases, or clauses—giving equal weight to each. The following revision links two of the original paragraph's choppy simple sentences with *and* to create a compound sentence.

> John Peter Zenger was a newspaper editor. He waged and won an important battle for freedom of the press in America. <u>He criticized the policies of the British governor, and as a result, he was charged with criminal libel.</u> Zenger's lawyers were disbarred. Andrew Hamilton defended him. Hamilton convinced the jury that Zenger's criticisms were true. Therefore, the statements were not libelous.

(2) Using Subordination

Subordination places the more important idea in the independent clause and the less important idea in the dependent clause. The following revision of the preceding paragraph uses subordination to change two simple sentences into dependent clauses, creating two **complex sentences**.

See
20b

> <u>John Peter Zenger was a newspaper editor who waged and won an important battle for freedom of the press in America.</u> He criticized the policies of the British governor, and as a result, he was charged with criminal libel. <u>When Zenger's lawyers were disbarred, Andrew Hamilton defended him.</u> Hamilton convinced the jury that Zenger's criticisms were true. Therefore, the statements were not libelous.

(3) Using Embedding

Embedding is the working of additional words and phrases into a sentence. In the following revision, the sentence *Hamilton convinced the jury . . .* has been reworded to create a phrase (*convincing the jury*) that is embedded into another sentence, where it now modifies the independent clause *Andrew Hamilton defended him.*

> John Peter Zenger was a newspaper editor who waged and won an important battle for freedom of the press in America. He criticized the policies of the British governor, and as a result, he was

charged with criminal libel. <u>When Zenger's lawyers were disbarred, Andrew Hamilton defended him, convincing the jury that Zenger's criticisms were true.</u> Therefore, the statements were not libelous.

This final revision of the original string of choppy sentences is a varied, readable paragraph that uses coordination, subordination, and embedding to vary sentence length. (It retains the final short simple sentence for emphasis.)

EXERCISE 2

Using coordination, subordination, and embedding, revise this string of choppy simple sentences into a more varied and interesting paragraph.

> The first modern miniature golf course was built in New York in 1925. It was an indoor course with 18 holes. Entrepreneurs Drake Delanoy and John Ledbetter built 150 more indoor and outdoor courses. Garnet Carter made miniature golf a worldwide fad. Carter built an elaborate miniature golf course. He later joined with Delanoy and Ledbetter. Together they built more miniature golf courses. They abbreviated playing distances. They highlighted the game's hazards at the expense of skill. This made the game much more popular. By 1930 there were 25,000 miniature golf courses in the United States. Courses grew more elaborate. Hazards grew more bizarre. The craze spread to London and Hong Kong. The expansion of miniature golf grew out of control. Then, interest in the game declined. By 1931 most miniature golf courses were out of business. The game was revived in the early 1950s. Today, there are between eight and ten thousand miniature golf courses. The architecture of miniature golf remains an enduring form of American folk art. (Adapted from *Games*)

❓ 23c Breaking Up Strings of Compound Sentences

An unbroken series of compound sentences can be dull. Moreover, when you connect clauses only with coordinating conjunctions, you do not indicate exactly how ideas are related or which is most important.

ALL COMPOUND SENTENCES: A volcano that is erupting is considered *active,* but one that may erupt is designated *dormant,* and one that has not erupted for a long time is called *extinct.* Most active volcanoes are located in "The Ring of Fire," a belt that circles the Pacific Ocean, and they can be extremely destructive. Italy's Vesuvius erupted in AD 79, and it destroyed the town of Pompeii. In 1883, Krakatoa, located between the Indonesian islands of Java and Sumatra, erupted, and it caused a tidal wave, and more than 36,000 people were killed. Martinique's Mont Pelée erupted in 1902, and its hot gas and ash killed 30,000 people, and this completely wiped out the town of St. Pierre.

VARIED SENTENCES: A volcano that is erupting is considered *active.* **(simple sentence)** One that may erupt is designated *dormant,* and one that has not erupted for a long time is called *extinct.* **(compound sentence)** Most active volcanoes are located in "The Ring of Fire," a belt that circles the Pacific Ocean. **(simple sentence with modifier)** Active volcanoes can be extremely destructive. **(simple sentence)** Erupting in AD 79, Italy's Vesuvius destroyed the town of Pompeii. **(simple sentence with modifier)** When Krakatoa, located between the Indonesian islands of Java and Sumatra, erupted in 1883, it caused a tidal wave that killed 36,000 people. **(compound-complex sentence with modifier)** The eruption of Martinique's Mont Pelée in 1902 produced hot gas and ash that killed 30,000 people, completely wiping out the town of St. Pierre. **(complex sentence with modifier)**

EXERCISE 3

Revise the compound sentences in this passage so the sentence structure is varied. Be sure that the writer's emphasis and the relationships between ideas are clear.

Dr. Alice I. Baumgartner and her colleagues at the Institute for Equality in Education at the University of Colorado surveyed two thousand Colorado schoolchildren, and they found some startling results. They asked, "If you woke up tomorrow and discovered that you were a (boy) (girl), how would your life be different?" and the answers were sad and shocking. The researchers assumed they would find that boys and girls would see advantages in being either male or female, but instead they found that both boys and girls had a fundamental contempt for females. Many elementary schoolboys titled their answers "The

Disaster" or "Doomsday," and they described the terrible lives they would lead as girls, but the girls seemed to feel they would be better off as boys, and they expressed feelings that they would be able to do more and have easier lives. (Adapted from *Redbook*)

23d   Varying Sentence Types

To achieve sentence variety, mix **declarative sentences** (statements) with occasional **imperative sentences** (commands or requests), **exclamations,** and **rhetorical questions** (questions that readers are not expected to answer).

Local television newscasts seem to be delivering less and less news. Although we stay awake for the late news hoping to be updated on local, national, and world events, only about 30 percent of most newscasts is devoted to news. Up to 25 percent of the typical program—even more during "sweeps weeks"—can be devoted to feature stories, with another 25 percent reserved for advertising. The remaining time is spent on weather, sports, and casual conversation between anchors. Given this focus on "soft" material, what options do those of us wishing to find out what happened in the world have? **(rhetorical question)** Critics of local television have a few suggestions. First, write to your local station's management voicing your concern and threatening to boycott the news if changes are not made; then, try to get others who feel the way you do to sign a petition. **(imperatives)** If changes are not made, try turning off your television and reading the newspaper! **(exclamation)**

Other options for varying sentence types include mixing simple, compound, and complex sentences (see **23b** and **c**); mixing cumulative and periodic sentences (see **21b**); and using balanced sentences (see **21c**).

EXERCISE 4

The following paragraph is composed entirely of declarative sentences. To make it more varied, add three sentences—one exclamation, one rhetorical question, and one imperative—anywhere in the paragraph. Be sure the new sentences are consistent with the paragraph's purpose and tone.

When the Fourth of July comes around, the nation explodes with patriotism. Everywhere we look we see parades and picnics, firecrackers and fireworks. An outsider might wonder what all the fuss is about. We could explain that this is America's birthday party, and all the candles are being lit at once. There is no reason for us to hold back our enthusiasm—or to limit the noise that celebrates it. The Fourth of July is watermelon and corn on the cob, American flags and sparklers, brass bands and more. Everyone looks forward to this celebration, and everyone has a good time.

23e Varying Sentence Openings

Rather than begin every sentence with the subject, add interest and variety by beginning with a modifying word, phrase, or clause.

(1) Beginning with an Adjective, an Adverb, or a Dependent Clause

<u>Proud</u> and <u>relieved</u>, they watched their daughter receive her diploma. (adjectives)

<u>Hungrily</u>, he devoured his lunch. (adverb)

<u>After Woodrow Wilson was incapacitated by a stroke</u>, his wife unofficially performed many presidential duties. (dependent clause)

(2) Beginning with a Prepositional Phrase, a Participial Phrase, or an Absolute Phrase

<u>For better or worse</u>, credit cards are now readily available to college students. (prepositional phrase)

<u>Located on the west coast of Great Britain</u>, Wales is part of the United Kingdom. (participial phrase)

<u>His interests widening</u>, Picasso designed ballet sets and illustrated books. (absolute phrase)

(3) Beginning with a Coordinating Conjunction or a Transitional Word or Phrase

The Big Bang may be the beginning of the universe, or it may be a discontinuity in which information about the earlier history of the universe was destroyed. <u>But</u> it is certainly the earliest event about which we have any record. (coordinating conjunction) (Carl Sagan, *The Dragons of Eden*)

Pantomime was first performed in ancient Rome. <u>However</u>, it remains a popular dramatic form today. (transitional word)

See Ch. 24

NOTE: If you begin a sentence with a coordinating conjunction, be sure that it is a complete sentence and not a **fragment**.

(4) Beginning with an Appositive

<u>A British scientist</u>, Alexander Fleming is best known for having discovered penicillin. (appositive)

EXERCISE 5

Each of these sentences begins with the subject. Revise each so that it has a different opening; then, identify your opening strategy.

EXAMPLE: N. Scott Momaday, the prominent Native American writer, tells the story of his first fourteen years in *The Names*.

REVISED: Prominent Native American writer N. Scott Momaday tells the story of his first fourteen years in *The Names*. (appositive)

1. Momaday was taken as a very young child to Devil's Tower, the geological formation in Wyoming that is called Tsoai (Bear Tree) in Kiowa, and there he was given the name Tsoai-talee (Bear Tree Boy).
2. The Kiowa myth of the origin of Tsoai is about a boy who playfully chases his seven sisters up a tree, which rises into the air as the boy is transformed into a bear.
3. The boy-bear becomes increasingly ferocious and claws the bark of the tree, which becomes a great rock with a flat top and deeply scored sides.
4. The sisters climb higher and higher to escape their brother's wrath, and eventually they become the seven stars of the Big Dipper.
5. This story, from which Momaday received one of his names, appears as a constant in his works *The Way to Rainy Mountain*, *House Made of Dawn*, and *The Ancient Child*.

23f   Varying   Standard Word Order

You can vary standard word order (subject-verb-object or subject-verb-complement) either by intentionally inverting this usual order or by placing words between subject and verb.

(1) Inverting Word Order

Sometimes, you can place the complement or direct object *before* the verb instead of in its conventional position after the verb, or place the verb *before* the subject instead of after it. These strategies draw attention to the word or word group that appears in an unexpected place.

(object)   (subject) (verb)
A cheery smile he had for everyone.

(complement)(verb)   (subject)
Hardest hit were the coastal areas.

NOTE: Be careful to use inverted word order in moderation; when overused, it becomes monotonous and can sound pretentious.

(2) Separating Subject from Verb

You can also place words or phrases between subject and verb—but be sure that the word group does not obscure the connection between subject and verb or create an **agreement** error.

See
35a

Many <u>states</u> <u>require</u> that infants and young children ride in government-approved child safety seats because they hope this will reduce needless fatalities. (subject and verb together)

Many <u>states</u>, hoping to reduce needless fatalities, <u>require</u> that infants and young children ride in government-approved child safety seats. (subject and verb separated)

EXERCISE 6

The following sentences use conventional word order. Revise each in one of two ways: either invert the sentence, or vary the word order by placing words between subject and verb. After you have completed your revisions, create a varied five-sentence paragraph by linking the sentences together.

EXAMPLE: Dada was an artistic and literary rebellion that defied the conventional values of the early twentieth century.

REVISION: Dada, an artistic and literary rebellion, defied the conventional values of the early twentieth century.

1. The Dada movement first appeared in 1915 and effectively ended in 1925 with the rise of Surrealism.
2. The name *Dada,* French for "hobby horse," was selected at random from a dictionary and was meant to symbolize the antirational, anti-aesthetic stance taken by its practitioners, who were in part rebelling against the militarism of World War I.
3. The Dadaists abandoned their original antimilitarist protest, and they ultimately rejected all traditional values, especially of culture, which was seen as symptomatic of the falseness and hypocrisy of society, and their goal became to destroy art as an aesthetic cult and replace it with "antiart" and "nonart."
4. The Dadaists rejected the artifact as art, and they substituted the nonsense poem, the ready-made object, and the collage, all of which depended more on the arbitrary and the accidental than on conscious artistry for the crafted design.
5. The most notorious example of Dada art is the sculpture *Fountain* (1917), which was a urinal Marcel Duchamp found and signed *R. Mutt* and entered into a gallery exhibit.

STUDENT WRITER AT WORK

Writing Varied Sentences

Read this draft of a student essay carefully. Then, revise it by varying the length, type, openings, and word order of the sentences. After you have done so, revise further, if necessary, to strengthen coherence, unity, and style.

The American Dream

Although I was only seven at the time, I can vividly recall my family's escape from Vietnam to America. My mother, brother, and I came to America together. My father had fought against the communists during the war. As a result, my brother and I were forbidden from obtaining any education beyond the high school level. Also, Vietnam was an impoverished nation. It seemed as if we had no choice but to leave.

The boat we left in was small. It held only fifty-two people. We left at two o'clock in the morning. At that time, passage by boat cost a sum equal to fifteen hundred American dollars for each child and three thousand dollars for each adult. This was a great deal of money, and very few families could afford to escape. My family was fairly well off in Vietnam. Still, this was a lot of money for us.

Unlike many other "boat people," we were rescued only three days after we left Vietnam. When we saw this ship, all the men in our boat hid. They told the women and children to sit up and stay in the ship's view. They hoped the crew would feel sorry for the women and children and rescue us. This is exactly what happened. When we first boarded the ship, the crew asked us if we wanted anything. We cupped our hands and brought them to our lips. This showed them we were thirsty.

The Norwegian ship left us in Japan at a United Nations refugee camp. We stayed there nearly a year. Then, United Nations staff came to pick up people who had sponsors in other countries. My father had come to the United States two years earlier, so he was our sponsor.

When my mother, brother, and I arrived in America, we stayed for two months in a boardinghouse with my father. Then, we all moved into an apartment of our own. My mother found a job as a housekeeper in a hospital. This was hard for her at first because she could not speak or understand English. It was frustrating to her when she was accused of not doing her work. She couldn't defend herself. My brother and I were more fortunate. At our school, there were many people to help us adjust to American life. When we came home from school, however, we had to fend for ourselves. Both of our parents worked until 6 p.m.

Before they arrived in America, my parents expected life to be much easier in America than it was in Vietnam. They were surprised to find out just how hard life could be here. Because of their limited education, my parents cannot expect a life much better than what they currently have. However, they do expect more for their children. We left Vietnam so my brother and I could have a better education and a better life. Now we are in America. The rest is up to us.

PART 4

SOLVING COMMON SENTENCE PROBLEMS

CHAPTER 24

REVISING SENTENCE FRAGMENTS

? FREQUENTLY ASKED QUESTIONS

What is a sentence fragment?   (p. 412)
How do I turn a fragment into a complete
    sentence?   (p. 413)
Can a list stand alone as a sentence?
    (p. 419)
Are sentence fragments ever acceptable?
    (p. 422)

A **sentence fragment** is an incomplete sentence—a phrase or clause that is punctuated as if it were a complete sentence. A sentence may be incomplete for any of the following reasons.

- **It lacks a subject.**

  Many astrophysicists now believe that galaxies are distributed in clusters. And even form supercluster complexes.

- **It lacks a verb.**

  Three key events defined my generation. The Gulf War, the Oklahoma City bombing, and the Rodney King verdict.

- **It lacks both a subject and a verb.**

  Researchers are engaged in a variety of studies. Suggesting a link between alcoholism and heredity. (*Suggesting* is a **verbal,** which cannot serve as a sentence's main verb.)

- **It is a dependent clause.**

  Bishop Desmond Tutu was awarded the 1984 Nobel Peace Prize. Because he struggled to end apartheid.

MAINTAINING SENTENCE BOUNDARIES

When readers cannot see where sentences begin and end, they have difficulty understanding what you have written. For instance, it is impossible to tell to which independent clause the fragment in each of the following sequences belongs.

The course requirements were changed last year. <u>Because a new professor was hired at the very end of the spring semester.</u> I was unable to find out about this change until after preregistration.

In *The Ox-Bow Incident,* the crowd is convinced that the men are guilty. <u>Even though the men insist they are innocent and Davies pleads for their lives.</u> They are hanged.

✔ CHECKLIST: REVISING SENTENCE FRAGMENTS

To determine whether a sentence is complete, ask these three questions.

✔ Does the word group have a subject?
✔ Does the word group have a verb?
✔ Is the word group a dependent clause? (A sentence cannot consist of a single clause that begins with a subordinating conjunction or a relative pronoun; moreover, unless it is a question, it cannot consist of a single clause beginning with *when, where, who, which, what, why,* or *how.*)

If you cannot answer yes to all three questions, the word group is a fragment, and you will need to use one or more of the following strategies to revise it.

✔ Attach the fragment to an adjacent independent clause.

FRAGMENT: According to German legend, Lohengrin is the son of Parzival. <u>And a knight of the Holy Grail.</u>

REVISED: According to German legend, Lohengrin is the son of Parzival and a knight of the Holy Grail.

continued on the following page

---

continued from the previous page

✔ Supply the missing subject or verb (or both).

FRAGMENT: Lancaster County, Pennsylvania, is home to many Pennsylvania Dutch. <u>Descended from eighteenth-century settlers from southwest Germany.</u>

REVISED: Lancaster County, Pennsylvania, is home to many Pennsylvania Dutch. They are descended from eighteenth-century settlers from southwest Germany.

✔ Delete the subordinating conjunction or relative pronoun.

FRAGMENT: Property taxes rose sharply. <u>Although city services showed no improvement.</u>

REVISED: Property taxes rose sharply. City services showed no improvement.

The following sections identify the grammatical structures most likely to appear as fragments and illustrate the most effective ways of revising each.

24a   Revising Dependent Clauses

A **dependent clause** contains a subject and a verb, but it cannot stand alone as a sentence. Because it needs an independent clause to complete its meaning, a **dependent clause** (also called a *subordinate clause*) must always be attached to at least one independent clause to form a complete sentence. You can recognize a dependent clause because it is always introduced by a **subordinating conjunction** (*although, because,* and so on) or a **relative pronoun** (*that, which, who,* and so on).

To correct a dependent clause fragment, you can join the dependent clause to a neighboring independent clause (creating a complex sentence), or you can delete the subordinating conjunction or relative pro-

---

noun. (You may have to replace the relative pronoun with another word that can serve as the subject.)

FRAGMENT: The United States declared war. <u>Because the Japanese bombed Pearl Harbor.</u> (Dependent clause is incorrectly punctuated as a sentence.)

REVISED: The United States declared war because the Japanese bombed Pearl Harbor. (Dependent clause has been attached to an independent clause to create a complex sentence.)

REVISED: The Japanese bombed Pearl Harbor. The United States declared war. (Subordinating conjunction *because* has been deleted; the result is a complete sentence.)

FRAGMENT: The battery is dead. <u>Which means the car won't start.</u> (Dependent clause is incorrectly punctuated as a sentence.)

REVISED: The battery is dead, which means the car won't start. (Dependent clause has been attached to an independent clause to create a complex sentence.)

REVISED: The battery is dead. This means the car won't start. (Relative pronoun *which* has been replaced by *this,* an acceptable subject, to create a complete sentence.)

EXERCISE 1

Identify the sentence fragments in the following paragraph and correct each, either by attaching the fragment to an independent clause or by deleting the subordinating conjunction or relative pronoun to create a sentence that can stand alone. (In some cases, you will have to replace a relative pronoun with another word that can serve as the subject.)

The drive-in movie came into being just after World War II. When both movies and cars were central to the lives of many Americans. Drive-ins were especially popular with teenagers and young families during the 1950s. When cars and gas were relatively inexpensive. Theaters charged by the carload. Which meant that a group of teenagers or a family with several children could spend an evening at the movies for a few dollars. In 1958, when the fad peaked, there were over four thousand drive-ins in the United States. While today there are fewer than three thousand. Many of these are in the Sunbelt, with most in California. Although many Sunbelt drive-ins continue to thrive because of the year-round warm weather. Many northern drive-ins are in financial trouble.

Because land is so expensive. Some drive-in owners break even only by operating flea markets or swap meets in daylight hours. While others, unable to attract customers, are selling their theaters to land developers. Soon drive-ins may be a part of our nostalgic past. Which will be a great loss for many who enjoy them.

24b Revising Phrases

A **phrase** works as part of a sentence, providing information—description, examples, and so on—about other words or word groups in the sentence. However, a phrase cannot stand alone. Many fragments are created when a phrase is incorrectly punctuated as a sentence.

(1) Prepositional Phrases

A prepositional phrase consists of a preposition, its object, and any modifiers of the object.

To correct a prepositional phrase fragment, attach it to the independent clause that contains the word or word group modified by the prepositional phrase.

FRAGMENT: President Lyndon Johnson decided not to seek reelection. <u>For a number of reasons.</u> (Prepositional phrase is incorrectly punctuated as a sentence.)

REVISED: President Lyndon Johnson decided not to seek reelection for a number of reasons. (Prepositional phrase has been attached to an independent clause.)

FRAGMENT: He ran sixty yards for a touchdown. <u>In the final minutes of the game.</u> (Prepositional phrase is incorrectly punctuated as a sentence.)

REVISED: He ran sixty yards for a touchdown in the final minutes of the game. (Prepositional phrase has been attached to an independent clause.)

EXERCISE 2

Read the following passage and identify the sentence fragments. Then, correct each one by attaching it to the independent clause that contains the word or word group it modifies.

Most college athletes are caught in a conflict. Between their athletic and academic careers. Sometimes college athletes' responsibilities on the playing field make it hard for them to be good students. Often athletes must make a choice. Between sports and a degree. Some athletes would not be able to afford college. Without athletic scholarships. But, ironically, their commitments (training, exercise, practice, and travel to out-of-town games, for example) deprive athletes. Of valuable classroom time. The role of college athletes is constantly being questioned. Critics suggest that athletes exist only to participate in and promote college athletics. Because of the importance of this role to academic institutions, scandals occasionally develop. With coaches and even faculty members arranging to inflate athletes' grades to help them remain eligible. For participation in sports. Some universities even lower admissions standards. To help remedy this and other inequities. The controversial Proposition 48, passed at the NCAA convention in 1982, established minimum College Board scores and grade standards for college students. But many people feel that the NCAA remains overly concerned. With profits rather than with education. As a result, college athletic competition is increasingly coming to resemble pro sports. From the coaches' pressure on the players to win to the network television exposure to the wagers on the games' outcomes.

(2) Verbal Phrases

A verbal phrase consists of a **verbal**—a present participle (*walking*), past participle (*walked*), infinitive (*to walk*), or gerund—plus related objects and modifiers (*walking along the lonely beach*). Because a verbal cannot serve as a sentence's main verb, a verbal phrase is not a complete sentence and should not be punctuated as one.

To correct a verbal phrase fragment, either attach the verbal phrase to a related independent clause or change the verbal to a verb and add a subject.

FRAGMENT: In 1948, India became independent. <u>Divided into the nations of India and Pakistan</u>. (Verbal phrase is incorrectly punctuated as a sentence.)

REVISED: Divided into the nations of India and Pakistan, India became independent in 1948. (Verbal phrase has been attached to the related independent clause to create a complete sentence.)

REVISED: In 1948, India became independent. It was divided into the nations of India and Pakistan. (Verbal *divided* has been changed to verb *was divided,* and subject *it* has been added; the result is a new independent clause.)

FRAGMENT: The pilot changed course. <u>Realizing the weather was worsening</u>. (Verbal phrase is incorrectly punctuated as a sentence.)

REVISED: The pilot changed course, realizing the weather was worsening. (Verbal phrase has been attached to the related independent clause to create a complete sentence.)

REVISED: The pilot changed course. She realized the weather was worsening. (Verb *realized* has been substituted for verbal *realizing,* and subject *she* has been added; the result is a new independent clause.)

EXERCISE 3

Identify the sentence fragments in the following paragraph and correct each. Either attach the fragment to a related independent clause or add a subject and a verb to create a new independent clause.

Many food products have well-known trademarks. Identified by familiar faces on product labels. Some of these symbols have remained the same, while others have changed considerably. Products like Sun-Maid Raisins, Betty Crocker potato mixes, Quaker Oats, and Uncle Ben's Rice use faces. To create a sense of quality and tradition and to encourage shopper recognition of the products. Many of the portraits have been updated several times. To reflect changes in society. Betty Crocker's portrait, for instance, has changed five times since its creation in 1936. Symbolizing women's changing roles. The original Chef Boy-ar-dee has also changed. Turning from the young Italian chef Hector Boiardi into a white-haired senior citizen. Miss Sunbeam, trademark of Sunbeam Bread, has had her hairdo modified several times since her first appearance in 1942; the Blue Bonnet girl, also created in 1942, now has a more modern look, and Aunt Jemima has also been changed. Slimmed down a bit in 1965. Similarly, the Campbell's Soup kids are less chubby now than in the 1920s when they first appeared. But manufacturers are very careful about selecting a trademark or modifying an existing one. Typically spending a good deal of time and money on research before a change is made.

(3) Appositives

An appositive—a noun or noun phrase that identifies or renames an adjacent noun or pronoun—cannot stand alone as a sentence.

To correct an appositive fragment, attach the appositive to the independent clause that contains the word or word group the appositive renames.

FRAGMENT: Piero della Francesca was a leader of the Umbrian school of painting. <u>A school that remained close to the traditions of Gothic art</u>. (Appositive, a fragment that identifies *the Umbrian school of painting,* is incorrectly punctuated as a complete sentence.)

REVISED: Piero della Francesca was a leader of the Umbrian school of painting, a school that remained close to the traditions of Gothic art. (Appositive has been attached to the word group it identifies.)

 REVISING SENTENCE FRAGMENTS: LISTS

Sometimes, an appositive fragment takes the form of a list. To correct this kind of fragment, add a colon to connect the list to the sentence that introduces it.

FRAGMENT: Tourists often outnumber residents in four European cities. <u>Venice, Florence, Canterbury, and Bath.</u>

REVISED: Tourists often outnumber residents in four European cities: Venice, Florence, Canterbury, and Bath.

Appositives are also sometimes introduced by a word or phrase like *that is, for example, for instance, namely,* or *such as.* These phrases do not change anything: appositives still cannot stand alone as sentences. To correct this kind of fragment, attach the appositive to the preceding independent clause.

FRAGMENT: Fairy tales are full of damsels in distress. <u>Such as Snow White, Cinderella, and Rapunzel</u>. (Appositive, a phrase that identifies *damsels in distress,* is incorrectly punctuated as a sentence.)

REVISED: Fairy tales are full of damsels in distress, such as Snow White, Cinderella, and Rapunzel. (Appositive has been attached to the word group it identifies.)

REVISING APPOSITIVE FRAGMENTS

You can also correct an appositive fragment by embedding the appositive within the related independent clause.

FRAGMENT: Some popular novelists are highly respected by later generations. <u>For example, Mark Twain and Charles Dickens</u>. (Appositive, a phrase that identifies *some popular novelists,* is incorrectly punctuated as a sentence.)

REVISED: Some popular novelists—for example, Mark Twain and Charles Dickens—are highly respected by later generations. (Appositive has been embedded within the related independent clause, directly following the word group it identifies.)

Note that a **nonrestrictive** appositive is set off by commas but that a **restrictive** appositive takes no commas.

See
38d1

EXERCISE 4

Identify the fragments in this paragraph and correct them by attaching each to the independent clause containing the word or word group the appositive modifies.

Until the early 1900s, communities in West Virginia, Tennessee, and Kentucky were isolated by the mountains that surrounded them. The great chain of the Appalachian Mountains. Set apart from the emerging culture of a growing America and American language, these communities retained a language rich with the dialect of Elizabethan English. Sprinkled with hints of a Scotch-Irish influence. In the 1910s and '20s, the communities in these mountains began to long for a better future for their children. The key to that future, as they saw it, was education. In some communities, that education took the form of Settlement Schools. Schools led by the new rash of idealistic young graduates of eastern women's colleges. These teachers taught the basic academic subjects. Such as reading, writing, and mathematics. They also schooled their students in the culture of the mountains. For example, the crafts, music, and folklore of the Appalachians. In addition, they taught them skills that would help them survive when the coal market began to decline. The Settlement Schools attracted artisans from around the world. Quilters, luthiers, weavers, basketmakers, and carpenters. The schools also opened the mountains to the world, causing the Elizabethan dialect to fade.

24c Revising Compounds

The last part of a **compound predicate, compound object,** or **compound complement** cannot stand alone as a sentence.

To correct this kind of fragment, connect the detached part of the compound to the rest of the sentence.

FRAGMENT: People with dyslexia have trouble reading. <u>And may also find it difficult to write.</u> (Fragment, part of the compound predicate *have . . . and may also find,* is incorrectly punctuated as a sentence.)

REVISED: People with dyslexia have trouble reading and may also find it difficult to write. (Detached part of the compound predicate has been connected to the rest of the sentence.)

FRAGMENT: They took only a compass and a canteen of water. <u>And some trail mix.</u> (Fragment, part of the compound object *compass . . . canteen . . . trail mix,* is incorrectly punctuated as a sentence.)

REVISED: They took only a compass, a canteen of water, and some trail mix. (Detached part of the compound object has been connected to the rest of the sentence.)

FRAGMENT: When their supplies ran out, they were surprised. <u>And hungry.</u> (Fragment, part of the compound complement *surprised and hungry,* is incorrectly punctuated as a sentence.)

REVISED: When their supplies ran out, they were surprised and hungry. (Detached part of the compound complement has been connected to the rest of the sentence.)

EXERCISE 5

Identify the sentence fragments in this passage and correct them by attaching each detached compound to the rest of the sentence.

As more and more Americans discover the pleasures of the wilderness, our national parks are feeling the stress. Wanting to get away for a weekend or a week, hikers and backpackers stream from the cities into nearby state and national parks. They bring with them a hunger for wilderness. But very little knowledge about how to behave ethically in the wild. They also don't know how to keep themselves safe. Some of them think of the national parks as inexpensive amusement parks. Without proper camping supplies and lacking enough food and water for their trip, they are putting at risk their lives and the lives of those who will be called on to save them. One family went for a hike up a desert canyon with an eight-month-old infant. And their seventy-eight-year-old grandmother. Although the terrain was difficult, they weren't wearing the proper shoes. Or good socks. Nor did they carry a first aid kit. Or a map or compass. They were on an unmarked trail in a little-used section of Bureau of Land Management lands. And following vague directions from a friend. They were soon lost. They hadn't brought water or food. Or even rain gear or warm clothes. Luckily for them, they had brought a cell phone. By the time they called for help, however, it was getting dark and a storm was building. The pilot and his crew safely located the family. And rescued them. Still, a little planning before they hiked in an inhospitable area, and a little awareness and preparedness for the terrain they were traveling in, would have saved this family much worry. And the taxpayers a lot of money.

 REVISING SENTENCE FRAGMENTS

    Sentence fragments are often used in speech and informal writing as well as in journalism, advertising, and creative writing. In most college writing situations, however, sentence fragments are not acceptable.

STUDENT WRITER AT WORK

Revising Sentence Fragments

Carefully read this excerpt from a draft of a student essay. Identify all the sentence fragments and determine why each is a fragment. Correct each sentence fragment by adding, deleting, or modifying words to create a sentence or by attaching the fragment to a neighboring independent clause. Finally, go over the draft again and, if necessary, revise further to strengthen coherence, unity, and style.

Ab Snopes: A Trapped Man

Abner (Ab) Snopes, the father in William Faulkner's story "Barn Burning," is trapped in a hopeless situation. Disgusted with his lack of status yet unable to do much to remedy his dissatisfaction. He has little control over his life, but he still struggles. Fighting his useless battle as best he can.

Ab is a family man. Responsible for a wife, children, and his wife's sister. Unfortunately, he is unable to meet his responsibilities. Such as providing a stable home for his family. Evicted because of Ab's "barn burnings," the family constantly moves from town to town. With all its belongings piled on a wagon. Still, Ab continues to burn barns. Because he hopes that these acts will give him power as well as revenge.

To the rich landowners he works for, Ab is of little significance. Poor, uneducated, uncultured. There are many men just like him. Who can work the land. Ab understands this situation. But is unwilling to accept his inferior status. Consequently, he approaches new employers with arrogance, and his actions and manner soon causing trouble. This behavior, of course, ensures his eventual dismissal. Ab feels that because he can never gain their respect. He should not even bother behaving in a civilized manner. So he insists on playing the role. Of a belligerent, raging man.

Ab's behavior sets in motion a self-fulfilling prophecy. Each time Ab's actions cause an employer to ask him to leave, his prophecy that he will be mistreated is fulfilled. He pretends that the failure is his employer's, not his own. And vents his frustration. By destroying the employer's property with fire. He also feels that such actions will earn him respect. People will be frightened of him, and he will create a name for himself. Only Ab's son, Sarty, sees the truth. That Ab is to his employers "no more [. . .] than a buzzing wasp."

CHAPTER 25

REVISING COMMA SPLICES AND FUSED SENTENCES

? FREQUENTLY ASKED QUESTIONS

What are comma splices and fused sentences, and how are they different from run-ons?   (p. 424)

How can I tell if I've created a comma splice or a fused sentence?   (p. 424)

How do I revise a comma splice or fused sentence?   (p. 425)

A **run-on sentence** is created when two independent clauses are joined without the necessary punctuation or connective word. A run-on sentence is not just a long sentence—in fact, run-ons can be quite short—but a grammatically incorrect construction. *Comma splices* and *fused sentences* are two kinds of run-on sentences.

A **comma splice** is an error that occurs when two independent clauses are joined by a comma. A **fused sentence** is an error that occurs when two independent clauses are joined with no punctuation.

COMMA SPLICE: Charles Dickens created the character of Mr. Micawber, he also created Uriah Heep.

FUSED SENTENCE: Charles Dickens created the character of Mr. Micawber he also created Uriah Heep.

✔ CHECKLIST: REVISING COMMA SPLICES AND FUSED SENTENCES

To find out if you have created a comma splice or fused sentence, ask yourself these two questions:
1. Have you joined two independent clauses with just a comma? If so, you have created a comma splice.
2. Have you joined two independent clauses with no punctuation? If so, you have created a fused sentence.

> To revise a comma splice or fused sentence, use one of the following strategies:
>
> ✔ Use a period to separate the clauses.
> ✔ Use a semicolon to separate the clauses.
> ✔ Add an appropriate coordinating conjunction.
> ✔ Subordinate one clause to the other, creating a complex sentence.

25a   Revising with Periods

You can revise a comma splice or fused sentence by using a period to separate the independent clauses, creating two separate sentences. This is a good strategy when the clauses are long or when they are not closely related.

COMMA SPLICE: In 1894, Frenchman Alfred Dreyfus was falsely convicted of treason, his struggle for justice pitted the army against the civil libertarians.

FUSED SENTENCE: In 1894, Frenchman Alfred Dreyfus was falsely convicted of treason his struggle for justice pitted the army against the civil libertarians.

REVISED: In 1894, Frenchman Alfred Dreyfus was falsely convicted of treason. His struggle for justice pitted the army against the civil libertarians.

 PUNCTUATING INTERRUPTED QUOTATIONS

Use a period—not a comma—to punctuate an interrupted quotation that consists of two complete sentences.

COMMA SPLICE: "This is a good course," Eric said, "in fact, I wish I'd taken it sooner."

REVISED: "This is a good course," Eric said. "In fact, I wish I'd taken it sooner."

Run-Ons/Comma Splices/Fused Sentences
   http://owl.english. purdue. edu/handouts/grammar/g_sentpr.html
   http://CAL.bemidji.msus.edu/WRC/Handouts/ROCSfused.html

25b Revising with Semicolons

See 39a

Use a semicolon between two closely related **independent clauses** that convey parallel or contrasting information.

COMMA SPLICE: Chippendale chairs have straight legs, Queen Anne chairs have curved legs.

FUSED SENTENCE: Chippendale chairs have straight legs Queen Anne chairs have curved legs.

REVISED: Chippendale chairs have straight legs; Queen Anne chairs have curved legs.

COMMA SPLICE: In pre–World War II western Europe, only a small elite had access to a university education, this situation changed dramatically after the war.

FUSED SENTENCE: In pre–World War II western Europe, only a small elite had access to a university education this situation changed dramatically after the war.

REVISED: In pre–World War II western Europe, only a small elite had access to a university education; this situation changed dramatically after the war.

 COMMA SPLICES AND FUSED SENTENCES

See 39b

When you use a **transitional word or phrase** (such as *thus, however, therefore,* or *for example*) to connect two independent clauses within a sentence, the transitional element must be preceded by a semicolon and followed by a comma. If you use a comma before the transitional element, you create a comma splice. If you omit punctuation entirely, you create a fused sentence.

COMMA SPLICE: The international date line is drawn north and south through the Pacific Ocean, thus, it separates Wake and Midway islands.

FUSED SENTENCE: The international date line is drawn north and south through the Pacific Ocean thus it separates Wake and Midway islands.

REVISED: The international date line is drawn north and south through the Pacific Ocean; thus, it separates Wake and Midway islands. (Semicolon is added before transitional word.)

> **REVISED:** The international date line is drawn north and south through the Pacific Ocean, largely at the 180th meridian. Thus, it separates Wake and Midway islands. (Period is added before transitional word.)

25c Revising with Coordinating Conjunctions

If two closely related clauses are of equal importance, you can join them into one compound sentence, using a **coordinating conjunction** to indicate whether the clauses are linked by addition (*and*), contrast (*but, yet*), causality (*for, so*), or a choice of alternatives (*or, nor*). Be sure to add a comma before the coordinating conjunction.

COMMA SPLICE: Elias Howe invented the sewing machine, Julia Ward Howe was a poet and social reformer.

FUSED SENTENCE: Elias Howe invented the sewing machine Julia Ward Howe was a poet and social reformer.

REVISED: Elias Howe invented the sewing machine, but Julia Ward Howe was a poet and social reformer. (Coordinating conjunction *but* shows that emphasis is on contrast.)

25d Revising with Subordinating Conjunctions or Relative Pronouns

When the ideas in two clauses are not of equal importance, correct the comma splice or fused sentence by creating a **complex sentence**, placing the less important idea in a dependent clause. The subordinating conjunction or relative pronoun establishes the specific relationship between the clauses.

COMMA SPLICE: Stravinsky's ballet *The Rite of Spring* shocked Parisians in 1913, its rhythms and the dancers' movements seemed erotic.

FUSED SENTENCE: Stravinsky's ballet *The Rite of Spring* shocked Parisians in 1913 its rhythms and the dancers' movements seemed erotic.

REVISED: Because its rhythms and the dancers' movements seemed erotic, Stravinsky's ballet *The Rite of Spring* shocked Parisians in 1913. (Subordinating conjunction *because* has been added to subordinate the second clause to the first; the result is one complex sentence.)

COMMA SPLICE: Lady Mary Wortley Montagu had suffered from smallpox herself, she helped spread the practice of inoculation against the disease in eighteenth-century England.

FUSED SENTENCE: Lady Mary Wortley Montagu had suffered from smallpox herself she helped spread the practice of inoculation against the disease in eighteenth-century England.

REVISED: Lady Mary Wortley Montagu, who had suffered from smallpox herself, helped spread the practice of inoculation against the disease in eighteenth-century England. (Relative pronoun *who* has been added to subordinate the first clause to the second; the result is a complex sentence.)

 ACCEPTABLE COMMA SPLICES

In a few cases, comma splices may be acceptable. For instance, a comma is used in dialogue between a statement and a tag question, even though each is a separate independent clause.

This is Ron's house, isn't it?

I'm not late, am I?

In addition, commas may be used to connect two short, balanced independent clauses or two or more short, parallel independent clauses, especially when one clause contradicts the other.

Commencement isn't the end, it's the beginning.

EXERCISE 1

Find the comma splices and fused sentences in the following paragraph. Correct each in *two* of the four possible ways listed on page 425. If a sentence is correct, leave it alone.

EXAMPLE: The fans rose in their seats, the game was almost over.

REVISED: The fans rose in their seats; the game was almost over.

The fans rose in their seats, for the game was almost over.

Entrepreneurship is the study of small businesses, college students are embracing it enthusiastically. Many schools offer one or more courses in entrepreneurship these courses teach the theory and practice of starting a small business. Students are signing up for courses, moreover, they are starting their own businesses. One student started with a car-waxing business, now he sells condominiums. Other students are setting up catering services they supply everything from waiters to bartenders. One student has a thriving cake-decorating business, in fact, she employs fifteen students to deliver the cakes. All over the country, student businesses are selling everything from tennis balls to bagels, the student owners are making impressive profits. Formal courses at the graduate as well as undergraduate level are attracting more business students than ever, several business schools (such as Baylor University, the University of Southern California, and Babson College) even offer degree programs in entrepreneurship. Many business school students are no longer planning to be corporate executives instead, they plan to become entrepreneurs.

EXERCISE 2

Combine each of the following sentence pairs into one sentence without creating comma splices or fused sentences. In each case, connect the clauses into a compound sentence with a semicolon or with a comma and a coordinating conjunction. Use each method at least twice. You may have to add, delete, reorder, or change words or punctuation.

EXAMPLE: People think of spring when they see crocuses blooming and robins hopping along on their lawns. I have less traditional methods for telling when spring is imminent.

REVISED: People think of spring when they see crocuses blooming and robins hopping along on their lawns, but I have less traditional methods for telling when spring is imminent.

1. Tiny fragments of broken eggshells are one sign. Dog hair clumping in the corners of my rooms is another.
2. I know it's time to break out the light-blocking shades in mid-March. I move my bed across the room, away from the window.
3. The sound of geese retreating is another clue. The woodpeckers begin searching for termites again in the sides of my wood-shingled house.
4. The baby mice start to rustle around in the old newspapers in the garage. I have to hide the sugar bowl from the ants.
5. I think T. S. Eliot was right. April is the cruelest month.

EXERCISE 3

Combine each of the following sentence pairs into one sentence without creating comma-splice or fused-sentence errors. In each case, subordinate one clause to the other to create a complex sentence. You may have to add, delete, reorder, or change words or punctuation.

EXAMPLE: I grew up on the beach in Florida. People think I'm lucky.

REVISED: Because I grew up on the beach in Florida, people think I'm lucky.

1. Other beach rats know better than to envy me. Inlanders romanticize life by the ocean.
2. The sound of the waves is comforting. The sand gets into everything.
3. In the summer, tourists clog the roads. In the winter, many of the locals are out of work.
4. Beach towns have a difficult time attracting any stable industry. Taxes are often prohibitive.
5. After a while, going to the beach in the summer loses its charm. The beach in winter, empty of other people, is a beautiful sight.

EXERCISE 4

Combine each of the following sentence pairs into one sentence without creating comma splices or fused sentences. In each case, either connect the clauses into a compound sentence with a semicolon or with a comma and a coordinating conjunction, or subordinate one clause to the other to create a complex sentence. You may have to add, delete, reorder, or change words or punctuation.

1. Several recent studies indicate that many American high school students have a poor sense of history. This is affecting our future as a democratic nation and as individuals.
2. Surveys show that nearly one-third of American seventeen-year-olds cannot identify the countries the United States fought against in World War II. One-third think Columbus reached the New World after 1750.
3. Several reasons have been given for this decline in historical literacy. The main reason is the way history is taught.
4. This problem is bad news. The good news is that there is increasing agreement among educators about what is wrong with current methods of teaching history.
5. History can be exciting and engaging. Too often it is presented in a boring manner.

6. Students are typically expected to memorize dates, facts, and names. History as adventure—as a "good story"—is frequently neglected.
7. One way to avoid this problem is to use good textbooks. Textbooks should be accurate, lively, and focused.
8. Another way to create student interest in historical events is to use primary sources instead of so-called comprehensive textbooks. Autobiographies, journals, and diaries can give students insight into larger issues.
9. Students can also be challenged to think about history by taking sides in a debate. They can learn more about connections among historical events by writing essays than by taking multiple-choice tests.
10. Finally, history teachers should be less concerned about specific historical details. They should be more concerned about conveying the wonder of history.

STUDENT WRITER AT WORK

Revising Comma Splices and Fused Sentences

Read the following answer to an economics examination question that asked students to discuss the provisions of the 1935 Social Security Act; then, correct all comma splices and fused sentences. After you have corrected the errors, go over the answer again and, if necessary, revise further to strengthen coherence, unity, and style.

In June of 1934, Franklin D. Roosevelt selected Frances Perkins to head the new Committee on Economic Security, its report was the basis of our current Social Security program. The committee formulated two policies, one dealt with the employable the other with the unemployable. Roosevelt insisted that these programs be self-financing, as a result both employer insurance and employee social insurance were required. In 1935 the Social Security Act was passed it attempted to categorize the poor and provided for federal sharing of the cost, but under local control. (The Social Security Act did not include a public works program, this feature of the New Deal was eliminated.)

Unemployment insurance was one major part of the act. Funds were to be payable through public employment offices, also the money was to be paid into a trust fund. It was to be used solely for benefits an individual could not be denied funds even if work were available. The program provided for payroll taxes, in addition separate records were to be kept by each state. Old Age Survivor Insurance, another major provision of the act, was for individuals over sixty-five it was amended in 1939 to cover dependents. One-quarter of the recipients were disabled. Public Assistance was the third major part of the act this program was designed to help children left alone by the death or absence of the parents and children with mental or physical disabilities. General assistance covered everything not included under the Public Assistance Program this coverage varied from state to state.

The Social Security Act stressed public administration of federal emergency relief assistance thus, it forced reorganization of public assistance. These efforts differed from previous efforts earlier there were no clear guidelines defining which individuals should get aid and why. The Social Security Act attempted to eliminate gaps and overlaps in services.

CHAPTER 26

REVISING FAULTY MODIFICATION

? FREQUENTLY ASKED QUESTIONS

What are misplaced modifiers, and how do I
revise them?   (p. 433)
What are dangling modifiers, and how do I
revise them?   (p. 440)

A **modifier** is a word, phrase, or clause that describes, limits, or qualifies another word or word group in the sentence. A modifier is generally placed close to its **headword,** the word or word group it modifies, and readers expect to find it there.

Wendy watched the storm, <u>dark and threatening</u>.

Faulty modification, the awkward or confusing placement of modifiers or the modification of nonexistent words, takes two forms: *misplaced modifiers* and *dangling modifiers*.

26a   Revising Misplaced Modifiers

A **misplaced modifier** is a word or word group whose placement suggests that it modifies one word or phrase when it is intended to modify another.

<u>Faster than a speeding bullet</u>, the citizens of Metropolis saw Superman flying overhead.

This introductory phrase appears to modify *citizens* when it should logically modify *Superman*. Here is a corrected version.

The citizens of Metropolis saw Superman flying overhead, <u>faster than a speeding bullet</u>.

When writing and revising, place modifying words, phrases, and clauses in a position that clearly identifies the headword and that does not awkwardly interrupt a sentence.

(1) Placing Modifying Words Precisely

Limiting modifiers—such as *almost, only, even, hardly, merely, nearly, exactly, scarcely, just,* and *simply*—should always immediately precede the words they modify. A different placement changes the meaning of the sentence.

> Nick *just* set up camp at the edge of the burned-out town. (He set up camp just now.)

> *Just* Nick set up camp at the edge of the burned-out town. (He set up camp alone.)

> Nick set up camp *just* at the edge of the burned-out town. (His camp was precisely at the edge.)

When a limiting modifier is placed so that it is not clear whether it modifies a word before it or one after it, it is called a **squinting modifier.** To avoid ambiguity, place the modifier so it clearly modifies its headword.

SQUINTING:
The life that everyone thought would fulfill her <u>totally</u> bored her. (Was she supposed to be totally fulfilled, or is she totally bored?)

REVISED:
The life that everyone thought would <u>totally</u> fulfill her bored her. (Everyone expected her to be totally fulfilled.)

REVISED:
The life that everyone thought would fulfill her bored her <u>totally</u>. (She was totally bored.)

EXERCISE 1

In the following sentence pairs, the modifier in each sentence points to a different headword. Underline the modifier and draw an arrow to the word it modifies. Then, explain the meaning of each sentence.

EXAMPLE: She <u>just</u> came in wearing a hat. (She just now entered.)

She came in wearing <u>just</u> a hat. (She wore only a hat.)

1. He wore his almost new jeans.
   He almost wore his new jeans.
2. He had only three dollars in his pocket.
   Only he had three dollars in his pocket.
3. I don't even like freshwater fish.
   I don't like even freshwater fish.
4. I go only to the beach on Saturdays.
   I go to the beach only on Saturdays.
5. He simply hated living.
   He hated simply living.

(2) Relocating Misplaced Phrases

Placing a modifying phrase incorrectly can change the meaning of a sentence or create an unclear or confusing sentence.

Misplaced Verbal Phrases   A **verbal phrase** that acts as a modifier should be placed directly *before* or directly *after* the nouns or pronoun it modifies. The incorrect placement of a verbal phrase can make a sentence convey an entirely different meaning or make no sense at all.

MISPLACED: Jane watched the boats <u>roller-skating along the shore</u>. (Were the boats roller-skating?)

REVISED: <u>Roller-skating along the shore</u>, Jane watched the boats.

MISPLACED: <u>Rolling down the hill</u>, she watched the car. (Was she rolling down the hill?)

REVISED: She watched the car <u>rolling down the hill</u>.

Misplaced Prepositional Phrases   A **prepositional phrase** used as an adjective nearly always directly *follows* the word it modifies.

This is a Dresden figurine <u>from Germany</u>.

Created by a famous artist, *Venus de Milo* is a statue <u>with no arms</u>.

Modifier Placement
   http://webster.commnet.edu/grammar/modifiers.htm

Incorrect placement of such modifiers can give rise to confusion or even unintended humor.

> *Venus de Milo* is a statue created by a famous artist <u>with no arms</u>. (Did the artist have no arms?)

A prepositional phrase used as an adverb also usually *follows* its headword.

> Cassandra looked <u>into the future</u>.

Be careful to avoid ambiguous placement of such phrases.

> MISPLACED: She saw the house she built <u>in her mind</u>. (Did she build the house in her mind?)

> REVISED: <u>In her mind</u>, she saw the house she built.

As long as the meaning of the sentence is clear, however, and as long as the headword is clearly identified, you can place an adverbial modifier in other positions.

> He had been waiting anxiously at the bus stop <u>for a long time</u>.

EXERCISE 2

Underline the modifying verbal phrases or prepositional phrases in each sentence and draw arrows to their headwords.

> EXAMPLE:　Calvin is the democrat <u>running for town council</u>.

1. The bridge across the river swayed in the wind.
2. The spectators on the shore were involved in the action.
3. Mesmerized by the spectacle, they watched the drama unfold.
4. The spectators were afraid of a disaster.
5. Within the hour, the state police arrived to save the day.
6. They closed off the area with roadblocks.
7. Drivers approaching the bridge were asked to stop.
8. Meanwhile, on the bridge, the scene was chaos.
9. Motorists in their cars were paralyzed with fear.
10. Struggling against the weather, the police managed to rescue everyone.

EXERCISE 3

Use the word or phrase that follows each sentence as a modifier in that sentence. Then draw an arrow to indicate its headword.

EXAMPLE: He approached the lion. (timid)

Timidly, he approached the lion.

1. The lion paced up and down in his cage, ignoring the crowd. (watching Jack)
2. Jack stared back at the lion. (nervous yet curious)
3. The crowd around them grew. (anxious to see what would happen)
4. Suddenly Jack heard a growl from deep in the lion's throat. (terrifying)
5. Jack ran from the zoo, leaving the lion behind. (scared to death)

(3) Revising Misplaced Dependent Clauses

A dependent clause that serves as a modifier must be clearly related to its headword. An adjective clause usually appears immediately *after* the word it modifies.

During the Civil War, Lincoln was the president <u>who governed the United States</u>.

An adverb clause can appear in any of several positions, as long as the relationship to the word or word group it modifies is clear and as long as its position conveys the intended emphasis.

<u>During the Civil War</u>, Lincoln was president.

Lincoln was president <u>during the Civil War</u>.

Correct misplaced dependent clauses by making the relationship between modifier and headword clear.

MISPLACED ADJECTIVE CLAUSE: This diet program will limit the consumption of possible carcinogens, <u>which will benefit everyone</u>. (Will carcinogens benefit everyone?)

Misplaced and Dangling Modifiers
   http://www.clearcf.uvic.ca/writersguide/Pages/SentMispMods.html

Revised: This diet program, <u>which will benefit everyone</u>, will limit the consumption of possible carcinogens.

Misplaced Adverb Clause: The parents checked to see that the children were sleeping <u>after they had a glass of wine</u>. (Did the children drink the wine?)

Revised: <u>After they had a glass of wine</u>, the parents checked to see that the children were sleeping.

EXERCISE 4

Relocate the misplaced verbal phrases, prepositional phrases, or dependent clauses so that they clearly point to the words or word groups they modify.

> **Example:** *Silent Running* is a film about a scientist left alone in space with Bruce Dern.
>
> *Silent Running* is a film with Bruce Dern about a scientist left alone in space.

1. She realized that she had married the wrong man after the wedding.
2. *The Prince and the Pauper* is a novel about an exchange of identities by Mark Twain.
3. The energy was used up in the ten-kilometer race that he was saving for the marathon.
4. He loaded the bottles and cans into his new Porsche, which he planned to leave at the recycling center.
5. The manager explained the sales figures to the board members using a graph.

(4) Revising Intrusive Modifiers

An **intrusive modifier** interrupts a sentence, making it difficult to understand.

Interrupted Verb Phrases Revise when a long modifying phrase comes between an auxiliary verb and a main verb.

Awkward: She <u>had</u>, without giving it a second thought or considering the consequences, <u>planned</u> to reenlist.

Revised: Without giving it a second thought or considering the consequences, she <u>had planned</u> to reenlist.

AWKWARD: He <u>will</u>, if he ever gets his act together, <u>be</u> ready to leave on Friday.

REVISED: If he ever gets his act together, he <u>will be</u> ready to leave on Friday.

A brief modifier, however, can usually interrupt a verb phrase.

She <u>had</u> always <u>planned</u> to reenlist.

He <u>will</u>, therefore, <u>be</u> ready to leave on Friday.

Split Infinitives   Revise when modifiers awkwardly interrupt an **infinitive** (*to* plus the base form of the verb).

AWKWARD: He hoped <u>to</u> quickly and easily <u>defeat</u> his opponent.

REVISED: He hoped <u>to defeat</u> his opponent quickly and easily.

When the intervening modifier is short, and when the alternative is awkward or ambiguous, a split infinitive is acceptable.

ACCEPTABLE: She expected <u>to</u> not quite <u>beat</u> her previous record.

Interrupted Subjects and Verbs or Verbs and Objects or Complements
Placing even a complex or lengthy adjective phrase or clause between a subject and a verb or between a verb and its object or complement will usually not cause confusion.

ACCEPTABLE: Major <u>films</u> that were financially successful in the 1930s <u>include</u> *Gone with the Wind* and *The Wizard of Oz*. (Adjective clause between subject and verb does not obscure sentence's meaning.)

However, an adverb phrase or clause in this position may not be clear or sound natural. Revise if you have any doubts about letting a modifier stand between subject and verb or between verb and object or complement.

CONFUSING: The <u>election</u>, because officials discovered that some people voted twice, <u>was</u> contested. (Adverb clause intrudes between subject and verb.)

REVISED: Because officials discovered that some people voted twice, the <u>election was</u> contested. (Subject and verb are no longer separated.)

CONFUSING: A. A. Milne <u>wrote</u>, when his son Christopher Robin was a child, <u>*Winnie the Pooh*</u>. (Adverb clause intrudes between verb and object.)

REVISED: When his son Christopher Robin was a child, A. A. Milne wrote *Winnie the Pooh*. (Verb and object are no longer separated.)

EXERCISE 5

Revise these sentences so that the modifying phrases or clauses do not interrupt the parts of a verb phrase or an infinitive or separate a subject from a verb or a verb from its object or complement.

EXAMPLE: A play can sometimes be, despite the playwright's best efforts, mystifying to the audience.

REVISED: Despite the playwright's best efforts, a play can sometimes be mystifying to the audience.

1. The people in the audience, when they saw the play was about to begin and realized the orchestra had finished tuning up and had begun the overture, finally quieted down.
2. They settled into their seats, expecting to very much enjoy the first act.
3. However, most people were, even after watching and listening for twenty minutes and paying close attention to the drama, completely baffled.
4. In fact, the play, because it had nameless characters, no scenery, and a rambling plot that didn't seem to be heading anywhere, puzzled even the drama critics.
5. Finally, one of the three major characters explained, speaking directly to the audience, what the play was really about.

26b Revising Dangling Modifiers

A **dangling modifier** is a word or phrase that cannot logically modify any word or word group in the sentence. In fact, its true headword does not appear in the sentence. In the following sentence, *using this drug* is a dangling modifier.

Using this drug, many undesirable side effects are experienced.

See
34d1

There are two ways to correct this dangling modifier. The first way is to *create a new subject* by supplying a word or word group that it can logically modify. (Note that this option changes **passive to active voice**.)

Dangling Modifiers (U.Vic)
http://www.vic.uh.edu/ac/grammar/dangling.html

REVISED: Using this drug, <u>patients</u> experience many undesirable side effects.

The second way to correct the dangling modifier is to reword it to *create a dependent clause.*

REVISED: Many undesirable side effects are experienced <u>when this drug is used</u>.

These two options for correcting dangling modifiers are further explained and illustrated in **26b1** and **26b2**.

(1) Creating a New Subject

DANGLING: <u>Using a pair of forceps</u>, the skin of the rat's abdomen was lifted, and a small cut was made into the body with scissors. (Modifier cannot logically modify *skin.*)

REVISED: <u>Using a pair of forceps</u>, the technician lifted the skin of the rat's abdomen and made a small cut into the body with scissors. (Subject of main clause has been changed from *the skin* to *the technician,* a logical headword.)

DANGLING: <u>With fifty pages left to read</u>, *War and Peace* was absorbing. (Modifier cannot logically modify *War and Peace.*)

REVISED: <u>With fifty pages left to read</u>, Meg found *War and Peace* absorbing. (Subject of main clause has been changed from *War and Peace* to *Meg,* a logical headword.)

(2) Creating a Dependent Clause

DANGLING PHRASE: <u>To implement a plus/minus grading system</u>, all students were polled. (Modifier cannot logically modify *students.*)

REVISED: <u>Before a plus/minus grading system was implemented</u>, all students were polled. (Modifying phrase is now a dependent clause.)

DANGLING: <u>On the newsstands only an hour</u>, its sales surprised everyone. (Modifier cannot logically modify *sales.*)

REVISED: <u>Because the magazine had been on the newsstands only an hour</u>, its sales surprised everyone. (Modifying phrase is now a dependent clause.)

 REVISING DANGLING ELLIPTICAL CLAUSES

 See 19b2

Elliptical clauses are incomplete constructions. Typically, the writer has intentionally omitted part of the subject or predicate (or the entire subject or predicate) from a dependent clause in order to create a more concise sentence. When such a clause cannot logically modify the subject of the sentence's main clause, it dangles. To revise a dangling elliptical clause, either create a new subject or create a complete dependent clause.

DANGLING: <u>While still in the Buchner funnel,</u> you should press the crystals with a clear stopper to eliminate any residual solvent. (Elliptical clause cannot logically modify *you*.)

REVISED: <u>While still in the Buchner funnel,</u> the crystals should be pressed with a clear stopper to eliminate any residual solvent. (Subject of main clause has been changed from *you* to *crystals*, a word the elliptical clause can logically modify.)

EXERCISE 6

Eliminate the dangling modifier from each of the following sentences. Either supply a word or word group the dangling modifier can logically modify, or change the dangling modifier into a dependent clause.

EXAMPLE: Skiing down the mountain, my hat flew off. (dangling modifier)

REVISED: Skiing down the mountain, <u>I</u> lost my hat. (logical headword added)

<u>As I skied down the mountain,</u> my hat flew off. (dependent clause)

1. Writing for eight hours every day, her lengthy books are published every year or so.

2. As an out-of-state student without a car, it was difficult to get to off-campus cultural events.
3. To build a campfire, kindling is necessary.
4. With every step upward, the trees became sparser.
5. Being an amateur tennis player, my backhand is weaker than my forehand.
6. When exiting the train, the station will be on your right.
7. Driving through the Mojave, the bleak landscape was oppressive.
8. By requiring auto manufacturers to further improve emission-control devices, the air quality will get better.
9. Using a piece of filter paper, the ball of sodium is dried as much as possible and placed in a test tube.
10. Having missed work for seven days straight, my job was in jeopardy.

STUDENT WRITER AT WORK

Revising Faulty Modification

Read this draft of a student's technical writing exercise, a description of a 10cc syringe. Correct misplaced and dangling modifiers and revise again if necessary to strengthen coherence, unity, and style.

Designed to inject liquids into, or withdraw them from, any vessel or cavity, the function of a syringe is often to inject drugs into the body or withdraw blood from it. Syringes are also used to precisely measure amounts of drugs or electrolytes that must be added to intravenous solutions.

There are available on the market today many different types of syringes, but the one most commonly used in hospitals is the 10-cubic centimeter (cc) disposable syringe. Approximately 5 inches long, the primary composition of this particular syringe is transparent polyethylene plastic. The 10cc syringe and the majority of other syringes all have a round plunger or piston within a barrel.

The barrel of a syringe is a round hollow cylinder about 4 1/2" long with a diameter of 3/8". The bottom end of the barrel has two extensions on its opposite sides, which are perpendicular to the cylinder. With a width equal to the diameter of the barrel, the length of these extensions is about 1/2". The purpose of these extensions is to enable one to hold with the index finger and middle finger the barrel of the syringe while depressing the plunger with the thumb.

The barrel of the syringe is calibrated on the side in black ink subdivided into gradations of 2cc. At the top of the syringe the barrel abruptly narrows to a very small cylinder, 1/8" in diameter and 1/4" in length. This small cylinder is surrounded by another hollow cylinder with a slightly larger diameter. The inside wall of the outer cylinder is threaded like a corkscrew. The purpose of this thread is to keep the needle in place.

The other major part of the syringe is the plunger. The plunger is a solid round cylinder that fits snugly into the barrel made of plastic. At the bottom of the plunger is a plastic ring the size of a dime, which provides something to grasp while withdrawing the plunger. The body of the plunger connects the bottom rim with the tip of the plunger, which is made of black rubber.

CHAPTER 27

REVISING FAULTY PARALLELISM

? FREQUENTLY ASKED QUESTIONS

What is parallelism?   (p. 445)
Why is parallelism a good strategy for me to
use in my writing?   (p. 445)
What is faulty parallelism, and how do I fix
it?   (p. 448)

Parallelism is the use of matching words, phrases, or clauses, or sentence structures to express equivalent ideas. Effective parallelism adds unity, balance, and force to your writing.

27a   Using Parallelism

Effective parallelism makes sentences clear and easy to follow and emphasizes relationships among equivalent ideas. Parallelism highlights the correspondence between *items in a series, paired items,* and elements in *lists and outlines.*

(1) With Items in a Series

Coordinate elements—words, phrases, or clauses—in a series should be presented in parallel form. (For information on punctuating elements in a series, see **38b** and **39c.**)

Eat, <u>drink</u>, and <u>be</u> merry.

<u>I came</u>; <u>I saw</u>; <u>I conquered</u>.

<u>Baby food consumption</u>, <u>toy production</u>, and <u>marijuana use</u> are likely to decline as the US population grows older.

Parallelism(U. Vic)
   http://www.clearcf.uvic.ca/writersguide/Pages/SentParallel.html
Parallel Structure
   http://www.bcc.ctc.edu/writinglab/Parallel.html

Three factors influenced his decision to seek new employment: <u>his desire to relocate</u>, <u>his need for greater responsibility</u>, and <u>his dissatisfaction with his current job</u>.

(2) With Paired Items

Paired points or ideas (words, phrases, or clauses) should be presented in parallel terms. Parallelism emphasizes their equivalence and relates the two ideas to each other.

The thank-you note was <u>short</u> but <u>sweet</u>.

<u>Roosevelt represented the United States</u>, and <u>Churchill represented Great Britain</u>.

The research focused on <u>muscle tissue</u> and <u>nerve cells</u>.

<u>Ask not what your country can do you</u>; <u>ask what you can do for your country</u>. (John F. Kennedy, inaugural address)

Paired items linked by **correlative conjunctions** (such as *not only/but also, both/and, either/or, neither/nor,* and *whether/or*) should be parallel.

The design team paid close attention not only <u>to color</u> but also <u>to texture</u>.

Either <u>repeat physics</u> or <u>take calculus</u>.

Both <u>cable television</u> and <u>videocassette recorders</u> continue to threaten the dominance of the major television networks.

Parallelism is also used with paired elements linked by *than* or *as*. In such cases, parallel structure stresses the contrast between the paired elements.

Richard Wright and James Baldwin chose <u>to live in Paris</u> rather than <u>to remain in the United States</u>.

Success is as much <u>a matter of hard work</u> as <u>a matter of luck</u>.

(3) In Lists and Outlines

Elements in a list should be expressed in parallel terms.

The Irish potato famine had four major causes:
1. The establishment of the landlord-tenant system
2. The failure of the potato crop
3. The reluctance of England to offer adequate financial assistance
4. The passage of the Corn Laws

See 3c3

Elements in a **formal outline** also should be parallel.

EXERCISE 1

Identify the parallel elements in these sentences by underlining parallel words and bracketing parallel phrases and clauses.

EXAMPLE: Manek spent six years in America [going to school] and [working for a computer company].

1. Manek returned to India after he completed his engineering degree to visit his large extended family and to find a wife.
2. Unfamiliar with marriage practices in India and accustomed to American notions of marriage for love, Manek's American friends frowned on his plans.
3. Not only Manek but also his parents wanted an arranged marriage.
4. He didn't believe that either you married for love or you had a loveless marriage.
5. His parents' marriage, an arranged one, continues happily; his aunt's marriage, also arranged, has lasted thirty years.

EXERCISE 2

Combine each of the following sentence pairs or sentence groups into one sentence that uses parallel structure. Be sure all parallel words, phrases, and clauses are expressed in parallel terms.

1. Originally, there were five performing Marx Brothers. One was nicknamed Groucho. The others were called Chico, Harpo, Gummo, and Zeppo.
2. Groucho was very well known. So were Chico and Harpo. Gummo soon dropped out of the act. And later Zeppo did too.
3. They began in vaudeville. That was before World War I. Their first show was called *I'll Say She Is.* It opened in New York in 1924.
4. The Marx Brothers' first movie was *The Cocoanuts.* The next was *Animal Crackers.* And this was followed by *Monkey Business, Horse Feathers,* and *Duck Soup.* Then came *A Night at the Opera.*
5. In each of these movies, the Marx Brothers make people laugh. They also exhibit a unique, zany comic style.
6. In their movies, each brother has a set of familiar trademarks. Groucho has a mustache and a long coat. He wiggles his eyebrows and smokes a cigar. There is a funny hat that Chico always wears. And he affects a phony Italian accent. Harpo never speaks.
7. Groucho is always cast as a sly operator. He always tries to cheat people out of their money. He always tries to charm women.

8. In *The Cocoanuts,* he plays Mr. Hammer, proprietor of the run-down Coconut Manor, a Florida hotel. In *Horse Feathers,* his character is named Professor Quincy Adams Wagstaff. Wagstaff is president of Huxley College. Huxley also has financial problems.
9. In *Duck Soup,* Groucho plays Rufus T. Firefly, president of the country of Fredonia. Fredonia was formerly ruled by the late husband of a Mrs. Teasdale. Fredonia is now at war with the country of Sylvania.
10. Margaret Dumont is often Groucho's leading lady. She plays Mrs. Teasdale in *Duck Soup.* In *A Night at the Opera,* she plays Mrs. Claypool. Her character in *The Cocoanuts* is named Mrs. Potter.

❷ 27b Revising Faulty Parallelism

Faulty parallelism occurs when elements that have the same function in a sentence are not presented in parallel terms.

> FAULTY PARALLELISM: Many people in developing countries suffer because the countries lack sufficient housing to accommodate them, sufficient food to feed them, and their health-care facilities are inadequate.

Because the three reasons in the preceding sentence are presented in a series, readers expect them to be expressed in parallel terms. The first two elements satisfy this expectation.

> sufficient housing to accommodate them . . .
>
> sufficient food to feed them . . .

The third item in the series, however, breaks this pattern.

> their health-care facilities are inadequate.

To correct the faulty parallelism and create a clear, emphatic sentence, all three elements must be presented in the same terms.

> Many people in developing countries suffer because the countries lack <u>sufficient housing to accommodate them</u>, <u>sufficient food to feed them</u>, and <u>sufficient health-care facilities to serve them</u>.

(1) Using Parallel Elements

Avoid faulty parallelism by matching nouns with nouns, verbs with verbs, and phrases and clauses with similarly constructed phrases and clauses.

Faulty Parallelism	*Revised*
Popular exercises for men and women include aerobic dancing, weight lifters, and jogging.	Popular exercises for men and women include aerobic <u>dancing</u>, weight <u>lifting</u>, and <u>jogging</u>.
Some of the side effects are skin irritation and eye irritation, and mucous membrane irritation may also develop.	Some of the side effects that may develop are <u>skin</u>, <u>eye</u>, and <u>mucous membrane</u> irritation.
I look forward to hearing from you and to have an opportunity to tell you more about myself.	I look forward to <u>hearing from you</u> and to <u>having an opportunity</u> to tell you more about myself.

(2) Repeating Signals of Parallelism

Faulty parallelism also occurs when a writer does not repeat words that signal parallelism: prepositions, articles, the *to* of the infinitive, and so on. Although the use of similar grammatical structures may sometimes be enough to convey parallelism, sentences are even clearer and more emphatic if other key words in parallel constructions are also parallel.

Faulty Parallelism	*Revised*
Computerization has helped industry by not allowing labor costs to skyrocket, increasing the speed of production, and improving efficiency. (Does *not* apply to all three phrases, or only the first?)	Computerization has helped industry <u>by not allowing labor costs to skyrocket</u>, <u>by increasing the speed of production</u>, and <u>by improving efficiency</u>. (Preposition *by* is repeated to clarify the boundaries of the three parallel phrases.)

(3) Repeating Relative Pronouns

Like correlative conjunctions, *who . . . and who, whom . . . and whom,* and *which . . . and which* are always paired and always introduce parallel clauses. To avoid faulty parallelism, be sure to include both parts of the correlative conjunction.

FAULTY: *The Thing,* directed by Howard Hawks, and which was released in 1951, featured James Arness as the monster.

REVISED: *The Thing,* <u>which</u> was directed by Howard Hawks <u>and</u> <u>which</u> was released in 1951, featured James Arness as the monster.

EXERCISE 3

Identify and correct faulty parallelism in these sentences. Then, underline the parallel elements—words, phrases, and clauses—in your corrected sentences. If a sentence is already correct, mark it with a *C* and underline the parallel elements.

EXAMPLE: Alfred Hitchcock's films include *North by Northwest, Vertigo, Psycho,* and he also directed *Notorious* and *Saboteur.*

REVISED: Films directed by Alfred Hitchcock include <u>*North by Northwest*</u>, <u>*Vertigo*</u>, <u>*Psycho*</u>, <u>*Notorious*</u>, and <u>*Saboteur*</u>.

1. The world is divided between those with galoshes on and those who discover continents.
2. Soviet leaders, members of Congress, and the American Catholic bishops all pressed the president to limit the arms race.
3. A national task force on education recommended improving public education by making the school day longer, higher teachers' salaries, and integrating more technology into the curriculum.
4. The fast-food industry is expanding to include many kinds of restaurants: those that serve pizza, fried-chicken chains, some offering Mexican-style menus, and hamburger franchises.
5. The consumption of Scotch in the United States is declining because of high prices, tastes are changing, and increased health awareness has led many whiskey drinkers to switch to wine or beer.

STUDENT WRITER AT WORK

Revising Faulty Parallelism

In the following section of a draft of a paper written for a class in public health, a student discusses factors that must be taken into account by medical practitioners at the Indian Health Service. Correct the faulty parallelism and revise again if necessary to strengthen coherence, unity, and style.

The average life span of Native Americans is considerably

lower than that of the general population. Not only is their infant mortality rate four times higher than that of the general population, but they also have a suicide rate that is twice as high as that of other races. Moreover, Native Americans both die in homicides more often than people of other races do and there are more alcohol-related deaths among Native Americans than among people of other races. Medical care available for them does not meet their needs and is presenting a challenge for the health professionals who serve them.

The Indian Health Service (IHS), a branch of the US Public Health Service, is responsible for providing medical care to Native Americans who live on reservations. The IHS has been criticized for its inability to deal with cultural differences between health professionals and Native Americans—cultural differences that interfere with adequate medical care. In order to diagnose disease states, for prescribing drug therapy, and to counsel patients, health professionals need to acquire an understanding of Native American culture. They must gain a working knowledge of Native Americans' ideas and feelings toward health and also God, relationships, and death. Only then can health professionals communicate their goals, provide quality medical care, and in addition they will be able to achieve patient compliance.

There are many obstacles to effective communication: hostility to white authority and whites' structured, organized society; language is another obvious barrier to communication; Native Americans' view of sickness, which may be different from Anglos'; and some Indian cultures' concept of time is also different from that of the Anglo health workers. Other problems are more basic: a physician cannot expect a patient to refrigerate medication if no refrigerators are available or dilute dosage forms at home or be changing wet dressings several times a day if clean water is not readily available nor quart/pint measuring devices to dilute stock solutions.

The problems in Native American health care cannot be completely solved by the improvement of communication channels or making these channels stronger. But the health professionals' communication with the Native American patient can be effective enough so that medical staff can acquire an adequate medical history, monitor drug use, be alert for possible drug interactions, and to provide useful discharge counseling. If health professionals can communicate understanding and respect for Native American culture and concern for their welfare, they may be able to meet the needs of their Native American patients more effectively.

CHAPTER 28

REVISING AWKWARD OR CONFUSING SENTENCES

❓ FREQUENTLY ASKED QUESTIONS

What is the difference between direct and indirect discourse? (p. 456)
What is wrong with using the phrase "the reason is because"? (p. 459)
How do I correct an incomplete or illogical comparison? (p. 460)

The most common causes of awkward or confusing sentences are *unwarranted shifts, mixed constructions, faulty predication,* and *illogical comparisons.*

28a Shifts in Tense

Verb tenses in a sentence or in a related group of sentences should shift only with good reason—to indicate changes of time, for example.

See 34b

The Wizard of Oz is a film that has enchanted audiences since it was made in 1939. (acceptable shift from present to past)

Unwarranted shifts can mislead readers and obscure your meaning.

FAULTY: The prisoner told the parole board that he promises to stay out of trouble. (unwarranted shift from past to present)

REVISED: The prisoner told the parole board that he promised to stay out of trouble. (both verbs in past tense)

Improving Sentence Clarity (Purdue)
   http://owl.english.purdue.edu/handouts/general/gl_sentclar.html
Consistency in Verb Tense and Pronouns/Point of View (includes self-test)
   http://gabiscott.com/bigdog/consistency.htm

See
53b

FAULTY: *On the Road* <u>is</u> a novel about friends who <u>drove</u> across the United States in the 1950s. (unwarranted shift from present to past)

REVISED: *On the Road* <u>is</u> a novel about friends who <u>drive</u> across the United States in the 1950s. (**literary work** discussed in both clauses; both verbs in present tense)

28b Shifts in Voice

Unwarranted shifts from active to passive voice (or from passive to active) can be confusing. In the following sentence, for instance, the shift from active (*wrote*) to passive (*was written*) makes it unclear who wrote *The Great Gatsby:*

FAULTY: F. Scott Fitzgerald <u>wrote</u> *This Side of Paradise,* and later *The Great Gatsby* <u>was written</u>.

REVISED: F. Scott Fitzgerald wrote *This Side of Paradise* and later wrote *The Great Gatsby.* (consistent use of active voice)

NOTE: Sometimes a shift from active to passive voice within a sentence may be necessary to give the sentence proper emphasis.

Even though consumers protested, the gasoline tax was increased.

28c Shifts in Mood

See
34c

<u>Mood</u> indicates whether a writer is making a statement or asking a question (**indicative mood**), issuing a command or making a request (**imperative mood**), or expressing a wish or hypothetical condition (**subjunctive mood**). Unnecessary shifts in mood can create awkward sentences.

FAULTY: <u>Heat</u> the mixture in a test tube, and <u>you should make</u> sure it <u>does</u> not boil. (shift from imperative to indicative mood)

REVISED: <u>Heat</u> the mixture in a test tube and <u>make sure</u> it does not boil. (both verbs in imperative mood)

28d Shifts in Person and Number

Person indicates who is speaking (first person—*I, we*), who is spoken to (second person—*you*), and who is spoken about (third person—*he,* *she, it,* and *they*). Unwarranted shifts between second- and third-person pronouns cause most errors.

> **FAULTY:** When <u>one</u> looks for a car loan, <u>you</u> compare the interest rates of several banks. (shift from third to second person)

> **REVISED:** When <u>you</u> look for a car loan, <u>you</u> compare the interest rates of several banks. (consistent use of second person)

Number indicates one (singular—*novel, it*) or more than one (plural— *novels, they, them*). Number should be consistent within a sentence.

> **FAULTY:** The <u>students</u> all turned in their <u>paper</u>. (shift from plural noun to singular noun)

> **REVISED:** The <u>students</u> all turned in their <u>papers</u>. (consistent use of plural nouns)

EXERCISE 1

Read the following sentences and eliminate any shifts in tense, voice, mood, person, or number. Some sentences are correct, and some can be revised in more than one way.

> EXAMPLE: When one examines at the history of the women's movement, you see that it had many different beginnings.

> REVISED: When you examine at the history of the women's movement, you see that it had many different beginnings.

1. Some historians see World War II and women's work in the factories as the beginning of the push toward equal rights for women.
2. Women went to work in the fabric mills of Lowell, Massachusetts, in the late 1800s, and her efforts at reforming the workplace are seen by many as the beginning of the equal rights movement.
3. Farm girls from New Hampshire, Vermont, and western Massachusetts came to Lowell to make money for their trousseaus, and they wanted to experience life in the city.
4. The factories promised the girls decent wages, and parents were promised that their daughters would live in a safe, wholesome environment.
5. Dormitories were built by the factory owners; they are supposed to ensure a safe environment for the girls.
6. First, visit the loom rooms at the Boot Mills Factory, and then you should tour a replica of a dormitory.

7. When one visits the working loom room at the factory, you are overcome with a sense of the risks and dangers the girls faced in the mills.
8. For a mill girl, moving to the city meant freedom and an escape from the drudgery of farm life; it also meant they had to face many new social situations for which they were not always prepared.
9. Harriet Robinson wrote *Loom and Spindle,* the story of her life as a mill girl, and then a book of poems was published.
10. When you look at the lives of the loom girls, one can see that their work laid part of the foundation for women's later demands for equal rights.

❓ 28e   Shifts from Direct to Indirect Discourse

Direct discourse reports the exact words of a speaker or writer. It is always enclosed in quotation marks and often accompanied by an identifying tag (*he says, she asked*). **Indirect discourse** summarizes the words of a speaker or writer. No quotation marks are used, and the reported words are often introduced with the word *that* or, in the case of questions, with *who, what, why, whether, how,* or *if.*

> Direct Discourse: My instructor said, "<u>I want</u> your paper by this Friday."

> Indirect Discourse: My instructor said that <u>he wanted</u> my paper by this Friday.

Statements and questions that shift between indirect and direct discourse are often confusing.

> Faulty: During his trial, John Brown repeatedly said that <u>I am not guilty</u>. (shift from indirect to direct discourse)

> Revised: During his trial, John Brown repeatedly said, "<u>I am not guilty</u>." (consistent use of direct discourse)

> Revised: During his trial, John Brown repeatedly said <u>that he was not guilty</u>. (consistent use of indirect discourse)

> Faulty: My mother asked <u>was I ever going to get a job</u>. (blends direct and indirect discourse)

> Revised: My mother asked <u>whether I was ever going to get a job</u>. (consistent use of indirect discourse)

> Revised: My mother asked, "<u>Are you ever going to get a job?</u>" (consistent use of direct discourse)

EXERCISE 2

Change the direct discourse in the following sentences to indirect discourse.

> EXAMPLE: Anna Quindlen explained why she kept her maiden name
> when she married: "It was a political decision, a simple
> statement that I was somebody and not an adjunct of
> anybody, especially a husband."
>
> Anna Quindlen explained that she made a decision to
> keep her maiden name when she married because it was a
> simple political statement that she was somebody and not
> an adjunct to anybody, especially not to a husband.

1. Sally Thane Christensen, advocating the use of an endangered species of tree, the yew, as a treatment for cancer, asked, "Is a tree worth a life?"
2. Stephen Nathanson, considering the morality of the death penalty, asked, "What if the death penalty did save lives?"
3. Martin Luther King, Jr., said, "I have a dream that one day this nation will rise up and live out the true meaning of its creed."
4. Benjamin Franklin once stated, "The older I grow, the more apt I am to doubt my own judgment of others."
5. Thoreau said, "The finest qualities of our nature, like the bloom on fruits, can be preserved only by the most delicate handling."

28f   Mixed Constructions

A **mixed construction** occurs when a prepositional, dependent clause, or indendent clause is used as the subject of a sentence.

MIXED: <u>By calling for information</u> is the way to learn more about the benefits of ROTC. (Prepositional phrase cannot logically serve as subject.)

REVISED: By calling for information, you can learn more about the benefits of ROTC. (Subject *you* is provided.)

MIXED: <u>Even though he published a paper on the subject</u> does not mean he should get credit for the discovery. (Dependent clause cannot logically serve as subject.)

REVISED: Even though he published a paper on the subject, he should not get credit for the discovery. (Subject *he* is provided.)

MIXED: <u>He was late</u> was what made him miss Act 1. (Independent clause cannot logically serve as subject.)

REVISED: Because he was late, he missed Act 1. (Independent clause has been changed to a dependent clause, creating a complex sentence.)

EXERCISE 3

Revise the following mixed constructions so their parts fit together both grammatically and logically.

EXAMPLE: By investing in commodities made her rich.

Investing in commodities made her rich.

1. In implementing the "motor voter" bill has made it easier for people to register to vote.
2. She sank the basket was the reason they won the game.
3. Just because situations change, doesn't change the characters' hopes and dreams.
4. By dropping the course would be his only chance to avoid a low GPA.
5. Even though she works for a tobacco company does not mean that she should be against laws prohibiting smoking in restaurants.

28g   Faulty Predication

Faulty predication (sometimes called *illogical predication*) occurs when a sentence's predicate does not logically complete its subject. Faulty predication is especially common in sentences that contain a *linking verb*—a form of the verb *be,* for example—and a subject complement.

FAULTY: Mounting costs and decreasing revenues <u>were the downfall</u> of the hospital.

This sentence incorrectly states that mounting costs and decreasing revenues were the *downfall* of the hospital when, in fact, they were the *reasons* for its downfall. You can correct this problem by providing a subject complement that relates logically to the subject.

REVISED: Mounting costs and decreasing revenues <u>were the reasons</u> for the downfall of the hospital.

Faulty parallelism most often occurs in the following situations.

(1) *Is When* or *Is Where*

Faulty predication occurs when a sentence that presents a definition contains a construction like *is where* or *is when.*

FAULTY: Taxidermy is where you construct a lifelike representation of an animal from its preserved skin. (In a definition, *is* must be preceded and followed by nouns or noun phrases.)

REVISED: Taxidermy is the construction of a lifelike representation of an animal from its preserved skin.

(2) *The Reason . . . Is Because*

Faulty predication occurs when the phrase *the reason is* precedes *because.* In this situation, *because* (which means "for the reason that") is redundant and can be deleted.

FAULTY: The reason we drive is because we are afraid to fly.

REVISED: The reason we drive is that we are afraid to fly.

REVISED: We drive because we are afraid to fly.

(3) Faulty Appositive

A **faulty appositive** is a type of faulty predication in which an appositive is equated with a noun or pronoun it cannot logically modify.

FAULTY: The salaries are high in professional athletics, such as baseball players. (*Professional athletics* is not the same as *baseball players.*)

REVISED: The salaries are high for professional athletes, such as baseball players. (*baseball players = professional athletes*)

EXERCISE 4

Revise the following sentences to eliminate faulty predication. Keep in mind that each sentence may be revised in more than one way.

EXAMPLE: The reason traffic jams occur at 9 a.m. and 5 p.m. is because too many people work traditional rather than staggered hours.

REVISED: Traffic jams occur at 9 a.m. and 5 p.m. because too many people work traditional rather than staggered hours.

1. Inflation is when the purchasing power of currency declines.
2. Hypertension is where the blood pressure is elevated.

3. Computers have become part of our everyday lives, such as instant cash machines.
4. Some people say the reason for the increasing violence in American cities is because guns are too easily available.
5. The reason for all the congestion in American cities is because too many people live too close together.

28h Incomplete or Illogical Comparisons

A comparison tells how two things are alike or unlike. When you make a comparison, be sure it is both **complete** (that readers can tell what two items are being compared) and **logical** (that it equates two comparable items).

> **INCOMPLETE:** My communications course is harder. (What two things are being compared?)

> **COMPLETE:** My communications course is harder <u>than Nina's</u>. (Comparison is now complete.)

> **ILLOGICAL:** The intelligence of a pig is greater than a dog. (illogically compares the intelligence of a pig to a dog)

> **LOGICAL:** The intelligence of a pig is greater than <u>that of</u> a dog.

EXERCISE 5

Revise the following sentences to correct any incomplete or illogical comparisons.

> INCOMPLETE: Technology-based industries are concerned about inflation as much as service industries.

> COMPLETE: Technology-based industries are concerned about inflation as much as service industries are.

1. Opportunities in technical writing are more promising than business writing.
2. Technical writing is more challenging.
3. In some ways, technical writing requires more attention to detail and is, therefore, more difficult.
4. Business writers are concerned about clarity as much as technical writers.
5. Technology-based industries may one day create more writing opportunities than any industry.

STUDENT WRITER AT WORK

Revising Awkward or Confusing Sentences

Following is an excerpt from a draft of a student's research paper on immigrant factory workers in New York City in the early twentieth century. In this section of her paper, the student focuses on a devastating fire that eventually contributed to the creation of stricter fire safety codes. Read the paragraphs and correct any mixed constructions, faulty predication, unwarranted grammatical shifts, or incomplete or illogical comparisons. If necessary, revise further to strengthen coherence, unity, and style.

In one particularly compelling section of World of Our Fathers, Irving Howe describes the devastating 1911 fire at the Triangle Shirtwaist Company (304-6). By quoting an eyewitness account and contemporary reactions and by reproducing graphic photographs is how he added drama to his account of an already dramatic event. For instance, Howe quotes labor activist Rose Schneiderman, who said this is not the first time girls have been burned alive in this city, and "The life of men and women is so cheap and property is so sacred" (305).

In his book The Triangle Fire, Leon Stein suggests that the fire, in the ten-story Asch Building near Washington Square in New York City, probably began with a cigarette or spark in a rag bin. Some people in the building apparently tried dousing the flames, but because of rotted hoses and rusted water valves made their efforts useless (15).

The announcement of the many causes of the fire deaths was obvious. According to the investigating committee, the one fire escape visible from Greene Street collapsed after fewer than twenty people escaped. In addition, although sprinkler systems had been invented in 1895 did not mean any were present in the Asch Building. They were considered more expensive. Records show that six months before the fire, the building was cited as a firetrap by the city. The owners failed to make alterations was what the report identified as a cause of the fire. Failure to have regular fire drills and a lack of clearly marked exits also contributed to the high death toll (Stein 117-19).

Because it was 4:30 p.m. on a Saturday—a work day—when the fire broke out meant that there were 650 workers in the building. The majority of these were young Jewish and Italian women, and there was no common language spoken by them. By not sharing a common language was one reason for the chaos among the workers (Stein 14-15). When those on the ninth floor found the fire exit doors locked, their panic peaked. With their exit blocked forced everyone to jump from the windows to avoid the intense fire that swept through the building. Although it took firefighters only eighteen minutes to bring the fire under control, 146 workers died.

PART 5

USING WORDS EFFECTIVELY

CHAPTER 29

CHOOSING WORDS

29a Choosing an Appropriate Level of Diction

Diction means the choice and use of words. Different audiences and situations call for different levels of diction.

(1) Formal Diction

Formal diction is grammatically correct and uses words familiar to an educated audience. For example, a writer using formal diction may choose *impoverished* rather than *poor, wealthy* or *affluent* rather than *rich, intelligent* rather than *smart,* and *automobile* rather than *car.* A writer of formal diction often maintains emotional distance from the audience by using the impersonal *one* rather than the more personal *I* and *you.* In addition, the tone of the writing—as determined by word choice, sentence structure, and choice of subject—is dignified and objective.

> We learn to perceive in the sense that we learn to respond to things in particular ways because of the contingencies of which they are a part. We may perceive the sun, for example, simply because it is

Roget's Thesaurus
  http://www.thesaurus.com/
Dictionary.com's List of Online Dictionaries
  http://www.dictionary.com/Dir/Reference/Dictionaries/

an extremely powerful stimulus, but it has been a permanent part of the environment of the species throughout its evolution, and more specific behavior with respect to it could have been selected by contingencies of survival (as it has been in many other species). (B. F. Skinner, *Beyond Freedom and Dignity*)

(2) Informal Diction

Informal diction is the language people use in conversation. You should use informal diction in your college writing only to imitate speech or dialect or to give a paper a conversational tone.

Colloquial Diction   **Colloquial diction** is the language of everyday speech. Contractions—*isn't, I'm*—are typical colloquialisms, as are **clipped forms**—*phone* for *telephone, dorm* for *dormitory.* Other colloquialisms include placeholders like *kind of* and utility words like *nice* for *acceptable, funny* for *odd,* and *great* for almost anything. Colloquial English also includes verb forms like *get across* for *communicate, come up with* for *find,* and *check out* for *investigate.*

Slang   **Slang** is a vivid and forceful use of language that calls attention to itself. It is often restricted to a single group of people—urban teenagers, rock musicians, or computer users, for example. Slang is constantly changing. Words like *uptight, groovy,* and *hippie* emerged in the 1960s. During the 1970s, technology, music, politics, and feminism influenced slang, giving us words like *hacker, disco, stonewalling,* and *macho.* The 1980s contributed expressions like *sound bite, yuppie,* and *chocoholic;* slang additions in the 1990s included such expressions as *wonk, hip-hop, downsize,* and *flame.*

Regionalisms   **Regionalisms** are words, expressions, and idiomatic forms that are used in particular geographical areas but may not be understood by a general audience. In eastern Tennessee, for example, a paper bag is a *poke,* and empty soda bottles are *dope bottles.* In Lancaster, Pennsylvania, which has a large Amish population, it is not unusual to hear an elderly person saying *daresome* for *adventurous.* And New Yorkers stand *on line* for a movie, whereas people in most other parts of the country stand *in line.*

Nonstandard Diction   **Nonstandard diction** refers to words and expressions not considered a part of standard English—words like *ain't, nohow, anywheres, nowheres, hisself,* and *theirselves.*

(3) College Writing

The level of diction appropriate for college writing depends on your assignment and your audience. A personal experience essay calls for a natural, informal style, but a research paper, an exam, or a report requires a more formal vocabulary and a more objective tone. In general, most college writing falls somewhere between formal and informal English, using a conversational tone but maintaining grammatical correctness and using a specialized vocabulary when the situation requires it. (Keep in mind that colloquial expressions are almost always inappropriate in your college writing, as are slang, regionalisms, and other nonstandard usages.)

EXERCISE 1

The diction of this paragraph, from Toni Cade Bambara's short story "The Hammer Man," is informal. In order to represent the speech of a young girl, the writer intentionally uses slang expressions and nonstandard grammar. Underline the words that identify the diction of this paragraph as informal. Then rewrite the paragraph, using standard diction.

Manny was supposed to be crazy. That was his story. To say you were bad put some people off. But to say you were crazy, well, you were officially not to be messed with. So that was his story. On the other hand, after I called him what I called him and said a few choice things about his mother, his face did go through some piercing changes. And I did kind of wonder if maybe he sure was nuts. I didn't wait to find out. I got in the wind. And then he waited for me on my stoop all day and all night, not hardly speaking to the people going in and out. And he was there all day Saturday, with his sister bringing him peanut-butter sandwiches and cream sodas. He must've gone to the bathroom right there cause every time I looked out the kitchen window, there he was. And Sunday, too. I got to thinking the boy was mad.

EXERCISE 2

After reading the following paragraph, underline the words and phrases that identify it as formal diction. Then, choose one paragraph and rewrite it using the level of diction that you would use in your college writing. Use a dictionary if necessary.

In looking at many small points of difference between species, which, as far as our ignorance permits us to judge, seem quite unimportant, we must not forget that climate, food, etc., have no doubt produced some direct effect. It is also necessary to bear in mind that owing to the law of correlation, when one part varies and the variations are accumulated through natural selection, other modifications, often of the most unexpected nature, will ensue. (Charles Darwin, *The Origin of Species*)

29b Choosing the Right Word

Choosing the right word to use in a particular context is very important. If you use the wrong word—or even *almost* the right one—you run the risk of misrepresenting your ideas.

(1) Denotation and Connotation

A word's **denotation** is its explicit dictionary meaning, what it stands for without any emotional associations. A word's **connotations** are the emotional, social, and political associations it has in addition to its denotative meaning.

Word	*Denotation*	*Connotation*
politician	someone who holds a political office	opportunist; wheeler-dealer

Selecting a word with the appropriate connotation can be challenging. For example, the word *skinny* has negative connotations, whereas *thin* is neutral, and *slender* is positive. And *mentally ill, insane, neurotic, crazy, psychopathic,* and *emotionally disturbed* have different emotional, social, and political connotations that affect the way people respond. If you use terms without considering their connotations, you run the risk of confusing and possibly angering your readers.

EXERCISE 3

The following words have negative connotations. For each, list one word with a similar meaning whose connotation is neutral and another whose connotation is favorable.

EXAMPLE: *Negative*   skinny
          Neutral   thin
          Favorable   slender

1. deceive
2. antiquated
3. egghead
4. pathetic
5. cheap
6. blunder
7. weird
8. politician
9. shack
10. stench

(2) Euphemisms

A **euphemism** is a term used in place of a blunt or impolite term that describes a subject society considers offensive or distasteful. College writing is no place for euphemisms. Say what you mean—*pregnant,* not *expecting; died,* not *passed away;* and *strike,* not *work stoppage.*

(3) Specific and General Words

Specific words refer to particular persons, items, or events; **general** words denote entire classes or groups. *Queen Elizabeth II,* for example, is more specific than *monarch; jeans* is more specific than *clothing;* and *Jeep* is more specific than *vehicle.* You can use general words to describe entire classes of items, but you must use specific words to clarify such generalizations.

(4) Abstract and Concrete Words

Abstract words—*beauty, truth, justice,* and so on—refer to ideas, qualities, or conditions that cannot be perceived by the senses. **Concrete** words name things that readers can *see, hear, taste, smell,* or *touch.* As with general and specific words, whether a word is abstract or concrete is relative. The more concrete your words and phrases, the more vivid the image you evoke in the reader.

 UTILITY WORDS

 See 22a2

Avoid abstract terms, such as *nice, great,* and *terrific,* that say nothing and could be used in almost any sentence. These **utility words** convey only emotions, not precise meanings. Replace them with more specific words.

VAGUE: The book was good.

BETTER: The book was a complex and suspensefully plotted mystery.

 EXERCISE 4

Revise the following paragraph from a job application letter by substituting specific, concrete language for general or abstract words and phrases.

I have had several part-time jobs lately. Some of them would qualify me for the position you advertised. In my most recent job, I sold products in a store. My supervisor said I was a good worker who possessed a number of valuable qualities. I am used to dealing with different types of people in various kinds of settings. I feel that my qualifications would make me a good candidate for your job opening.

29c   Avoiding Unoriginal Language

(1) Jargon

Jargon refers to the specialized or technical vocabulary of a trade, a profession, or an academic discipline when it is used outside the field for which it was developed. Within a particular field, a term may be easily understood, but outside that field, it is often imprecise and confusing. For example, medical doctors may say that a procedure is *contraindicated* or that they are going to carry out a *differential diagnosis.* Business executives may want departments to *interface* effectively, and sociologists may identify the need for *perspectivistic thinking* to achieve organizational goals. If they are addressing other professionals in their respective fields, the use of these terms is perfectly appropriate. If, however, they are addressing a lay audience, the terms become jargon.

(2) Neologisms

Neologisms are newly coined words that are not part of standard English. New situations call for new words, and such words often become a part of the language—*e-mail, carjack,* and *outsource,* for example.

Some coined words, however, may never be considered part of standard English. For example, questionable neologisms are created when the suffix *-wise* is added to existing words—creating new words like *weatherwise, sportswise, timewise,* and *productwise.*

If you are not sure whether to use a word, look it up in a current college **dictionary**. If it is not there, you probably should not use it.

See Ch. 30

(3) Pretentious Diction

Pretentious diction is language that is inappropriately elevated and wordy. In an effort to impress readers, some writers overuse adjectives and adverbs, polysyllabic words, complex sentences, and poetic devices.

> PRETENTIOUS DICTION: As I fell into slumber, I cogitated about my day ambling through the splendor of the Appalachian Mountains.

> REVISED: As I fell asleep, I thought about my day hiking through the Appalachian Mountains.

Pretentious diction is not formal diction used in an inappropriate situation; it is always out of place. By calling attention to itself, it gets in the way of communication and draws readers away from the point you are making.

❓ (4) Clichés

Clichés are trite expressions that have lost their impact because they have been so overused. Familiar sayings like "rush to judgment," and "what goes around comes around," for example, do little to enhance your writing.

The purpose of college writing is always to convey information clearly; clichés do just the opposite. Take the time to think of fresh expressions.

EXERCISE 5

Rewrite the following passage, eliminating jargon, neologisms, pretentious diction, and clichés. Feel free to add words and phrases and to reorganize sentences to make their meaning clear. If you are not certain about the meaning or status of a word, consult a dictionary.

At a given point in time, there coexisted a hare and a tortoise. The aforementioned rabbit was overheard by the tortoise to be blowing his horn about the degree of speed he could attain. The latter quadruped thereupon put forth a challenge to the former by advancing the suggestion that they interact in a running competition. The hare acquiesced, laughing to himself. The animals concurred in the decision to acquire the services of a certain fox to act in the capacity of judicial referee. This particular fox was in agreement, and, consequently, implementation of the plan was facilitated. In a relatively small amount of time, the hare had considerably outdistanced the tortoise and, after ascertaining that he himself was in a more optimized position distancewise than the tortoise, he arrived at the unilateral decision to avail himself of a respite. He made the implicit assumption in so doing that he would anticipate no difficulty in overtaking the tortoise when his suspension of activity ceased. An unfortunate development racewise occurred when the hare's somnolent state endured for a longer-than-anticipated time frame, facilitating the tortoise's victory in the contest and affirming the concept of unhurriedness and firmness triumphing in competitive situations. Thus, the hare was unable to snatch victory out of the jaws of defeat.

EXERCISE 6

Go through a newspaper or magazine and list the jargon, neologisms, pretentious diction, or clichés you find. Then, substitute more original words for the ones you identified. Be prepared to discuss your interpretation of each word and of the word you chose to put in its place.

29d   Using Figures of Speech

Writers often go beyond the literal meanings of words to achieve special effects through **figures of speech.** Although you should not overuse figures of speech, do not be afraid to use them when you think they will help you communicate your ideas to your readers.

CLOSE UP   COMMONLY USED FIGURES OF SPEECH

A **simile** is a comparison between two essentially unlike things on the basis of a shared quality. A simile is introduced by *like* and *as.*

<u>Like</u> travelers with exotic destinations on their minds, the graduates were remarkably forgetful. (Maya Angelou, *I Know Why the Caged Bird Sings*)

A **metaphor** also compares two essentially dissimilar things, but instead of saying that one thing is *like* another, it *equates* them.

Perhaps it is easy for those who have never felt the stings and darts of segregation to say, "Wait." (Martin Luther King, Jr., "Letter from Birmingham Jail")

continued on the following page

continued from the previous page

An **analogy** explains an unfamiliar concept or thing by comparing it to a more familiar one.

According to Robert Frost, writing free verse is like playing tennis without a net.

Personification gives an idea or inanimate object human attributes, feelings, or powers.

Truth strikes us from behind, and in the dark, as well as from before in broad daylight. (Henry David Thoreau, *Journals*)

A **hyperbole** (or overstatement) is an intentional exaggeration for emphasis. For example, Jonathan Swift uses hyperbole in his essay "A Modest Proposal" when he suggests that eating Irish babies would help the English solve their food shortage.

Understatement intentionally downplays the seriousness of a situation or sentiment by saying less than is really meant.

According to Mao Tse-tung, a revolution is not a tea party.

EXERCISE 7

Read the following paragraph from Mark Twain's *Life on the Mississippi* and identify as many figures of speech as you can.

Now when I had mastered the language of this water, and had come to know every trifling feature that bordered the great river as familiarly as I knew the letters of the alphabet, I had made a valuable acquisition. But I had lost something, too. I had lost something which could never be restored to me while I lived. All the grace, the beauty, the poetry, had gone out of the majestic river! I still keep in mind a certain wonderful sunset which I witnessed when steamboating was new to me. A broad expanse of the river was turned to blood; in the middle distance the red hue brightened into gold, through which a solitary log came floating black and

Avoiding Clichés
   http://www.urich.edu/~writing/wweb/cliche.html
Cliché Finder
   http://www.westegg.com/cliche/

conspicuous; in one place a long, slanting mark lay sparkling upon the water; in another the surface was broken by boiling, tumbling rings, that were as many-tinted as an opal; where the ruddy flush was faintest, was a smooth spot that was covered with graceful circles and radiating lines, ever so delicately traced; the shore on our left was densely wooded, and the somber shadow that fell from this forest was broken in one place by a long, ruffled trail that shone like silver; and high above the forest wall a clean-stemmed dead tree waved a single leafy bough that glowed like a flame in the unobstructed splendor that was flowing from the sun. There were graceful curves, reflected images, woody heights, soft distances; and over the whole scene, far and near, the dissolving lights drifted steadily, enriching it every passing moment with new marvels of coloring.

29e Avoiding Ineffective Figures of Speech

(1) Dead Metaphors and Similes

Metaphors and similes stimulate thought by calling up vivid images in a reader's mind. A **dead metaphor** or **simile,** however, has been used so often that it has become a pat, meaningless phrase.

off the beaten path	happy as a clam
sit on the fence	a shot in the arm
free as a bird	smooth sailing
spread like wildfire	fit like a glove
Herculean efforts	fighting like cats and dogs

Avoid dead metaphors and similes; instead, take the time to think of images that make your writing fresher and more vivid.

(2) Mixed Metaphors

A **mixed metaphor** results when you combine two or more incompatible images. Always revise mixed metaphors to make your imagery consistent.

MIXED: Management <u>extended an olive branch</u> in an attempt <u>to break some of the ice</u> between the company and the striking workers.

REVISED: Management extended an olive branch with the hope that the striking workers would pick it up.

EXERCISE 8

Rewrite the following sentences, adding figurative language to each sentence to make the ideas more vivid and exciting. Identify each figure of speech you use. Be careful to avoid ineffective figures of speech.

EXAMPLE:　The room was cool and still.

The room was cool and still like the inside of a cathedral. (simile)

1. The last of the marathon runners limped toward the finish line.
2. The breeze gently stirred the wind chimes.
3. Jeremy has shoulder-length hair and a high forehead and wears small, red glasses.
4. The computer classroom was quiet.
5. The demolition crew worked slowly but efficiently.
6. Interstate highways often make for tedious driving.
7. Diego found calculus hard.
8. Music is essentially mathematical.
9. Katrina claims her dog is far more intelligent than her brother.
10. Emotions are curious.

29f Avoiding Offensive Language

The language we use not only expresses our ideas but also shapes our thinking. For this reason, we all should be aware of the influence of language on our perceptions. Although we may not be able to change the language, we can avoid using words that insult or degrade others.

(1) Stereotypes

Racial and Ethnic　When referring to any racial, ethnic, or religious group, use words with neutral connotations or words that the group uses in *formal* speech or writing to refer to itself. Deciding which term to use is not always easy because the preferred names for specific groups change over time. For example, *African American* is now preferred by many Americans of African ancestry over *black,* which itself replaced *Negro* in the 1960s. People from East Asia—once called *Orientals*—now generally refer to themselves as *Asian* or *Asian American,* or by their country of origin (*Korean,* for example). Many of America's native peoples prefer *Native American,* although some call themselves *Indian,* and others identify themselves as members of a particular tribe—for example, *Kiowa* or *Navajo.* Native Americans in Canada and Alaska, who consider *Eskimo* demeaning, have adopted *Inuit.* The preferences of people of Spanish descent vary according to their national origin. *Hispanic*—a term coined by the US Bureau of the Census—is often used to refer to anyone of Spanish descent, as are *Latino* and *Latina.* But many individuals prefer other designations—for example, *Chicano* and *Chicana* for people from Mexico. A large number of Americans of Spanish descent, however, prefer to use names that emphasize their dual heritages—*Cuban American, Mexican American, Dominican American,* and so on.

Age   Unwarranted assumptions based on age can offend readers. Do not assume, for example, that all people over a certain age are forgetful, sickly, or inactive. Also, do not express surprise or shock at the ability of an older person to do something that would be perfectly natural for someone younger to do. Many older people like to call themselves "senior citizens" or "seniors," and these terms are commonly used by the media and the government.

Class   Your readers may not share your background or your assumptions about particular groups of people. Do not demean certain jobs because they are low paying or praise others because they have impressive titles. Similarly, do not use words—*hick, cracker, redneck,* or *white trash,* for example—that denigrate people based on their class.

Sexual Orientation   Here too, use neutral terms (like *gay* and *lesbian*). Do not mention a person's sexual orientation unless it is relevant to your discussion.

(2) Sexist Language

Sexist language entails much more than the use of derogatory words, such as *hunk, chick,* and *bimbo.* Assuming that some professions are exclusive to one gender—for instance, that *nurse* denotes only women and that *doctor* denotes only men—is also sexist. So is the use of such outdated job titles as *postman* for *letter carrier, fireman* for *firefighter,* and *stewardess* for *flight attendant.*

Sexist language also occurs when a writer fails to apply the same terminology to both men and women. For example, refer to two scientists with PhDs not as Dr. Sagan and Mrs. Yallow, but as Dr. Sagan and Dr. Yallow. Refer to two writers as James and Wharton, or Henry James and Edith Wharton, not James and Mrs. Wharton.

In your writing, always use *women*—not *girls, gals,* or *ladies*—when referring to adult females. Use *Ms.* as the form of address when a woman's marital status is unknown or irrelevant. (If the woman you are addressing refers to herself as *Mrs.* or *Miss,* however, use the form of address she prefers.) Finally, avoid using the generic *he* or *him* when your subject could be either male or female. Use the third-person plural or the phrase *he or she* (not *he/she*).

SEXIST: Before boarding, each passenger should make certain that <u>he</u> has <u>his</u> ticket.

REVISED: Before boarding, <u>passengers</u> should make certain that <u>they</u> have <u>their</u> tickets.

REVISED: Before boarding, each <u>passenger</u> should make certain that <u>he or she</u> has a ticket.

NOTE: Remember not to overuse *his or her* or *he or she* constructions, which can make your writing repetitious and wordy.

SEXIST LANGUAGE

When trying to avoid sexist use of *he* and *him*, be careful not to create ungrammatical constructions.

UNGRAMMATICAL: Before the publication of Richard Wright's novel *Native Son,* any unknown African-American <u>writer</u> had trouble getting <u>their</u> work published.

Although many people do use *they* or *their* in speech to refer to a singular noun, you should avoid this usage in your college writing.

REVISED: Before the publication of Richard Wright's novel *Native Son,* unknown African-American <u>writers</u> had trouble getting <u>their</u> work published.

Avoiding Gender-Biased Language (Harvard U.)
http://www.fas.harvard.edu/~wricntr/gender.html

✔ ELIMINATING SEXIST LANGUAGE

SEXIST USAGE	POSSIBLE REVISIONS
Mankind	People, human beings
Man's accomplishments	Human accomplishments
Man-made	Synthetic
Female engineer (lawyer, accountant, etc.), male model	Engineer (lawyer, accountant, etc.), model
Policeman/woman	Police officer
Salesman/woman/girl	Salesperson/representative
Businessman/woman	Businessperson/executive
<u>Everyone</u> should complete <u>his</u> application by Tuesday.	<u>Everyone</u> should complete <u>his or her</u> application by Tuesday. <u>All students</u> should complete <u>their</u> applications by Tuesday.

EXERCISE 9

Suggest alternative forms for any of the following constructions you consider sexist. In each case, comment on the advantages and disadvantages of the alternative you recommend. If you feel that a particular term is not sexist, explain why.

forefathers	(to) man the battle stations
man-eating shark	Girl Friday
manpower	point man
workman's compensation	stock boy
men at work	cowboy
copy boy	man overboard
bus boy	fisherman
first baseman	foreman
corpsman	manned space program
congressman	gentleman's agreement
advance man	no-man's-land
manhunt	spinster
longshoreman	old maid
committeeman	old wives' tale

EXERCISE 10

Each of the following pairs of terms includes a feminine form that was at one time in wide use; all are still used to some extent. Which do you think are likely to remain in our language for some time, and which do you think will disappear? Explain your reasoning.

heir/heiress author/authoress
benefactor/benefactress poet/poetess
murderer/murderess tailor/seamstress
actor/actress comedian/comedienne
hero/heroine villain/villainess
host/hostess prince/princess
aviator/aviatrix widow/widower
executor/executrix

STUDENT WRITER AT WORK

Choosing Words

The following excerpt is from a draft written for a communications class. Underline any words and phrases you think are not appropriate, accurate, or fresh. Then, revise the essay, changing words and sentences as you see fit. If necessary, revise again to strengthen coherence, unity, and style.

Saying It with a Smile

Our first impressions of a local television news program come from the newscasters, those smiling people who converse with us every evening. Undoubtedly, there are many qualifications local reporters must have, including a superlative educational background and some experience in broadcasting. They should also be sharp and have a keen interest in exposing the real truth. Above all, however, broadcasters must have a pleasing appearance.

Using familiar faces has become an effective marketing strategy for the news . A number of station managers have seen their market share increase and their negatives decrease when they slotted a newscaster with whom the audience identified. Market research has shown that viewers like to visualize the newscaster as if he were one of the family. Therefore, people chosen for the job must look nice— just like the boy or girl next door. Promos for the local news reinforce this squeaky clean image. In one spot, we see a newsman walking through a deteriorating urban neighborhood playing ball with lower-class kids and shaking hands with their moms and dads. In another, we see a female anchor bringing her son and some schoolmates to the station. Their eyes are as big as saucers as they look around. These kids are in seventh grade, and they use words like "cool" and "awesome" as they talk about the evening news. Clearly, this rather blatant tactic is calculated to present the reporters to the viewers as everyday people.

Just as tranquilizers calm someone's nerves, these newscasters lull us into not caring and then feed us empty calories. We are so conditioned to identify with the reporters that we never think about the actual content of the news. Beyond a shadow of a doubt, we are inclined to remember those stories that consume the most time in the half-hour broadcast. Except for national emergencies, the "big" stories are happy talk about local issues. Many of these have almost no news value—a rock concert, ice skating at a pond, and a pizza-eating contest, for example. This is obviously what we want to know and why we tune in. It must be, for ratings have never been higher. There is no mention of the unsolved hit-and-run murder of a young boy in my neighborhood. This is outrageous! But what the heck, that's what we expect anyhow. Tomorrow night we will ritualistically tune in and hear our favorite newsman tell us the big story: "Beer drinking banned at the baseball stadium."

CHAPTER 30

USING A DICTIONARY

? FREQUENTLY ASKED QUESTIONS

What kind of dictionary should I use?
  (p. 480)
Should I use a thesaurus? (p. 483)
Is an electronic dictionary better than a
  print dictionary? (p. 483)

? Every student should own a dictionary. The most widely used type of dictionary is a one-volume **desk dictionary** or **college dictionary.**

To fit a lot of information into a small space, dictionaries use a system of symbols, abbreviations, and typefaces. Each dictionary uses a slightly different system, so consult the preface of your dictionary to determine how its system operates. (A labeled entry from *The American Heritage College Dictionary* appears on p. 482.)

30a Understanding a Dictionary Entry

Dictionary entries typically include all or most of the following items.

(1) Entry Word

The **entry word,** which appears in boldface at the beginning of the entry, gives the spelling of the word and indicates how the word is divided into syllables.

col · or n. Also chiefly British **col · our**

Webster's Dictionary Online
  http://www.m-w.com/dictionary.htm
How Does a Word Get into the Dictionary?
  http://www.m-w.com/about/wordin.htm
D. Wilton's Etymology Page
  http://www.wordorigins.org/home.htm

(2) Pronunciation Guide

The **pronunciation guide** appears in parentheses or between slashes after the main entry. Dictionaries use symbols to represent sounds, and an explanation of these symbols usually appears at the bottom of each page or across the bottom of facing pages throughout the alphabetical listing.

(3) Part-of-Speech Label

Abbreviations called **part-of-speech labels** indicate parts of speech and grammatical forms. If a verb is **regular**, the entry provides only the base form of the verb. If a verb is **irregular**, the part-of-speech label indicates the irregular principal parts of the verb.

with · draw . . . v. -drew; -drawn; -drawing

In addition, the label indicates whether a verb is **transitive** (*tr.*), **intransitive** (*intr.*), or both.

Part-of-speech labels also indicate the plural forms of irregular nouns. (When the plural form is regular, it is not shown.)

child . . . n. pl. children

moth · er-in-law . . . n. pl. moth · ers-in-law

Finally, part-of-speech labels usually indicate the **comparative** and **superlative** forms of both regular and irregular adjectives and adverbs.

red . . . adj. redder; reddest

bad . . . adv. worse; worst

EXERCISE 1

Use your college dictionary to help you answer the following questions about grammatical forms.

1. What are the principal parts of the following verbs: *drink, deify, carol, draw,* and *ring?*
2. Which of the following nouns can be used as verbs: *canter, minister, council, command, magistrate, mother,* and *lord?*
3. What are the plural forms of these nouns: *silo, sheep, seed, scissors, genetics,* and *alchemy?*
4. What are the comparative and superlative forms of the following adverbs and adjectives: *fast, airy, good, mere, homey,* and *unlucky?*

5. Are the following verbs transitive, intransitive, or both: *bias, halt, dissatisfy, die,* and *turn?* Copy from the dictionary the phrase or sentence that illustrates the use of each verb.

(4) Etymology

The **etymology** of a word—its history over the years—appears in brackets either before or after the list of meanings. It traces a word to its roots and shows its form when it entered English. For instance, *The American Heritage Dictionary* (see Figure 1) shows that *couple* came into Middle English (ME) from Old French (OFr.) and into Old French from Latin (Lat.).

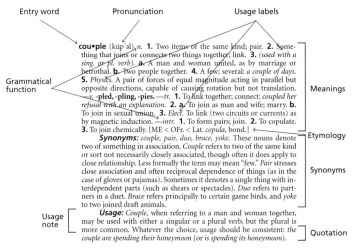

Figure 1 Entry from The American Heritage Dictionary, *College Edition*

(5) Meanings

Some dictionaries give the most common meaning first and then list less common ones. Others begin with the oldest meaning and move to the most current one. Check the preface of your dictionary to find out how its meanings are arranged.

Remember that if a word is in the process of acquiring new meanings, the dictionary may not yet include them. Also, remember that a dictionary meaning is primarily a record of the **denotations**, or exact meanings, of a word. A word's emotional associations, or **connotations**, are not always listed.

See
29b1

(6) Synonyms and Antonyms

A dictionary entry often lists synonyms and occasionally antonyms in addition to definitions. **Synonyms** are words that have similar meanings, such as *well* and *healthy.* **Antonyms** are words that have opposite meanings, such as *courage* and *cowardice.*

NOTE: When you consult a **thesaurus,** a book or computer program that lists synonyms and antonyms, remember that no two words have exactly the same meanings. Use synonyms carefully, checking your dictionary to make sure that the connotation of the synonym is close to that of the original word.

(7) Idioms

Dictionary entries often show how certain words are used in set expressions called **idioms.** The meaning of such expressions cannot always be determined from the words alone. For example, what are **speakers of other languages** to make of the expressions "catch a cold," "shut the light," and "take a walk"?

See
Ch. 56

Dictionaries also indicate the idiomatic use of **prepositions**. For example, we do not say that we *abide with* a decision or that we *interfere on* an election; we say that we *abide by* and *interfere with.*

See
56j

ELECTRONIC DICTIONARIES

Electronic dictionaries include the same amount of information that one-volume desk dictionaries have. Electronic dictionaries come in two forms—CD-ROM and online. Typically, you have to download a CD-ROM dictionary onto your hard drive before you can use it with your word-processing program. To use an online dictionary, you have to log on to a Web site, such as <http://www.m-w.com/dictionary.htm>.

(8) Usage Labels

Dictionaries use **usage labels** to indicate in what contexts words are acceptable. Where such labels involve value judgments, dictionaries differ.

USAGE LABELS

Label	Definition	Example
Nonstandard	A word in wide use but not considered standard usage	*ain't*
Informal/ Colloquial	A word used in conversation and acceptable in informal writing	*I've* for *I have* *sure* for *surely* *prof* for *professor*
Slang	A word appropriate only in extremely informal situations	*rip off*
Regional	A word or meaning of a word limited to a certain geographical region	*arroyo* (used in the Southwest), meaning "deep gully"
Obsolete	A word no longer in use	*egal,* meaning "equal"
Archaic/Rare	A once-common word or meaning that is now seldom used	*affright,* meaning "to arouse fear or terror" (archaic)
Poetic	A word used commonly only in poetry	*eve* for *evening* *o'er* for *over*
Biology/Physics/ Military/etc.	A word or meaning of a word limited to a particular field or discipline	*couple* (in electricity), meaning "to link by magnetic induction"

EXERCISE 2

Use your college dictionary to find the restrictions on the use of the following words.

1. irregardless
2. apse
3. flunk
4. lorry
5. kirk

6. gofer
7. whilst
8. sine
9. bannock
10. blowhard

(9) General Information

Dictionaries can be excellent sources of general information. If you want to find out the year in which John Glenn orbited the earth, you can look up the entry *Glenn, John*. If you need to find out for whom the Davis Cup is named, you can look up *Davis Cup*.

EXERCISE 3

To test the research capability of your dictionary, use it to answer the following questions.

1. What is moo goo gai pan?
2. In what year did William Faulkner win the Nobel Prize in literature?
3. When was Sandra Day O'Connor appointed to the Supreme Court?
4. What is Dadaism?
5. From which language is Yiddish primarily derived?
6. When was the King James Version of the Bible published?
7. What was novelist George Eliot's given name?
8. What does the abbreviation *FRB* stand for?
9. What two oceans border the continent of Africa?
10. When did Desmond Tutu win the Nobel Peace Prize?

30b   Surveying Abridged Dictionaries

An **abridged dictionary** is one that is condensed from a more complete collection of words and meanings. Still, a good hardback abridged dictionary will contain about 1,500 pages and about 150,000 entries. A paperback dictionary—which contains fewer entries, treated in less detail—is adequate for checking spelling, but for reference, you should consult a hardback abridged dictionary, such as *The American Heritage*

College Dictionary, The Concise Oxford Dictionary of Current English, The Random House College Dictionary, Merriam-Webster's Collegiate Dictionary, or *Webster's New World College Dictionary.*

NOTE: The name *Webster,* referring to the great lexicographer Noah Webster, is in the public domain. Because it cannot be copyrighted, it appears in the titles of many dictionaries of varying quality.

30c Surveying Unabridged Dictionaries

When you are looking for a detailed history of a word or when you want to look up a rare usage, you will need to consult an **unabridged dictionary,** which presents a comprehensive survey of all words in a language. *The Random House Unabridged Dictionary* and *Webster's Third New International Dictionary of the English Language* are two good unabridged dictionaries.

 CLOSE UP

THE OXFORD ENGLISH DICTIONARY *(OED)*

Consisting of twenty volumes plus four supplements, *The Oxford English Dictionary* (also available on CD-ROM) offers over 500,000 definitions, chronologically arranged, and more than two million supporting quotations. The quotations begin with the earliest recorded use of a word and progress to its current meaning.

courage ('kʌridʒ), *sb.* Forms: 4-7 corage, curage, (4-6 corrage, 5 curag, coreage, 6 currage, courra(d)ge, 7 corege), 5- courage. [ME. *corage,* a. OF. *corage, curage,* later *courage* = Pr. and Cat. *coratge,* Sp. *corage,* It. *coraggio,* a Common Romanic word, answering to a L. type **corāticum,* f. *cor* heart. Cf. the parallel *ætāticum* from *ætāt-em* (AGE); and see -AGE.]

†**1.** The heart as the seat of feeling, thought, etc.; spirit, mind, disposition, nature. *Obs.*
c **1300** K. *Alis.* 3559 Archelaus, of proud corage. *c* **1386** CHAUCER *Prol.* 11 Smale fowles maken melodie . . So priketh hem nature in here corages. *c* **1430** *Pilgr. Lyf Manhode* 1. xxxiii. (1869) 20 What thinkest in thi corage? *c* **1430** *Stans Puer* 5 To all norture thi corage to enclyne. *c* **1500** *Knt. Curtesy* 407 in Ritson *Met. Rom.* III. 213 in his courage he was full sad. **1593** SHAKS. *3*

Hen. VI, II. ii. 57 This soft courage makes your Followers faint. **1638** DRUMM. OF HAWTH. *Irene* Wks. (1711) 163 Men's courages were growing hot, their hatred kindled. **1659** B. HARRIS *Parival's Iron Age* 41 The Spaniards .. attacked it with all the force and maistry the greatest courages were able to invent.

†**b.** *transf.* Of a plant. *Obs.* (Cf. 'To bring a thing into *good heart.*')
c **1420** *Palladius on Husb.* XI. 90 In this courage Hem forto graffe is goode.

†**c.** Applied to a person: of. *spirit. Obs.*
1561 T. Hoby tr. *Castiglione's Courtyer* (1577) V j b, The prowes of those diuine courages [viz. Marquesse of Mantua, etc.]. **1647** W. BROWNE *Polex.* II 197 These two great courages being met, and followed by a small companie of the most resolute pirates.

CHAPTER 31

IMPROVING SPELLING

? FREQUENTLY ASKED QUESTIONS

Why I still need to proofread if I use a spell
   checker?   (p. 488)
How do I find the correct spelling of a
   word if I don't know how to spell it?
   (p. 490)
Are there any rules I can memorize?
   (p. 490)

Most people can spell even difficult words "almost" correctly; usually
only a letter or two are wrong. For this reason, memorizing a few simple
rules and their exceptions and learning the correct spelling of the most
commonly misspelled words can make a big difference.

31a   Understanding Spelling and Pronunciation

Sound alone does not necessarily indicate a word's spelling in English,
and the inconsistency between sound and spelling creates a number of
problems. Because pronunciation often provides no clues to spelling,
you must memorize the spellings of many words and use a dictionary or
spell checker regularly.

Words Commonly Misspelled (from Strunk's *Elements of Style*)
   http://www.bartleby.com/141/strunk4.html
Spelling Test and Tips
   http://www.sentex.net/~mmcadams/spelling.html
Spelling Tips
   http://owl.english.purdue.edu/handouts/grammar/
American vs. British Spelling
   http://www.gsu.edu/~wwwesl/egw/jones/differences.htm

USING A SPELL CHECKER

If you use a spell checker, remember that spell checkers will not identify a word spelled correctly but used incorrectly—*its* for *it's*, for example—or a typo that creates another word, such as *form* for *from*. For this reason, you still need to proofread your papers even after you have run a spell check.

(1) Vowels in Unstressed Positions

Many unstressed vowels sound exactly alike when we say them. For instance, it is hard to tell from pronunciation alone that the *i* in *terrible* is not an *a*. In addition, the unstressed vowels *a, e,* and *i* are impossible to distinguish in the suffixes **-able and -ible**, *-ance* and *-ence,* and *-ant* and *-ent*.

See
31b7

| comfort*able* | brilli*ance* | serv*ant* |
| compat*ible* | excell*ence* | independ*ent* |

(2) Silent Letters

Some English words contain silent letters. The *b* in *climb* is silent, as is the *t* in *mortgage*. You have to memorize the spellings of such words.

ai_s_le	dum_b_	_p_neumonia
condem_n_	_k_nife	sil_h_ouette
depo_t_	_k_ni_gh_t	sovereign

(3) Words That Are Often Pronounced Carelessly

Most of us pronounce words rather carelessly in everyday speech. Consequently, when spelling, we may leave out, add, or transpose letters. The following words are often misspelled because they are pronounced incorrectly.

Feb_r_uary	recognize	proba_bl_y
can_d_idate	nu_c_lear	_s_pecific
lib_r_ary	enviro_n_ment	su_r_prise
gove_rn_ment	hund_r_ed	suppose_d_ to
quan_t_ity	light_n_ing	use_d_ to

(4) Variant Forms of the Same Word

Some words are spelled one way in the United States and another way in Great Britain and the Commonwealth nations.

American	*British*	*American*	*British*
color	colour	judgment	judgement
defense	defence	theater	theatre
honor	honour	traveled	travelled

(5) Homophones

Homophones are words—such as *accept* and *except*—that are pronounced alike but spelled differently.

SPELLING: ONE WORD OR TWO?

Some words may be written as one word or two. The form you use is determined by meaning.

any way versus *anyway*
It began to rain, but the game continued *anyway*.
The early pioneers made the trip West *any way* they could.

every day versus *everyday*
Every day brings new opportunities.
John thought of himself as an *everyday* type of person.

One Word	*Two Words*
already	a lot
cannot	all right
classroom	even though
overweight	no one

Consult a dictionary if you have any doubts about whether a word is written as one word or two.

SPELLING AN UNFAMILIAR WORD

Most spell checkers have a "guess" function that enables you to look up a word even if you do not know how to spell it. You select the word in question and the computer lists the word or words to which you might be referring.

31b Learning Spelling Rules

Knowing a few reliable rules and their most common exceptions can help you overcome problems caused by the general inconsistency between pronunciation and spelling.

(1) The *ie/ei* Combinations

The old rule still stands: use *i* before *e* except after *c* (or when pronounced *ay*, as in *neighbor*).

i *before* e	ei *after* c	ei *pronounced* ay
belief	ceiling	neighbor
chief	deceit	weigh
niece	receive	freight
friend	perceive	eight

Exceptions: *either, neither, foreign, leisure, weird, seize.* In addition, if the *ie* combination is not pronounced as a unit, the rule does not apply: *atheist, science.*

EXERCISE 1

Fill in the blanks with the proper *ie* or *ei* combination. After completing the exercise, use your dictionary or spell checker to check your answers.

EXAMPLE: conc__*ei*__ve

1. rec_____pt
2. var_____ty
3. caff_____ne
4. ach_____ve
5. kal_____doscope
6. misch_____f

7. effic_____nt   9. spec_____s

8. v_____n   10. suffic_____nt

(2) Doubling Final Consonants

The only words that double their consonants before a suffix that begins with a vowel (*-ed, -ing*) are those that pass the following three tests.

1. They have one syllable or are stressed on the last syllable.
2. They contain only one vowel in the last syllable.
3. They end in a single consonant.

The word *tap* satisfies all three conditions: it has only one syllable, it contains only one vowel (*a*), and it ends in a single consonant (*p*). Therefore, the final consonant doubles before a suffix beginning with a vowel (*tapped, tapping*). The word *relent* meets two of the conditions (it is stressed on the last syllable, and it has one vowel in the last syllable), but it does not end in a single consonant. Therefore, its final consonant is not doubled (*relented, relenting*).

(3) Prefixes

The addition of a prefix never affects the spelling of the root (*mis* + *spell* = *misspell*). Some prefixes can cause spelling problems, however, because they are pronounced alike although they are not spelled alike: *ante-/anti-, en-/in-, per-/pre-,* and *de-/di-*.

antebellum   antiaircraft
encircle   integrate
perceive   prescribe
deduct   direct

(4) Silent *e* before a Suffix

When a suffix that begins with a consonant is added to a word that ends in silent *e*, the *e* is generally kept: *hope/hopeful; lame/lamely; bore/boredom.* **Exceptions:** *argument, truly, ninth, judgment,* and *abridgment.*

When a suffix that starts with a vowel is added to a word that ends in silent *e*, the *e* is generally dropped: *hope/hoping; trace/traced; grieve/grievance; love/lovable.* **Exceptions:** *changeable, noticeable, courageous.*

EXERCISE 2

Combine the following words with the suffixes in parentheses. Keep or drop the silent *e* as you see fit; be prepared to explain your choices.

EXAMPLE: fate (al)

   fatal

1. surprise (ing)
2. sure (ly)
3. force (ible)
4. manage (able)
5. due (ly)

6. outrage (ous)
7. service (able)
8. awe (ful)
9. shame (ing)
10. shame (less)

(5) *y* before a Suffix

When a word ends in a consonant plus *y*, the *y* generally changes to an *i* when a suffix is added (*beauty + ful = beautiful*). The *y* is retained, however, when the suffix *-ing* is added (*tally + ing = tallying*) and in some one-syllable words (*dry + ness = dryness*).

When a word ends in a vowel plus *y*, the *y* is retained (*joy + ful = joyful; employ + er = employer*). Exception: *day + ly = daily.*

EXERCISE 3

Add the endings in parentheses to the following words. Change or keep the final *y* as you see fit; be prepared to explain your choices.

EXAMPLE: party (ing)

   partying

1. journey (ing)
2. study (ed)
3. carry (ing)
4. shy (ly)
5. study (ing)

6. sturdy (ness)
7. merry (ment)
8. likely (hood)
9. plenty (ful)
10. supply (er)

(6) *seed* Endings

Endings with the sound *seed* are nearly always spelled *cede*, as in *precede, intercede, concede,* and so on. **Exceptions:** *supersede, exceed, proceed, succeed.*

(7) *-able, -ible*

If the root of a word is itself an independent word, the suffix *-able* is most commonly used. If the root of a word is not an independent word, the suffix *-ible* is most often used.

comfort<u>able</u>   *compat*<u>ible</u>
agree<u>able</u>   *incred*<u>ible</u>
dry<u>able</u>   *plaus*<u>ible</u>

(8) Plurals

Most nouns form plurals by adding *s: savage/savages, tortilla/tortillas, boat/boats* There are, however, a number of exceptions.

Words Ending in f *or* fe   Some words ending in *f* or *fe* form plurals by changing the *f* to *v* and adding *es* or *s: life/lives, self/selves.* Others add just *s: belief/beliefs, safe/safes.* Words ending in double *f* take *s* to form plurals: *tariff/tariffs.*

Words Ending in y   Most words that end in a consonant followed by *y* form plurals by changing the *y* to *i* and adding *es: baby/babies.* **Exceptions:** proper nouns, such as the *Kennedys* (never the *Kennedies*).
Words that end in a vowel followed by a *y* form plurals by adding *s: day/days, monkey/monkeys.*

Words Ending in o   Words that end in a vowel followed by *o* form the plural by adding *s: radio/radios, stereo/stereos, zoo/zoos.* Most words that end in a consonant followed by *o* add *es* to form the plural: *tomato/tomatoes, hero/heroes.* **Exceptions:** *silo/silos, piano/pianos, memo/memos, soprano/sopranos.*

Words Ending in s, ss, sh, ch, x, *and* z   These words form plurals by adding *es: Jones/Joneses, mass/masses, rash/rashes, lunch/lunches, box/boxes, buzz/buzzes.*

NOTE: Some one-syllable words that end in *s* or *z* double their final consonants when forming plurals: *quiz/quizzes.*

Compound Nouns   **Compound nouns**—nouns formed from two or more words—usually conform to the rules governing the last word in the compound construction: *welfare state/welfare states; snowball/snowballs.* However, where the first element of the compound noun is more important than the others, the plural is formed with the first element: *sister-in-law/sisters-in-law, attorney general/attorneys general.*

Foreign Plurals Some words, especially those borrowed from Latin or Greek, keep their foreign plurals. Look up a foreign word's plural form in a dictionary if you do not know it.

Singular	*Plural*
basis	bases
criterion	criteria
datum	data
larva	larvae
medium	media
memorandum	memoranda
stimulus	stimuli

31c Distinguishing Commonly Confused Words

Following is a list of commonly confused **homophones** (words that sound exactly alike but have different spellings and meanings, such as *night* and *knight*) and near-homophones (words that sound similar, such as *accept* and *except*).

NOTE: A spell checker will not identify an incorrectly used homophone.

accept	to receive
except	other than
advice	recommendation
advise	to recommend
affect	to have an influence on (*verb*)
effect	result (*noun*); to cause (*verb*)
all ready	prepared
already	by or before this or that time
allude	to refer to indirectly
elude	to avoid

allusion	indirect reference
illusion	false belief or perception
bare	uncovered
bear	to carry (*verb*); an animal (*noun*)
board	a wooden plank (*noun*); to get on an airplane, etc. (*verb*)
bored	uninterested
buy	purchase
by	next to; near
capital	the seat of government; monetary assets
capitol	government building
Capitol	the building in Washington, DC, where the US Congress meets
cite	to quote, refer to
sight	the ability to see
site	a place
coarse	rough
course	path; class
complement	to complete or add to (*verb*); something that completes (*noun*)
compliment	praise
conscience	sense of right and wrong
conscious	mentally awake
council	governing body
counsel	advice (*noun*); to give advice (*verb*)
desert	to abandon
dessert	sweet course at the end of a meal
device	an implement; a plan
devise	to invent
die	to lose life
dye	to change the color of something
elicit	to draw out, evoke
illicit	unlawful; forbidden

eminent	prominent
immanent	inherent
imminent	about to happen
forth	forward
fourth	referring to the number 4
gorilla	the animal
guerrilla	a type of soldier or warfare
hear	to perceive by ear
here	in this place
heard	past tense of *hear*
herd	group of animals
its	possessive of *it*
it's	contraction of *it is*
later	after a time
latter	the last in a series
lead	a metal (*noun*)
led	past tense of *lead*
lessen	to reduce
lesson	something learned
loose	not tight; unbound
lose	to misplace
maybe	perhaps
may be	might be
no	negative
know	to be certain
passed	past tense of *pass*
past	a previous time; a time gone by
patience	calm endurance
patients	persons receiving medical care
peace	the absence of war; quiet
piece	a portion of something

persecute	to harass or worry
prosecute	to institute criminal proceedings against
personal	private; one's own
personnel	employees
plain	unadorned
plane	an aircraft; a carpenter's tool
precede	to come before
proceed	to continue
principal	most important (*adjective*); head of a school (*noun*)
principle	a basic truth; rule of conduct
quiet	silent
quite	very
raise	to build up
raze	to tear down
right	correct
rite	a ritual
write	to put words on paper
road	street, highway
rode	past tense of *ride*
scene	place of action; section of a play
seen	viewed
sense	perception, understanding
since	from a time in the past up to the present
stationary	standing still
stationery	writing paper
than	as compared with
then	at that time; next
their	possessive of *they*
there	in that place
they're	contraction of *they are*

through	finished; into and out of
threw	past tense of *throw*
thorough	complete
to	toward
too	also; more than sufficient
two	the number
waist	the middle of the body
waste	discarded material (*noun*); to squander (*verb*)
weather	atmospheric conditions
whether	in either case
which	one of a group
witch	female sorcerer
who's	contraction of *who is*
whose	possessive of *who*
your	possessive of *you*
you're	contraction of *you are*

PART 6

UNDERSTANDING GRAMMAR

CHAPTER 32

PARTS OF SPEECH

? FREQUENTLY ASKED QUESTIONS

How does a noun function in a sentence? (p. 500)

How does a pronoun function in a sentence? (p. 501)

How does a verb function in a sentence? (p. 502)

How does an adjective function in a sentence? (p. 505)

How does an adverb function in a sentence? (p. 506)

How does a preposition function in a sentence? (p. 507)

How does a conjunction function in a sentence? (p. 508)

How does a interjection function in a sentence? (p. 509)

The eight basic **parts of speech**—the building blocks for all English sentences—are *nouns, pronouns, verbs, adjectives, adverbs, prepositions, conjunctions,* and *interjections.* How a word is classified depends on its function in a sentence.

32a Nouns

Nouns name people, animals, places, things, ideas, actions, or qualities.

A **common noun** names any one of a class of people, places, or things: *artist, judge, building, event, city.*

A **proper noun,** always **capitalized**, refers to a particular person, place, or thing: *Mary Cassatt, World Trade Center, Crimean War.*

A **count noun** names something that can be counted: five *dogs,* two dozen *grapes.*

A **noncount noun** names a quantity that is not countable: *time, dust, work, gold.* Noncount nouns generally have only a singular form.

A **collective noun** designates a group thought of as a unit: *committee, class, navy, band, family.* <u>**Collective nouns**</u> are generally singular unless the members of the group are referred to as individuals.

An **abstract noun** refers to an intangible idea or quality: *love, hate, justice, anger, fear, prejudice.*

32b   Pronouns

Pronouns are words used in place of nouns. The noun for which a pronoun stands is called its **antecedent.**

> If you use a <u>quotation</u>, you must document it. (Pronoun *it* refers to antecedent *quotation.*)

Although different types of pronouns may have exactly the same forms, they are distinguished from one another by their functions in a sentence.

A **personal pronoun** stands for a person or thing. Personal pronouns include *I, me, we, us, my, mine, our, ours, you, your, yours, he, she, it, its, him, his, her, hers, they, them, their,* and *theirs.*

> <u>They</u> made <u>her</u> an offer <u>she</u> couldn't refuse.

An **indefinite pronoun** does not refer to any particular person or thing. For this reason, indefinite pronouns do not require antecedents. Indefinite pronouns include another, any, each, few, many, some, nothing, one, anyone, everyone, everybody, everything, someone, something, either, and neither.

> <u>Many</u> are called, but <u>few</u> are chosen.

A **reflexive pronoun** ends with *-self* and refers to a recipient of the action that is the same as the actor. The reflexive pronouns are *myself, yourself, himself, herself, itself, oneself, themselves, ourselves,* and *yourselves.*

> They found <u>themselves</u> in downtown Pittsburgh.

Intensive pronouns have the same forms as reflexive pronouns; an intensive pronoun emphasizes a noun or pronoun that directly precedes it.

> Darrow <u>himself</u> was sure his client was innocent.

A **relative pronoun** introduces an adjective clause or a noun clause in a sentence. Relative pronouns include *which, who, whom, that, what, whose, whatever, whoever, whomever,* and *whichever.*

Gandhi was the charismatic man <u>who</u> helped lead India to independence. (introduces adjective clause)

<u>Whatever</u> happens will be a surprise. (introduces noun clause)

An **interrogative pronoun** introduces a question. Interrogative pronouns include *who, which, what, whom, whose, whoever, whatever,* and *whichever.*

<u>Who</u> was that masked man?

A **demonstrative pronoun** points to a particular thing or group of things. *This, that, these,* and *those* are demonstrative pronouns.

<u>This</u> is one of Shakespeare's early plays.

A **reciprocal pronoun** denotes a mutual relationship. The reciprocal pronouns are *each other* and *one another.*
Each other indicates a relationship between two individuals; *one another* denotes a relationship among more than two.

Romeo and Juliet declared their love for <u>each other</u>.

Concertgoers jostled <u>one another</u> in the ticket line.

32c　Verbs

(1) Recognizing Verbs

A verb may express either action or a state of being.

He <u>ran</u> for the train. (action)

Elizabeth II <u>became</u> queen after the death of her father, George VI. (state of being)

Verbs can be classified into two groups: *main verbs* and *auxiliary verbs.*

Main Verbs　**Main verbs** carry most of the meaning in the sentences or clauses in which they appear.
Some main verbs are action verbs.

Emily Dickinson <u>wrote</u> poetry.

Other main verbs function as linking verbs. A **linking verb** does not show any physical or emotional action. Its function is to link the sentence's subject to a **subject complement,** a word or phrase that renames or describes the subject.

Carbon disulfide <u>smells</u> bad.

FREQUENTLY USED LINKING VERBS

appear	believe	look	seem	taste
be	feel	prove	smell	turn
become	grow	remain	sound	

Auxiliary Verbs **Auxiliary verbs** (also called **helping verbs**), such as *be* and *have,* combine with main verbs to form **verb phrases.** Auxiliary verbs indicate tense, voice, or mood.

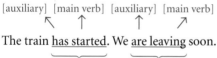

The train <u>has started</u>. We <u>are leaving</u> soon.

       [verb phrase]   [verb phrase]

Certain auxiliary verbs, known as **modal auxiliaries,** indicate necessity, possibility, willingness, obligation, or ability.

In the future, farmers <u>might</u> cultivate seaweed as a food crop.

Coal mining <u>would</u> be safer if dust were controlled in the mines.

MODAL AUXILIARIES

can	might	ought [to]	will
could	must	shall	would
may	need [to]	should	

---

(2) Recognizing Verbals

Verbals, such as *known* or *swimming* or *to go,* are verb forms that act as adjectives, adverbs, or nouns. A verbal can never serve as a sentence's main verb unless it is used with one or more auxiliary verbs (*has known, should be swimming*). Verbals include *participles, infinitives,* and *gerunds.*

Participles Virtually every verb has a **present participle,** which ends in *-ing* (*loving, learning, going, writing*), and a **past participle,** which usually ends in *-d* or *-ed* (*agreed, learned*). Some verbs have **irregular** past participles (*gone, begun, written*). Participles may function in a sentence as adjectives or as nouns.

> See
> 34a2

Twenty brands of <u>running</u> shoes were displayed at the exhibition. (Present participle *running* serves as adjective modifying noun *shoes.*)

The <u>crowded</u> bus went right by those waiting at the corner. (Past participle *crowded* serves as adjective modifying noun *bus.*)

The <u>wounded</u> were given emergency first aid. (Past participle *wounded* serves as a noun, the sentence's subject.)

Infinitives An **infinitive**—*to* plus the base form of the verb—may function as an adjective, an adverb, or a noun.

Ann Arbor was clearly the place <u>to be</u>. (Infinitive *to be* serves as adjective modifying noun *place.*)

They say that breaking up is hard <u>to do</u>. (Infinitive *to do* serves as adverb modifying adjective *hard.*)

Carla went outside <u>to think</u>. (Infinitive *to think* serves as adverb modifying verb *went.*)

<u>To win</u> was everything. (Infinitive *to win* serves as a noun, the sentence's subject.)

Gerunds **Gerunds,** special forms of verbs ending in *-ing,* are always used as nouns.

<u>Seeing</u> is <u>believing</u>. (Gerund *seeing* serves as sentence's subject; gerund *believing* serves as subject complement.)

He worried about <u>interrupting</u>. (Gerund *interrupting* is object of preposition *about.*)

Andrew loves <u>skiing</u>. (Gerund *skiing* is direct object of verb *loves.*)

NOTE: When the *-ing* form of a verb is used as a noun, it is considered a *gerund;* when it is used as an adjective, it is a *present participle.*

32d Adjectives

Adjectives describe, limit, qualify, or in some other way modify nouns or pronouns.

(1) Descriptive Adjectives

Descriptive adjectives name a quality of the noun or pronoun they modify.

After the game, they were <u>exhausted</u>.

They ordered a <u>chocolate</u> soda and a <u>butterscotch</u> sundae.

Some descriptive adjectives are formed from common nouns or from verbs (*friend/friendly, agree/agreeable*). Others, called **proper adjectives,** are formed from proper nouns.

The <u>Shakespearean</u> sonnet consists of an octave and a sestet.

Two or more words may be joined, with or without a hyphen, to form a **compound adjective** (*foreign born, well-read*).

(2) Determiners

When articles, pronouns, numbers, and the like function as adjectives, limiting or qualifying nouns or pronouns, they are referred to as **determiners**.

Articles (*a, an, the*)

<u>The</u> boy found <u>a</u> four-leaf clover.

Possessive nouns

<u>Lesley's</u> mother lives in New Jersey.

Possessive pronouns (the personal pronouns *my, your, his, her, its, our, their*)

<u>Their</u> lives depended on <u>my</u> skill.

Demonstrative pronouns (*this, these, that, those*)

<u>This</u> song reminds me of <u>that</u> song we heard yesterday.

Interrogative pronouns (*what, which, whose*)

Whose book is this?

Indefinite pronouns (*another, each, both, many, any, some,* and so on)

Both candidates agreed to return another day.

Relative pronouns (*what, whatever, which, whichever, whose, whoever*)

I forgot whatever reasons I had for leaving.

Numbers (*one, two, first, second,* and so on)

The first time I played baseball, I got only one hit.

32e Adverbs

Adverbs describe the action of verbs or modify adjectives; other adverbs; or complete phrases, clauses, or sentences. They answer the questions "How?" "Why?" "Where?" "When?" "Under what conditions?" and "To what extent?"

He walked rather hesitantly toward the front of the room. (walked *how?*)

Let's meet tomorrow for coffee. (meet *when?*)

Adverbs that modify other adverbs or adjectives limit or qualify the words they modify.

He pitched an almost perfect game.

Interrogative adverbs—*how, when, why,* and *where*—introduce questions.

Why did the compound darken?

Conjunctive adverbs act as transitional words, joining and relating independent clauses.

Conjunctive adverbs may appear in any of several positions in a sentence.

Jason forgot to register for chemistry. However, he managed to sign up during the drop/add period. (conjunctive adverb at beginning of sentence)

Jason forgot to register for chemistry; however, he managed to sign up during the drop/add period. (conjunctive adverb at beginning of clause)

Jason forgot to register for chemistry. He managed, <u>however</u>, to sign up during the drop/add period. (conjunctive adverb within sentence)

Jason forgot to register for chemistry. He managed to sign up during the drop/add period, <u>however</u>. (conjunctive adverb at end of sentence)

FREQUENTLY USED CONJUNCTIVE ADVERBS

accordingly	furthermore	meanwhile	similarly
also	hence	moreover	still
anyway	however	nevertheless	then
besides	incidentally	next	thereafter
certainly	indeed	nonetheless	therefore
consequently	instead	now	thus
finally	likewise	otherwise	undoubtedly

32f Prepositions

A **preposition** introduces a noun or pronoun (or a phrase or clause functioning in the sentence as a noun), linking it to other words in the sentence. The word or word group the preposition introduces is called its **object**.

See 56j

prep   obj   prep   obj prep obj

They received a postcard <u>from</u> Bobby telling <u>about</u> his trip <u>to</u> Canada.

FREQUENTLY USED PREPOSITIONS

about	beneath	inside	since
above	beside	into	through
across	between	like	throughout
after	beyond	near	to
against	by	of	toward
along	concerning	off	under
among	despite	on	underneath
around	down	onto	until
as	during	out	up
at	except	outside	upon
before	for	over	with
behind	from	past	within
below	in	regarding	without

32g Conjunctions

Conjunctions connect words, phrases, clauses, or sentences. Different conjunctions establish different relationships between the items they connect.

Coordinating conjunctions (*and, or, but, nor, for, so, yet*) connect words, phrases, or clauses that are grammatically equivalent.

We could choose pheasant <u>or</u> venison. (*Or* links two nouns.)

The United States is a government "of the people, by the people, <u>and</u> for the people." (*And* links three prepositional phrases.)

Thoreau wrote *Walden* in 1854, <u>and</u> he died in 1862. (*And* links two independent clauses.)

<u>Correlative conjunctions</u>, always used in pairs, also link grammatically equivalent items.

FREQUENTLY USED CORRELATIVE CONJUNCTIONS

both . . . and	neither . . . nor
either . . . or	not only . . . but also
just as . . . so	whether . . . or

<u>Both</u> Hancock <u>and</u> Jefferson signed the Declaration of Independence. (Correlative conjunctions link two nouns.)

<u>Either</u> I will renew my lease, <u>or</u> I will move. (Correlative conjunctions link two independent clauses.)

Subordinating conjunctions include *since, because, although, if, after, when, while, before, unless,* and so on. A subordinating conjunction introduces a dependent (subordinate) clause, connecting it to the sentence's independent (main) clause to form a **complex sentence**. The subordinating conjunction indicates the relationship between the clauses.

<u>Although</u> drug use is a serious concern for parents, many parents are afraid to discuss it with their children.

It is best to diagram your garden <u>before</u> you start to plant it.

Conjunctive adverbs, also known as *adverbial conjunctions,* are discussed in **32e.**

32h   Interjections

Interjections are words used as exclamations: *Oh! Ouch! Wow! Alas! Hey!* These words, which express emotion, are grammatically independent; that is, they do not have a grammatical function in a sentence. Interjections may be set off in a sentence by commas.

The message, alas, arrived too late.

For greater emphasis, interjections can be punctuated as independent units, set off with an exclamation point.

Alas! The message arrived too late.

Other kinds of words may also be used in isolation. These include *yes, no, hello, good-bye, please,* and *thank you.* All such words, including interjections, are collectively referred to as **isolates.**

CHAPTER 33

NOUNS AND PRONOUNS

? FREQUENTLY ASKED QUESTIONS

Is *I* always more appropriate than *me*?   (p. 511)
How do I know whether to use *who* or
   whom?   (p. 512)
What is an antecedent?   (p. 514)
How do I know whether to use *who, which,*
   or *that*?   (p. 515)

33a   Case

Case is the form a noun or pronoun takes to indicate its function in a sentence. English has three cases: *subjective, objective,* and *possessive.* Nouns change form only in the possessive case: the *cat's* eyes, *Molly's* book. Pronouns, however, have many case forms.

PRONOUN CASE FORMS

Subjective

I	he, she	it	we	you	they	who
						whoever

Objective

me	him, her	it	us	you	them	whom
						whomever

Possessive

my	his, her	its	our	your	their	whose
mine	hers		ours	yours	theirs	

---

(1) Using Subjective Case

A pronoun takes the **subjective case** in the following situations:

SUBJECT OF A VERB: I bought a mountain bike.

SUBJECT COMPLEMENT: It was <u>he</u> for whom the men were looking.

(2) Using Objective Case

A pronoun takes the **objective case** in these situations:

DIRECT OBJECT: Our sociology teacher likes Adam and <u>me</u>.

INDIRECT OBJECT: The plumber's bill gave <u>him</u> quite a shock.

OBJECT OF A PREPOSITION: Between <u>us</u>, we own ten shares of stock.

NOTE: *I* is not necessarily more appropriate than *me*. In compound constructions like the following, *me* is correct.

Just between you and <u>me</u> [not *I*], I think we're going to have a quiz. (*Me* is the object of the preposition *between*.)

(3) Using Possessive Case

A pronoun takes the **possessive case** when it indicates ownership (*our* car, *your* book). Remember to use the possessive, not the objective, case before a **gerund**.

Napoleon approved of <u>their</u> [not *them*] ruling Naples. (*Ruling* is a gerund.)

See 32c2

EXERCISE 1

Choose the correct form of the pronoun within the parentheses. Be prepared to explain why you chose each form.

EXAMPLE: Toni Morrison, Alice Walker, and (<u>she</u>, her) are perhaps the most widely recognized African-American women writing today.

1. Both Walt Whitman and (he, him) wrote a great deal of poetry about nature.
2. Our instructor gave Matthew and (me, I) an excellent idea for our project.
3. The sales clerk objected to (me, my) returning the sweater.
4. I understand (you, your) being unavailable to work tonight.
5. The waiter asked Michael and (me, I) to move to another table.

Using Pronouns Clearly
   http://owl.english. purdue. edu/handouts/grammar/g_pronuse.html
Pronouns and Names (M. Browning)
   http://www.princeton.edu/~browning/binding.html
Pronoun Types and Common Mistakes (Emory U.)
   http://www.emory.edu/ENGLISH/WC/pronounref.html

33b Determining Pronoun Case in Special Situations

(1) Implied Comparisons with *Than* or *As*

When a sentence containing an implied comparison ends with a pronoun, your meaning dictates your choice of pronoun case.

Darcy likes John more than I. (more than I like John)

Darcy likes John more than me. (more than she likes me)

(2) *Who* and *Whom*

 The case of the pronouns *who* and *whom* depends on their function *within their own clause.* When a pronoun serves as the subject of its clause, use *who* or *whoever;* when it functions as an object, use *whom* or *whomever.*

The Salvation Army gives food and shelter to whoever is in need. (*Whoever* is the subject of the dependent clause *whoever is in need.*)

I wonder whom jazz musician Miles Davis influenced. (*Whom* is the object of *influenced* in the dependent clause *whom jazz musician Miles Davis influenced.*)

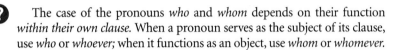 **PRONOUN CASE IN QUESTIONS**

To determine the case of *who* at the beginning of a question, use a personal pronoun to answer the question. The case of *who* should be the same as the case of the personal pronoun.

Who wrote *The Age of Innocence?* She wrote it. (subject)

Whom do you support for mayor? I support her. (object)

In all but the most formal situations, current usage accepts *who* at the beginning of questions (Who do you support for mayor?).

 EXERCISE 2

Using the word in parentheses, combine each pair of sentences into a single sentence. You may change word order and add or delete words.

EXAMPLE: Even after he left the band The Police, bass player Sting's musical career continued to thrive. He once taught middle-school English. (who)

REVISED: Even after he left the band The Police, bass player Sting, who once taught middle-school English, continued to have a thriving musical career.

1. The photographs of Herb Ritts of world leaders, leading artistic figures in dance and drama, and a vanishing African tribe are technically beautiful and emotionally compelling. He got his start by taking photographs of Hollywood stars. (who)
2. Tim Green has written several novels about a fictional football team. He played for the Atlanta Hawks and has a degree in law. (who)
3. Some say Carl Sagan did more to further science education in America than any other person. He wrote many books on science and narrated many popular television shows. (who)
4. Jodie Foster has won two Academy Awards for her acting. She was a child star. (who)
5. Sylvia Plath met the poet Ted Hughes at Cambridge University in England. She later married him. (whom)

(3) Appositives

An **appositive** is a noun or noun phrase that identifies or renames an adjacent noun or pronoun. The case of a pronoun in an appositive depends on the function of the word it describes.

We heard two Motown recording artists, Smokey Robinson and <u>him</u>. (*Recording artists* is the object of the verb *heard,* so the pronoun in the appositive *Smokey Robinson and him* takes the objective case.)

Two recording artists, Smokey Robinson and <u>he</u>, recorded for Motown Records. (*Recording artists* is the subject of the sentence, so the pronoun in the appositive *Smokey Robinson and he* takes the subjective case.)

(4) *We* and *Us* before a Noun

When a first-person plural pronoun directly precedes a noun, the case of the pronoun depends on the way the noun functions in the sentence.

<u>We</u> women must stick together. (*Women* is the subject of the sentence, so the pronoun *we* must be in the subjective case.)

Teachers make learning easy for <u>us</u> students. (*Students* is the object of the preposition *for,* so the pronoun *us* must be in the objective case.)

33c Pronoun Reference

An **antecedent** is the word or word group to which a pronoun refers. **Pronoun reference** is clear when readers can easily identify the pronoun's antecedent. Pronoun reference is not clear, however, when a pronoun's antecedent is *ambiguous, remote,* or *nonexistent.* In such cases, substitute a noun or noun phrase for the pronoun.

(1) Ambiguous Antecedents

Sometimes a pronoun—for example, *this, that, which* or *it*—could refer to more than one antecedent in a sentence.

AMBIGUOUS: The accountant took out his calculator and completed the tax return. Then, he put <u>it</u> in his briefcase. (The pronoun *it* can refer either to *calculator* or to *tax return.*)

CLEAR: The accountant took out his calculator and completed the tax return. Then, he put <u>the calculator</u> into his briefcase.

Sometimes a pronoun does not seem to refer to any specific antecedent. In such cases, supply a noun to clarify the ambiguous reference.

AMBIGUOUS: Some one-celled organisms contain chlorophyll yet are considered animals. <u>This</u> illustrates the difficulty of classifying single-celled organisms. (Exactly what does *this* refer to?)

CLEAR: Some one-celled organisms contain chlorophyll yet are considered animals. <u>This paradox</u> illustrates the difficulty of classifying single-celled organisms.

(2) Remote Antecedents

The farther a pronoun is from its antecedent, the more difficult it is for readers to make a connection between them.

UNCLEAR: During the mid-1800s, many Czechs began to immigrate to America. By 1860, about 23,000 Czechs had left their country. By 1900, 13,000 Czech immigrants were coming to <u>its</u> shores each year. (The pronoun *its* in the last sentence is so far removed from its antecedent, *America,* that this reference cannot be easily understood.)

CLEAR: During the mid-1800s, many Czechs began to immigrate to America. By 1860, about 23,000 Czechs had left their country. By 1900, 13,000 Czech immigrants were coming to <u>America's</u> shores each year.

(3) Nonexistent Antecedents

Sometimes a pronoun refers to a nonexistent antecedent.

UNCLEAR: Our township has decided to build a computer lab in the school because they feel fourth graders should begin using computers. (*They* refers to an antecedent that the writer has neglected to mention.)

CLEAR: Our township has decided to build a computer lab in the school because <u>teachers</u> feel that fourth graders should begin using computers.

PRONOUN REFERENCE

Familiar expressions like "*It* says in the paper" and "*They* said on the news" include pronouns that refer to nonexistent antecedents. To clarify such a reference, substitute an appropriate noun for the pronoun: "*The article* in the paper says . . ." and "On the news, *Cokie Roberts* said. . . ."

(4) *Who, Which,* and *That*

In general, the pronoun *who* refers to people or to animals that have names. The pronouns *which* and *that* refer to objects, events, or unnamed animals and sometimes to groups of people.

David Henry Hwang, <u>who</u> wrote the Tony Award–winning play *M. Butterfly,* also wrote *Family Devotions* and *FOB.*

The spotted owl, <u>which</u> lives in old-growth forests, is in danger of extinction.

Houses <u>that</u> are built today are more energy efficient than those built twenty years ago.

NOTE: Make certain that you use *which* in nonrestrictive clauses, which are always set off with commas. In most cases, use *that* in restrictive clauses. *Who* may be used in both **restrictive and nonrestrictive clauses**.

See
38d1

EXERCISE 3

Analyze the pronoun reference errors in each of the following sentences. After doing so, revise each sentence by substituting an appropriate noun or noun phrase for the underlined pronoun.

EXAMPLE: Jefferson asked Lewis to head the expedition, and Lewis selected <u>him</u> as his associate.

ANALYSIS: *Him* refers to a nonexistent antecedent.

REVISION: Jefferson asked Lewis to head the expedition, and Lewis selected Clark as his associate.

1. The purpose of the expedition was to search out a land route to the Pacific and to gather information about the West. The Louisiana Purchase increased the need for <u>it</u>.
2. The expedition was going to be difficult. <u>They</u> trained the men in Illinois, the starting point.
3. Clark and most of the men who descended the Yellowstone River camped on the bank. <u>It</u> was beautiful and wild.
4. Both Jefferson and Lewis had faith that <u>he</u> would be successful in this transcontinental journey.
5. The expedition was efficient, and only one man was lost. <u>This</u> was extraordinary.

STUDENT WRITER AT WORK

Nouns and Pronouns

Following is part of a draft of a student essay about John Updike. This section of the essay gives a plot summary of Updike's short story "A & P." Read the draft and revise it to correct errors in case and to eliminate unclear pronoun reference. After you have corrected the errors, go over the draft again and, if necessary, revise further to strengthen coherence, unity, and style.

John Updike's "A & P," a short story that appears in the collection <u>Pigeon Feathers and Other Stories</u>, takes place in a small town similar to Updike's hometown. The character which has the significant role in "A & P" is Sammy, a cashier at the supermarket. Sammy is a nineteen-year-old boy that is just out of high school. He analyzes everyone who comes to the A & P to shop. It is him who is the narrator of the story.

The story takes place on a Thursday afternoon when three girls in bathing suits walk into the store. They are different from the other shoppers. Their manner and the way they walk make them different from them. Sammy notices that one of the girls, who he calls Queenie, leads the other girls. This appeals to him. He identifies with her because he feels that he too is a leader.

When the girls come to his check-out counter, he rings up their purchase. Suddenly the store manager, Lengel, begins scolding the girls for coming into the store in bathing suits. Sammy feels sorry for them, and in a gesture of defiance he quits. Sammy feels that him quitting is a rejection of him and all that he stands for. To Sammy, Lengel is a person that represents the narrow morality of the town.

Sammy's quitting is the climax of the story. Sammy chooses to follow his conscience and in doing so pays the price. He feels that not following his ideals would be bad. Because he is young, however, he does not realize the significance of the act which he commits. For a moment Lengel and Sammy face each other, but he does not change his mind. Sammy feels that he has won his freedom. His confidence is short-lived, though. When he walks out into the parking lot, the girls are gone, and he is alone. It is then he realizes that the world is going to be hard for him from this point on.

CHAPTER 34

VERBS

? FREQUENTLY ASKED QUESTIONS

Which verbs are irregular? (p. 519)
How do I use *lie* and *lay* correctly? (p. 522)
Which is correct, "I wish I were" or "I wish I was"? (p. 529)
Should I always use the active voice? (p. 530)

VERBS: KEY TERMS

Form   The spelling of a verb that conveys tense, person, number, and so on.

Tense   The form a verb takes to indicate when an action occurs or when a condition exists—*present, past, future,* and so on.

Person   The form a verb takes to indicate whether someone is speaking (*first person*), is spoken to (*second person*), or is spoken about (*third person*).

Number   The form a verb takes to indicate whether the subject is singular (The child *writes*) or plural (The children *write*).

Mood   The form a verb takes to indicate the writer's attitude—for example, whether he or she is making a statement, giving a command, or making a recommendation (I *read* the book; *Read* the book!; I suggest you *read* the book).

Voice   The form a verb takes to indicate whether the subject acts or is acted upon (He *wrote* the book; The book *was written* by him).

34a   Verb Forms

Every verb has four **principal parts: a base form** (the form of the verb used with *I, we, you,* and *they* in the present tense),* a **present**

Regular and Irregular Verbs (U. Illinois)
   http://www.english.uiuc.edu/cws/wworkshop/grammar/regularverbs.htm

participle, (the *-ing* form of the verb), a **past tense form,** and a **past participle.**

(1) Regular Verbs

A **regular verb** forms both its past tense and its past participle by adding *-d* or *-ed.*

PRINCIPAL PARTS OF REGULAR VERBS		
Base Form	*Past Tense Form*	*Past Participle*
smile	smiled	smiled
talk	talked	talked
jump	jumped	jumped

(2) Irregular Verbs

Irregular verbs do not follow the pattern just discussed. The chart that follows lists the principal parts of the most frequently used irregular verbs.

FREQUENTLY USED IRREGULAR VERBS		
Base Form	*Past Tense Form*	*Past Participle*
arise	arose	arisen
awake	awoke, awaked	awoke, awaked
be	was/were	been
beat	beat	beaten
begin	began	begun
bend	bent	bent
bet	bet, betted	bet
bite	bit	bitten
blow	blew	blown
break	broke	broken

continued on the following page

*Note: The verb *be* is so irregular that it is the one exception to this definition; its base form is *be.*

continued from the previous page

Base Form	Past Tense Form	Past Participle
bring	brought	brought
build	built	built
burst	burst	burst
buy	bought	bought
catch	caught	caught
choose	chose	chosen
cling	clung	clung
come	came	come
cost	cost	cost
deal	dealt	dealt
dig	dug	dug
dive	dived, dove	dived
do	did	done
drag	dragged	dragged
draw	drew	drawn
drink	drank	drunk
drive	drove	driven
eat	ate	eaten
fall	fell	fallen
fight	fought	fought
find	found	found
fly	flew	flown
forget	forgot	forgotten, forgot
freeze	froze	frozen
get	got	gotten
give	gave	given
go	went	gone
grow	grew	grown
hang (execute)	hanged	hanged
hang (suspend)	hung	hung
have	had	had
hear	heard	heard
keep	kept	kept
know	knew	known

Base Form	Past Tense Form	Past Participle
lay	laid	laid
lead	led	led
lend	lent	lent
let	let	let
lie (recline)	lay	lain
lie (tell an untruth)	lied	lied
make	made	made
prove	proved	proved, proven
read	read	read
ride	rode	ridden
ring	rang	rung
rise	rose	risen
run	ran	run
say	said	said
see	saw	seen
sell	sold	sold
set (place)	set	set
shake	shook	shaken
shrink	shrank, shrunk,	shrunk, shrunken
sing	sang	sung
sink	sank	sunk
sit	sat	sat
sneak	sneaked	sneaked
speak	spoke	spoken
speed	sped, speeded	sped, speeded
spin	spun	spun
spring	sprang	sprung
stand	stood	stood
steal	stole	stolen
strike	struck	struck, stricken
swear	swore	sworn
swim	swam	swum
swing	swung	swung
take	took	taken

continued on the following page

continued from the previous page

Base Form	Past Tense Form	Past Participle
teach	taught	taught
throw	threw	thrown
wake	woke, waked	waked, woken
wear	wore	worn
wring	wrung	wrung
write	wrote	written

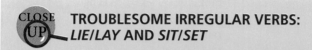

TROUBLESOME IRREGULAR VERBS: *LIE/LAY* AND *SIT/SET*

Lie means "to recline" and does not take an object ("He likes to *lie* on the floor"); *lay* means "to place" or "to put" and does take an object ("He wants to *lay* a rug on the floor"):

Base Form	Past Tense Form	Past Participle
lie	lay	lain
lay	laid	laid

Sit means "to assume a seated position" and does not take an object ("She wants to *sit* on the table"); *set* means "to place" or "to put" and usually takes an object ("She wants to *set* a vase on the table"):

Base Form	Past Tense Form	Past Participle
sit	sat	sat
set	set	set

EXERCISE 1

Complete the sentences in the following paragraph with an appropriate form of the verbs in parentheses.

EXAMPLE: An air of mystery surrounds many of those who have
_____ (sing) and played the blues.

An air of mystery surrounds many of those who have
<u>sung</u> and played the blues.

The legendary bluesman Robert Johnson supposedly
_____ (sell) his soul to the devil in order to become a
guitar virtuoso. Myth has it that the young Johnson could barely
chord his instrument and annoyed other musicians by trying to sit
in at clubs, where he _____ (sneak) onto the bandstand
to play every chance he got. He disappeared for a short time, the
story goes, and when he returned he was a phenomenal guitarist,
having _____ (swear) a Faustian oath to Satan. Johnson's
song "Crossroads Blues"—rearranged and recorded by the sixties
supergroup Cream as simply "Crossroads"—supposedly recounts
this exchange, telling how Johnson _____ (deal) with the
devil. Some of his other songs, such as "Hellhound on My Trail,"
are allegedly about the torment he suffered as he _____
(fight) for his soul.

EXERCISE 2

Complete the following sentences with appropriate forms of the verbs in
parentheses.

EXAMPLE: Mary Cassatt _____ down her paintbrush. (lie,
lay)

Mary Cassatt <u>lay</u> down her paintbrush.

1. Impressionist artists of the nineteenth century preferred everyday
   subjects and used to _____ fruit on a table to paint. (sit,
   set)
2. They were known for their technique of _____ dabs of
   paint quickly on canvas, giving an "impression" of a scene, not extensive detail. (lying, laying)
3. Claude Monet's *Women in the Garden* featured one woman in the
   foreground who _____ on the grass in a garden. (sat, set)
4. In Pierre Auguste Renoir's *Nymphs,* two nude figures talk while
   _____ on flowers in a garden. (lying, laying)
5. Paul Cézanne liked to _____ in front of his subject as he
   painted and often completed paintings out of doors rather than in a
   studio. (sit, set)

34b Tense

Tense is the form that a verb takes to indicate when an action occurred or when a condition existed.

ENGLISH VERB TENSES

Simple Tenses

 Present (I *finish,* she or he *finishes*)

 Past (I *finished*)

 Future (I *will finish*)

Perfect Tenses

 Present perfect (I *have finished,* she or he *has finished*)

 Past perfect (I *had finished*)

 Future perfect (I *will have finished*)

Progressive Tenses

 Present progressive (I *am finishing,* she or he *is finishing*)

 Past progressive (I *was finishing*)

 Future progressive (I *will be finishing*)

 Present perfect progressive (I *have been finishing*)

 Past perfect progressive (I *had been finishing*)

 Future perfect progressive (I *will have been finishing*)

---

(1) Using the Simple Tenses

The **simple tenses** include *present, past,* and *future.*

The **present tense** usually indicates an action taking place at the time it is expressed in speech or writing or an action that occurs regularly.

 I <u>see</u> your point. (an action taking place when it is expressed)

 He <u>wears</u> wool in the winter. (an action that occurs regularly)

SPECIAL USES OF THE PRESENT TENSE

In addition to expressing an action that takes place in the present, the present tense has four special uses.

TO INDICATE FUTURE TIME: The grades <u>arrive</u> next Thursday.

TO STATE A GENERALLY HELD BELIEF: Studying <u>pays</u> off.

TO STATE A SCIENTIFIC TRUTH: An object at rest <u>tends</u> to stay at rest.

TO DISCUSS A LITERARY WORK: *Family Installments* <u>tells</u> the story of a Puerto Rican family.

The **past tense** indicates that an action has already taken place.

John Glenn <u>orbited</u> the earth three times on February 20, 1962. (an action completed in the past)

As a young man, Mark Twain <u>traveled</u> through the Southwest. (an action that recurred in the past but did not extend into the present)

The **future tense** indicates that an action will or is likely to take place. The future tense is formed with the auxiliary verbs *will* or *shall* plus the present tense.

Halley's Comet <u>will reappear</u> in 2061. (a future action that will definitely occur)

The land boom in Nevada <u>will</u> probably <u>continue</u>. (a future action that is likely to occur)

(2) Using the Perfect Tenses

The **perfect tenses** designate actions that were or will be completed before other actions or conditions. The perfect tenses are formed with the appropriate tense form of the auxiliary verb *have* plus the past participle.

Verb tense (U. Ottawa)
http://www.uottawa.ca/academic/arts/writcent/hypergrammar/usetense.html

The **present perfect** tense can indicate two types of continuing action beginning in the past.

Dr. Kim <u>has finished</u> studying the effects of BHA on rats. (an action that began in the past and is finished at the present time)

My mother <u>has invested</u> her money wisely. (an action that began in the past and extends into the present)

The **past perfect** tense indicates an action occurring before a certain time in the past.

By 1946, engineers <u>had built</u> the first electronic digital computer.

The **future perfect** tense indicates that an action will be finished by a certain future time.

By Tuesday, the transit authority <u>will have run</u> out of money.

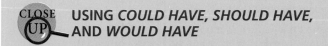 **CLOSE UP** **USING *COULD HAVE, SHOULD HAVE, AND WOULD HAVE***

Do not use the preposition *of* after *would, should, could,* and *might.* Use the auxiliary verb *have* after these words.

INCORRECT: I should <u>of</u> left for class earlier.

CORRECT: I should <u>have</u> left for class earlier.

---

(3) Using the Progressive Tenses

The **progressive tenses** express continuing action. They are formed with the appropriate tense of the verb *be* plus the present participle.

The **present progressive** tense indicates that something is happening at the time it is expressed in speech or writing.

The volcano <u>is erupting</u>, and lava <u>is flowing</u> toward the town.

Verb Tense Consistency (Emory U.)
http://www.emory.edu/ENGLISH/WC/verbconsist.html

The **past progressive** tense indicates two kinds of past action.

Roderick Usher's actions <u>were becoming</u> increasingly bizarre. (a continuing action in the past)

The French revolutionary Marat was stabbed to death while he <u>was bathing</u>. (an action occurring at the same time in the past as another action)

The **future progressive** tense indicates a continuing action in the future.

The treasury secretary <u>will be</u> carefully <u>monitoring</u> the money supply.

The **present perfect progressive** tense indicates action continuing from the past into the present and possibly into the future.

Rescuers <u>have been working</u> around the clock.

The **past perfect progressive** tense indicates that a past action went on until another one occurred.

Before President Kennedy was assassinated, he <u>had been working</u> on civil rights legislation.

The **future perfect progressive** tense indicates that an action will continue until a certain future time.

By eleven o'clock, we <u>will have been driving</u> for seven hours.

EXERCISE 3

A verb is missing from each of the following sentences. Fill in the form of the verb indicated in parentheses after each sentence.

EXAMPLE: The Outer Banks _____ (stretch: present) along the North Carolina coast for more than 175 miles.

The Outer Banks <u>stretch</u> along the North Carolina coast for more than 175 miles.

1. Many portions of the Outer Banks of North Carolina _____ (give: present) the visitor a sense of history and timelessness.
2. Many students of history _____ (read: present perfect) about the Outer Banks and its mysteries.
3. It was on Roanoke Island in the 1580s that English colonists _____ (establish: past) the first settlement in the New World.

4. That colony vanished soon after it was settled, _____ (become: present participle) known as the famous "lost colony."
5. By 1718, the pirate Blackbeard _____ (made: past perfect) the Outer Banks a hiding place for his treasures.
6. It was at Ocracoke, in fact, that Blackbeard _____ (meet: past) his death.
7. Even today, fortune hunters _____ (search: present progressive) the Outer Banks for Blackbeard's hidden treasures.
8. The Outer Banks are also famous for Kitty Hawk and Kill Devil Hills; even as technology has advanced into the space age, the number of tourists flocking to the site of the Wright brothers' epic flight _____. (grow: present perfect progressive)
9. Long before that famous flight occurred, however, the Outer Banks _____ (claim: past perfect) countless ships along its ever-shifting shores, resulting in its nickname—the "Graveyard of the Atlantic."
10. If the Outer Banks continue to be protected from the ravages of overdevelopment and commercialization, visitors _____ (enjoy: future progressive) the mysteries of this tiny finger of land for years to come.

34c Mood

Mood is the form a verb takes to indicate whether a writer is making a statement, asking a question, giving a command, or expressing a wish or a contrary-to-fact statement. The three moods in English are the *indicative,* the *imperative,* and the *subjunctive.*

The **indicative** mood expresses an opinion, states a fact, or asks a question: Jackie Robinson <u>had</u> an impact on professional baseball.

The **imperative** mood is used in commands and direct requests. Usually, the imperative includes only the base form of the verb without a subject: <u>Use</u> a dictionary.

(1) Forming the Subjunctive Mood

The **subjunctive** mood causes the greatest difficulty for writers. The **present subjunctive** uses the base form of the verb, regardless of the subject.

Dr. Gorman suggested that he <u>study</u> the Cambrian period. (present subjunctive)

In the subjunctive mood, the auxiliary verb *be* always takes the form *were*—regardless of the number or person of the subject.

I wish I <u>were</u> going to Europe; I wish they <u>were</u> going too.

(2) Using the Subjunctive Mood

Use the present subjunctive in *that* clauses after such words as *ask, suggest, require, recommend,* and *demand.*

The report recommended that juveniles <u>be</u> given mandatory counseling.

Captain Ahab insisted that his crew <u>hunt</u> the white whale.

Use the past subjunctive in **conditional statements** (statements beginning with *if* that are contrary to fact, including statements that express a wish).

If John <u>were</u> here, he could see Marsha. (John is not here.)

The father acted as if he <u>were</u> having the baby. (The father couldn't be having the baby.)

I wish I <u>were</u> more organized. (expresses a wish)

NOTE: If an *if* clause expresses a condition that is possible, use the indicative mood, not the subjunctive.

If a peace treaty <u>is</u> signed, the world will be safer. (A peace treaty is possible.)

The subjunctive is also used in some idiomatic expressions.

If need <u>be</u>, we will stay up all night to finish the report.

<u>Come</u> what may, they will increase their steel production.

Special interest groups have, as it <u>were</u>, shifted the balance of power.

EXERCISE 4

Complete the sentences in the following paragraph by inserting the appropriate form (indicative, imperative, or subjunctive) of the verb in parentheses. Be prepared to explain your choices.

Harry Houdini was a famous escape artist. He _____ (perform) escapes from every type of bond imaginable: handcuffs, locks, straitjackets, ropes, sacks, and sealed chests underwater. In Germany, workers _____ (challenge) Houdini to escape from a packing box. If he _____ (be) to escape, they would admit that he _____ (be) the best escape artist in the world. Houdini accepted. Before getting into the box, he asked that the observers _____ (give) it a thorough examination. He then asked that a worker _____ (nail) him into the box. "_____ (place) a screen around the box," he ordered after he had been sealed inside. In a few minutes, Houdini _____ (step) from behind the screen. When the workers demanded that they _____ (see) the box, Houdini pulled down the screen. To their surprise, they saw the box with the lid still nailed tightly in place.

34d Voice

Voice is the form a verb takes to indicate whether its subject acts or is acted upon. When the subject of a verb does something—that is, acts—the verb is in the **active voice.** When the subject of a verb receives the action—that is, is acted upon—the verb is in the **passive voice.**

ACTIVE VOICE: <u>Hart Crane wrote</u> *The Bridge.*

PASSIVE VOICE: *The Bridge* <u>was written</u> by Hart Crane.

 **VOICE**

Because the active voice emphasizes the person or thing performing an action, it is usually briefer, clearer, and more emphatic than the passive voice. Whenever possible, use active constructions in your college writing. Some situations, however, require use of the passive voice. For example, you should use passive constructions when the actor is unknown or unimportant or when the recipient of an action should logically receive the emphasis.

DDT <u>was found</u> in soil samples. (Passive voice emphasizes finding DDT; who found it is not important.)

Grits <u>are eaten</u> throughout the South. (Passive voice emphasizes fact that grits are eaten, not those who eat them.)

(1) Changing from Passive to Active Voice

You can change a verb from passive to active voice by making the subject of the passive verb the object of the active verb. The person or thing performing the action then becomes the subject of the new sentence.

> **PASSIVE:** The novel *Frankenstein* <u>was written</u> by Mary Shelley.
>
> **ACTIVE:** Mary Shelley <u>wrote</u> the novel *Frankenstein.*

If a passive verb has no object, you must supply one that will become the subject of the active verb.

> **PASSIVE:** Baby elephants are taught to avoid humans. (By whom are baby elephants taught?)
>
> **ACTIVE:** <u>Adult elephants</u> teach baby elephants to avoid humans.

EXERCISE 5

Determine which verbs in the following paragraph should be changed from the passive to the active voice. Rewrite the sentences containing these verbs.

> Rockets were invented by the Chinese about AD 1000. Gunpowder was packed into bamboo tubes and ignited by means of a fuse. These rockets were fired by soldiers at enemy armies and usually caused panic. In thirteenth-century England, an improved form of gunpowder was introduced by Roger Bacon. As a result, rockets were used in battles and were a common—although unreliable— weapon. In the early eighteenth century, a twenty-pound rocket that traveled almost two miles was constructed by William Congreve, an English artillery expert. By the late nineteenth century, thought was given to supersonic speeds by the physicist Ernst Mach. The sonic boom was predicted by him. The first liquid-fuel rocket was launched by the American Robert Goddard in 1926. A pamphlet written by him anticipated almost all future rocket developments. As a result of his pioneering work, he is called the father of modern rocketry.

(2) Changing from Active to Passive Voice

You can change a verb from active to passive voice by making the object of the active verb the subject of the passive verb. The subject of the active verb then becomes the object of the passive verb.

> **ACTIVE:** Sir James Murray <u>compiled</u> *The Oxford English Dictionary.*
>
> **PASSIVE:** *The Oxford English Dictionary* <u>was compiled</u> by Sir James Murray.

Remember that an active verb must have an object or else it cannot be put into the passive voice. If an active verb has no object, supply one. This will become the subject of the passive sentence.

ACTIVE: Jacques Cousteau invented.
Cousteau invented _____?_____ .

PASSIVE: _____?_____ was invented by Jacques Cousteau.
The scuba was invented by Jacques Cousteau.

EXERCISE 6

Determine which sentences in the following paragraph should be in the passive voice. Rewrite those sentences, making sure that you can explain the reasons for your choices.

The Regent Diamond is one of the world's most famous and coveted jewels. A slave discovered the 410-carat diamond in 1701 in an Indian mine. Over the years, people stole and sold the diamond several times. In 1717, the regent of France bought the diamond for an enormous sum, but during the French Revolution, it disappeared again. Someone later found it in a ditch in Paris. Eventually, Napoleon had the diamond set into his ceremonial sword. At last, when the French monarch fell, the government placed the Regent Diamond in the Louvre, where it remains to be enjoyed by all.

STUDENT WRITER AT WORK

Verbs

This is a draft of a paper written for a technical writing class. The student was told to write an essay in which she explained a basic scientific principle to readers who had little or no understanding of science. As you read, look for inaccuracies or inconsistencies in verb form, tense, and mood; in addition, make sure the writer has made effective use of both passive and active voice. You may add and delete words and phrases as well as rearrange sentences. After you have corrected this draft, go over it again and, if necessary, revise further for coherence, unity, and style.

How Fast Did That Piece of Paper Fall?

Most people who never studied physics assume that heavier

objects fall faster than light objects will. This assumption was also made by Aristotle, the brilliant philosopher of ancient Greece. He believed that heavy objects naturally tended to be closer to the ground than light objects. For this reason, they must have fell faster than light objects. This explanation was assumed by Aristotle to conform to common sense. Was it true that heavier bodies fell faster than lighter ones did?

In the seventeenth century, Galileo Galilei, an Italian scientist, laid the groundwork for modern physics. It was recognized by him that heavier objects did not always fall faster than lighter objects. As a result of Galileo's analysis of falling bodies, it is now known by students that in the absence of air resistance, all objects fall at the same rate.

By repeating his experiments in the classroom, you can test Galileo's principle. At the same time you prove the validity of Galileo's ideas, Aristotle's assumptions can be disproved. When you raise two objects—a stone and a flat piece of paper—that were laying on a table to equal distances above the ground and let go, you should see the heavier object reach the ground first. This experiment would seem to confirm Aristotle's belief that heavier objects fall faster than light ones. Repeat the experiment, this time crumpling the flat piece of paper into a wad. Now the two objects should reach the ground at almost the same time. How is this difference explained?

The key to explaining the difference lies in Galileo's principle. The paper, whose weight was the same whether it was flat or crumpled up, falls faster when it is in a wad because it has a smaller cross-sectional area. It is the cross-sectional area of an object that determines the rate at which it will drop: the larger the area, the more air resistance the object encountered and the slower it will have dropped. If the flat piece of paper was dropped in a vacuum—where there is no air resistance—it would have dropped as fast as the heavy object. This, then, is why the phrase "in the absence of air resistance" is added to Galileo's principle.

CHAPTER 35

AGREEMENT

? FREQUENTLY ASKED QUESTIONS

What do I do if a phrase like *along with* comes between the subject and the verb? (p. 535)

If one part of a subject is singular and one is plural, is the verb singular or plural? (p. 535)

Do subjects like *anyone* take singular or plural verbs? (p. 536)

Can I use *they* to refer to a word like *everyone*? (p. 542)

Agreement is the correspondence between words in number, gender, or person. Subjects and verbs agree in **number** (singular or plural) and **person** (first, second, or third); pronouns and their antecedents agree in number, person, and **gender** (masculine, feminine, or neuter).

35a Subject-Verb Agreement

Singular subjects take singular verbs, and plural subjects take plural verbs.

SINGULAR: <u>Hydrogen peroxide</u> <u>is</u> an unstable compound.

PLURAL: <u>Characters</u> <u>are</u> not well developed in O. Henry's short stories.

See 34b1

Present tense verbs, except *be* and *have,* add *-s* or *-es* when the subject is third-person singular. (Third-person singular subjects include

Subject-Verb Agreement
http://www.unm.edu/~seceas/sva.htm
Agreement
http://andromeda.rutgers.edu/~jlynch/Writing/a.html#agreement

nouns; the personal pronouns *he, she, it,* and *one;* and many indefinite pronouns.)

> <u>She</u> frequently <u>cites</u> statistics to support her assertions.
>
> In every group, <u>somebody</u> <u>emerges</u> as a natural leader.
>
> The <u>president</u> <u>has</u> the power to veto congressional legislation.

Present tense verbs do not add *-s* or *-es* when the subject is a plural noun, a first-person or second-person pronoun (*I, we, you*), or third-person plural pronoun (*they*).

> <u>Experts</u> <u>recommend</u> that dieters avoid salty processed meat.
>
> In our Bill of Rights, <u>we</u> <u>guarantee</u> all defendants the right to a speedy trial.
>
> At this stratum, <u>you</u> <u>see</u> rocks dating back fifteen million years.
>
> <u>They</u> <u>say</u> that some wealthy people default on their student loans.

In some situations, subject-verb agreement can be troublesome.

(1) Words between Subject and Verb

If a modifying phrase comes between subject and verb, the verb should agree with the subject, not with a word in the modifying phrase.

> The <u>sound</u> of the drumbeats <u>builds</u> in intensity in *The Emperor Jones.*
>
> The <u>games</u> won by the intramural team <u>are</u> usually few and far between.

When phrases introduced by *along with, as well as, in addition to, including,* and *together with* come between subject and verb, these phrases do not change the subject's number. ❓

> Heavy <u>rain</u>, together with high winds, <u>causes</u> hazardous driving conditions.

(2) Compound Subjects Joined by *And* ❓

Compound subjects joined by *and* usually take plural verbs.

> <u>Air bags and antilock brakes</u> <u>are</u> standard on all new models.

There are, however, two exceptions to this rule. First, compound subjects joined by *and* that stand for a single idea or person are treated as a unit and used with singular verbs.

Rhythm and blues is a forerunner of rock and roll.

Second, when *each* or *every* precedes a compound subject joined by *and,* the subject takes a singular verb.

Every desk and file cabinet was searched before the letter was found.

(3) Compound Subjects Joined by *Or*

Compound subjects joined by *or* or by *either . . . or* or *neither . . . nor* may take singular or plural verbs.

If both subjects are singular, use a singular verb; if both subjects are plural, use a plural verb.

Either radiation or chemotherapy is combined with surgery for the most effective results. (Both *radiation* and *chemotherapy* are singular, so the verb is singular.)

Either radiation treatments or chemotherapy sessions are combined with surgery for the most effective results. (Both *treatments* and *sessions* are plural, so the verb is plural.)

When a singular and a plural subject are linked by *or,* or by *either . . . or, neither . . . nor,* or *not only . . . but also,* the verb agrees with the subject that is nearer to it.

Either radiation treatments or chemotherapy is combined with surgery for the most effective results. (Singular verb agrees with *chemotherapy.*)

Either chemotherapy or radiation treatments are combined with surgery for the most effective results. (Plural verb agrees with *treatments.*)

(4) Indefinite Pronouns

Some **indefinite pronouns**—*both, many, few, several, others*—are always plural and take plural verbs. Most others—*another, anyone, everyone, one, each, either, neither, anything, everything, something, nothing, nobody,* and *somebody*—are singular and take singular verbs.

Anyone is welcome to apply for this grant.

Each of the chapters includes a review exercise.

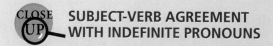

SUBJECT-VERB AGREEMENT WITH INDEFINITE PRONOUNS

A few indefinite pronouns—*some, all, any, more, most,* and *none*—can be singular or plural, depending on the noun they refer to.

Of course, <u>some</u> of this trouble <u>is</u> to be expected. (*Some* refers to *trouble;* therefore, the verb is singular.)

<u>Some</u> of the spectators <u>are</u> getting restless. (*Some* refers to *spectators;* therefore, the verb is plural.)

(5) Collective Nouns

A **collective noun** names a group of persons or things—for instance, *navy, union, association, band.* When it refers to a group as a unit, as it usually does, a collective noun takes a singular verb; when it refers to the individuals or items that make up the group, it takes a plural verb.

To many people, <u>the royal family symbolizes</u> Great Britain. (The family, as a unit, is the symbol.)

<u>The family</u> all <u>eat</u> at different times. (Each member eats separately.)

If a plural verb sounds awkward with a collective noun, reword the sentence.

<u>The family members</u> all <u>eat</u> at different times.

Phrases that name a fixed amount—*three-quarters, twenty dollars, the majority*—are treated like collective nouns. When the amount denotes a unit, it takes a singular verb; when it denotes part of the whole, it takes a plural verb.

<u>Three-quarters</u> of his usual salary <u>is</u> not enough. (*Three-quarters* denotes a unit.)

<u>Three-quarters</u> of workshop participants <u>improve</u> dramatically. (*Three-quarters* denotes part of the group.)

CLOSE
UP
SUBJECT-VERB AGREEMENT WITH COLLECTIVE NOUNS

The number is always singular, and *a number* is always plural.

The number of voters <u>has</u> declined.

A number of students <u>have</u> missed the opportunity to preregister.

(6) Singular Subjects with Plural Forms

A singular verb takes a singular subject, even if the form of the subject is plural.

Politics <u>makes</u> strange bedfellows.

Statistics <u>deals</u> with the collection, classification, analysis, and interpretation of data.

When such words have plural meanings, however, use a plural verb.

Her politics <u>are</u> too radical for her parents. (*Politics* refers not to the science of political government but, rather, to political principles or opinions.)

The statistics <u>prove</u> him wrong. (*Statistics* denotes not a body of knowledge but the numerical facts or data themselves.)

The title of an individual work takes a singular verb even if the title's form is plural.

The Grapes of Wrath <u>describes</u> the journey of migrant workers and their families from the Dust Bowl to California.

See
31b8
NOTE: Some words retain their Latin **plural** forms, which are not like English plural forms. Be particularly careful to use the correct verbs with such words: *criterion is, criteria are; medium is, media are.*

(7) Inverted Subject-Verb Order

Even if the verb comes before the subject (as it does in questions and in sentences beginning with *there is* or *there are*), the subject and verb must agree.

Is either answer correct?

There is a monument to Emiliano Zapata in Mexico City.

There are currently twelve federal circuit courts of appeal.

(8) LinkingVerbs

A **linking verb** should agree with its subject, not with the subject complement.

See 32c1

The problem was termites.

Here, the verb *was* correctly agrees with the subject *problem*, not with the subject complement *termites*. If *termites* were the subject, the verb would be plural.

Termites were the problem.

(9) Relative Pronouns

When a **relative pronoun** (*who, which, that,* and so on) introduces a dependent clause, the verb in that clause should agree in number with the pronoun's **antecedent** (the word to which the pronoun refers).

The farmer is among the ones who suffer during a grain embargo.
(Verb *suffer* agrees with plural antecedent *ones*.)

The farmer is the only one who suffers during the grain embargo.
(Verb agrees with singular antecedent *one*.)

EXERCISE 1

Each of these ten correct sentences illustrates one of the conventions just explained. Read each sentence carefully, and explain why each verb form is used.

EXAMPLE: *Harold and Maude* is a popular cult film. (The verb is singular because the subject *Harold and Maude* is the title of an individual work, even though it is plural in form.)

1. Jack Kerouac, along with Allen Ginsberg and William S. Burroughs, was a major figure in the "beat" movement.
2. Every American boy and girl needs to learn basic computational skills.

3. Aesthetics is not an exact science.
4. The audience was restless.
5. The Beatles' *Sergeant Pepper* album is one of those albums that remain popular long after the time they are issued.
6. All is quiet.
7. The subject was roses.
8. When he was young, Benjamin Franklin's primary concern was books.
9. Fifty dollars is too much to spend on one concert ticket.
10. "There are more things in heaven and earth, Horatio, than are dreamt of in your philosophy."

EXERCISE 2

Some of the following sentences are correct, but others contain common errors in subject-verb agreement. If a sentence is correct, mark it with a *C*; if it has an error, correct it.

1. *I Love Lucy* is one of those television shows that almost all Americans have seen at least once.
2. The committee presented its findings to the president.
3. Neither Western novels nor science fiction appeal to me.
4. Stage presence and musical ability makes a rock performer successful today.
5. *It's a Wonderful Life,* like many old Christmas movies, seems to be shown on television every year.
6. Hearts are my grandmother's favorite card game.
7. The best part of B. B. King's songs are the guitar solos.
8. Time and tide waits for no man.
9. Sports are my main pastime.
10. *Vincent and Theo* is Robert Altman's movie about the French Impressionist painter van Gogh and his brother.

35b Pronoun-Antecedent Agreement

See 32b

A **pronoun** must agree with its **antecedent**—the word or word group to which the pronoun refers. Singular pronouns—such as *he, him, she, her, it, me, myself,* and *oneself*—should refer to singular antecedents. Plural pronouns—such as *we, us, they, them,* and *their*—should refer to plural antecedents.

(1) Compound Antecedents

In most cases, use a plural pronoun to refer to a **compound antecedent** (two or more antecedents connected by *and*) even if one or more of the antecedents are singular.

Mormonism and Christian Science were influenced in their beginnings by Shaker doctrines.

However, if a compound antecedent denotes a single unit—one person or thing or idea—use a singular pronoun to refer to the compound antecedent.

In 1904, the husband and father brought his family from Germany to the United States.

Use a singular pronoun when a compound antecedent is preceded by *each* or *every*.

Every programming language and software package has its limitations.

Use a singular pronoun to refer to two or more singular antecedents linked by *or* or *nor*.

Neither Thoreau nor Whitman lived to see his work read widely.

When one part of a compound antecedent is singular and one part is plural, the pronoun agrees in person and number with the closer antecedent.

Neither Great Britain nor the Benelux nations have experienced changes in their borders in recent years.

(2) Collective Noun Antecedents

If the meaning of the collective noun antecedent is singular (as it will be in most cases), use a singular pronoun. If the meaning is plural, use a plural pronoun.

The teachers' union was ready to strike for the new contract its members had been promised. (All the members act as one.)

When the whistle blew, the <u>team</u> left <u>their</u> seats and moved toward the court. (Each member acts individually.)

(3) Indefinite Pronoun Antecedents

See 35a4

Most **indefinite pronouns**—*each, either, neither, one, anyone,* and the like—are singular and require singular pronouns.

<u>Neither</u> of the men had <u>his</u> proposal ready by the deadline.

<u>Each</u> of the neighborhoods is like a separate nation, with <u>its</u> own traditions and values.

CLOSE UP   **PRONOUN-ANTECEDENT AGREEMENT**

In speech and in informal writing, many people use the plural pronouns *they* or *their* with singular indefinite pronouns that refer to people, such as *someone, everyone,* and *nobody.*

> <u>Everyone</u> can present <u>their</u> own viewpoint.

In college writing, however, you should never use a plural pronoun to refer to a singular subject. Instead, you can use both the masculine and the feminine pronoun.

> <u>Everyone</u> can present <u>his or her</u> own viewpoint.

Or, you can make the sentence's subject plural.

> <u>All participants</u> can present <u>their</u> own viewpoints.

See 29f2

The use of *his* alone to refer to a singular indefinite pronoun (Everyone can present *his* own viewpoint) is considered **sexist language**.

EXERCISE 3

In the following sentences, find and correct any errors in subject-verb or pronoun-antecedent agreement.

1. The core of a computer is a collection of electronic circuits that are called the central processing unit.
2. Computers, because of advanced technology that allows the central processing unit to be placed on a chip, a thin square of semiconducting material about one-quarter of an inch on each side, has been greatly reduced in size.
3. Computers can "talk" to each other over phone lines through a modem, an acronym for *modulator-demodulator.*
4. Pressing of keys on keyboards resembling typewriter keyboards generate electronic signals that are input for the computer.
5. Computers have built-in memory storage, and equipment such as disks or tapes provide external memory.
6. RAM (random-access memory), the erasable and reusable computer memory, hold the computer program, the computations executed by the program, and the results.
7. After computer programs are "read" from a disk or tape, the computer uses the instructions as needed to execute the program.
8. ROM (read-only memory), the permanent memory that is "read" by the computer but cannot be changed, are used to store programs that are needed frequently.
9. A number of arcade-style video games with sound and color is available for home computers.
10. Although some computer users write their own programs, most buy ready-made software programs such as the ones that allows a computer to be used as a word processor.

EXERCISE 4

The following ten sentences illustrate correct subject-verb and pronoun-antecedent agreement. Following the instructions in parentheses after each sentence, revise each so its verbs and pronouns agree with the newly created subject.

> EXAMPLE: One child in ten suffers from a learning disability.
> (Change *One child in ten* to *Ten percent of all children.*)
>
> Ten percent of all children suffer from a learning disability.

1. The governess is seemingly pursued by evil as she tries to protect Miles and Flora from those she feels seek to possess the children's souls. (Change *The governess* to *The governess and the cook.*)
2. Insulin-dependent diabetics are now able to take advantage of new technology that can help alleviate their symptoms. (Change *diabetics* to *the diabetic.*)

3. All homeowners in coastal regions worry about the possible effects of a hurricane on their property. (Change *All homeowners* to *Every homeowner.*)
4. Federally funded job-training programs offer unskilled workers an opportunity to acquire skills they can use to secure employment. (Change *workers* to *the worker.*)
5. Foreign imports pose a major challenge to the American automobile market. (Change *Foreign imports* to *The foreign import.*)
6. *Brideshead Revisited* tells how one family and its devotion to its Catholic faith affect Charles Ryder. (Delete *and its devotion to its Catholic faith.*)
7. *Writer's Digest* and *The Writer* are designed to aid writers as they seek markets for their work. (Change *writers* to *the writer.*)
8. Most American families have access to television; in fact, more have televisions than have indoor plumbing. (Change *Most American families* to *Almost every American family.*)
9. In Montana, it seems as though every town's elevation is higher than its population. (Change *every town's elevation* to *all the towns' elevations.*)
10. A woman without a man is like a fish without a bicycle. (Change *A woman/a man* to *Women/men.*)

STUDENT WRITER AT WORK

Agreement

Read the following draft of an English composition essay carefully, correcting all errors in subject-verb and pronoun-antecedent agreement. After you have corrected the errors, go over the draft again and, if necessary, revise further to strengthen coherence, unity, and style.

Marriage in the Ashanti Tribe

The Ashanti tribe is the largest in the small West African country of Ghana. The language of the Ashantis, Akan, is the most widely spoken in the country. The unity in the Ashanti tribe is derived from a golden stool that the Ashantis believe descended from the skies at the command of their chief priest. This unity has encouraged the Ashantis to create a system in which the family is so strong that the tribe has little need for formal support services. For instance, the tribe need few institutions to care for their orphans or homeless people. Among the

Ashanti people, home and family means plenty of relatives living and working as well-knit units who live in single or neighboring households. Marriage among members of the Ashanti tribe is therefore a union of two families as well as of two individuals.

In Ashanti, marriage is less an agreement entered into by two individuals before God or the justice of the peace than it is a social contract between two families, each of which are represented by a partner to the marriage. Because a marriage binds two families together, it is not to be entered into hurriedly. In fact, everyone in the tribe fear the social consequences of an ill-conceived union. The families of both of the young people are active counselors during the courtship, and its wholehearted approval and endorsement is essential to the success of the marriage. The family seek the answers to many questions. For instance, are the bride and bridegroom of similar age? Have either been married before? If so, why did the previous marriage fail? What is the history of the family? Is the family in debt? Most important, of what clan is the family?

When all the questions have been answered satisfactorily, the man and the woman are married. The crucial part of the wedding ceremony is the giving of a small sum of money and various gifts and drinks by the family of the groom to that of the bride. The actual value of such payments are often small, amounting to about fifty dollars. (A royal family gives more and receives more.) This money is sometimes referred to as "bridewealth." It constitutes only a token of the agreement reached between bride and groom and between their families. In the giving and receiving of the gifts, the young people and their families mutually pledge their faithfulness and support. When this transaction has been witnessed by both families, the man and woman are joined together as husband and wife. For better or for worse, they are married.

CHAPTER 36

ADJECTIVES AND ADVERBS

? FREQUENTLY ASKED QUESTIONS

What is the difference between an
adjective and an adverb?   (p. 546)
How do I know when to use *more*
and when to use an *-er* ending?
(p. 550)
How do I know when to use *most* and
when to use an *-est* ending?   (p. 550)
What is wrong with *most unique*?
(p. 551)
What is a double negative?   (p. 552)

36a   Understanding Adjectives and Adverbs

Adjectives modify nouns and pronouns. **Adverbs** modify verbs; adjectives; other adverbs; or entire phrases, clauses, or sentences. Both adjectives and adverbs describe, limit, or qualify other words, phrases, or clauses.

The *function* of a word, not its *form*, determines whether it is as an adjective or an adverb. Although many adverbs (like *immediately* and *hopelessly*) end in *-ly*, others (such as *almost* and *very*) do not. Moreover, some adjectives (such as *lively*) end in *-ly*. Only by locating the modified word and determining what part of speech it is can you identify a modifier as an adjective or an adverb.

> Adjectives
>   http://webster.commnet.edu/grammar/adjectives.htm
> Adjectives (Bowling Green)
>   http://www.bgsu.edu/departments/writing-lab/uses_of_adjectives.html

36b   Using Adjectives

Be sure to use an **adjective**—not an adverb—as a subject complement. A **subject complement** is a word that follows a linking verb and modifies the sentence's subject, not its verb. (A **linking verb** does not show physical or emotional action. *See, appear, believe, become, grow, turn, remain, prove, look, sound, smell, taste, feel,* and the forms of the verb *be* are or can be used as linking verbs.)

Michelle seemed <u>brave</u>. (*Seemed* shows no action and is, therefore, a linking verb. Because *brave* is a subject complement that modifies the subject *Michelle,* it takes the adjective form.)

Michelle smiled <u>bravely</u>. (*Smiled* shows action, so it is not a linking verb. *Bravely* modifies *smiled,* so it takes the adverb form.)

NOTE: Sometimes the same verb can function as either a linking verb or an action verb.

He remained <u>stubborn</u>. (He was still stubborn.) He remained <u>stubbornly</u>. (He remained, in a stubborn manner.)

Also, be sure to use an adjective as an **object complement,** a word that follows a sentence's direct object and modifies that object and not the verb. Objects are nouns or pronouns, so their modifiers must be adjectives.

Most people called him <u>timid</u>. (People consider him to be timid; here *timid* is an object complement that modifies *him,* the sentence's direct object, so the adjective form is correct.)

Most people called him <u>timidly</u>. (People were timid when they called him; here *timidly* modifies the verb *called*—not the object—so the adverb form is correct.)

(For information on placement of adjectives in a sentence, see **56i1**.)

36c   Using Adverbs

Be sure to use an **adverb**—not an adjective—to modify verbs; adjectives; other adverbs; or entire phrases, clauses, or sentences.

FAULTY: Most students did <u>great</u> on the midterm. (adjective form incorrectly used to modify verb *did*)

REVISED: Most students did <u>well</u> (or <u>very well</u>) on the midterm.

FAULTY: My parents dress a lot more <u>conservative</u> than my friends do. (adjective form incorrectly used to modify verb *dressed*)

REVISED: My parents dress a lot more <u>conservatively</u> than my friends do.

(For information on placement of adverbs in a sentence, see **56i1.**)

 USING ADJECTIVES AND ADVERBS

In informal speech, adjective forms, such as *good, bad, sure, real, slow, quick,* and *loud,* are often used to modify verbs, adjectives, and adverbs. Avoid these informal modifiers in college writing.

INFORMAL: The program ran <u>good</u> the first time we tried it, but the new system performed <u>bad</u>.

REVISED: The program ran <u>well</u> the first time we tried it, but the new system performed <u>badly</u>.

EXERCISE 1

Revise each of the incorrect sentences in the following paragraph so that only adjectives modify nouns and pronouns and only adverbs modify verbs, adjectives, or other adverbs.

A popular self-help trend in the United States today is subliminal tapes. These tapes, with titles like "How to Attract Love," "Freedom from Acne," and "I Am a Genius," are intended to solve every

Adverbs
    http://webster.commnet.edu/grammar/adverbs.htm
Adverbs (Bowling Green)
    http://www.bgsu.edu/departments/writing-lab/uses_of_adverbs.html

problem known to modern society—quick and easy. The tapes are said to work because their "hidden messages" bypass conscious defense mechanisms. The listener hears only music or relaxing sounds, like waves rolling slow and steady. At decibel levels perceived only subconsciously, positive words and phrases are embedded, usually by someone who speaks deep and rhythmic. The top-selling cassettes are those that help listeners lose weight or quit smoking. The popularity of such tapes is not hard to understand. They promise easy solutions to complex problems. But the main benefit of these tapes appears to be for the sellers, who are accumulating profits real fast.

EXERCISE 2

Being careful to use adjectives—not adverbs—as subject complements and object complements, write five sentences in imitation of each of the following sentences. Consult the list of linking verbs in **32c1,** and use a different linking verb in each of your sentences.

1. Julie looked worried.
2. Dan considers his collection valuable.

36d Using Comparatives and Superlatives

COMPARATIVE AND SUPERLATIVE FORMS

Form	Function	Example
Positive	Describes a quality; indicates no comparison	big
Comparative	Indicates comparison between *two* qualities (greater or lesser)	bigger
Superlative	Indicates comparison among *more than two* qualities (greatest or least)	biggest

NOTE: Some adverbs, particularly those indicating time, place, and degree (*almost, very, here, yesterday,* and *immediately*), do not have comparative or superlative forms.

---

(1) Comparative Forms

To form the comparative, all one-syllable adjectives and many two-syllable adjectives (particularly those that end in *-y, -ly, -le, -er,* and *-ow*) add *-er*: slow<u>er</u>, funni<u>er</u>. (Note that a final *y* becomes *i* before *-er* is added.)

Other two-syllable adjectives and all long adjectives form the comparative with *more*: <u>more</u> famous, <u>more</u> incredible.

Adverbs ending in *-ly* also form the comparative with *more*: <u>more</u> slowly. Other adverbs use the *-er* ending to form the comparative: soon<u>er</u>.

All adjectives and adverbs indicate a lesser degree with *less*: <u>less</u> lovely, <u>less</u> slowly.

(2) Superlative Forms

Adjectives that form the comparative with *-er* add *-est* to form the superlative: nic<u>est</u>, funni<u>est</u>. Adjectives that indicate the comparative with *more* use *most* to indicate the superlative: <u>most</u> famous, <u>most</u> challenging.

The majority of adverbs use *most* to indicate the superlative: <u>most</u> quickly. Others use the *-est* ending: soon<u>est</u>.

All adjectives and adverbs use *least* to indicate the least degree: <u>least</u> interesting, <u>least</u> willingly.

 CLOSE UP **USING COMPARATIVES AND SUPERLATIVES**

- Never use both *more* and *-er* to form the comparative or both *most* and *-est* to form the superlative.

  FAULTY: Nothing could have been <u>more easier</u>.
  REVISED: Nothing could have been <u>easier</u>.

  FAULTY: Jack is the <u>most meanest</u> person in town.
  REVISED: Jack is the <u>meanest</u> person in town.

- Never use the superlative when comparing only two things.

  FAULTY: Stacy is the <u>tallest</u> of the two sisters.
  REVISED: Stacy is the <u>taller</u> of the two sisters.

> • Never use the comparative when comparing more than two things.
>
> FAULTY: We chose the <u>earlier</u> of the four appointments.
>
> REVISED: We chose the <u>earliest</u> of the four appointments.

(3) Irregular Comparatives and Superlatives

Some adjectives and adverbs have irregular comparative and superlative forms. Instead of adding a word or an ending to the positive form, they use different words to indicate the comparative and the superlative.

IRREGULAR COMPARATIVES AND SUPERLATIVES			
	Positive	*Comparative*	*Superlative*
Adjectives:	good	better	best
	bad	worse	worst
	a little	less	least
	many, some, much	more	most
Adverbs:	well	better	best
	badly	worse	worst

(4) Illogical Comparisons

Many adjectives and adverbs can logically exist only in the positive degree. For example, words like *perfect, unique, excellent, impossible,* and *dead* can never be used in the comparative or superlative degree.

FAULTY: The vase is the <u>most unique</u> piece in her collection.

REVISED: The vase in her collection is <u>unique</u>. (It is one of a kind.)

These words can, however, be modified by words that suggest approaching the absolute state—*nearly* or *almost,* for example.

He revised until his draft was <u>almost perfect</u>.

EXERCISE 3

Supply the correct comparative and superlative forms for each of the following adjectives or adverbs. Then, use each form in a sentence.

>   EXAMPLE: strange   stranger   strangest
>
>   The story had a *strange* ending.
>   The explanation sounded *stranger* each time I heard it.
>   This is the *strangest* gadget I have ever seen.

1. many
2. eccentric
3. confusing
4. bad
5. mysterious
6. softly
7. embarrassing
8. well
9. often
10. tiny

36e Avoiding Double Negatives

Be careful not to create a **double negative** by using a negative modifier (such as *never, no,* or *not*) with another negative word, such as *nearly, hardly, none,* or *nothing*.

DOUBLE NEGATIVE: Old dogs can<u>not</u> learn <u>no</u> new tricks.

REVISED: Old dogs cannot learn new tricks.

NOTE: Remember that many **contractions** include the negative word *not*.

DOUBLE NEGATIVE: The instructor <u>doesn't</u> give <u>no</u> partial credit.

REVISED: The instructor doesn't give partial credit.

STUDENT WRITER AT WORK

Adjectives and Adverbs

Read this draft of an essay, and correct errors in the use of adjectives and adverbs. Check to be sure adjectives modify nouns or pronouns and adverbs modify verbs, adjectives, or other adverbs; also make sure the correct comparative and superlative forms are used, and eliminate any double negatives. After you have corrected the errors, go over the draft again and, if necessary, revise further to strengthen coherence, unity, and style.

Working

My attitude toward work was shaped by my grandfather when I was real young, around the age of four. He did everything he could to encourage me to choose a job where I would use my brain, not my hands or my back. He tried hard to make his feelings real clearly to me. Still, it took a long time before I realized what he was telling me. Eventually, I learned that I had two choices: I could take it easy and drift into a job, or I could work hard and train for a career. I chose the most difficult of the two alternatives.

Every morning, my mother would drop me off at my grandparents' house real early, on her way to work. I would eat breakfast, and my grandfather would tell me stories about his life in the mines. He would tell me about his three friends who were crushed by a cave-in and about a terrifying gas explosion incident that nearly took his life. His most commonest stories were about the long, hard hours he had spent in the mines working for minimum wage, which was just a couple of cents an hour at that time. He didn't tell me none of these stories to scare me, but to make me think hard about the kind of job I might get when I grew up.

Years later, around the time of my sixteenth birthday, I needed money quick. I needed spending money when I went out with my friends, and I had to start saving regular for college. I decided to get a job, and I soon found one at Insalaco's supermarket. There I hauled heavy boxes of canned goods and unpacked them, stocked shelves, and labeled cans and boxes. This work was monotonous, and as time went on it grew more and more tediously. At the end of each day, I really felt very badly. In fact, every bone in my body ached. This was without a doubt the worse job I could imagine.

Everyone in my family had always considered me intelligently, and they thought I should go to college. To me, the thought of studying and doing homework for four more years after high school hadn't never been very appealing. After working at Insalaco's, however, I knew my family was right, and I understood what my grandfather had been trying to tell me.

PART 7

UNDERSTANDING PUNCTUATION AND MECHANICS

OVERVIEW OF SENTENCE PUNCTUATION: COMMAS, SEMICOLONS, COLONS, DASHES, PARENTHESES

(Further explanations and examples are located in the sections listed in parentheses after each example.)

SEPARATING INDEPENDENT CLAUSES

With a Comma and a Coordinating Conjunction
The House approved the bill, but the Senate rejected it. **(38a)**

With a Semicolon
Paul Revere's *The Boston Massacre* is traditional American protest art; Edward Hicks's paintings are socially conscious art with a religious strain. **(39a)**

With a Semicolon and a Transitional Word or Phrase
Thomas Jefferson brought two hundred vanilla beans and a recipe for vanilla ice cream back from France; thus, he gave America its all-time favorite ice-cream flavor. **(39b)**

With a Colon
A *U.S. News & Word Report* survey revealed a surprising fact: Americans spend more time at malls than anywhere else except at home and at work. **(42a2)**

SEPARATING ITEMS IN A SERIES

With Commas
Chipmunk, raccoon, and *Mugwump* are Native American words. **(38b)**

With Semicolons
As ballooning became established, a series of firsts ensued: The first balloonist in the United States was 13-year-old Edward Warren, 1784; the first woman aeronaut was a Madame Thible who, depending on your source, either recited poetry or sang as she lifted off; the first airmail letter, written by Ben Franklin's grandson, was carried by balloon; and the first bird's-eye photograph of Paris was taken from a balloon. (Elaine B. Steiner, *Games*) **(39c)**

SETTING OFF EXAMPLES, EXPLANATIONS, OR SUMMARIES

With a Colon
She had a dream: to play professional basketball. **(42a2)**

With a Dash
Walking to school by myself, spending the night at a friend's house, getting my ears pierced, and starting to wear makeup—these were some of the milestones of my childhood and adolescence. **(42b2)**

SETTING OFF NONESSENTIAL MATERIAL

With a Single Comma
His fear increasing, he waited to enter the haunted house. **(38d4)**

With a Pair of Commas
Mark McGwire, not Sammy Sosa, was the first to break Roger Maris's record. **(38d3)**

With Dashes
Neither of the boys—both nine-year-olds—had any history of violence **(42b1)**

With Parentheses
In some European countries (notably Sweden and France), high-quality day care is offered at little or no cost to parents. **(42c1)**

CHAPTER 37

USING END PUNCTUATION

? FREQUENTLY ASKED QUESTIONS

Do abbreviations always include periods?
(p. 560)
How are periods used in electronic
addresses?   (p. 561)
Can I use exclamation points for emphasis?
(p. 563)

37a   Using Periods

(1) Ending a Sentence

Periods signal the end of a statement, a mild command or polite request, or an indirect question.

Something is rotten in Denmark. (statement)

Be sure to have the oil checked before you start out. (mild command)

When the bell rings, please exit in an orderly fashion. (polite request)

They wondered whether the water was safe to drink. (indirect question)

(2) Marking an Abbreviation

Periods are used in most abbreviations.

Mr. Spock	221B Baker St.	9 p.m.
Dr. Who	Aug.	etc.

If the abbreviation falls at the end of a sentence, do not add another period.

FAULTY: He promised to be there at 6 a.m..

REVISED: He promised to be there at 6 a.m.

NASA's Guide to Punctuation
  http://stipo.larc.nasa.gov/sp7084/sp7084ch3.html
Punctuation Guide (Purdue)
  http://owl.english.purdue.edu/handouts/grammar/

However, do add a question mark if the sentence is a question.

Did he arrive at 6 p.m.?

If the abbreviation falls *within* a sentence, use normal punctuation after the abbreviation's final period.

FAULTY: He promised to be there at 6 p.m. but he forgot.

REVISED: He promised to be there at 6 p.m., but he forgot.

ABBREVIATIONS WITHOUT PERIODS

Abbreviations composed of all capital letters do not usually require periods unless they stand for initials of people's names (E. B. White).

MD   RN   BC

Familiar abbreviations of the names of corporations or government agencies and abbreviations of scientific and technical terms do not require periods.

IBM   EPA   DNA   CD-ROM

Acronyms—new words formed from the initial letters or first few letters of a series of words—do not include periods.

modem   op-ed   scuba   radar
OSHA   AIDS   NAFTA   CAT scan

Clipped forms (commonly accepted shortened forms of words, such as *flu, dorm, math,* and *fax*) do not use periods.

Postal abbreviations do not include periods.

NY   CA   MS   FL   TX

(3) Marking Divisions in Dramatic, Poetic, and Biblical References

Periods separate act, scene, and line numbers in plays; book and line numbers in long poems; and chapter and verse numbers in biblical references. (Do not space between the periods and the elements they separate.)

Dramatic Reference: *Hamlet* 2.2.1–5

Poetic Reference: *Paradise Lost* 7.163–67

Biblical Reference: Judges 4.14

(4) Marking Divisions in Electronic Addresses

Periods, along with other punctuation marks (such as slashes and colons), are frequently used in electronic addresses (URLs).

g.mckay@smu.edu

http://www.nwu.org/nwu

NOTE: When you type an electronic address, do not end it with a period or add spaces after periods within the address.

EXERCISE 1

Correct these sentences by adding missing periods and deleting unnecessary ones. If a sentence is correct, mark it with a *C.*

Example: Their mission changed the war

Their mission changed the war.

1. Julius Caesar was killed in 44 B.C.
2. Dr. McLaughlin worked hard to earn his Ph.D..
3. Carmen was supposed to be at A.F.L.-C.I.O. headquarters by 2 p.m.; however, she didn't get there until 10 p.m.
4. After she studied the fall lineup proposed by N.B.C., she decided to work for C.B.S.
5. Representatives from the U.M.W. began collective bargaining after an unsuccessful meeting with Mr. L Pritchard, the coal company's representative.

37b Using Question Marks

(1) Marking the End of a Direct Question

Use a question mark to signal the end of a direct question.

Who was that masked man? (direct question)

"Is this a silver bullet?" they asked. (declarative sentence opening with a direct question)

(2) Marking Questionable Dates or Numbers

Use a question mark in parentheses to indicate that a date or number is uncertain.

Aristophanes, the Greek playwright, was born in 448 (?) BC and died in 380 (?) BC.

(3) Editing Misused Question Marks

Do not use question marks in the following situations.

After an Indirect Question Use a period, not a question mark, with an **indirect question** (a question that is not quoted directly).

FAULTY: The personnel officer asked whether he knew how to type?

REVISED: The personnel officer asked whether he knew how to type.

With Other Punctuation Do not use other punctuation marks along with question marks.

FAULTY: "Can it be true?," he asked.

REVISED: "Can it be true?" he asked.

With Another Question Mark Do not end a sentence with more than one question mark.

FAULTY: You did what?? Are you crazy??

REVISED: You did what? Are you crazy?

To Convey Sarcasm Do not use question marks to convey sarcasm. Instead, suggest your attitude through word choice.

FAULTY: I refused his generous (?) offer.

REVISED: I refused his not-very-generous offer.

In an Exclamation Do not use a question mark after an exclamation phrased as a question.

FAULTY: Will you please stop that at once?

REVISED: Will you please stop that at once!

EXERCISE 2

Correct the use of question marks and other punctuation in the following sentences.

EXAMPLE: She asked whether Freud's theories were accepted during his lifetime?

She asked whether Freud's theories were accepted during his lifetime.

1. He wondered whether he should take a nine o'clock class?
2. The instructor asked, "Was the Spanish-American War a victory for America?"?
3. Are they really going to China??!!
4. He took a modest (?) portion of dessert—half a pie.
5. "Is *data* the plural of *datum*?," he inquired.

37c Using Exclamation Points

Use an exclamation point to signal the end of an emotional or emphatic statement, an emphatic interjection, or a forceful command.

Remember the *Maine*!

No! Don't leave!

Finish this job at once!

NOTE: Except for recording dialogue, exclamation points are almost never appropriate in college writing. Even in informal writing, use exclamation points sparingly.

EXERCISE 3

Add appropriate punctuation to this passage.

Dr Craig and his group of divers paused at the shore, staring respectfully at the enormous lake Who could imagine what terrors lay beneath its surface Which of them might not emerge alive from this adventure Would it be Col Cathcart Capt Wilks, the MD from the naval base Her husband, P L Fox Or would they all survive the task ahead Dr Craig decided some encouraging remarks were in order

"Attention divers," he said in a loud, forceful voice "May I please have your attention The project which we are about to undertake—"

"Oh, no" screamed Mr Fox suddenly "Look out It's the Loch Ness Monster"

"Quick" shouted Dr Craig "Move away from the shore" But his warning came too late

CHAPTER 38

USING COMMAS

? FREQUENTLY ASKED QUESTIONS

Should I use a comma before *and* when it comes between the last two items in a series?   (p. 566)

How do I know whether to put a comma after a word or group of words that opens a sentence?   (p. 568)

How do I use commas with *that* and *which?* (p. 571)

How do I use commas with words and phrases like *however* and *in fact?* (p. 572)

How do I use commas with quotations? (p. 574)

Should I always use a comma before *and* and *but?*   (p. 580)

38a Setting Off Independent Clauses

Use a comma when you form a compound sentence by linking two independent clauses with a **coordinating conjunction** (*and, but, or, nor, for, yet, so*) or a pair of **correlative conjunctions**.

The House approved the bill, but the Senate rejected it.

Either the hard drive is full, or the modem is too slow.

NOTE: You may omit the comma if two clauses connected by a coordinating conjunction are very short.

Seek and ye shall find.

Love it or leave it.

SEPARATING INDEPENDENT CLAUSES

*See
39b*

Use a **semicolon**—not a comma—to separate two independent clauses linked by a coordinating conjunction when at least one of the clauses already contains a comma or when the clauses are especially complex.

The tourists visited Melbourne, the capital of Australia, for three days; and they toured Wellington, New Zealand, for two.

EXERCISE 1

Combine each of the following sentence pairs into one compound sentence, adding commas where necessary.

EXAMPLE: Emergency medicine became an approved medical specialty in 1979. Now, pediatric emergency medicine is becoming increasingly important. (and)

Emergency medicine became an approved medical specialty in 1979, and now, pediatric emergency medicine is becoming increasingly important.

1. The Pope did not hesitate to visit his native Poland. He did not hesitate to meet with Solidarity leader Lech Walesa. (nor)
2. Agents place brand-name products in prominent positions in films. The products will be seen and recognized by large audiences. (so)
3. Unisex insurance rates may have some drawbacks for women. These rates may be very beneficial. (or)
4. Cigarette advertising no longer appears on television. It does appear in print media. (but)
5. Dorothy Day founded the Catholic Worker movement more than fifty years ago. Her followers still dispense free food, medical care, and legal advice to the needy. (and)

Commas, Commas, and More Commas
   http://www.unc.edu/depts/wcweb/handouts/commas.html

38b Setting Off Items in a Series

(1) Coordinate Elements

Use commas between items in a series of three or more **coordinate elements** (words, phrases, or clauses joined by a coordinating conjunction).

> *Chipmunk*, *raccoon*, and *Mugwump* are Native American words.
>
> You may pay <u>by check</u>, <u>with a credit card</u>, or <u>in cash</u>.
>
> <u>Brazilians speak Portuguese</u>, <u>Colombians speak Spanish</u>, and <u>Haitians speak French and Creole</u>.

Do not use a comma to introduce or to close a series.

> FAULTY: Three important criteria are, fat content, salt content, and taste.
>
> REVISED: Three important criteria are fat content, salt content, and taste.
>
> FAULTY: Quebec, Ontario, and Alberta, are Canadian provinces.
>
> REVISED: Quebec, Ontario, and Alberta are Canadian provinces.

See 39c

If phrases or clauses in a **series** already contain commas, use semicolons to separate the items.

?

NOTE: To avoid ambiguity, always use a comma before the *and* (or other coordinating conjunction) that separates the last two items in a series.

> AMBIGUOUS: The party was made special by the company, the subdued light from the hundreds of twinkling candles and the excellent hors d'oeuvres. (Did the hors d'oeuvres give off light?)
>
> REVISED: The party was made special by the company, the subdued light from the hundreds of twinkling candles, and the excellent hors d'oeuvres.

(2) Coordinate Adjectives

Use a comma between items in a series of two or more **coordinate adjectives**—adjectives that modify the same word or word group—unless they are joined by a conjunction.

She brushed her <u>long</u>, <u>shining</u> hair.

The baby was <u>tired</u> and <u>cranky</u> and <u>wet</u>. (adjectives joined by conjunctions; no commas required)

✔ CHECKLIST: PUNCTUATING ADJECTIVES IN A SERIES

✔ If you can reverse the order of the adjectives or insert *and* between the adjectives without changing the meaning, the adjectives are coordinate, and you should use a comma.

She brushed her long, shining hair.

She brushed her shining, long hair.

She brushed her long [and] shining hair.

✔ If you cannot reverse the order of the adjectives or insert *and,* the adjectives are not coordinate, and you should not use a comma.

Ten red balloons fell from the ceiling.

Red ten balloons fell from the ceiling.

Ten [and] red balloons fell from the ceiling.

NOTE: Numbers—such as *ten*—are not coordinate with other adjectives.

EXERCISE 2

Correct the use of commas in the following sentences, adding or deleting commas where necessary. If a sentence is punctuated correctly, mark it with a *C*.

EXAMPLE: Neither dogs snakes bees nor dragons frighten her.

Neither dogs, snakes, bees, nor dragons frighten her.

1. Seals, whales, dogs, lions, and horses, all are mammals.
2. Mammals are warm-blooded vertebrates that bear live young, nurse them, and usually have fur.
3. Seals are mammals but lizards, and snakes, and iguanas are reptiles, and salamanders are amphibians.
4. Amphibians also include frogs, and toads and newts.
5. Eagles geese ostriches turkeys chickens and ducks are classified as birds.

■ **EXERCISE 3**

Add two coordinate adjectives to modify each of the following combinations, inserting commas where required.

EXAMPLE: classical music

strong, beautiful classical music

1. distant thunder
2. silver spoon
3. New York Yankees
4. miniature golf
5. Rolling Stones
6. loving couple
7. computer science
8. wheat bread
9. art museum
10. new math

❓ 38c   Setting Off Introductory Elements

(1) Dependent Clauses

An introductory dependent clause is generally set off from the rest of the sentence by a comma.

Although the CIA used to call undercover agents *penetration agents*, they now routinely refer to them as *moles*.

When war came to Beirut and Londonderry and Saigon, the victims were the children.

If the dependent clause is short, you may omit the comma—*provided the sentence will be clear without it.*

When I exercise I drink plenty of water.

NOTE: Do not use a comma to set off a dependent clause at the *end* of a sentence.

(2) Verbal and Prepositional Phrases

Introductory verbal and prepositional phrases are usually set off by commas.

Thinking that this might be his last chance, Scott struggled toward the Pole. (participial phrase)

<u>To write well</u>, one must read a lot. (infinitive phrase)
<u>During the Depression</u>, movie attendance rose. (prepositional phrase)

If the introductory phrase is short and no ambiguity is possible, you may omit the comma.

<u>After the exam</u> I took a four-hour nap.

 USING COMMAS

> <u>**Gerund phrases**</u> and <u>**infinitive phrases**</u> that serve as subjects are not set off by commas.
>
> **FAULTY (GERUND PHRASE):** Laughing out loud, can release tension.
>
> **REVISED:** Laughing out loud can release tension.
>
> **FAULTY (INFINITIVE PHRASE):** To know him, is to love him.
>
> **REVISED:** To know him is to love him.

See
19b1

(3) Transitional Words and Phrases

When a <u>**transitional word or phrase**</u> begins a sentence, it is usually set off from the rest of the sentence with a comma.

<u>However</u>, any plan that is enacted must be fair.

See
6c2

EXERCISE 4

Add commas in the following paragraph where needed to set off introductory elements from the rest of the sentence.

    While childhood is shrinking adolescence is expanding. Whatever the reason girls are maturing earlier. The average onset of puberty is now two years earlier than it was only forty years ago. What's more both boys and girls are staying in the nest longer. At present, it isn't unusual for children to stay in their parents' home until they're twenty or twenty-one, delaying adulthood and extending adolescence. To some who study the culture this increase in adolescence portends dire consequences. With teenage hormones running amuck for longer the problems of teenage pregnancy and sexually transmitted diseases loom large. Young boys' spending long periods of their lives without responsibilities is also a recipe for disaster. Others see this "youthing" of American culture in a more positive light. Without a doubt adolescents are creative, lively, more willing to take risks. If we channel their energies carefully they could contribute, even in their extended adolescence, to American culture and technology.

38d Setting Off Nonessential Material

Sometimes words, phrases, or clauses *contribute* to the meaning of the sentence but are not *essential* to the meaning. That is, deleting the material would not substantially change the sentence's main point or emphasis. Commas should set off such nonessential material whether it appears at the beginning, in the middle, or at the end of a sentence.

(1) Nonrestrictive Modifiers

Restrictive modifiers, which supply information essential to the meaning of the word or word group they modify, are *not* set off from it by commas. However, **nonrestrictive modifiers,** which supply information not essential to the meaning of the word or word group they modify, *are* set off by commas.

Compare these two sentences.

Actors who have inflated egos are often insecure.

Actors, who have inflated egos, are often insecure.

In the first sentence, *who have inflated egos* is **restrictive.** The sentence indicates that only those actors with inflated egos—not all actors—are insecure. In the second sentence, the modifying phrase *who have inflated egos* is **nonrestrictive.** The sentence indicates that *all* actors—not just those with inflated egos—are insecure.

As the following examples illustrate, commas set off only nonrestrictive modifiers—those that supply nonessential information—never restrictive modifiers, which supply essential information.

Adjective Clauses

> **RESTRICTIVE:** Speaking in public is something <u>that most people fear</u>.
> **NONRESTRICTIVE:** He ran for the bus, <u>which was late as usual</u>.

Prepositional Phrases

> **RESTRICTIVE:** The man <u>with the gun</u> demanded their money.
> **NONRESTRICTIVE:** The clerk, with a nod, dismissed me.

Verbal Phrases

> **RESTRICTIVE:** The candidates <u>running for mayor</u> have agreed to a debate.
> **NONRESTRICTIVE:** The marathoner, <u>running her fastest</u>, beat her previous record.

Appositives

> **RESTRICTIVE:** The film <u>*Citizen Kane*</u> made Orson Welles famous.
> **NONRESTRICTIVE:** *Citizen Kane*, <u>Orson Welles's first film</u>, made him famous.

 USING COMMAS WITH *THAT* AND *WHICH* ❓

That introduces only restrictive clauses.

I bought a used car <u>that</u> cost $2,000.

Which introduces both restrictive and nonrestrictive clauses.

RESTRICTIVE: I bought a used car <u>which</u> cost $2,000.
NONRESTRICTIVE: The used car I bought, <u>which</u> cost $2,000, broke down after a week.

Many writers, however, prefer to use *which* only to introduce non-restrictive clauses.

> ✔ **CHECKLIST: RESTRICTIVE AND NONRESTRICTIVE MODIFIERS**
>
> To determine whether a modifier is restrictive or nonrestrictive, ask these questions:
>
> ✔ Is the modifier essential to the meaning of the noun it modifies (*The man with the gun,* not just any man)? If so, it is restrictive and does not take commas.
> ✔ Is the modifier introduced by *that* (*something that most people fear*)? If so, it is restrictive. *That* cannot introduce a nonrestrictive clause.
> ✔ Can you delete the relative pronoun without causing ambiguity or confusion (*something [that] most people fear*)? If so, the clause is restrictive.
> ✔ Is the appositive more specific than the noun that precedes it (*the film* Citizen Kane)? If so, it is restrictive.

EXERCISE 5

Insert commas where necessary to set off nonrestrictive modifiers.

The Statue of Liberty which was dedicated in 1886 has undergone extensive renovation. Its supporting structure whose designer was the French engineer Alexandre Gustave Eiffel is made of iron. The Statue of Liberty created over a period of nine years by sculptor Frédéric-Auguste Bartholdi stands 151 feet tall. The people of France who were grateful for American help in the French Revolution raised the money to pay the sculptor who created the statue. The people of the United States contributing over $100,000 raised the money for the pedestal on which the statue stands.

(2) Transitional Words and Phrases

See
6c2

Transitional words and phrases—which include conjunctive adverbs like *however, therefore, thus,* and *nevertheless* as well as expressions like *for example* and *on the other hand*—qualify, clarify, and make connections. However, they are not essential to meaning. For this reason, they are always set off from the rest of the clause by commas.

The Outward Bound program⹁ for example⹁ is extremely safe.

Other programs are not so safe⹁ however.

NOTE: A transitional word or phrase is also usually set off by commas when it occurs at the *beginning* of a clause.

Still, Outward Bound has a good reputation.

 TRANSITIONAL WORDS AND PHRASES

When a transitional word or phrase joins two independent clauses, it must be preceded by a semicolon and followed by a comma.

Laughter is the best medicine; of course, penicillin also comes in handy sometimes.

(3) Contradictory Phrases

A phrase that expresses contrast is usually set off by commas.

This medicine is taken after meals, never on an empty stomach.

Mark McGwire, not Sammy Sosa, was the first to break Roger Maris's record.

(4) Absolute Phrases

An **absolute phrase,** which usually consists of a noun and a participle, is always set off by commas from the sentence it modifies.

His fear increasing, he waited to enter the haunted house.

Many soldiers were lost in Southeast Asia, their bodies never recovered.

(5) Miscellaneous Nonessential Material

Other nonessential material usually set off by commas includes tag questions, names in direct address, mild interjections, and *yes* and *no.*

This is your first day on the job, isn't it?

I wonder, Mr. Honeywell, whether Mr. Albright deserves a raise.

Well, it's about time.

Yes, we have no bananas.

EXERCISE 6

Set off the nonessential elements in these sentences with commas. If a sentence is correct, mark it with a *C*.

EXAMPLE: Piranhas like sharks will attack and eat almost anything if the opportunity arises.

Piranhas, like sharks, will attack and eat almost anything if the opportunity arises.

1. Kermit the Frog is a Muppet a cross between a marionette and a puppet.
2. The common cold a virus is frequently spread by hand contact not by mouth.
3. The account in the Bible of Noah's Ark and the forty-day flood may be based on an actual deluge.
4. Many US welfare recipients, such as children, the aged, and the severely disabled, are unable to work.
5. The submarine *Nautilus* was the first to cross under the North Pole wasn't it?
6. The 1958 Ford Edsel was advertised with the slogan "Once you've seen it, you'll never forget it."
7. Superman was called Kal-El on the planet Krypton; on earth however he was known as Clark Kent not Kal-El.
8. Its sales topping any of his previous singles "Heartbreak Hotel" was Elvis Presley's first million-seller.
9. Two companies Nash and Hudson joined in 1954 to form American Motors.
10. A firefly is a beetle not a fly and a prairie dog is a rodent not a dog.

38e Using Commas in Other Conventional Contexts

❓ (1) With Direct Quotations

In most cases, use commas to set off a direct quotation from the **identifying tag**—the phrase that identifies the speaker (*he said, she answered*).

Emerson said to Whitman, "I greet you at the beginning of a great career."

"I greet you at the beginning of a great career," Emerson said to Whitman.

"I greet you," Emerson said to Whitman, "at the beginning of a great career."

When the identifying tag comes between two complete sentences, however, the tag is introduced by a comma but followed by a period.

"Winning isn't everything," Vince Lombardi said. "It's the only thing."

If the first sentence of an interrupted quotation ends with a question mark or exclamation point, do not use commas.

"Should we hold the front page?" she asked. "After all, it's a slow news day."

"Hold the front page!" he cried. "This is the biggest story of the decade."

(2) With Titles or Degrees Following a Name

Hamlet, prince of Denmark, is Shakespeare's most famous character.

Michael Crichton, MD, wrote *Jurassic Park.*

(3) In Addresses and Dates

Her address is 600 West End Avenue, New York, NY 10024.

On August 30, 1983, the space shuttle *Challenger* was launched.

When a date or an address falls within a sentence, a comma follows the last element. No comma separates the street number from the street or the state name from the ZIP Code.

NOTE: When only the month and year are given, no commas are used (August 1983).

(4) In Salutations and Closings

Use commas in informal correspondence following salutations and closings and following the complimentary close in personal or business correspondence.

| Dear John, | Love, |
| Dear Aunt Sophie, | Sincerely, |

In **business letters**, always use a colon, not a comma, after the salutation.

See
54a

(5) In Long Numbers

For a number of four digits or more, place a comma before every third digit, counting from the right.

1,200   120,000

12,000   1,200,000

NOTE: Commas are not required in long numbers used in page and line numbers, addresses, telephone numbers, ZIP Codes, or four-digit year numbers.

EXERCISE 7

Add commas where necessary to set off quotations, names, dates, addresses, and numbers.

1. India became independent on August 15 1947.
2. The UAW has more than 1500000 dues-paying members.
3. Nikita Khrushchev, former Soviet premier, said "We will bury you!"
4. Mount St. Helens, northeast of Portland Oregon, began erupting on March 27 1980 and eventually killed at least thirty people.
5. Located at 1600 Pennsylvania Avenue Washington DC, the White House is a popular tourist attraction.
6. In 1956, playing before a crowd of 64519 fans in Yankee Stadium in New York New York, Don Larsen pitched the first perfect game in World Series history.
7. Lewis Thomas MD was born in Flushing New York and attended Harvard Medical School in Cambridge Massachusetts.
8. In 1967 2000000 people worldwide died of smallpox, but in 1977 only about twenty died.
9. "The reports of my death" Mark Twain remarked "have been greatly exaggerated."
10. The French explorer Jean Nicolet landed at Green Bay Wisconsin in 1634, and in 1848 Wisconsin became the thirtieth state; it has 10355 lakes and a population of more than 4700000.

38f   Using Commas to Prevent Misreading

In some cases, you must use a comma to avoid ambiguity. Consider the following sentence.

Those who can, sprint the final lap.

Without the comma, *can* appears to be an auxiliary verb ("Those who can sprint . . ."), and the sentence seems incomplete. The comma tells readers to pause, preventing confusion.

Also use a comma to acknowledge the omission of a repeated word, usually a verb, and to separate words repeated consecutively.

> Pam carried the box; Tim, the suitcase.

> Everything bad that could have happened, happened.

EXERCISE 8

Add commas where necessary to prevent misreading.

> EXAMPLE: Whatever will be will be.
>
> Whatever will be, will be.

1. According to Bob Frank's computer has three disk drives.
2. Da Gama explored Florida; Pizarro Peru.
3. By Monday evening students must begin preregistration for fall classes.
4. Whatever they built they built with care.
5. When batting practice carefully.
6. Brunch includes warm muffins topped with whipped butter and freshly brewed coffee.
7. Students go to school to learn not to play sports.
8. Technology has made what once seemed impossible possible.

EXERCISE 9

Add commas to the following sentences where needed, and be prepared to explain why each is necessary. If a sentence is correct, mark it with a *C*.

> EXAMPLE: Once again Congress is looking to make changes in immigration law.
>
> REVISED: Once again, Congress is looking to make changes in immigration law.

1. According to some critics the test which new citizens must take before they are naturalized is simple and shallow.
2. Others claim that making the test more difficult would be unfair because many graduates of American high schools cannot answer the basic civics questions about the design of the American flag the structure of the US government and the events of American political history required by the test.

3. Some fear that too many new citizens from foreign countries will undermine core American values but others argue that those values came from earlier immigrants and that change is not necessarily bad.
4. Fear of immigrants while seemingly unfounded is not new.
5. In the 1940s the American government forced immigrants from Japan and their American-born children into internment camps after the Japanese bombed Pearl Harbor initiating America's involvement in World War II.

38g   Editing Misused Commas

Do not use commas in the following situations.

(1) To Join Two Independent Clauses

A comma alone cannot join two independent clauses; it must be preceded by a coordinating conjunction. Using just a comma to connect two independent clauses creates a **comma splice**.

FAULTY: The season was unusually cool, nevertheless the orange crop was not seriously harmed.

REVISED: The season was unusually cool; nevertheless, the orange crop was not seriously harmed.

REVISED: The season was unusually cool. Nevertheless, the orange crop was not seriously harmed.

REVISED: The season was unusually cool, but the orange crop was not seriously harmed.

REVISED: Although the season was unusually cool, the orange crop was not seriously harmed.

(2) To Set Off Restrictive Modifiers

Commas are not used to set off **restrictive modifiers**.

FAULTY: Women, who seek to be equal to men, lack ambition.

REVISED: Women who seek to be equal to men lack ambition.

FAULTY: The film, *Malcolm X,* was directed by Spike Lee.

REVISED: The film *Malcolm X* was directed by Spike Lee.

(3) Between Inseparable Grammatical Constructions

Do not place a comma between grammatical elements that cannot be logically separated: a subject and its predicate, a verb and its complement or direct object, a preposition and its object, or an adjective and the word or phrase it modifies.

FAULTY (COMMA BETWEEN SUBJECT AND PREDICATE): A woman with dark red hair, opened the door

REVISED: A woman with dark red hair opened the door.

FAULTY (COMMA BETWEEN VERB AND OBJECT): Louis Braille developed, an alphabet of raised dots for the blind.

REVISED: Louis Braille developed an alphabet of raised dots for the blind.

FAULTY (COMMA BETWEEN PREPOSITION AND OBJECT): They relaxed somewhat during, the last part of the obstacle course.

REVISED: They relaxed somewhat during the last part of the obstacle course.

FAULTY (COMMA BETWEEN ADJECTIVE AND WORDS IT MODIFIES): Wind-dispersed weeds include the well-known and plentiful, dandelions, milkweed, and thistle.

REVISED: Wind-dispersed weeds include the well-known and plentiful dandelions, milkweed, and thistle.

(4) Between a Verb and an Indirect Quotation or Indirect Question

Do not use commas between verbs and indirect quotations or indirect questions.

FAULTY: Humorist Art Buchwald once said, that the problem with television news is that it has no second page.

REVISED: Humorist Art Buchwald once said that the problem with television news is that it has no second page.

FAULTY: The landlord asked, if we would sign a two-year lease.

REVISED: The landlord asked if we would sign a two-year lease.

(5) Between Phrases Linked by Correlative Conjunctions

See
32g

Commas are not used to separate phrases linked by **correlative conjunctions**.

FAULTY: Forty years ago, most college students had access to neither photocopiers, nor pocket calculators.

REVISED: Forty years ago, most college students had access to neither photocopiers nor pocket calculators.

FAULTY: Both typewriters, and tape recorders were generally available, however.

REVISED: Both typewriters and tape recorders were generally available, however.

❓ (6) In Compounds That Are Not Independent Clauses

Do not use commas between two elements of a compound subject, predicate, object, complement, or auxiliary verb.

FAULTY (COMMA INTERRUPTS COMPOUND SUBJECT): Plagues, and pestilence were common during the Middle Ages.

REVISED: Plagues and pestilence were common during the Middle Ages.

FAULTY (COMMA INTERRUPTS COMPOUND PREDICATE): Many women thirty-five and older are returning to college, and tend to be good students.

REVISED: Many women thirty-five and older are returning to college and tend to be good students.

FAULTY (COMMA INTERRUPTS COMPOUND OBJECT): Mattel has marketed a doctor's lab coat, and an astronaut suit for its Barbie doll.

REVISED: Mattel has marketed a doctor's lab coat and an astronaut suit for its Barbie doll.

FAULTY (COMMA INTERRUPTS COMPOUND COMPLEMENT): People buy bottled water because it is pure, and fashionable.

REVISED: People buy bottled water because it is pure and fashionable.

FAULTY (COMMA INTERRUPTS COMPOUND AUXILIARY VERB): She can, and will be ready to run in the primary.

REVISED: She can and will be ready to run in the primary.

REVISED: She can‸ and will‸ be ready to run in the primary.

(7) Before a Dependent Clause at the End of a Sentence

Commas are generally not used before a dependent clause that falls at the end of a sentence.

FAULTY: Jane Addams founded Hull House, because she wanted to help Chicago's poor.

REVISED: Jane Addams founded Hull House because she wanted to help Chicago's poor.

EXERCISE 10

Unnecessary commas have been intentionally added to some of the sentences that follow. Delete any unnecessary commas. If a sentence is correct, mark it with a *C*.

EXAMPLE: Spring fever, is a common ailment.

Spring fever is a common ailment.

1. A book is like a garden, carried in the pocket. (Arab proverb)
2. Like the iodine content of kelp, air freight, is something most Americans have never pondered. (*Time*)
3. Charles Rolls, and Frederick Royce manufactured the first Rolls-Royce Silver Ghost, in 1907.
4. The hills ahead of him were rounded domes of grey granite, smooth as a bald man's pate, and completely free of vegetation. (Wilbur Smith, *Flight of the Falcon*)
5. Food here is scarce, and cafeteria food is vile, but the great advantage to Russian raw materials, when one can get hold of them, is that they are always fresh and untampered with. (Andrea Lee, *Russian Journal*)

CHAPTER 39

USING SEMICOLONS

? FREQUENTLY ASKED QUESTIONS

When do I use a semicolon?   (p. 582)
Do I introduce a list with a semicolon or a
   colon?   (p. 588)

? The **semicolon** is used only between items of equal grammatical rank: two independent clauses, two phrases, and so on.

39a   Separating Independent Clauses

Use a semicolon between closely related independent clauses that convey parallel or contrasting information but are not joined by a coordinating conjunction.

Paul Revere's *The Boston Massacre* is traditional American protest art; Edward Hicks's paintings are socially conscious art with a religious strain.

**See
Ch. 25**

NOTE: Using only a comma or no punctuation at all between independent clauses creates a **comma splice** or **fused sentence**.

EXERCISE 1

Add semicolons, periods, or commas plus coordinating conjunctions where necessary to separate independent clauses. Then, reread the paragraph to make certain no comma splices or fused sentences remain.

EXAMPLE: *Birth of a Nation* was one of the earliest epic movies it was based on the book *The Klansman.*

Birth of a Nation was one of the earliest epic movies; it was based on the book *The Klansman.*

Semicolons (U. of Wisc.)
   http://www.wisc.edu/writing/Handbook/Semicolons.html

During the 1950s movie attendance declined because of the increasing popularity of television. As a result, numerous gimmicks were introduced to draw audiences into theaters. One of the first of these was Cinerama, in this technique three pictures were shot side by side and projected onto a curved screen. Next came 3-D, complete with special glasses, *Bwana Devil* and *The Creature from the Black Lagoon* were two early 3-D ventures. *The Robe* was the first picture filmed in Cinemascope in this technique a shrunken image was projected on a screen twice as wide as it was tall. Smell-O-Vision (or Aroma-rama) was a short-lived gimmick that enabled audiences to smell what they were viewing problems developed when it became impossible to get one odor out of the theater in time for the next smell to be introduced. William Castle's *Thirteen Ghosts* introduced special glasses for cowardly viewers who wanted to be able to control what they saw, the red part of the glasses was the "ghost viewer" and the green part was the "ghost remover." Perhaps the ultimate in movie gimmicks accompanied the film *The Tingler* when this film was shown seats in the theater were wired to generate mild electric shocks. Unfortunately, the shocks set off a chain reaction that led to hysteria in the theater. During the 1960s such gimmicks all but disappeared, viewers were able once again to simply sit back and enjoy a movie. In 1997 *Mr. Payback*, a short interactive film that contained elements of a videogame, brought back the gimmick, it allowed viewers to vote on how they wanted the plot to unfold.

EXERCISE 2

Combine each of the following sentence groups into one sentence that contains only two independent clauses. Use a semicolon to join the two clauses. You will need to add, delete, relocate, or change some words; keep experimenting until you find the arrangement that best conveys the sentence's meaning.

> EXAMPLE: The Congo River Rapids is a ride at the Dark Continent in Tampa, Florida. Riders raft down the river. They glide alongside jungle plants and animals.
>
>   The Congo River Rapids is a ride at the Dark Continent in Tampa, Florida; riders raft down the river, gliding alongside jungle plants and animals.

1. Theme parks offer exciting rides. They are thrill packed. They flirt with danger.

2. Free Fall is located in Atlanta's Six Flags over Georgia. In this ride, riders travel up a 128-foot-tall tower. They plunge down at fifty-five miles per hour.

3. In the Sky Whirl riders go 115 feet up in the air and circle about seventy-five times. This ride is located in Great America. Great America parks are in Gurnee, Illinois, and Santa Clara, California.

4. The Kamikaze Slide can be found at the Wet 'n Wild parks in Arlington, Texas, and Orlando, Florida. This ride is a slide three hundred feet long. It extends sixty feet in the air.

5. Viper is an exciting ride. It is found at Six Flags Great Adventure in Jackson, New Jersey. Its outside loop has a 360-degree spiral.

6. Astroworld in Houston, Texas, boasts Greezed Lightnin'. This ride is an eighty-foot-high loop. The ride goes from zero to sixty miles per hour in four seconds and moves forward and backward.

7. The Beast is at Kings Island near Cincinnati, Ohio. The Beast is a wooden roller coaster. It has a 7,400-foot track and goes seventy miles per hour.

8. Busch Gardens in Williamsburg, Virginia, features Escape from Pompeii. This is a water ride. It allows riders to explore ruins and see Mount Vesuvius.

9. Wild Arctic is at Sea World in Orlando, Florida. This ride includes a simulated helicopter flight. The flight goes to Base Station Wild Arctic. The ride also goes to a wrecked ship.

10. At Busch Gardens Tampa Bay in Tampa, Florida, Egypt is a thrill-packed attraction. It features an inverted roller coaster with cars hanging from the top. A replica of King Tut's tomb is also featured.

39b Separating Independent Clauses Introduced by Transitional Words and Phrases

Use a semicolon between two independent clauses when the second clause is introduced by a **transitional word or phrase**. (The transitional element is followed by a comma.)

Thomas Jefferson brought two hundred vanilla beans and a recipe for vanilla ice cream back from France; thus, he gave America its all-time favorite ice-cream flavor.

Using Semicolons (U. Richmond)
http://www.urich.edu/~writing/wweb/semicolon.html

EXERCISE 3

Combine each of the following sentence groups into one sentence that contains only two independent clauses. Use a semicolon and the transitional word or phrase in parentheses to join the two clauses, adding commas within clauses where necessary. You will need to add, delete, relocate, or change some words. There is no one correct version; keep experimenting until you find the arrangement you feel is most effective.

EXAMPLE: The Aleutian Islands are located off the west coast of Alaska. They are an extremely remote chain of islands. They are sometimes called America's Siberia. (in fact)

The Aleutian Islands, located off the west coast of Alaska, are an extremely remote chain of islands; in fact, they are sometimes called America's Siberia.

1. The Aleutians lie between the North Pacific Ocean and the Bering Sea. The weather there is harsh. Dense fog, 100-mph winds, and even tidal waves and earthquakes are not uncommon. (for example)
2. These islands constitute North America's largest network of active volcanoes. The Aleutians boast some beautiful scenery. The islands are relatively unexplored. (still)
3. The Aleutians are home to a wide variety of birds. Numerous animals, such as fur seals and whales, are found there. These islands may house the largest concentration of marine animals in the world. (in fact)
4. During World War II, thousands of American soldiers were stationed on Attu Island. They were stationed on Adak Island. The Japanese eventually occupied both islands. (however)
5. The islands' original population of native Aleuts was drastically reduced in the eighteenth century by Russian fur traders. Today the total population is only about 8,500. US military employees comprise more than half of this. (consequently)

(Adapted from *National Geographic*)

39c   Separating Items in a Series

Use semicolons between items in a series when one or more of these items include commas.

Three papers are posted on the bulletin board outside the building: a description of the exams; a list of appeal procedures for students who fail; and an employment ad from an automobile factory, addressed specifically to candidates whose appeals are turned down. (Andrea Lee, *Russian Journal*)

Laramie, Wyoming; Wyoming, Delaware; and Delaware, Ohio, were three of the places they visited.

EXERCISE 4

Replace commas with semicolons where necessary to separate internally punctuated items in a series. (For information on use of semicolons with quotation marks, see **41d2.**)

> EXAMPLE: Luxury automobiles have some strong selling points: they are status symbols, some, such as the Corvette, appreciate in value, and they are usually comfortable and well appointed.
>
> Luxury automobiles have some strong selling points: they are status symbols; some, such as the Corvette, appreciate in value; and they are usually comfortable and well appointed.

1. The history of modern art seems at times to be a collection of "isms": Impressionism, a term that applies to a variety of painters who attempted to depict contemporary life in a new objective manner by reproducing an "impression" of what the eye sees, Abstract Expressionism, which applies to a wide-ranging group of artists who stress emotion and the unconscious in their nonrepresentational works, and, more recently, Minimalism, which applies to a group of painters and sculptors whose work reasserts the physical reality of the object.

2. Although the term *Internet* is widely used to refer only to the World Wide Web and e-mail, the Internet consists of a variety of discrete elements, including network news, which allows users to post and receive messages dealing with an unbelievably broad range of topics, Gopher, *Archie,* and WAIS, which allow users to track and retrieve information from a variety of sources in different ways, and FTP, which lets users download material from remote computers.

3. Three of rock and roll's best-known guitar heroes played with the "British Invasion" group The Yardbirds: Eric Clapton, the group's first lead guitarist, went on to play with John Mayall's Bluesbreakers, Cream, and Blind Faith, and still enjoys popularity as a solo act, Jeff Beck, the group's second guitarist, though not as visible as Clapton, made rock history with the Jeff Beck Group and inventive solo albums, and Jimmy Page, the group's third and final guitarist, transformed the remnants of the original group into the premier heavy metal band, Led Zeppelin.

4. Some of the most commonly confused words in English are *aggravate,* which means "to worsen," and *irritate,* which means "to annoy," *continual,* which means "recurring at intervals," and *continuous,* which means "an action occurring without interruption," *imply,* which means "to hint, suggest," and *infer,* which means "to conclude from," and *compliment,* which means "to praise," and *complement,* which means "to complete or add to."

5. Tennessee Williams wrote *The Glass Menagerie,* which is about Laura Wingfield, a disabled young woman, and her family, *A Streetcar Named Desire,* which starred Marlon Brando, and *Cat on a Hot Tin Roof,* which won a Pulitzer Prize.

EXERCISE 5

Combine each of the following sentence groups into one sentence that includes a series of items separated by semicolons. You will need to add, delete, relocate, or change words. Try several versions of each sentence until you find the most effective arrangement.

> EXAMPLE: Collecting baseball cards is a worthwhile hobby. It helps children learn how to bargain and trade. It also encourages them to compare data about ballplayers. Most important, it introduces them to role models.
>
> Collecting baseball cards is a worthwhile hobby because it helps children learn how to bargain and trade; encourages them to compare data about ballplayers; and, most important, introduces them to role models.

1. A good dictionary offers definitions of words, including some obsolete and nonstandard words. It provides information about synonyms, usage, and word origins. It also offers information on pronunciation and syllabication.

2. The flags of the Scandinavian countries all depict a cross on a solid background. Denmark's flag is red with a white cross. Norway's flag is also red, but its cross is blue, outlined in white. Sweden's flag is blue with a yellow cross.

3. Over one hundred international collectors' clubs are thriving today. One of these associations is the Cola Clan, whose members buy, sell, and trade Coca-Cola memorabilia. Another is the Citrus Label Society. There is also a Cookie Cutter Collectors' Club.

4. Listening to the radio special, we heard "Shuffle Off to Buffalo" and "Moon over Miami," both of which are about eastern cities. We heard "By the Time I Get to Phoenix" and "I Left My Heart in

San Francisco," which mention western cities. Finally, we heard "The Star-Spangled Banner," which seemed to be an appropriate finale.

5. There are three principal types of contact lenses. Hard contact lenses, also called "conventional lenses," are easy to clean and handle and quite sturdy. Soft lenses, which are easily contaminated and must be cleaned and disinfected daily, are less durable. Gas-permeable lenses, sometimes advertised as "semihard" or "semisoft" lenses, look and feel like hard lenses but are more easily contaminated and less durable.

39d   Editing Misused Semicolons

Do not use semicolons in the following situations.

(1) Between a Dependent and an Independent Clause

Use a comma, not a semicolon, between a dependent and an independent clause.

FAULTY: Because new drugs can now suppress the body's immune reaction; fewer organ transplants are rejected by the body.

REVISED: Because new drugs can now suppress the body's immune reaction, fewer organ transplants are rejected by the body.

(2) Between a Phrase and a Clause

Use a comma, not a semicolon, between a phrase and a clause.

FAULTY: Increasing rapidly; computer crime poses a challenge for government, financial, and military agencies.

REVISED: Increasing rapidly, computer crime poses a challenge for government, financial, and military agencies.

(3) To Introduce a List

Use a colon, not a semicolon, to introduce a **list**.

FAULTY: The evening news is a battleground for the three major television networks; CBS, NBC, and ABC.

REVISED: The evening news is a battleground for the three major television networks: CBS, NBC, and ABC.

(4) To Introduce a Quotation

Do not use a semicolon to introduce a **quoted speech or writing**.

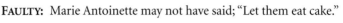

See 41a

FAULTY: Marie Antoinette may not have said; "Let them eat cake."

REVISED: Marie Antoinette may not have said, "Let them eat cake."

EXERCISE 6

Read the following paragraph carefully. Then, add semicolons where necessary and delete incorrectly used ones, substituting other punctuation where necessary.

> Barnstormers were aviators; who toured the country after World War I, giving people short airplane rides and exhibitions of stunt flying, in fact, the name *barnstormer* was derived from the use of barns as airplane hangars. Americans' interest in airplanes had all but disappeared after the war. The barnstormers helped popularize flying; especially in rural areas. Some were pilots who had flown in the war; others were just young men with a thirst for adventure. They gave people rides in airplanes; sometimes charging a dollar a minute. For most passengers, this was their first ride in an airplane, in fact, sometimes it was their first sight of one. After Lindbergh's 1927 flight across the Atlantic; Americans suddenly needed no encouragement to embrace aviation. The barnstormers had outlived their usefulness; and an era ended. (Adapted from William Goldman, *Adventures in the Screen Trade*)

CHAPTER 40

USING APOSTROPHES

? FREQUENTLY ASKED QUESTIONS

How do I form the possessive if a singular
word already ends in -s? (p. 590)
How do I form the possessive with plural
words that end in -s? (p. 591)
What's the difference between *its* and *it's*?
(p. 594)

Use an apostrophe to form the possessive case, to indicate omissions in contractions, and to form certain plurals.

40a Forming the Possessive Case

The possessive case indicates ownership. In English, the possessive case of nouns and indefinite pronouns is indicated either with a phrase that includes the word *of* (the hands *of* the clock) or with an apostrophe and, in most cases, an *s* (the clock's hands).

(1) Singular Nouns and Indefinite Pronouns

To form the possessive case of singular nouns and indefinite pronouns, add *'s*.

"The Monk's Tale" is one of Chaucer's *Canterbury Tales.*

When we would arrive was anyone's guess.

? (2) Singular Nouns Ending in -s

To form the possessive case of singular nouns that end in -s, add *'s* in most cases.

Reading Henry James's *The Ambassadors* was not Maris's idea of fun.

The class's time was changed to 8 a.m.

The Uses of the Apostrophe
http://webster.commnet.edu/grammar/marks/apostrophe.htm

NOTE: With some singular nouns that end in -*s,* pronouncing the possessive ending as a separate syllable can sound awkward; in such cases, it is acceptable to use just an apostrophe: Crispus Attucks' death, Aristophanes' *Lysistrata.*

An apostrophe is not used to form the possessive case of a title that already contains an *'s* ending; use a phrase instead.

> **FAULTY:** *A Midsummer Night's Dream*'s staging
> **REVISED:** the staging of *A Midsummer Night's Dream*

(3) Plural Nouns Ending in -*s*

To form the possessive case of regular plural nouns (those that end in -*s* or -*es*), add only an apostrophe.

> *The Readers' Guide to Periodical Literature* is available online.
> Laid-off employees received two weeks' severance pay and three months' medical benefits.
> The Lopezes' three children are triplets.

(4) Irregular Plural Nouns

To form the possessive case of nouns that have irregular plurals, add *'s.*

> Long after they were gone, the geese's honking could still be heard.
> *The Children's Hour* is a play by Lillian Hellman; *The Women's Room* is a novel by Marilyn French.
> The two oxen's yokes were securely attached to the cart.

(5) Compound Nouns or Groups of Words

To form the possessive case of compound nouns or of word groups, add *'s* to the last word.

> The editor-in-chief's position is open.
> He accepted the secretary of state's resignation under protest.
> This is someone else's responsibility.

(6) Two or More Items

To indicate individual ownership of two or more items, add *'s* to each item. To indicate joint ownership, add *'s* only to the last item.

INDIVIDUAL OWNERSHIP: Ernest Hemingway's and Gertrude Stein's writing styles have some similarities. (Hemingway and Stein have two separate writing styles.)

JOINT OWNERSHIP: Gilbert and Sullivan's operettas include *The Pirates of Penzance* and *The Mikado.* (Gilbert and Sullivan collaborated on both operettas.)

EXERCISE 1

Change the modifying phrases that follow the nouns to possessive forms that precede the nouns.

> EXAMPLE: the pen belonging to my aunt
>
> my aunt's pen

1. the songs recorded by Ray Charles
2. the red glare of the rockets
3. the idea Warren had
4. the housekeeper Rick and Leslie hired
5. the first choice of everyone
6. the dinner given by Harris
7. furniture designed by William Morris
8. the climate of the Virgin Islands
9. the sport the Russells play
10. the role created by the French actress

EXERCISE 2

Change each word or phrase in parentheses to its possessive form. In some cases, you may have to use a phrase to indicate the possessive.

> EXAMPLE: The (children) toys were scattered all over their (parents) bedroom.
>
> The children's toys were scattered all over their parents' bedroom.

1. Jane (Addams) settlement house was called Hull House.
2. (*A Room of One's Own*) popularity increased with the rise of feminism.
3. The (chief petty officer) responsibilities are varied.
4. Vietnamese (restaurants) numbers have grown dramatically in ten (years) time.
5. (Charles Dickens) and (Mark Twain) works have sold millions of copies.

40b Avoiding Apostrophes with Plural Nouns and Personal Pronouns

Do not use apostrophes with plural nouns that are not possessive.

Faulty:	*Revised:*
The <u>Thompson❜</u>s are not at home.	The <u>Thompsons</u> are not at home.
The down <u>vest❜</u>s are very warm.	The down <u>vests</u> are very warm.
The Philadelphia Seventy <u>Sixer❜</u>s sometimes play well.	The Philadelphia Seventy <u>Sixers</u> sometimes play well.

Do not use apostrophes to form the possessive case of personal pronouns.

Faulty:	*Revised:*
This ticket must be <u>your❜</u>s or <u>her❜</u>s.	This ticket must be <u>yours</u> or <u>hers</u>.
The next turn is <u>their❜</u>s.	The next turn is <u>theirs</u>.
The doll had lost <u>it❜</u>s right eye.	The doll had lost <u>its</u> right eye.
The next great moment in history is <u>our❜</u>s.	The next great moment in history is <u>ours</u>.

See
40c1

Be especially careful not to confuse the possessive forms of personal pronouns with **contractions**.

EXERCISE 3

In the following sentences, correct any errors in the use of apostrophes to form noun plurals or the possessive case of personal pronouns. If a sentence is correct, mark it with a *C*.

> EXAMPLE: Dr. Sampson's lecture's were more interesting than her's.
>
> Dr. Sampson❜s lectures were more interesting than hers.

1. The Schaefer's seats are right next to our's.
2. Most of the college's in the area offer computer courses open to outsider's as well as to their own students.
3. The network completely revamped its daytime programming.
4. Is the responsibility for the hot dog concession Cynthia's or your's?
5. Romantic poets are his favorite's.
6. Debbie returned the books to the library, forgetting they were her's.
7. Cultural revolution's do not occur very often, but when they do they bring sweeping change's.

8. Roll-top desk's are eagerly sought by antique dealer's.
9. A flexible schedule is one of their priorities, but it isn't one of our's.
10. Is yours the red house or the brown one?

40c Indicating Omissions in Contractions

(1) Omitted Letters

Apostrophes replace omitted letters in contractions that combine a pronoun and a verb (*he* + *will* = *he'll*) or the elements of a verb phrase (*do* + *not* = *don't*).

FREQUENTLY USED CONTRACTIONS

it's (it is)	let's (let us)
he's (he is)	we've (we have)
she's (she has)	they're (they are)
who's (who is)	we'll (we will)
isn't (is not)	I'm (I am)
wouldn't (would not)	we're (we are)
couldn't (could not)	you'd (you would)
don't (do not)	we'd (we would)
won't (will not)	they'd (they had)

 USING APOSTROPHES

Be careful not to confuse contractions (which always include apostrophes) with the possessive forms of personal pronouns (which never include apostrophes).

Contractions	*Possessive Forms*
Who's on first?	Whose book is this?
They're playing our song.	Their team is winning.
It's raining.	Its paws were muddy.
You're a real pal.	Your résumé is very impressive.

NOTE: Contractions are generally not used in college writing.

(2) Omitted Numbers

In informal writing, an apostrophe may be used to represent the century in a year.

Crash of '29   class of '97   '57 Chevy

In college writing, however, write out the year in full: *the Crash of 1929, the class of 1997, a 1957 Chevrolet.*

EXERCISE 4

In the following sentences, correct any errors in the use of standard contractions or personal pronouns. If a sentence is correct, mark it with a *C*.

> EXAMPLE: Who's troops were sent to Korea?
>
> <u>Whose</u> troops were sent to Korea?

1. Its never easy to choose a major; whatever you decide, your bound to have second thoughts.
2. Olive Oyl asked, "Whose that knocking at my door?"
3. Their watching too much television; in fact, they're eyes are glazed.
4. Whose coming along on the backpacking trip?
5. The horse had been badly treated; it's spirit was broken.
6. Your correct in assuming its a challenging course.
7. Sometimes even you're best friends won't tell you your boring.
8. They're training had not prepared them for the hardships they faced.
9. It's too early to make a positive diagnosis.
10. Robert Frost wrote the poem that begins, "Who's woods these are I think I know."

40d   Forming Plurals

In a few special situations, add *'s* to form plurals.

FORMING PLURALS WITH APOSTROPHES

Plurals of Letters

The Italian language has no *j*'s or *k*'s.

continued on the following page

---

continued from the previous page

Plurals of Words Referred To as Words

The supervisor would accept no *if*'s, *and*'s, or *but*'s.

See 44c

NOTE: **Elements spoken of as themselves** (letters, numerals, or words) are set in italic type; the plural ending, however, is not.

EXERCISE 5

In the following sentences, form correct plurals for the letters and words in parentheses. Underline to indicate italics where necessary.

EXAMPLE: The word *bubbles* contains three (b).

The word *bubbles* contains three *b*'s.

1. She closed her letter with a row of (x) and (o) to indicate kisses and hugs.
2. The three (R) are reading, writing, and 'rithmetic.
3. The report included far too many (maybe) and too few (definitely).
4. The word bookkeeper contains two (o), two (k), and three (e).
5. His letter included many (please) and (thank you).

CHAPTER 41

USING QUOTATION MARKS

Use quotation marks to set off brief passages of quoted speech or writing, to set off titles, and to set off words used in special ways. Do not use quotation marks with long passages of prose or poetry.

41a   Setting Off Quoted Speech or Writing

When you quote a word, phrase, or brief passage from someone else's speech or writing, enclose the quoted material in a pair of quotation marks.

Gloria Steinem said, "We are becoming the men we once hoped to marry."

In an essay about advertising in women's magazines, Gloria Steinem wrote, "When *Ms.* began, we didn't even consider *not* taking ads."

Gallery of Misused Quotation Marks
   http://www.juvalamu.com/qmarks/
Quotation Marks Exercises
   http://owl.english.purdue.edu/handouts/grammar/g_quoteEX1.html

---

CLOSE UP   USING QUOTATION MARKS WITH DIALOGUE

When you record dialogue, enclose the quoted words in quotation marks. Begin a new paragraph each time a new speaker is introduced.

When you are quoting several paragraphs of dialogue by one speaker, begin each new paragraph with quotation marks. However, use closing quotation marks only at the end of the *entire quoted passage,* not at the end of each paragraph.

Special rules govern the punctuation of a quotation when it is used with an **identifying tag,** a phrase (such as *he said*) that identifies the speaker or writer.

(1) Identifying Tag in the Middle of a Quoted Passage

Use a pair of commas to set off an identifying tag that interrupts a quoted passage.

"In the future," pop artist Andy Warhol once said, "everyone will be world famous for fifteen minutes."

If the identifying tag follows a completed sentence but the quoted passage continues, use a period after the tag, and begin the new sentence with a capital letter and quotation marks.

"Be careful," Erin warned. "Reptiles can be tricky."

(2) Identifying Tag at the Beginning of a Quoted Passage

Use a comma after an identifying tag that introduces quoted speech or writing.

The Raven repeated, "Nevermore."

See 42a3

Use a **colon** instead of a comma before a quotation if the identifying tag is a complete sentence.

She gave her final answer: "No."

Also, use a colon—not a comma—to introduce a **long prose passage** (a quotation of more than four typed lines).

(3) Identifying Tag at the End of a Quoted Passage

Use a comma to set off a quotation from an identifying tag that follows it.

"Be careful out there," the sergeant warned.

If the quotation ends with a question mark or an exclamation point, use that punctuation mark instead of the comma. In this situation, the tag begins with a lowercase letter even though it follows end punctuation.

"Is Ankara the capital of Turkey?" she asked.

"Oh boy!" he cried.

NOTE: Commas and periods are always placed *inside* quotation marks. For information on placement of other punctuation marks with quotation marks, see **41d.**

EXERCISE 1

Add quotation marks to these sentences where necessary to set off quotations from identifying tags.

EXAMPLE: Wordsworth's phrase splendour in the grass was used as the title of a movie about young lovers.

Wordsworth's phrase "splendour in the grass" was used as the title of a movie about young lovers.

1. Few people can explain what Descartes's words I think, therefore I am actually mean.
2. Gertrude Stein said, You are all a lost generation.
3. Freedom of speech does not guarantee anyone the right to yell fire in a crowded theater, she explained.
4. There's no place like home, Dorothy insisted.
5. If everyone will sit down the teacher announced the exam will begin.

41b   Setting Off Titles

Titles of short works and titles of parts of long works are enclosed in quotation marks. Other titles are italicized.

NOTE: MLA style recommends underlining to indicate **italics**.

TITLES REQUIRING QUOTATION MARKS

Articles in Magazines, Newspapers, and Professional Journals
   "Why Johnny Can't Write"

Essays, Short Stories, Short Poems, and Songs
   "Fenimore Cooper's Literary Offenses"   "Flying Home"

   "The Road Not Taken"   "The Star-Spangled Banner"

Chapters or Sections of Books
   "Miss Sharp Begins to Make Friends"

Episodes of Radio or Television Series
   "Lucy Goes to the Hospital"

EXERCISE 2

Add quotation marks to the following sentences where necessary to set off titles. If italics are incorrectly used, substitute quotation marks.

EXAMPLE: Canadian author Margaret Atwood has written stories, such as *Rape Fantasies;* poems, such as You Fit Into Me; and novels, such as *Alias Grace.*

Canadian author Margaret Atwood has written stories, such as "Rape Fantasies"; poems, such as "You Fit Into Me"; and novels, such as *Alias Grace.*

1. One of the essays from her new book *Good Bones and Simple Murder* was originally published in *Harper's* magazine.
2. Her latest collection of poems, *Morning in the Burned House,* contains the moving poem *In the Secular Night.*

3. You may have seen the movie *The Handmaid's Tale,* starring Robert Duvall, based on her best-selling novel.
4. *Surfacing* was the first book of hers I read, but my favorite work of hers is the short story Hair Ball.
5. I wasn't surprised to find her poems The Animals in the Country and This Is a Photograph of Me in our English textbook last year.

WORDS USED IN SPECIAL WAYS

A word used in a special or unusual way is enclosed in quotation marks.

It was clear that adults approved of children who were "readers," but it was not at all clear why this was so. (Annie Dillard)

NOTE: If you use the expression *so-called* before an unusual usage, do not also use quotation marks.

A **coinage**—an invented word—is also enclosed in quotation marks.

After the twins were born, the minivan became a "babymobile."

41c Setting Off Long Prose Passages and Poetry

(1) Long Prose Passages

When you quote a short prose passage, set it off in quotation marks and run it into text.

Galsworthy describes Aunt Juley as "prostrated by the blow" (329).

However, do not enclose a **long prose passage** (a passage of more than four lines) in quotation marks. Instead, set it off by indenting the entire passage one inch (or ten spaces) from the left-hand margin. Double-space above and below the quoted passage, and double-space between lines within it. Introduce the passage with a colon.

The following portrait of Aunt Juley illustrates several of the

devices Galsworthy uses throughout The Forsyte Saga, such as a journalistic detachment that is almost cruel in its scrutiny, a subtle sense of the grotesque, and an ironic stance:

> Aunt Juley stayed in her room, prostrated by the blow. Her face, discoloured by tears, was divided into compartments by the little ridges of pouting flesh which had swollen with emotion [. . .]. At fixed intervals she went to her drawer, and took from beneath the lavender bags a fresh pocket-handkerchief. Her warm heart could not bear the thought that Ann was lying there so cold. (329)

Many similar portraits of characters appear throughout the novel.

NOTE: With long prose passages, parenthetical documentation is placed one space *after* the end punctuation. (With short prose passages, parenthetical documentation goes *before* the end punctuation.)

QUOTING LONG PROSE PASSAGES

When you quote a long prose passage that is a single paragraph, do not indent the first line. When quoting two or more paragraphs, however, indent the first line of each paragraph (including the first) three additional spaces. If the first sentence of the quoted passage does not begin a paragraph in the source, do not indent—but do indent the first line of each subsequent paragraph. If the passage you are quoting includes material set in quotation marks, keep the quotation marks.

❓ (2) Poetry

One line of poetry is treated like a short prose passage: it is enclosed in quotation marks and run into the text.

One of John Donne's best-known poems begins with the line, "Go and catch a falling star."

Two or three lines of poetry are run into the text and separated by **slashes** (/).

See 42e2

> Alexander Pope writes, "True Ease in Writing comes from Art, not Chance, / As those move easiest who have learned to dance."

More than three lines of poetry should be set off like a **long prose passage**. (For special emphasis, fewer lines may also be set off in this manner.) Punctuation, spelling, capitalization, and indentation are reproduced *exactly.*

See 41c1

> Wilfred Owen, a poet who was killed in action in World War I,
>
> expressed the horrors of war with vivid imagery:
>
> > Bent double, like old beggars under sacks.
> >
> > Knock-kneed, coughing like hags, we cursed through sludge.
> >
> > Till on the haunting flares we turned our backs
> >
> > And towards our distant rest began to trudge. (1-4)

41d Using Quotation Marks with Other Punctuation

At the end of a quotation, other punctuation is sometimes placed before quotation marks and sometimes placed after them.

(1) With Final Commas or Periods

Quotation marks come *after* the comma or period at the end of a quotation.

> Many, like Frost, think about "the road not taken," but not many have taken "the one less traveled by."

(2) With Final Semicolons or Colons

Quotation marks come *before* a semicolon or colon at the end of a quotation.

> Students who do not pass the test receive "certificates of completion"; those who pass are awarded diplomas.

> Taxpayers were pleased with the first of the candidate's promised "sweeping new reforms": a balanced budget.

(3) With Question Marks, Exclamation Points, and Dashes

If a question mark, exclamation point, or dash is part of the quotation, place the quotation marks *after* the punctuation.

"Who's there?" she demanded.

"Stop!" he cried.

"Should we leave now, or—" Vicki paused, unable to continue.

If a question mark, exclamation point, or dash is *not* part of the quotation, place the quotation marks *before* the punctuation.

Did you finish reading "The Black Cat"?

Whatever you do, don't yell "Uncle"!

The first story—Updike's "A & P"—provoked discussion.

If both the quotation and the sentence are questions or exclamations, place the quotation marks *before* the punctuation.

Who asked, "Is Paris burning"?

QUOTATIONS WITHIN QUOTATIONS

Use *single* quotation marks to enclose a quotation within a quotation.

Claire noted, "Liberace always said, 'I cried all the way to the bank.'"

Also, use single quotation marks within a quotation to indicate a title that would normally be enclosed in double quotation marks.

I think what she said was, "Play it, Sam. Play 'As Time Goes By.'"

Use double quotation marks around quotations or titles within a **long prose passage**.

See
41c1

41e   Editing Misused Quotation Marks

Quotation marks should not be used in the following situations.

(1) To Convey Emphasis

FAULTY: William Randolph Hearst's "fabulous" home is a castle called San Simeon.

REVISED: William Randolph Hearst's fabulous home is a castle called San Simeon.

(2) To Set Off Slang or Technical Terms

FAULTY: Dawn is "into" running.

REVISED: Dawn is very involved in running.

FAULTY: "Biofeedback" is sometimes used to treat migraine headaches.

REVISED: Biofeedback is sometimes used to treat migraine headaches.

(3) To Enclose Titles of Long Works

FAULTY: "War and Peace" is even longer than "Paradise Lost."

REVISED: *War and Peace* is even longer than *Paradise Lost.*

NOTE: **Titles** of long works are italicized.

See
44a

  TITLES OF YOUR OWN PAPERS

Do not use quotation marks (or italics) to set off the title on the title page or the first page of your own papers. See **55c.**

(4) To Set Off Terms Being Defined

FAULTY: The word "tintinnabulation," meaning the ringing sound of bells, was used by Poe in his poem "The Bells."

REVISED: The word *tintinnabulation,* meaning the ringing sound of bells, was used by Poe in his poem "The Bells."

(5) To Set Off Indirect Quotations

FAULTY: Freud wondered "what a woman wanted."

REVISED: Freud wondered what a woman wanted.

REVISED: Freud wondered, "What does a woman want?"

EXERCISE 3

In the following paragraph, correct the use of single and double quotation marks to set off direct quotations, titles, and words used in special ways. Supply quotation marks where required and delete those not required, substituting italics where necessary.

In her essay 'The Obligation to Endure' from the book "Silent Spring," Rachel Carson writes: As Albert Schweitzer has said, 'Man can hardly even recognize the devils of his own creation.' Carson goes on to point out that many chemicals have been used to kill insects and other organisms which, she writes, are "described in the modern vernacular as pests." Carson believes such "advanced" chemicals, by contaminating our environment, do more harm than good. In addition to "Silent Spring," Carson is also the author of the book "The Sea Around Us." This work, divided into three sections (Mother Sea, The Restless Sea, and Man and the Sea About Him), was published in 1951.

EXERCISE 4

Correct the use of quotation marks in the following sentences. If a sentence is correct, mark it with a *C*.

EXAMPLE: The "Watergate" incident brought many new expressions into the English language.

The Watergate incident brought many new expressions into the English language.

1. Kilroy was here and Women and children first are two expressions *Bartlett's Familiar Quotations* attributes to "Anon."
2. Neil Armstrong said he was making a small step for man but a giant leap for mankind.
3. "The answer, my friend", Bob Dylan sang, "is blowin' in the wind".
4. The novel was a real "thriller," complete with spies and counterspies, mysterious women, and exotic international chases.
5. The sign said, Road liable to subsidence; it meant that we should look out for potholes.
6. One of William Blake's best-known lines—To see a world in a grain of sand—opens his poem Auguries of Innocence.
7. In James Thurber's short story The Catbird Seat, Mrs. Barrows annoys Mr. Martin by asking him silly questions like Are you tearing up the pea patch? Are you scraping around the bottom of the pickle barrel? and Are you lifting the oxcart out of the ditch?
8. I'll make him an offer he can't refuse, promised "the godfather" in Mario Puzo's novel.
9. What did Timothy Leary mean by "Turn on, tune in, drop out?"
10. George, the protagonist of Bernard Malamud's short story, A Summer's Reading, is something of an "underachiever."

CHAPTER 42

USING OTHER PUNCTUATION MARKS

42a   Using Colons

The **colon** is a strong punctuation mark that points readers ahead to the rest of the sentence. When a colon introduces a list or series, explanatory material, or a quotation, it must be preceded by a complete sentence.

(1) Introducing Lists or Series

Colons set off lists or series, including those introduced by phrases like *the following* or *as follows.*

Waiting tables requires three skills memory, speed, and balance.

(2) Introducing Explanatory Material

Colons often introduce material that explains, exemplifies, or summarizes. Frequently, this material is presented in the form of an **appositive,** a word group that identifies or renames an adjacent noun or pronoun.

Diego Rivera painted a controversial mural the one commissioned for Rockefeller Center in the 1930s.

She had one dream to play professional basketball.

Sometimes a colon separates two independent clauses, the second illustrating or explaining the first.

A *U.S. News & World Report* survey revealed a surprising fact: Americans spend more time at malls than anywhere else except at home and at work.

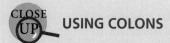 **USING COLONS**

When a complete sentence follows a colon, it may begin with either a capital or a lowercase letter. However, if it is a quotation, the first word is always capitalized (unless it was not capitalized in the source).

(3) Introducing Quotations

When a **long prose passage** is quoted, it is always introduced by a colon. In addition, a colon is used before a short quotation when it is introduced by a complete independent clause.

With dignity, Bartleby repeated the words: "I prefer not to."

OTHER CONVENTIONAL USES OF COLONS

To Separate Titles from Subtitles
Family Installments: Memories of Growing Up Hispanic

To Separate Minutes from Hours
6:15 a.m.

After Salutations in **Business Letters**
Dear Dr. Evans:

To Separate Place of Publication from Name of Publisher in a **Works Cited** *List*
Fort Worth: Harcourt, 2001

Punctuation Marks (other than commas)
http://cctc2.commnet.edu/grammar/marks/marks.htm

(4) Editing Misused Colons

Do not use colons in these situations.

After Certain Expressions　Colons are not used after expressions like *such as, namely, for example,* or *that is.* Remember that when a colon introduces a list or series, a complete sentence must precede it.

FAULTY: The Eye Institute treats patients with a wide variety of conditions, such as: myopia, glaucoma, and cataracts.

REVISED: The Eye Institute treats patients with a wide variety of conditions, such as myopia, glaucoma, and cataracts.

In Verb and Prepositional Constructions　Colons should not be placed between verbs and their objects or complements or between prepositions and their objects.

FAULTY: James A. Michener wrote: *Hawaii, Centennial, Space,* and *Poland.*

REVISED: James A. Michener wrote *Hawaii, Centennial, Space,* and *Poland.*

FAULTY: Hitler's armies marched through: the Netherlands, Belgium, and France.

REVISED: Hitler's armies marched through the Netherlands, Belgium, and France.

EXERCISE 1

Add colons where required in the following sentences. If necessary, delete excess colons.

EXAMPLE:　There was one thing he really hated getting up at 700 every morning.

There was one thing he really hated: getting up at 7:00 every morning.

1. Books about the late John F. Kennedy include the following *A Hero for Our Time; Johnny, We Hardly Knew Ye; One Brief Shining Moment;* and *JFK: Reckless Youth.*
2. Only one task remained to tell his boss he was quitting.
3. The story closed with a familiar phrase "And they all lived happily ever after."
4. The sergeant requested: reinforcements, medical supplies, and more ammunition.

5. She kept only four souvenirs a photograph, a matchbook, a theater program, and a daisy pressed between the pages of *William Shakespeare The Complete Works.*

42b Using Dashes

(1) Setting Off Nonessential Material

Like commas, **dashes** can set off <u>nonessential material</u>, but unlike commas, dashes tend to call attention to the material they set off. Indicate a dash with two unspaced hyphens (unless your word-processing program has a dash function).

Explanations, qualifications, examples, definitions, and appositives may be set off by dashes for emphasis or clarity.

Neither of the boys—both nine-year-olds—had any history of violence.

Too many parents learn the dangers of swimming pools the hard way—after their toddler has drowned.

(2) Introducing a Summary

A dash is used to introduce a statement that summarizes a list or series before it.

"Study hard," "Respect your elders," "Don't talk with your mouth full"—Sharon had often heard her parents say these things.

(3) Indicating an Interruption

In dialogue, a dash may mark a hesitation or an unfinished thought.

"I think—no, I know—this is the worst day of my life," Julie sighed.

(4) Editing Overused Dashes

Because too many dashes can make a passage seem disorganized and out of control, they should not be overused.

Faulty (Overuse of Dashes): Registration was a nightmare—most of the courses I wanted to take—geology and conversational Spanish, for instance—met at inconvenient times—or were closed by the time I tried to sign up for them—it was really depressing—even for registration.

Revised (Moderate Use of Dashes): Registration was a nightmare. Most of the courses I wanted to take—geology and conversational

Spanish, for instance—met at inconvenient times or were closed by the time I tried to sign up for them. It was really depressing—even for registration.

EXERCISE 2

Add dashes where needed in the following sentences. If a sentence is correct, mark it with a *C*.

> EXAMPLE: World War I called "the war to end all wars" was, unfortunately, no such thing.
>
> World War I—called "the war to end all wars"—was, unfortunately, no such thing.

1. Tulips, daffodils, hyacinths, lilies all these flowers grow from bulbs.
2. St. Kitts and Nevis two tiny island nations are now independent after 360 years of British rule.
3. "But it's not" She paused and reconsidered her next words.
4. He considered several different majors history, English, political science, and business before deciding on journalism.
5. The two words added to the Pledge of Allegiance in the 1950s "under God" remain part of the Pledge today.

❓ 42c Using Parentheses

(1) Setting Off Nonessential Material

Parentheses enclose material that is relatively unimportant in a sentence—for example, material that expands, clarifies, illustrates, or supplements.

In some European countries (notably Sweden and France), high-quality day care is offered at little or no cost to parents.

When a complete sentence set off by parentheses falls within another sentence, it should not begin with a capital letter or end with a period.

The area is so cold (temperatures average in the low twenties) that it is virtually uninhabitable.

If the parenthetical sentence does *not* fall within another sentence, however, it must begin with a capital letter and end with appropriate punctuation.

The area is very cold. (Temperatures average in the low twenties.)

(2) Using Parentheses in Other Situations

Parentheses are used around letters and numbers that identify points on a list, dates, cross-references, and documentation.

All reports must include the following components: (1) an opening summary, (2) a background statement, and (3) a list of conclusions.

Russia defeated Sweden in the Great Northern War (1700–1721).

Other scholars also make this point (see p. 54).

One critic has called the novel "puerile" (Arvin 72).

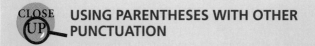

CLOSE UP **USING PARENTHESES WITH OTHER PUNCTUATION**

When parentheses fall within a sentence, punctuation never precedes the opening parenthesis. Punctuation may follow the closing parenthesis, however.

INCORRECT: George Orwell's *1984*, (1949), which focuses on the dangers of a totalitarian society, is required reading.

REVISED: George Orwell's *1984* (1949), which focuses on the dangers of a totalitarian society, is required reading.

EXERCISE 3

Add parentheses where necessary in the following sentences. If a sentence is correct, mark it with a *C*.

EXAMPLE: The greatest battle of the War of 1812 the Battle of New Orleans was fought after the war was declared over.

The greatest battle of the War of 1812 (the Battle of New Orleans) was fought after the war was declared over.

1. During the Great War 1914–1918, Britain censored letters written from the front lines.

2. Those who lived in towns on the southern coast like Dover could often hear the mortar shells across the channel in France.
3. Wilfred Owen wrote his most famous poem "Dulce et Decorum Est" in the trenches in France.
4. The British uniforms with bright red tabs right at the neck were responsible for many British deaths.
5. It was difficult for the War Poets as they are now called to return to writing about subjects other than the horrors of war.

② 42d Using Brackets

(1) Setting Off Comments within Quotations

Brackets within quotations tell readers that the enclosed words are yours and not those of your source. You can bracket an explanation, a clarification, a correction, or an opinion.

"Even at Princeton he [F. Scott Fitzgerald] felt like an outsider."

If a quotation contains an error, indicate that the error is not yours by following the error with the italicized Latin word *sic* ("thus") in brackets.

"The octopuss [*sic*] is a cephalopod mollusk with eight arms."

 USING BRACKETS TO EDIT QUOTATIONS

See 14d1

Use brackets to indicate changes that enable you to fit a **quotation** smoothly into your sentence. If you use ellipses to indicate omitted words, enclose the ellipses in brackets.

---

(2) In Place of Parentheses within Parentheses

When one set of parentheses falls within another, use brackets in place of the inner set.

In her study of American education between 1945 and 1960 (*The Trouble Crusade* [New York: Basic, 1963]), Diane Ravitch addresses issues like progressive education, race, educational reforms, and campus unrest.

42e　Using Slashes

(1) Separating One Option from Another

The either/or fallacy is a common error in logic.

Writer/director Spike Lee will speak at the film festival.

Notice that in this case, there is no space before or after the slash.

(2) Separating Lines of Poetry Run into the Text

The poet James Schevill writes, "I study my defects / And learn how to perfect them."

In this case, leave a space both before and after the slash.

42f　Using Ellipses

Use ellipses in the following situations.

(1) Indicating an Omission in Quoted Prose

Use an ellipsis—three *spaced* periods—to indicate that you have omitted material from a quotation. Enclose the ellipsis in brackets to distinguish your ellipsis from ellipses that might have appeared in the original text. When deleting material, be careful not to change the meaning of the original passage.

ORIGINAL: "When I was a young man, being anxious to distinguish myself, I was perpetually starting new propositions." (Samuel Johnson)

WITH OMISSIONS: "When I was a young man, [. . .] I was perpetually starting new propositions." (Three spaced periods indicate omissions.)

When you delete material at the end of a sentence, place the sentence's end punctuation after the bracketed ellipsis.

According to humorist Dave Barry, "From outer space Europe appears to be shaped like a large ketchup stain [. . .]."

NOTE: Never begin a quoted passage with an ellipsis.

When you delete material from a quotation of more than one sentence, where to place the end punctuation—before or after the bracketed ellipses—is determined by where you have deleted material.

? *Deletion from Middle of One Sentence to End of Another*

> According to Donald Hall, "Everywhere one meets the idea that reading is an activity desirable in itself [...]. People surround the idea of reading with piety and do not take into account the purpose of reading."

Deletion from Middle of One Sentence to Middle of Another

> "When I was a young man, [...] I found that generally what was new was false." (Samuel Johnson)

NOTE: An ellipsis in the middle of a quoted passage can indicate the omission of a word, a sentence or two, or even a whole paragraph or more.

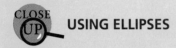

USING ELLIPSES

If a quotation ending with an ellipsis is followed by parenthetical documentation, the final punctuation follows the documentation.

As Jarman argues, "Compromise was impossible [...]" (161).

(2)   Indicating an Omission in Quoted Poetry

Use an ellipsis within brackets when you omit a word or phase from a line of poetry. When you omit one or more lines of poetry, use a complete line of spaced periods within brackets.

ORIGINAL:

> Stitch! Stitch! Stitch!
> In poverty, hunger, and dirt,
> And still with a voice of dolorous pitch,
> Would that its tone could reach the Rich,
> She sang this "Song of the Shirt!"
>
> (Thomas Hood)

WITH OMISSION:

Stitch! Stitch! Stitch!
In poverty, hunger, and dirt,
[.............................]
She sang this "Song of the Shirt!"

EXERCISE 4

Read the following paragraph and follow the instructions after it, taking care in each case not to delete essential information.

> The most important thing about research is to know when to stop. How does one recognize the moment? When I was eighteen or thereabouts, my mother told me that when out with a young man I should always leave a half-hour before I wanted to. Although I was not sure how this might be accomplished, I recognized the advice as sound, and exactly the same rule applies to research. One must stop *before* one has finished; otherwise, one will never stop and never finish. (Barbara Tuchman, *Practicing History*)

1. Delete a phrase from the middle of one sentence, and mark the omission with ellipses and brackets.
2. Delete words from the middle of one sentence to the middle of another, and mark the omission with ellipses and brackets.
3. Delete words at the end of any sentence, and mark the omission with ellipses and brackets.
4. Delete one complete sentence from the middle of the passage, and mark the omission with ellipses and brackets.

EXERCISE 5

Add appropriate punctuation—colons, dashes, parentheses, brackets, or slashes—to the following sentences. If a sentence is correct, mark it with a *C*.

EXAMPLE: There was one thing she was sure of if she did well at the interview, the job would be hers.

There was one thing she was sure of: if she did well at the interview, the job would be hers.

1. Mark Twain Samuel L. Clemens made the following statement "I can live for two months on a good compliment."

2. Liza Minnelli, the actress singer who starred in several films, is the daughter of Judy Garland.
3. Saudi Arabia, Oman, Yemen, Qatar, and the United Arab Emirates all these are located on the Arabian Peninsula.
4. John Adams 1735–1826 was the second president of the United States; John Quincy Adams 1767–1848 was the sixth.
5. The sign said "No tresspassing *sic.*"
6. *Checkmate* a term derived from the Persian phrase meaning "the king is dead" announces victory in chess.
7. The following people were present at the meeting the president of the board of trustees, three trustees, and twenty reporters.
8. Before the introduction of the potato in Europe, the parsnip was a major source of carbohydrates in fact, it was a dietary staple.
9. In this well-researched book (*Crime Movies* New York Norton, 1980), Carlos Clarens studies the gangster genre in film.
10. I remember reading though I can't remember where that Upton Sinclair sold plots to Jack London.

STUDENT WRITER AT WORK

Punctuation

Review Chapters 37–42. Then, read this student essay. Commas, semicolons, quotation marks, apostrophes, parentheses, and dashes have been intentionally deleted; only the end punctuation has been retained. When you have read the essay carefully, add all appropriate punctuation marks.

The dry pine needles crunched like eggshells under our thick boots.

Wont the noise scare them away Dad?

He smiled knowingly and said No deer rely mostly on smell and sight.

I thought That must be why were wearing fluorescent orange jumpsuits but I didn't feel like arguing the point.

It was a perfect day for my first hunting experience. The biting winds were caught by the thick bushy arms of the tall pines and I could feel a numbing redness in my face. Now I realized why Dad always grew that ugly gray beard that made him look ten years older. A few sunbeams managed to carve their way through the layers of branches and leaves creating pools of white light on the dark earth.

How far have we come? I asked.

Oh only a couple of miles. We should be meeting Joe up ahead.

Joe was one of Dads hunting buddies. He always managed to go off on his own for a few hours and come back with at least a four-pointer. Dad was envious of Joe and liked to tell people what he called the real story.

You know Joe paid a fortune for that buck at the checking station hed tell his friends. Dad was sure that this would be his lucky year.

We trudged up a densely wooded hill for what seemed like hours. The sharp-needled branches whipped my bare face as I followed close behind my father occasionally I wiped my cheeks to discover a new cut in my frozen flesh.

All this for a deer I thought.

The still pine air was suddenly shattered by four rapid gunshots echoing across the vast green valley below us.

Joes got another one. Come on! Dad yelled. It seemed as if I were following a young kid as I watched my father take leaping strides down the path we had just ascended. I had never seen him so enthusiastic before. I plodded breathlessly along trying to keep up with my father.

Suddenly out of the corner of my eye I caught sight of an object that didnt fit in with the monotony of trunks and branches and leaves and needles. I froze and observed the largest most majestic buck I had ever seen. It too stood motionless apparently grazing on some leaves or berries. Its coloring was beautiful with alternating patches of tan brown and snow-white fur. The massive antlers towered proudly above its head as it looked up and took notice of me. What struck me most were the tearful brown eyes almost feminine in their gaze.

Once again the silence was smashed this time by my fathers thundering call and I watched as the huge deer scampered gracefully off through the trees. I turned and scurried down the path after my father. I decided not to mention a word of my encounter to him. I hoped the deer was far away by now.

Finally I reached the clearing from where the shots had rung out. There stood Dad and Joe smiling over a fallen six-point buck. The purple-red blood dripped from the wounds to form a puddle in the dirt. The bucks sad brown eyes gleamed in the sun but no longer smiled and blinked.

Where have you been? asked Dad. Before I could answer he continued Do you believe this guy? Every year he bags the biggest deer in the whole state!

While they laughed and talked I sat on a tree stump to rest my aching legs. Maybe now we can go home I thought.

But before long I heard Dad say Come on Bob I know theres one out there for us.

We headed right back up that same path and sure enough that same big beautiful buck was grazing in that same spot on the same berry bush. The only difference was that this time Dad saw him.

This is our lucky day he whispered.

I froze as Dad lifted the barrel of his rifle and took careful aim at the silently grazing deer. I closed my eyes as he squeezed the trigger but instead of the deadly gun blast I heard only a harmless click. His rifle had jammed.

Use your rifle quick he whispered.

As I took aim through my scope the deer looked up at me. Its soulful brown eyes were magnified in my sight like two glassy bulls-eyes. My finger froze on the trigger.

Shoot him! Shoot him!

But instead I aimed for the clouds and fired. The deer vanished along with my fathers dreams. Dad never understood why this was the proudest moment of my life.

CHAPTER 43

CAPITALIZATION

? FREQUENTLY ASKED QUESTIONS

Is the first word of a line of poetry always
capitalized?   (p. 623)
Are *east* and *west* capitalized?   (p. 624)
Are *black* and *white* capitalized when they
denote races?   (p. 625)
Are brand names always capitalized?
(p. 626)
Which words in titles are *not* capitalized?
(p. 627)
Are the names of seasons capitalized?
(p. 628)

43a   Capitalizing the First Word of a Sentence

Capitalize the first word of a sentence, including a sentence of quoted speech or writing.

As Shakespeare wrote, "Who steals my purse steals trash."

Do not capitalize a sentence set off within another sentence by dashes or parentheses.

Finding the store closed—it was a holiday—they went home.

The candidates are Frank Lester and Jane Lester (they are not related).

Capitalization is optional when a complete sentence follows a colon.

Using Capitals
    http://www.clearcf.uvic.ca/writersguide/Pages/Capitals.html
Steve Tripp's Capitalization Page + Exercises
    http://www.u-aizu.ac.jp/~tripp/cap.html

CLOSE UP　USING CAPITAL LETTERS IN POETRY

Remember that the first word of a line of poetry is generally capitalized. If the poet uses a lowercase letter to begin a line, however, follow that style when you quote the line.

43b　Capitalizing Proper Nouns

Proper nouns—the names of specific persons, places, or things—are capitalized, and so are adjectives formed from proper nouns.

(1) Specific People's Names

Eleanor Roosevelt	Elvis Presley
Jackie Robinson	William the Conqueror

When a title precedes a person's name or is used instead of the name, it, too, is capitalized.

Dad	Pope John XXIII
Count Dracula	Justice Ruth Bader Ginsburg

Titles that *follow* names or those that refer to a general position, not the particular person who holds it, are usually not capitalized. A title denoting a family relationship is never capitalized when it follows an article or a possessive pronoun.

Capitalize:	*Do Not Capitalize:*
Grandma	my grandmother
Private Hargrove	Mr. Hargrove, a private in the army
Queen Mother Elizabeth	a popular queen mother
Sen. Barbara Boxer	Barbara Boxer, the senator from California
Uncle Harry	my uncle
Gen. Pattong	a four-star general

Titles or abbreviations of academic degrees are always capitalized, even when they follow a name.

Perry Mason, Attorney-at-Law   Michelle Russo, PhD

Benjamin Spock, MD

Titles that indicate high-ranking positions may be capitalized even when they are used alone or when they follow a name.

the Pope

Abraham Lincoln, President of the United States

(2) Names of Particular Structures, Special Events, Monuments, Vehicles, and So On

the *Titanic*   the Taj Mahal

the Brooklyn Bridge   Mount Rushmore

the World Series   the Eiffel Tower

NOTE: Capitalize a common noun, such as *bridge, river, county,* or *lake,* when it is part of a proper noun (Lake Erie, Kings County).

(3) Places, Geographical Regions, and Directions

Saturn   the Straits of Magellan

Budapest   the Western Hemisphere

Walden Pond   the Fiji Islands

Capitalize *north, east, south,* and *west* when they denote particular geographical regions, but not when they designate directions.

There are more tornadoes in Kansas than in the <u>East</u>. (*East* refers to a specific region.)

Turn <u>west</u> at Broad Street and continue <u>north</u> to Market. (*West* and *north* refer to directions, not specific regions.)

(4) Days of the Week, Months, and Holidays

Saturday   Cinco de Mayo

January   Rosh Hashanah

(5) Historical Periods, Events, Documents, and Names of Legal Cases

the Battle of Gettysburg   the Treaty of Versailles

the Industrial Revolution   the Voting Rights Act

the Reformation   *Brown v. Board of Education*

NOTE: Names of court cases are underlined to indicate italics in the text of your papers but not in bibliographic entries.

(6) Philosophic, Literary, and Artistic Movements

Naturalism   Dadaism

Neoclassicism   Expressionism

(7) Races, Ethnic Groups, Nationalities, and Languages

African American   Korean

Latino/Latina   Dutch

NOTE: When the words *black* and *white* denote races, they have traditionally not been capitalized. Current usage is divided on whether to capitalize *black*.

(8) Religions and Their Followers; Sacred Books and Figures

Islam   the Koran   Buddha

the Talmud   God   the Scriptures

NOTE: It is not necessary to capitalize pronouns referring to God (although some people do so as a sign of respect).

(9) Political, Social, Athletic, Civic, and Other Groups and Their Members

the New York Yankees

the Democratic Party

the International Brotherhood of Electrical Workers

the American Civil Liberties Union

the National Council of Teachers of English

the Rolling Stones

NOTE: When the name of a group or institution is abbreviated, the **abbreviation** uses capital letters in place of the capitalized words.

IBEW   ACLU   NCTE

(10) Businesses; Government Agencies; and Medical, Educational, and Other Institutions

Congress	Lincoln High School
the Environmental Protection Agency	the University of Maryland

(11) Brand Names and Words Formed from Them

Velcro   Coke   Post-it   Rollerblades   Astroturf

NOTE: Brand names that over long use have become synonymous with the product—for example, *nylon* and *aspirin*—are no longer capitalized. (Consult a dictionary to determine whether to capitalize a familiar brand name.)

 USING BRAND NAMES

In general, use generic references, not brand names, in college writing—*photocopy*, not *Xerox*, for example. These generic names are not capitalized.

(12) Specific Academic Courses

Sociology 201   English 101

NOTE: Do not capitalize a general subject area unless it is the name of a language.

FAULTY: He had a double major in English and <u>Accounting</u>.

REVISED: He had a double major in English and <u>accounting</u>.

(13) Adjectives Formed from Proper Nouns

Freudian slip   Elizabethan era

Platonic ideal   Shakespearean sonnet

Aristotelian logic   Marxist ideology

When words derived from proper nouns have lost their original associations, do not capitalize them.

The <u>china</u> pattern was very elaborate.

We need a 75-<u>watt</u> bulb.

43c Capitalizing Important Words in Titles

In general, capitalize all words in titles with the exception of articles (*a, an,* and *the*), prepositions, coordinating conjunctions, and the *to* in infinitives. If an article, preposition, or coordinating conjunction is the *first* or *last* word in the title, however, do capitalize it.

"Dover Beach"   *On the Waterfront*

The Declaration of Independence   *The Skin of Our Teeth*

Across the River and into the Trees   *What Friends Are For*

43d Capitalizing the Pronoun *I*, the Interjection *O*, and Other Single Letters in Special Constructions

Always capitalize the pronoun *I* even if it is part of a contraction (*I'm, I'll, I've*).

Sam and <u>I</u> finally went to the Grand Canyon, and <u>I'm</u> glad we did.

Always capitalize the interjection *O*.

Give us peace in our time, <u>O</u> Lord.

However, capitalize the interjection *oh* only when it begins a sentence.

NOTE: Many other single letters are capitalized in certain usages: U-boat, D day, Model T, vitamin B, an *A* in history, C major. Consult your dictionary to determine whether to use a capital letter.

43e   Capitalizing Salutations and Closings of Letters

Always capitalize the first word of the salutation of a personal or **business letter**.

> Dear Fred,   Dear Mr. Reynolds:

Always capitalize the first word of the complimentary close.

> Sincerely,   Very truly yours,

43f   Editing Misused Capitals

Do not capitalize in the following cases.

(1) Seasons

Do not capitalize the names of the seasons—summer, fall, winter, spring—unless they are personified, as in *Old Man Winter.*

(2) Centuries and Loosely Defined Historical Periods

Do not capitalize the names of centuries or general historical periods.

> seventeenth-century poetry   the automobile age

Do, however, capitalize names of specific historical, anthropological, and geological periods.

> Iron Age   Paleozoic Era

(3) Diseases and Other Medical Terms

Do not capitalize names of diseases or medical tests or conditions unless a proper noun is part of the name or unless the disease is an **acronym**.

> polio   Apgar test   AIDS
>
> Reye's syndrome   mumps   SIDS

EXERCISE

Capitalize words where necessary in these sentences.

> EXAMPLE: John F. Kennedy won the pulitzer prize for his book
> *profiles in courage.*
>
> John F. Kennedy won the <u>P</u>ulitzer <u>P</u>rize for his book <u>P</u>
> *rofiles in <u>C</u>ourage.*

1. Two of the brontë sisters wrote *jane eyre* and *wuthering heights,* nineteenth-century novels that are required reading in many english classes that study victorian literature.
2. It was a beautiful day in the spring—it was april 15, to be exact—but all Ted could think about was the check he had to write to the internal revenue service and the bills he had to pay by friday.
3. Traveling north, they hiked through british columbia, planning a leisurely return on the cruise ship *canadian princess.*
4. Alice liked her mom's apple pie better than aunt nellie's rhubarb pie; but she liked grandpa's punch best of all.
5. A new elective, political science 30, covers the vietnam war from the gulf of tonkin to the fall of saigon, including the roles of ho chi minh, the viet cong, and the buddhist monks; the positions of presidents johnson and nixon; and the influence of groups like the student mobilization committee and vietnam veterans against the war.
6. When the central high school drama club put on a production of shaw's *pygmalion,* the director xeroxed extra copies of the parts for eliza doolittle and professor henry higgins so he could give them to the understudies.
7. Shaking all over, Bill admitted, "driving on the los angeles freeway is a frightening experience for a kid from the bronx, even in a bmw."
8. The new united federation of teachers contract guarantees teachers many paid holidays, including columbus day, veterans day, and washington's birthday; a week each at christmas and easter; and two full months (july and august) in the summer.
9. The sociology syllabus included the books *beyond the best interests of the child, regulating the poor,* and *a welfare mother;* in anthropology, we were to begin by studying the stone age; and in geology, we were to focus on the Mesozoic era.
10. Winners of the nobel peace prize include lech walesa, former leader of the polish trade union solidarity; the reverend dr. martin luther king, jr., founder of the southern christian leadership conference; and bishop despond tutu of south africa.

CHAPTER 44

ITALICS

? FREQUENTLY ASKED QUESTIONS

What kinds of titles are italicized?
(p. 630)
Is it acceptable to underline to indicate
italics in my papers? (p. 631)
Is it acceptable to use italics to emphasize
certain words or phrases? (p. 632)

44a Setting Off Titles and Names

Use italics for the titles and names listed in the following box. All other titles are set off with **quotation marks**.

TITLES AND NAMES SET IN ITALICS

BOOKS: *David Copperfield, The Bluest Eye*

NEWSPAPERS: the *Washington Post,* the *Philadelphia Inquirer* (Articles and names of cities are italicized only when they are part of a title.)

MAGAZINES AND JOURNALS: *Rolling Stone, Scientific American*

ONLINE JOURNAL: *Web del Sol*

WEB SITE OR HOME PAGE: *Africana.com, Wilton's Etymology Page*

PAMPHLETS: *Common Sense*

FILMS: *Casablanca, Schindler's List*

TELEVISION PROGRAMS: *The Simpsons, The Sopranos*

RADIO PROGRAMS: *All Things Considered, A Prairie Home Companion*

LONG POEMS: *John Brown's Body, The Faerie Queen*

PLAYS: *Macbeth, A Raisin in the Sun*

LONG MUSICAL WORKS: *Rigoletto, Eroica*

SOFTWARE PROGRAMS: *Word, PowerPoint*

PAINTINGS AND SCULPTURE: *Guërnica, Pietà*

SHIPS: *Lusitania,* USS *Saratoga* (SS and USS are not italicized.)

TRAINS: *City of New Orleans,* the *Orient Express*

AIRCRAFT: the *Hindenburg, Enola Gay* (Only particular aircraft, not makes or types—such as Piper Cub or Boeing 757—are italicized.

SPACECRAFT: *Challenger, Enterprise*

NOTE: Names of sacred books, such as the Bible, and well-known documents, such as the Constitution and the Declaration of Independence, are neither italicized nor placed within quotation marks.

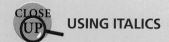

USING ITALICS

MLA style recommends that you underline to indicate italics. However, you may italicize if your instructor prefers.

44b Setting Off Foreign Words and Phrases

Italics are often used to set off foreign words and phrases that have not become part of the English language.

"*C'est la vie,*" Madeline said when she missed the bus.

Spirochaeta plicatilis is a corkscrew-like bacterium.

If you are not sure whether a foreign word has been assimilated into English, consult a dictionary.

44c Setting Off Elements Spoken of as Themselves and Terms Being Defined

Italics are used to set off letters, numerals, and words that refer to the letters, numerals, and words themselves.

Is that a *p* or a *g*?

I forget the exact address, but I know it has a *3* in it.

Does *through* rhyme with *cough*?

Italics also set off words and phrases that you go on to define.

A *closet drama* is a play meant to be read, not performed.

NOTE: When you quote a dictionary definition, put the word you are defining in italics and the definition itself in quotation marks.

To *infer* means "to draw a conclusion"; to *imply* means "to suggest."

❓ 44d Using Italics for Emphasis

Italics can occasionally be used for emphasis.

Initially, poetry might be defined as a kind of language that says *more* and says it *more intensely* than does ordinary language. (Lawrence Perrine, *Sound and Sense*)

However, overuse of italics is distracting. Instead of italicizing, try to indicate emphasis with word choice and sentence structure.

EXERCISE

Underline to indicate italics where necessary, and delete any italics that are incorrectly used. If a sentence is correct, mark it with a *C*.

EXAMPLE: However is a conjunctive adverb, not a coordinating conjunction.

However is a conjunctive adverb, not a coordinating conjunction.

1. I said Carol, not Darryl.
2. A *deus ex machina,* an improbable device used to resolve the plot of a fictional work, is used in Charles Dickens's novel Oliver Twist.
3. He dotted every i and crossed every t.
4. The Metropolitan Opera's production of Carmen was a tour de force for the principal performers.
5. *Laissez-faire* is a doctrine holding that government should not interfere with trade.
6. Antidote and anecdote are often confused because their pronunciations are similar.
7. Hawthorne's novels include Fanshawe, The House of the Seven Gables, The Blithedale Romance, and The Scarlet Letter.
8. Words like mailman, policeman, and fireman have been replaced by nonsexist terms like letter carrier, police officer, and firefighter.
9. A classic black tuxedo was considered de rigueur at the charity ball, but Jason preferred to wear his *dashiki.*
10. Thomas Mann's novel Buddenbrooks is a bildungsroman.

CHAPTER 45

HYPHENS

? FREQUENTLY ASKED QUESTIONS

Should I use a hyphen to divide an electronic
address at the end of a line?   (p. 634)
When do I hyphenate a compound word?
(p. 635)

Hyphens have two conventional uses: to break a word at the end of a line and to link words in certain compounds.

45a   Breaking a Word at the End of a Line

A computer never breaks a word at the end of a line unless you select that option. Sometimes you will want to hyphenate—for example, to fill in space at the end of a line. When you break a word at the end of a line, divide it only between syllables, consulting a dictionary if necessary. Never divide a word at the end of a page, and never hyphenate one-syllable words. In addition, never leave a single letter at the end of a line or carry only one or two letters to the next line.

If you must divide a **compound word** at the end of a line, put the hyphen between the elements of the compound (*snow-mobile*, not *snowmo-bile*).

See
45b

DIVIDING ELECTRONIC ADDRESSES (URLs)

Do not use a hyphen to divide an electronic address (URL) at the end of a line. (Readers might think the hyphen is part of the address.) MLA style requires that you break the URL at a slash. If this is not possible, break it in a logical place—after a period, for example—or avoid the problem entirely by moving the entire URL to the next line.

Using Hyphens
   http://owl.english.purdue.edu/handouts/grammar/g_hyphen.html

45b Dividing Compound Words

A **compound word** is composed of two or more words. Some familiar compound words are always hyphenated: *no-hitter, helter-skelter.* Other compounds are always written as one word: *fireplace, peacetime.* Finally, some compounds are always written as two separate words: *labor relations, bunk bed.* Your dictionary can tell you whether a particular compound requires a hyphen.

Hyphens are generally used in the following compounds.

(1) Hyphenating with Compound Adjectives

When a **compound adjective** *precedes* the noun it modifies, its elements are joined by hyphens.

The research team tried to use <u>nineteenth-century</u> technology to design a <u>space-age</u> project.

When a compound adjective *follows* the noun it modifies, it does not include hyphens.

The three government-operated programs were run smoothly, but the one that was not <u>government operated</u> was short of funds.

NOTE: A compound adjective formed with an adverb ending in *-ly* is not hyphenated, even when it precedes the noun.

Many <u>upwardly mobile</u> families are on tight budgets.

Use **suspended hyphens**—hyphens followed by a space or by appropriate punctuation and a space—in a series of compounds that have the same principal elements.

The <u>three-</u>, <u>four-</u>, and <u>five-year-old</u> children sang songs.

(2) Hyphenating with Certain Prefixes and Suffixes

Use a hyphen between a prefix and a proper noun or proper adjective.

mid-July   pre-Columbian

Use a hyphen to connect the prefixes *all-, ex-, half-, quarter-, quasi-,* and *self-* and the suffixes *-elect* to a noun.

ex-senator   self-centered   president-elect

NOTE: The words *selfhood, selfish,* and *selfless* do not include hyphens. In these cases, *self* is the root, not a prefix.

(3) Hyphenating in Compound Numerals and Fractions

Hyphenate compounds that represent numbers below one hundred, even if they are part of a larger number.

the twenty-first century　　　three hundred sixty-five days

Also, hyphenate the written form of a fraction when it modifies a noun.

a two-thirds share of the business

(4) Hyphenating for Clarity

Hyphenate to prevent readers from misreading one word for another.

In order to reform criminals, we must re-form our ideas about prisons.

Hyphenate to avoid hard-to-read combinations, such as two *i*'s (*semi-illiterate*).

Hyphenate in most cases between a capital initial and a word when the two combine to form a compound: *A-frame, T-shirt.*

(5) Hyphenating in Coined Compounds

A **coined compound,** one that uses a new combination of words as a unit, requires hyphens.

He looked up with a who-do-you-think-you-are expression.

EXERCISE 1

Form compound adjectives from the following word groups, inserting hyphens where necessary.

EXAMPLE:　A contract for three years

　　　　　　a three-year contract

1. a relative who has long been lost
2. someone who is addicted to video games
3. a salesperson who goes from door to door
4. a display calculated to catch the eye

5. friends who are dearly beloved
6. a household that is centered on a child
7. a line of reasoning that is hard to follow
8. the border between New York and New Jersey
9. a candidate who is thirty-two years old
10. a computer that is friendly to its users

EXERCISE 2

Add hyphens to the compounds in these sentences wherever they are required. Consult a dictionary if necessary.

EXAMPLE: Alaska was the forty ninth state to join the United States.

Alaska was the <u>forty•ninth</u> state to join the United States.

1. One of the restaurant's blue plate specials is chicken fried steak.
2. Virginia and Texas are both right to work states.
3. He stood on tiptoe to see the near perfect statue, which was well hidden by the security fence.
4. The five and ten cent store had a self service makeup counter and stocked many up to the minute gadgets.
5. The so called Saturday night special is opposed by pro gun control groups.
6. He ordered two all beef patties with special sauce, lettuce, cheese, pickles, and onions on a sesame seed bun.
7. The material was extremely thought provoking, but it hardly presented any earth shattering conclusions.
8. The Dodgers Phillies game was rained out, so the long suffering fans left for home.
9. Bone marrow transplants carry the risk of what is known as a graft versus host reaction.
10. The state funded child care program was considered a highly desirable alternative to family day care.

CHAPTER 46

ABBREVIATIONS

? FREQUENTLY ASKED QUESTIONS

When can I abbreviate the titles used with
   people's names?   (p. 638)
Is it acceptable to use abbreviations for
   technical terms?   (p. 639)
Are abbreviations like *e.g.* and *etc.*
   acceptable in college writing?   (p. 640)

Abbreviations are generally not appropriate in college writing except in tables, charts, and works cited lists. Some abbreviations are only acceptable in scientific, technical, or business writing, or only in a particular discipline. If you have any questions about the appropriateness of a particular abbreviation, check a style manual in your field.

? 46a   Abbreviating Titles

Titles before and after proper names are usually abbreviated.

Mr. Homer Simpson   Dr. Mathilde Krim

Henry Kissinger, PhD   St. Jude

Rep. Chaka Fattah   Prof. Elie Weisel

Do not, however, use an abbreviated title without a name.

FAULTY: The <u>Dr.</u> diagnosed hepatitis.

REVISED: The <u>doctor</u> diagnosed hepatitis.

46b   Abbreviating Organization Names and Technical Terms

You may refer to well-known businesses and government, social, and civic organizations by capitalized initials. These abbreviations fall into two categories: those in which the initials are pronounced as separate units (MTV) and **acronyms**, in which the initials are pronounced as a word (NATO).

To save space, you may use accepted abbreviations for complex technical terms that are not well known, but be sure to spell out the full term the first time you mention it, followed by the abbreviation in parentheses.

> Citrus farmers have been using ethylene dibromide (EDB), a chemical pesticide, for more than twenty years. Now, however, EDB has contaminated water supplies.

NOTE: Spell out a term if you think the abbreviation will confuse readers.

46c Abbreviating Dates, Times of Day, Temperatures, and Numbers

50 BC (*BC* follows the date.)	AD 432 (*AD* precedes the date.)
6 a.m.	3:03 p.m.
20°C (Centigrade or Celsius)	180°F (Fahrenheit)

Always capitalize *BC* and *AD*. (The more neutral alternatives *BCE*, for "before the common era," and *CE*, for "common era," are also capitalized.) Use lowercase letters for a.m. and p.m. These abbreviations are used only when they are accompanied by numbers.

FAULTY: We will see you in the <u>a.m.</u>

REVISED: We will see you in the <u>morning</u>.

REVISED: We will see you <u>at 8 a.m.</u>

Avoid the abbreviation *no.* (written either *no.* or *No.*), except in technical writing, and then use it only before a specific number.

FAULTY: The <u>no.</u> on the label of the unidentified substance wasn't clear.

REVISED: The unidentified substance was labeled <u>no. 52</u>.

Abbreviations and Acronyms (U. Colorado)
  http://www.colorado.edu/Publications/styleguide/abbrev.html

46d   Editing Misused Abbreviations

In college writing, abbreviations are not used in the following cases.

(1) Latin Expressions

Abbreviations of the common Latin phrases *i.e.* ("that is"), *e.g.* ("for example"), and *etc.* ("and so forth") are sometimes appropriate for informal writing. In college writing, however, write out an equivalent phrase.

INFORMAL: Poe wrote "The Gold Bug," "The Tell-Tale Heart," etc.

PREFERABLE: Poe wrote "The Gold Bug," "The Tell-Tale Heart," and other stories.

INFORMAL: Other musicians (e.g., Springsteen) have been influenced by Dylan.

PREFERABLE: Other musicians (for example, Springsteen) have been influenced by Dylan.

(2) The Names of Days, Months, or Holidays

FAULTY: Sat., Aug. 9, was the hottest day of the year.

REVISED: Saturday, August 9, was the hottest day of the year.

FAULTY: Only twenty-three shopping days remain until Xmas.

REVISED: Only twenty-three shopping days remain until Christmas.

(3) Units of Measurement

In informal or technical writing, some units of measurement are abbreviated when preceded by a numeral.

The hurricane had winds of 35 mph.

One Honda gets over 50 mpg.

In college writing, however, write out such expressions, and spell out such words as *inches, feet, years, miles, pints, quarts,* and *gallons.*

However, even in informal or technical writing, abbreviations for units of measurement are not used in the absence of a numeral.

FAULTY: The laboratory equipment included pt. and qt. measures and a beaker that could hold a gal. of liquid.

REVISED: The laboratory equipment included pint and quart measures and a beaker that could hold a gallon of liquid.

(4) Names of Streets and Places

Abbreviations of names of streets, cities, states, countries, and geographical regions are common in informal writing and in correspondence. In college writing, however, these words should be spelled out. However, the abbreviation *US* is often acceptable (US Coast Guard), as is *DC* in *Washington, DC.* It is also permissible to use the abbreviation *Mt.* before the name of a mountain (*Mt. Etna*) and St. in a place name (*St. Albans*).

(5) Names of Academic Subjects

Names of academic subjects are not abbreviated in college writing.

FAULTY: <u>Psych.</u>, <u>soc.</u>, and English <u>lit.</u> are required courses.

REVISED: <u>Psychology</u>, <u>sociology</u>, and English <u>literature</u> are required courses.

(6) Parts of Books

Although abbreviations that designate parts of written works (*ch. 3, sec. 7*) may be used in the Works Cited list and in parenthetical documentation, they should not be used elsewhere in a paper.

(7) People's Names

FAULTY: Mr. Harris's five children were named <u>Robt.</u>, <u>Eliz.</u>, <u>Jas.</u>, <u>Chas.</u>, and <u>Wm.</u>

REVISED: Mr. Harris's five children were named <u>Robert</u>, <u>Elizabeth</u>, <u>James</u>, <u>Charles</u>, and <u>William</u>.

(8) Names of Businesses

The abbreviations *Inc., Bros., Co.,* or *Corp.* and the **ampersand** (*&*) are not used unless they are part of a firm's official name.

Company names are written exactly as the firms themselves write them.

Western Union Telegraph Company	AT&T
Santini Bros.	Charles Schwab & Co., Inc.

Exception: <u>MLA documentation format</u> requires abbreviations of publishers' company names—for example, *Harcourt* for *Harcourt College Publishers.*

See Ch. 16

Abbreviations for *company, corporation,* and the like are not used in the absence of a company name.

FAULTY: The <u>corp.</u> merged with a small <u>co.</u> in Pittsburgh.

REVISED: The <u>corporation</u> merged with a small <u>company</u> in Pittsburgh.

The ampersand is used in college writing only in the name of a company that requires it or in citations that follow APA documentation style.

(9) Symbols

The symbols %, =, +, #, and ¢ are acceptable in technical and scientific writing but not in nontechnical college writing.

FAULTY: The price of admission has increased <u>50%</u>.

REVISED: The price of admission has increased <u>fifty percent</u>.

The symbol *$* is acceptable before specific numbers, but not as a substitute for the words *money* or *dollars.*

CORRECT: The book of poetry cost only <u>$4.25</u>.

FAULTY: The value of the <u>$</u> declined steadily in the 1930s.

REVISED: The value of the <u>dollar</u> declined steadily in the 1930s.

EXERCISE

Correct any incorrectly used abbreviations in the following sentences, assuming that all are intended for a college audience. If a sentence is correct, mark it with a *C.*

EXAMPLE: *Romeo & Juliet* is a play by Wm. Shakespeare.

Romeo and Juliet is a play by <u>William</u> Shakespeare.

1. The committee meeting, attended by representatives from Action for Children's Television (ACT) and NOW, Sen. Putnam, & the pres. of ABC, convened at 8 A.M. on Mon. Feb. 24 at the YWCA on Germantown Ave.
2. An econ. prof. was suspended after he encouraged his students to speculate on securities issued by a corp. under investigation by the SEC.

3. Benjamin Spock, the MD who wrote *Baby and Child Care,* was a respected dr. known throughout the USA.

4. The FDA banned the use of Red Dye no. 2 in food in 1976, but other food additives are still in use.

5. The Rev. Dr. Martin Luther King, Jr., leader of the SCLC, led the famous Selma, Ala., march.

6. Wm. Golding, a novelist from the U.K., won the Nobel Prize in lit.

7. The adult education center, financed by a major computer corp., offers courses in basic subjects like introductory bio. and tech. writing as well as teaching programming languages, such as PASCAL.

8. All the bros. in the fraternity agreed to write to Pres. Dexter appealing their disciplinary probation under Ch. 4, Sec. 3, of the IFC constitution.

9. A 4 qt. (i.e., 1 gal.) container is needed to hold the salt solution.

10. According to Prof. Morrison, all those taking the exam should bring two sharpened no. 2 pencils to the St. Joseph's University auditorium on Sat.

CHAPTER 47

NUMBERS

? FREQUENTLY ASKED QUESTIONS

When do I spell out a number, and when do I use a numeral?   (p. 644)

Convention determines when to use a **numeral** (22) and when to spell out a number (twenty-two). Numerals are commonly used in scientific and technical writing and in journalism, but less often in academic or literary writing.

NOTE: The guidelines in this chapter are based on the *MLA Handbook for Writers of Research Papers*. **APA style** style requires that all numbers below ten be spelled out if they do not represent specific measurements and that numbers ten and above be expressed in numerals.

? 47a Spelled-Out Numbers versus Numerals

Unless a number falls into one of the categories listed in **47b,** spell it out if you can do so *in one or two words*.

The Hawaiian alphabet has only <u>twelve</u> letters.

Class size stabilized at <u>twenty-eight</u> students.

The subsidies are expected to total about <u>two million</u> dollars.

Numbers *more than two words* long are expressed in figures.

The dietitian prepared <u>125</u> sample menus.

The developer of the community purchased <u>300,000</u> doorknobs, <u>153,000</u> faucets, and <u>4,000</u> manhole covers.

NOTE: Numerals and spelled-out numbers should generally not be mixed in the same passage. For consistency, then, the number 4,000 in the preceding example is expressed in figures even though it could be written in just two words.

Never begin a sentence with a numeral. If necessary, try to reword the sentence.

FAULTY: 250 students are currently enrolled in World History 106.

REVISED: Current enrollment in World History 106 is 250 students.

47b Conventional Uses of Numerals

(1) Addresses

111 Fifth Avenue, New York, NY 10003

(2) Dates

January 15, 1929   1914–1919

(3) Exact Times

9:16   10 a.m. (or 10:00 a.m.)

Exceptions: Spell out times of day when they are used with *o'clock: eleven o'clock,* not *11 o'clock.* Also, spell out times expressed as round numbers: *They were in bed by ten.*

(4) Exact Sums of Money

$25.11 $6,752.00

NOTE: You may spell out a round sum of money if you use sums infrequently in your paper, provided you can do so in two or three words.

five dollars   two thousand dollars

(5) Divisions of Written Works

Use arabic (not roman) numerals for chapter and volume numbers; acts, scenes, and lines of plays; chapters and verses of the Bible; and line numbers of long poems.

Steve Tripp's "Numbers in Formal English"
   http://www.u-aizu.ac.jp/~tripp/numbers.html

(6) Measurements before an Abbreviation or a Symbol

12″   55 mph

32°   15 cc

(7) Percentages, Decimals, and Fractions

80%   3.14   6¾

NOTE: You may spell out a percentage (eighty percent) if you use percentages infrequently in your paper and if they can be expressed in two or three words.

(8) Ratios, Scores, and Statistics

Children preferred Fun Flakes over Graino by a ratio of 20 to 1.

The Orioles defeated the Phillies 6 to 0.

The median age of the voters was 42; the mean age was 40.

(9) Identification Numbers

Route 66   Track 8   Channel 12

EXERCISE

Revise the use of numbers in these sentences, making sure usage is correct and consistent. If a sentence uses numbers correctly, mark it with a C.

EXAMPLE: The Empire State Building is one hundred and two stories high.

The Empire State Building is <u>102</u> stories high.

1. *1984,* a novel by George Orwell, is set in a totalitarian society.
2. The English placement examination included a 30-minute personal-experience essay, a 45-minute expository essay, and a 150-item objective test of grammar and usage.
3. In a control group of two hundred forty-seven patients, almost three out of four suffered serious adverse reactions to the new drug.
4. Before the Thirteenth Amendment to the Constitution, slaves were counted as ⅗ of a person.
5. The intensive membership drive netted 2,608 new members and additional dues of over 5 thousand dollars.

6. They had only 2 choices: either they could take the yacht at Pier Fourteen, or they could return home to the penthouse at Twenty-seven Harbor View Drive.
7. The atomic number of lithium is three.
8. Approximately 3 hundred thousand schoolchildren in District 6 were given hearing and vision examinations between May third and June 26.
9. The United States was drawn into the war by the Japanese attack on Pearl Harbor on December seventh, 1941.
10. An upper-middle-class family can spend over 250,000 dollars to raise each child up to age 18.

PART 8

WRITING IN THE DISCIPLINES

CHAPTER 48

UNDERSTANDING THE DISCIPLINES

? FREQUENTLY ASKED QUESTIONS

What do my instructors expect from my
papers?   (p. 651)
How formal should my papers be?   (p. 654)
What documentation style should I use?
(p. 655)

All instructors, regardless of academic discipline, have certain expec- **?**
tations when they read a paper. They expect to see standard English, correct grammar and spelling, logical thinking, and clear documentation of
sources. In addition, they expect to see sensible organization, convincing
support, and careful editing. Despite these similarities, however, instructors in various disciplines have different expectations about a paper—for
example, different documentation styles and different specialized vocabularies. To a large extent, then, learning to write in a particular discipline
involves learning the conventions that scholars in that field have agreed
to follow.

48a   Research Sources

Gathering information is basic to all disciplines, but not all disciplines
rely on the same kinds of resources. In the humanities, for example, print
sources—whether found on shelves in the library or accessed from a
database—are central to most studies. Although some historians will
conduct interviews and some literary scholars will collect quantifiable
data, most people who do research in the humanities spend a great
amount of time reading print sources.

Those who work in the social sciences also spend a lot of time examining the literature on a particular topic. But they also rely heavily on observation of behavior, interviews, and surveys, for example. Because of
the kinds of data they generate, social scientists typically use statistical
methodology and record their results in charts, graphs, and tables. Those

who work in the natural sciences (such as biology, chemistry, and physics) and the applied sciences (engineering and computer science, for example) rely almost exclusively on **empirical data**—information obtained through controlled laboratory experiments or from mathematical models. They use the data they collect to formulate theories that explain their observations.

The information you gather from print and electronic resources in the library, in the field, on the Internet, or in the laboratory will help you support the points you make when you write. Whether you want to make a point about the color gray in a work by Herman Melville or about the effect of a particular amino acid on the respiratory system, your intent is the same: to find the support you need to convince readers that what you are saying is reasonable.

The kind of support that is acceptable and persuasive, however, varies from discipline to discipline. Students of literature often use quotations from fiction or poetry to support their statements, whereas historians are likely to refer to original documents, such as court or church records. Social scientists frequently rely on statistics to support their conclusions; those in the natural sciences use the empirical data they derive from controlled experiments.

48b   Writing Assignments

Because each discipline has a different set of concerns, writing assignments vary from course to course. A sociology course, for example, may require a statistical analysis; a literature course may require a literary analysis. Therefore, it is not enough simply to know the material about which you are asked to write. You must also be aware of what the instructor in a particular discipline expects of you. For example, when your art history instructor asks you to write a paper on the Brooklyn Bridge, she does not expect you to write an analysis of Hart Crane's long poem *The Bridge* (a topic suitable for a literature class) nor does she want a detailed discussion of the steel cables used in bridge building (a topic suitable for a materials engineering class). What she might expect is for you to discuss the use of the bridge as an artistic subject—as it is in the paintings of Joseph Stella and the photographs of Alfred Stieglitz, for example.

When you get any assignment, be sure you understand exactly what you are being asked to do; if you are not sure, ask your instructor for clarification. Then, acquaint yourself with the ideas that are of interest to those who publish on your topic. Take the time to look through your textbook and class notes or do some **exploratory research** to get a sense of the theories, concerns, and controversies pertinent to your topic. (See **49a, 50a,** and **51a** for lists of specialized research sources used in each discipline.)

See 11a

48c   Conventions of Style, Format, and Documentation

(1) Style

Specialized Vocabulary   Learning the vocabulary of a discipline is like going to a foreign country and learning a new language. At first, you observe native speakers from a distance. Eventually, as you learn a few words, you begin to communicate—if only slightly. Finally, after you can speak the language well, you become actively involved with those around you and, if you are lucky, participate in the life of the community. Only by learning the specialized vocabulary of a field can you communicate with those who work in it.

When you write a paper for a particular course, you use the specialized vocabulary of those who publish in the discipline. When you write a paper for a literature course, for example, you use the literary terms you hear in class and read in your textbook—*point of view, persona, imagery,* and so on. It makes no sense to use inexact words or colloquial phrases when the discipline offers a vocabulary that will enable you to express concepts accurately and concisely. What other word, for example, would you use to denote *metaphor?*

WRITING IN THE DISCIPLINES

Although technical terms facilitate communication within a discipline, outside that discipline they become **jargon** and do exactly the opposite. Moreover, in many disciplines, scholars are often so narrowly specialized that even those in the same field may have difficulty understanding their colleagues' technical vocabulary. Therefore, when you write for a general audience, some basic definitions may be helpful.

See 29c1

Level of Diction   Within any field, particular assignments call for different **levels of diction**. Regardless of discipline, research papers tend to be formal: they use learned words, are grammatically correct, avoid contractions and colloquialisms, and use third-person pronouns. Proposals—whether they are in the humanities, social sciences, or natural sciences—also are relatively formal.

Other assignments, by their very nature, are less formal than proposals and research papers. For example, because its purpose is to present an individual's personal reactions, a response statement uses subjective language, first person, and active voice ("I see a lot of weaknesses I didn't notice last time"). A lab report is also informal, but because its purpose is to report the observations themselves—not the observer's reactions—it frequently uses objective language and passive voice ("The acid was poured" rather than "I poured the acid"). For the most part, then, it is an assignment's purpose and audience, not its discipline, that determines its level of diction.

(2) Format

Each discipline has certain formatting conventions that govern the way written information is presented on the page. A **format** is an accepted way of displaying material in a document. A format may govern the arrangement of an entire document (such as a lab report, which has certain prescribed sections) or determine whether writers use internal headings in their papers. Formatting conventions also determine how certain kinds of information are presented or displayed *within* a document. For example, social scientists expect statistical data to be

presented in **tables or graphs**. Specific mechanical concerns, such as whether to spell out a number or use numerals, also differ from discipline to discipline.

Professional organizations, such as the Modern Language Association, define the guidelines that govern document formats within their disciplines. Typically, a professional organization will issue or recommend a handbook or **style sheet** that defines the standards for spelling, mechanics, punctuation, and capitalization. This style sheet also gives explicit guidelines for the use and placement of information in diagrams, graphs, tables, and photographs within a paper as well as for typing conventions, such as the placement of page numbers and the arrangement of information on a title page. Because significant differences in format exist between disciplines, you should consult the appropriate style sheet before you begin your paper.

(3) Documentation

Different disciplines use different styles of **documentation**. Four of the most widely used styles are those recommended by the Modern Language Association (MLA), the American Psychological Association (APA), *The Chicago Manual of Style* (CMS), and the Council of Biology Editors (CBE).

See
Chs.
16–17

Instructors in the humanities usually prefer MLA style, which uses parenthetical references within the text to refer to a Works Cited list at the end of the paper, or CMS style, which uses footnotes or endnotes keyed to bibliographic citations at the end of the paper. Instructors in some of the social sciences, such as psychology and education, prefer APA style, which uses parenthetical references that differ from MLA references. Other disciplines—the physical and biological sciences, for example—prefer a number-reference format, such as CBE style, which uses raised numbers or numbers in parentheses in the text that refer to a numbered list of works at the end of the paper.

Because of the lack of uniformity among the disciplines, it is especially important that you consult your instructor to see which documentation style is required. Your instructor may expect you to use a certain style sheet. If this is not the case, however, it is your responsibility to determine which style to use—possibly by looking at an important journal in the field and following its documentation style.

✔ CHECKLIST: DOCUMENTATION

- ✔ Make sure you understand what information must be documented (see **16a**).
- ✔ Do not assume the documentation style you use in one class is appropriate for another class.
- ✔ Use one documentation style consistently throughout the paper.
- ✔ Make sure you have a copy of the appropriate style sheet or journal so that you can consult it as you write.
- ✔ Follow *exactly* the conventions of the style you decide to use.
- ✔ When you proofread the final draft of your paper, make certain that you have documented all information that needs documentation and that you have punctuated all entries correctly.

Writing in the Disciplines

	Disciplines	Research Sources	Assignments
HUMANITIES	Languages Literature Philosophy History Linguistics Religion Art history Music	Library sources (print and electronic) Interviews Observations (museums, concerts) Oral history Internet	Response statement Book review Art, music, dance, or film review Bibliographic essay Annotated bibliography Literary analysis Research paper
SOCIAL SCIENCES	Anthropology Psychology Economics Business Education Sociology Political science Social work Criminal justice	Library sources (print and electronic) Surveys Observation (behavior of groups and individuals) Internet	Experience paper Case study Literature review Proposal Research paper
NATURAL AND APPLIED SCIENCES	*Natural sciences* Biology Chemistry Physics Astronomy Geology Mathematics *Applied sciences* Engineering Computer science Nursing Pharmacy	Library sources (print and electronic) Observations Experiments Surveys Internet	Abstract Literature survey Laboratory report Research paper

	Style and Format	Documentation

HUMANITIES	***Style***
	Specialized vocabulary
	Direct quotations
	
	Format
	Little use of internal headings,
	  visuals, etc.
		English, languages, philosophy:
		  MLA
		History, art: CMS

SOCIAL SCIENCES	***Style***
	Specialized vocabulary, including
	  statistical terminology
	
	Format
	Internal headings
	Use of visuals (graphs, maps,
	  flowcharts, photographs)
	Numerical data (in tabular form)
		APA

NATURAL AND APPLIED SCIENCES	***Style***
	Frequent use of passive voice
	Few direct quotations
	
	Format
	Internal headings
	Use of tables, graphs, and
	  illustrations (exact formats vary)
		Biology: CBE
		Other scientific disciplines use a
		  variety of different
		  documentation styles.

CHAPTER 49

WRITING IN THE HUMANITIES

? FREQUENTLY ASKED QUESTIONS

What research sources should I use in the humanities? (p. 658)
How do I write a response statement? (p. 664)
What does a paper that uses *The Chicago Manual of Style* (CMS) format look like? (p. 675)

The **humanities** include art, film, music, literature, languages, philosophy, and religion. In these disciplines, research often involves analyzing or interpreting a **primary source**—a literary work, a historical document, a musical composition, or a painting or piece of sculpture—or making connections between one work and another. Scholars in humanities disciplines may also cite **secondary sources**—commentaries on primary sources—to support their points or develop new interpretations.

See
10f2

49a Research Sources

Library research is an important part of study in many humanities disciplines. When you begin your research in any subject area, the *Humanities Index* is one general source you can use. This index lists articles from more than two hundred scholarly journals in such areas as history, language, literary criticism, and religion. It is available in print—with entries arranged alphabetically in yearly volumes according to author and subject—and in electronic form.

Many specialized sources are also available to help you with your research.

(1) Print Sources

The following reference sources, many of which are available on CD-ROM or online as well as in print, are used in various humanities disciplines.

Art

Art Index
Artwords: A Glossary of Contemporary Art Theory
Contemporary Artists
The Dictionary of Art
Dictionary of Women Artists
Encyclopedia of Aesthetics
Encyclopedia of Comparative Iconography: Themes Depicted in Works of Art
Encyclopedia of World Art
Index to Art Reproductions in Books
New Dictionary of Modern Sculpture
Oxford Companion to Art
Praeger Encyclopedia of Art
Thames and Hudson Dictionary of Art and Artists

Drama

Cambridge Guide to Theatre
The Crown Guide to the World's Great Plays from Ancient Greece to Rome
A Guide to Critical Reviews
International Dictionary of Theatre
McGraw-Hill Encyclopedia of World Drama
Modern World Drama: An Encyclopedia
New York Times Theatre Reviews
Oxford Companion to the Theatre
The Performing Arts: A Guide to the Reference Literature
Play Index
World Encyclopedia of Contemporary Theatre

Film

Film Comment
The Film Encyclopedia
Film Review Annual
Guide to Critical Reviews
International Dictionary of Film and Filmmakers
International Index to Film Periodicals
International Index to Multimedia Information
Magill's Survey of Cinema
The Motion Picture Guide
The Movie List Book: A Reference Guide to Film Themes, Settings, and Series

New York Times Film Reviews
Oxford History of World Cinema
Variety Film Reviews

History
America: History and Life
Cambridge Ancient History
Cambridge Medieval History
CRIS (Combined Retrospective Index to Journals in History)
A Dictionary of American History
Encyclopedia of Africa South of the Sahara
Encyclopedia of Latin American History and Culture
Encyclopedia of the Renaissance
Encyclopedia of the Vietnam War
Encyclopedia of Urban America: The Cities and Suburbs
Growing Up in America
Guide to Historical Literature (AHA)
Handbook to Life in Ancient Greece
Harvard Guide to American History
Historical Abstracts
History of the Internet: A Chronology
Medieval England: An Encyclopedia
New Cambridge Modern History

Language and Literature
Annual Bibliography of English Language and Literature
Biography Index
Book Review Digest
Book Review Index
Cassell's Encyclopedia of World Literature
Children's Literature Review
Contemporary Authors
Current Biography
Dictionary of Languages: The Definitive Reference to More Than 400 Languages
Dictionary of Literary Biography
Dictionary of Modern American Usage
Encyclopedia of Folklore and Literature
Encyclopedia of Latin American Literature
Encyclopedia of the Essay
Encyclopedia of the Novel

Essay and General Literature Index
European Writers
Language and Language Behavior Abstracts (LLBA)
Literary History of the United States (LHUS)
MLA International Bibliography
Native American Literatures
New Princeton Encyclopedia of Poetry and Poetics
Oxford Companion to American Literature
Oxford Companion to Classical Literature
Oxford Companion to English Literature
Oxford English Dictionary
Reference Guide to Short Fiction
Salem Press Critical Surveys of Poetry, Fiction, Long Fiction, and Drama
Twentieth Century Authors
World Literature Criticism

Music

Baker's Biographical Dictionary of 20th Century Classical Musicians
The Garland Encyclopedia of World Music
International Dictionary of Black Composers
Music Article Guide
Music Index
Music Reference and Research Materials
New Grove Dictionary of Music and Musicians
New Harvard Dictionary of Music
New Oxford Companion to Music
Popular Musicians

Philosophy

The Cambridge Dictionary of Philosophy
The Concise Encyclopedia of Western Philosophy and Philosophers
Dictionary of the History of Ideas
Encyclopedia of Philosophy
Masterpieces of World Philosophy in Summary Form
Modern Philosophy: An Introduction and Survey
Oxford Companion to Philosophy
Philosopher's Index
The Philosopher's Index: An International Index to Philosophical Periodicals and Books
Routledge Encyclopedia of Philosophy

Religion
> *The Cambridge Companion to the Bible*
> *Encyclopedia of Christianity*
> *Encyclopedia of Ethics*
> *Encyclopedia of Islam*
> *Encyclopedia of Judaica*
> *Encyclopedia of Religion*
> *Encyclopedia of Women and World Religion*
> *HarperCollins Dictionary of Religion*
> *The Hutchinson Encyclopedia of Living Faiths*
> *New Catholic Encyclopedia*
> *Oxford Dictionary of Religion*
> *Oxford Dictionary of the Christian Church*
> *Religion Index*

(2) Databases for Computer Searches

Some of the most helpful databases for humanities disciplines include *Art Index, MLA Bibliography, Religion Index, Philosopher's Index, Music Literature International (RRM), Essay and General Literature Index, Artbibliographies Modern, Historical Abstracts,* the *LLBA Index, Dissertation Abstracts, Arts and Humanities Search,* and *OnLine.* Ask your librarian about the availability of these and other databases.

(3) Internet Sites

Art History
> Art History Network
> http://www.arthistory.net

> Art History Resources on the Web
> http://witcombe.sbc.edu/ARTHLinks.html

> Voice of the Shuttle Art and Art History Page
> http://vos.ucsb.edu/shuttle/art.html

Drama
> The English Server Drama Collection
> http://www.eserver.org/drama/default.html

> Inter-Play
> http://www.portals.org/interplay/

The WWW Virtual Library: Theatre and Drama
http://www.vl-theatre.com

Film

Academic Film Studies Gateway
http://www.academicinfo.net/film.html

The Internet Movie Database
http://us.imdb.com

Movie Review Query Engine
http://www.mrqe.com

History

Horus' Web Links to History Resources
http://www.ucr.edu/h-gig/horuslinks.html

Hyper History Online
http://www.hyperhistory.com/online_n2/History_n2/a.html

Internet History Sourcebooks Project
http://www.fordham.edu/halsall/

Literature and Languages

iLoveLanguages
http://www.ilovelanguages.com/

The On-Line Books Page
http://digital.library. upenn.edu/books/

Online Literary Criticism Collection
http://www.ipl.org/ref/

VCU Trail Guide to International Sites and Language Resources
http://www.fln.vcu.edu/

Music

The Classical Music Pages
http://w3.rz-berlin.mpg.de/cmp/classmus.html

Music Libraries and Music Archives
http://www.siba.fi/Kulttuuripalvelut/music.html

Worldwide Internet Music Resources
http://www.music.indiana.edu/music_resources/

Philosophy

Guide to Philosophy on the Internet
http://www.earlham.edu/~peters/philinks.htm

Philosophy Pages from Garth Kemerling
http://www.philosophypages.com

Stanford Encyclopedia of Philosophy
http://plato.stanford.edu

Religion

Academic Info Religion Gateway
http://www.academicinfo.net/religindex.html

Religion-Online.org
http://www.religion-online.org

Rutgers University Virtual Religion Index
http://religion.rutgers.edu/vri/america.html

(4) Other Sources of Information

Research in the humanities is not limited to print and electronic sources. For example, historians may do interviews and archival work or consult records collected in town halls, churches, or courthouses; art historians visit museums and galleries; and music scholars attend concerts.

In addition, nonprint sources, such as **interviews** and **surveys**, can be important resources for a paper in any humanities discipline.

49b Assignments in the Humanities

(1) The Response Statement

In some disciplines, particularly literature, you may write a **response statement,** an informal reaction to a literary work, a painting, a film, a dance performance, or a concert. Such an assignment requires you to write a first-person account of your feelings and to explore the factors that influenced your reactions. The following response statement was written in a journal kept for an Introduction to Literature course.

Sample Response Statement

   Rereading <u>The Catcher in the Rye</u> after two years, I see a lot of weaknesses I didn't notice last time. The style is too cute and too repetitive, and it calls attention to itself. Salinger has Holden Caulfield say things like "I mean" and "if you know what I mean" too many times, and he seems to use bad language for no particular reason. Also, I don't like Holden as much as I did the first time I read the book. Before, I saw him as isolated and misunderstood, a pathetic character who could have been happy if only he had stayed a child forever. Now, he gets on my nerves. I keep thinking he could do something to help himself if he didn't have to blame everything on the "phonies." All this probably says more about how I've changed in two years than about how good or bad the book is.

(2) The Book Review

  A **book review,** which may be assigned in any humanities discipline, asks you to **respond critically** to a book, judging it according to a particular set of criteria. (Reviews of performances or nonprint works are similar to book reviews.) The book review that follows was written for a cross-disciplinary composition class.

See
7c

Excerpt from a Book Review

   In his thought-provoking book <u>Chaos: Making a New Science</u>, James Gleick presents recent events that have shaped chaos theory and introduces the individuals responsible for these events. He begins with the starting point of the new science, Edward Lorenz's Butterfly Effect, and ends with a comprehensive discussion of the newest discoveries and the future of chaos theory. Most important, he explains the equations, theories, and concepts that are the heart of chaos theory. One example of how this new science is applied is Mitchell Feigenbaum's theory of universality. Using only a handheld calculator, Feigenbaum proved that simple equations from a simple system can be applied to a totally unrelated system to produce a complicated solution. Although Feigenbaum's theory was at first greeted with skepticism, it soon became the basis for finding order in otherwise unrelated systems. Gleick's clear analysis of this and other theories makes his explanation of chaos theory appropriate for readers with little scientific background as well as for more knowledgeable readers.

(3) The Bibliographic Essay

A **bibliographic essay** surveys research in a particular field and assesses the usefulness of various sources. Several publications include annual bibliographic essays to inform scholars of recent developments in a particular humanities discipline. Students in advanced literature or history classes may also be asked to write this type of essay. The following excerpt, written by a student in an American literature class, comes from a bibliographic essay on Mark Twain's novel *Pudd'nhead Wilson*.

Excerpt from a Bibliographic Essay

Most early critics analyze the novel in terms of racial issues and the doctrine of environmental determinism. Langston Hughes, for instance, writes that "the basic theme [of Pudd'nhead Wilson] is slavery [. . .] and its main thread concerns the absurdity of man-made differentials, whether of caste or 'race'" (viii). James M. Cox also focuses on the racial issue, specifically on miscegenation, but in a more symbolic way than Hughes does. Cox's analysis of the novel is very similar to Fiedler's. Like Fiedler, Cox believes that the novel deals with American guilt; it is a "final unmasking of the heart of darkness beneath the American dream" (361). Tom serves as the white man's nemesis, spawned by the guilt of miscegenation, a violation of the black race. According to Cox, he is "the instrument of an avenging destiny which has overtaken Dawson's Landing" (353).

(4) The Annotated Bibliography

Each entry in an **annotated bibliography** includes full source information and a *brief* summary of the source's main points or arguments. The following example is an entry from a student's annotated bibliography of *Pudd'nhead Wilson*.

Excerpt from an Annotated Bibliography

Chellis, Barbara A. "Those Extraordinary Twins: Negroes and Whites." American Quarterly 21 (1969): 100-12. Chellis sees Pudd'nhead Wilson as an exposé of "the fiction of law and custom" that has justified distinctions between blacks and whites. Twain develops his theme through his characterizations of Roxy, Tom, and Chambers. According to Chellis, Roxy's "crime"—condemning the real Tom to slavery—stems not from the influence of her race but from her white values. Tom is spoiled and selfish—the kind of person produced by white society's values. The invalidity of race distinctions is further pointed out through the servility of Chambers, who is white. Thus, black "servility" is ultimately seen to be nothing more than the result of training.

(5) The Literary Analysis

Students in literature classes frequently analyze poems, plays, short stories, or novels. For a detailed discussion of how to write a **literary analysis,** as well as three sample papers—illustrating an analysis of a short story, a poem, and a one-act play—see Chapter **53**. See **49d1** for an example of a literary analysis that uses secondary source material.

49c Conventions of Style, Format, and Documentation

(1) Style and Format

Each humanities discipline has its own specialized vocabulary, and you should use the terms used in the field; be careful, however, not to overuse technical terminology. You can use the first person (*I*) when you are expressing your own reactions and convictions—for example, in a response statement. In other situations, use the third person (*he, she,* and so on).

Although papers in the humanities do not usually include abstracts, internal headings, tables, or graphs, this situation is changing. Be sure you know what your instructor expects.

NOTE: When you write papers about **literature**, follow the special conventions of literary analysis.

(2) Documentation

Literature and modern and classical language scholars use **MLA format**; history scholars use *The Chicago Manual of Style*.

49d Sample Humanities Research Papers

(1) Modern Language Association (MLA) Format: A Literary Analysis

The following literary analysis, "Assertive Men and Passive Women: A Comparison of Adrienne Rich's 'Aunt Jennifer's Tigers' and 'Mathilde in Normandy,'" focuses on two of Adrienne Rich's poems. It uses MLA documentation style and cites several critical articles. Because the instructor did not require a separate title page, the student included her name, her instructor's name, the course number, and the date on the first page of her paper. For a detailed discussion of the process of writing a research paper in the humanities, see Chapter **10**.

Cathy Thomason

Composition 102

Dr. Alvarez-Goldstein

9 May 2001

Assertive Men and Passive Women: A Comparison

of Adrienne Rich's "Aunt Jennifer's Tigers" and

"Mathilde in Normandy"

Adrienne Rich began her poetic career in the 1950s as

an undergraduate at Radcliffe College. The product of a

conservative Southern family, Rich was greatly influenced by

her father, who encouraged the young poet to seek higher

standards for her work. However, her early work shows

evidence of Rich's future struggle with this upbringing.

Although she used styles and subjects that gained approval

from both her father and the almost all-male literary world,

some of her early works suggest an inner struggle with the

status quo of male dominance (Bennett 178). "Aunt Jennifer's

Tigers" and "Mathilde in Normandy" clearly reflect this

struggle.

Both "Aunt Jennifer's Tigers" and "Mathilde in

Normandy" tell the story of women living in the shadow of

men's accomplishments. The central figures of the two poems

display their creativity and intelligence through a traditional

female occupation, embroidery. Although the poems are set in

different time periods ("Mathilde in Normandy" in the Middle

Margin annotations:

Student's name and page number are on every page

Center title

Double-space

Background

Thesis statement

Paragraph summarizes similarities between two poems

Thomason 2

Ages and "Aunt Jennifer's Tigers" in the 1950s), their focus is the same: both are about women who recognize their subordinate positions but are powerless to change their situations. The difference between the two, however, lies in the fact that Mathilde does not suffer the inner conflict that Aunt Jennifer does.

"Aunt Jennifer's Tigers" is the story of a woman trapped in a conventional and apparently boring marriage. Her outlet is her needlework; through her embroidery, she creates a fantasy world of tigers as an escape from her real life. In 1972, in her essay "When We Dead Awaken," Rich said, "In writing this poem, composed and apparently cool as it is, I thought I was creating a portrait of an imaginary woman" (469). What she later discovered was that Aunt Jennifer was probably typical of many married women in the 1950s. These women, Rich observed, "didn't talk to each other much in the fifties—not about their secret emptiness, their frustrations [. . .]" (470).

    Standing in opposition to the timid and frustrated Aunt Jennifer are the tigers in the first stanza:

> Aunt Jennifer's tigers prance across a screen,
> Bright topaz denizens of a world of green.
> They do not fear the men beneath the tree;
> They pace in sleek chivalric certainty. (1-4)

Unlike Aunt Jennifer, the tigers move with confidence and "chivalric certainty." They are not dominated by men, as Aunt

[Margin annotations:]

Running acknowledgement introduces quotation

Parenthetical documentation

Long quotation indented 10 spaces (1") from left-hand margin; no quotation marks necessary

Parenthetical documentation identifies quoted lines

Jennifer is. According to Claire Keyes, this stanza contains the dominant voice (24). Although Aunt Jennifer is not assertive or forceful, her creations—the tigers—are. In other words, Aunt Jennifer's work is more interesting than she is. Even so, the tigers are a part of Aunt Jennifer's imagination, and they show there is more to Aunt Jennifer than her existence as a housewife would suggest.

"Mathilde in Normandy" is based on the folktale that William the Conqueror's wife, Queen Mathilde, created the Bordeaux Tapestry to tell the story of the Norman invasion of England (Keyes 24). The men in this poem are as powerful as the men who dominate Aunt Jennifer, showing their masculinity in their attack on another country. Although Rich acknowledges Mathilde's position as a woman who may never see her husband again—"Say what you will, anxiety there too / Played havoc with the skein" (21-22)—Mathilde, unlike Aunt Jennifer, has no problem with the notion that women should stay home. According to the speaker, "Yours was a time when women sat at home" (17). Therefore, Mathilde does not suffer inner turmoil about her role in life as a subordinate wife.

Mathilde is separated from her husband's world because she is female and considered unable to fight, to compete in a male world. Aunt Jennifer, however, is held back from the male world by a different barrier:

Short quotation run in with text; slash separates two lines of poetry

Aunt Jennifer's fingers fluttering through her wool

Find even the ivory needle hard to pull.

The massive weight of Uncle's wedding band

Sits heavily upon Aunt Jennifer's hand. (5-8)

Her marriage is not a happy one; her wedding band holds her

down (Keyes 23). Thus, in accepting her role as housewife,

Aunt Jennifer is denied a satisfying existence. She is reduced

to maintaining a household for a husband who dominates all

aspects of her life. Even Aunt Jennifer's pursuit of art is made

difficult by her marriage. The "weight" of her wedding band

makes it difficult to embroider.

For Mathilde, life is objectionable only because she fears

that her husband and the men of the kingdom will not return.

She identifies with her husband's cause and accepts the fact

that the life men lead is dangerous. Unlike Mathilde, Aunt

Jennifer sees her marriage as imprisonment; she will be free

only when she dies:

When Aunt is dead, her terrified hands will lie

Still ringed with the ordeals she was mastered by.

The tigers in the panel that she made

Will go on prancing, proud and unafraid. (9-12)

Aunt Jennifer's hands are "terrified," overwhelmed by

the power that her husband, and society, have over her. Aunt

Jennifer, who is "mastered" by her situation, stands in

opposition to the tigers, who flaunt their independence,

Thomason 5

forever "prancing, proud and unafraid." Mathilde's experience
with male power is also terrifying. She is in the vulnerable
position of being a queen whose husband and court are away
at war. If her husband does not return, she can be subjugated
by another man, one wishing to take over the kingdom.

Conclusion   Both "Aunt Jennifer's Tigers" and "Mathilde in
Normandy" present stories of women bound to men.
Although both poems suggest that conventional relationships
between men and women are unsatisfactory, Mathilde does
not struggle against her role as Aunt Jennifer does. As Claire
Keyes points out, although these poems are "well mannered
and feminine on the surface," they "speak differently in their
muted stories" (28). Although only "Aunt Jennifer's Tigers"
openly criticizes the status quo, both poems reflect the inner
conflicts of women and express their buried desires subtly.

Thomason 6

Works Cited ← Center
← Double-
space

Bennett, Paula. "Dutiful Daughter." <u>My Life a Loaded Gun:</u>

Indent →
5 spaces
(or ½")
<u>Female Creativity and Feminist Politics</u>. Boston: Beacon,

1986. 171-76.

Keyes, Claire. <u>The Aesthetics of Power: The Story of Adrienne</u>

<u>Rich</u>. Athens: U of Georgia P, 1986.

Rich, Adrienne. "Aunt Jennifer's Tigers." <u>Poems: Selected and</u>

<u>New</u>. New York: Norton, 1974. 81.

---. "Mathilde in Normandy." <u>Poems: Selected and New</u>. New

York: Norton, 1974. 94-95.

Three →
unspaced
hyphens used
instead of
repeating
author's name
---. "When We Dead Awaken." <u>Ways of Reading: An</u>

<u>Anthology for Writers</u>. Ed. David Bartholomae and

Anthony Petrowsky. Boston: Bedford, 1993. 461-76.

(2) *The Chicago Manual of Style* (CMS) Format: Excerpts from a History Research Paper

The following pages are excerpted from a history research paper, "Native Americans and the Reservation System," which uses Chicago Style. Because the instructor did not require a separate title page, the student included the necessary identifying information in a heading on the first page of her paper.

1   Page number on every page

Angela M. Womack

American History 301

3 December 2000

Double-space ⟶ Native Americans and the Reservation System

It is July 7th, and ten thousand Navajo Indians make ready to leave land in Arizona that they have called home for generations. This land has been assigned to the Hopi tribe by the U.S. government to settle a boundary dispute between the two tribes.[1] Ella Bedonie, a member of the Navajo tribe, says, "The Navajo and the Hopi people have no dispute. It's the government that's doing this to us. I think the Hopis may have the land for a while, but then the government . . . will step in."[2] The Hopis are receiving 250,000 acres to compensate them for the 900,000 acres they will lose in this land deal; however, the groundwater on this land is suspect because of possible contamination by a uranium mine upstream. To mitigate this situation, the government has sweetened the deal with incentives of livestock.[3]

Superscripts (raised numerals) refer to endnotes listed on "Notes" page

2

This was the fate many Native Americans faced as western expansion swept across the North American continent. Now consider that the incident mentioned occurred not on July 7, 1886, but on July 7, 1986. Indian relations with the U.S. government are as problematic today as ever before, for the federal government's administration of the reservation

Thesis statement

system both promotes and restricts the development of the Native American culture.

A reservation is an area of land reserved for Indian use. There are approximately 260 reservations in the United States at present.[4] The term *reservation* can be traced back to the time when land was "reserved" for Indian use in treaties between whites and Native Americans. Figures from 1978

10

Notes

1. Trebbe Johnson, "Indian Land, White Greed," *Nation,* 4 July 1987, 15.

2. Johnson, 17.

3. Johnson, 16.

4. Ted Williams, "On the Reservation: America's Apartheid," *National Review,* 8 May 1987, 28.

Sources listed in order in which they appear in paper. Second and subsequent references to sources include only author's last name and page number.

11

Bibliography ← Center
← Double-
space

"Adrift in Their Own Land." *Time,* 6 July 1987, 89.

Entries are
listed
alphabetically
according to
author's last
name

Arrandale, Tom. "American Indian Economic Development."

Editorial Research Reports, 17 Feb. 1984, 127–142.

Battise, Carol. Personal interview, 25 Sept. 1987.

Cook, J. "Help Wanted—Work, Not Handouts." *Forbes,* 4

May 1987, 68–71.

Horswell, Cindy. "Alabama-Coushattas See Hope in U.S.

Guardianship." *Houston Chronicle,* 26 May 1987, 11.

First line of
each entry is
flush with left-
hand margin;
subsequent
lines indented
3 spaces

Johnson, Trebbe. "Indian Land, White Greed." *Nation,* 4 July

1987, 15–18.

Martin, Howard N. "Alabama-Coushatta Indians of Texas:

Alabama-Coushatta Historical Highlights." Brochure,

Alabama-Coushatta Indian Reservation: Livingston, Tex., n.d.

Article has no
listed author;
alphabetized
according to
first significant
word of title

"A New Brand of Tribal Tycoons." *Time,* 16 March 1987, 56.

Philp, K. R. "Dillon S. Myer and the Advent of Termination:

1950–1953." *Western Historical Quarterly* 3 (January

1988): 37–59.

U.S. Bureau of Indian Affairs. "Information About . . . The Indian

People." Washington, D.C.: GPO, 1981. Mimeographed.

Williams, Ted. "On the Reservation: America's Apartheid."

National Review, 8 May 1987, 28–30.

Young, J., and T. Williams. *American Realities: Historical*

Realities from the First Settlements to the Civil War. Boston:

Little, Brown, 1981.

CHAPTER 50

WRITING IN THE SOCIAL SCIENCES

The **social sciences** include anthropology, business, criminal justice, economics, education, political science, psychology, social work, and sociology. When you approach an assignment in the social sciences, your purpose is often to study the behavior of individuals or groups. You may be seeking to understand causes; predict results; define a policy, habit, or trend; or analyze a problem. Before you can approach a problem in the social sciences, you must develop a **hypothesis,** an educated guess about what you believe your research will suggest. Then, you can gather the data that will either prove or disprove that hypothesis. Data may be quantitative or qualitative. **Quantitative data** are numerical—the "countable" results of surveys and polls. **Qualitative data** are less exact and more descriptive—the results of interviews or observations, for example.

❷ 50a   Research Sources

Although library research is an important component of research in the social sciences, researchers also engage in field research. In the library, social scientists consult print and electronic versions of compilations of statistics, government documents, and newspaper articles, in addition to scholarly books and articles. Outside the library, social scientists conduct interviews and surveys and observe individuals and groups. Because so much of their data are quantitative, social scientists must know how to analyze statistics and how to read and interpret tables.

(1) Print Sources

The following reference sources, many of which are available on CD-ROM or online as well as in print, are useful in a variety of social science disciplines.

African American Encyclopedia
American Statistics Index
Bibliografía Chicana: A Guide to Information Sources
CQ Researcher
Dictionary of Mexican American History
Encyclopedia of Black America
Handbook of North American Indians
Harvard Encyclopedia of American Ethnic Groups
Human Resources Abstracts
Index to International Statistics
International Bibliography of the Social Sciences
International Encyclopedia of the Social Sciences
Population Index
Public Affairs Information Service (PAIS)
Reference Encyclopedia of the American Indian
Reference Library of Black America
Social Sciences Citation Index
Social Sciences Index
Statistical Reference Index (SRI)
Women's Studies: A Guide to Information Sources

Anthropology
Abstracts in Anthropology
Anthropological Literature
Companion Encyclopedia of Anthropology: Humanity, Culture and Social Life
Cultural Anthropology: A Guide to Reference and Information Sources
Dictionary of Anthropology
Encyclopedia of Cultural Anthropology
Encyclopedia of World Cultures
International Bibliography of Social and Cultural Anthropology
Worldmark Encyclopedia of Cultures and Daily Life

Business and Economics
ABI Inform
Accounting and Tax Index

Business Information Sources
Business Periodicals Index
Dictionary of Economics
The Encyclopedia of Banking and Finance
The Encyclopedia of Management
Handbook of North American Industry: NAFTA and the Economies of Its Members
Handbook of U.S. Labor Statistics
International Encyclopedia of the Stock Market
Journal of Economic Literature
The McGraw-Hill Dictionary of Modern Economics
Personnel Management Abstracts
Rand McNally Commercial Atlas and Marketing Guide
Wall Street Journal Index

Criminal Justice
American Justice
Criminal Justice Abstracts
Criminal Justice Periodical Index
Criminal Justice Research in Libraries and on the Internet
Criminology, Penology, and Police Science Abstracts
Dictionary of Crime
Encyclopedia of American Prisons
Encyclopedia of Crime and Justice
Encyclopedia of World Crime
Index to Legal Periodicals

Education
Critical Dictionary of Educational Concepts
Current Index to Journals in Education
Dictionary of Education
Education Index
Encyclopedia of American Education
Encyclopedia of Educational Research
Facts on File
Historical Dictionary of Women's Education in the United States
Resources in Education
Review of Research in Education
Yearbook of the National Society for the Study of Education

Political Science
ABC Political Science
American Political Dictionary
CIS Index (Congressional Information Service)
CRIS: The Combined Retrospective Index to Journals in Political Science
Dictionary of Modern Politics
Dictionary of Political Thought
Encyclopedia of Constitutional Amendments, Proposed Amendments and Amending
Encyclopedia of Modern World Politics
Encyclopedia of the Third World
Encyclopedia of the United Nations and International Agreements
Encyclopedia of U.S. Foreign Relations
Europa World Year Book
Facts about the Congress
Facts about the Supreme Court
Foreign Affairs Bibliography
International Encyclopedia of Public Policy and Administration
International Political Science Abstracts
ISLA (Information Services on Latin America)
Worldmark Encyclopedia of the Nations

Psychology
Biographical Dictionary of Psychology
The Blackwell Dictionary of Cognitive Psychology
The Companion Encyclopedia of Psychology
Contemporary Psychology
Encyclopedia of Human Behavior
Encyclopedia of Mental Health
Encyclopedia of Psychology
International Encyclopedia of Psychiatry, Psychology, Psychoanalysis and Neurology
Psychological Abstracts
Psychology Basics

Sociology and Social Work
Critical Dictionary of Sociology
Encyclopedia of Social Work
Encyclopedia of Sociology
Family Studies Abstracts

Handbook of Sociology
International Handbook of Contemporary Developments in Sociology
Poverty and Human Resources Abstracts
Sage Encyclopedia of Social Work
Social Work Research and Abstracts
Sociological Abstracts
Statistical Handbook on Poverty in the Developing World
Survey of Social Science

Government Documents   Government documents are important resources for social scientists because they contain complete and up-to-
date facts and figures on a wide variety of subjects.

Government documents can be located through the *Monthly Catalog,*
which contains the list of documents (in print, microfiche, and electronic formats) published each month. Other useful indexes include *The
Congressional Information Service Index, The American Statistics Index,*
and *The Index to U.S. Government Periodicals.*

Newspaper Articles   Newspaper articles are particularly good
sources for researching subjects in political science, economics, and
business. For information from newspapers from across the country, a
useful source is *Newsbank,* which provides subject headings under the
appropriate government agencies. For instance, articles on child abuse
are likely to be listed under "Health and Human Services." Another useful source of information from newspapers is *InfoTrac's National Newspaper Index.*

(2) Databases for Computer Searches

Some of the more widely used databases for social science disci-
plines are *Cendata, Business Index ASAP, Social Sciences Index,
PsycINFO, ERIC, Social Scisearch, Sociological Abstracts, Information
Science Abstracts, PAIS International, Population Bibliography, Economic
Literature Index, ABI/INFORM, Legal Resource Index, Management
Contents, Trade & Industry Index, PTSF + S Indexes,* and *Facts on File.*
Check with your librarian about the availability of these and other
databases in your library.

Lexis/Nexis is a powerful database that enables you not only to survey
thousands of newspapers from across the country but also to view and
reprint the articles. *Lexis/Nexis* also has a special section that contains articles focusing on legal matters and tax issues.

(3) Internet Sites

Anthropology

Anthropology Resources on the Internet
http://home.worldnet.fr/~clist/Anthro/

Anthropology Resources on the Internet
http://www.aaanet.org/resinet.htm

A Guide to Internet Resources in Anthropology
http://faculty.plattsburgh.edu/richard.robbins/legacy/anth_on_www.html

Business and Economics

Business and Economics Numeric Data
http://www.mnsfld.edu/depts/lib/ecostats.html

Fed in Print: An Index to Federal Reserve Economic Research
http://www.frbsf.org/publications/fedinprint/index.html

The Internet Public Library: Business and Economics Reference
http://www.ipl.org/ref/RR/static/bus00.00.00.html

The Scout Report
http://scout.cs.wisc.edu/report/bus-econ/current/

Criminal Justice

Bureau of Justice Statistics
Sourcebook of Criminal Justice Statistics Online
http://www.albany.edu/sourcebook/

FSU School Criminology Criminal Justice Links
http://www.criminology.fsu.edu/cj.html

Links to Other Criminal Justice Sites
http://astro.temple.edu/~rkane/cjlinks.html

Education

Education World
http://www.education-world.com/

US Department of Education
http://www.ed.gov.

Yahoo Education: Theory and Methods
http://dir.yahoo.com/education/theory_and_methods/

Political Science
Governments on the WWW
http://www.gksoft.com/govt/en/

Political Resources on the Net
http://www.politicalresources.net

Political Science Research Sources
http://www.mbc.edu/academic/disciplines/polsci/research.html

Psychology
Dr. Michael Fenichel's Current Topics in Psychology
http://www.fenichel.com/Current.shtml

Psych Central
http://www.grohol.com/resources/

PsychCrawler
http://www.psychcrawler.com

Sociology and Social Work
Social Work and Social Services Web Sites
http://gwbweb.wustl.edu/websites.html

Social Work Search.com
http://www.socialworksearch.com

Sociology Weblinks
http://www.usi.edu/libarts/socio/sd_wblnk.htm

Western Connecticut State University List: Sociology Internet Resource
http://www.wcsu.ctstateu.edu/socialsci/socres.html

(4) Other Sources of Information

Interviews, surveys, and observations of the behavior of various groups and individuals are important nonlibrary sources for social science research. Assignments may ask you to use your classmates as subjects for surveys or interviews. For example, in a political science class, your instructor may ask you to interview a sample of college students and classify them as conservative, liberal, or moderate. You may be asked to poll each group to find out college students' attitudes on such issues as the death penalty, affirmative action, or the problems of the homeless. If you were writing a paper on educational programs for the mentally gifted, in addition to library research you might observe two classes—one of gifted students and one of average students. You might also interview students, teachers, or parents. Similarly, research in psychology and social work may rely on your observations of clients and their families.

50b Assignments in the Social Sciences

(1) The Experience Paper

Instructors in the social sciences often ask students to do hands-on **field research** outside the library; one typical assignment is the **experience paper,** in which students record their observations and reactions to a field trip or site visit. For example, students in an education class might write up their observations of a class of hearing-impaired students, criminal justice students might record their reactions to a juvenile detention facility, business majors might write about their impressions of how a particular small business operates, and students in a psychology class could write an experience paper about a visit to a state-run psychiatric facility.

See 11d

The following excerpt, written by a student in a sociology of religion class, describes visits to two different churches.

Excerpt from an Experience Paper

The Pentecostal church service I observed was full of self-expression, movement, and emotion. People sang and praised the Lord in loud voices. In an atmosphere similar to that of a revival, people spontaneously expressed their joy and their reactions to the sermon. Each word the preacher spoke elicited responses like "Praise the Lord," "Hallelujah," "Thank the Lord," and "Amen." Rather than focusing on religious doctrine, the sermon focused on the problems of everyday life. The Presbyterian service I observed was very different. Compared to the Pentecostal service it seemed structured and traditional. The sanctuary was quiet; organ music was the only sound. Worshippers did not shout or clap. They prayed in low voices and sometimes engaged in silent prayers; even their hymns were restrained and solemn. Finally, the sermon was less pragmatic than the Pentecostal sermon; it focused on theological doctrine and only tangentially discussed the doctrine's relevance to everyday life.

❓ (2) The Case Study

The **case study** is important in psychology, sociology, anthropology, and political science, where it can examine an individual case, the dynamics of a group, or the operations of a political organization. Case studies are usually informative rather than persuasive, describing a problem and suggesting solutions or treatments. They generally include the following components: the statement of the problem, the background of the problem, the observations of the behavior of the individual or group being studied, the conclusions, and the suggestions for improvement or future recommendations.

Different disciplines use case studies in different ways. In political science, case studies can examine foreign policy negotiations or analyze such issues as "Should government control the media?" In psychology, social work, and educational psychology or counseling, the case study typically focuses on an individual and his or her interaction with peers or with agency professionals. Such a case study usually describes behavior and outlines the steps that should be taken to solve the problem that the caseworker or researcher observes.

Excerpt from a Case Study (Social Work)

Mona Freeman, a 14-year-old girl, was brought to the Denver Children's Residential Treatment Center by her 70-year-old, devoutly religious adoptive mother. Both were personable, verbal, and neatly groomed. The presenting problem was seen differently by the two clients. Mrs. Freeman described Mona's "several years of behavior problems," including "lying, stealing, and being boy crazy." Mona viewed herself as a "disappointment" and wanted "time to think." She had been expelled from the local Seventh-day Adventist School for being truant and defiant several months earlier and had been attending public school. The examining psychiatrist diagnosed a conduct disorder but saw no intellectual, physical, or emotional disabilities. He predicted that Mona probably would not be able to continue to live in "such an extreme disciplinary environment" as the home of Mrs. Freeman because she had lived from age seven until twelve with her natural father in Boston, Massachusetts—a situation that was described as a "kidnapping" by Mrs. Freeman. The psychiatrist mentioned some "depression" and attributed it to Mona's inability to fit into her current environment and to the loss of her life with her father in Boston.

(3) The Literature Review

The **literature review** (similar in purpose and format to the **bibliographic essay** assigned in the humanities) is often part of the background section of a social science research paper. By commenting on recent scholarship on a particular topic, students demonstrate knowledge of a topic as well as an understanding of different critical approaches to that topic. The following excerpt, written for an introductory psychology class, is from a literature review on depression among college students.

See 49b3

Excerpt from a Literature Review

Negative events and outlook are not the only causes of depression among college students (Brown & Silberschatz, 1988; Cochran & Hammen, 1985). In fact, some students do not become depressed as a result of one or more negative events, while others are depressed even if no negative event takes place (Billings et al., 1983). Depression can arise from a range of social and environmental factors, which can appear as a combination of stressful life events, poor coping style, and a lack of social resources (Cochran & Hammen, 1985; Vrendenburg et al., 1985).

(4) The Proposal

A **proposal,** often the first stage of a research project, can clarify and focus a project's direction and goals. In a proposal, you define your research project and make a convincing case for it. In the process, you adhere strictly to any specifications outlined by your instructor or in the request for proposals issued by the grant-giving agency.

Along with a proposal, you usually send a *letter of transmittal* and a **résumé**, which lists your specific qualifications for the project and summarizes your relevant work experience and accomplishments.

Many proposals include some or all of the following components.

Cover Sheet   The cover sheet includes your name, the title of your project, and the person or agency to which your proposal is submitted. It also provides a short title that expresses your subject concisely. Usually, another line on this sheet states the reason for the submission of the proposal—for example, to satisfy a course requirement or to request funding or facilities.

Abstract   Usually on a separate page, the abstract provides a short summary of your proposal. (See **51b1** for information on writing abstracts; for a sample, see **50d.**)

Statement of Purpose   This section tells why you are conducting your research and what you hope to accomplish—for example, "The Maquiladora Project is an industrial development program that relies on international cooperation with Mexican industries to utilize Mexican labor while boosting the employment of US white-collar workers."

Background of the Problem   This section summarizes previous research on the problem you are addressing.

Rationale   In this section, you explain as persuasively as possible why your research project is necessary and what makes it important at this time.

Statement of Qualification   This section enumerates the special qualifications you bring to your work.

Literature Review   The **literature review** contains a brief description of each source you have consulted.

Research Methods   This section describes the exact methods you will use in carrying out your research and the materials you will need; its purpose is to demonstrate the soundness of your method.

Timetable   This section presents the schedule you will follow as you carry out the project.

Budget   This section estimates the costs for carrying out the research.

Conclusion   In this section, you restate the importance of your project.

50c   Conventions of Style, Format, and Documentation

(1) Style and Format

Like other disciplines, social science uses a technical vocabulary. For instance, the social work case study excerpted in **50b2** identifies "the presenting problem"—that is, the reason the "subject," Mona, was brought to the Denver Children's Residential Treatment Center. Because you are addressing specialists, you should use the specialized vocabulary of the discipline and, when you discuss charts and tables, you should use statistical terms, such as *mean, percentage,* and *chi square.* Keep in mind, however, that you should use plain English to explain what percentages, means, and standard deviations signify in terms of your analysis.

A social science research paper has a title page that includes a **running head,** a title, and a **byline** (your name, school, and so on). Every page of the paper, including the title page, has a **page header,** an abbreviated title and page number printed at the top. Social science papers also include **internal headings** (for example, *Method, Results, Background of Problem, Description of Problem, Solutions,* and *Conclusion*). Each section of a social science paper is a complete unit with a beginning and an end so that it can be read separately, out of context, and still make sense. The body of the paper may present and discuss graphs, maps, photographs, flowcharts, or tables.

(2) Documentation

Many of the journals in the various social science disciplines use the documentation style of the American Psychological Association's *Publication Manual.*

50d   American Psychological Association (APA) Format: Social Science Research Paper

The following excerpts are from a psychology research paper, "Impression Formation in Customer-Clerk Interactions," which uses **APA documentation style**.

See 17a

Page header,
page number

Impression Formation   1

Type running
head flush
with left-hand
margin

Running head: IMPRESSION FORMATION

Title

Impression Formation in

Customer-Clerk Interactions

Jennifer Humble

Byline

Dr. Barbara Bremer

December 11, 2000

Page header
and number
on every page

|

Center

Abstract

The present study examined the extent to which physical appearance and dress affect the quality of customer-clerk interactions. An observational study was conducted in which a well-dressed actor and a poorly dressed actor posed as customers and engaged in customer-clerk interactions at nine different stores in a suburban shopping mall. The sociability of the clerk, time of initiation of interaction, duration of interaction, and prices of the first two watches shown were recorded. In support of the proposed hypothesis that dress and physical appearance will affect the quality of social interactions, the results indicated that the sociability of each clerk was significantly higher when interacting with the well-dressed actor than when interacting with the poorly dressed actor.

Full title
(centered)

Impression Formation in

Customer-Clerk Interactions

Introduction

In an attempt to understand the factors that influence

the quality of social interactions between customers and

Literature
review
(¶s 1–3)

clerks, some theorists have proposed that the sociability

of the customer is the critical factor in determining the

Authors'
names in
parentheses
when not
mentioned in
text

sociability of the interaction (Hester, Koger, & McCauley,

1985). Hester et al. (1985) reported that the customer's

sociability will determine the sociability of the salesperson

because the salesperson appears to adapt to and mimic

the sociability of the customer. Furthermore, Segal and

Year in
parentheses,
authors'
names in text

McCauley (1986) reported that sociability of customer-clerk

interactions is only minimally affected by such factors

as urbanism of location of interaction and business of

the location. Thus, they, too, indicated that customer

sociability plays a crucial role in determining the quality

of customer-clerk interactions.

Although customer sociability is believed to be a

key factor in determining the quality of social interactions, one

must also consider the effect of first impressions as

a determinant of the quality of these interactions. Past

research indicates that individuals tend to form impressions

and make judgments of others on the basis of cues, including

facial expression, gestures, and dress (Hamid, 1972). Hamid

Impression Formation   9

Results

Internal Heading

Analysis of the results of the sociability scale indicated significant differences in each of the six behavioral ratings of the clerk's sociability with respect to Actor 1 and Actor 2. In Actor 1/Actor 2 evaluation of the clerk's interaction with both Actor 1 and Actor 2, significant differences were seen with respect to the clerk's greeting ($\underline{t}(16) = 4.81$, $\underline{p}<.000$), conversation ($\underline{t}(16) = 2.98$, $\underline{p}<.009$), farewell ($\underline{t}(16) = 3.58$, $\underline{p}<.003$), smile ($\underline{t}(16) = 5.41$, $\underline{p}<.000$), facial regard ($\underline{t}(16) = 8.50$, $\underline{p}<.000$), and overall tone ($\underline{t}(16) = 3.50$, $\underline{p}<.008$), using two-tailed $\underline{t}$-tests for independent samples. Each clerk's sociability rating tended to be higher when interacting with Actor 1 than when interacting with Actor 2. Means and standard deviations of the six behavioral scores are presented in Table 1.

Statistical findings reported.

The results of the Stable Observer's evaluation of the clerk's behavior when interacting with Actor 1 and Actor 2 also indicated significant differences in the clerk's greeting ($\overline{t}(16) = 4.81$, $\overline{p}<.001$), conversation ($\overline{t}(16) = 2.98$, $\overline{p}<.009$), farewell ($\overline{t}(16) = 4.37$, $\overline{p}<.000$), smile ($\overline{t}(16) = 6.43$, $\overline{p}<.000$), facial regard ($\overline{t}(16) = 8.50$, $\overline{p}<.000$), and overall tone ($\overline{t}(16) = 4.38$, $\overline{p}<.000$), using two-tailed $\overline{t}$-tests for independent samples. The Stable Observer also rated the Clerk as being more sociable when interacting with Actor 1 than when

Tables, included as appendix, are discussed in text of paper. See **55d** for format.

Impression Formation   15

Center

References

Double-space → Francis, S. K., & Evans, P. K. (1987). Effects of hue, value,

Journal article by two authors   and style of garment and personal coloring of model on

person perception. Perceptual and Motor Skills, 64, 383-390.

Items listed alphabetically by first author's last name. Use initials for first names.   Hamid, P. N. (1972). Some effects of dress cues on

observational accuracy, a perceptual estimate, and impression

formation. Journal of Social Psychology, 86, 279-289.

Hester, L., Koger, P., & McCauley, C. (1985). Individual

differences in customer sociability. European Journal of Social

Psychology, 15, 453-456.

Indent first line of each entry 5 to 7 spaces.* Type subsequent lines flush with left-hand margin.   Lennon, S. J., & Davis, L. L. (1989). Categorization in first

impressions. Journal of Psychology, 123(5), 439-446.

Segal, M. E., & McCauley, C. R. (1986). The sociability of

commercial exchange in rural, suburban, and urban locations:

A test of the urban overload hypothesis. Basic and Applied

Social Psychology, 7(2), 115-135.

Tetlock, P. E. (1983). Accountability and the perseverance

of first impressions. Social Psychology Quarterly, 46(4),

285-292.

*This format is now recommended by the APA for all manuscripts submitted for publication. If your instructor prefers, you may instead type the first line of each entry flush with the left-hand margin and indent subsequent lines.

Table 1
Mean (S.D.) Scores and Correlations of Interrater Reliability of Actor 1/Actor 2 and Stable Observer's Rating of Salesperson Sociability

| | Actor 1/Actor 2 Rating | | | | Stable Observer's Rating | | | | Interrater Reliability |
| | Clerk 1 | | Clerk 2 | | Clerk 1 | | Clerk 2 | | Correlation Coefficient |
	$\bar{x}$	S.D.	$\bar{x}$	S.D.	$\bar{x}$	S.D.	$\bar{x}$	S.D.	
Greeting	1.78	0.44	0.78	0.44	1.78	0.44	0.78	0.44	0.87
Conversation	1.67	0.50	0.89	0.60	1.67	0.50	0.89	0.60	1.00
Farewell	1.78	0.44	0.89	0.60	1.89	0.33	0.89	0.60	0.94
Smile	2.56	0.53	0.78	0.83	2.56	0.53	0.67	0.71	0.98
Facial regard	2.67	0.50	0.78	0.44	2.67	0.50	0.78	0.44	1.00
Overall tone	2.78	0.67	1.44	1.13	2.89	0.60	1.22	0.97	0.93

$N = 9$ for both Clerk 1 and Clerk 2.

CHAPTER 51

WRITING IN THE NATURAL AND APPLIED SCIENCES

? FREQUENTLY ASKED QUESTIONS

What research sources should I use
in the natural and applied sciences?
(p. 697)
How do I write an abstract? (p. 702)
What does a paper that uses the Council of
Biological Editors (CBE) style look like?
(p. 707)

Writing in the natural and applied sciences relies on **empirical data**—information derived from observations or experiments. Although science writing is usually concerned with accurately reporting observations and experimental data, it may also be persuasive.

Basic to research in the natural and applied sciences is the **scientific method,** a process by which scientists gather and interpret information.

✔ CHECKLIST: THE SCIENTIFIC METHOD

✔ Define a problem you want to solve or an event you want to explain. Conduct a literature search to find out what previous work has been done on the problem.
✔ Formulate a hypothesis that attempts to explain the problem.
✔ Plan a method of investigation that will allow you to test your hypothesis.
✔ Carry out your experiment. Make careful observations, and record your data.
✔ Analyze the results of your experiment, and determine whether they support your initial hypothesis. Revise your hypothesis, if you can, to account for any discrepancies. If you cannot, plan further research that may help you explain the phenomena you have observed.

51a Research Sources ❓

The data used in the sciences are the result of observation and experimental research. In addition to being discussed, most results are tabulated and displayed graphically. In addition, scientists often carry out literature searches to determine what other work has been done in their areas of interest.

(1) Print Sources

Because scientists are interested in the number of times and the variety of sources in which a study is cited, they frequently consult the *Science Citation Index.* The following reference sources, many of which are available on CD-ROM or online as well as in print, are used in various science disciplines.

General Science
> *A to Z of Women in Science and Math*
> *Applied Science and Technology Index*
> *CRC Handbook of Chemistry*
> *Current Contents, Address Directory*
> *General Science Index*
> *Instruments of Science: An Historical Encyclopedia*
> *McGraw-Hill Encyclopedia of Science and Technology*
> *Reference Sources in Science, Engineering, Medicine, and Agriculture*
> *Science and Technology Almanac*
> *Sciences of the Earth: An Encyclopedia of Events, People, and Phenomena*
> *Scientific and Technical Information Sources*
> *UXL Encyclopedia of Science*
> *UXL Science Fact Finder*
> *Van Nostrand's Scientific Encyclopedia*

Chemistry
> *Analytical Abstracts*
> *Chemical Abstracts*
> *Chemical Technology*
> *Comprehensive Natural Products Chemistry*
> *Concise Encyclopedia of Biochemistry and Molecular Biology*
> *Dictionary of Chemistry*
> *Dictionary of Organic Compounds*
> *History and Use of Our Earth's Chemical Elements: A Reference*

How to Find Chemical Information: A Guide for Practicing Chemists,
  Educators, and Students
Information Sources in Chemistry
Kirk-Othmer Encyclopedia of Chemical Technology
McGraw-Hill Encyclopedia of Chemistry

Earth Sciences
  Abstracts of North American Geology
  Annotated Bibliography of Economic Geology
  Bibliography and Index of Geology
  Bibliography of North American Geology
  Climatology and Data
  Encyclopedia of Climate and Weather
  Encyclopedia of Earth Systems Science
  Geological Abstracts
  Geology
  Geophysical Abstracts
  Guide to USGA Publications
  Macmillan Encyclopedia of Earth Sciences
  Weather America

Engineering
  Chemical Engineers' Condensed Encyclopedia of Process Equipment
  Engineering Index
  Environment Abstracts
  Genetic Engineering: A Documentary History
  Government Reports Announcements and Index (NTIS)
  Handbook of Mechanical Engineering Calculations
  Marks' Standard Handbook for Mechanical Engineers
  Pollution Abstracts
  Selected Water Resources Abstracts
  Wiley Encyclopedia of Electrical and Electronics Engineering

Life Sciences
  Animals: A Macmillan Illustrated Encyclopedia
  Bibliography of Agriculture
  Biological Abstracts
  Biological and Agricultural Index
  Biology Digest
  Concise Encyclopedia of Biochemistry and Molecular Biology

Cumulative Index to Nursing and Allied Health Literature
Dictionary of Genetics
Encyclopedia of Bioethics
Encyclopedia of Environmental Biology
Encyclopedia of Genetics
Environment Abstracts Annual
G. Zimek's Animal Life Encyclopedia
Gale Encyclopedia of Medicine
Hospital Literature Index
Index Medicus
International Dictionary of Medicine and Biology
International Nursing Index
Smithsonian Book of North American Mammals
Zoological Record

Mathematics
Computer and Control Abstracts
Concise Encyclopedia of Mathematics
Current Index to Statistics
Encyclopedia of Mathematics
Encyclopedia of Statistical Sciences
Encyclopedic Dictionary of Mathematics
Handbook of Mathematics
Mathematical Reviews
Notable Mathematicians: From Ancient Times to the Present
Notable Women in Mathematics: A Biographical Dictionary
Recognizing Excellence in the Mathematical Sciences: An International
    Compilation of Awards, Prizes, and Recipients
Universal Encyclopedia of Mathematics

Physics
Astronomy and Astrophysics Abstracts
CRC Handbook of Chemistry and Physics
Encyclopedia of Physics
Encyclopedic Dictionary of Physics
Handbook of Physical Quantities
History of Astronomy: An Encyclopedia
NASA Atlas of the Solar System
Physics Abstracts
Q Is for Quantum: An Encyclopedia of Particle Physics
Solid State and Superconductivity Abstracts

(2) Databases for Computer Searches

Helpful databases for research in the sciences include *BIO-SIS Previews, CASearch, SCISEARCH, Agricola, CAB Abstracts, CINAHL, Compendex, Environmental Route Net, NTIS, Inspec, MEDLINE, MATHSCI, Life Sciences Collection, GEOREF, Zoological Record Online, Wildlife Review and Fisheries Review,* and *World Patents Index.* Check with your librarian about the availability of these databases in your library.

(3) Internet Sites

General Science

The Best Information on the Net (BIOTN): General Science
http://vweb.sau.edu/bestinfo/Majors/Science/sciindex.htm

General Science Reference Sources: Michigan State University Libraries
http://www.lib.msu.edu/science/general.htm

Science Reference Shelf
http://physics.hallym.ac.kr/dir/ed/sciref.html

Biology

Bio Online
http://www.bio.com

Biodiversity and Biological Collections Web Server
http://biodiversity.uno.edu

Vaughan Memorial Library: Biology Reference Shelf
http://www.acadiau.ca/vaughan/guides/biology/eref.html

Chemistry

ChemistryWeb Home Page
http://www.ssc.ntu.edu.sg:8000/chemweb/htmlj/

Classic Chemistry
http://webserver.lemoyne.edu/faculty/giunta/

General Chemistry Online
http://antoine.frostburg.edu/chem/senese/101/index.shtml

Earth Sciences

Links to Great Earth-Science Resources
http://www.unige.ch/sciences/terre/admin/terre_link.html

National Centre for Petroleum Geology and Geophysics:
On-line Earth Science Journals
http://www.ncpgg.adelaide.edu.au/journals.htm

United States Geological Survey: Earth and Environmental Science
http://geology.usgs.gov/index/shtml

Engineering

The Edinburgh Engineering Virtual Library
http://www.eevl.ac.uk/wwwvl.html

Engineering News Record
http://www.enr.com

The Engineer's Reference
http://www.eng-sol.com

Life Science

Internet Travels in the Life Science
http://www.life.uiuc.edu/bio100/Life_Sci_Links.html

Mathematics

The Mac Tutor History of Mathematics Archive
http://www-groups.dcs.st-and.ac.uk/~history/

Math Archives: Topics in Mathematics
http://archives.math.utk.edu/topics/

Physics

Physics Reference Guide
http://www.library.ucsb.edu/guides/phys-gd.html

Physics Web
http://physicsweb.org/resources/

Physlink
http://www.physlink.com

(4) Other Sources of Information

Opportunities for research outside the library vary widely because of the many ways in which scientists can gather information. In agronomy, for example, researchers collect soil samples; in toxicology, they test air or water quality. In marine biology, they might conduct research in a particular aquatic environment, and in chemistry, they conduct experiments to identify an unknown substance. Scientists also conduct surveys: epidemiologists study the spread of communicable diseases, and cancer researchers question populations to determine how environmental or dietary factors influence the likelihood of contracting cancer. The Internet can be an important source of up-to-date scientific information. In fact, scientists have used the Internet for years to communicate and share information about their research.

51b Assignments in the Sciences

Many writing assignments in the sciences are similar to those in other disciplines. Others, such as the laboratory report, are unique to the sciences.

❓ (1) The Abstract

Most scientific articles begin with **abstracts,** technical summaries that serve as guides for readers. In addition, many scientific indexes include abstracts of articles so researchers can determine whether an article is of use to them. An **indicative abstract** gives a general sense of the content of an article, helping readers decide whether they want to read it in full. (An annotated bibliography includes short indicative abstracts following each complete citation.) An **informative abstract** includes enough detail so that readers can obtain essential information without reading the article itself. (Some scientific abstracts, called **structured abstracts,** include internal headings.)

When writing an abstract, follow the organization of your paper, devoting a sentence or two to each of its major sections. State the purpose, method of research, results, and conclusion in the order in which they appear in the paper, but include only essential information. Avoid quoting from your paper or repeating its title.

Abstract: Biology

"Purification to Near Homogeneity of Bovine Transforming Epithelial Growth Factor," by Stephen McManus, Cooperative Education Student, Smith, Kline & French Labs.

The control of cellular proliferation is known to be mediated at an extracellular level by polypeptide growth factors; examples include epidermal growth factor (EGF), platelet-derived growth factor (PDGF), and transforming growth factors alpha and beta (TGF-a, TGF-ß). The transforming growth factors are so called because of their ability to induce anchorage-independent growth of selected target cell lines. Our studies have identified an apparently novel growth factor activity associated with epithelial cells and tissues. This activity, called *epithelial transforming growth factor* (TGF-e), is identified by the anchorage-independent growth of the SW13 epithelial cell line, derived from human adrenocortical carcinoma. The purification of this factor was accomplished by a multistep chromatography and electrophoretic process. The total purification was estimated as 6×10^5-fold with 1% recovery, corresponding to a yield of 0.1 µg TGf-e/kg bovine kidney.

(2) The Literature Survey

Literature surveys are common in the sciences, most often appearing as a section of a proposal or as part of a research paper. Unlike an abstract, which summarizes a single source, a literature survey summarizes a number of studies and sometimes compares and contrasts them. By doing so, the literature survey provides a theoretical context for the paper's discussion.

Literature Survey: Parasitology

Ultrastructural studies of micro- and macrogametes have included relatively few of the numerous Eimerian species. Major early studies include the following (hosts are listed in parentheses): micro- and macrogametes of *E. performans* (rabbits), *E. stiedae* (rabbits), *E. bovis* (cattle), and *E. auburnensis* (cattle) (Hammond et al., 1967; Scholtyseck et al., 1966), macrogametogenesis in *E. magna* (rabbits) and *E. intestinalis* (rabbits) (Kheysin, 1965), macrogametogony of *E. tenella* (chickens) (McLaren, 1969), and the microgametocytes and macrogametes of *E. neischulzi* (rats) (Colley, 1967). More recent investigations have included macrogametogony of *E. acervulina* (chickens) (Pitillo and Ball, 1984).

(3) The Laboratory Report

A laboratory report, the most common assignment for students taking courses in the sciences, is divided into sections that reflect the stages of the scientific method. Not every section will be necessary for every experiment, and some experiments may call for additional components, such as an abstract or a reference list. In addition, lab experiments may include tables, charts, graphs, and illustrations. The exact format of a student lab report is usually defined by the specific course's lab manual.

A lab report is an explanation of a process. Because its purpose is to enable readers to understand a complex series of tasks, it must present stages clearly and completely, in exact chronological order, and illustrate the purpose of each step. In addition, a lab report must provide descriptions of the equipment used in an experiment.

Laboratory Report: Chemistry

Purpose   In this section, you describe the goal of the experiment, presenting the hypothesis you tested or examined.

> The purpose of this lab experiment is to determine the iron
> content of an unknown mixture containing an iron salt by titration
> with potassium permanganate solution.
>
> Equation to find % of Fe: $5Fe^{2+} + MnO_{4-} + 8H^+ = 5Fe^{3+} + Mn^{2+} + 4H_2O$

Equipment   In this section, you list the equipment you used in the experiment. Often, this section also identifies and explains your methodology.

> Equipment includes two 60 ml beakers, a graduated cylinder, a
> scale, 600 ml of distilled water, 2 grams of H_2SO_4, 5 grams of $KMnO_4$,
> 100 ml of $H_2C_2O_4 \cdot 2H_2O$, and a Bunsen burner.

Procedure   In this section, you describe the steps of the experiment in the order in which they occur, usually numbering the steps.

> 1) A $KMnO_4$ solution was prepared by dissolving 1.5 grams of $KMnO_4$
> in 500 ml of distilled water.
>
> 2) Two samples $H_2C_2O_4 \cdot 2H_2O$ of about 0.2 grams each were weighed.

3) Each sample was dissolved in 60 ml of H_2O and 30 ml of H_2SO_4 in a 250 ml beaker.

4) The mixture was heated to 80°C and titrated slowly with $KMnO_4$ until the mixture turned pink.

5) The procedure was repeated twice.

Results   In this section, you present the results—observations, measurements, or equations—that you obtained from your experiments.

Percentage of iron: 1st run = 12.51 ml

2nd run = 11.2 ml

Conclusion or Discussion of Results   In this section, you explain your results or justify them in terms of the initial questions asked in the *Purpose* section.

Calculation for % of iron

$$\frac{12.5 \text{ ml} \times .0894 \text{ M}}{100 \text{ ml}/1} \times \frac{5 \text{ moles Fe}}{1 \text{ mole MnO}_4} \times \frac{55.85 \text{ g/mol}}{.5 \text{ g}} \times 100 = \frac{66.11}{500}$$

$$= 13.22\% \text{ Fe}$$

51c   Conventions of Style, Format, and Documentation

(1) Style and Format

Because writing in the sciences focuses on the experiment, not on those conducting the experiment, writers often use the passive voice. For example, in a lab report, you would say, "The mixture was heated for forty-five minutes" rather than "I heated the mixture for forty-five minutes." Another stylistic convention to remember concerns verb tense: a conclusion or a statement of generally accepted fact should be in the present tense ("Objects in motion *tend* to stay in motion"); a summary of a study, however, should be in the past tense ("Watson and Crick *discovered* the structure of DNA"). Finally, note that direct quotations are seldom used in scientific papers.

Because you are writing to inform or persuade other scientists, you should write clearly and concisely. Remember to use technical terms only when they are necessary to convey your meaning. Too many terms can make your paper difficult to understand—even for scientists familiar with your discipline. Often, a scientific paper will include a glossary that lists and defines terms that may be unfamiliar to readers.

Tables and illustrations are an important part of scientific papers. Be careful to place tables as close to your discussion of them as possible and to number and label any type of illustration or diagram so you can refer to it in your text. Keep in mind that each professional society prescribes formats for **tables** and other visuals and the way they are to be presented. Therefore, you cannot use a single format for all your scientific writing.

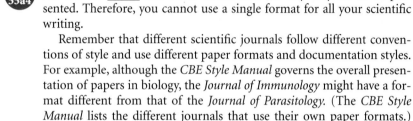

See
55a4

Remember that different scientific journals follow different conventions of style and use different paper formats and documentation styles. For example, although the *CBE Style Manual* governs the overall presentation of papers in biology, the *Journal of Immunology* might have a format different from that of the *Journal of Parasitology*. (The *CBE Style Manual* lists the different journals that use their own paper formats.) Your instructor may ask you to prepare your paper according to the style sheet of the journal to which you could submit your work. Although publication may seem a remote possibility to you, following a style sheet reminds you that writing in the sciences involves writing for a specific audience.

You should also learn the various abbreviations by which journals are referred to in the reference sections of science papers. For example, *The American Journal of Physiology* is abbreviated "Amer. J. Physiol.," and *The Journal of Physiological Chemistry* is abbreviated "J. of Physiol. Chemistry." Note that in CBE style, the abbreviated forms of journal titles are *not* underlined in the reference list.

(2) Documentation

Documentation style varies from one scientific discipline to another; even within each discipline, documentation style may vary from one journal to another. For this reason, ask your instructor which documentation style is required. Most disciplines in the sciences use a number-reference format prescribed by their professional societies. For instance, electrical engineers use the format of the Institute for Electronics and Electrical Engineers, chemists use the format of the American Chemical Society, physicists use the format of the American Institute of Physics, and mathematicians use the format of the American Mathematical Society.

51d Council of Biology Editors (CBE) Format: Excerpts from a Science Research Paper

The following excerpts from a biology research paper, "Maternal Smoking: Deleterious Effects on the Fetus," use the **CBE** number-reference format recommended by the *CBE Style Manual*.

See 17c

Maternal Smoking   Running Head

1

June M. Fahrman

Biology 306

April 17, 1997

Maternal Smoking: Deleterious   Title

Effects on the Fetus

Introduction   Internal Heading

The placenta, lifeline between fetus and mother, has been the subject of various studies aimed at determining the mechanisms by which substances in the mother's bloodstream affect the fetus. For example, cigarette smoking is clearly associated with an increased risk in the incidence of low-birthweight infants,[1] due both to prematurity and to intrauterine growth retardation.[2]

Development of the Placenta

At the morula stage of development, less than one week after fertilization, two types of cells can be distinguished. . . .

References

1. Rakel RE. Conn's current therapy 1988. Philadelphia: W. B. Saunders; 1988. 360 p.

2. Meberg A, Sande H, Foss, OP, Stenwig JT. Smoking during pregnancy—effects on the fetus and on thiocyanate levels in mother and baby. Acta. Paediatr Scand 1979; 68:547-552.

3. Lehtovirta P, Forss M. The acute effect of smoking on intervillous blood flow of the placenta. Brit Obs Gyn 1978; 85:729-731.

4. Phelan JP. Diminished fetal reactivity with smoking. Amer Obs Gyn 1980;136:230-233.

5. VanDerVelde WJ. Structural changes in the placenta of smoking mothers: a quantitative study. Placenta 1983; 4:231-240.

6. Asmussen I. Ultrastructure of the villi and fetal capillaries in placentas from smoking and nonsmoking mothers. Brit Obs Gyn 1980;87:239-245.

7. Meyer M. Perinatal events associated with maternal smoking during pregnancy. Amer Epid 1976; 103(5):464-476.

CHAPTER 52

WRITING ESSAY EXAMS

? FREQUENTLY ASKED QUESTIONS

How do I know what an exam question is
   really asking me to do?   (p. 711)
How do I organize an essay exam answer?
   (p. 712)
What should I look for when I reread my
   answer?   (p. 714)

Taking exams is a skill, one you have been developing throughout
your life as a student. Although both short-answer and essay exams require you to study, to recall what you know, and to budget your time
carefully as you write your answers, only essay questions ask you to
synthesize information and to arrange ideas in a series of clear, logically connected sentences and paragraphs. To write an essay examination, or even a paragraph-length answer, you must do more than
memorize facts; you must see the relationships among them. In other
words, you must **think critically** about your subject.

52a   Planning an Essay Exam Answer

Because you are under pressure during an exam and tend to write
quickly, you may be tempted to skip the planning and revision stages
of the writing process. But if you write in a frenzy and hand in your
exam without a second glance, you are likely to produce a disorganized or even incoherent answer. With careful planning and editing,
you can write an answer that demonstrates your understanding of the
material.

Answer Essay Questions (successatschool.com)
   http://www.successatschool.com/EssayQ.html
Tips on Essay Exams (UNC)
   http://www.unc.edu/depts/wcweb/handouts/essay-exams.html

(1) Review Your Material

Be sure you know beforehand the scope and format of the exam. How much of your text and class notes will be covered—the entire semester's work or only the material covered since the last test? Will you have to answer every question, or will you be able to choose among alternatives? Will the exam be composed entirely of fill-in, multiple-choice, or true/false questions, or will it call for sentence-, paragraph-, or essay-length answers? Will the exam test your ability to recall specific facts, or will it require you to demonstrate your understanding of the course material by drawing conclusions?

Exams challenge you to recall and express in writing what you already know—what you have read, what you have heard in class, what you have reviewed in your notes. Before you even take any exam, then, you must study: reread your text and class notes, highlight key points, and perhaps outline particularly important sections of your notes. When you prepare for a short-answer exam, you may memorize facts without analyzing their relationship to one another or their relationship to a body of knowledge as a whole: the definition of *pointillism,* the date of Queen Victoria's death, the formula for a quadratic equation, three reasons for the fall of Rome, two examples of conditioned reflexes, four features of a feudal economy, six steps in the process of synthesizing Vitamin C. When you prepare for an essay exam, however, you must do more than remember bits of information; you must also make connections among ideas.

When you are sure you know what to expect, see if you can anticipate the essay questions your instructor might ask. Try out likely questions on classmates, and see whether you can do some collaborative brainstorming to outline answers to possible questions. If you have time, you might even practice answering one or two in writing.

(2) Consider Your Audience and Purpose

The audience for an exam is the instructor who prepared it. As you read the questions, then, think about what your instructor has emphasized in class. Keep in mind that your purpose is to demonstrate that you understand the material, not to make clever remarks or introduce irrelevant information. Also, make every effort to use the vocabulary of the particular academic discipline and to follow any discipline-specific stylistic **conventions** your instructor has discussed.

(3) Read through the Entire Exam

Before you begin to write, read the questions carefully to determine your priorities and your strategy. First, be sure that your copy of the test is complete and that you understand exactly what each question requires. If you need clarification, ask your instructor or proctor for help. Then, plan carefully, deciding how much time you should devote to answering each question. Often, the point value of each question or the number of questions on the exam determines how much time you should spend on each answer. If an essay question is worth fifty out of one hundred points, for example, you will probably have to spend at least half (and perhaps more) of your time planning, writing, and proofreading your answer.

Next, decide where to start. Responding first to questions whose answers you are sure of is usually a good strategy. This tactic ensures that you will not become bogged down in a question that baffles you, left with too little time to write a strong answer to a question that you understand well. Moreover, starting with the questions that you are sure of can help build your confidence.

(4) Read Each Question Carefully

To write an effective answer, you need to understand the question. As you read any essay question, you may find it helpful to underline keywords and important terms.

Sociology: Distinguish among Social Darwinism, instinct theory, and sociobiology, giving examples of each.

Music: Explain how Milton Babbitt used the computer to expand Schoenberg's twelve-tone method.

Philosophy: Define existentialism and identify three influential existentialist works, explaining why they are important.

Look carefully at the wording of each question. If the question calls for a *comparison and contrast* of *two* styles of management, a *description* or *analysis* of *one* style, no matter how comprehensive, will not be acceptable. If the question asks for causes *and* effects, a discussion of causes alone will not do.

The wording of the question suggests what you should emphasize. For instance, an American history instructor would expect very different answers to the following two exam questions:

- Give a detailed explanation of the major causes of the Great Depression, noting briefly some of the effects of the economic collapse on the United States.
- Give a detailed summary of the effects of the Great Depression on the United States, briefly discussing the major causes of the economic collapse.

Although the preceding questions look somewhat alike, the first calls for an essay that stresses *causes,* whereas the second calls for one that stresses *effects.*

The following question on a literature exam also requires a very specific treatment of the topic.

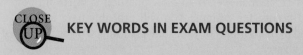

KEY WORDS IN EXAM QUESTIONS

Pay careful attention to the words used in exam questions.

- Explain
- Compare
- Contrast
- Trace
- Evaluate
- Discuss

- Clarify
- Relate
- Justify
- Analyze
- Interpret
- Describe

- Classify
- Identify
- Illustrate
- Define
- Support
- Summarize

(5) Brainstorm to Find Ideas

See 1b6

Once you understand the question, you need to **find something to say**. Begin by **brainstorming,** quickly listing all the relevant ideas you can remember. Then, identify the most important points on your list, and delete the others. A quick review of the exam question and your supporting ideas should lead you toward a workable thesis for your essay answer.

❓ 52b   Shaping an Essay Exam Answer

Like an essay, an effective exam answer has a definite structure.

See 2b2

(1) Stating a Thesis

Often, you can rephrase the exam question as a **thesis statement**. For example, the American history exam question "Give a detailed summary of the effects of the Great Depression on the United States, briefly discussing the major causes of the economic collapse" suggests the following thesis statement.

> **EFFECTIVE THESIS STATEMENT:** The Great Depression, caused by the American government's economic policies, had major political, economic, and social effects on the United States.

An effective thesis statement addresses all aspects of the question but highlights only relevant concerns. The following thesis statements are not effective.

VAGUE THESIS STATEMENT: The Great Depression, caused largely by profligate spending patterns, had a number of very important results.

INCOMPLETE THESIS STATEMENT: The Great Depression caused major upheaval in the United States.

IRRELEVANT THESIS STATEMENT: The Great Depression, caused largely by America's poor response to the 1929 stock market crash, had more important consequences than World War II did.

(2) Making an Informal Outline

Because time is limited, you should plan your answer before you write it. Therefore, once you have decided on a suitable thesis, you should make an **informal outline** of your major points.

Write on the inside cover of your exam book or on its last sheet. Use the **essay pattern** suggested by the question—definition, comparison and contrast, or cause and effect, for instance—to shape your outline, and list your supporting points in the order in which you plan to discuss them. Once you have completed your outline, check it against the exam question to make certain it covers everything the question calls for—and *only* what the question calls for.

An informal outline for an answer to the American history question ("Give a detailed summary of the effects of the Great Depression on the United States, briefly discussing the major causes of the economic collapse.") might look like this.

THESIS STATEMENT: The Great Depression, caused by the American government's economic policies, had major political, economic, and social effects on the United States.

SUPPORTING POINTS:
Causes
American economic policies: income poorly distributed, factories expanded too much, more goods produced than could be purchased
Effects
1. Economic situation worsened—farmers, businesses, workers, and stock market all affected.
2. Roosevelt elected—closed banks, worked with Congress to enact emergency measures.
3. Reform—TVA, AAA, NIRA, etc.
4. Social Security Act, WPA, PWA

See 5e An answer based on this outline will follow a **cause-and-effect** pattern, with an emphasis on effects, not causes.

52c   Writing and Revising an Essay Exam Answer

Referring to your outline, you can now begin to draft your answer. Don't bother crafting an elaborate or unusual **introduction;** your time is precious, and so is your reader's. A simple statement of your thesis that summarizes your answer is your best introductory strategy: this approach is efficient, and it reminds you to address the question directly.

To develop the **body** of the essay, follow your outline point by point, using clear topic sentences and transitions to indicate your progression and to help your instructor see that you are answering the question in full. Such signals, along with parallel sentence structure and repeated key words, make your answer easy to follow.

The most effective **conclusion** for an essay examination is a clear, simple restatement of the thesis or a summary of the essay's main points.

Essay answers should be complete and detailed, but they should not contain irrelevant material. Every unnecessary fact or opinion increases your chance of error, so don't repeat yourself or volunteer unrequested information, and don't express your own feelings or opinions unless such information is specifically called for. In addition, be sure to support all your general statements with specific examples.

Leave enough time to reread and revise what you have written. Try to view your answer from a fresh perspective. Is your thesis statement clearly worded? Does your essay support your thesis and answer the question? Are your facts correct, and are your ideas presented in a logical order? Review your topic sentences and transitions. Check sentence structure and word choice, spelling and punctuation. If a sentence—or even a whole paragraph—seems irrelevant, cross it out. If you suddenly remember something you want to add, you can insert a few additional words with a caret (^). Neatly insert a longer addition at the end of your answer, box it, and label it so your instructor will know where it belongs. Finally, be sure that you have written legibly and that you have not inadvertently left out any words.

The following one-hour essay answer conforms to the outline in **52b2.** Notice how the student restates the question in her thesis statement and keeps the question in focus by repeating keywords like *cause, effect, result, response,* and *impact.*

EFFECTIVE ESSAY EXAM ANSWER

QUESTION: Give a detailed summary of the effects of the Great Depression on the United States, briefly discussing the major causes of the economic collapse.

The Great Depression, caused by the American government's economic policies, had major political, economic, and social effects on the United States.

Introduction—thesis statement rephrases exam question

The Depression was precipitated by the stock market crash of October 1929, but its actual causes were more subtle: they lay in the US government's economic policies. First, personal income was not well distributed. Although production rose during the 1920s, the farmers and other workers got too little of the profits; instead, a disproportionate amount of income went to the richest 5 percent of the population. The tax policies at this time made inequalities in income even worse. A good deal of income also went into development of new manufacturing plants. This expansion stimulated the economy but encouraged the production of more goods than consumers could purchase. Finally, during the economic boom of the 1920s, the government did not attempt to limit speculation or impose regulations on the securities market; it also did little to help build up farmers' buying power. Even after the crash began, the government made mistakes: instead of trying to counter the country's deflationary economy, the government focused on keeping the budget balanced and making sure the United States adhered to the gold standard.

Summarizes policies leading to Depression (causes)

The Depression, devastating to millions of individuals, had a tremendous impact on the nation as a whole. Its political, economic, and social consequences were great.

Transition from causes to effects

Early effects
(¶s 4–8
summarize
important
results in
chronological
order)

Between October 1929 and Roosevelt's inauguration on March 4, 1932, the economic situation grew worse. Businesses were going bankrupt, banks were failing, and stock prices were falling. Farm prices fell drastically, and hungry farmers were forced to burn their corn to heat their homes. There was massive unemployment, with millions of workers jobless and humiliated, losing skills and self-respect. President Hoover's Reconstruction Finance Corporation made loans available to banks, railroads, and businesses, but Hoover felt state and local funds (not the federal government) should finance public works programs and relief. Confidence in the president declined as the country's economic situation worsened.

Additional
effects:
Roosevelt's
emergency
measures

One result of the Depression was the election of Franklin Delano Roosevelt. By the time of his inauguration, most American banks had closed, thirteen million workers were unemployed, and millions of farmers were threatened by foreclosure. Roosevelt's response was immediate: two days after he took office, he closed all banks and took steps to support the stronger ones with loans and to prevent the weaker ones from reopening. During the first hundred days of his administration, he kept Congress in special session. Under his leadership, Congress enacted emergency measures designed to provide "Relief, Recovery, and Reform."

In response to the problems caused by the Depression, Roosevelt set up agencies to reform some of the conditions that had helped to cause the Depression in the first place. The Tennessee Valley Authority, created in May of 1933, was one of these. Its purposes were to control floods by building new dams and improving old ones and to provide cheap, plentiful electricity. The TVA improved the standard of living of area farmers and drove down the price of power all over the country. The Agricultural Adjustment Administration, created the

Additional
effects:
Roosevelt's
reform
measures

same month as the TVA, provided for taxes on basic commodities, with the tax revenues used to subsidize farmers to produce less. This reform measure caused prices to rise.

Another response to the problems of the Depression was the National Industrial Recovery Act. This act established the National Recovery Administration, an agency that set minimum wages and maximum hours for workers and set limits on production and prices. Other laws passed by Congress between 1935 and 1940 strengthened federal regulation of power, interstate commerce, and air traffic. Roosevelt also changed the federal tax structure to redistribute American income.

Additional effects: NIRA, other laws, etc.

One of the most important results of the Depression was the Social Security Act of 1935, which established unemployment insurance and provided financial aid for the blind and disabled and for dependent children and their mothers. The Works Progress Administration (WPA) gave jobs to over two million workers, who built public buildings, roads, streets, bridges, and sewers. The WPA also employed artists, musicians, actors, and writers. The Public Works Administration (PWA) cleared slums and created public housing. In the National Labor Relations Act (1935), workers received a guarantee of government protection for their unions against unfair labor practices by management.

Additional effects: Social Security, WPA, etc.

nclusion   As a result of the economic collapse known as the Great Depression, Americans saw their government take responsibility for providing immediate relief, for helping the economy recover, and for taking steps to ensure that the situation would not be repeated. The economic, political, and social impact of the laws passed during the 1930s is still with us, helping to keep our government and our economy stable.

Notice that in her answer the student does not include any irrelevant material: she does not, for example, describe the conditions of people's lives in detail, blame anyone in particular, discuss the president's friends and enemies, or consider parallel events in other countries. She covers only what the question asks for. Notice, too, how topic sentences ("One result of the Depression . . ."; "In response to the problems caused by the Depression . . ."; "One of the most important results of the Depression . . .") keep the primary purpose of the discussion in focus and guide her instructor through the essay.

A well-planned essay like the preceding one is not easy to write. Consider the following ineffective answer to the same question.

INEFFECTIVE ESSAY EXAM ANSWER

The Great Depression is generally considered to have begun with the stock market crash of October 1929 and to have lasted until the defense buildup for World War II. It was a terrible time for millions of Americans, who were not used to being hungry or out of work. Perhaps

No clear thesis. Vague, subjective impressions of the Depression

the worst economic disaster in our history, the Depression left its scars on millions of once-proud workers and farmers who found themselves reduced to poverty. We all have heard stories of businessmen committing suicide when their investments failed, of people selling apples on the street, and of farmers and their families leaving the Dust Bowl in desperate search of work. My own grandfather, laid off from his job, had to support my grandmother and their four children on what he could make from odd carpentry jobs. This was the Depression at its worst.

What else did the Depression produce? One result of the Depression was the election of Franklin Delano Roosevelt. Roosevelt immediately closed all banks. Then Congress set up the Federal Emergency Relief Administration, the Civilian Conservation Corps, the Farm Credit Administration, and the Home Owners' Loan Corporation. The Reconstruction Finance Corporation and the Civil Works

Administration were two other agencies designed to provide "Relief, Recovery, and Reform." All these agencies helped Roosevelt in his efforts to lead the nation to recovery while providing relief and reform.

Along with these emergency measures, Roosevelt set out to reform some of the conditions he felt were responsible for the economic collapse. Accordingly, he created the Tennessee Valley Authority (TVA) to control floods and provide electricity in the Tennessee Valley. The Agricultural Adjustment Agency levied taxes and got the farmers to grow less, causing prices to rise. Thus, these agencies, the TVA and the AAA, helped to ease things for the farmers.

The National Industrial Recovery Act established the National Recovery Administration, which was designed to help workers. It established minimum wages and maximum hours, both of which made conditions better for workers. Other important agencies included the Federal Power Commission, the Interstate Commerce Commission, the Maritime Commission, and the Civil Aeronautics Authority. Changes in the tax structure at about this time made the tax system fairer and eliminated some inequities. Roosevelt, working smoothly with his cabinet and with Congress, took many important steps to ease the nation's economic burden.

Despite the fact that he was handicapped by polio, Roosevelt was a dynamic president. His fireside chats, which millions of Americans heard on the radio every week, helped to reassure Americans that things would be fine. This increased his popularity. But he had problems, too. Not everyone agreed with him. Private electric companies opposed the TVA, big business disagreed with his support of labor unions, the rich did not like the way he restructured the tax system, and many people saw him as dangerously radical. Still, he was one of the most popular presidents ever.

Margin annotations:

Gratuitous summary

Unsupported generalization

Why were these agencies important? What did they do?

...ression: ...ssion of ...sevelt is ...evant to topic.

Undeveloped
information

—Social Security Act: unemployment insurance, aid to blind and

    disabled and children

—WPA: built public projects

—PWA: public housing

—National Labor Relations Act: strengthened labor unions

This essay only indirectly answers the exam question. It devotes too much space to unnecessary elements: an emotional introduction, needlessly repeated words and phrases, gratuitous summaries, and unsupported generalizations. Without a thesis statement to guide her, the writer slips into a discussion of only the immediate impact of the Depression and never discusses its causes or long-term effects. Although the body paragraphs do provide the names of many agencies created by the Roosevelt administration, they do not explain the purpose of most of them. Consequently, the student seems to consider the formation of the agencies, not their contributions, to be the Depression's most significant result.

Because the student took a time-consuming detour, she had to list points at the end of the essay without discussing them fully; moreover, she was left with no time to sum up her main points, even in a one-sentence conclusion. Although it is better to include undeveloped information than to skip it altogether, an undeveloped list has shortcomings. Many instructors will not give credit if you do not write out your answer in full. More important, you cannot effectively show logical or causal relationships in a list.

52d   Writing Paragraph-Length Essay Exam Answers

Some essay questions ask for a paragraph-length answer, not a full essay. A paragraph should be just that: not one or two sentences, not a list of points, not more than one paragraph.

A paragraph-length answer should be **<u>unified</u>** by a clear topic sentence. Just as an essay answer begins with a thesis statement, a paragraph answer opens with a topic sentence that summarizes what the paragraph will cover. You should generally word this sentence so that it echoes the exam question. The paragraph should also be **<u>coherent</u>**—that is, its statements should be linked by transitions that move the reader along. And, the paragraph should be **<u>well developed</u>**, with enough relevant detail to convince your reader that you know what you are talking about.

EFFECTIVE PARAGRAPH-LENGTH EXAM ANSWER

QUESTION: In one paragraph, define the term *management by objectives*, give an example of how it works, and briefly discuss an advantage of this approach.

As defined by Horngren, <u>management by objectives</u> is an | Definition
approach by which a manager and his or her superior together
formulate goals, and plans by which they can achieve these goals,
for a forthcoming period. For example, a manager and a superior | Example
can formulate a responsibility accounting budget, and the
manager's performance can then be measured according to how
well he or she meets the objectives defined by the budget. The
advantage of this approach is that the goals set are attainable | Advantage
because they are not formulated in a vacuum. Rather, the objectives
are based on what the entire team reasonably expects to
accomplish. As a result, the burden of responsibility is shifted from
the superior to the team: the goal itself defines all the steps needed
for its completion.

In this answer, key phrases ("As *defined* by . . ."; "For *example* . . .";
"The *advantage* of this approach . . .") clearly identify the various parts
of the question being addressed. The writer includes just what the question asks for, and no more. His use of the wording of the question helps
make the paragraph orderly, coherent, and emphatic.

The student who wrote the following response may know what *management by objectives* is, but his paragraph sounds more like a casual explanation to a friend than an answer to an exam question.

INEFFECTIVE PARAGRAPH-LENGTH EXAM ANSWER

Sketchy,   Management by objectives is when managers and their bosses
casual
definition get together to formulate their goals. This is a good system of

No example
given

management because it cuts down on hard feelings between

managers and their superiors. Because they set the goals together,

they can make sure they're attainable by considering all possible

influences, constraints, etc., that might occur. This way neither the

Vague manager nor the superior gets all the blame when things go

wrong.

Remember, no response to an exam question will be effective unless you take the time to read the question carefully, plan your response, and outline your answer before you begin to write. It is always a good idea to use the wording of the question in your answer and to reread your answer to make sure it explicitly answers the question.

CHAPTER 53

WRITING ABOUT LITERATURE

? FREQUENTLY ASKED QUESTIONS

How do I find the real meaning of a literary
work?   (p. 723)
Do I put a title in quotation marks or
underline it?   (p. 725)

53a   Reading Literature

When you read a literary work about which you plan to write, use the
same critical thinking skills and **active reading** strategies you apply to
other works you read: preview the work, and highlight it to identify key
ideas and cues to meaning; then, annotate it carefully.

See
7b

As you read and take notes, focus on the special concerns of literary
analysis, considering elements like a short story's plot, a poem's rhyme or
meter, or a play's characters. Look for *patterns,* related groups of words,
images, or ideas that run through a work. Look for *anomalies,* unusual
forms, unique uses of language, unexpected actions by characters, or unusual treatments of topics. Finally, look for *connections,* links with other
literary works, with historical events, or with biographical information.

READING LITERATURE

When you read a work of literature, keep in mind that you do
not read to magically discover the one correct meaning the writer

❓

continued on the following page

Reading Poetry (U. Wisc.)
   http://www.wisc.edu/writing/Handbook/ReadingPoetry.html
Some Basic Guidelines for Reading Literature (Texas)
   http://uwc-server.fac.utexas.edu/stu/handouts/reading.html
Guide to Literacy Resources on the Net (J. Lynch)
   http://andromeda.rutgers.edu/~jlynch/Lit/

continued from the previoius page

has hidden between the lines. The "meaning" of a literary work is created by the interaction between a text and its readers. Do not assume, however, that a work can mean whatever you want it to mean; ultimately, your interpretation must be consistent with the stylistic signals, thematic suggestions, and patterns of imagery in the text.

53b   Writing about Literature

When you write about literature, your goal is to make a point and support it with appropriate references to the work under discussion or to related works or secondary sources. (For an example of a literary analysis that uses outside sources, see **49d1.**) As you write, you observe the conventions of literary criticism, which has its own specialized vocabulary and formats. You also respond to discipline-specific assignments. For instance, you may be asked to **analyze** a work, to take it apart and consider one or more of its elements—perhaps the plot or characters in a story or the use of language in a poem. Or, you may be asked to **interpret** a work, to try to explore its possible meanings. Less often, you may be called on to **evaluate** a work, to judge its strengths and weaknesses.

More specifically, you may be asked to trace the critical or popular reception to a work; to compare two works by a single writer (or by two different writers); or to consider the relationship between a work of literature and a literary movement or historical period. You may also be asked to analyze a character's motives or the relationship between two characters, or to comment on a story's setting or tone. In any case, understanding exactly what you are expected to do will make your writing task easier.

✔ CHECKLIST: WRITING ABOUT LITERATURE

✔ Use present-tense verbs when discussing works of literature: "The character of Mrs. Mallard's husband is not developed. . . ."
✔ Use past-tense verbs only when discussing historical events ("Owen's poem conveys the destructiveness of World War I, which at the time the poem *was* written *was* considered to be . . ."),

when presenting historical or biographical data ("Her first novel, *published* in 1811 when Austen *was* thirty-six, . . ."), or when identifying events that occurred prior to the time of the story's main action ("Miss Emily is a recluse; since her father *died* she has lived alone except for a servant.").

✔ Support all points with specific, concrete examples from the work you are discussing, briefly summarizing key events, quoting dialogue or description, describing characters or setting, or paraphrasing ideas.

✔ Combine paraphrase, summary, and quotation with your own interpretations, weaving quotations smoothly into your paper (see **14d**).

✔ Be careful to acknowledge all sources, including the work or works under discussion. Make sure you have introduced the words or ideas of others with a reference to the source and followed borrowed material with appropriate parenthetical documentation. Also, be sure you have quoted accurately and enclosed the words of others in quotation marks.

✔ Use parenthetical documentation (see **16a**) and include a Works Cited list (see **16b**) in accordance with MLA documentation style.

✔ When citing a part of a short story or novel, supply the page number (168). For a poem, give the line numbers (2–4). For a classic verse play, include act, scene, and line numbers (1.4.29–31). For other plays, supply act and/or scene numbers. (When quoting more than four lines of prose or more than three lines of poetry, be sure to follow the guidelines outlined in **41c.**)

✔ Avoid subjective expressions like *I feel, I believe, it seems to me,* and *in my opinion.* These weaken your paper by suggesting that its ideas are "only" your opinion and have no validity in themselves.

✔ Avoid unnecessary plot summary. Your goal is to draw a conclusion about one or more works and to support that conclusion with pertinent details. If a plot development supports a point you wish to make, a *brief* summary is acceptable. But plot summary is no substitute for analysis.

✔ Use **literary terms** accurately. For example, be careful not to confuse *narrator* or *speaker* with *writer* (feelings or opinions expressed by a narrator or character do not necessarily represent those of the writer). You should not say, "In the poem's last stanza, *Frost* expresses his indecision" when you mean the poem's *speaker* is indecisive.

✔ Underline titles of novels and plays (see **44a**); enclose titles of short stories and poems within quotation marks (see **41b**).

See
53f

53c Writing about Fiction

When you write a **literary analysis** of a work of fiction, you follow the same process you use when you write any paper about literature. However, you concentrate on elements—such as plot, character, setting, and point of view—characteristic of works of fiction.

✔ CHECKLIST: WRITING ABOUT FICTION

✔ **Plot**   What happens in the story? What conflicts can you identify? Are they resolved? In what order are the events arranged? Why are they arranged in this way?

✔ **Character**   Who is the protagonist? The antagonist? What role do minor characters play? What are each character's most striking traits? Does the protagonist grow and change during the story? Are the characters portrayed sympathetically? How do characters interact with one another? What motivates the characters?

✔ **Setting**   Where and when is the story set? How does the setting influence the plot? How does it affect the characters?

✔ **Point of View**   Is the story told by an anonymous third-person narrator or by a character, using first-person (*I* or *we*) point of view? Is the first-person narrator trustworthy? Is the narrator a participant in the action or just a witness to the story's events? How would a different point of view change the story?

✔ **Style, Tone, and Language**   Is the level of diction formal? Informal? Is the style simple or complex? Is the tone intimate or distant? What kind of imagery is used?

✔ **Theme**   What central theme or themes does the story explore?

Carla Watts, a student in an introductory literature course, was asked to select a short story from the literature anthology her class was using and to write an essay about it, basing her analysis solely on her own reactions to the story, not on literary criticism. The following story, written in 1983 by Gary Gildner, is the one she decided to write about.

Writing about Literature (The Citadel)
    http://www.citadel.edu/citadel/otherserv/wctr/writinglit/html
Sample Literary Essay (U. Victoria)
    http://www.clearcf.uvic.ca/writersguide/Pages/SampleEssaysLit.html

SLEEPY TIME GAL

In the small town in northern Michigan where my father lived as a young man, he had an Italian friend who worked in a restaurant. I will call his friend Phil. Phil's job in the restaurant was as ordinary as you can imagine—from making coffee in the morning to sweeping up at night. But what was not ordinary about Phil was his piano playing. On Saturday nights my father and Phil and their girlfriends would drive ten or fifteen miles to a roadhouse by a lake where they would drink beer from schooners and dance and Phil would play an old beat-up piano. He could play any song you named, my father said, but the song everyone waited for was the one he wrote, which he would always play at the end before they left to go back to the town. And everyone knew of course that he had written the song for his girl, who was as pretty as she was rich. Her father was the banker in their town, and he was a tough old German, and he didn't like Phil going around with his daughter.

My father, when he told the story, which was not often, would tell it in an offhand way and emphasize the Depression and not having much, instead of the important parts. I will try to tell it the way he did, if I can.

So they would go to the roadhouse by the lake, and finally Phil would play his song, and everyone would say, Phil, that's a great song, you could make a lot of money from it. But Phil would only shake his head and smile and look at his girl. I have to break in here and say that my father, a gentle but practical man, was not inclined to emphasize the part about Phil looking at his girl. It was my mother who said the girl would rest her head on Phil's shoulder while he played, and that he got the idea for the song from the pretty way she looked when she got sleepy. My mother was not part of the story, but she had heard it when she and my father were younger and therefore had that information. I would like to intrude further and add something about Phil writing the song, maybe show him whistling the tune and going over the words slowly and carefully to get the best ones, while peeling onions or potatoes in the restaurant; but my father is already driving them home from the roadhouse, and saying how patched up his tires were, and how his car's engine was a gingerbread of parts from different makes, and some parts were his own invention as well. And my mother is saying that the old German had made his daughter promise not to get involved with any man until after college, and they couldn't be late. Also my mother likes the sad parts and is eager to get to their last night before the girl goes away to college.

continued on the following page

continued from the previous page

So they all went out to the roadhouse, and it was sad. The women got tears in their eyes when Phil played her song, my mother said. My father said that Phil spent his week's pay on a new shirt and tie, the first tie he ever owned, and people kidded him. Somebody piped up and said, Phil, you ought to take that song down to Bay City—which was like saying New York City to them, only more realistic—and sell it and take the money and go to college too. Which was not meant to be cruel, but that was the result because Phil had never even got to high school. But you can see people were trying to cheer him up, my mother said.

Well, she'd come home for Thanksgiving and Christmas and Easter and they'd all sneak out to the roadhouse and drink beer from schooners and dance and everything would be like always. And of course there were the summers. And everyone knew Phil and the girl would get married after she made good her promise to her father because you could see it in their eyes when he sat at the old beat-up piano and played her song.

That last part about their eyes was not, of course, in my father's telling, but I couldn't help putting it in there even though I know it is making some of you impatient. Remember that this happened many years ago in the woods by a lake in northern Michigan, before television. I wish I could put more in, especially about the song and how it felt to Phil to sing it and how the girl felt when hearing it and knowing it was hers, but I've already intruded too much in a simple story that isn't even mine.

Well, here's the kicker part. Probably by now many of you have guessed that one vacation near the end she doesn't come home to see Phil, because she meets some guy at college who is good-looking and as rich as she is and, because her father knew about Phil all along and was pressuring her into forgetting about him, she gives in to this new guy and goes to his hometown during the vacation and falls in love with him. That's how the people in town figured it, because after she graduates they turn up, already married, and right away he takes over the old German's bank—and buys a new Pontiac at the place where my father is the mechanic and pays cash for it. The paying cash always made my father pause and shake his head and mention again that times were tough, but here comes this guy in a spiffy white shirt (with French cuffs, my mother said) and pays the full price in cash.

And this made my father shake his head too: Phil took the song down to Bay City and sold it for twenty-five dollars, the only money he ever got for it. It was the same song we'd just heard on the radio

> and which reminded my father of the story I just told you. What happened to Phil? Well, he stayed in Bay City and got a job managing a movie theater. My father saw him there after the Depression when he was on his way to Detroit to work for Ford. He stopped and Phil gave him a box of popcorn. The song he wrote for the girl has sold many millions of records, and if I told you the name of it you could probably sing it, or at least whistle the tune. I wonder what the girl thinks when she hears it. Oh yes, my father met Phil's wife too. She worked in the movie theater with him, selling tickets and cleaning the carpet after the show with one of those sweepers you push. She was also big and loud and nothing like the other one, my mother said.

Carla began by reading the story through quickly. Then she reread it more carefully, highlighting and annotating as she read. A portion of the highlighted and annotated story follows.

When do events take place?

In the small town in northern Michigan where my father lived as a young man, he had an Italian friend who worked in a restaurant. I will call his friend Phil. Phil's job in the restaurant was as ordinary as you can imagine—from making coffee in the morning to sweeping up at night. But what was not ordinary about Phil was his piano playing. On Saturday nights my father and Phil and the girlfriends would drive ten or fifteen miles to a roadhouse by a lake where they would drink beer from schooners and dance and Phil would play *[Sat. nights = special-dancing, beer, etc.]* an old beat-up piano. He could play any song you named, my father *[?]* said, but the song everyone waited for was the one he wrote, which he would always play at the end before they left to go back to the town. And everyone knew of course that he had written the song for his girl, who was as pretty as she was rich. Her father was the *[Sounds like fairy tale]* banker in their town, and he was a tough old German, and he didn't like Phil going around with his daughter.

My father, when he told the story, which was not often, would tell it in an offhand way and emphasize the Depression and not having much, instead of the important parts. I will try to tell it the way he did, if I can.

Carla's next task was to brainstorm to find ideas. As she searched for a topic for her essay, she found it helpful to brainstorm separately on plot, character, setting, point of view, tone and style, and theme to see which suggested the most promising possibilities. Her brainstorming list follows on the next page.

Brainstorming List

<u>Plot</u>
Flashback — narrator remembers story father told.
Story: Phil loved rich banker's daughter, wrote song for
        her, girl married someone else, Phil sold song for
        $25.00, married another woman.
Ordinary, predictable story of "star-crossed lovers" from
        different backgrounds ("Probably by now many of
        you have guessed . . ."), but what actually happened
        isn't important.

<u>Character</u>
Phil — Italian, never went to high school, ordinary job in
        restaurant, extraordinary piano player.
Girl — no name, pretty, rich, educated
Narrator — ?
Mother — romantic
Father — mechanic; gentle, practical

<u>Setting</u>
"small town in northern Michigan"
Past — when narrator's father was a young man
In woods — near lake
Roadhouse — dancing, drinking, beat-up piano

<u>Point of View</u>
Narrator tells story to reader, but there's a story
        inside the story.
Father tells his story, mother qualifies his version (she's
        "not part of the story" but has heard it), narrator
        tells how they told it.
Point of view keeps shifting — characters compete to tell
        the story ("I would like to intrude further . . .").
Father's version: stresses Depression, hard times
Mother's version: stresses relationship, "sad parts"
Readers encouraged to find own point of view; narrator of
        story addresses readers.
Three characters invent and reinvent and embellish story
        each time they tell it.

Tone and Style
Conversational style — narrator talks to reader ("Well,
  here's the kicker part.").
Like a fairy tale (girl = "as pretty as she was rich";
  father = "a gentle but practical man")
Casual speech, contractions; "Well," "some guy," etc.

Theme
Which is "real" story?
  Subject of Phil's story = missed chances, failure.
  Subject of narrator's story = the past?
  Values of different characters? Conflict between real
  events and memory?

When Carla looked over her brainstorming list, she saw at once that character and point of view suggested the most interesting possibilities for her paper. Still, she found herself unwilling to start drafting her essay until she could find out more about the story's title, which she thought must be significant. She asked around until she found someone who told her that the title was the name of an actual song—and supplied the lyrics. She recorded her reactions to this information in a journal entry.

Journal Entry

"Sleepy Time Gal" = name of song
Mother says Phil got inspiration for song from the way
  his girl looked when she got sleepy. ** Does title of
  story refer to girl or to song? **
Song = fantasy about the perfect married life that should
  follow the evenings of dancing: in a "cottage for two"
  wife will be happy cooking and sewing for her husband
  and will end her evenings early. She'll be happy to
  forget about dancing and be a stay-at-home wife.
Maybe lyrics describe what Phil wants and never gets?

At this point, Carla decided to arrange some of the most useful material from her brainstorming list, journal entry, and annotations into categories. She gave these categories headings that corresponded to the three versions of Phil's story presented in "Sleepy Time Gal," and she added related supporting details as they occurred to her.

Three Versions of Phil's Story

Mother's Version

"Likes the sad parts" and the details of the romance:
   the way the father made the daughter promise not to
   get involved with a man until she finished college, the
   way the women got tears in their eyes when Phil
   played his song.
Remembers girl's husband had French cuffs.
Remembers Phil's wife = "big and loud."
Notes people were trying to cheer Phil up.
Remembers girl resting head on Phil's shoulder, and how he
   got idea for song.

Father's Version

Depression/money: mentions Phil's patched tires and engine,
   how he spent a week's pay on new clothes, how girl's
   husband pays cash for a new Pontiac.
"Times were tough"

Narrator's Version

Facts of story — but wants to add more about Phil's
   process of writing song (because he, like Phil, = artist?),
   more about romance ("you could see it in their eyes").
Wants to embellish story.
("I wish I could put more in . . .")

Carla's notes and lists eventually suggested the following thesis statement for her paper: "'Sleepy Time Gal' is a story that is not about the 'gal'
of the title or about the man the narrator calls Phil but rather about the
different viewpoints of its three narrators." Guided by this tentative thesis statement, she went on to write and revise her paper, following the
process detailed in Chapter **3**. The final draft of Carla's paper follows.
Annotations have been added to identify the conventions that apply to
writing essays about works of fiction. (Note that because all students in
the class selected stories from the same text, Carla's instructor did not require a Works Cited page.)

Watts 1

Carla Watts

Professor Sierra

English 1001

12 March 2001

Whose Story?

Midway through Gary Gildner's short story "Sleepy Time
Gal," the narrator acknowledges, "I've already intruded too
much in a simple story that isn't even mine" (215). But whose
story <u>is</u> "Sleepy Time Gal"? It is presented as the tale of Phil,
an ordinary young man of modest means who falls in love with
a rich young woman, writes a song for her, and loses both
the woman and the song, as well as the fame and fortune
the song could have brought him, apparently because he is
unwilling to fight for either. But actually, "Sleepy Time Gal" is
not Phil's story, and it is not the story of the girl he loves; the
story belongs to the three characters who compete to tell it.

The story these characters tell is a simple one; it is also
familiar. Phil is a young man with an ordinary job. He has little
education and no real prospects of doing anything beyond
working in a restaurant doing menial jobs. He is in love with a
girl whose father is a rich banker, a girl who goes to college.
Phil has no more chance of marrying the girl than he has of
becoming educated or becoming a millionaire. He has written
a song for her, but he is doomed to sell the rights to it for
twenty-five dollars. Phil may be a man with dreams and

Right margin annotations:

Paper title is
centered

Title is in
quotation
marks

Parenthetical
documentation
identifies page
on which
quotation
appeared

Thesis
statement

Brief plot
summary is
combined
with
interpretation

expectations that go beyond the small Michigan town
and the roadhouse, but he does not seem to be willing to
struggle to make his dreams come true. Ironically, he never
achieves the happy married life his song describes; his dreams
remain just dreams, and he settles for life in the dream world
of a movie theater.

Father's
perspective

|

Past tense
used to
identify events
that occurred
before story's
main action

The character who seems to be the author of Phil's story is
the narrator's father: he is the only one who knew Phil and
witnessed the story's events, and he has told it again and again
to his family. But the story he tells reveals more than just what
happened to Phil; it says a lot about his own life too. The father
is a mechanic who eventually leaves his small Michigan town for
Detroit. As the narrator observes, he is "a gentle but practical
man" (214). We can assume he has seen some hard times; he
sees Phil's story only in the context of the times, and "times
were tough" (216). The narrator says, "My father, when he told

Ellipsis (set in
brackets)
indicates
words omitted
from
quotation

the story, [. . .] would tell it in an offhand way and emphasize
the Depression and not having much, instead of the important
parts" (214). In the father's version, seemingly minor details are
important: Phil's often-mended car engine, "a gingerbread of
parts from different makes" (215), and incidents like how Phil
spent a week's pay on a new shirt and tie, "the first tie he ever
owned" (215), and how the girl's husband paid cash for a new
Pontiac. These details are important to the father because they
have to do with money. He sees Phil's story as more about

Watts 3

a particular time (the Depression era) than about particular
people. Whenever he hears Phil's song on the radio, he
remembers that time.

The narrator's mother, however, sees Phil's story as a
romantic, timeless story of hopelessly doomed lovers. She did
not witness the story's events, but she has heard the story
often. According to the narrator, she "likes the sad parts and
is eager to get to their last night before the girl goes away
to college" (215). She remembers how the women in the
roadhouse got tears in their eyes when Phil played the song
he wrote. The mother's selective memory helps to characterize
her as somewhat romantic and sentimental, interested in
people and their relationships (the way the girl's father made
her promise to avoid romantic entanglements until after
college; the way Phil's friends tried to cheer him up) and in
visual details (the way the girl rested her head on Phil's
shoulder; the French cuffs on her husband's shirt). In the
interaction between the characters, she sees drama and
even tragedy. The sentimental story of lost love appeals to
her just as the story of lost opportunity appeals to the father.

The narrator knows the story only through his father's
telling and retelling of it, and he says, "I will try to tell it the
way he did, if I can" (214). But this is impossible: as he tells
the story, he embellishes it, and he makes it his own. He is the
one who communicates the story to readers, and he ultimately

(margin note, right) Mother's perspective

(margin note, right) Point is supported by specific references to story

(margin note, left) Narrator's perspective

Watts 4

decides what to include and what to leave out. His story reflects both his parents' points of view: the focus on both characters and events, both romance and history. In telling Phil's story, he tells the story of a time, re-creating a Depression-era struggle of a man who could have made it big but wound up a failure; however, he also recounts a story about people, a romantic, sentimentalized story of lost love. And, he tells a story about his own parents.

The narrator, like Phil, is creative; he needs to convey the facts of the story, but he must struggle to resist the temptation to add to them—to add more about how Phil went about writing the song, "maybe show him whistling the tune and going over the words slowly and carefully to get the best ones" (214-15), more about the romance itself. The narrator is clearly embellishing the story—for instance, when he says everyone knew Phil and the girl would get married because "you could see it in their eyes" (215), he admits that this detail is not in his father's version of the story—but he is careful to identify his own contributions, explaining, "I couldn't help putting it in there" (215). The narrator cannot help wondering about the parts his father did not tell, and he struggles to avoid rewriting the story to include them. Sometimes he cannot help himself, and he apologizes for his lapses with a phrase like "I have to break in here [. . .]" (214). But, for the most part, the narrator knows his place, knows it is not really his story to tell:

Narrator's perspective continued

Watts 5

"I wish I could put more in, especially about the song
and how it felt to Phil to sing it and how the girl felt
when hearing it and knowing it was hers, but I've already
intruded too much in a simple story that isn't even
mine" (215).

Phil's story is, as the narrator acknowledges, a simple
one, almost a cliché. But Gary Gildner's story, "Sleepy Time
Gal," is more complex. In it, three characters create and
re-create a story of love and loss, ambition and failure, all
contributing the details they feel should be stressed and, in
the process, revealing something about themselves and about
their own hopes and dreams.

Conclusion
reinforces
thesis

Carla's paper focuses on the story's shifting point of view and the contributions of the three central characters to Phil's story. She supports her thesis with specific references to "Sleepy Time Gal"—in the form of quotation, summary, and paraphrase—and interprets the story's events in light of the points she is making. Her paper does not include every idea in her notes, nor should it: she selects only those details that support her thesis.

53d Writing about Poetry

When you write a paper about poetry, you follow the same process discussed in **53c.** However, you concentrate on the elements poets use to create and enrich their work—for example, voice, form, sound, meter, language, and tone.

✔ CHECKLIST: WRITING ABOUT POETRY

✔ **Voice** Who is the poem's speaker? What is the speaker's attitude toward the poem's subject? How would you characterize the speaker's tone?

✔ **Word Choice and Word Order** What words seem important? Why? What does each word say? What does it suggest? Are any words repeated? Why? Is the poem's diction formal or informal? Is the arrangement of words conventional or unconventional?

✔ **Imagery** What images are used in the poem? To what senses (sight, sound, smell, taste, or touch) do they appeal? Is one central image important? Why? Is there a pattern of related images?

✔ **Figures of Speech** Does the poet use simile? Metaphor? Personification? What do figures of speech contribute to the poem?

✔ **Sound** Does the poem include rhyme? Where? Does it have regular meter (that is, a regular pattern of stressed and unstressed syllables)? Does the poem include repeated consonant or vowel sounds? What do these elements contribute to the poem?

✔ **Form** Is the poem written in open form (with no definite pattern of line length, rhyme, or meter) or in closed form (conforming to a pattern)? Why do you think this kind of form is used?

✔ **Theme** What central theme or themes does the poem explore?

Daniel Johanssen, a student in an introductory literature course, followed this process as he planned an essay about Delmore Schwartz's 1959 poem "The True-Blue American," which follows. Daniel's essay appears on pages 740–42. (Note that because all students in the class selected poems from the same text, Daniel's instructor did not require a Works Cited page.)

THE TRUE-BLUE AMERICAN

Jeremiah Dickson was a true-blue American,
 For he was a little boy who understood America, for he felt that he must
Think about *everything*; because that's *all* there is to think about,
Knowing immediately the intimacy of truth and comedy,
Knowing intuitively how a sense of humor was a necessity   5
For one and for all who live in America. Thus, natively, and
Naturally when on an April Sunday in an ice cream parlor Jeremiah
Was requested to choose between a chocolate sundae and a banana split
He answered unhesitatingly, having no need to think of it
Being a true-blue American, determined to continue as he began: 10
Rejecting the either-or of Kierkegaard,[1] and many another European;
Refusing to accept alternatives, refusing to believe the choice of between;
Rejecting selection; denying dilemma; electing absolute affirmation:
    knowing
      in his breast   15
        The infinite and the gold
        Of the endless frontier, the deathless West.
"Both: I will have them both!" declared this true-blue American
In Cambridge, Massachusetts, on an April Sunday, instructed
      By the great department stores, by the Five-and-Ten,   20
Taught by Christmas, by the circus, by the vulgarity and grandeur of
      Niagara Falls and the Grand Canyon,
Tutored by the grandeur, vulgarity, and infinite appetite gratified and
      Shining in the darkness, of the light
On Saturdays at the double bills of the moon pictures,   25
The consummation of the advertisements of the imagination of the light
Which is as it was—the infinite belief in infinite hope—
    of Columbus, Barnum, Edison, and Jeremiah Dickson.

---

[1]Søren Kierkegaard (1813–1855)—Danish philosopher who greatly influenced twentieth-century existentialism. *Either-Or* (1841) is one of his best-known works.

Johanssen 1

Daniel Johanssen

Professor Stang

English 1001

8 April 2001

Paper title is
centered

Title of poem
is in quotation
marks

Thesis
statement

Slash
separates
lines of
poetry

Parenthetical
documentation
indicates line
numbers

Irony in "The True-Blue American"

The poem "The True-Blue American" by Delmore
Schwartz is not as simple and direct as its title suggests. In
fact, the title is extremely ironic. At first, the poem seems
patriotic, but actually the flag-waving strengthens the
speaker's criticism. Even though the poem seems to support
and celebrate America, it is actually a bitter critique of the
negative aspects of American culture.

According to the speaker, the primary problem with
America is that its citizens falsely believe themselves to be
authorities on everything. The following lines introduce the
theme of the "know-it-all" American: "For he was a little boy
who understood America, for he felt that he must / Think
about everything; because that's all there is to think about"
(2-3). This theme is developed later in a series of parallel
phrases that seem to celebrate the value of immediate
intuitive knowledge and a refusal to accept or to believe
anything other than what is American (4-6).

Americans are ambitious and determined, but these
qualities are not seen in the poem as virtues. According to the
speaker, Americans reject sophisticated "European" concepts

Johanssen 2

like doubt and choices and alternatives and instead insist on "absolute affirmation" (13)—simple solutions to complex problems. This unwillingness to compromise translates into stubbornness and materialistic greed. This tendency is illustrated by the boy's asking for <u>both</u> a chocolate sundae <u>and</u> a banana split at the ice cream parlor—not "either-or" (11). Americans are characterized as pioneers who want it all, who will stop at nothing to achieve "The infinite and the gold / Of the endless frontier, the deathless West" (16-17). For the speaker, the pioneers and their "endless frontier" are not noble or self-sacrificing; they are like a greedy little boy at an ice cream parlor.

According to the speaker, the greed and materialism of America began as grandeur but ultimately became mere vulgarity. Similarly, the "true-blue American" is not born a vulgar parody of grandeur; he learns it from his true-blue fellows:

More than 3 lines of poetry are set off from text. Quotation is indented 10 spaces (or 1″) from left margin; no quotation marks are used.

>   instructed
> By the great department stores, by the Five-
>   and-Ten,
> Taught by Christmas, by the circus, by the vulgarity
>   and grandeur of
> Niagara Falls and the Grand Canyon,
> Tutored by the grandeur, vulgarity, and infinite
>   appetite gratified [. . .]. (19-23)

Among the "tutors" the speaker lists are such American institutions as department stores and national monuments.

Johanssen 3

Within these institutions, grandeur and vulgarity coexist; in a sense, they are one and the same.

The speaker's negativity climaxes in the phrase "Shining in the darkness, of the light" (24). This paradoxical statement suggests the negative truths hidden beneath America's glamorous surface. All the grand and illustrious things of which Americans are so proud are personified by Jeremiah Dickson, the spoiled brat in the ice cream parlor.

Conclusion reinforces thesis

Like America, Jeremiah has unlimited potential. He has native intuition, curiosity, courage, and a pioneer spirit. Unfortunately, however, both America and Jeremiah Dickson are limited by their willingness to be led by others, by their greed and impatience, and by their preference for quick, easy, unambiguous answers rather than careful philosophical analysis. Regardless of his—and America's—potential, Jeremiah Dickson is doomed to be hypnotized and seduced by glittering superficialities, light without substance, and to settle for the "double bills of the moon pictures" (25) rather than the enduring truths of a philosopher like Kierkegaard.

53e   Writing about Drama

When you write a paper about a play, you focus on the special conventions of drama. Here, for example, you might consider not just the play's plot and characters but also its staging.

✔ CHECKLIST: WRITING ABOUT DRAMA

✔ **Plot**   What happens in the play? What conflicts are developed? How are they resolved? Are there any subplots? What events, if any, occur offstage?

✔ **Character**   Who are the major characters? The minor characters? What relationships exist among them? What are their most distinctive traits? What do we learn about characters from their words and actions? From the play's stage directions? From what other characters tell us? Does the main character change or grow during the course of the play? What motivates the characters?

✔ **Staging**   When and where is the play set? How do the scenery, props, costumes, lighting, and music work together to establish this setting? What else do these elements contribute to the play?

✔ **Theme**   What central theme or themes does the play explore?

Kimberly Allison, a student in an introductory literature class, was assigned to write a short paper on one element—plot, character, staging, or theme—in a one-act play. She chose to write about the characters in Susan Glaspell's 1916 play *Trifles*. Her completed paper, annotated to highlight some conventions of writing about drama, appears on pages 744–48. (Note that because all students in the class selected plays from the same text, Kimberly's instructor did not require a Works Cited page.)

Allison 1

Kimberly Allison

English 1013

Professor Johnson

1 March 2001

Double-space

Desperate Measures:

Acts of Defiance in <u>Trifles</u>

Opening
sentence
identifies
author and
work

Susan Glaspell wrote her best-known play, <u>Trifles</u>, in

1916, at a time when women were beginning to challenge

their socially defined roles, realizing that their identities as

wives and domestics kept them in a subordinate position in

society. Because women were demanding more autonomy,

Introduction
places play in
historical
context

traditional institutions such as marriage, which confined

women to the home and made them mere extensions of their

husbands, were beginning to be reexamined.

As a married woman, Glaspell was evidently touched by

these concerns, perhaps because when she wrote <u>Trifles</u> she

was at the mercy of her husband's wishes and encountered

barriers in pursuing her career. But for whatever reason, Glaspell

chose as the play's protagonist a married woman, Minnie Foster

(Mrs. Wright), who has challenged society's expectations in a

very extreme way: by murdering her husband. Minnie's defiant

act has occurred before the action begins, and as the play

unfolds, two women, Mrs. Peters and Mrs. Hale, piece together

the details of the situation surrounding the murder. As the

events unfold, however, it becomes clear that the focus

Allison 2

of <u>Trifles</u> is not on who killed John Wright, but on the

themes of the subordinate role of women, the confinement

of the wife in the home, and the experiences all women

share; through these themes, Glaspell shows her audience

the desperate measures women had to take to achieve

autonomy.

    The subordinate role of women, particularly Minnie's role

in her marriage, becomes evident in the first few minutes of

the play when Mr. Hale observes that the victim, John Wright,

had little concern for his wife's opinions: "I didn't know as

what his wife wanted made much difference to John" (1164).

Here Mr. Hale suggests that Minnie was powerless against the

wishes of her husband. Indeed, as these characters imply,

Minnie's every act and thought were controlled by her

husband. Minnie only had power in her kitchen, and Mrs.

Peters and Mrs. Hale understand this situation because their

behavior is controlled by their husbands. Therefore, when

Sheriff Peters condemns Minnie's concern about her

preserves, saying, "Well, can you beat the women! Held for

murder and worrying about her preserves" (1166), he is, in a

sense, condemning all three of the women for worrying about

domestic matters rather than about the murder that has been

committed. Indeed, the sheriff's comment suggests that he

assumes women's lives are trivial, an assumption that pervades

the thoughts and speech of all three men.

Thesis
statement

Topic sentence
identifies first
point paper
will discuss:
women's
subordinate
role

Allison 3

Topic sentence
introduces
second point
paper will
discuss:
women's
confinement

Mrs. Peters and Mrs. Hale are similar to Minnie in another way as well: throughout the play, they are confined to the kitchen of the Wrights' house, while their husbands enter and exit the house at will. This scenario mirrors Minnie's daily life, as she remained in the home while her husband went to work and into town. The two women discuss Minnie's isolation in being housebound: "Not having children makes less work— but it makes a quiet house, and Wright out to work all day, and no company when he did come in" (1171). Beginning to identify with Minnie's loneliness, Mrs. Peters and Mrs. Hale recognize that, busy in their own homes, they have, in fact, participated in isolating and confining Minnie. Mrs. Hale declares, "I wish I had come over once in a while! That was a crime! That was a crime! Who's going to punish that? [. . .] I might have known she needed help" (1173)!

Transitional
paragraph
discusses
women's
observations
and
conclusions

Soon the two women discover that Minnie's only connection to the outside world was her bird, the symbol of her confinement; Minnie was a caged bird who was kept from singing and communicating with others because of her restrictive husband. And piecing together the evidence—the disorderly kitchen, the poorly stitched quilt pieces, and the dead canary—the women come to believe that John Wright broke the bird's neck just as he had broken Minnie's spirit. Now, Mrs. Peters and Mrs. Hale see the connection between the dead canary and Minnie's situation. The stage directions

Allison 4

describe the moment when the women become aware

of the truth: "<u>Their eyes meet</u>," and the women share

"<u>A look of growing comprehension, of horror</u>" (1172).

Through their observations and discussions in Mrs.

Wright's kitchen, Mrs. Hale and Mrs. Peters come to understand

the commonality of women's experiences. Mrs. Hale speaks for

both of them when she says, "I know how things can be—for

women. [. . .] We all go through the same things—it's all just a

different kind of the same thing" (1173). And, once the two

women realize the experiences they share, they begin to

recognize that they must join together in order to challenge a

male-oriented society; although their experiences may seem

trivial to the men, the "trifles" of their lives are significant to

them. They realize that Minnie's independence and identity

were crushed by her husband and that their own husbands

have asserted that women's lives are trivial and unimportant as

well. This realization leads them to commit an act as defiant as

the one that has gotten Minnie into trouble: they conceal their

discovery from their husbands and from the law.

Significantly, Mrs. Peters does acknowledge that "the

law is the law," but she also understands that because Mr.

Wright treated his wife badly, Minnie is justified in killing him.

They also realize, however, that for men the law is black and

white and that an all-male jury will not take into account the

extenuating circumstances that prompted Minnie to kill her

Topic sentence
introduces
third point
paper will
discuss:
commonality
of women's
experiences

Allison 5

husband. And even if Minnie were allowed to communicate to the all-male court the abuses she has suffered, the law would undoubtedly view her experience as trivial.

Nevertheless, because Mrs. Hale and Mrs. Peters empathize with Minnie's condition, they suppress the evidence they find, enduring their husbands' condescension rather than standing up to them. Through this desperate action, the women attempt to break through the boundaries of their social role, just as Minnie has done. Although Minnie is imprisoned for her crime, she has freed herself; and, although Mrs. Peters and Mrs. Hale conceal their knowledge, fearing the men will laugh at them, these women are really challenging society and freeing themselves as well.

Conclusion places play in historical context

In Trifles, Susan Glaspell addresses many of the problems shared by early twentieth-century women, including their subordinate status and their confinement in the home. In order to emphasize the pervasiveness of these problems, and the desperate measures women had to take to break out of restrictive social roles, Glaspell does more than focus on the plight of the woman who has ended her isolation and loneliness by committing a heinous crime against society. By illustrating the vast differences between male and female experience, she shows how men define the roles of women and how women can challenge these roles in search of their own significance in society and their eventual independence.

53f Using Literary Terms

When you write about literature, you use a vocabulary appropriate to the discipline. The following glossary defines some of the terms you will use.

alliteration   Repetition of initial sounds in a series of words, as in "dark, damp dungeon."

allusion   A reference to a historical event, a work of literature, a biblical passage, or the like that the author expects readers to recognize.

antagonist   The character who is in conflict with or in opposition to the *protagonist.* Sometimes the antagonist is a force or situation, such as war or poverty.

assonance   Repetition of vowel sounds in a series of words, as in "fine slide on the ice."

blank verse   Lines of unrhymed iambic pentameter in no particular stanzaic form; approximates the rhythms of ordinary English speech.

character   The fictional representation of a person. Characters may be *round* (well developed) or *flat* (undeveloped stereotypes), *dynamic* (changing and growing during the course of the story) or *static* (remaining essentially unchanged by the story's events).

climax   The point of greatest tension or importance in a play or story; the point at which the story's decisive action takes place.

closed form   A kind of poetic structure characterized by a consistent pattern of rhyme, meter, or stanzaic form.

conflict   The opposition between two or more characters, between a character and a natural force, or between contrasting tendencies or motives or ideas within one character.

consonance   Repetition of consonant sounds in a series of words, as in "the gnarled fingers of his nervous hands."

denouement   The point in the plot of a work of fiction or drama at which the action comes to an end and loose ends are tied up.

exposition   The initial stage of the plot of a work of fiction or drama, in which the author presents basic information readers need to understand the story's characters and events.

figurative language   Language whose meaning is not to be taken literally. The most commonly used figures of speech are *metaphor, personification,* and *simile.*

free verse   Poetry that does not follow a fixed meter or rhyme scheme.

hyperbole Intentional overstatement or exaggeration.

imagery Use of sensory description (description that relies on sight, sound, smell, taste, or touch) to make what is being described more vivid. A *pattern of imagery* combines a group of related images in order to create a single effect.

irony Language that suggests a discrepancy or incongruity between what is said and what is meant (*verbal irony*), between what actually happens and what we expected to happen (*situational irony*), or between what a character knows or believes and what the reader knows (*dramatic irony;* also called *tragic irony*).

metaphor A comparison that equates two things that are essentially unlike. Unlike a *simile,* a metaphor does not use *like* or *as.*

meter The pattern of stressed and unstressed syllables in a line of poetry; each repeated unit of meter is called a *foot.* An *anapest* has three syllables, the first two unstressed and the third stressed; a *dactyl* has three syllables, the first stressed and subsequent ones unstressed; an *iamb* has two syllables, of which the second is stressed; a *spondee* has two syllables, both stressed; and a *trochee* has two syllables, the first stressed and the second unstressed. A poem's meter is described by the kind of foot (iamb, dactyl, and so on) and the number of feet in each line (one foot per line = monometer, two feet per line = dimeter, three feet = trimeter, four = tetrameter, five = pentameter, and so on). Thus, a poetic line containing five feet, each of which contains an unstressed syllable followed by a stressed syllable, would be described as *iambic pentameter.*

monologue An extended speech by one character.

narration The recounting of events—for example, in a work of fiction. When an event that has already occurred is recounted in a later sequence of events, it is called a *flashback;* when something that will occur later in a narration is suggested earlier, the suggestion is called a *foreshadowing.*

open form A kind of poetic structure not characterized by any consistent pattern of rhyme, meter, or stanzaic form.

paradox A seemingly contradictory statement.

persona The narrator or speaker of a story or poem; the persona's attitudes and opinions are not necessarily those of the author.

personification The assigning of human qualities to nonhuman things.

plot The arrangement of events in a work of literature.

point of view   The perspective from which a story is told. A story may have a *first-person narrator,* who may be a major or minor character in the story. Alternatively, a story may have a *third-person narrator,* who is not a character in the story. Such a narrator may be an *omniscient narrator,* who knows the thoughts and motives of all the story's characters, or a *limited omniscient narrator,* who sees into the minds of only some of the characters. A narrator who cannot be trusted—because he or she is naive, evil, stupid, or self-serving—is called an *unreliable narrator.* The objective perspective that presents only information an audience would get from watching the action unfold on stage is called the *dramatic* point of view.

protagonist   The principal character of a work of drama or fiction.

rhyme   The repetition of the last stressed vowel sound and all subsequent sounds. *End rhyme* occurs at the ends of poetic lines; *internal rhyme* occurs within a line of poetry.

rhythm   The regular repetition of stresses and pauses.

setting   The background against which the action of a work of literature takes place: the historical period, locale, season, time of day, etc.

simile   A comparison that equates two essentially unlike things using the words *like* or *as.*

soliloquy   A convention of drama in which a character speaks directly to the audience, revealing thoughts and feelings that the play's other characters, even if they are present on the stage, are assumed not to hear.

stanza   A group of lines in a poem, separated from others by a blank space on the page, which forms a unit of thought, mood, or meter. Common stanzaic forms include the *couplet* (two lines), *tercet* (three lines), *quatrain* (four lines), *sestet* (six lines), and *octave* (eight lines).

stock character   A character who behaves consistently and predictably and who is instantly recognizable and familiar to the audience.

symbol   An image whose meaning transcends its literal or denotative sense in a complex way. Its multiple associations give it significance beyond what it could carry on its own.

theme   An idea expressed by a work of literature.

tone   The attitude of the speaker toward a work's subject, characters, or audience, conveyed by the work's word choice and arrangement of words.

understatement   Intentional downplaying of a situation's significance.

CHAPTER 54

WRITING FOR THE WORKPLACE

? FREQUENTLY ASKED QUESTIONS

How do I address a business letter to a woman? (p. 752)

What should a business letter look like? (p. 753)

Is my e-mail at work private? (p. 754)

How should I design a résumé so that it can be scanned or posted on the Internet? (p. 759)

54a Writing Business Letters

Business letters should be brief and to the point, with important information placed early in the letter. Be concise, avoid digressions, and try to sound as natural as possible.

The first paragraph of your letter should introduce your subject and mention any pertinent previous correspondence. The body of your letter should present the facts readers will need in order to understand your points. (If your ideas are complicated, present your points in a bulleted or numbered **list**.) Your conclusion should reinforce your message.

See 55a3

CLOSE UP   BUSINESS LETTER SALUTATIONS

If you are writing to a woman, consult previous correspondence, and use the title she uses. If you do not know her preference, use *Ms.* If you know a person's last name and first initial and do not know whether the person is male or female (or if you do not have a specific person to whom to address your letter), call the company and ask for the full name of the person who should receive your letter. If you are unable to determine the name of the person who will receive your letter, use a neutral form of address—*Dear Editor* or *Dear Personnel Director,* for example. Keep in mind that generic salutations, such as *Gentlemen, Dear Sirs,* and *Dear Madam,* are both **sexist** and outdated. Whenever possible, use a person's name.

See 29f2

SAMPLE LETTER ❓

6732 Wyncote Avenue
Houston, TX 77004
May 3, 2000

Heading

Mr. William S. Price, Jr., Director
Division of Archives and History
Department of Cultural Resources
109 East Jones Street
Raleigh, NC 27611

Inside address

Dear Mr. Price:

Salutation

Thank you for sending me the material I requested about pirates in colonial North Carolina.

Both the pamphlets and the bibliography were extremely useful for my research. Without your help, I am sure my paper would not have been so well received.

Body

I have enclosed a copy of my paper, and I would appreciate any comments you may have. Again, thank you for your time and trouble.

Sincerely yours,

Complimentary close

Written signature

Kevin Wolk

Typed signature

Kevin Wolk

Copy sent

cc: Dr. N. Provisor, Professor of History

Additional data

Enc.: Research paper

SENDING MESSAGES BY FAX AND E-MAIL

The standards for electronic messages are the same as those for any other form of business correspondence.

Faxes Remember that faxes are often received not by an individual but at a central location, so you must include a cover sheet that contains the recipient's name and title, the date, the company and department, the fax and telephone numbers, and the total number of pages faxed. In addition, supply your own name and telephone and fax numbers. (It is also a good idea to call ahead to alert the addressee that a fax is coming.)

E-mail In many workplaces, virtually all internal communications are in the form of e-mail. Although personal e-mail can be quite informal, you should treat your business e-mail as if it were a standard written letter. Include a salutation and a subject line, and be sure to state your purpose and to present your ideas clearly and succinctly. Avoid slang and imprecise diction, and proofread carefully. Also, keep in mind that e-mail composed at work is the property of the employer, who has the legal right to access it. For this reason, e-mail at work is never private or completely secure.

54b Writing Letters of Application and Résumés

When you apply for employment, your goal is to get an interview. The **letter of application** summarizes your qualifications for a specific position; the **résumé** provides a general overview of your accomplishments.

(1) Letters of Application

Begin your letter of application by identifying the job you are applying for and stating where you heard about it—in a newspaper, in a professional journal, on the Internet, or from your school's job placement service, for example. Be sure to include the date of the advertisement and the exact title of the position. End your introduction with your thesis: a statement of your ability to do the job.

SAMPLE LETTER OF APPLICATION: SEMIBLOCK FORMAT

246 Hillside Drive
Urbana, IL 61801   Heading
October 20, 2000
kr237@metropolis.105.com

Mr. Maurice Snyder, Personnel Director
Guilford, Fox, and Morris
22 Hamilton Street   Inside address
Urbana, IL 61822

Dear Mr. Snyder: Salutation

My college advisor, Dr. Raymond Walsh, has told me that you
are interested in hiring a part-time accounting assistant. I believe that my academic background and my work experience
qualify me for this position.

I am presently a junior accounting major at the University of   Body
Illinois. During the past year, I have taken courses in taxation,
trusts, and business law. I am also proficient in *Lotus* and
ClarisWorks. Last spring, I gained practical accounting experience by working in our department's tax clinic.

←— Double-
space

After I graduate, I hope to get a master's degree in taxation
and then return to the Urbana area. I believe that my experience in taxation as well as my familiarity with the local busi-   ←— Single-
ness community would enable me to contribute to your firm.   space

I have enclosed a résumé for your examination. I will be available for an interview any time after midterm examinations,
which end October 25. I look forward to hearing from you.

Complimentary   Sincerely yours,
close
                       Sandra Kraft

                       Sandra Kraft   Typed
                       Enc.: Résumé   signature
                                                    Additional
                                                    data

In the body of your letter, provide the information that will convince your reader of your qualifications—for example, relevant courses you have taken and pertinent job experience. Be sure to address any specific criteria mentioned in the advertisement. Above all, emphasize your strengths, and explain how they relate to the specific job for which you are applying.

Conclude by saying that you have enclosed your résumé. State that you are available for an interview, noting any dates on which you cannot be available.

EXERCISE 1

Look through the employment advertisements in your local newspaper or in the files of your college placement service. Choose one job, and write a letter of application in which you outline your achievements and discuss your qualifications for the position.

(2) Print Résumés

A résumé lists relevant information about your education, your job experience, your goals, and your personal interests.

There is no single correct format for a résumé. You may decide to arrange your résumé in **chronological order,** listing your education and work experience in sequence (beginning with the most recent), or in **emphatic order,** presenting first the material that will be of most interest to a particular employer. Whatever a résumé's arrangement, it should be brief—one page is sufficient for an undergraduate—easy to read, and clearly and logically organized.

 PRINT RÉSUMÉS

Use strong action verbs to describe your duties, responsibilities, and accomplishments.

accomplished	achieved	supervised
communicated	collaborated	instructed
completed	implemented	proposed
performed	organized	trained

Application Letters: How to Sell Yourself (Purdue)
http://owl.english.purdue.edu/handouts/pw/p_applettr.html

SAMPLE RÉSUMÉ: CHRONOLOGICAL ORDER

KAREN L. OLSON

SCHOOL
3312 Hamilton St. Apt. 18
Philadelphia, PA 19104
215-382-0831
olsonk@durm.ocs.drexel.edu

HOME
110 Ascot Ct.
Harmony, PA 16037
412-452-2944

EDUCATION

DREXEL UNIVERSITY, Philadelphia, PA 19104
Bachelor of Science in Graphic Design
Anticipated Graduation: June 2001
Cumulative Grade Point Average: 3.2 on a 4.0 scale

COMPUTER SKILLS AND COURSE WORK

HARDWARE
Operate both Macintosh computer and PCs.
SOFTWARE
Adobe Illustrator, Photoshop, and *TypeAlign; QuarkXPress; CorelDRAW; Micrografx Designer*
COURSES
Corporate Identity, Environmental Graphics, Typography, Photography, Painting and Printmaking, Sculpture, Computer Imaging, Art History

EMPLOYMENT EXPERIENCE

UNISYS CORPORATION, Blue Bell, PA 19124
June–September 2000, Cooperative Education
Graphic Designer. Designed interior pages as well as covers for target marketing brochures. Created various logos and spot art designed for use on interoffice memos and departmental publications.

CHARMING SHOPPES, INC., Bensalem, PA 19020
June–December 1999, Cooperative Education
Graphic Designer/Fashion Illustrator. Created graphics for future placement on garments. Did some textile designing. Drew flat illustrations of garments to scale in computer. Prepared presentation boards.

THE TRIANGLE. Drexel University, Philadelphia, PA 19104
January 2000–present
Graphics Editor. Design all display advertisements submitted to Drexel's student newspaper.

DESIGN AND IMAGING STUDIO, Drexel University, Philadelphia, PA 19104
October 1998–June 2000
Monitor. Supervised computer activity in studio. Answered telephone. Assisted other graphic design students in using computer programs.

ACTIVITIES AND AWARDS

The Triangle, Graphics Editor: 1999–present
Kappa Omicron Nu Honor Society, vice president: 1998–present
Dean's List: Spring 1996, fall and winter 1998
Graphics Group, vice president: 1998–present

REFERENCES AND PORTFOLIO

Available upon request.

SAMPLE RÉSUMÉ: EMPHATIC ORDER

MICHAEL D. FULLER

SCHOOL	HOME
27 College Avenue	1203 Hampton Road
University of Maryland	Joppa, MD 21085
College Park, MD 20742	(301) 877-1437
(301) 357-0732	
mful532@aol.com	

RESTAURANT EXPERIENCE

McDonald's Restaurant, Pikesville, MD. Cook.
Prepared hamburgers. Acted as assistant manager for two weeks while manager was on vacation. Supervised employees, helped prepare payroll and work schedules. Was named employee of the month. Summer 1999.

University of Maryland Cafeteria, College Park, MD. Busboy.
Cleaned tables, set up cafeteria, and prepared hot trays. September 1998–May 1999.

OTHER WORK EXPERIENCE

University of Maryland Library, College Park, MD. Reference assistant. Filed, sorted, typed, shelved, and cataloged. Earnings offset college expenses. September 1997–May 1998.

EDUCATION

University of Maryland, College Park, MD (sophomore).
Biology major. Expected date of graduation: June 2001.
Forest Park High School, Baltimore, MD.

INTERESTS

Member of University Debating Society.
Tutor in University's Academic Enrichment Program.

REFERENCES

Mr. Arthur Sanducci, Manager
McDonald's Restaurant
5712 Avery Road
Pikesville, MD 22513

Mr. William Czernick, Manager
Cafeteria
University of Maryland
College Park, MD 20742

Ms. Stephanie Young, Librarian
Library
University of Maryland
College Park, MD 20742

(3) Electronic Résumés

Many employers now request résumés that they can scan into a database for future reference. If you have to prepare such a résumé, you must
format it accordingly. Because scanners will not pick up columns, bullets, or italics, you should not use them in a scannable résumé.

Whereas in a print résumé you use strong action verbs to describe
your accomplishments, in a scannable résumé, you use key nouns or adjectives that can be entered into a company database. These words will
help employers find your résumé when they carry out a keyword search
for applicants with certain skills. (To facilitate a keyword search, some
applicants even include a Keyword section at the top of their résumés,
before Education and Experience.) In addition, scannable résumés
should include a separate section that lists skills.

 ELECTRONIC RÉSUMÉS

Use strong adjectives and nouns to describe your duties, responsibilities, and accomplishments.

capable	communicator	leader
dedicated	competent	creative
flexible	diversified	motivated
responsible	efficient	well traveled

Increasingly, résumés are posted on electronic bulletin boards or on
Web sites, such as Monster.com., and, frequently, these résumés contain
hyperlinks to other sites. (These links are underlined and highlighted in
blue.) For example, your name could be a link to your home page, which
might include a biographical sketch, or the title of your senior thesis
could be a link to a site that contains the text of the thesis itself. Presently,
most résumés are still submitted on paper, but electronic résumés are
gaining in popularity.

Writing Cover Letters (Illinois)
   http://www.english.uiuc.edu/cws/wworkshop/tips/writtech.cover.htm
Action Words for Better Résumés
   http://www.msajobs.com/actionwords.html

SAMPLE RÉSUMÉ: SCANNABLE

CONSTANTINE G. DOUKAKIS

2000 Clover Lane   Phone: (817) 735-9120
Fort Worth, TX 76107   E-Mail: Douk@aol.com

Employment Objective: Entry level position in an organization that will enable me to use my academic knowledge and the skills that I learned in my work experience.

EDUCATION:

University of Texas at Arlington, Bachelor of Science in Civil Engineering. June 2001. Major: Structural Engineering. Graduated Magna Cum Laude. Overall GPA: 3.754 on a 4.0 base.

SCHOLASTIC HONORS AND AWARDS:

Member of Phi Eta Sigma First-Year Academic Honor Society, Chi Epsilon Civil Engineering Academic Society, Tau Beta Pi Engineering Academic Society, Golden Key National Honor Society

Jack Woolf Memorial Scholarship for Outstanding Academic Performance

COOPERATIVE EMPLOYMENT EXPERIENCE:

Dallas-Fort Worth International Airport, Tarrant County, TX, Dec. 1999 to June 2000. Assistant Engineer. Supervised and inspected airfield paving, drainage, and utility projects as well as terminal building renovations. Performed on-site and laboratory soil tests. Prepared concrete samples for load testing.

Dallas-Fort Worth International Airport, Tarrant County, TX, Jan. 2000 to June 2000. Draftsman in Design Office. Prepared contract drawings and updated base plans as well as designed and estimated costs for small construction projects.

Johnson County Electric Cooperative, Cleburne, TX, Jan. 1999 to June 1999. Junior Engineer in Plant Dept. of Maintenance and Construction Division. Inspected and supervised in-plant construction. Devised solutions to construction problems. Estimated costs of materials for small construction projects. Presented historical data relating to the function of the department.

SKILLS:

Strong organizational and leadership skills. Technical knowledge of IBM microcomputer hardware. Knowledge of DOS, Windows 2000, and MacOs. Proficiency in Word, Excel, FileMaker Pro, PowerPoint, WordPerfect, and various Internet client software.

> ### ✔ CHECKLIST: COMPONENTS OF A RÉSUMÉ
>
> ✔ The **heading** includes your name, school address, home address, telephone number, and e-mail address.
>
> ✔ A statement of your **career objective** (optional), placed at the top of the page, identifies your professional goals.
>
> ✔ The **education section** includes the schools you have attended, starting with the most recent one and moving back in time. (After graduation from college, do not list your high school unless you have a compelling reason to do so—for instance, if it is nationally recognized for its academic standards or it has an active alumni network in your field.)
>
> ✔ The **summary of work experience** generally starts with your most recent job and moves backward in time.
>
> ✔ The **background** or **interests section** lists your most important (or most relevant) special interests and community activities.
>
> ✔ The **honors section** lists academic achievements and awards.
>
> ✔ The **references section** lists the full names and addresses of at least three references. If your résumé is already one full page long, a line saying that your references will be sent upon request is sufficient.

EXERCISE 2

Prepare a résumé to include with the letter of application you wrote for Exercise 1.

54c Writing Memos

Memos communicate information within a business organization, transmitting brief messages of a paragraph or two or short reports or proposals. Their function may be either to convey information or to persuade.

Writing in the Job Search (Purdue)
  http://owl.english.purdue.edu/handouts/pw/index.html
Business Letters: Accentuating the Positive (Purdue)
  http://owl.english.purdue.edu/handouts/pw/p_subnegmess.html
Business English Hangman
  http://www.better-english.com/hangman/hangone.htm
Business English Crosswords
  http://www.better-english.com/crosswords/test.htm

SAMPLE MEMO

Opening
component

TO: Ina Ellen, Senior Counselor
FROM: Kim Williams, Student Tutor Supervisor
SUBJECT: Construction of a Tutoring Center
DATE: November 10, 2000

Purpose
statement

This memo proposes the establishment of a tutoring center in the Office of Student Affairs.

BACKGROUND
Under the present system, tutors must work with students at a number of facilities scattered across the university campus. As a result, tutors waste a lot of time running from one facility to another and are often late for appointments.

NEW FACILITY

Body

I propose that we establish a tutoring facility adjacent to the Office of Student Affairs. The two empty classrooms next to the office, presently used for storage of office furniture, would be ideal for this use. We could furnish these offices with the desks and file cabinets already stored in these rooms.

BENEFITS
The benefits of this facility would be the centralizing of the tutoring services and the proximity of the facility to the Office of Student Affairs. The tutoring facility could also use the secretarial services of the Office of Student Affairs.

Conclusion

RECOMMENDATIONS
To implement this project we would need to do the following:

1. Clean up and paint rooms 331 and 333
2. Use folding partitions to divide each room into five single-desk offices
3. Use stored office equipment to furnish the center

I am certain these changes would do much to improve the tutoring service. I look forward to discussing this matter with you in more detail.

EXERCISE 3

Your duties at your summer job with a public utility include reading correspondence sent from your division to the public. While reading a pamphlet that discusses energy conservation, you notice repeated use of the word *repairmen,* and you come across the sentences "Each consumer must do *his* part" and "*Mothers* should teach their children about conservation." With the approval of your supervisor, you decide to write a memo to John Durand, public relations manager, explaining that some customers might perceive this language as **sexist**—and, therefore, offensive. In your memo, explain to Mr. Durand why the language should be changed, and suggest some words and phrases he could use in their place. Mr. Durand is your superior, so maintain a reasonable and respectful tone.

See
29f2

CHAPTER 55

DOCUMENT DESIGN AND MANUSCRIPT FORMAT

This chapter presents general guidelines for document design as well as specific formatting conventions followed in the humanities and the social sciences and specified by MLA and APA, respectively.

55a   Document Design

Document design refers to the conventions that determine the way a document—a research paper, memo, report, business letter, or résumé, for example—looks on a page. Designing a document often involves making choices that will emphasize key ideas and make your paper easier to read. In many college writing situations, the **format** of your paper—including such matters as how you use headings, how you construct tables and charts, and how you arrange information on a title page—is defined by the discipline in which you are writing. Although formatting conventions differ from discipline to discipline, the basic principles of document design are the same. In general, well-designed documents have the following characteristics:

- Effective format
- Clear headings
- Useful lists
- Attractive visuals

(1) Creating an Effective Format

Margins   Your document should be double-spaced (unless your instructor tells you otherwise) with at least a one-inch margin on all sides. You can either leave a ragged edge on the right, or you can justify your text so that all the words are aligned evenly at the right margin. A ragged edge is recommended because it varies the visual landscape of your document, making it easier to read.

Fonts   To create a readable document, use a 10- or 12-point font. Avoid fonts that distract readers (script or cursive fonts, for example).

(2) Using Headings

Headings tell readers what to expect in a section before they actually read it. By breaking up a text and eliminating long, uninterrupted blocks of prose, headings make a document inviting and readable.

Number of Headings   You should have enough headings to highlight the most important points of your document. A long, complicated document needs more headings than a shorter, less complex document. Keep in mind, however, that although too few headings may not be of much use, too many headings will make your document look like an outline.

Phrasing   Headings should be brief, descriptive, specific, and to the point. They can be single words—*Summary* or *Introduction,* for example—or phrases (always stated in **parallel** terms). Headings can be phrased as questions or statements.

See
27a

Format   Headings and subheadings may be *centered,* placed *flush left,* or *indented.* The most important thing to remember is that headings at the same level should have the same format—for example, if one first-level heading is boldfaced and centered, all other first-level headings must be boldfaced and centered.

Typographical Emphasis   You can emphasize headings by using **boldface,** *italics,* or ALL CAPITAL LETTERS. Used in moderation, these distinctive typefaces make a text more readable. (Notice, for example, how these typefaces are used in this handbook.) Used excessively, however, they slow readers down and make reading more difficult.

SAMPLE HEADING FORMATS

Centered, Boldfaced, Uppercase and Lowercase

<u>Flush Left, Underlined, Uppercase and Lowercase</u>

   <u>Indented, underlined, lowercase paragraph heading ending with a period</u>.

ALL CAPITAL LETTERS, CENTERED

(3) Constructing Lists

A list moves material out of a text, where it may be difficult to read, and enables readers to see it easily. A list can also break up complicated statements into a series of key ideas. Lists are easiest to read when all the elements are **parallel** and about the same length. When rank is important, number the items on the list; when it isn't, use **bullets** (as in the following list). Make sure you introduce the list with a complete sentence followed by a colon.

We should take several steps to reduce our spending:
- We should cut our workforce by 10 percent.
- We should utilize less-expensive vendors.
- We should decrease overtime.
- We should replace our present health plan with a less-expensive HMO.

Because the items on the preceding list are complete sentences, each ends with a period. Do not use periods if the items are not sentences.

   NOTE: Lists are useful because they make items stand out from the text around them. Too many lists, however, have the opposite effect, making a document seem choppy and difficult to read.

(4) Tables, Graphs, Diagrams, and Photographs

Visuals, such as tables, graphs, diagrams, and photographs, can enhance your document by enabling you to present a great deal of information in a limited space. You can create your own tables and graphs by using a computer program like *Excel, Lotus,* or *Microsoft Word.* In addition, you can get diagrams and photographs by photocopying or scanning them from a print source or by downloading them from the Internet or CD-ROMs. Remember, however, that if you use a visual from a source, you *must* use appropriate documentation.

Tables   Tables present data in a condensed, visual format—arranged in rows and columns. Tables most often contain numerical data, although occasionally they contain words as well as numbers. When you plan your table, make sure you include only the data that you will need; discard information that is too detailed or difficult to understand (this material is best presented in an appendix). Keep in mind that tables may distract readers, so include only those necessary to support your discussion. The following table summarizes personnel data.

McVay 3

As the following table shows, the Madison location now employs more workers in every site than the St. Paul location.

Table 1   *Heading*

Number of Employees at Each Location   *Descriptive caption*

Employees	Location	
	Madison	St. Paul
Plant	461	254
Warehouse	45	23
Outlet Stores	15	9

Data

Because the Madison location has grown so quickly, steps must be taken to . . .

Graphs   Like tables, graphs present data in visual form. Whereas tables present specific numerical data, graphs convey the general pattern or trend that the data suggest. Because graphs tend to be more general (and, therefore, less accurate) than tables, they are frequently accompanied by tables. The following is an example of a bar graph:

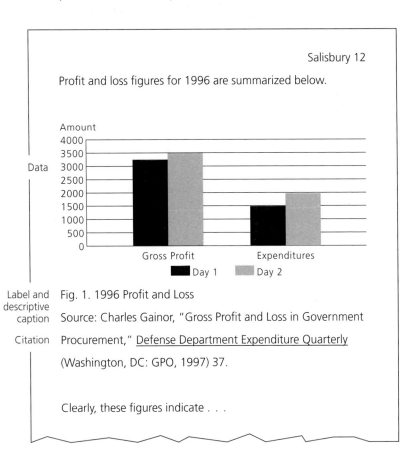

Salisbury 12

Profit and loss figures for 1996 are summarized below.

Data

Label and descriptive caption   Fig. 1. 1996 Profit and Loss

Source: Charles Gainor, "Gross Profit and Loss in Government

Citation   Procurement," <u>Defense Department Expenditure Quarterly</u>

(Washington, DC: GPO, 1997) 37.

Clearly, these figures indicate . . .

Diagrams A diagram enables you to focus on specific details of a mechanism or object. Diagrams are often used in scientific and technical writing to clarify concepts while eliminating paragraphs of detailed and confusing description. The following diagram, which illustrates the ancient Greek theater, serves a similar purpose in a literature paper.

Dixon 10

The design of the ancient Greek theater is similar to that of a present-day sports stadium, as figure 2 illustrates.

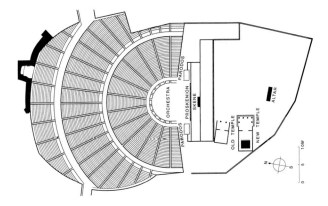

Fig. 2. The Theater of Dionysus at Athens, from W. B. Worthen, <u>The Harcourt Brace Anthology of Drama</u>, 3rd Edition (Fort Worth: Harcourt, 2000) 16.

Label and descriptive caption

Citation

This design, with its tiered seats, enabled the audience to view the actors onstage as well as . . .

Photographs   Photographs enable you to show exactly what something or someone looks like—an animal in its natural habitat, a work of fine art, or an actor in costume, for example. Although computer technology that enables you to paste photographs directly into a text is widely available, use it with restraint. Not every photograph will support or enhance your written text; in fact, an irrelevant photograph distracts readers.

Robes 3

In the later years of his life, Twain was seen more as a personality than as a writer. Figure 3 shows him in a characteristic pose.

Fig. 3. Mark Twain, <u>On Porch with Kitten, Mark Twain and His Times</u>, 17 April 1999, U of Virginia, 18 June 2000 <http://etext.virginia.edu/railton/index2html>.

Label and descriptive caption

The white suit he wears in this photograph . . .

✔ CHECKLIST: USING VISUALS IN THE TEXT

✔ Use a visual only when it contributes something important to the discussion, not for embellishment.

✔ Use the visual in the text only if you plan to discuss it in your paper (place the visual in an appendix if you do not).

✔ Introduce each visual with a complete sentence.

✔ Follow each visual with a discussion of its significance.

✔ Leave wide margins around each visual.

✔ Place the visual as close as possible to the section of your document in which it is discussed.

✔ Label each visual appropriately.

✔ Document each visual that is borrowed from a source.

55b Creating a Web Site ❓

Because many colleges and universities now provide students with a full range of Internet services, it is possible that over the course of your college career you will have the opportunity to create a Web page or a full Web site. You may even be asked to do so as part of the requirements for a course. Like other documents, Web pages are subject to specific conventions of document design.

Essentially, there are two ways to create Web pages. You can create a Web page from scratch using HTML (hypertext markup language), the programming language by which standard documents are converted to World Wide Web hypertext documents. Or (and this is by far the easier way), you can use Web page creation software that automatically converts text and graphics into HTML so that they can be posted on the Web. Even though these programs allow you to create Web pages quickly and easily, you will still need to devote time to learning them, just as you would with any new software program.

(1) Building a Home Page

A personal **home page** usually contains information about how to contact the author, a brief biography, and links to other Web sites. A home page can be expanded into a full **Web site** (a group of related Web pages).

A Beginner's Guide to HTML
   http://www.ncsa.uiuc.edu/General/Internet/WWW/HTMLPrimerAll.html

To create a simple home page from scratch, you will need to know a few of the most basic HTML tags. (**Tags** tell your Web browser how to display text and images.) If you have a document that you want to turn into a Web page, you must code it by placing the proper HTML tags as needed.

 BASIC HTML TAGS

<HTML> Indicates the beginning of an HTML document

<BODY> Indicates the start of a document's body text

<P>, </P> Indicates begin paragraph and end paragraph, respectively

<H1>, <H2>, <H3>, <H4> Heading tags, from largest to smallest

<A HREF= "(Web address here)"> Tag used to create a link to another Web page

</A> Ends linked text

 Indicates a line break

<B> Indicates that the word following will appear in bold

</B> Indicates the end of a word that will appear in bold

</BODY> Indicates the end of a document's body text

</HTML> Indicates the end of a document

If you examine a coded home page, you will notice that it begins with an <HTML> tag at the top and ends with an </HTML> tag at the bottom. Similarly, <BODY> and </BODY> tags indicate the beginning and end of a document's text. Paragraph <P> and heading <H> tags organize body text into headings, subheadings, and paragraphs.

Once you have mastered simple text-only pages, you can move on to design Web pages that include tables, charts, photographs, animation, and film clips. One way to learn how to do this is to examine the HTML codes for your favorite Web pages. Do this by clicking on *view* in your browser's main menu (at the top of your computer screen) and selecting *page source* from the pull-down menu. Your browser will then display the

HTML code for the page you are viewing. You can then "save" the source code in a word-processing document and borrow it later as you create pages of your own. Note that although you may borrow code from a Web site, it is never acceptable to **plagiarize** a site's content.

WEB SITES AND COPYRIGHT

Copyright gives an author the legal right to control the copying of his or her work. As a rule, you should assume that any material—text or pictures—on the Web is copyrighted unless the author makes an explicit statement to the contrary. This means that you must receive permission if you are going to reproduce this material on your Web site. The only exception to this rule is the **fair use doctrine** that allows the use of material for the purpose of commentary, parody, or research and education. Thus, you can quote a small part of an article from the *New York Times* for the purpose of criticizing it, but you must get permission from the *New York Times* to reproduce the article in its entirety on your Web site. You do not, however, have to get permission to provide a link to the article at the *New York Times*'s Web site. (The material you quote in a research paper falls under the fair use doctrine and does not require permission.)

(2) Organizing Information

Before creating a Web site, sketch a basic plan on a piece of paper. Consider how your Web pages will be connected and what links you will provide to other Web sites. Your home page should provide an overview of your site and give readers a clear sense of what material the site will contain. Beginning with the home page, users will navigate from one piece of information to another.

As you plan your Web site, consider how your pages will be organized. If your site is relatively uncomplicated, you can arrange pages so that one page leads sequentially to the next. For example, your personal Web site could begin with a home page and then progress to a page that presents your interest in sports, then to one that presents your volunteer work, and finally to your résumé. If your site is relatively complicated, however, you will have to group pages according to their order of importance or according to their relevance to a particular category. *The Holt Handbook*'s Web site, for example, presents a great deal of information under various headings—Using Your Brief Holt Handbook, Succeeding in First-Year Composition, and Tip of the Day, for example (see Figure 1).

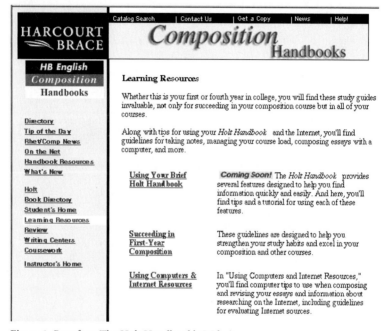

Figure 1 *Page from* The Holt Handbook's *Web site*

(3) Designing a Web Site

When you design your Web site, lay out text and graphics so that they present your ideas clearly and logically. Because your home page is the first thing readers will encounter, it should be clear and easy to follow. If it is not, readers will lose interest and move on to some other site. Present related items next to each other, and use text sparingly. Make sure you identify items on the same topic by highlighting them in the same color or by using the same font or graphic. Remember, however, that using too many graphics or fancy type styles will confuse readers. In addition, do not use graphics that take too long to download (25K to 30K is a reasonable upper limit).

(4) Providing Links

Your home page will contain buttons or links. **Buttons**—graphic icons, such as arrows or pictures—enable readers to move from one page of a Web site to another. **Links** (short for *hyperlinks*)—words or URLs (electronic addresses) highlighted and underlined in blue—enable readers to navigate from one site to another. When you provide a link, you are directing people to the Web site to which the link refers. For this reason, be certain that the site is up and running and that the information is reliable. In addition, only include links that are relevant to your Web site.

(5) Proofreading Your Text

Before you post your site on the Web, proofread the text of your Web pages just as you would any other document. (Even if you run a spell check and grammar check, you should still proofread carefully.) Then, make sure you have provided both *begin* and *end* tags. If you have included links on your Web site, be sure you have entered the full Web address (beginning with *http://*). If you have used a colored background or text, be sure you have avoided color combinations that make your pages difficult to read (purple on black, for example). Finally, make certain you have received permission for and acknowledged all material—graphics as well as text—that you have borrowed from a source.

(6) Posting a Web Site

Once you have designed a Web site, you will need to upload, or post, it so that others can view it on the Web. Most commonly, Web pages are posted with **ftp** (file transfer protocol) software programs, such as Fetch for Macintosh. Recent versions of the most popular Internet browsers contain software for posting pages to the Web.

See
12a4

To post a Web page, open your program and enter the ftp address of your Internet Service Provider. You will also need a user name and password that you will enter when you have established communication with your host server. Once you have established communication, you can post your Web site almost instantly. (If you have made any mistakes in coding your page, the errors will be apparent as soon as you view the page on the Web.)

55c MLA Manuscript Guidelines

MLA guidelines are used for papers in the humanities. The following guidelines are based on the *MLA Handbook for Writers of Research Papers*, Fifth Edition. (For an example of a paper that uses MLA manuscript format, see **18m.**)

1. Type your paper with a one-inch margin at the top, bottom and on both sides. Indent the first line of every paragraph, as well as the first line of every item on the Works Cited list, five spaces (or one-half inch). Set off a **long prose quotation** (more than four lines) by indenting ten spaces (or one inch) from the left-hand margin. Double-space your paper throughout.

2. If your instructor does not require a separate title page, use the model on page 777. Capitalize all important words in the title, but not prepositions, coordinating conjunctions, articles, or the *to* in infinitives, unless they begin or end the title. Do not underline the title or enclose it in quotation marks, but do underline words in the title if they would otherwise be underlined (for example, book titles). Never put a period after a title, even it is a sentence. Double-space between the last line of the title and the first line of your paper. If the title is longer than a single line, double-space and center the second line below the first.

3. If your instructor requires a separate title page, use a format like the one used in the paper in **18m.**

4. Number all pages of your paper consecutively—including the first—in the upper right-hand corner, one-half inch from the top, flush right. (Do not put *p.* before the page numbers, and do not put periods or any other punctuation after them.) Type your name before the page number on every page.

5. The *MLA Handbook* does not mention **headings**. Traditionally, papers in the humanities do not use headings; instead, strong topic sentences or transitional paragraphs introduce ideas. This trend seems to be changing, however. If you want to use headings, check with your instructor to make sure they are acceptable.

6. Tables and illustrations should be placed as close as possible to the part of the paper in which they are discussed.

   Tables should be headed *Table* and given an arabic numeral and a descriptive caption. Type the heading and the descriptive caption flush left on separate lines above the table. Capitalize the heading

MLA Style Document Formatting (Capital Com. & Tech. College, CT)
http://webster.commnet.edu/mla/format.htm

and the caption as if they were titles. If the table is borrowed from a source, give the full citation below the table beginning at the left-hand margin. Double-space the table's text and the notes.

Other visuals, such as graphs, diagrams, and photographs, should be labeled *Figure* (abbreviated *Fig.*) and given an arabic number. The label, a descriptive caption, and the full citation are typed below the illustration beginning at the left-hand margin.

7. If you use source material in your paper, follow the MLA documentation style discussed and illustrated in **16a.**

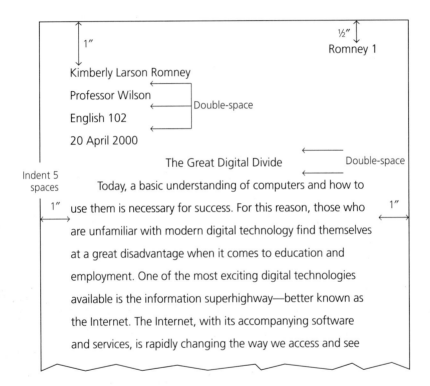

55d   APA Manuscript Guidelines

APA guidelines are used for papers in the social sciences. The following list is based on the *Publication Manual of the American Psychological Association* (4th ed.). For an example of a paper that uses APA manuscript format, see **50d.**

1. Type your paper with at least a one-inch margin at the top, bottom, and sides of the paper. Do not hyphenate words at the end of a line. Double-space between all lines of the manuscript. (You may use triple- or quadruple-spacing before and after a table.)

2. Indent the first line of every paragraph, as well as the first line of every item on the Reference List, five to seven spaces. Set off quotations of forty or more words in a block format placed five to seven spaces from the left-hand margin. If the quotation is one paragraph or less, do not indent; if it is more than one paragraph, indent the first line of the second and subsequent paragraphs five to seven spaces from the new margin.

3. The title page should follow the model on page 690.

4. Papers in the social sciences often contain an **abstract,** a short summary of approximately one hundred words. If your instructor requires an abstract, it should appear as a separate numbered page (labeled *Abstract*) after the title page.

5. Number all pages of your paper consecutively. Each page should include a **page header** (a shortened form of the title) as well as the page number in the upper right-hand corner. Begin the text of your paper on a new page. Center the title of the paper at the top of the page; if the title is more than one line, double-space between the lines and center. Skip two spaces and begin typing the text.

6. Major __headings__ should be centered and typed with uppercase and lowercase letters. Minor headings should be flush left, typed with uppercase and lowercase letters, and underlined.

7. Items in a series should be formatted as a numbered __list__.

8. __Tables__ (numerical values displayed in columns and rows) should be numbered consecutively in the order in which they are mentioned in the paper (Table 1, Table 2, and so on). Double-space each table and include a brief identifying title (*Table 1. Population Figures for 1995*) directly above it. Begin each table on a separate page after the reference list. Refer to each table by number in the text of your paper—for example, "Table 3 summarizes this study."

   Other types of visuals (charts, graphs, diagrams, and so on) are also numbered consecutively. The label *Figure* and an identifying caption are typed beneath the visual beginning at the left-hand margin.

   APA recommends that tables and figures be placed in an appendix at the end of the paper; however, your instructor may want you to include this material in the body of the paper.

9. If you use source material in your paper, follow the APA documentation style in **17a.**

See 55a2

See 55a3

See 55a4

PART 9

ESL AND GLOSSARIES

CHAPTER 56

ENGLISH FOR SPEAKERS OF OTHER LANGUAGES (ESL)

? FREQUENTLY ASKED QUESTIONS

56a   Writing for Native English Speakers

Writing for a native English-speaking audience involves much more than writing correct English sentences. Native and nonnative speakers of English may have very different expectations about logic, organization, support, and even purpose and audience. In order to meet the expectations of an English-speaking audience, writers need to understand these differences. Scholars in the field of **contrastive rhetoric,** which is devoted to the study of the contrasting rhetorical and stylistic characteristics of various languages, have identified some of these differences.

Native English speakers are direct. English speakers tend to follow a straight line of logic, from clear statement to supporting examples, without irrelevancies or digressions. Compared to speakers of other languages, native speakers of English can seem curt and businesslike, even blunt and rude. Whereas business letters in many Asian languages may begin with observations about the weather or even with inquires about the health of the recipient's family, business letters in English usually begin by stating the main point of the letter. Many English sayings express the direct quality of the language: "Get to the point," "Say what you mean," "Stop beating around the bush."

Native speakers of English value originality. In many cultures, the point of speaking in public or writing for an audience is to imitate the style of famous orators and writers, both ancient and modern. Native speakers of English, however, generally expect writers to be original in their opinions, choice of supporting details, and even style. Readers of English want to see new twists on old ideas and original uses of language. Therefore, they object to the use of clichés and overly familiar language.

Native speakers of English expect audiences to disagree. In many cultures, audiences are expected to agree with the speaker or writer. By contrast, writers in English may invite questions, criticism, or even disagreement from the audience. In some cultures, such responses by the audience might be considered inappropriate or rude, but they show English-speaking writers that the audience is reading closely and taking their ideas seriously.

Native speakers of English question authority. Native speakers of English assume they are operating within a democratic society that encourages open debate. Every belief the audience holds, no matter how ancient or cherished, can be challenged. The English speaker's skeptical attitude may disturb some members of some cultural groups. To them, English speakers may appear to have no firm beliefs of their own at all

---

The ESL Study Hall (George Washington U.)
   http://gwis2.circ.gwu.edu/~gwvcusas/
Dave Sperling's ESL (English as a Second Language) Café
   http://www.eslcafe.com
Self-Study Quizzes for ESL Students (TESL)
   http://www.aitech.ac.jp/~iteslj/quizzes/
Activities for ESL Students (TESL)
   http:www.aitech.ac.jp/~iteslj/s/

and may seem not to respect the beliefs of their audience. However, English speakers often use skepticism not to destroy belief, but rather to investigate it, refine it, and reinforce it.

EXERCISE 1

Newspaper editorials or letters to the editor are often good examples of the qualities of English discussed in this section. Find a letter or an editorial in a local newspaper and see how many of these qualities it displays. (For example, does it come to the point immediately? Does it challenge the truth of accepted ideas?) Does it display qualities that are different from those of a writer discussing the same subject in your native language?

56b   Choosing a Topic

What **topics** do native speakers of English choose to write about? In general, they try either to *inform* their readers, giving new information that readers may not already know, or to *persuade* their readers, offering opinions that may not be popular and then convincing their readers to accept these opinions as valid. Therefore, they will choose a topic about which they believe they know more than their audience does, or they will choose a topic about which there is public debate.

Such topics may be quite different from those chosen by nonnative speakers of English. In some cultures, it is rude for a writer to claim to know more than an audience about a topic; a writer must be humble and perhaps even apologize to the audience for not knowing enough. In other cultures, controversial topics are intentionally avoided for complex social and political reasons. However, too much humility may cause English audiences to lose their trust in the writer; avoiding controversial topics may make the writer seem indecisive.

56c   Stating and Supporting a Thesis

(1) Stating a Thesis

When writing in English, state your **thesis**—your main idea or point of view—as quickly as possible. You need not worry about offending or insulting your readers by doing this; in fact, your readers expect you to state your thesis as soon as you can.

You should also be quite specific in **stating your thesis**. You may begin with general statements, but keep in mind that an English-speaking audience will look for a specific thesis statement that expresses what you have to say about the topic.

See 2b2

 STATING A THESIS

See 2b2

An **effective thesis statement** has the following characteristics.

- It is a statement of opinion or conjecture, not a self-evident statement or a statement of fact.
- It is not a familiar platitude, such as "Honesty is the best policy" or "Look before you leap," but a more original, even unique, idea.
- It is narrow enough to be supported within the scope of the essay.
- It can be supported with concrete examples.

---

(2) Supporting a Thesis

Native speakers of English usually demand a very tight connection between an essay's thesis and its support. The thesis states the writer's main point, and the support answers the question "Why?" or "How?" by giving reasons or examples. English speakers expect that all the support will be directly related to the thesis.

Native speakers of English may have little patience for what they see as digressions or indirect discussions of the subject. In the classic essay patterns of many languages—the *ba-gu-wen* pattern of Chinese rhetoric, for example—the writer is supposed to digress. In the eyes of Chinese essay writers, English essays may seem less imaginative, less creative, than the Chinese ideal. Nevertheless, it is important that you meet the native-speaking audience's expectations of a direct, businesslike discussion.

Native speakers of English support a thesis statement in one of two ways: ❓

- With *facts and statistics:* Native English speakers reject the strategy of supporting one personal opinion with only other personal opinions (which is an accepted pattern of logic in many cultures).

- With the *opinions of authorities:* The criteria that make a person an authority for English speakers may be different from those used in other cultures. It is not simply a person's social status or position as a political or religious leader that matters, but rather the person's expertise in the subject. Even the highest-ranking officials still must support their beliefs with factual information.

SUPPORTING A THESIS

- Examples must be real and not hypothetical. It is better to point to the experiences of real people than to make up examples. It is better to say, "Eighty-six percent of Americans on welfare say they would prefer to have a job" than to say, "Few people would choose welfare over working if they had a choice."
- Examples must be relevant to the thesis. Speakers of English want to see a direct connection between factual evidence and the position the writer is taking. If a writer asserts, for example, that cats make better pets than dogs, it makes no sense to say that pigs are also becoming popular pets in America. Instead, the writer can point out that cats are quieter and easier to care for than dogs.
- Examples must be sufficient to convince readers that a statement is true. Beware of false generalizations based on too few details. For example, the fact that your friend got a good job without going to college does not mean that no one needs to go to college to get a good job. Do enough people who do not go to college get good jobs to justify the assertion that college is not necessary?

EXERCISE 2

After each of the following thesis statements are statements of fact meant to support it. In each group, which factual statements best support the writer's position? Why?

1. Eating too much beef is bad for your health.
   a. People who eat a lot of beef have more heart attacks than people who do not.
   b. American beef in particular is full of unhealthful chemicals.
   c. Raising animals just to eat them is cruel.
   d. People who eat a lot of beef tend not to eat other foods that they need, such as grains and vegetables.

2. Standardized tests are a poor means of determining a student's academic abilities.
   a. Many students who perform well at other academic tasks do poorly on standardized tests.
   b. Standardized tests are too difficult.
   c. Other kinds of academic work are much more important than standardized tests.
   d. The conditions under which students take standardized tests may damage the students' performance.
   e. Standardized tests may have content that is unfamiliar to some groups of otherwise able students.
3. Engineering is a very good field to enter today.
   a. There are too many doctors.
   b. There are many jobs open to engineers.
   c. Engineering is fun,
   d. Engineers are well paid.
   e. Engineers build things.

EXERCISE 3

For each of the following thesis statements, write at least three statements of fact that support it. If you disagree with any of the statements, rewrite it so that you can better support it.

1. American women are the freest women in the world.
2. Knowing English well is a very important business skill.
3. Americans do not know enough about other countries.
4. Recycling alone will not solve our pollution problems.

56d   Organizing Ideas

(1) Using an Introduction, a Body, and a Conclusion

Native speakers of English are likely to expect to find a **thesis-and-support** organization of ideas. In addition, most native speakers learn to use a very specific organizational pattern in their essays.

See 2b1

- The **introduction** introduces the topic and states the thesis.
- The **body** presents the support for the thesis statement.
- The **conclusion** sums up the writer's position.

> Introduction   Thesis statement: Languages contain a lot of
>   cultural information.

Body

    Support: For example, a language can tell a lot about social relations among the people who speak it.

    Support: A language can also reveal the social values of particular groups.

    Support: Learning a language can even tell us about the material possessions of its speakers.

    Support: On the deepest level, a language can contain ingrained cultural attitudes about time and space.

Conclusion

    Summary: Therefore, when we study a language, we are also studying the cultural attitudes of the people who speak it.

EXERCISE 4

Is there a specific strategy for organizing essays in your native language? If so, what is it? Is it similar to the English method for organizing ideas, or is it quite different from it? Make a list of similarities and differences.

(2) Writing in Paragraphs

See
Ch. 6

    The **paragraph** is a basic unit of communication in English. Many other languages use paragraphs, of course, but some do not. Some languages are not even written, as English is, horizontally from left to right. Some other languages, even those that are written as English is, have no convention of bringing together groups of sentences into a paragraph.

  WRITING IN PARAGRAPHS

- The first line of a paragraph is indented, giving the paragraph its characteristic shape on a page.
- Paragraphs vary in length, from a single sentence to many sentences, from a few lines to a page or more. Regardless of the paragraph's length, however, all its sentences focus on a single idea.
- A paragraph's main idea is often stated explicitly as a topic sentence, most often (though not always) at the beginning.

- All the other sentences in the paragraph provide further explanation of the topic sentence or concrete examples to illustrate the topic sentence.
- The sentences in a paragraph are often linked by connecting devices, such as the repetition of key words and the use of **transitional words or phrases**.

See
6c2

EXERCISE 5

In each of the following paragraphs, look for these elements: a clearly stated main idea; examples that illustrate the topic sentence; and connecting devices, such as transitional phrases. If the main idea is not clearly stated, try stating it in your own words. Is every sentence in the paragraph clearly focused on that main idea?

1. Asian Americans are not one people but several—Chinese Americans, Japanese Americans, and Filipino Americans. Chinese and Japanese Americans have been separated by geography, culture, and history from China and Japan for seven and four generations, respectively. They have evolved cultures and sensibilities distinctly not Chinese or Japanese and distinctly not white American. Even the Asian languages as they exist today in America have been adjusted and developed to express a sensitivity created by a new experience. In America, Chinese and Japanese American culture and history have been inextricably linked by confusion, the popularization of their hatred for each other, and World War II. (Frank Chin, Jeffery Paul Chan, Lawson Fusao Inada, Shawn Wong, Preface to *Aiiieeeee*)

2. The sex differences in personality formation that Chodorow describes in early childhood appear during the middle childhood years in studies of children's games. Children's games are considered by George Herbert Mead and Jean Piaget as the crucible of social development during the school years. In games, children learn to take the role of the other and come to see themselves through another's eyes. In games, they learn respect for rules and come to understand the ways rules can be made and changed. (Carol Gilligan, *In a Different Voice*)

56e Writing Correct English

Grammatical errors can become a serious problem for native as well as nonnative speakers when such errors get in the way of efficient communication. Therefore, although you may not be able to eliminate all grammatical errors from your English, you should try to make it as correct as possible.

In addition to the cultural and logical patterns discussed so far, English differs from other languages in its grammar. The study of grammatical differences among various languages is called **contrastive linguistics.** Scholars in the field of contrastive linguistics have identified a number of differences between English and other languages.

In English, words may change their form according to their function. In some languages, words never change form, or they change form according to rules different from those of English. For example, English verbs change form to communicate whether an action is taking place in the past, in the present, or in the future; in Chinese, however, other words may be added to the sentence to indicate when in the past the action took place (yesterday, last month, ten years ago), but the verb itself does not change form to indicate past action.

In English, context is extremely important to understanding function. Sometimes, it is impossible to identify the function of an English word without noting its context. In the following sentences, for instance, the very same words perform different functions according to their relation to other words.

Juan and I are taking a <u>walk</u>. (*Walk* is a noun, a direct object of the verb *taking,* with an article, *a,* attached to it.)

If you <u>walk</u> instead of drive, you will help conserve the earth's resources. (*Walk* is a verb, the predicate of the subject *you.*)

Jie was <u>walking</u> across campus when she met her chemistry professor. (*Walking* is part of the verb, the predicate of the subject *Jie.*)

<u>Walking</u> a few miles a day will make you healthier. (*Walking* is a noun, the subject of the verb *will make.*)

Next summer, we'll take a <u>walking</u> tour of southern Italy. (*Walking* is an adjective describing *tour.*)

See Ch. 31

<u>Spelling</u> **in English is not perfectly phonetic and may sometimes seem illogical.** In many languages that use a phonetic alphabet or syllabary, such as Japanese, Korean, or Persian script, words are spelled exactly as they are pronounced. Spelling in English, however, is often a matter of memorization, not sounding out the words phonetically. For example, the "ough" sound in the words *tough, though,* and *thought* is pronounced quite differently in each case. In fact, spelling in English is

related more to the history of the word and its origins in other languages than to the way the word is pronounced.

Word order is extremely important in English sentences.

See 56k

EXERCISE 6

As a nonnative speaker of English, you may have more conscious knowledge of English grammar than a native speaker who has never studied it as a foreign language. Moreover, as a speaker of at least two languages, you probably have a good sense of grammatical differences between languages.

Make a list of a few major differences between the grammar of English and the grammar of your native language and of any other languages you know. Be prepared to explain these differences to your classmates.

56f Nouns

A **noun** *names* things: people, objects, places, feelings, ideas.

See 32a

Nouns can be quite different in different languages. In some languages, nouns have gender; that is, they may be *masculine* or *feminine*. In Spanish, the word for *moon* (*la luna*) is feminine, whereas the word for *sun* (*el sol*) is masculine. In other languages, there is no difference between the singular and plural forms of nouns. In Japanese, one person is *hito*, whereas many people are still *hito*. In some languages (including English), nouns may be used as adjectives: "She ate a *cheese* sandwich."

(1) Singular, Plural, and Noncount Nouns

In English, nouns may have number; that is, they may change in form according to whether they name one thing or more than one thing. If a noun names only one thing, it is a singular noun; if a noun names more than one thing, it is a **plural** noun.

See 31b8

Glossary of Grammatical Terms (Rhodes College)
    http://www.rhodes.edu/kamhi/center/glossary.html
Ask a Grammar Expert (E-Mailed Responses to Grammar Questions)
    http://www.grammarnow.com/
University of Illinois's "Grammar Safari"
    http://deil.lang.uiuc.edu/web.pages/grammarsafari.html
Nouns Defined
    http://www.english.uiuc.edu/cws/wworkshop/grammar/nounsdefined.htm
Common and Proper Nouns (Illinois)
    http://www.english.uiuc.edu/cws/wworkshop/grammar/commonproper.htm

Some English nouns, called **noncount nouns,** do not have a plural form because the things they name cannot be counted. (**Count nouns** name items that can be counted, such as *book* or *child*.) Understanding the distinction between count and noncount nouns is important in determining the correct use of **articles** with nouns.

See
56f2

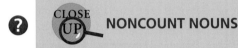 **NONCOUNT NOUNS**

The following commonly used nouns are noncount nouns. These words have no plural forms. Therefore, you should never add -*s* to them.

advice	evidence	knowledge
clothing	furniture	luggage
education	homework	merchandise
equipment	information	revenge

EXERCISE 7

Underline all the nouns in the following passage. Then, list the nouns in three columns (singular, plural, noncount).

The highway took me through Danville, where I saw a pillared antebellum mansion with a trailer court on the front lawn. Route 127 ran down a long valley of pastures and fields edged by low, rocky bluffs and split by a stream the color of muskmelon. In the distance rose the foothills of the Appalachians, old mountains that once separated the Atlantic from the shallow inland sea now the middle of America. The licks came out of the hills, the fields got smaller, and there were little sawmills cutting hardwoods into pallets, crates, and fenceposts. The houses shrank, and their colors changed from white to pastels, to iridescents, to no paint at all. The lawns went from Vertagreen bluegrass to thin fescue to hard-packed dirt glinting with fragments of glass, and the lawn ornaments changed from birdbaths to plastic flamingos and donkeys to broken-down automobiles with raised hoods like tombstones. On the porches stood long-legged wringer washers and ruined sofas, and, by the front doors, washtubs hung like coats of arms. (William Least Heat Moon, *Blue Highways*)

EXERCISE 8

Each of the following sentences has one number error in a noun. Underline each noun in the sentence. Then, located the noun that has the incorrect number and correct it. Be prepared to explain the error and how you corrected it.

1. Donald arrived in New York with three suitcase and his aunt's telephone number.
2. Where is the magazines I lent you last month?
3. The United States has fifty state, one special district, and territories, such as the Virgin Islands, Guam, and American Samoa.
4. There are more woman in the American military today than at any time in the past.
5. When Françoise came back from vacation, she was filled with happinesses.
6. The journey of a thousand mile begins with just one step.
7. John F. Kennedy was president of the United States for only three year.
8. Why do so many man say they are superior to women?
9. Most rock-and-roll bands have three guitar and one set of drums.
10. Except for Native Americans, every American citizens is the descendant of immigrants or slaves.

(2) Using Articles with Nouns

English has two **articles:** *a* and *the*. *A* is called the **indefinite** article; *the* is the **definite** article. *A* is replaced by *an* if the word that follows begins with a *vowel* (*a, e, i, o,* or *u*) or with a *vowel sound:* <u>a</u> book, <u>an</u> apple, <u>an</u> honor. If the vowel is pronounced like a consonant, use *a:* <u>a</u> onetime offer.

The primary function of articles is to signal to the audience whether the noun being referred to is new to the discussion or has already been mentioned.

Use an **indefinite article** (*a* or *an*) with a noun when readers have no reason to be familiar with the noun you are naming—when you are introducing the noun for the first time, for example. To say "Jatin entered <u>a</u> building" signals to the audience that you are introducing the idea of the building into your speech or writing for the first time. The building is indefinite, or not specific, until it has been identified.

Use the **definite article** (*the*) when the noun you are naming has already been introduced. The definite article indicates that the noun introduced may already be familiar to readers. To say "Jatin entered <u>the</u> building," signals to readers that you are referring to the same building you mentioned earlier. The building has now become specific and may be referred to by the definite article.

USING ARTICLES WITH NOUNS

There are two main exceptions to the rules governing the use of articles with nouns.

1. Plural nouns do not require indefinite articles: "I love horses," not "I love a horses." (Plural nouns do, however, require definite articles: "I love the horses in the national park near my house.")
2. Noncount nouns may not require articles: "Love conquers all," not "A love conquers all" or "The love conquers all."

EXERCISE 9

In the following passage, underline every noun and circle the article that accompanies it. Do your best to explain why the noun requires that article, or, if there is no article, why it does not require one.

Close about the plaza and the cathedral were the townhouses that intrigued me greatly. These were the homes of the rich, *los ricos.* The high front walls were neatly painted brown, grey, pink, or light cream. The street windows were even with the sidewalk with long iron bars that reached also to the roof. Lace curtains, drapes, and wooden screens behind the bars kept people from looking in. Every townhouse had a *zaguán* and a driveway cutting across the sidewalk, ramped and grooved so the carriages could roll in and out. On hot days the *zaguanes* were left wide open, showing a part of the patios with their fountains, rose gardens, and trees. The walls and the floors of the corridors were decorated with colored tile in solid colors and complicated designs. Between the open *zaguán* and the patio there was the *cancel,* a grill of wrought iron that was always kept closed and locked. (Ernesto Galarza, *Barrio Boy*)

(3) Using Other Determiners with Nouns

 Determiners are words that function as **adjectives** to limit or qualify the meaning of nouns. In addition to articles, nouns may be identified by other determiners that function in ways similar to articles, such as

demonstrative pronouns, possessive nouns and pronouns, numbers (both **cardinal** and **ordinal**), and other words indicating number and order.

1. **Demonstrative pronouns** (*this, that, these, those*) communicate

   • the relative nearness or farness of the noun from the speaker's position (*this* and *these* for things that are *near, that* and *those* for things that are *far*): *this* book on my desk, *that* book on your desk; *these* shoes on my feet, *those* shoes in my closet
   • the *number* of things indicated (*this* and *that* for *singular* nouns, *these* and *those* for *plural* nouns): *this* (or *that*) flower in the vase, *these* (or *those*) flowers in the garden.

2. **Possessive nouns** and **possessive pronouns** (*Ashraf's, his, their*) show who or what the noun belongs to: *Maria's* courage, *everybody's* fears, the *country's* natural resources, *my* personality, *our* groceries.

3. **Cardinal** numbers (*three, fifty, a thousand*) and **ordinal** numbers (*first, tenth, thirtieth*) indicate how many of the noun you mean and in what order the noun appears among other items: *seven* continents, *third* planet.

4. Words other than numbers may indicate **amount** (*many, few*) and **order** (*next, last*) and function in the same ways as cardinal and ordinal numbers: *few* opportunities, *last* chance.

For information on the order of adjectives in a series, see **56i2.**

56g Pronouns

Any English noun may be replaced by a pronoun. For example, *doctor* may be replaced by *he* or *she*, *books* by *them*, and *computer* by *it*.

Pronouns must be in proper grammatical **case:** *subjective, objective,* or *possessive.* (Possessive **case** in nouns is often indicated by an apostrophe followed by an *s*: Philip's beard, England's weather, a computer's keyboard. These nouns, too, may be replaced by pronouns called *possessive pronouns: my, his/her/its, your, their.*)

See
33a

Pronounds Defined (Illinois)
   http://www.english.uiuc.edu/cws/wworkshop/grammar/pronoundef.htm
Jack Lynch's Guide to Grammar and Style (much on mechanics)
   http://andromeda.rutgers.edu/~jlynch/Writing/contents.html

Pronouns must **agree** with the nouns they replace; that is, they must be the same *number* (singular or plural) and *gender* (male, female, or neuter).

Finally, pronouns must clearly **refer** to the nouns they replace.

EXERCISE 10

Underline all the pronouns in the following passage. Identify the noun each pronoun replaces.

> In the olden days, both Land and Heaven were tight friends as they were once human-beings. So one day, Heaven came down from heaven to Land his friend and he told him to let them go to the bush and hunt for the bush animals; Land agreed to what Heaven told him. After that they went into a bush with their bows and arrows, but after they had reached the bush, they were hunting for animals from morning till 12 o'clock a.m., but nothing was killed in that bush, then they left that bush and went to a big field and were hunting till 5 o'clock in the evening and nothing was killed there as well. After that, they left there again to go to a forest and it was 7 o'clock before they could find a mouse and started to hunt for another, so that they might share them one by one, because the one they had killed already was too small to share, but they did not kill any more. After that they came back to a certain place with the one they had killed and both of them were thinking how to share it. But as this mouse was too small to divide into two and these friends were also greedy, Land said that he would take it away and Heaven said that he would take it away. (Amos Tutuola, *The Palm-Wine Drunkard*)

EXERCISE 11

There are no pronouns in the following passage. The repetition of the nouns again and again would seem strange to a native speaker of English. Rewrite the passage, replacing as many of the nouns as possible with appropriate pronouns. Be sure that the connection between the pronouns and the nouns they replace is clear.

> The young couple seated across from Daniel at dinner the night before were newlyweds from Tokyo. The young couple and Daniel ate together with other guests of the inn at long, low tables in a large dining room with straw mat flooring. The man introduced himself immediately in English, shook Daniel's hand firmly, and,

after learning that Daniel was not a tourist but a resident working in Osaka, gave Daniel a business card. The man had just finished college and was working at the man's first real job, clerking in a bank. Even in a sweatsuit, the man looked ready for the office: chin closely shaven, bristly hair neatly clipped, nails clean and buffed. After a while the man and Daniel exhausted the man's store of English and drifted into Japanese.

The man's wife, shy up until then, took over as the man fell silent. The woman and Daniel talked about the new popularity of hot springs spas in the countryside around the inn, the difficulty of finding good schools for the children the woman hoped to have soon, the differences between food in Tokyo and Osaka. The woman's husband ate busily with an air of tolerating the woman's prattling. From time to time the woman refilled the man's beer glass or served the man radish pickles from a china bowl in the middle of the table, and then returned to the conversation.

56h Verbs

Although **verbs** in different languages perform similar functions, they differ in form and usage from language to language perhaps more than any other speech or grammatical unit.

See 32c1

Although all languages use verbs to express **states of being,** some languages use two different verbs to describe permanent and impermanent states of being—for example, *ser* and *estar* in Spanish. Other languages use two different verbs to describe animate and inanimate objects—for example, *aru* and *iru* in Japanese. With its single verb *be*, English is in this respect simpler than many other languages.

Languages may also differ in the ways they use verbs to communicate **action.** In Arabic, verbs change form to indicate whether the action they describe is complete or not. In Japanese, verbs can be conjugated to communicate the speaker's feelings about the action of the verb—for example, whether the action was overdone or "too much." Again, because English communicates such concepts in other words, the forms of its action verbs are simpler in these contexts than are the forms of action verbs in other languages.

(1) Tense, Person, and Number

English verbs change their form according to *tense, person,* and *number.* **Tense** refers to when the action described by the verb takes place.

See 34b

Person refers to who or what is performing the action described by the verb (*I, you, she*), and **number** refers to how many people or things are performing the action (one or more than one).

In other languages, verbs may change their appearance according to different rules. In Japanese, for example, verbs are not conjugated according to the person performing the action, but, rather, according to the social relationship between the speaker and the listener. In Chinese, verbs themselves do not change form to express tense; the time when the action is performed is communicated through other words.

Many **irregular** English verbs do not change their form according to the usual rules governing tense and person, but instead change in idiosyncratic ways. Unless you use the correct forms of the verbs in your sentences, you will confuse your English-speaking reader by communicating meanings you do not intend.

(2) Subject-Verb Agreement

The **subject** of a verb is the person or thing that performs the action expressed by the verb. Verbs must match, or **agree** with, their subjects in *person* (I, you, he) and *number* (he, they) so that in English we say *I read* but *she reads.* Be especially careful with irregular verbs: "I *am,* it *is,* they *are.*"

(3) Auxiliary Verbs

Meaning is also communicated in English by **auxiliary verbs** (also known as *helping verbs*), such as forms of the verbs *be* and *have:* "Julio *is* taking* a vacation." These auxiliary verbs change form to indicate tense, person, and number: "Julio and Ana *were* taking* a vacation." Other auxiliary verbs, called **modal auxiliaries**, include *would, should,* and *can.*

Model auxiliaries do not change form to indicate tense, person, and number: "I *should* save some money"; We *should* have saved* some money."

(4) Progressive and Perfect Tenses

Some nonnative speakers of English use **verb tenses** that are more complicated than they need to be. Such speakers may do this because their native language uses a more complicated tense where English does not, or because they "overcorrect" their verbs into complicated tenses.

Specifically, nonnative speakers tend to use **progressive** (present and past) verb forms instead of **simple** (present and past) verb forms, and **perfect** (present and past) verb forms instead of simple (present and past) verb forms. To communicate your ideas clearly to an English-speaking audience, choose the simplest possible verb tense.

(5) Double Negatives

The meaning of a verb may be made negative in English in a variety of ways, chiefly by adding the words *not* or *does not* to the verb (is, *is not;* can ski, *can't* ski; drives a car, *does not* drive a car).

Nonnative speakers (and some native speakers of English) sometimes use **double negatives**. A double negative occurs when the meaning of a verb is negated not just once but twice in a single sentence. In some languages, a double structure is actually required in order to negate a verb; for example, the French phrase "Je ne sais pas" ("I don't know") uses the double structure *ne + pas* around the verb *sais*. However, a double negative is incorrect in English.

See 36e

CLOSE UP   **AVOIDING DOUBLE NEGATIVES WITH CONTRACTIONS**

Be especially careful to avoid using double negatives with contractions that include the word *not.*

INCORRECT: Henry <u>doesn't</u> have <u>no</u> friends at all.

CORRECT: Henry <u>doesn't</u> have <u>any</u> friends at all.

CORRECT: Henry has <u>no</u> friends at all.

INCORRECT: I looked for articles in the library, but there <u>weren't none</u>.

CORRECT: I looked for articles in the library, but there <u>weren't any</u>.

CORRECT: I looked for articles in the library, but there were <u>none</u>.

---

(6) Verbs as Nouns and Adjectives

When English verbs are used as nouns or adjectives, speakers of other languages may be confused, particularly if in their native language, words do not change their function according to the way they are used in a sentence. Two verb forms may be used as nouns: **infinitives** (which always begin with *to,* as in *to work, to sleep, to eat*) and **gerunds** (which always end in *-ing,* as in *working, sleeping, eating*).

Present participles (which also end in -*ing*) and **past participles** (which often end in -*ed*, -*t*, or -*en*, as in *worked, slept, eaten*) are frequently used as adjectives.

> To bite into this steak takes better teeth than mine. (infinitive used as noun)

> Cooking is one of my favorite hobbies. (gerund used as noun)

> Some people think raw fish is more healthful than cooked fish. (past participle used as adjective)

> According to the Bible, God spoke to Moses from a burning bush. (present participle used as adjective)

EXERCISE 12

Identify all the infinitives (*to* _____), gerunds (_____ *ing*), present participles (_____ *ing*), and past participles (_____ *ed*, _____ *t*, _____ *en*) in the following passage. Define their function as either noun or adjective.

> The car is the quintessential American possession. The car, not the home, is the center of American life. Despite its central place in the mystique of the American Dream, the individually owned home is actually anti-American in many ways. Owning a car means freedom, progress, and individual initiative, the most basic American values. To own a house means rusting pipes and rotting roof beams. Staying in one place implies stagnation and decay, whereas moving (always "forward") connotes energy, creativity, never-ending youth: "Moss doesn't grow on a rolling stone." And the way Americans move is in their cars, their personalized, self-contained, mobile units.

56i   Adjectives and Adverbs

<u>Adjectives and adverbs</u> are words that modify other words, such as nouns and verbs.

Adjectives describe the qualities of nouns or modify other adjectives. A book might be *large* or *small, blue* or *red, difficult* or *easy, expensive* or *cheap.* Unlike adjectives in other languages, English adjectives change their form only to indicate degree (*fast, faster, fastest*). In English, adjectives do not have to agree in gender with the noun they describe, as adjectives must in French and German, for example. In Japanese, some

See
36c

adjectives are conjugated in past and present tenses, something English adjectives do not require.

Adverbs in English are easily identified: nearly all end in *-ly* (*calmly, loudly, rapidly*), except for a small number of "intensifiers," such as *very, rather,* and *quite*. Adverbs generally describe the qualities of verbs. A person may walk *slowly* or *quickly, shyly* or *confidently, elegantly* or *clumsily*. Adverbs may also modify adjectives (*very blue* eyes, *truly religious* man) or other adverbs (answer *rather stupidly,* investigate *extremely thoroughly*).

(1) Position of Adjectives and Adverbs

In Arabic and in Romance languages, such as Spanish, French, and Italian, adjectives typically follow the nouns they describe. In other languages, such as Japanese, Chinese, and English, adjectives usually appear *before* the nouns they describe. A native speaker of English would not say, "Cars red and black are involved in more accidents than cars blue, green, or white," but would say instead, "Red and black cars are involved in more accidents than blue, green, or white cars." However, adjectives may appear *after* linking verbs, direct objects, and indefinite pronouns.

PLACEMENT OF ADJECTIVES

They bought <u>two</u> shrubs for the yard. (before noun)

The name seemed <u>familiar</u>. (after linking verb)

The coach ran them <u>ragged</u>. (after direct object)

Anything <u>sad</u> makes me cry. (after indefinite pronoun)

Adverbs may appear before or after the verbs they describe, but they should be placed as close to the verb as possible: not "I *told* John that I couldn't meet him for lunch *politely*," but "I *politely told* John that I couldn't meet him for lunch" or "I *told* John *politely* that I couldn't meet him for lunch." When an adverb modifies an adjective, it usually comes before the adjective: "The logic is *basically sound*." However, adverbs may appear in a greater variety of positions than adjectives do.

PLACEMENT OF ADVERBS

He walked <u>slowly</u> across the room.

<u>Slowly</u> he walked across the room.

He <u>slowly</u> walked across the room.

He walked across the room <u>slowly</u>.

EXERCISE 13

Each of these sentences is followed by a list of adjectives and adverbs that can be used in the sentence. Place the adjectives and adverbs where they belong in each sentence. (Adjectives and adverbs are listed in the order in which they should appear in the sentences.)

1. Researchers believe that tests are not reliable. (most, now, IQ, entirely)
2. Just as culture is derived from Greece, culture is derived from China. (European, ancient, Asian, ancient)
3. According to the Japanese proverb, for a lid there's a pot. (old, cracked, chipped)
4. The people of Louisiana play a music called zydeco. (Cajun, southern, lively)
5. When you begin to exercise, start and build up to levels. (slowly, steadily, strenuous)
6. Because I transferred credits from my school, I was able to graduate. (many, previous, early)
7. Signers of the Declaration of Independence, which proclaimed the rights of people, owned slaves. (many, American, "unalienable," all, African)
8. Often, feminists feel they are describing the condition of women in the world, when they are describing women in America. (too, American, all, really, only)
9. I work hours on essays, but I remember to take breaks. (usually, many, periodic)
10. The word can have meanings in contexts. (same, different, different)

(2) Order of Adjectives

A single noun may be modified by more than one adjective, perhaps even by a whole list of adjectives in a row. Given a list of three or four modifiers, most native speakers would arrange them in a sentence in the same order. If shoes are to be described as *green* and *big*, numbering *two*, and of the type worn for playing *tennis*, a native speaker would say "two big green tennis shoes." However, determining the order in which these modifiers should be listed before the noun can be troublesome for speakers of languages other than English.

Generally, the modifiers that are most important in completing the meaning of the noun are placed closest to that noun. For example, the most important fact in characterizing the shoes just described is that they are tennis shoes; their size and color are less important. Details about size generally precede details about the color and texture. Details about number nearly always precede all others.

Another way of determining the correct order of modifiers is to make sure that each word describes all the words that follow. For example, in the phrase *fat black cat, black* describes *cat*, whereas *fat* describes *black cat*.

 ORDER OF ADJECTIVES

1. articles (*a, the*), demonstratives (*this, those*), and possessives (*his, our, Maria's, everybody's*)
2. amounts (*one, five, many, few*), order (*first, next, last*)
3. personal opinions (*nice, ugly, crowded, pitiful*)
4. sizes and shapes (*small, tall, straight, crooked*)
5. age (*young, old, modern, ancient*)
6. colors (*black, white, red, blue, dark, light*)
7. nouns functioning as adjectives to form a unit with the noun (*soccer* ball, *cardboard* box, *history* class)

EXERCISE 14

Write five original sentences in which two or three adjectives describe one noun. Be sure that the adjectives are in the right order.

56j Prepositions

In English, **prepositions** (such as *to, at, from, with,* and *between*) give meaning to nouns by linking them with other words and other parts of the sentence: "I got a book *of* poetry *for* my birthday." **Prepositions** convey several different kinds of information.

- relations to **time** (*at* nine o'clock, *in* five minutes, *for* a month)
- relations of **place** (*in* the classroom, *at* the library, *beside* the chair) and **direction** (*to* the market, *onto* the stage, *toward* the freeway)
- relations of **association** (go *with* someone, the tip *of* the iceberg)
- relations of **purpose** (working *for* money, dieting *to* lose weight)

In some languages, prepositions may be used in quite different ways, may exist in forms quite different from those in English, or may not exist at all. Therefore, speakers of those languages may have a lot of difficulty with English prepositions. Speakers of language with prepositions very similar to those in English—especially Romance languages, such as Spanish, French, and Italian—have a different problem. They may be tempted to translate prepositional phrases directly into English, although idiomatic use of prepositions varies widely among languages.

CLOSE UP — PREPOSITIONS IN IDIOMATIC EXPRESSIONS

Nonnative speakers of English may have trouble with prepositions in the following expressions.

Common Nonnative Speaker Usage	*Native Speaker Usage*
according *with*	according *to*
apologize *at*	apologize *to*
appeal *at*	appeal *to*
apply *with*	apply *to*
believe *at*	believe *in*
different *to*	different *from*
for least, *for* most	*at* least, *at* most
refer *at*	refer *to*
relevant *with*	relevant *to*
similar *with*	similar *to*
subscribe *with*	subscribe *to*

Remember also that more than one preposition may be combined with a given word, but the combinations create different expressions with different meanings.

> agree *with*, agree *to*
> care *for*, take care *of*
> *from* the beginning, *at* the beginning
> look *for*, look *at*, look *after*
> talk *to*, talk *with*
> *to* the end, *at* the end
> unfamiliar *with*, unfamiliar *to*

NOTE: There is one construction incorporating a preposition that is peculiar to English. Infinitive forms of verbs are formed in English by adding *to* to the base form of the verb: *to write, to read, to sleep, to eat.* When these verbs are combined with other verbs, confusion may result. In the sentence, "Ali is learning to play tennis," *to* is part of the verb *play,* not part of the verb *learning.* Thus, a native speaker would know to say, "Ali is learning tennis," not "Ali is learning to tennis," but a nonnative speaker might not.

EXERCISE 15

Identify as many prepositions as you can in the following passage. How might similar information be communicated in your native language?

In retrospect, the distinguishing feature of the post–World War II era was its remarkable affluence. From 1950 through 1970, by fits and starts, the American Gross National Product grew at an average annual rate of 3.9 percent, perhaps the best performance in the nation's history. Autos, chemicals, and electrically powered consumer durables were the leading sectors driving the economy forward in the 1950s; housing, aerospace, and the computer industry, in the 1960s. In consequence, the average American commanded 50 percent more real income at the end of the period than at the beginning. Exuberant growth and

---

Articles, Determiners, and Qualifiers
   http://cctc2.commnet.edu/grammar/determiners/determiners.htm
Prepositions
   http://cctc2.commnet.edu/grammar/prepositions.htm

dramatic changes in the standard of living were hardly novel in the American experience, and it was possible to view postwar economic developments as a mere extension of historic trends. But in one crucial respect the era was indeed different. Past increases in real income had mainly purchased improvements in the necessities of life—more and better food, clothing, shelter. After 1950 rising income meant that the mass of Americans, including many blue-collar workers, could, for the first time, enjoy substantial amounts of discretionary income—i.e., income spent not for essentials but for amenities. (Allen J. Matusow, *The Unraveling of America*)

EXERCISE 16

In the following passage, provide appropriate prepositions in the positions indicated.

Everyone knows what is supposed to happen when two Englishmen who have never met before come face _____ face _____ a railway compartment—they start talking _____ the weather. _____ some cases this may simply be because they happen to find the subject interesting. Most people, though, are not particularly interested _____ analyses _____ climatic conditions, so there must be other reasons _____ conversations _____ this kind. One explanation is that it can often be quite embarrassing to be alone _____ the company _____ someone you are not acquainted _____ and *not* speak to them. If no conversation takes place the atmosphere can become rather strained. However, by talking _____ the other person _____ some neutral topic like the weather, it is possible to strike up a relationship _____ him without actually having to say very much. Railway-compartment conversations _____ this kind—and they do happen, although not of course as often as the popular myth supposes—are good examples of the sort _____ important social function that is often fulfilled _____ language. Language is not simply a means of communicating information _____ the weather or any other subject. It is also a very important means _____ establishing and maintaining relationships _____ other people. (Adapted from Peter Trudgill, *Sociolinguistics: An Introduction to Language and Society*)

56k   Word Order

(1) Standard Word Order

The importance of word order varies from language to language. In English, word order is extremely important, contributing a good deal to the meaning of a sentence. Like Chinese, English is an "SVO" language, or one in which the most typical sentence pattern is "subject-verb-object." (Arabic, by contrast, is a "VSO" language.) A native speaker of English will understand that in the sentence "Dog bites man," the dog is doing the biting and the man is getting bitten, whereas in the sentence "Man bites dog," the opposite is true.

Of course, there is some flexibility in the word order of English sentences. For example, adjectives and adverbs (or phrases that function as adjectives or adverbs) may be placed in various positions in a sentence, depending on the sentence's intended emphasis or meaning.

(2) Word Order in Questions

Word order in questions can be particularly troublesome for speakers of languages other than English, partly because there are so many different ways to form questions in English.

 CLOSE UP   WORD ORDER IN QUESTIONS

1. To create a yes/no question from a statement using the verb *to be,* simply invert the order of the subject and the verb:

   <u>Rasheem is</u> researching the depletion of the ozone layer.

   <u>Is Rasheem</u> researching the depletion of the ozone layer?

2. To create a yes/no question from a statement using a verb other than *to be,* use a form of the auxiliary verb *do* before the sentence without inverting the subject and verb:

   <u>Does</u> Rasheem want to research the depletion of the ozone layer?

   <u>Do</u> Rasheem's friends want to help him with his research?

   <u>Did</u> Rasheem's professors approve his research proposal?

continued on the following page

continued from the previous page

3. A question can also be formed by adding a **tag question** (such as *won't he?* or *didn't I?*) to the end of a statement. If the verb of the main statement is *positive*, then the verb of the tag question is *negative*; if the verb of the main statement is *negative*, then the verb of the tag question is *positive*:

Rasheem <u>is</u> researching the depletion of the ozone layer, <u>isn't</u> he?

Rasheem <u>doesn't</u> intend to write his dissertation about the depletion of the ozone layer, <u>does</u> he?

4. To create a question asking for information, use **interrogative** words (*who, what, where, when, why, how*), and invert the order of the subject and verb (note that *who* functions as the subject of the question in which it appears):

<u>Who is</u> researching the depletion of the ozone layer?

<u>What is Rasheem</u> researching?

<u>Where is Rasheem</u> researching the depletion of the ozone layer?

56l Common Sentence Errors

Even native speakers of English make errors in their writing—in particular, common errors, such as *sentence fragments, comma splices,* and *fused sentences,* and excessive or unnecessary passive constructions.

For information on some of the most common sentence errors in English, see Chapter **24,** "Revising Sentence Fragments"; Chapter **25,** "Revising Comma Splices and Fused Sentences"; and **34d1,** "Changing from Passive to Active Voice."

Phrases
http://cctc2.commnet.edu/grammar/phrases.htm
Clauses
http://cctc2.commnet.edu/grammar/clauses.htm
Elementary Rules of Composition from Strunk's *Elements of Style*
http://www.bartleby.com/141/strunk.html#III
Sentence Craft (L. Behrens, UCSB)
http://www.writing.ucsb.edu/faculty/behrens/sentcomb.htm
Sentence Combining Basics (Bowling Green)
http://www.bgsu.edu/departments/writing-lab/sentence_combining_b.html

CHAPTER 57

GLOSSARY OF USAGE

? FREQUENTLY ASKED QUESTIONS

Is *criteria* singular or plural? (p. 810)
Which is correct, *everyday* or *every day*?
 (p. 811)
What is the difference between *imply* and
 infer? (p. 813)
How do I decide whether to use *who* or
 whom in a sentence? (p. 818)

This glossary of usage lists words and phrases that are often trouble-some for writers.

a, an Use *a* before words that begin with consonants and words with initial vowels that sound like consonants: *a* person, *a* historical document, *a* one-horse carriage, *a* uniform. Use *an* before words that begin with vowels and words that begin with a silent *h: an* artist, *an* honest person.

accept, except *Accept* is a verb that means "to receive"; *except* as a preposition to conjunction means "other than" and as a verb means "to leave out": The auditors will *accept* all your claims *except* the last two. Some businesses are *excepted* from the regulation.

advice, advise *Advice* is a noun meaning "opinion or information of-fered"; *advise* is a verb that means "to offer advice to": The broker *advised* her client to take his attorney's *advice.*

affect, effect *Affect* is a verb meaning "to influence"; *effect* can be a verb or a noun—as a verb it means "to bring about," and as a noun it means "result": We know how the drug *affects* patients immediately, but little is known of its long-term *effects*. The arbitrator tried to *effect* a settlement between the parties.

Words or Expressions Commonly Misused (Strunk's *Elements of Style*)
 http://www.bartleby.com/141/strunk3.html
A Word a Day (wordsmith.org; new word defined, with examples, each day)
 http://www.wordsmith.org/words/today.html

all ready, already *All ready* means "completely prepared"; *already* means "by or before this or that time": I was *all ready* to help, but it was *already* too late.

all right, alright Although the use of *alright* is increasing, current usage calls for all right.

allusion, illusion An *allusion* is a reference or hint; an *illusion* is something that is not what it seems: The poem makes an *allusion* to the Pandora myth. The shadows created an optical *illusion*.

a lot *A lot* is always two words.

among, between *Among* refers to groups of more than two things; *between* refers to just two things: The three parties agreed *among* themselves to settle the case. There will be a brief intermission *between* the two acts. Note that *amongst* is British, not American, usage.

amount, number *Amount* refers to a quantity that cannot be counted; *number* refers to things that can be counted: Even a small *amount* of caffeine can be harmful. Seeing their commander fall, a large *number* of troops ran to her aid.

an, a See **a, an.**

and/or In business or technical writing, use *and/or* when either or both of the items it connects can apply. In college writing, however, avoid the use of *and/or.*

as . . . as . . . In such constructions, *as* signals a comparison; therefore, you must always use the second *as: East of Eden* is *as* long *as* if not longer than *The Grapes of Wrath.*

as, like *As* can be used as a conjunction (to introduce a complete clause) or as a preposition; *like* should be used as a preposition only: In *The Scarlet Letter,* Hawthorne uses imagery *as* (not *like*) he does in his other works. After classes, Nancy works *as* a manager of a fast-food restaurant. Writers *like* Carl Sandburg appear once in a generation.

at, to Many people use the prepositions *at* and *to* after *where* in conversation: *Where* are you working *at? Where* are you going *to?* This is redundant and should not be used in college writing.

awhile, a while *Awhile* is an adverb; *a while,* which consists of an article and a noun, is used as the object of a preposition: Before we continue, we will rest *awhile.* (modifies the verb *rest*); Before we continue, we will rest for *a while.* (object of the preposition *for*)

bad, badly   *Bad* is an adjective, and *badly* is an adverb: The school board decided that *Huckleberry Finn* was a *bad* book. American automobile makers did not do *badly* this year. After verbs that refer to any of the senses or after any other linking verb, use the adjective form: He looked *bad*. He felt *bad*. It seemed *bad*.

being as, being that   These awkward phrases add unnecessary words and weaken your writing. Use *because* instead.

beside, besides   *Beside* is a preposition meaning "next to"; *besides* can be either a preposition meaning "except" or "other than" or an adverb meaning "as well": *Beside* the tower was a wall that ran the length of the city. *Besides* its industrial uses, laser technology has many other applications. Edison invented not only the lightbulb but the phonograph *besides*.

between, among   See **among, between.**

bring, take   *Bring* means to transport from a farther place to a nearer place; *take* means to carry or convey from a nearer place to a farther one: *Bring* me a souvenir from your trip. *Take* this message to the general and wait for a reply.

can, may   *Can* denotes ability, and *may* indicates permission: If you *can* play, you *may* use my piano.

capital, capitol   *Capital* refers to a city that is an official seat of government; *capitol* refers to a building in which a legislature meets: Washington, DC, is the *capital* of the United States. When we were there, we visited the *Capitol* building.

center around   This imprecise phrase is acceptable in speech and informal writing but not in college writing. Use *center on* instead.

cite, site   *Cite* is a verb meaning "to quote as an authority or example"; *site* is a noun meaning "a place or setting": Akemi *cited* five sources in her research paper. The builder cleared the *site* for the new bank.

climactic, climatic   *Climactic* means "of or related to a climax"; *climatic* means "of or related to climate": The *climactic* moment of the movie occured unexpectedly. If scientists are correct, the *climatic* conditions of Earth are changing.

coarse, course   *Coarse* is an adjective meaning "inferior" or "having a rough, uneven texture"; *course* is a noun meaning "a route or path," "an area on which a sport is played," or "a unit of study": *Coarse* sandpaper is used to smooth the surface. The *course* of true love never runs smoothly. Last semester I had to drop a *course*.

compare to, compare with   *Compare to* means "to liken" or "to represent as similar"; *compare with* means "to examine in order to find ways in which two things are similar or different": Shall I *compare* you *to* a summer's day? Jane *compared* the paintings of Cézanne *with* those of Magritte.

complement, compliment   *Complement* means "to complete or add to"; *compliment* means "to give praise": A double-blind study would *complement* their preliminary research. My instructor *complimented* me on my improvement.

conscious, conscience   *Conscious* is an adjective meaning "having one's mental faculties awake"; *conscience* is a noun that means the moral sense of right and wrong: The patient will remain *conscious* during the procedure. His *conscience* would not allow him to lie.

continual, continuous   *Continual* means "recurring at intervals"; *continuous* refers to an action that occurs without interruption: A pulsar is a star that emits a *continual* stream of electromagnetic radiation. (It emits radiation at regular intervals.) A small battery allows the watch to run *continuously* for five years. (It runs without stopping.)

could of, should of, would of   The contractions *could've, should've,* and *would've* are often misspelled as the nonstandard constructions *could of, should of,* and *would of.* Use *could have, should have,* and *would have* in college writing.

council, counsel   A *council* is "a body of people who serve in a legislative or advisory capacity"; *counsel* means "to offer advice or guidance": The city *council* argued about the proposed ban on smoking. The judge *counseled* the couple to settle their differences.

couple of   *Couple* means "a pair," but *couple of* is often used colloquially to mean "several" or "a few." In your college writing, specify "four points" or "two examples" rather than using "a couple of."

? *criterion, criteria*   *Criteria,* from the Greek, is the plural of *criterion,* meaning "standard for judgment": Of all the *criteria* for hiring graduating seniors, class rank is the most important *criterion.*

data   *Data* is the plural of the Latin *datum,* meaning "fact." In everyday speech and writing, *data* is used for both singular and plural. In college writing, use *data* only for the plural: The *data* discussed in this section are summarized in Appendix A.

different from, different than   *Different than* is widely used in American speech. In college writing, use *different from.*

discreet, discrete   *Discreet* means "careful or prudent"; *discrete* means "separate or individually distinct": Because Madame Bovary was not *discreet*, her reputation suffered. Atoms can be broken into hundreds of *discrete* particles.

disinterested, uninterested   *Disinterested* means "objective" or "capable of making an impartial judgment"; *uninterested* means "indifferent or unconcerned": The American judicial system depends on *disinterested* jurors. Finding no treasure, Hernando de Soto was *uninterested* in going farther.

don't, doesn't   *Don't* is the contraction of *do not; doesn't* is the contraction of *does not*. Do not confuse the two: My dog *doesn't* (not *don't*) like to walk in the rain.

effect, affect   See **affect, effect.**

e.g.   *E.g.* is an abbreviation for the Latin *exempli gratia,* meaning "for example" or "for instance." In college writing, do not use *e.g.* Instead, use its English equivalent.

emigrate from, immigrate to   To *emigrate* is "to leave one's country and settle in another"; to *immigrate* is "to come to another country and reside there." The noun forms of these words are *emigrant* and *immigrant*: My great-grandfather *emigrated from* Warsaw along with many other *emigrants* from Poland. Many people *immigrate* to the United States for economic reasons, but such *immigrants* still face great challenges.

eminent, imminent   *Eminent* is an adjective meaning "standing above others" or "prominent"; *imminent* means "about to occur": Oliver Wendell Holmes, Jr., was an *eminent* jurist. In ancient times, a comet signaled *imminent* disaster.

enthused   *Enthused,* a colloquial form of *enthusiastic,* should not be used in college writing.

etc.   *Etc.,* the abbreviation of *et cetera,* means "and the rest." Do not use it in your college writing. Instead, say "and so on"—or, better yet, specify exactly what *etc.* stands for.

everyday, every day   *Everyday* is an adjective that means "ordinary" or "commonplace"; *every day* means "occurring daily": In the Gettysburg Address, Lincoln used *everyday* language. She exercises almost *every day.*

everyone, every one   *Everyone* is an indefinite pronoun meaning "every person"; *every one* means "every individual or thing in a particular group": *Everyone* seems happier in the spring. *Every one* of the packages had been opened.

except, accept   See **accept, except.**

explicit, implicit   *Explicit* means "expressed or stated directly"; *implicit* means "implied" or "expressed or stated indirectly": The director *explicitly* warned the actors to be on time for rehearsals. Her *implicit* message was that lateness would not be tolerated.

farther, further   *Farther* designates distance; *further* designates degree: I have traveled *farther* from home than any of my relatives. Critics charge that welfare subsidies encourage *further* dependence.

fewer, less   Use *fewer* with nouns that can be counted: *fewer* books, *fewer* people, *fewer* dollars. Use *less* with quantities that cannot be counted: *less* pain, *less* power, *less* enthusiasm.

firstly (secondly, thirdly, . . .)   Archaic forms meaning "in the first . . . second . . . third place." Use *first, second, third.*

further, farther   See **farther, further.**

good, well   *Good* is an adjective, never an adverb: She is a *good* swimmer. *Well* can function as an adverb or as an adjective. As an adverb, it means "in a good manner": She swam *well* (not *good*) in the meet. *Well* is used as an adjective with verbs that denote a state of being or feeling. Here, *well* can mean "in good health": I feel *well.*

got to   *Got to* is not acceptable in college writing. To indicate obligation, use *have to, has to,* or *must.*

hanged, hung   Both *hanged* and *hung* are past participles of *hang. Hanged* is used to refer to executions; *hung* is used to mean "suspended": Billy Budd was *hanged* for killing the master-at-arms. The stockings were *hung* by the chimney with care.

he, she   Traditionally, *he* has been used in the generic sense to refer to both males and females. To acknowledge the equality of the sexes, however, avoid the generic *he.* Use plural pronouns whenever possible. See **29f2.**

hopefully   The adverb *hopefully,* meaning "in a hopeful manner," should modify a verb, an adjective, or another adverb. Do not use *hopefully* as a sentence modifier meaning "it is hoped." Rather than "*Hopefully,* scientists will soon discover a cure for AIDS," write "Scientists *hope* they will soon discover a cure for AIDS."

i.e.   *I.e.* is an abbreviation for the latin *id est,* meaning "that is." In college writing, do not use *i.e.* Instead, use its English equivalent.

if, whether   When asking indirect questions or expressing doubt, use *whether:* He asked *whether* (not *if*) the flight would be delayed. The flight attendant was not sure *whether* (not *if*) it would be delayed.

illusion, allusion   See **allusion, illusion.**

immigrate to, emigrate from   See **emigrate from, immigrate to.**

implicit, explicit   See **explicit, implicit.**

imply, infer   *Imply* means "to hint" or "to suggest"; *infer* means "to con- ❓ clude from": Mark Antony *implied* that the conspirators had murdered Caesar. The crowd *inferred* his meaning and called for justice.

infer, imply   See **imply, infer.**

inside of, outside of   *Of* is unnecessary when *inside* and *outside* are used as prepositions. *Inside of* is colloquial in references to time: He waited *inside* (not *inside of*) the coffee shop. He could run a mile in *under* (not *inside of*) eight minutes.

irregardless, regardless   *Irregardless* is a nonstandard version of *regardless.* Use *regardless* instead.

is when, is where   These constructions are faulty when they appear in definitions: A playoff *is* an additional game played to establish the winner of a tie. (not "A playoff *is when* an additional game is played . . .")

its, it's   *Its* is a possessive pronoun; *it's* is a contraction of *it is*: It's no secret that the bank is out to protect *its* assets.

kind of, sort of   *Kind of* and *sort of* to mean "rather" or "somewhat" are colloquial and should not appear in college writing: It is well known that Napoleon was *rather* (not *kind of*) short.

lay, lie   See **lie, lay.**

leave, let   *Leave* means "to go away from" or "to let remain"; *let* means "to allow" or "to permit": *Let* (not *leave*) me give you a hand.

less, fewer   See **fewer, less.**

let, leave   See **leave, let.**

lie, lay   *Lie* is an intransitive verb (one that does not take an object) meaning "to recline." Its principal forms are *lie, lay, lain, lying*: Each afternoon she would *lie* in the sun and listen to the surf. *As I Lay Dying* is a novel by William Faulkner. By 1871, Troy had *lain* undisturbed for two thousand years. The painting shows a nude *lying* on a couch. *Lay* is a transitive verb (one that takes an object) meaning "to put" or "to place." Its principal forms are *lay, laid, laid, laying*: The Federalist Papers *lay* the foundation for American conservatism. In October 1781, the British *laid* down their arms and surrendered. He had *laid* his money on the counter before leaving. We watched the stonemasons *laying* a wall.

like, as   See **as, like.**

loose, lose　*Loose* is an adjective meaning "not rigidly fastened or securely attached"; *lose* is a verb meaning "to misplace": The marble facing of the building became *loose* and fell to the sidewalk. After only two drinks, most people *lose* their ability to judge distance.

lots, lots of, a lot of　These words are colloquial substitutes for *many, much,* or *a great deal of.* Avoid their use in college writing: The students had *many* (not *lots of* or *a lot* of) options for essay topics.

man　Like the generic pronoun *he, man* has been used in English to denote members of both sexes. This usage is being replaced by *human beings, people,* or similar terms that do not specify gender. See **29f2.**

may be, maybe　*May be* is a verb phrase; *maybe* is an adverb meaning "perhaps": She may be the smartest student in the class. *Maybe* her experience has given her an advantage.

may, can　See **can, may.**

media, medium　*Medium,* meaning a "means of conveying or broadcasting something," is singular; *media* is the plural form and requires a plural verb: The *media* have distorted the issue.

might have, might of　*Might of* is a nonstandard spelling of the contraction of *might have* (*might've*). Use *might have* in college writing.

number, amount　See **amount, number.**

OK, O.K., okay　All three spellings are acceptable, but this term should be avoided in college writing. Replace it with a more specific word or words: The instructor's lecture was *adequate* (not *okay*), if uninspiring.

outside of, inside of　See **inside of, outside of.**

passed, past　*Passed* is the past tense of the verb *pass; past* means "belonging to a former time" or "no longer current": The car must have been going eighty miles per hour when it *passed* us. In the envelope was a bill marked *past* due.

percent, percentage　*Percent* indicates a part of a hundred when a specific number is referred to: "*10 percent* of his salary." *Percentage* is used when no specific number is referred to: "a *percentage* of next year's receipts." In technical and business writing, it is permissible to use the % sign after percentages you are comparing. Write out the word *percent* in college writing.

phenomenon, phenomena　A *phenomenon* is a single observable fact or event. It can also refer to a rare or significant occurrence. *Phenomena* is the plural form and requires a plural verb: Many supposedly paranormal *phenomena* are easily explained.

plus As a preposition, *plus* means "in addition to." Avoid using *plus* as a substitute for *and:* Include the principal, *plus* the interest, in your calculations. Your quote was too high; *moreover* (not *plus*), it was inaccurate.

precede, proceed *Precede* means "to go or come before"; *proceed* means "to go forward in an orderly way": Robert Frost's *North of Boston* was *preceded* by an earlier volume. In 1532, Francisco Pizarro landed at Tumbes and *proceeded* south.

principal, principle As a noun, *principal* means "a sum of money (minus interet) invested or lent" or "a person in the leading position"; as an adjective, it means "most important." A *principle* is a rule of conduct or a basic truth: He wanted to reduce the *principal* of the loan. The principal of the high school is a talented administrator. Women are the *principal* wage earners in many American households. The Constitution embodies certain fundamental *principles.*

quote, quotation *Quote* is a verb. *Quotation* is a noun. In college writing, do not use *quote* as a shortened form of *quotation:* He included several *quotations* (not *quotes*) from experts.

raise, rise *Raise* is a transitive verb, and *rise* is an intransitive verb—that is, *raise* takes an object, and *rise* does not: My grandparents *raised* a large family. The sun will *rise* at 6:12 this morning.

real, really *Real* means "genuine" or "authentic"; *really* means "actually." In your college writing, do not use *real* as an adjective meaning "very."

reason is that, reason is because *Reason* should be used with *that* and not with *because,* which is redundant: The *reason* he left *is that* (not *is because*) you insulted him.

regardless, irregardless See **irregardless, regardless.**

respectably, respectfully, respectively *Respectably* means "worthy of respect"; *respectfully* means "giving honor or deference"; *respectively* means "in the order given": He skated quite *respectably* at his first Olympics. The seminar taught us to treat others *respectfully.* The first- and second-place winners were Tai and Kim, *respectively.*

rise, raise See **raise, rise.**

set, sit *Set* means "to put down" or "to lay." Its principal forms are *set* and *setting:* After rocking the baby to sleep, he *set* her down carefully in her crib. After *setting* her down, he took a nap. *Sit* means "to assume a sitting position." Its principal forms are *sit, sat,* and *sitting:* Many children *sit* in front of the television five to six hours a day. The dog *sat* by the fire. We were *sitting* in the airport when the flight was cancelled.

shall, will   *Will* has all but replaced *shall* to express all future action.

should of   See **could of, should of, would of.**

since   Do not use *since* for *because* if there is any chance of confusion. In the sentence "*Since* President Nixon traveled to China, trade between China and the United States has increased," *since* could mean either "from the time that" or "because." To be clear, use *because.*

sit, set   See **set, sit.**

so   Avoid using *so* alone as a vague intensifier meaning "very" or "extremely." Follow *so* with *that* and a clause that describes the result: She was *so* pleased with their work *that* she took them out to lunch.

sometime, sometimes, some time   *Sometime* means "at some time in the future"; *sometimes* means "now and then"; *some time* means "a period of time": The president will address Congress *sometime* next week. All automobiles, no matter how reliable, *sometimes* need repairs. It has been *some time* since I read that book.

sort of, kind of   See **kind of, sort of.**

stationary, stationery   *Stationary* means "staying in one place"; *stationery* means "materials for writing" or "letter paper": The communications satellite appears to be *stationary* in the sky. The secretaries supply departmental offices with *stationery.*

supposed to, used to   *Supposed* to and *used to* are often misspelled. Both verbs require the final *d* to indicate past tense.

take, bring   See **bring, take.**

than, then   *Than* is a conjunction used to indicate a comparison; *then* is an adverb indicating time: The new shopping center is bigger *than* the old one. He did his research; *then* he wrote a report.

that, which, who   Use *that* or *which* when referring to a thing; use *who* when referring to a person: It was a speech *that* inspired many. The movie, *which* was a huge success, failed to impress her. Anyone *who* (not *that*) takes the course will benefit.

their, there, they're   *Their* is a possessive pronoun; *there* indicates place and is also used in the expressions *there is* and *there are*; *they're* is a contraction of *they are*: Watson and Crick did *their* DNA work at Cambridge University. I love New York, but I wouldn't want to live *there*. *There is* nothing we can do to resurrect an extinct species. When *they're* well treated, ferrets make excellent pets.

themselves; theirselves, theirself   *Theirselves* and *theirself* are nonstandard variants of *themselves.*

then, than   See **than, then.**

till, until, 'til   *Till* and *until* have the same meaning, and both are acceptable. *Until* is preferred in college writing. *'Til,* a contraction of *until,* should be avoided.

to, at   See **at, to.**

to, too, two   *To* is a preposition that indicates direction; *too* is an adverb that means "also" or "more than is needed"; *two* expresses the number 2: Last year, we flew from New York *to* California. "Tippecanoe and Tyler, *too*" was William Henry Harrison's campaign slogan. The plot was *too* complicated for the average reader. Just north of *Two* Rivers, Wisconsin, is a petrified forest.

try to, try and   *Try and* is the colloquial equivalent of the more formal try to: He decided to *try to* (not *try and*) do better. In college writing, use *try to.*

-type   Deleting this empty suffix eliminates clutter and clarifies meaning: Found in the wreckage was an *incendiary* (not *incendiary-type*) device.

uninterested, disinterested   See **disinterested, uninterested.**

unique   Because *unique* means "the only one," not "remarkable" or "unusual," never use constructions like "the most unique" or "very unique."

until   See **till, until, 'til.**

used to   See **supposed to, used to.**

utilize   In most cases, replace *utilize* with *use* (*utilize* often sounds pretentious).

wait for, wait on   To *wait for* means "to defer action until something occurs." To *wait on* means "to act as a waiter": I am *waiting for* (not *on*) dinner.

weather, whether   *Weather* is a noun meaning "the state of the atmosphere"; *whether* is a conjunction used to introduce an alternative: The *weather* outside is frightful, but the fire inside is delightful. It is doubtful *whether* we will be able to ski tomorrow.

well, good   See **good, well.**

were, we're   *Were* is a verb; *we're* is the contraction of *we are:* The Trojans *were* asleep when the Greeks attacked. We must act now if *we're* going to succeed.

whether, if   See **if, whether.**

which, who, that   See **that, which, who.**

who, whom When a pronoun serves as the subject of its clause, use *who* or *whoever;* when it functions in a clause as an object, use *whom* or *whomever:* Sarah, *who* is studying ancient civilizations, would like to visit Greece. Sarah, *whom* I met in France, wants me to travel to Greece with her. To determine which to use at the beginning of a question, use a personal pronoun to answer the question: *Who* tried to call me? *He* called. (subject); *Whom* do you want for the job? I want *her.* (object)

who's, whose *Who's* means "who is"; *whose* indicates possession: *Who's* going to take calculus? The writer *whose* book was in the window was autographing copies.

will, shall See **shall, will.**

would of See **could of, should of, would of.**

your, you're *Your* indicates possession, and *you're* is the contraction of *you are:* You can improve *your* stamina by jogging two miles a day. *You're* certain to be the winner.

CHAPTER 58

GLOSSARY OF GRAMMATICAL AND RHETORICAL TERMS

absolute phrase   See **phrase.**

abstract noun   See **noun.**

acronym   A word formed from the first letters or initial sounds of a group of words: <u>NATO</u> = <u>N</u>orth <u>A</u>tlantic <u>T</u>reaty <u>O</u>rganization.

active voice   See **voice.**

adjective   A word that describes, limits, qualifies, or in any other way modifies a noun or pronoun. A **descriptive adjective** names a quality of the noun or pronoun it modifies: *junior year.* A **proper adjective** is formed from a proper noun: *Hegelian philosophy.* **32d, 36b**

adjective clause   See **clause.**

adverb   A word that describes the action of verbs or modifies adjectives, other adverbs, or complete phrases, clauses, or sentences. Adverbs answer the questions "How?" "Why?" "Where?" "When?" and "To what extent?" Adverbs are formed from adjectives, many by adding *-ly* to the adjective form (*dark/darkly, solemn/solemnly*), and may also be derived from prepositions (*Joe carried on.*). Other adverbs that indicate time, place, condition, cause, or degree are not derived from other parts of speech: *then, never, very,* and *often,* for example. The words *how, why, where,* and *when* are classified as **interrogative adverbs** when they ask questions (<u>*How* did we get into this mess?</u>). See also **conjunctive adverb. 32e, 36c**

adverb clause   See **clause.**

adverbial conjunction   See **conjunctive adverb.**

agreement   The correspondence between words in number, person, and gender. Subjects and verbs must agree in number (singular or plural) and person (first, second, or third): <u>*Soccer is* a popular European sport;</u> <u>*I play*</u> soccer too. **35a** Pronouns and their antecedents must agree in number, person, and gender (masculine, feminine, neuter): <u>*Lucy* loaned Charlie *her* car.</u> **35b**

allusion   A reference to a well-known historical, literary, or biblical person or event that readers are expected to recognize.

analogy   A kind of comparison in which the writer explains an unfamiliar idea or object by comparing it to a more familiar one: *Sensory pathways of the central nervous system are bundles of nerves rather like telephone cables that feed information about the outside world into the brain for processing.*

antecedent   The word or word group to which a pronoun refers: <u>*Brian*</u> *finally bought the stereo he had always wanted.* (*Brian* is the antecedent of the pronoun *he.*)

appositive   A noun or noun phrase that identifies or renames the noun or pronoun it follows: *Columbus,* <u>*the capital of Ohio,*</u> *is in the central part of the state.* Appositives may be used without special introductory phrases, as in the preceding example, or they may be introduced by *such as, or, that is, for example,* or *in other words: Japanese cars,* <u>*such as Hondas,*</u> *now have a large share of the US automobile market.* **19c5** In a **restrictive appositive,** the appositive precedes the noun or pronoun it modifies: <u>*Singing cowboy*</u> *Gene Autry became the owner of the California Angels.* **38d1**

article   The word *a, an,* or *the.* Articles signal that a noun follows and are classified as **determiners. 56f2–3**

auxiliary verb   See **verb.**

balanced sentence   A sentence neatly divided between two parallel structures. Balanced sentences are typically **compound sentences** made up of two parallel clauses (*The telephone rang, and I answered.*), but the parallel clauses of a **complex sentence** can also be balanced. **21c**

base form   See **principle parts.**

cardinal number   A number that expresses quantity—*seven, thirty, one hundred.* (Contrast **ordinal number.**)

case   The form a noun or pronoun takes to indicate how it functions in a sentence. English has three cases. A pronoun takes the **subjective** (or **nominative**) **case** when it acts as the subject of a sentence or a clause: <u>*I*</u> *am an American.* **33a1** A pronoun takes the **objective case** when it acts as the object of a verb or of a preposition: *Fran gave* <u>*me*</u> *her dog.* **33a2** Both nouns and pronouns take the **possessive case** when they indicate ownership: <u>*My*</u> *house is brick,* <u>*Brandon's*</u> *T-shirt is red.* This is the only case in which nouns change form. **33a3**

clause   A group of related words that includes a subject and a predicate. An **independent (main) clause** may stand alone as a sentence (*Yellowstone is a national park in the West.*), but a **dependent (subordinate) clause** must always be accompanied by an independent clause

(*Yellowstone is a national park in the West that is known for its geysers.*). Dependent clauses are classified according to their function in a sentence. An **adjective clause** (sometimes called a **relative clause**) modifies nouns or pronouns: *The philodendron, which grew to be twelve feet tall finally died* (the clause modifies *philodendron*). An **adverb clause** modifies single words (verbs, adjectives, or adverbs) or an entire phrase or clause: *The film was exposed when Bill opened the camera* (the clause modifies *exposed*). A **noun clause** acts as a noun (as subject, direct object, indirect object, or complement) in a sentence: *Whoever arrives first wins the prize* (the clause is the subject of the sentence). An **elliptical clause** is grammatically incomplete—that is, part or all of the subject or predicate is missing. If the missing part can be inferred from the context of the sentence, such a construction is acceptable: *When (they are) pressed, the committee members will act.* **19b2**

climactic word order   The writing strategy of moving from the least important to the most important point in a sentence and ending with the key idea. **21a2**

collective noun   See **noun.**

comma splice   An error created when two independent clauses are incorrectly joined by a comma. **Ch. 25**

> **COMMA SPLICE:** The Mississippi River flows south, the Nile River flows north.
>
> **REVISED:** The Mississippi River flows south. The Nile River flows north.
>
> **REVISED:** The Mississippi River flows south; the Nile River flows north.
>
> **REVISED:** The Mississippi River flows south, and the Nile River flows north.
>
> **REVISED:** Although the Mississippi River flows south, the Nile River flows north.

common noun   See **noun.**

comparative degree   See **comparison.**

comparison   The forms taken by an adjective or an adverb to indicate degree. The **positive degree** describes a quality without indicating comparison (*Frank is tall.*). The **comparative degree** indicates comparison between two persons or things (*Frank is taller than John.*). The **superlative degree** indicates comparison between one person or thing and two or more others (*Frank is the tallest boy in his scout troop.*). **36d** *complement*   A word or word group that describes or renames a subject, an object, or a verb. A **subject complement** is a word or phrase that follows a linking verb and renames the subject. It can be an adjective (called a **predicate adjective**) or a noun (called a **predicate nominative**): *Clark Gable was a movie star*. An **object complement** is a word or phrase that describes or renames a direct object. Object complements can be either adjectives or nouns: *We call the treehouse the hideout*.

complete predicate   See **predicate**.

complete subject   See **subject**.

complex sentence   See **sentence**.

compound   Two or more words that function as a unit, such as **compound nouns**: *attorney-at-law, boardwalk;* **compound adjectives**: *hardhitting editorial;* **compound prepositions**: *by way of, in addition to;* **compound subjects**: *April and May are spring months.;* **compound predicates**: *Many try and fail to climb Mount Everest.*

compound adjective   See **compound**.

compound noun   See **compound**.

compound predicate   See **compound**.

compound preposition   See **compound**.

compound sentence   See **sentence**.

compound subject   See **compound**.

compound-complex sentence   See *sentence*.

conjunction   A word or words used to connect single words, phrases, clauses, and sentences. **Coordinating conjunctions** (*and, or, but, nor, for, so, yet*) connect words, phrases, or clauses of equal weight: *crime and punishment* (coordinating conjunction *and* connects two words). **Correlative conjunctions** (*both . . . and, either . . . or, neither . . . nor,* and so on), always used in pairs, also link items of equal weight: *Neither Texas nor Florida crosses the Tropic of Cancer.* **Subordinating conjunctions** (*since, because, although, if, after,* and so on) introduce adverb clauses: *You will have to pay for the tickets now because I will not be here later.* **32g**

conjunctive adverb   An adverb that joins and relates independent clauses in a sentence (*also, anyway, besides, hence, however, nevertheless, still,* and so on): *Howard tried out for the Yankees; however, he didn't make the team.* **32e**

connotation   The emotional associations that surround a word. (Contrast **denotation.**) **29b1**

contraction   The combination of two words with an apostrophe replacing the missing letters: *We + will = we'll; was + not = wasn't.*

coordinate adjective   One of a series of adjectives that modify the same word or word group: *The park was quiet, shady,* and *cool.* **38b2**

coordinating conjunction   See **conjunction.**

coordination   The pairing of similar elements (words, phrases, or clauses) to give equal weight to each. Coordination is used in simple sentences to link similar elements into compound subjects, predicates, complements, or modifiers. It can also link two independent clauses to form a compound sentence: *The sky was cloudy, and it looked like rain.* (Contrast **subordination.**)

correlative conjunction   See **conjunction.**

count noun   See **noun.**

cumulative sentence   A sentence that begins with a main clause followed by additional words, phrases, or clauses that expand or develop it: *On the hill stood a schoolhouse, paint peeling, windows boarded, playground overgrown with weeds.* **21b1**

dangling modifier   A modifier for which no logical headword appears in the sentence. To correct dangling modifiers, either create a new subject that can logically serve as the headword of the dangling modifier, or change the dangling modifier into a dependent clause. **26b**

DANGLING: Pumping up the tire, the trip continued.

REVISED: After pumping up the tire, they continued the trip.

dead metaphor   A metaphor so overused that it has become a meaningless cliché. **29e1**

deductive argument   An argument that begins with a general statement or proposition and establishes a chain of reasoning that leads to a conclusion. **8b**

demonstrative pronoun   See **pronoun;** see also **determiner.**

denotation   The dictionary meaning of a word. (Contrast **connotation.**) **29b1**

dependent clause   See **clause.**

descriptive adjective   See **adjective.**

determiner   Determiners are words that function as adjectives to limit or qualify nouns. Determiners include **articles** (*a, an, the*): *the book, a peanut;* **possessive nouns** (*Janet's*): *Janet's dog;* **possessive pronouns** (*my, your, his,* and so on): *their apartment, my house;* **demonstrative pronouns** (*this, these, that, those*): *that table, these chairs;* **interrogative pronouns** (*what, which, whose,* and so on): *Which car is yours?;* **indefinite pronouns** (*another, each, both, many,* and so on): *any minute, some day;* **relative pronouns** (*what, whatever, which, whichever, whose, whosoever*): *Bed rest was what the doctor ordered.;* and **ordinal** and **cardinal numbers** (*one, two, first, second,* and so on): *Claire saw two robins.* **32d2; 36a; 56f3**

direct object   See **object.**

direct quotation   See **quotation.**

documentation   The formal acknowledgment of the sources used in a piece of writing. **Chs. 16–17**

documentation style   A format for providing information about the sources used in a piece of writing. Documentation formats vary from discipline to discipline. **Chs. 16–17**

double negative   A nonstandard combination of two negative words:

DOUBLE NEGATIVE: *She didn't have no time.*

REVISED: *She had no time* or *She didn't have any time.* **36e; 56h5**

ellipsis   Three spaced periods used to indicate the omission of a word or words from a quotation: *"The time has come [. . .] and we must part."* **42f**

elliptical clause   See **clause.**

embedding   A strategy for varying sentence structure that involves changing some sentences into modifying phrases and working them into other sentences. **23b3**

enthymeme   A syllogism in which one of the premises—usually the major premise—is implied rather than stated. **8b2**

expletive   A construction in which *there* or *it* is used with a form of the verb *be: There is no one here by that name.*

faulty parallelism   See **parallelism.**

figurative language   Language that departs from the literal meaning or order or words to create striking effects or new meanings. Types of figurative language (called **figures of speech**) include **simile, metaphor,** and **personification. 29d**

figure of speech   See **figurative language.**

finite verb   A verb that can serve as the main verb of a sentence. Unlike **participles, gerunds,** and **infinitives** (see also **verbal**), finite verbs do not require an auxiliary in order to function as the main verb: *The rooster* <u>crowed</u>.

fragment   See **sentence fragment.**

function word   An article, a preposition, a conjunction, or an auxiliary verb that indicates the function of and the grammatical relationships among the nouns, verbs, and modifiers in a sentence.

fused sentence   A type of **run-on sentence** that occurs when two independent clauses are joined without punctuation. Correct fused sentences by separating the independent clauses with a period, a semicolon, or a comma and a coordinating conjunction, or by using subordination. **Ch. 25**

> FUSED SENTENCE: Protein is needed for good nutrition lipids and carbohydrates are too.
>
> REVISED: Protein is needed for good nutrition. Lipids and carbohydrates are, too.
>
> REVISED: Protein is needed for good nutrition; lipids and carbohydrates are, too.
>
> REVISED: Protein is needed for good nutrition, but lipids and carbohydrates are, too.
>
> REVISED: Although protein is needed for good nutrition, lipids and carbohydrates are, too.

gender   The classification of nouns and pronouns as masculine *(father, boy, he)*, feminine *(mother, girl, she)*, or neuter *(radio, kitten, them)*.

gerund   A special form of verb ending in *-ing* that is always used as a noun: <u>*Fishing is* <u>relaxing</u></u> (gerund *fishing* serves as subject; gerund *relaxing* serves as subject complement). Note: When the *-ing* form of a verb is used as a modifier, it is considered a **present participle.** See also **verbal.**

gerund phrase   See **phrase.**

headword   The word or phrase in a sentence that is described, defined, or limited by a modifier.

helping verb   See **verb.**

idiom An expression that is characteristic of a particular language and whose meaning cannot be predicted from the meaning of its individual words: *lend a hand.*

imperative mood See **mood.**

indefinite pronoun See **pronoun;** see also **determiner.**

independent clause See **clause.**

indicative mood See **mood.**

indirect object See **object.**

indirect question A question that tells what has been asked but, because it does not report the speaker's exact words, does not take quotation marks or end with a question mark: *He asked whether he could use the family car.*

indirect quotation See **quotation.**

inductive argument An argument that begins with observations or experiences and moves toward a conclusion. **8a**

infinitive The base form of the verb preceded by *to.* An infinitive can serve as an adjective (*He is the man to watch.*), an adverb (*Chris hoped to break the record.*), or a noun (*To err is human.*). See also **verbal.**

infinitive phrase See **phrase.**

intensifier A word that adds emphasis but not additional meaning to words it modifies. *Much, really, too, very,* and *so* are typical intensifiers.

intensive pronoun See **pronoun.**

interjection A grammatically independent word, expressing emotion, that is used as an exclamation. An interjection can be set off by a comma, or, for greater emphasis, it can be punctuated as an independent unit, set off by an exclamation point: *Ouch! That hurt.* **32h**

interrogative adverb See **adverb.**

interrogative pronoun See **pronoun;** see also **determiner.**

intransitive verb See **verb.**

irregular verb A verb that does not form both its past tense and past participle by adding *-d* or *-ed* to the base form of the verb. **34a2**

isolate Any word, including **interjections,** that can be used in isolation: *Yes. No. Hello. Good-bye. Please. Thanks.*

linking verb A verb that connects a subject to its complement: *The crowd became quiet.* Words that can be used as linking verbs include *seem, appear, believe, become, grow, turn, remain, prove, look, sound, smell, taste, feel,* and forms of the verb *be.*

main clause   See **clause.**

main verb   See **verb.**

metaphor   A form of **figurative language** in which the writer makes an implied comparison between two unlike items, equating them in an unexpected way: *The subway coursed through the arteries of the city.* **29d**

misplaced modifier   A modifier that has no clear relationship with its headword, usually because it is placed too far from it. **26a**

MISPLACED: By changing his diapers, Dan learned much about his new baby son.

REVISED: Dan learned much about his new baby son by changing his diapers.

mixed construction   A sentence made up of two or more parts that do not fit together grammatically. **28f**

MIXED: The Great Chicago Fire caused terrible destruction was what prompted changes in the fire code. (independent clause used as a subject)

REVISED: The terrible destruction of the Great Chicago Fire prompted changes in the fire code.

REVISED: Because of the terrible destruction of the Great Chicago Fire, the fire code was changed.

mixed metaphor   The combination of two or more incompatible images in a single figure of speech: *During the race, John kept a stiff upper lip as he ran like the wind.* **29e2**

modal auxiliary   See **verb.**

modifier   A word, phrase, or clause that acts as an adjective or an adverb, describing, limiting, or qualifying another word or word group in the sentence.

mood   The verb form that indicates the writer's basic attitude. There are three moods in English. The **indicative mood** is used for statements and questions: *Nebraska <u>became</u> a state in 1867.* The **imperative mood** specifies commands or requests and is often used without a subject: *(You) <u>Pay</u> the rent.* The **subjunctive mood** expresses wishes or hypothetical conditions: *I wish the sun <u>were</u> shining.* **34c**

nominal   A word, phrase, or clause that functions as a noun.

nominative case   See **case.**

noncount noun   See **noun.**

nonfinite verb   See **verbal.**

nonrestrictive modifier   A modifying phrase or clause that does not limit or particularize the words it modifies, but rather supplies additional information about them. Nonrestrictive modifiers are set off by commas: *Oregano, also known as marjoram or suganda, is a member of the mint family.* **38d1** (Contrast **restrictive modifier.**)

noun   A word that names people, places, things, ideas, actions, or qualities. A **common noun** names any of a class of people, places, or things: *lawyer, town, bicycle.* A **proper noun,** always capitalized, refers to a particular person, place, or thing: *Anita Hill, Chicago, Schwinn.* A **count noun** names something that can be counted: a *a dozen eggs, two cats in the yard.* A **noncount noun** names a quantity that is not countable: *sand, time, work.* An **abstract noun** refers to an intangible idea or quality: *bravery, equality, hunger.* A **collective noun** designates a group of people, places, or things thought of as a unit: *Congress, police, family.* **32a**

noun clause   See **clause.**

noun phrase   See **phrase.**

number   The form taken by a noun, pronoun, or verb to indicate one (**singular**): *car, he, this, boast,* or many (**plural**): *cars, they, those, boasts.* **28d**

object   A noun, pronoun, or other noun substitute that receives the action of a **transitive verb, verbal,** or **preposition.** A **direct object** indicates where the verb's action is directed and who or what is affected by it: *John caught a butterfly.* An **indirect object** tells to or for whom the verb's action was done: *John gave Nancy the butterfly.* An **object of a preposition** is a word or word group introduced by a preposition: *John gave Nancy the butterfly for an hour.*

object complement   See **complement.**

object of a preposition   See **object.**

objective case   See **case.**

ordinal number   A number that indicates position in a series: *seventh, thirtieth, one-hundredth.* (Contrast **cardinal number.**)

parallelism   The use of similar grammatical elements in sentences or parts of sentences: *We serve beer, wine, and soft drinks.* Words, phrases, clauses, or complete sentences may be parallel, and parallel items may be paired or presented in a series. When elements that have the same function in a sentence are not presented in the same terms, the sentence is flawed by **faulty parallelism. 21c; Ch. 27** *participial phrase*   See **phrase.**

participle   A verb form that generally functions in a sentence as an adjective. Virtually every verb has a **present participle,** which ends in -*ing* (*breaking, leaking, taking*), and a **past participle,** which usually ends in -*d* or -*ed* (*agreed, walked, taken*). (See also **verbal.**) *The heaving seas swamped the dinghy* (present participle *heaving* modifies noun *seas*); *Aged people deserve respect* (past participle *aged* modifies noun *people*).

parts of speech   The eight basic building blocks for all English sentences: *nouns, pronouns, verbs, adjectives, adverbs, prepositions, conjunctions,* and *interjections.*

passive voice   See **voice.**

past participle   See **participle.**

periodic sentence   A sentence that moves from a number of specific examples to a conclusion, gradually building in intensity until a climax is reached in the main clause: *Sickly and pale and looking ready to crumble, the marathoner headed into the last mile of the race.* **21b2**

person   The form a pronoun or verb takes to indicate the speaker (**first person**): *I am/we are;* those spoken to (**second person**): *you are;* and those spoken about (**third person**): *he/she/it is; they are.* **28d**

personal pronoun   See **pronoun.**

personification   A form of **figurative language** in which the writer describes an idea or inanimate object in terms that imply human attributes, feelings, or powers: *The big feather bed beckoned to my tired body.* **29d**

phrase   A grammatically ordered group of related words that lacks a subject or a predicate or both and functions as a single part of speech. A **verb phrase** consists of an auxiliary (helping) verb and a main verb: *The wind was blowing hard.* A **noun phrase** includes a noun or pronoun plus all related modifiers: *She broke the track record.* A **prepositional phrase** consists of a preposition, its object, and any modifiers of that object: *The ball sailed over the fence.* A **verbal phrase** consists of a verbal and its related objects, modifiers, or complements. A verbal phrase may be a **participial phrase** (*Undaunted by the sheer cliff, the climber scaled the rock.*), a **gerund phrase** (*Swinging from trees is a monkey's favorite way to travel.*), or an **infinitive phrase** (*Wednesday is Bill's night to cook spaghetti.*). An **absolute phrase** usually consists of a noun or pronoun and a participle, accompanied by modifiers: *His heart racing, he dialed her number.* **19b1** *plural*   See **number.**

positive degree   See **comparison.**

possessive case   See **case.**

possessive noun   See **determiner.**

possessive pronoun   See **determiner.**

predicate   A verb or verb phrase that tells or asks something about the subject of a sentence is called a **simple predicate:** *Well-tended lawns grow green and thick.* (*Grow* is the simple predicate.) A **complete predicate** includes all the words associated with the predicate: *Well-tended lawns grow green and thick.* (*Grow green and thick* is the complete predicate.)

predicate adjective   See **complement.**

predicate nominative   See **complement.**

prefix   A letter or group of letters put before a root or word that adds to, changes, or modifies it.

preposition   A part of speech that introduces a noun or pronoun (or a phrase or clause functioning in the sentence as a noun), linking it to other words in the sentence: *Jeremy crawled under the bed.* **32f**

prepositional phrase   See **phrase.**

present participle   See **participle.**

principal parts   The forms of a verb from which all other forms can be derived. The principal parts are the **base form** (*give*), the **present participle** (*giving*), the **past tense** (*gave*), and the **past participle** (*given*).

pronoun   A word that may be used in place of a noun in a sentence. The noun for which a pronoun stands is called its **antecedent.** There are eight types of pronouns. Some have the same form but are distinguished by their function in the sentence. A **personal pronoun** stands for a person or thing: *I, me, we, us, my,* and so on (*They broke his window.*). A **reflexive pronoun** ends in *self* or *selves* and refers to the subject of the sentence or clause: *myself, yourself, himself,* and so on (*They painted the house themselves.*). An **intensive pronoun** ends in *self* or *selves* and emphasizes a preceding noun or pronoun (*Custer himself died in the battle.*). A **relative pronoun** introduces an adjective or noun clause in a sentence: *which, who, whom,* and so on (*Sitting Bull was the Sioux chief who defeated Custer.*). An **interrogative pronoun** introduces a question: *who, which, what, whom,* and so on (*Who won the lottery?*). A **demonstrative pronoun** points to a particular thing or group of things: *this, that, these, those* (*Who was that masked man?*). A **reciprocal pronoun** denotes a mutual relationship: *each other, one another* (*We still have each other.*). An **indefinite pronoun** refers to persons or things in general, not to specific individuals. Most indefinite pronouns are singular—*anyone, everyone, one, each*—but some are always plural—*both, many, several* (*Many are called, but few are chosen.*). **32b**

proper adjective   See **adjective.**

proper noun   See **noun.**

quotation   The use of the written or spoken words of others. A **direct quotation** is a passage borrowed word for word from another source. Quotation marks (" ") establish the boundaries of a direct quotation: *"Those tortillas taste like cardboard," complained Beth.* **41a** An **indirect quotation** reports someone else's written or spoken words without quoting that person directly. Quotation marks are not used: *Beth complained that the tortillas tasted like cardboard.*

reciprocal pronoun   See **pronoun.**

reflexive pronoun   See **pronoun.**

regular verb   A verb that forms both its past tense and past participle by the addition of *-d* or *-ed* to the base form of the verb. **34a1**

relative clause   See **clause.**

relative pronoun   See **pronoun.**

restrictive appositive   See **appositive.**

restrictive modifier   A modifying phrase or clause that limits the meaning of the word or word group it modifies. Restrictive modifiers are not set off by commas: *The Ferrari that ran over the fireplug was red.* (Contrast **nonrestrictive modifier.**) **38d1**

root   A word from which other words are formed. An understanding of a root word increases a reader's ability to understand unfamiliar words that incorporate the root.

run-on sentence   An incorrect construction that results when the proper connective or punctuation does not appear between independent clauses. A run-on occurs either as a **comma splice** or as a **fused sentence. Ch. 25**

sentence   An independent grammatical unit that contains a *subject* and a *predicate* and expresses a complete thought: *Carolyn sold her car.* A **simple sentence** consists of one subject and one predicate: *The* *season ended*. **19a;** a **compound sentence** is formed when two or more simple sentences are connected with coordinating conjunctions, conjunctive adverbs, semicolons, or colons: *The rain stopped, and the sun began to shine.* **20a;** a **complex sentence** consists of one simple sentence, which functions as an independent clause in the complex sentence, and at least one dependent clause, which is introduced by a subordinating conjunction or a relative pronoun: *When he had sold three boxes* [dependent clause], *he was halfway to his goal.* [independent clause] **20b;** and a **compound-complex sentence** consists of two or more independent clauses and at least one dependent clause: *After he prepared a shopping list* [dependent clause], *he went to the store* [independent clause], *but it was closed.* [independent clause]. **20b**

sentence fragment An incomplete sentence, phrase, or clause that is punctuated as if it were a complete sentence. **Ch. 24**

shift A change of *tense, voice, mood, person, number,* or *type of discourse* within or between sentences. Some shifts are necessary, but problems occur with unnecessary or illogical shifts. **28a–e**

simile A form of **figurative language** in which the writer makes a comparison, introduced by *like* or *as*, between two unlike items on the basis of a shared quality: *Like sands through the hourglass, so are the days of our lives. The wind was as savage as his neighbor's Doberman.* **29d**

simple predicate See **predicate.**

simple sentence See **sentence.**

simple subject See **subject.**

singular See **number.**

split infinitive An infinitive whose parts are separated by a modifier. **26a4**

SPLIT: She expected *to* ultimately *swim* the channel.

REVISED: She expected ultimately *to swim* the channel.

squinting modifier A modifier that seems to modify either a word before it or one after it and that conveys a different meaning in each case. **26a1**

SQUINTING: The task completed simply delighted him.

REVISED: He was delighted to have the task completed simply.

REVISED: He was simply delighted to have the task completed.

subject A noun or noun substitute that tells who or what a sentence is about is called a **simple subject:** *Healthy thoroughbred <u>horses</u> run like the wind.* (*Horses* is the simple subject.) The **complete subject** of a sentence includes all the words associated with the subject: <u>*Healthy thoroughbred horses*</u> *run like the wind.* (*Healthy thoroughbred horses* is the complete subject.) **19a**

subject complement See **complement.**

subjective case See **case.**

subjunctive mood See **mood.**

subordinate clause See **clause.**

subordinating conjunction See **conjunction.**

subordination Making one or more clauses of a sentence grammatically dependent upon another element in a sentence: *Preston was only eighteen when he joined the firm.* (Contrast **coordination.**) **20b**

suffix A syllable added at the end of a word or root that changes its part of speech.

superlative degree See **comparison.**

suspended hyphen A hyphen followed by a space or by the appropriate punctuation and a space: *The wagon was pulled by a two-, four-, or six-horse team.*

syllogism A three-part set of statements or propositions, devised by Aristole, that contains a major premise, a minor premise, and conclusion. **8b1**

tag question A question, consisting of an auxiliary verb plus a pronoun, that is added to a statement and set off by a comma: *You know it's going to rain, <u>don't you?</u>*

tense The form of a verb that indicates when an action occurred or when a condition existed. **34b**

transitive verb See **verb.**

verb A word or phrase that expresses action (*He <u>painted</u> the fence.*) or a state of being (*Henry <u>believes</u> in equality.*). A **main verb** carries most of the meaning in the sentence or clause in which it appears: *Winston Churchill <u>smoked</u> long, thick cigars.* A main verb is a **linking verb** when it is followed by a **subject complement:** *Dogs <u>are</u> good pets.* An **auxiliary verb** (sometimes called a **helping verb**) combines with the main verb to form a **verb phrase:** *Graduation day <u>has arrived</u>.* The auxiliaries *be* and *have* are used to indicate the tense and voice of the main verb. The auxiliary *do* is used for asking questions and forming negative statements. Other auxiliary verbs, known as **modal auxiliaries** (*must, will, can, could, may, might, ought* (*to*), *should,* and *would*), indicate necessity, possibility, willingness, obligation, and ability: *It might rain next Tuesday.* A **transitive verb** requires an **object** to complete its meaning in the sentence: *Pete drank all the wine* (*wine* is the direct object). An **intransitive verb** has no direct object: *The candle flame glowed.* **32c1; Ch. 34**

verb phrase   See **phrase.**

verbal   (**nonfinite verb**) Verb forms—**participles, infinitives,** and **gerunds**—that are used as nouns, adjectives, or adverbs. Verbals do not behave like verbs. Only when used with an auxiliary can such verb forms serve as the main verb of a sentence. *The wall painted* is not a sentence; *The wall was painted* is. **32c2**

verbal phrase   See **phrase.**

voice   The form that determines whether the subject of a verb is acting or is acted upon. When the subject of a verb performs the action, the verb is in the **active voice:** *Tiger Woods sank a thirty-foot putt.* When the subject of a verb receives the action—that is, is acted upon—the verb is in the **passive voice:** *A thirty-foot putt was sunk by Tiger Woods.* **21e; 28b; 34d**

ACKNOWLEDGMENTS

John Berger, excerpt from *About Looking* by John Berger. Copyright © 1980 by John Berger. Reprinted by permission of Pantheon Books, a division of Random House, Inc.

Michael Finkel, "Undecided and Proud of It" by Michael Finkel from *The New York Times*, 11/24/89. Copyright © 1989 by The New York Times Co. Reprinted by permission.

Victoria Fromkin, excerpt adapted from *An Introduction to Language*, Fourth Edition, by Victoria A. Fromkin and Robert Rodman. Copyright © 1988 by Holt, Rinehart and Winston. Reprinted by permission of the publisher. This material may not be reproduced, stored in a retrieval system, or transmitted in any form or by any means without the prior written permission of the publisher.

Duane Gall, "Multicultural Education" by Duane Gall from *UTNE Reader*, November/December 1990. Copyright © Duane Gall. Reprinted by permission of the author.

Gary Gildner, "Sleepy Time Gal" from *The Crush* by Gary Gildner. Copyright © 1983 by Gary Gildner. Reprinted by permission of the author.

Landon Y. Jones, courtesy Landon Y. Jones, *Great Expectations: America and the Babyboom Generation*. Copyright © 1980.

Ron Kovic, excerpt from *Born on the Fourth of July* by Ron Kovic. Copyright © 1976. Reprinted by permission of The McGraw-Hill Companies.

Jake Lamar, "Whose Legacy Is It Anyway?" by Jake Lamar from *The New York Times*, 09/09/91. Copyright © 1991 by The New York Times Co. Reprinted by permission.

Richard D. Lamm, "English Comes First" by Richard D. Lamm from *The New York Times*, 07/01/86. Copyright © 1986 by The New York Times Co. Reprinted by permission.

Joseph Nocera, "The Case against Joe Nocera: How People like Me Helped Ruin the Public Schools" by Joseph Nocera reprinted with permission from *The Washington Monthly*. Copyright by The Washington Monthly Company, 1611 Connecticut Ave., N.W., Washington, DC 20009, (202) 462-0128.

Bill Roberts, excerpt from the article "The World of Hunting" by WIlliam R. Quimby. From *Safari Magazine*, July/August 1992. Copyright © 1992 by William R. Quimby. Reprinted by permission of The Safari Club International.

Phyllis Schlafly, excerpt from the article "Comparable Worth Unfair to Men and Women" by Phyllis Schlafly from *The Humanist*, May/June 1986. Reprinted with permission of The American Humanist Association, copyright © 1986.

INDEX

Page numbers in blue refer to definitions. For Web sites on many of the topics in this index, check the pages in the text for that particular topic.